FIRE

With an insatiable appetite for travel, food and new experiences, Christine Manfield has traversed the globe in search of inspiration. Her quest has taken her from Tokyo to Istanbul, and from Hanoi to Marrakech.

Now, in *FIRE*, she shares her world of flavour: her favourite places, the memorable dishes she has enjoyed along the way, and the recipes they have inspired her to create. Her verve and irrepressible enthusiasm make her an excellent travelling companion, and she leaves no stone unturned in her quest for new tastes. With more than 300 recipes imbued with fire, spice and a sense of adventure, this rich and evocative volume is full of ideas and inspiration for your next meal – or your next big trip.

Christine Manfield is one of Australia's most celebrated chefs – a perfectionist inspired by strong flavours, and a writer whose successful books *Spice, Stir, Christine Manfield Originals* and *Christine Manfield Desserts* have spiced up the lives of keen cooks everywhere.

Her professional culinary life started in the mid-1980s and has culminated to date in three ground-breaking restaurants – Paramount in Sydney from 1993 to 2000, East@West in London from 2003 to early 2005, and now back in Sydney with Universal Restaurant, which opened its doors in August 2007.

An inveterate traveller, Christine continues to broaden her global food interests, working alongside respected chefs around the world and hosting gastronomic tours to exotic destinations including Morocco, India, Spain and Turkey.

For Margie, you constantly inspire and amaze me.
I am in awe of your insight, understanding and nurturing.
You offer meaning to every adventure in life.

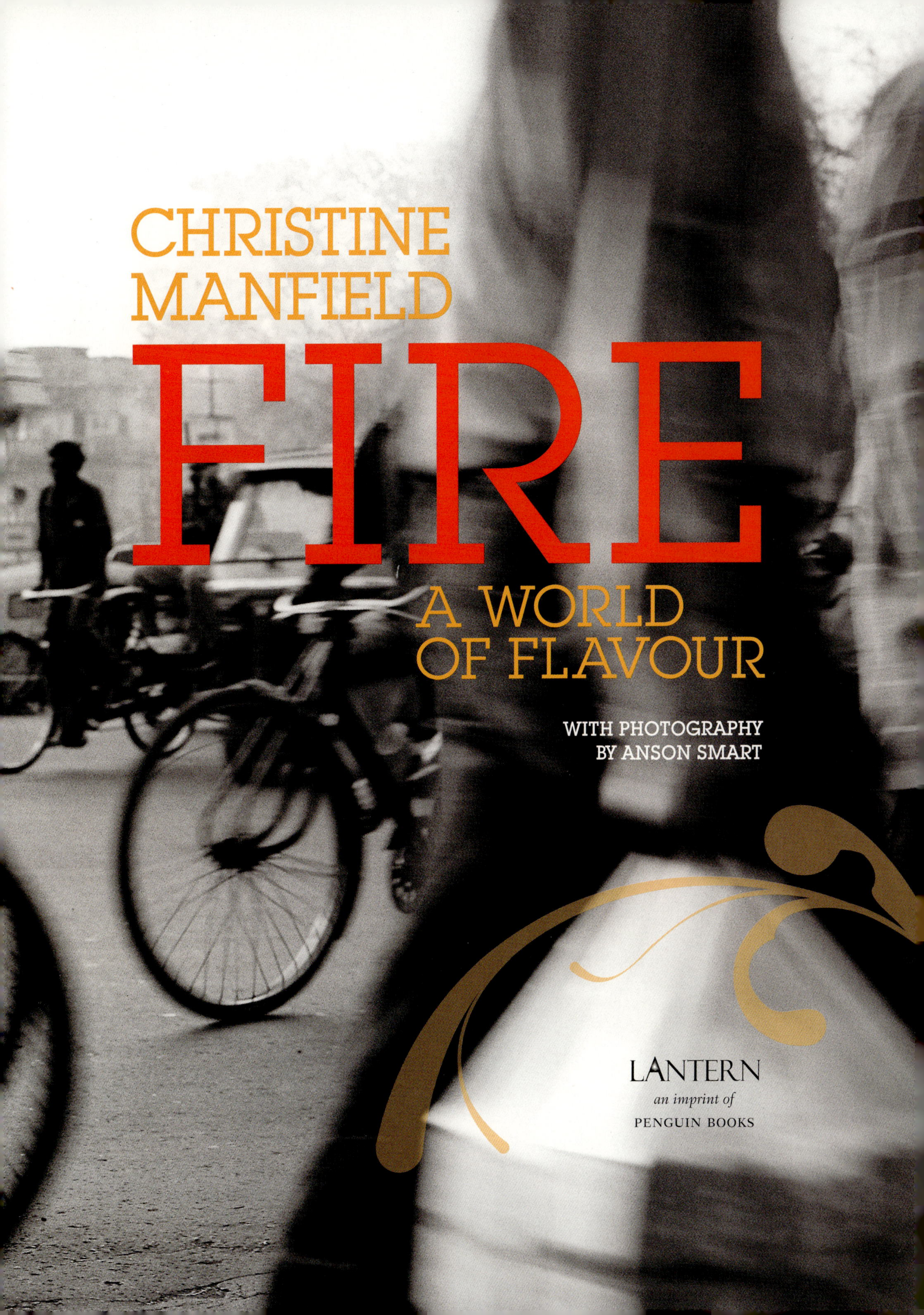

CHRISTINE MANFIELD

FIRE

A WORLD OF FLAVOUR

WITH PHOTOGRAPHY BY ANSON SMART

LANTERN
an imprint of
PENGUIN BOOKS

CONTENTS

TENUTA
IL CORNO
ITALIA
TENUTA
IL CORNO
ITALIA
TENUTA
IL CORNO
ITALIA
AGRINICO
TENUTA
IL CORNO
ITALIA

FOREWORD

The first time I became aware of Christine Manfield was in a photo taken at the Oasis Seros Restaurant in Sydney. It was in *The Weekend Australian Magazine* and it must have been during the late 1980s. For some reason I've kept the article tucked away in my recipe file all these years. I'm looking at it now. There's Christine: a shock of New Romantic white hair, large black earrings and braces on trousers that look as though they are made from a chef's apron.

In 1999, I finally experienced her extraordinary palate when I dined at Paramount, the legendary restaurant owned by Chris and her partner, Margie Harris. Up till then, I'd only heard about its revolutionary nature second-hand. The food I ate that night represented one of the few seminal moments I've experienced in a restaurant.

We've since become friends. We've enjoyed meals together on four continents; attended a washed-out cheese festival in Britain; holidayed on a 40-metre gulet off the Turkish Coast (co-cooking a meal for the skipper and his wife, Chris's eggplant dish won them over); and, individually and independently, contributed towards making flavourful food paramount.

Chris's palate is extraordinarily refined, but assertive, robust and balanced. I can still recall the flavours of her black pepper tea soup from East@West Restaurant in London, her turmeric lemongrass broth with chicken dumplings and spiced beetroot that she cooked to raise money for leukaemia in Auckland, and that fabulously camp ice-cream dessert I will always associate with her: Universal Gaytime.

This book in part encapsulates her philosophy on food, flavour and texture, but it also shows how some of the world's most vibrant culinary regions have inspired her to take their classic dishes into a new realm. Chris combines her love of travel, her understanding of flavours from many disciplines, and her appreciation of other cooks' skills, many of them time-honoured, to bring a fresh approach to dishes that seem both classic and contemporary. There is a great simplicity to her recipes, even if the shopping list does sometimes look a little daunting. A Sri Lankan curry powder may have seventeen ingredients, but then I like to think any foodie worth their salt would have most of these spices to hand anyway.

To bring even more life and relevance to the recipes, Chris has written beautifully evocative travel pieces, stories revolving around the craziness of life in Tokyo, the calm of duck-filled waterways in Kerala and the exotic scents emanating from the Fes medina. Her travel pieces conjure up colourful images, tantalising aromas and a myriad sounds, all seen through the eyes of a truly talented craftsperson.

I have purchased all of Chris's previous books both for myself and for others. *FIRE* will be no exception. It is a culinary world-view from a fiercely intelligent, appreciative and enquiring mind. It is all about her love of food and of differing cultures; about her respect for traditions, and her embracing of adventure. My only concern is whether it'll be too large for my hand luggage as I can't put it down.

Peter Gordon

INTRODUCTION

I have fire in my belly when it comes to all things culinary, and travelling the world. Driven by a deep-seated passion and a desire to explore and experiment, I aim to offer a personal account of the wonderful and exotic adventures that have been an intrinsic part of my life over the past three decades. It's about a life built around food: its source, inspiration, cultural differences and influences – a starting point for understanding time and place, and an illustration of how travel has affected and impacted on everything I do and the way I interpret the world. It has been these influences and diversity that have shaped my personal direction, with food that crosses cultural boundaries with confidence without being labelled 'fusion', and parallels the direction of what has become part of our own heritage, development and repertoire in Australia – a culinary freestyle that has enriched our food culture and given it maturity and world renown.

'Logic takes you from A to B . . .
Imagination takes you everywhere'
Albert Einstein

Travel challenges and offers life-changing experiences that broaden perceptions and knowledge. For me, travelling has become a life-long quest to expand the taste memory bank, to find different interpretations of what has already been learnt and tasted, with the hope of discovering something new, combined with the constant challenge and desire to take risks and evolve. These experiences have translated directly into my work – intellectually, emotionally and practically. I'll go anywhere where food is a celebration of everyday life, where conviviality and the pleasures of the table are cherished, and it is these places I rely on for constant and ongoing inspiration, like drawing breath. So many places, so many people, so little time, so many adventures to engage in, so much delicious food to taste, so many flavours to experiment with, so much to glean and learn. The more I see, the less I feel I know.

These experiences constantly invigorate and inspire me, each experience building on the last to create what has become my culinary passport. My cooking has evolved with my travels, so that how I cook is like an imprint of my personality and experience – translated onto the plate through flavour and texture and a confident understanding of the parameters of taste. Travel has an incredible ability to catapult me into another reality, into the world of others, and it is usually at the simplest point of contact – food – that an immediate connection is forged. The sharing of food knows no political boundaries; it is a reminder of remarkable places visited, with tastes that transport me immediately to any given place. It's as if I can taste the character and essence of a place through its food.

My driving ambition has always been to seek out those flavours and ingredients that dance together, to create a symphony of flavours that sing on the palate, a synergy that appears effortless and enticing. My primary motivation centres around encouraging the importance and value of pleasure, celebrating and sharing good food wherever I go, seducing the palate with exciting tastes and communicating through the medium of food. I have long defined my work by the 'adopt and adapt' principle – conducting investigative research into the kitchens of the world, to further understand process, technique, flavours, textures and culinary traditions, striving to achieve the elusive umami (a Japanese term for the 'tastiness' factor) with every flavour combination.

Travel and appreciation of different cultures, along with access to the global pantry have made it nigh on impossible to define how I cook in any conventional sense. Many chefs will say their food is produce driven, however this doesn't really say anything about the specific style of cooking or shed any light on an accurate definition. Simple, straightforward cooking and the use of fresh produce can fit into any cuisine of the world, so what makes that sentiment unique to Australia? As we continue to follow the global grab-bag approach to what we cook, it will remain very difficult to surmise in one simple paragraph the exact nature of Australian cooking, which I believe to be a healthy attitude and approach to have. Take off the blinkers and celebrate what makes us different! So it is within this context that my professional cooking life has developed, giving me the opportunity to play some part in our gastronomic life.

My professional culinary life started in the mid-1980s, and to date has culminated in three restaurants, which serve as benchmarks for my work: Paramount in Sydney, from 1993 to 2000; East@West in London, from 2003 to early 2005; and now back in Sydney, with Universal Restaurant, which opened in August 2007, each experience eclipsing the last. Throughout, I continue to strive for excellence, to evolve and consolidate; to remain dynamic, relevant and intrigued; to never become complacent or mediocre, nor take anything for granted; and to measure my achievements against those I admire, who offer continuing inspiration. Each place has given me an opportunity to fulfil my dreams and aspirations. More than ever, the menu at Universal reflects my culinary passport, a personal exploration and infectious interpretation of the infinite flavours of the world. With a working philosophy of 'global yet local', and featuring pure, clean flavours that are decisive and complex yet thoroughly refined, the menu reflects a brave new world inspired by exotic destinations and world travel.

'Cooking is forever a compromise with historical fact and fancy . . . there must be passionate leaders who know how to keep that compromise honest'
M.F.K. Fisher

First and foremost I am a curious cook, constantly intrigued by what I eat and how I cook and the way I think about food. I live for culinary adventure, to travel, explore, experiment and embrace change. The world is my oyster! Travel gives my work meaning and a sense of place, keeps me on my toes, my mind fresh and inspired; travel is the path of discovery, a renewal of my affinity with all that is exciting in the world of gastronomy. I cherish the culinary melting pot of flavours, tastes and delights I have at my disposal, in my own backyard and across the globe.

My cooking is instinctive and distinctive. For me, cooking is a pleasure, and I find kitchen life both contemplative and grounding. I remain fascinated by all that is new yet have a deep respect for all that is old, tried and true. Only from this point of understanding and knowledge can I move forward and embrace change with dynamic energy, enthusiasm and lust for life. The world of food has offered me inexhaustible opportunities of taste combinations, endless excitement and thrilling adventures, because I have never passed up the chance to widen my horizons and entertain every possibility.

Food and travel remain life-long obsessions, I adore every minute of this never-ending journey of discovery. The fire in my belly continues to burn strong and I am determined to never let it be extinguished. Travel, adventure, food and wine offer immense and intrinsic rewards, adding complexity and depth to every experience. I invite you to engage your imagination and explore the endless possibilities of a world of flavour.

LESS IS MORE TOKYO

Arriving in Tokyo for the first time can be a daunting prospect: it's so easy to be overwhelmed. I know I experience a 'what planet have I landed on?' moment every time I arrive in this crazy, congested metropolis. There is a dizzying surrealism about the endless blinking neon signs that bombard you from every direction. Trying to work out where to go can be baffling because there is no logical sequence to the street numbers (due to a complicated system of land titles being subdivided to pay death duties). It can even be a challenge for taxi drivers to deliver you to the correct location if you don't have the proper details written in Japanese. Despite this, Tokyo has to be one of the friendliest cities on earth, an enigmatic place that rewards exploration. But it is the food draws me here time and again. Each offering is a considered work of art, from a humble bowl of soba noodles or plate of yakitori (grilled chicken skewers) to the brilliance of a bento box lunch (several small dishes neatly arranged in a lacquered box) or the single-minded perfection of kaiseki (exquisitely presented, seasonally inspired cuisine). One of the essential characteristics of Japanese cuisine is a satisfying, savoury quality, umami, which is rapidly gaining recognition as one of the basic tastes alongside hot, sour, salty, sweet and bitter. Imparted by certain amino acids found in sake and ingredients such as soy sauce, miso, bonito, matsutake and shiitake mushrooms, konbu seaweed, green tea and parmesan cheese, umami has become a touchstone for chefs and gourmands around the world, not least for its ability to round out and enhance other flavours.

From Narita, Tokyo's main airport, it's a 70-kilometre trek to the centre of town, which takes about 2 hours by road, but a more time-efficient option is to take the JR Narita Express train to a main station close to where you are staying and then walk or grab a taxi from there. The cost of a taxi from the airport is quite exorbitant due to the distance involved and the volume of traffic, but they can be a viable option for zipping around town. Navigating the Tokyo subway system can be challenging, especially during the peak-hour frenzy when people are literally squeezed into the carriages, but you can generally count on the assistance of a friendly local – and there is English signage to help you find your way.

My first visit to Tokyo was in the depths of winter, and on the very first morning I awoke to falling snow. This was a beautiful thing – until it became apparent that our movements were going to be somewhat restricted. If we ventured outside for too long, we returned wet and frozen (not helped by our being unable to resist a childlike instinct to make and throw snowballs, which reduced us to hysterics on several occasions). Walking between rows of giant frozen tuna at Tsukiji fish market at six one morning, with the freezing air rising from the murky waters of the Sumida River, we weren't sure who was colder – us or the fish! In an attempt to warm ourselves from the inside we tried some coffee, dispensed hot in cans from a machine – not a taste experience I want to repeat any time soon. I have also visited Tokyo in the summer months, but have yet to witness hanami, the

SHOPPING IN TOKYO

YAMAYA WINE STORE
1F Onoko Shinjuku Bldg, 3-2-7 Nishi-Shinjuku, Shinjuku-ku
Fabulous selection of wines from around the globe, especially France.

SHO-CHU AUTHORITY
B2/F Caretta Shiodome, 1-8-2 Higashi-Shimbashi, Minato-ku
Tel +81 3 5537 2105
In the basement of the Shiodome Tower, this emporium of sake and shochu (a distilled spirit made with various grains or sweet potato) is a real treat, stocking thousands of brands and varieties of these seductive drinks.

KAPPABASHI DORI
Shinburi Dori, starting at Asakusa Dori (look for the chef's-head sign), Nishi-Asakusa, near Tawaramachi subway station
The place to come for kitchenware supplies and specialty knife shops, with the focus mainly on commercial sales.

AMEYA YOKOCHO MARKET
Taito-ku, from Marui City to Okachimachi station, Ueno
Get off at the Ueno subway station to find Tokyo's liveliest street market, where Asian, Korean (love the kim chee), African and Indian cuisines jostle for attention – a great way to try flavours other than Japanese. Running parallel to the train line, the street is packed with stalls selling edible treats, food vendors making all manner of snacks, produce and spices.

YOKU MOKU
5-3-3 Minami-Aoyama, Shibuya-ku
Tel +81 3 5485 3330
www.yokumoku.co.jp
The definitive confectioners, with exquisite pastries and chocolates, all beautifully packaged.

cherry-blossom season in April. During one of the most anticipated events of the Japanese calendar, the riot of soft-pink flowers is celebrated in a haze of drunken parties in the city's parks and gardens.

Tokyo itself has no real centre; it is more a collection of neighbourhoods and districts, like a patchwork of villages that have merged together. Homogeneous high-rises stand beside some of the most stunning and beautifully designed buildings I've ever seen. In spite of its dimensions and dense population, Tokyo actually feels like one of the safest cities you can visit; strangers are helpful, even with the language barrier. I find the best approach to exploring the city is to choose a district, jump on the subway and then walk around the streets. Tokyo is a shopping nirvana, and each district has its own unique character. Fashion stores are packed into the yuppie precinct of Harajuku, around Takeshita Dori, and more recently have spilt into the Daikanyama and Nakameguro districts, where many hours can be squandered ogling the groovy and anarchistic style of Tokyo's youth culture. This is definitely the birthplace of 'bling', and in a city obsessed with fashion, you'll see things you won't see anywhere else – quirky at times, extraordinarily beautiful and stylish at others, the diversity on the streets is amazing.

STAYING IN TOKYO

PARK HYATT TOKYO
3-7-1-2 Nishi Shinjuku, Shinjuku-ku
Tel +81 3 5322 1234
www.tokyo.park.hyatt.com
Staying in these state-of-the-art towers (which featured in the film *Lost in Translation*) is like being up in the clouds, with staggering views, an exclusive ambience and impeccable service. Make time to have dinner at the New York Grill, consistently rated as one of the world's best restaurants.

PARK HOTEL TOKYO
Shiodome Media Tower, 1-7-1 Higashi Shimbashi, Minato-ku
Tel +81 3 62521111
www.parkhoteltokyo.com
Designer boutique hotel in Shimbashi district, overlooking the river.

YOSHIMIZU
3-11-3 Ginza, Chuo-ku
Tel +81 3 3248 4432
www.yoshimizu.com
A small ryokan (Japanese inn) with traditional tatami floors, right in the heart of Ginza.

Omotesando Dori is one of the main thoroughfares – I walked along here one Sunday to watch teenagers busking and doing whacky Elvis impersonations. This main road leads to Minami Aoyama, where the high-end chic stores and international labels compete for attention; I always manage to do damage to my credit card here with some extravagant retail therapy. A must-see is the futuristic honeycomb-glass building that houses Prada, a womb-like, white glowing cocoon. A few doors down is the most divine pastry shop, Yoku Moku, with its distinctive blue-tiled wall, where I always buy tins of beautifully arranged paper-thin pastries and individually wrapped tuile wafers for presents. Throughout the city, trendy boutiques, shops and hotels sit comfortably alongside Buddhist and Shinto shrines, pagoda temples, sumo wrestlers and kabuki theatre. The Japanese are fanatical supporters of their national heroes – and sporting teams are no different. During one of my visits, World Cup fever had taken hold and thousands of people flooded the streets to watch the soccer on massive video screens that stretched several storeys high. It was impossible not to get caught up in the excitement. The Japanese have certainly cornered the market when it comes to inventiveness. From the Sony Building in Ginza to Electric City in Akihabara, it is impossible not to be dazzled by the incredible display of new gadgets and creations. Tokyo is a hi-tech metropolis with palpable energy, a place where computer nerds and techno-heads have become part of the landscape.

Roppongi has long been the hub for expat services and Western-style restaurants, and there's now the glamorous development of Roppongi Hills next door. One of my favourite places in this district is Shunju, with its contemporary, clean-tasting Japanese food. Dining here is like being in an elegant private home, so Zen and minimal; you remove your shoes at the door before sitting on tatami mats around a sunken table. On my first visit, I shared a tasting menu of tofu – starting with fresh house-made soy milk cooked at the table in a small clay pot to make silken tofu, which we ate fondue-style with pickled ginger, sesame and spring onions. Tofu steamed in bamboo tubes followed – fresh squares of tofu that were drizzled with shiro shoyu (white soy sauce) so the whiteness of the tofu was not stained by the darker regular soy sauce. It was served with shavings of smoke-dried bonito – sensational. We progressed through the rest of the tofu preparations (including an ethereal agedashi tofu), and each course was a textural revelation. On a return visit, I chose seasonal vegetable and seafood items, and was equally impressed by their inherent integrity and taste. By contrast, some friends took us to Tableaux in Shibuya – the whole place was so camp we felt as if we had stumbled onto the set of *La Cage aux Folles*. The menu was modern Californian and the waiters had perfectly manicured arched eyebrows; it was great fun, and showcased the extremes of this city.

Tokyo's ancient and mystical gardens are peaceful sanctuaries and offer a chance to escape from the claustrophobic frenzy of the streets. The beauty of bonsai, the arched wooden bridges over central ponds brimming with fish, and the natural rock formations reflect the harmonious blend of Taoist, Buddhist and Shinto traditions. We walked through the East Garden of the Imperial Palace (the rest of the palace grounds are off limits to the public), and strolled around the massive Yoyogi Koen gardens, near Shinjuku. Within Yoyogi Koen gardens is the Meiji Jingu shrine, the most significant Shinto shrine in Tokyo, which was reconstructed after being obliterated by American bombs during the Second World War. We could hardly hear the traffic noise as we wandered along the shaded paths. The older neighbourhoods of Asakusa and Ueno sit on either side of the Imperial Palace, and it's in this area that you'll find the lively Ameyoko Market and the intriguing kitchenware and restaurant supply stores along Kappabashi Dori. As we were walking along the streets and lanes lined with small wooden houses, all of a sudden a couple of kimono-clad women shuffled past us. What a thrill; it gave us the sensation of spotting a rare bird.

At the other end of the scale, Tokyo boasts the most lavish department stores in the world: Isetan in Shinjuku, Matsuya in Ginza, Takashimaya and Mitsukoshi in Chuo-ku and Seibu in Shibuya are among my favourites. Every department store has an enviable food hall, usually in its basement, with opulent displays. It's hard to know where to start, what to taste or what to buy, and the packaging is to die for. Many fruits and vegetables are individually wrapped in several layers of paper, like precious jewels. I love that attention to detail and respect for every little thing.

When my friend and colleague Rainer was executive chef at the Park Hyatt Tokyo's New York Grill (before he moved to London to establish Zuma and Roka restaurants), he invited me to be a guest chef in residence. The hotel is located in the district of Shinjuku, which is a bit like Gotham City on steroids, a forest of skyscrapers and elevated freeways. The Park Hyatt is spread across the top of three interconnecting towers that dominate the landscape. In my free time, I would wander around the back streets and lanes, finding little hole-in-the-wall joints and modest shopfronts that specialise in one type of cooking, whether it be yakitori, sushi, tempura or noodles, harking back to the pedlars who wandered the streets during Edo times. Although these have now largely disappeared, remnants of the tradition persist and near the exits to subway stations, especially late at night, you can often pick up taiyaki (sweet fish pancake wrapped in nori seaweed) or yaki soba (noodles fried on a wide teppan grill pan with shredded cabbage and pork, pickled ginger and bean sprouts). I also discovered the Japanese love for flavoured jellies, when the hotel pastry chefs made miniature replicas of some of my architecturally styled desserts (many based on fruit jellies) to sell in their patisserie. Each batch disappeared off the shelves as soon as it was made. On my travels around the city, I was to see many, many shops that specialised in sweet jellies struggling to keep up with the demand.

Rainer took me out to dinner when we had the time. One evening we had a memorable meal at a tiny seven-seat place in Azabujuban. We ate from the most delicious kaiseki menu: each tiny jewel-like dish of seasonal produce was notable for its well-defined, singular flavours, and its presentation was inspired by nature and evocative of the season – the essence of Japanese food. The only thing we were required to order was sake, the rest just flowed in a procession throughout the evening (just as well, as the owners did not speak a word of English). There are thousands of places like this dotted across town – so local, inviting and affordable. Tracing its origins back to shojin ryori, the refined vegetarian food of Buddhist temples, kaiseki is the epitome of Japanese haute cuisine, a sequence of immaculately prepared tastes defined by the four seasons that is the inspiration for many Western chefs, myself included. Omakase (literally meaning 'entrusting') is a menu of the chef's choice, a series of dishes displaying elaborate attention to detail that has been a major influence on recent restaurant trends internationally. Across the world, the same traditions are executed to perfection at Masa, a highly acclaimed Japanese restaurant in New York City, offering tastes such as tuna toro with caviar, a salad of Japanese eggplant with miso, sea urchin from Hokkaido with sweet corn risotto, and slivers of squid with sea salt and yuzu (a fragrant Japanese citrus fruit). Tetsuya in Sydney is another fine example, with a tasting menu that includes signature dishes of veal with wasabi and sea urchin butter and confit of Petuna ocean trout with fennel.

This style of eating exemplifies the sophistication of the Japanese tradition and, to me, is infinitely more appealing than lengthy a-la-carte menus and large plates of food. The food is clean and elegant, and the design and visual appeal are considered vital elements of any dish, just as important as flavour. In less formal eateries where you must order your dish, it's quite acceptable to point at coloured pictures on menus, plastic models in window displays, or what you see on someone else's plate. Either way, language is no barrier to enjoying your meal. My Japanese eating experiences have changed the way I prepare and serve food, and I have adopted the 'less

EATING IN TOKYO

GOEMON
1-1-26 Hin-Komagome, Bunkyo-ku
Tel +81 3 3811 2015
People flock here to enjoy a Tokyo wintertime ritual, the amazingly delicious yudofu (tofu in broth). Start early and be patient – nothing is rushed.

SHUNJU
B1 House 5302, 5-16-47 Roppongi, Minato-ku
Tel +81 3 3583 2611
www.shunju.com
A contemporary and sophisticated izakaya (sake bar that serves food) with an emphasis on organic and biodynamic produce and a thorough respect for seasonality – the tofu dishes are a revelation.

SAZANKA
11/F Okura Hotel
2-10-4 Toranomon, Minato-ku
www.okura.com/tokyo
Tel +81 3 3505 6071
Teppanyaki restaurant that cooks beef (try the premium Sendai) and fish to perfection.

BIRD LAND
Tsukamoto Sozan Building B1/F, 4-2-15 Ginza, Chuo-ku
Tel +81 3 5250 1081
Grilled chicken (free-range) and yakitori are the specialties here, and they're absolutely delicious.

CAFFE @ IDEE
6-1-6 Minami-Aoyama, Minato-ku
Tel +81 3 3409 6744
This cool cafe is part of the groovy design store Idee, so you can shop and eat at the same place. There's also a branch in the vast Roppongi Hills complex.

SEKISHIN-TEI
New Otani Hotel, 4-1 Kioi-cho, Chiyoda-ku
Tel +81 3 3238 0024
www.newotani.co.jp/en
Set in a beautiful 440-year-old garden, this restaurant serves terrific teppanyaki. Kitted out in white bibs and aprons, we had a great lunch here of Kobe beef and lobster as the snow fell outside.

KEIKA KUMAMOTO RAMEN
3-7-2 Shinjuku, Shinjuku-ku
Tel +81 3 3354 4591
The ramen noodles here are among the best in town, and I love the soup with sliced pork and ginger. Be prepared to join the queue and wait – it's worth it.

IPPUDO
1-3-13 Hiro-o, Daikanyama, Shibuya-ku
Tel +81 3 5420 2225
My other favourite ramen noodle shop, this place is always packed, but the queue moves fast. My pick is aka maru, pork noodles in broth with a splash of dark soy sauce and a dollop of red chilli paste, and the gyoza dumplings are pure heaven.

MUTSUKARI
6/F Ginza Pony Building, 5-5-19 Ginza
Tel +81 3 5568 6266
A good place to indulge in a seasonal kaiseki menu.

ARONIA DE TAKAZAWA
2/F Sanyo Building, 3-5-2 Akasaka, Minato-ku
Tel +81 3 3505 5052
Beautiful, intimate restaurant with only ten seats that offers a contemporary take on the classics – go for the set kaiseki menu.

GOKOKU
7-4-5 Minato-ku, Roppongi
Tel +81 3 3796 3356
If you're only visiting Tokyo, it's worth eating here to sample some Japanese regional specialties.

IROHA SUSHI
1-22-13 Kamimeguro, Meguro-ku
Tel +81 3 3794 6879
www.irohasushi.com
Rely on the chef's choice to enjoy some delicious sushi and seafood bites.

SUSHI SEI
near Tsukiji Fish Market, not far from the Namiyoke-jinja shrine
Here you'll find sublime tuna, toro (tuna belly), sea urchin, squid and crab sushi, served by particularly friendly staff.

KYUBEI
5/F Okura Hotel
2-10-4 Toranomon, Minato-ku
www.okura.com/tokyo
Tel +81 3 3505 6067
Terrific sushi restaurant.

is more' approach. I now see that small, elegant portions are far superior in every sense, and this has guided me ever since. Of course, Japanese food is not alone in this; consider the small plates of Spanish tapas and Middle Eastern or Greek mezes.

A dawn visit to Tsukiji fish market on the Sumida-gawa River is mandatory every time I'm in Tokyo – for me, it is like a pilgrimage, a rite of passage into the city. This wholesale market has the most unbelievable array of seafood and occupies a vast area, covering several blocks. It is the largest seafood market in the world, with aisles dedicated to sea urchins, oysters, eels, octopus and squid in all shapes and sizes, dazzling sides of dark and fleshy bluefin tuna and pearly white swordfish, and the potentially deadly fugu (puffer fish). I have never been surrounded by so much fish anywhere else; crucially, there's no smell, because everything is in such pristine condition. Traders, restaurateurs and chefs swarm around, eyeballing the fish, picking and choosing what will be needed for the day's trade. It makes me marvel at the volume of seafood that must be consumed in Japan on a daily basis. I quickly learn to stay out of the way of the fast-moving tarettos, motorised carts with crazed drivers on a mission to dispatch seafood to the thousands of eating houses and shops across the city before the start of the day's business – one false move and you'd be skittled.

Grab some breakfast at a sushi/sashimi bar near here, as the sun rises, and I promise you, fresh fish will take on a whole new meaning. Qualified sushi masters (taisho) train for many years to perfect their incredible knife skills and subtlety of hand, so sushi is regarded as restaurant and/or special-occasion food and is not usually prepared at home. There are several hole-in-the-wall sushi bars in the side streets around the market, but I usually head for Sushi Sei. It can be hard to find: my landmark is the Namiyoke-jinja shrine (the temple where the fishermen come to pray and be blessed), which is near the bonito section of the market. From here, walk a couple of streets away to the right and then ask a shopkeeper for directions if need be. Once you've taken your seat at the sushi bar, it's simply a matter of point-and order – from nigiri sushi, rice topped with a slice of raw fish to makizushi – sushi rice and fish rolled in nori seaweed. If raw fish for breakfast does not appeal, then do try a traditional breakfast of rice, miso soup, grilled salmon, dried fish, omelette, pickles, tofu, seaweed and salted umeboshi plum – it's hard to imagine a healthier start to the day.

One night we took the plunge and ordered fugu, or puffer fish. We happened to be there in winter, when fugu is in season, so we were in luck. It was not really what I was expecting, though. In fact, I was quite disappointed by its somewhat bland taste and slightly chewy texture. But that's not really the point. The thrill lies in getting the highly competent chef (a special licence is needed to carve these fish) to slice it as close as possible to the gills and liver, to give diners the desired tingling sensation in the mouth; if the chef errs by just one millimetre you'd be dead, your nervous system paralysed by poison. Some equate it to playing Russian roulette at the table. Special ceramic plates are hand-crafted by artisans for this delicacy, and its cost is about the same as an expensive cut of Wagyu or Kobe beef.

After this extravagance, we decided to eat noodles for a while; there are plenty of modest shops about where the noodles are hand-made in the front window. Who could resist that? To address the seasons appropriately, hearty udon or ramen noodles are served in broths and soups during winter, and in summer, the lighter soba and somen noodles are served cold in salads. The noodle shops or restaurants are usually quite small with tables or benchtops around a central kitchen so you can see the action. I love this sort of communal eating – it's a great way to observe the finer points of social interaction while practising your noodle-slurping technique. Another eating experience to look out for is the ever-popular robata grill cooking. In this traditional method of cooking, everything from vegetables and tofu to fish and meat are cooked over hot coals on an open grill and passed to diners on a large wooden paddle. It is a wonderfully interactive restaurant experience as it breaks down any barriers of shyness or formality. We also had a terrific lunch one day at a teppanyaki restaurant, where meat, vegetables and seafood are cooked by a chef on a hot plate in front of you. We sat there with large white bibs draped around us (to protect our clothes from splatters from the grill plate) and feasted on prime beef seared to melting tenderness. Other eating houses specialise in dishes cooked at the table, such as shabu-shabu and sukiyaki, where meat is cooked with jelly-like glass noodles called shirataki, or the winter comfort food of nabemono, a one-pot dish of meat, tofu and vegetables. For a snack to go with beer or sake, it's hard to beat kushiage, small breaded morsels of meat, fish or vegetables skewered and deep-fried until golden.

One taste I had an immediate affinity with was sake, Japan's elegant rice wine. Many times over, I worked my way through various cold sakes in an effort to understand and appreciate their specific characteristics. I still explore the different types wherever I go – it's fascinating to unravel their complexities. A good starting point is Honjozoshu, where a little alcohol is added to premium sake, producing a characteristically clean dry finish. Moving on, try the savoury, soft, delicate notes of Junmai, the pure Ginjoshu and the top-grade Daiginjoshu, which can be fruity, but is smooth, crisp and pristine in its purity. With alcohol levels around 15 per cent (only a degree or so more than wine), sake is a great accompaniment to meals and makes a versatile match for smoked and pickled food, such as tea-smoked oysters or ginger-pickled tuna, which can overpower wines. We chose a small selection for East @ West in London: the clean and crisp flavour of Kubota Senjyu, the lemony Kikusui Makantei and the full-bodied, viscous Tengumai Bunsei. Back in Sydney, at Universal, we stock Tosatsuru 'Azure' Ginjo-shu sake, with its distinctive blue bottle and pure, fresh taste with a dry finish.

The Buddhist ritual of Chanoya (the taking of tea) is a ceremonial affair, performed and hosted by a tea master who brews green tea, which is taken for relaxation, health and as a tonic. The focus is on simplicity and refinement, and the ceremony combines the art of ceramics, cooking, haiku (Japanese poetry), calligraphy and flower arrangement. Delicate sweetmeats are served to balance the naturally bitter taste of the green tea. Taking part in a traditional tea ceremony offers the perfect respite from the frenetic energy of Tokyo.

Tokyo is a treasure trove of secrets and surprises. The shopping is exceptional, the food is sublime, service is outstanding, the streets are clean, and the infrastructure is extraordinary. Japanese culture is complex and unique – even friends who have lived there for a long time continue to peel back the layers to discover yet another fascinating aspect. I long to return to this food-lover's paradise and explore further. Kyoto beckons.

STEAMED SEA URCHIN CUSTARDS

These ethereal custards in the style of Japanese chawan mushi must be served as soon as they are made. I use the purpose-made little porcelain bowls with fitted lids for cooking and serving them. The recipe makes eight small custards (two per person) using these cups; if you use larger vessels, increase the steaming time slightly.

200 ml Dashi Stock (see Essentials)
2 teaspoons sea salt
15 ml mirin
15 ml sake
2 teaspoons shiro (white) soy sauce
90 ml lightly beaten egg (about 1½ eggs)
12 large sea urchin roes, cut in half
1 tablespoon finely sliced green onion
2 teaspoons minced Pickled Ginger (see Essentials)
2 teaspoons finely chopped chives

Heat the dashi stock to simmering point, then season with salt, mirin, sake and soy sauce. Cool the liquid completely, then stir in the beaten egg. Don't whisk too much: you don't want air bubbles on the surface – the mixture should be smooth and even.

Divide the sea urchin roe and remaining ingredients equally among the cups, then ladle on the custard mixture until the cups are three-quarters full.

Place in a bamboo or metal steamer tray and steam, covered, over gently simmering water for 6 minutes. The custard should be just set and slightly wobbly in the centre when you gently shake the cup to test. To serve, cover each custard cup with its lid and serve immediately.

SERVES 4

SALMON AND NORI TEMPURA, GINGER BLOSSOM AND APPLE SALAD

An old favourite, this dish relies on incredible freshness and the symphony of textures and flavours. Other fish such as tuna, ocean trout, Hamachi or Hiramasa kingfish work just as well for the tempura.

4 roasted nori sheets
2 teaspoons wasabi paste
4 × 60 g salmon portions, cut from the middle of the fish into rectangular logs
2 teaspoons ponzu soy sauce
vegetable oil, for deep-frying
Tempura Batter (see Essentials)
4 teaspoons salmon roe

GINGER APPLE SALAD
1 green apple, sliced and cut into thin julienne strips
1 ginger blossom (myoga), finely sliced lengthways
1 small cucumber, peeled and cut into thin julienne strips
½ avocado, diced
2 teaspoons shredded Pickled Ginger (see Essentials)
2 green onions, finely sliced
1 punnet rocket cress, snipped
2 small fresh wasabi leaves, finely shredded
80 ml Sweet Ginger Dressing (see Essentials)

To prepare the salmon, lay out the nori sheets and spread with wasabi paste. Roll the salmon pieces in ponzu to season, then lay in the centre of the nori sheet and roll up to secure (trim the edges if necessary).

Heat the oil to 180°C. Dip the salmon nori rolls in tempura batter to lightly coat, then deep-fry for 1 minute exactly. Remove from the hot oil and drain on paper towel. Cut each salmon roll into three slices.

To make the salad, mix the ingredients together in a bowl, add the ginger dressing and toss gently to coat.

Arrange the salad on serving plates, sit the salmon slices on top and spoon on the salmon roe to serve.

SERVES 4

SALMON AND NORI TEMPURA, GINGER BLOSSOM AND APPLE SALAD >

HAMACHI TARTARE, PICKLED GINGER AND ROASTED SHIRO MISO

Hamachi is common in the northern hemisphere and prized in Japan, with a limited supply finding its way to London chefs with deep pockets. It's of the yellowtail family and closely related to Australia's Hiramasa, our premium-grade kingfish, organically farmed in the cold waters off the South Australian coast. Its dense and compact flesh make it ideal to serve as sashimi, tartare or tataki, rather than changing its unctuous character with unnecessary cooking. To show it to its best visual effect, I serve the tartare in elegant glassware.

2 tablespoons shiro (white) miso paste
250 g sashimi-grade Hamachi or Hiramasa fillet, skin and bones removed
120 g cooked Black-ink Noodles (see Essentials), cut into 5 cm lengths
2 tablespoons finely shredded yam bean
2 teaspoons shredded Pickled Ginger (see Essentials)
½ punnet daikon cress, snipped
2 red radishes, cut into fine julienne strips
2 green onions, sliced into fine rounds
½ punnet shiso cress, snipped
1 ginger blossom (myoga), finely sliced lengthways
1 tablespoon finely chopped chives
1 teaspoon black sesame seeds
1 teaspoon white sesame seeds, roasted
1 tablespoon finger lime pearls
1 tablespoon wasabi flying fish roe (tobiko)

TARTARE DRESSING
20 ml fresh lime juice, strained
20 ml Ginger Juice (see Essentials)
2 teaspoons Japanese rice vinegar
½ teaspoon Roasted Garlic Paste (see Essentials)
1 red shallot, minced
2 teaspoons fish sauce
2 teaspoons mirin
20 ml sunflower oil
40 ml extra virgin olive oil
¼ teaspoon freshly ground black pepper
50 ml Sweet-and-sour Pickle (see Essentials)

To toast the shiro miso, spread the paste in a thin layer on a baking tray lined with baking paper and leave in an oven for 3 hours with only the pilot light on (any more heat and it will burn). When the miso has dried enough and become toasty, crumble into small pieces and keep stored in an air-tight container until ready to serve.

To make the dressing, whisk all the ingredients together in a bowl until combined.

To prepare the fish, precision-cut the fillet into even 5 mm dice using a sharp knife. Add half the dressing to the diced fish and leave to pickle for 3 minutes while you assemble the salad.

Toss the noodle strips with the remaining ingredients, then add the fish tartare and some extra dressing to coat the salad. Arrange in glasses, top with crumbled roasted shiro miso and serve immediately.

SERVES 4

SPICY OCTOPUS WITH BLACK-INK NOODLES

Here I have adapted the principle of the Japanese sunomono (a salad dressed with rice vinegar), made it a more elaborate affair with the addition of noodles and turned up the heat a notch with a gently spiced dressing.

400 g large octopus tentacles, thoroughly rinsed under cold running water
2 tablespoons sea salt
2 teaspoons shichimi togarashi
½ teaspoon freshly ground black pepper
120 g cooked Black-ink Noodles (see Essentials)
½ punnet enoki mushrooms, trimmed
2 tablespoons finely shredded daikon radish
1 small cucumber, peeled, seeded and finely shredded
1 stick celery, shaved into tissue-thin slices on the diagonal
½ long red chilli, finely sliced
1 tablespoon chopped chives
½ punnet shiso cress, snipped
2 tablespoons mitsuba leaves
1 punnet onion cress (rock chives), snipped
½ punnet daikon radish cress, snipped

SPICY LIME DRESSING
2 teaspoons yuzu juice, strained
25 ml fresh lime juice, strained
50 ml shiro (white) soy sauce
25 ml fish sauce
2 teaspoons Ginger Juice (see Essentials)
1 teaspoon minced garlic
1 small red chilli, minced
1 teaspoon freshly ground black pepper
70 ml sunflower oil
2 teaspoons shellfish oil
1 teaspoon chilli oil

To cook the octopus tentacles, add the salt to 2 litres of boiling water and slowly lower the octopus tentacles into the water. Bring back to the boil then reduce the heat and simmer over very low heat for 30 minutes. The surface of the water should be gently ticking over, not rapidly boiling. Turn off the heat and leave the octopus in the water to cool.

To make the spicy lime dressing, whisk all the ingredients together until combined.

To make the salad, cut the octopus into thin round slices, season with the shichimi and pepper and toss with half the dressing. Leave to marinate for 15 minutes.

Mix the cooked noodles with the octopus, then add the remaining salad ingredients and dressing and toss to combine. Arrange the noodle salad on plates and serve immediately.

SERVES 4

SESAME MISO TOFU WITH GREEN BEANS AND SAMPHIRE

Tofu is a constant feature on our vegetarian menu, an ingredient that offers amazing diversity and possibilities for its preparation. I love it for its creamy texture and, when seasoned and deep-fried, it even manages to sway those who normally would not consider eating it. Fresh samphire is a seasonal sea vegetable which I love to use in many of my Japanese-inspired dishes.

300 g firm silken tofu, drained
20 ml ponzu soy sauce
1 teaspoon sesame oil
1 teaspoon chilli oil
20 ml Ginger Juice (see Essentials)
12 wild asparagus spears
160 g baby green beans, cut in half
100 g fresh samphire, picked
vegetable oil, for deep-frying
½ cup Chilli Salt Crust (see Essentials)
2 teaspoons white sesame seeds
1 teaspoon kinome leaves
1 teaspoon chopped chives

MISO DRESSING
2 tablespoons white sesame seeds, roasted
50 g shiro (white) miso paste
2 teaspoons Roasted Garlic Paste (see Essentials)
50 ml mirin
2 teaspoons castor sugar

To make the dressing, put half the sesame seeds in a mortar and pestle and crush to make a paste. Work the miso, garlic paste, mirin and sugar into the paste until smooth and thick.

To prepare the tofu, cut the block into 1 cm slices crossways and pat dry with paper towel. Mix the ponzu, sesame oil, chilli oil and ginger juice together in a bowl, pour over the tofu slices and leave to marinate for 2 hours.

Cut the stalks off the asparagus spears to make them the same length as the beans. Blanch the greens in boiling salted water for 1 minute then drain. Refresh in iced water and drain again. Combine with the miso dressing and samphire and toss until well coated.

Heat the oil in a large saucepan or wok to 180°C.

Mix the chilli salt crust, sesame seeds, kinome leaves and chives in a bowl. Remove the tofu slices from the marinade, then roll each slice in the mixture until lightly coated. Add the tofu slices, a few at a time, to the hot oil and deep-fry for 3 minutes until crisp. Drain on paper towel and continue with the remaining tofu.

To serve, arrange the beans, asparagus and samphire in the centre of each serving plate and sprinkle with the remaining roasted sesame seeds. Arrange the tofu slices on top and serve immediately.

SERVES 6

SCALLOP TATAKI, STEAMED SCALLOP ROE CUSTARD AND SEAWEED

The combination of flavours and textures in this dish is ethereal and elicits a wonderful response from everyone who tastes it.

10 large scallops
½ teaspoon sansho pepper
½ teaspoon freshly ground white pepper
1 teaspoon sea salt
20 ml sunflower oil
10 g hijiki (or arame) seaweed, soaked in warm water for 30 minutes, drained
40 g sesame seaweed salad
2 tablespoons fennel bulb shavings
1 small stick celery, finely sliced
2 green onions, finely sliced
½ punnet mizuna cress, snipped
Powdered Scallop Roe (see Essentials), for sprinkling
2 tablespoons shredded roasted nori seaweed
2 teaspoons Shiro Miso Flakes (see Essentials)
4 kinome leaves

SCALLOP ROE CUSTARDS
½ teaspoon minced ginger
1 teaspoon finely chopped chives
1 teaspoon Powdered Scallop Roe (see Essentials)
100 ml Dashi Stock (see Essentials)
1 teaspoon sea salt
1 teaspoon sake
1 teaspoon mirin
1 teaspoon shiro (white) soy sauce
50 ml lightly beaten egg (about 1 egg)

WASABI MISO DRESSING
20 ml sake
30 ml mirin
75 g shiro (white) miso paste
40 g castor sugar
2 teaspoons grated fresh wasabi
60 ml Japanese rice vinegar
1 teaspoon Ginger Juice (see Essentials)
½ teaspoon yuzu juice

To make the custards, place some minced ginger and chives in each of four sake cups, then add a sprinkling of the dried scallop roe powder.

Heat the dashi stock to simmering point, then season with the salt, sake, mirin and soy. Cool the liquid completely then stir in the beaten egg. Don't whisk too much: you don't want air bubbles on the surface – the mixture should be smooth and even. Pour the custard into the cups until they are full.

Sit the cups on a flat tray and place in a steamer over gently simmering water. Steam for 4 minutes until the custards are just set. Carefully remove from the steamer and leave to rest for a minute.

To make the dressing, bring the sake and mirin to simmering point and whisk in the miso. Bring back to boiling point and stir in the sugar. When the sugar has dissolved, remove from the heat and allow to cool. Whisk the cooled miso paste with the remaining ingredients until combined.

Remove the roes and intestinal tracts from the scallops. Mix the sansho, pepper and salt in a bowl, then roll the sides of the scallops in the pepper mix.

Heat the oil in a non-stick pan and sear the scallops on their seasoned sides, using tongs to roll. The entire cooking time should be 40–50 seconds. Do not lay the scallops on either of their flat sides as these should remain raw. Cut each scallop into four round slices – the seasoned edges will give the slices their definition. Arrange the scallop slices in a concentric circle in the centre of each plate.

Mix the hijiki with the seaweed salad, fennel, celery, green onion and mizuna cress. Add enough dressing to coat the salad, and toss to combine.

Arrange the salad on top of the scallops – do not completely cover them. Make a well in the middle of the salad, turn out the scallop custard and sit in the centre. Sprinkle with scallop roe powder, roasted nori and miso flakes. Lay a kinome leaf on top and serve.

SERVES 4

ASPARAGUS TEMPURA WITH GREEN TEA NOODLES AND LOTUS ROOT

A perennial favourite on our restaurant menus, this combination of vegetable textures captures the essence of Japanese cooking. If you prefer, slices of silken tofu or fish can be used instead of the asparagus.

80 g green tea noodles (cha soba)
olive oil, for tossing
½ fresh lotus root, peeled
120 g edamame, cooked and podded
1 tablespoon shredded Pickled Ginger (see Essentials)
½ small avocado, diced
¼ punnet soy bean sprouts, stems trimmed
2 tablespoons mitsuba leaves
1 punnet shiso cress, snipped
100 ml Soy Wasabi Dressing (see Essentials)
vegetable oil, for deep-frying
16 thin asparagus spears
Tempura Batter (see Essentials)
2 tablespoons Fried Leek Strips (see Essentials)

To cook the noodles, drop into boiling water with a pinch of salt and cook for 2 minutes until soft. Drain and refresh under cold running water, then toss through a little olive oil to prevent sticking.

To prepare the noodle salad, slice the lotus root into tissue-thin rounds using a mandoline. Mix the cooked noodles with the sliced lotus root, edamame, pickled ginger, avocado, soy bean sprouts, mitsuba leaves and shiso cress. Add the dressing and toss to combine.

Heat the oil in a wok or large saucepan to 180°C. Cut the stems off the asparagus spears to make 6 cm lengths. Coat the asparagus in tempura batter, shake off any excess and drop into the hot oil, a few at a time. Cook for 1 minute until the batter is crisp. Drain on paper towel and continue with the remaining asparagus.

Arrange some noodle salad in the centre of each serving plate and sit the asparagus tempura on top. Place the fried leek strips on top of the asparagus and serve immediately.

SERVES 4

SOY-GLAZED OCEAN TROUT AND TATSOI SALAD

This is one of my absolute favourite recipes over summer – so easy to prepare, with clean and distinct flavours that are a constant reminder of Japan.

20 ml vegetable oil
400 g piece ocean trout fillet, cut from the middle of the fish
20 ml sweet soy sauce (kecap manis)
20 ml light soy sauce
100 g small tatsoi leaves
3 sticks Asian celery, finely sliced
8 snowpeas (mange-tout), finely sliced
100 g bean sprouts, trimmed
3 green onions, finely sliced
2 small green chillies, finely sliced
1 tablespoon shredded Pickled Ginger (see Essentials)
1 bunch asparagus, sliced and blanched
1 avocado, finely diced
2 wasabi leaves, finely shredded
4 tablespoons coriander leaves
100 ml Soy Wasabi Dressing (see Essentials)

Brush a flat tray with the oil, cut the ocean trout into large chunks and brush the surfaces liberally with the sweet soy and soy sauces. Lay the fish on the tray and cook under a hot grill for 3 minutes until the fish is still rosy in the centre. Remove from the heat.

To make the salad, mix the remaining ingredients together in a bowl and toss with the soy wasabi dressing. Break the fish into flakes and gently mix through the salad.

Arrange the salad on serving plates, drizzle with any extra dressing and serve immediately.

SERVES 4

SESAME TUNA, AVOCADO AND CRESS SALAD

An easy-to-prepare salad that captures the essence of Japanese technique and taste. Regardless of season, it's always wise to have a salad like this in your repertoire for its clean and refreshing flavours.

350 g sashimi-grade bluefin or yellowfin tuna, trimmed
1 tablespoon sea salt
1 tablespoon freshly ground black pepper
1 teaspoon white sesame seeds, roasted
1 teaspoon black sesame seeds
20 ml vegetable oil

SESAME MISO DRESSING
20 ml light soy sauce
½ teaspoon sesame oil
20 ml Chinese black vinegar
¼ teaspoon chilli oil
1 tablespoon shiro (white) miso paste
20 ml mirin
20 ml Japanese rice vinegar
2 teaspoons fresh lime juice, strained
½ teaspoon freshly ground black pepper
250 ml vegetable oil

AVOCADO SALAD
1 punnet micro watercress
1 punnet chervil cress
1 punnet coriander cress
1 punnet shiso cress
1 large avocado, diced
1 small cucumber, finely sliced
4 green onions, finely sliced on the diagonal
1 long green chilli, finely sliced
2 teaspoons shredded Pickled Ginger (see Essentials)

To make the dressing, whisk all the ingredients together in a bowl until emulsified.

To prepare the tuna, mix the salt, pepper and sesame seeds together and rub into the tuna, then roll it in the oil.

Heat a frying pan and sear the tuna briefly to seal the sesame seasoning onto the surface. Remove from the heat and rest on ice for 30 seconds to stop the cooking process, then cut into thin slices.

To prepare the salad, snip the cress leaves and mix with the remaining salad ingredients in a bowl. Drizzle with enough salad dressing to wet. Add the tuna slices and toss to combine.

Arrange the salad on plates and serve with the remaining dressing.

SERVES 4

WAGYU BEEF TERIYAKI AND SESAME CUCUMBER SALAD

The premium grade of grain-fed beef is of paramount importance for the success of this dish. Wagyu is a current favourite in Australia, but other beef such as Kobe or the French Charolais works just as well as long as there is a discernible marbling of fat in the meat. A small portion of rich meat like this is all that is required to satisfy and thrill the tastebuds, and the clean flavours of the salad cut through the rich fattiness of the meat – making an ideal partnership.

320 g Wagyu (or similar) beef sirloin fillet, trimmed
80 ml Japanese dark soy sauce
40 ml mirin
30 ml sake
1 clove garlic, minced
1 teaspoon minced ginger
1 tablespoon demerara sugar
20 ml vegetable oil
1 small cucumber, peeled, seeded and finely diced
2 tablespoons finely diced daikon radish
½ red capsicum (pepper), finely diced
2 green onions, finely sliced
½ punnet daikon radish cress, snipped
½ punnet sorrel cress, snipped
2 teaspoons castor sugar
20 ml Japanese rice vinegar
½ teaspoon sesame oil
1 tablespoon white sesame seeds, roasted
2 tablespoons Fried Leek Strips (see Essentials)

To prepare the beef, slice the fillet into four portions crossways, to yield even medallions.

Combine the soy, mirin and sake in a saucepan and bring to the boil. Add the garlic and ginger and simmer for about 10 minutes until slightly reduced. Add the sugar and simmer for another 5 minutes until thickened and glossy. Allow to cool slightly.

Pour the sauce over the beef portions and leave to marinate for 10 minutes.

Heat the oil in a heavy-based frying pan or grill plate. Remove the beef from its marinade and cook over high heat for 2 minutes. Turn the meat over and cook for another 2 minutes until glazed. Remove the beef and leave to rest for 6 minutes.

Add the marinade to the pan and cook for 2–3 minutes until reduced. Pour the sauce over the meat.

Combine the cucumber, radish, capsicum, green onion, daikon and sorrel cress in a bowl, add the sugar, vinegar and sesame oil and toss well.

Slice each beef fillet into thin slices across the grain and arrange on serving plates. Spoon the cucumber salad on top of the beef and sprinkle with sesame seeds. Sit the fried leeks on top and serve immediately.

SERVES 4

WASABI-PICKLED HIRAMASA KINGFISH WITH SWEET GRILLED EEL

This is a magical combination of silky-textured kingfish (the prized Hiramasa from South Australian waters), the spicy heat of wasabi, the surprise citrus bursts from the pearls of finger lime and the luscious sweetness of grilled eel. The success of the dish lies in using premium-quality produce, dextrous knife skills and minimal cooking.

400 g Hiramasa kingfish (or Hamachi) fillet, skin and bones removed, cut from the middle of the fish
2 teaspoons Yamamoto wasabi oil
100 ml Soy Wasabi Dressing (see Essentials)
2 golden shallots, finely diced
60 g sesame seaweed salad
5 g dried arame seaweed, softened in warm water for 30 minutes then drained
2 tablespoons chopped chives
1 punnet shiso cress, snipped
1 tablespoon finger lime pearls
2 teaspoons wasabi flying fish roe (tobiko)
1 Japanese grilled eel fillet (unagi), cut into 4 pieces crossways
20 ml teriyaki sauce
8 green shiso leaves
6 tablespoons Sushi Rice (see Essentials)
2 tablespoons bonito flakes

Cut the kingfish into uniform fine dice with a sharp knife (this maintains the integrity of its texture).

Season the diced fish with wasabi oil then toss through the soy wasabi dressing with the diced shallots and stir to combine. Cover and leave to pickle for 20 minutes. Stand over a bowl of ice to keep cool.

When ready to serve, stir the sesame seaweed salad, arame seaweed, chopped chives, shiso sprouts, finger lime pearls and wasabi flying fish roe through the pickled fish.

Brush the eel fillet with teriyaki sauce and caramelise under a hot grill for 2 minutes.

Place two green shiso leaves in the centre of each plate to form a mat, spoon a mound of rice on top, then lay the grilled eel on the rice to cover it. Pile the fish on top neatly, sprinkle with bonito flakes and serve.

SERVES 4

TEA-SMOKED DUCK AND GINGER-PICKLED CHERRIES

Cherries have a short season in Japan and are a revered fruit. You'll often find that each cherry is individually wrapped in paper, making them appear like prized jewellery, with a price tag to match. The pickled cherries in this recipe are a perfect foil for the richness of duck and can also be served with slow-braised or roasted pork.

1 teaspoon sansho pepper
1 teaspoon freshly ground white pepper
2 teaspoons sea salt
2 duck breasts, trimmed
1 cup Tea-smoking Mix (see Essentials)
vegetable oil, for deep-frying
4 thin slices sourdough baguette, toasted
1 tablespoon Duck Liver Pate (see Essentials)
1 punnet swiss chard cress, snipped
1 punnet red garnet cress, snipped
1 punnet rocket cress, snipped
4 purple shiso leaves, torn
handful of dandelion leaves, trimmed
3 red shallots, finely sliced
2 red radishes, cut into fine julienne strips
80 ml Sweet Ginger Dressing (see Essentials)
2 slices speck (smoked bacon), cut into fine julienne strips and grilled until crisp

GINGER-PICKLED CHERRIES
200 ml Forum cabernet vinegar
50 ml Yamamoto sweet ginger vinegar
150 ml white wine (chenin blanc is ideal)
20 ml cherry liqueur
30 g ginger, finely shredded
100 g brown sugar
1 teaspoon sea salt
1 teaspoon freshly ground black pepper
400 g dark red cherries, pitted

To pickle the cherries, heat both the vinegars, wine, liqueur and shredded ginger and sugar in a saucepan to boiling point. Season with salt and pepper, reduce the heat and add the cherries. Simmer gently for 2 minutes then remove from the heat and allow the cherries to cool slightly in the liquid. Transfer to a jar, seal and refrigerate for a few days before using.

To tea-smoke the duck, mix the sansho, pepper and salt together and sprinkle over both sides of the duck fillets to season, reserving a little for later in the recipe. Lay the duck breasts on a steamer tray lined with baking paper, skin-side down, and cover the tray with a tightly fitting lid. Make sure the paper doesn't cover all the holes in the steamer as the smoke needs to have access. Line a wok with foil and place over high flame. Add the tea-smoking mix and when it starts to smoke (after about 30 seconds), sit the steamer tray with the duck over the wok and leave to smoke for 8 minutes. Open the lid, turn the duck breasts over, cover again and smoke for another 3–6 minutes or until the meat is cooked yet still medium–rare. Remove the duck from the heat. Allow the burnt tea mix to cool completely before discarding.

Heat the oil in a deep-fryer or wok to 180°C and fry the smoked duck breasts for 4 minutes until crisp. Slice the duck into thin slices across the fillet and sprinkle with the remaining salt and pepper mix.

Spread the toasted baguette slices with the duck pate and sit in the centre of each serving plate.

Strain 4 tablespoons of the pickled cherries from their liquid. Mix the strained cherries with the cress, leaves, shallots and radish. Mix 20 ml of the cherry-pickling liquid into the ginger dressing and stir to combine. Add enough dressing to the cress salad to season the leaves and toss gently to combine.

Arrange slices of smoked duck over the pate toasts then sit the cress salad on top. Drizzle with a little extra dressing and sprinkle the crisp speck on top. Serve immediately.

SERVES 4

CHOCOLATE CHERRY MERINGUE CLOUDS

This dessert is a tribute to the cherry blossom season, a highlight of the Japanese calendar that is cause for much celebration. This quantity will make 6–8 meringues, as it's too difficult to make the mix in a smaller quantity. I always make a few extra anyway so I can choose the very best-looking ones to serve. The meringues should be cloud-like in their texture, almost like biting into puffs of sweet air.

50 ml cherry liqueur
150 ml Sugar Syrup (see Essentials)
100 g Dark Chocolate Ganache (see Essentials)
250 g cherries, pitted
120 ml creme fraiche, lightly whipped
1 tablespoon icing sugar, sieved

MERINGUES
3 egg whites
pinch of salt
125 g castor sugar
2 teaspoons cornflour
½ teaspoon white vinegar
½ teaspoon vanilla extract

To make the meringues, whisk the egg whites and salt in an electric mixer until soft peaks form. With the beaters running, gradually add the sugar and continue to whisk until glossy and firm. Stir in the cornflour, vinegar and vanilla until just combined.

Preheat the oven to 100°C. Line ring moulds with baking paper and set them on a flat baking tray lined with baking paper. Pipe the meringue into the moulds and twist the piping bag to make little peaks on each meringue. Bake the meringues for 2 hours. Turn off the heat and leave the meringues in the oven to cool for a further 2–3 hours.

To make the syrup, heat the cherry liqueur and sugar syrup in a saucepan and simmer gently for 15 minutes until slightly reduced. Allow to cool completely before serving.

To prepare the cherries, put the chocolate ganache in a piping bag with a small round nozzle. Pipe the ganache into the pitted cherries.

To serve, unmould the meringues, peel off the paper and cut the top off each one about a third of the way down. Fill the meringue bases with creme fraiche and sit a few of the chocolate-stuffed cherries on top.

Spoon the cherry syrup onto plates, sit a meringue in the centre and scatter any remaining cherries around the meringue. Sit the meringue top over the cherries like a hat and dust with icing sugar to serve.

SERVES 6

SAUTERNES JELLY WITH MELON BALLS AND PRALINE

The melons in Japan are second to none; in fact, they are so precious they are individually wrapped in tissue for display and can fetch a very high price per kilo. The wine must be of premium quality in this dessert, so splurge and go for something spectacular. In the past I have made this with a 20-year-old Chateau d'Yquem and Muscat de Beaumes de Venise. In Australia, I go for something like Mount Horrocks Cordon Cut or Tempus Two's Noble Semillon – look for a wine that has good acidity and zestiness and is not overwhelmingly sweet or cloying on the palate.

375 ml sauternes
6 g gelatine leaves, softened in cold water, squeezed
1 sheet edible gold leaf
⅛ small watermelon
¼ rockmelon
¼ honeydew melon
¼ champagne melon
1 tablespoon mint cress, snipped (or tiny mint leaves)
2 tablespoons crushed Almond Praline (see Essentials)

Heat the sauternes until warm (you only want it hot enough to dissolve the gelatine), then stir in the gelatine. Allow to cool and just before it begins to set, stir through flecks of gold leaf so they are suspended in the jelly. Pour into glasses and refrigerate for about 4 hours until set. It may be necessary to stir the jelly just until it starts to set so the gold flecks remain properly suspended rather than floating on top or sinking to the bottom.

Scoop out small balls of each melon using a small parisienne cutter (melon baller). Mix together gently in a bowl with the mint cress.

Spoon the mixed melon balls onto the jellies, sprinkle with the crushed praline and serve.

SERVES 4

BLADE RUNNER UTOPIA CHINA

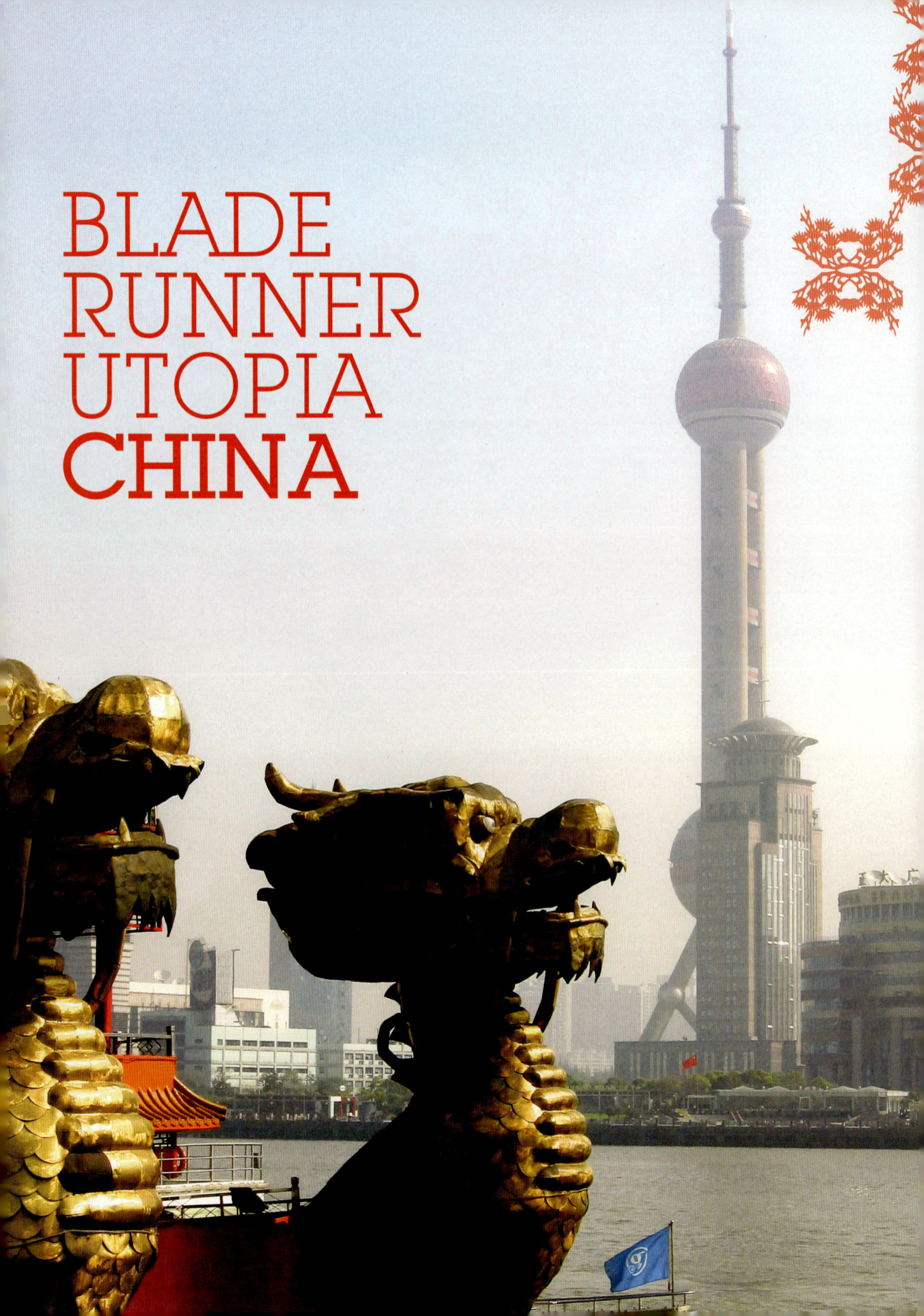

Arrive in Shanghai in the early evening and you will be completely dazzled by the postmodern neon landscape. After negotiating your way from the space-age airport into a taxi, you zoom into the city along a super freeway at breakneck speed through what used to be a vast swathe of crop fields and rice paddies. All around you, skyscrapers stretch for miles as you approach Puxi, on the western side of the Huangpu River, which is definitely the side where all the action is. You could opt for the Maglev (the bullet train from the airport) but it will only get you to the outskirts of Pudong, on the eastern side of the river, where you'll either have to find a taxi or take the metro to the city centre.

Shanghai has good bones; its bohemian charm provides a striking backdrop for the imposing architecture, a city wrapped in the emperor's new clothing. The level of development and construction beggars belief, and the skyline seems to change on a weekly basis. It is a city of contrasts and contradictions where the old is offset by the new. Sleazy opium dens have been transformed into elegant bars; the tea warehouses of Hongkou have become home to the latest modern art studios and galleries. For the most graphic contrast between old and new, stand in the historic Yu Gardens and peer across the ancient rooftops to see skyscrapers in every direction. The weather is something else again: the heat and humidity of summer makes even walking along the street a chore, while the icy winter adds a soft white veneer to the cityscape. I have braved both seasonal extremes, and could happily go with either.

I fell in love with this city the very first moment I arrived and the feeling intensifies with each visit. So much to see, so little time . . . Shanghai offers unlimited opportunities, it's just a matter of knowing where to start. Head first is always my rule! Any westerner who lives there or understands the culture will introduce you to the prevailing way of thinking: *TIC – This is China*, as a way of explaining the unexplainable or anything that doesn't happen quite as it should. It also explains why anything goes, why there are no limits. Before you know it, you'll be saying it yourself.

This is not a city for shrinking violets; it demands something of you. My usual practice when arriving anywhere is to check into a hotel, refresh with a shower then hit the streets, whatever the time is. Last time we went straight to the coolest bar in the French Concession: Face Bar, set in the grounds of the original 1920s Ruijin guesthouse with a sublime outdoor garden terrace. Other favourite haunts include Shintori for the ultimate design statement, People 7 Bar next door with its tricky entrance door – see if you can work it out – and the moody ambience of Manifesto Bar down the road. Of course it was the Glamour Bar at M on the Bund that paved the way for all these newcomers in the first place; the cocktails are of the moment and the atmosphere is electric, overseen by genial host, Bruno.

Getting to know the districts makes getting around easier. I always ask the hotel concierge to write the names of where I want to go in Chinese, then I carry a fistful of these cards around so I can show taxi drivers and (hopefully) not get too lost. If you're on foot, the maps are pretty easy to follow once you get your tongue around the unusual-sounding names. Shanghai central is based on the Puxi side of the river and there are six main districts to concentrate on. Foremost is the Bund, a broad boulevard that formed the heart of colonial Shanghai, its grandiose edifices facing the river. When you explore the back streets of this area, the echo of a bygone era prevails as you pass broken-down dusty doorways. This is a hive of activity – you can't miss the tangible energy, the pulsating beat. You have entered *Blade Runner* territory, a futuristic place that is hungry for both progress and survival.

Just south of the Bund across the Yan'an Dong Lu flyover is the Old City, also on the riverfront. Here you can catch a glimpse of how the city was originally constructed, with its beautiful gardens, bazaars, street markets and shikumen (tenements) between compact rows of houses. We have so many photos of unsuspecting friends walking along the streets through people's laundry hanging out on the footpaths – nothing like a pair of undies flapping in your face as you wait to cross the road. Not to mention the whole fish or gutted ducks that hang from hooks over the fence, being air-dried for later use. It's all unbelievably industrious; not an inch of space goes to waste.

STAYING IN SHANGHAI

88 XINTIANDI
380 Huang Pi Nan Lu, Shanghai
Tel +86 21 5383 8833
www.88xintiandi.com
Gorgeous boutique guesthouse in the redeveloped downtown area – great location that's within easy walking distance of every central district.

At the heart of the Old City lie the 18th-century Yu Gardens, with their massive rock sculptures and lily ponds full of carp. Just outside the gardens, across a zigzag bridge, the Huxin Ting Teahouse sits in the centre of an ornamental lake. Surrounding the lake is the Yu Gardens Bazaar, packed with restaurants and gift shops. Better-priced souvenirs can be found elsewhere but don't miss the Nan Xiang Steamed Bun Restaurant where you may witness the longest queue for food anywhere in the world. Most people are lining up for takeaway so if you decide to eat there, be brave, walk right past and go up the stairs to one of the three levels where you can sit and enjoy the signature xiao long bao (steamed Shanghai dumplings with their hidden liquid centres). On the way up we watched as three young girls shelled the tiny hairy crabs (da zha xie), each the size of a 50-cent piece, whose meat and roes are used as stuffing for the dumplings. The menu's quaint description of roe as 'crab ovaries' left my friend Jason feeling a touch apprehensive. Further upstairs, we observed four young cooks making dumplings, their hands moving like lightning as they stuffed and pleated the little pastry sheets into shape – a daunting task when you consider that each order has up to 12 dumplings on a plate, and they serve many thousands per day. This is one of the iconic restaurants of the city, a shrine to dumpling artistry. After stuffing our faces, we waddled around the narrow streets of the Old City past the antique markets and shopfronts along Fangbang Lu and Fuyou Lu to buy some fun souvenirs: Mao memorabilia, gorgeous little tea sets and colourful posters.

Shanghai is designed for retail therapy. The busiest strip along Nanjing Xi Lu to Nanjing Dong Lu has a mall that leads to the Bund from Renmin (People's) Square. The density of neon signs reminds me of Tokyo, and there seems to be stiff competition to see which shop can play the loudest and most distorted music. The fast and furious pace is a direct contrast to the early-morning rituals that take place in the local parks, where many people start the day practising tai chi or ballroom dancing. So calm and serene – then the spell is broken and the frenzy of activity takes over.

Pudong, on the other side of the river, is the new glitzy part of town, an emerging financial district that doesn't really do much for me. But getting there can be a blast! Just once, take a ride in the glass-walled capsules through the Bund Tourist Tunnel that goes under the Huangpu River. It's a total trip, a fantastic hallucinogenic light show that has to be seen to be believed. The other options are to catch the metro or jump on a ferry that crosses the busy river, dodging other ferries, ships, tankers and sampans (small boats). This is, after all, the busiest shipping and commercial port in China. If you have time to spare in Pudong, check out the Oriental Pearl Tower that houses the Shanghai History Museum in its basement (which is

EATING IN SHANGHAI

WHAMPOA CLUB
5th Floor, Three on the Bund (enter from Guangdong Lu), Shanghai
Tel +86 21 6321 3737
Chef Jereme Leung's postmodern Chinese food is sensational – his tasting menus are well considered and the lunch menu is a total indulgence.

1221
1221 Yanan Xi Lu (at Fanyu Lu), Shanghai
Tel +86 21 6213 6585
This place is hard to find (it's down an alleyway off Yanan Xi Lu) but once there, you'll enjoy terrific Shanghainese food with a modern twist.

DIN TAI FUNG
Taipei Steamed Dumpling House
2F House 6, South Block Xintiandi, Lane 123, Xinye Road, Shanghai
Tel +86 21 6385 8378
Go for the Shanghainese crab and pork steamed dumplings, the noodles with peanut and sesame, the fried rice with egg and shrimps, the double-boiled chicken soup with noodles, and the steamed cucumber with sesame and chilli oil.

NAN XIANG STEAMED BUN RESTAURANT
85 Yuyuan Lu, at Yu Gardens, Shanghai
At this perennial favourite there is always a long queue – mainly for the takeaway shopfront on street level. Go upstairs to sit down, but expect to wait. This is a shrine to dumplings.

GLAMOUR BAR
M on the Bund
6th Floor, 20 Guangdong Lu, Shanghai
Tel +86 21 6350 9988
The best-looking bar in town with terrific service under the watchful eye of manager Brùno and an interesting program of musical and literary events. Go upstairs to M on the 7th floor for lunch or supper served on the most glamorous roof terrace on the Bund.

worth a look) and marvel at the towering Jinmao Building with its futuristic pagoda shape. Then head straight back to where the action is.

Eating in this city is a dream – you'll find everything from the traditional to the regional, the experimental and international. The street food couldn't be fresher and all the ingredients are out on display. Some of the best street food can be found along Wujiang Lu just off Nanjing Xi Lu near Renmin Square – it's always crowded with locals so it's best to avoid peak eating times if you can. Try the clay-pot chicken or any of the noodle dishes – you can't really go wrong.

Shanghai boasts a world-class restaurant scene. If you're up for a treat, go to the Whampoa Club on the Bund for chef Jereme Leung's nine-course set lunch menu – a series of small dim sum-style treats served in succession rather than all together, as is the usual custom. Dinner is equally enticing: elegant morsels of smoked duck with lotus root; delicious pork ribs with Chinese five-spice; steamed prawn with ginger custard; or chilled noodle salad with freshly made tofu. Western chefs are also carving a place for themselves in the city; elegant restaurants like T8 and Laris are using local ingredients with interesting East–West interpretations. For me, being adventurous is part of the fun when travelling, and tasting new or reinterpreted dishes is something I love to do. On my first visit to Shanghai I was blown away by creations such as frogs legs with fennel pollen, beef and ginseng consommé and a salad of abalone and crisp pork. There are some fabulous restaurants that serve Shanghainese food with a modern touch. A local friend, Johnny, took us to one of his favourite haunts, a place called We Go (don't you just love the names?) where we ate a heavenly dish of steamed eggplant in a dark soy caramel-type sauce flavoured with black vinegar, together with dried shrimps soaked in Shaoxing wine and tossed with stir-fried minced pork and chilli. That has to be on the list of my all-time favourite eggplant dishes – I'm afraid no one else got much of a look in! Equally delicious was shredded pork stir-fried with soy, black vinegar and red chilli, and fermented bean curd served cold with shredded cloud-ear fungus, chilli and roasted peanuts.

A Shanghainese menu follows a certain order. Three or four 'cold' plates are served first, such as a shredded chicken salad with peanut sauce (think Bang Bang Chicken), a bean curd dish like the one I mentioned above, fresh soy beans (edamame) and a pickled vegetable. The hot dishes follow, all served together for communal sharing; there's always something with pork, and maybe prawns or crispy fish and duck. Vegetables are next (asparagus, Chinese broccoli or other greens) and they are usually steamed then served in a clear sauce that has been thickened with cornflour, followed by a clear broth or soup, then seasonal fruit. Rice is not customary for this sort of meal; it features more at breakfast when congee (a savoury rice pudding) is served. The traditional Chinese greeting 'Have you eaten rice yet?' should not be taken literally. Generally, there should be enough to eat without rice; indeed, the host may be considered to be lacking in generosity if rice is requested.

About one or two hours' drive west of Shanghai, you'll find the canal towns of Zhouzhuang, Tongli, Suzhou and Xitang, their streets draped with hanging willow trees. Built on water, they are like miniature versions of Venice. The 900-year-old village of Zhouzhuang, with its stone arched bridges and calm waterways, is now listed as a World Heritage site. Equally appealing and less crowded is Xitang, with its captivating covered walkways and ornate bridges, and some buildings that date back to the Ming dynasty. We chose to visit during the Dragon Boat Festival in June, which is celebrated by making zongzi, pyramid-shaped dumplings made of sticky rice, pork, lotus seeds and sweet sausage wrapped in banana leaf and steamed. I bought a bagful for a couple of dollars from one of the street vendors, and we munched happily as we searched for the perfect lunch stop. We settled on a modest place with views along the canal and ate some simply prepared fish and vegetable dishes. After lunch, we just went with the flow, not bothering with a map because you can always find your way out. We peered into tiny houses, seeing first-hand the life of these waterside dwellers. We stumbled on a place that made rice wine, so an impromptu wine tasting took place, making the drive back to Shanghai a bit of a blur.

China's cultural and political capital, Beijing, is just as beguiling as Shanghai, but in an entirely different way. The wide boulevards and sense of space make it a great walking city – although, having said that, it is a sprawling metropolis so it is essential to break it down into manageable areas. Just before summer hits, the dust storms blow down from the Gobi Desert and cover everything in a thick blanket of brown sandy dust. In summer, the city becomes stiflingly hot, which makes it difficult to get out and about with any real ease. And, as in Shanghai, the winter is bitingly cold with icy winds and lots of snow so the best months to visit Beijing are from September to December.

Beijing can keep you spellbound for days. I find the people incredibly friendly, approachable and helpful, and am enthralled by the array of interesting faces hailing from the north of China, the Mongolian border and from the remote north-west of the country. They do things big here and Tiananmen Square, the largest public square in the world, is no exception. It is packed with kite flyers, scammers, souvenir vendors (bargain hard!) and students who happily walk with you so they can practise their English – it takes an hour just to walk around its perimeter. There's the Mao Mausoleum with the imposing stone monuments to the People's heroes of the Long March in front, all presided over by an enormous portrait of Mao that sits high above the Gate of Heavenly Peace, which marks the entrance to the Forbidden City. Officially called the Palace Museum, this complex was the imperial palace of the emperors from the Ming and Qing dynasties, and it is impossible not to be overwhelmed by the scale of this most formidable place. Largely due to the foresight of political leader Zhou Enlai, it survived the ravages of the Cultural Revolution when many of Beijing's historical buildings were lost. The Forbidden City's courtyards and buildings boast fanciful names including the Palace of Earthly Tranquillity and the Hall of Mental Cultivation. Similarly elaborate descriptions are often used for traditional regional dishes, such as Sichuanese Fish with Strange Flavour, Yunnanese Rice Sticks Crossing the Bridge, and Jade Tree of Gold Coins. Perusing a menu in China can be akin to reading poetry.

To the south of Tiananmen, the Temple of Heaven is a must-see, with its marble terraces and impressive circular shape. Built during the Ming dynasty in the early 1400s, it shows that the architects of the time had incredible vision. An hour's drive from the centre of the city is the majestic Summer Palace, which was built as a retreat for the emperor's family so they could escape Beijing's summer heat. All pink and green, the palace temples and pavilions were built on a hill around a lake, surrounded by manicured gardens. It's an idyllic place to relax – no wonder the emperors loved it.

I think the most interesting parts of Beijing can be found by wandering down any of its remaining hutongs, the narrow lanes and alleyways that once criss-crossed the entire city. Many have been bulldozed in the rush to modernise, but pockets remain, including those in the historic Dongcheng district, just to the east of the city centre. A world away from the glitz and glamour of modern life, each hutong is a precinct and has a story to tell; they play a big part in bringing the traditional character and flavour of Beijing to life. We found steaming food stalls and bicycle vendors buzzing with activity (fantastic dumplings!), then moved on past all manner of industrious activity through these courtyard communities with their shops and services. Siheyuan are the traditional courtyard houses that form the walls of the hutongs, and many are now protected as cultural symbols. The lavishness of the gate – look for lots of red and gold – indicates the status of its inhabitants.

This is a city that celebrates its most prized delicacy – Peking Duck. Although it originated in the kitchens of the imperial court during the Yuan dynasty it only became available to the public after the fall of Qing (last) dynasty in 1911. Every time I come here, I try a couple of different places to find the ultimate rendition of this legendary dish, but my favourite remains Li Qun, buried in a maze of hutong off Qianmen Dong Dajie. The ducks are roasted in wood-fired ovens that burn fragrant apple-tree wood, and the kitchen is right by the entrance so you can watch the chefs while you wait for a table. We also ate a memorable eggplant dish here, braised in a hot bean sauce with chilli oil, garlic and ginger. It reminded me a little of the flavour and texture of ma po dou fu (which means pock-marked woman's bean curd!), a personal favourite that I order whenever I see it on a menu.

The regional restaurant culture in Beijing has really blossomed in recent years. Like any other big metropolis, the city attracts workers from rural towns or other cities who come to the big smoke to improve their earning capacity, so it is only natural that such a wide choice of food styles are on offer. Modern art is big in China,

STAYING IN BEIJING

RED CAPITAL RESIDENCE
9 Dongsi Jiutiao, Dongcheng, Beijing
Tel +86 10 8401 6152
www.redcapitalclub.com.cn
Quaint courtyard house in a local hutong that has been converted into a quirky boutique hotel. Its five rooms are small and all face the central open-air courtyard. The Bunker Bar in the basement is lots of fun – the whole place is themed on kitsch Mao memorabilia.

particularly in Beijing, and this preoccupation with all things modern flows through to its restaurants and their design. The downside is that design statements can sometimes outdo the food, turning fusion into confusion, but it's all part of the evolutionary process. We have happily eaten our way through several of China's regions at different restaurants here, from Yunnanese hot pots (perfect in winter when it's bone-chillingly cold outside) to the fiery western food of the Hunan and Sichuan provinces. Hunan was the home province of Mao and you will find dishes dedicated to him on some menus in Beijing – notably the Red Capital Club, with whimsical names that conjure up revolutionary images, such as Raising Red Lanterns (jumbo shrimp shaped like lanterns and bathed in a pungent spicy sauce).

Margie and I had a stand-out Sichuan dinner at Source, in a renovated courtyard house at the end of a narrow hutong. The passion and commitment to quality was evident the minute we arrived. With an emphasis on produce (much of it organic), the food is a modern interpretation of classic regional dishes. They offer one menu, a series of ten small tastes that can accommodate the vagaries of fussy eaters without skipping a beat. This is a seriously grown-up practice and one I applaud; I just love it when you can relax and trust the kitchen's direction and sensibility. We started with tiny pickled vegetables with toasted sesame seeds and chilli oil, then worked our way through the other courses: a chicken and tofu consomme; a couple of deliciously light raw vegetable salads (one with tiny river prawns, the other with smoked tempeh, black bean and chilli); melt-in-the-mouth braised chicken and mushrooms in a Sichuan pepper sauce that was steamed and presented in a bamboo tube; tangy noodles with ginger; an omelette and green onion cake to die for; then a little cast-iron hot pot of succulent pork, pumpkin and peanuts in an unctuous sweet and sour sauce. To finish, a waffle-like corn cake made from whole corn kernels cooked in an eggy yeast batter then drizzled with sugar syrup. To date, this has been my favourite food experience in China, and the restaurant's owner, Bing Bing, is as engaging and charming as she is modern.

Near the east wall of the Forbidden City is the Nanchizi area, and this is where you'll find the Donganmen Night Market, a row of food stalls lined up on the northern side of the street. The charcoal barbeques have an extraordinary array of things on sticks, including snakes and their peeled skins, crunchy crickets, tiny transparent white frogs, sparrows that look like miniature quail, and lamb kidneys encased in their fat. I settled on a plate of Beijing pot-sticker dumplings (jiaozi) filled with pork and green onion; some bean-skin pastry rolls with pork and cabbage; and little omelette rolls with vegetable stuffing. You can buy just a piece or a whole plate. Nearby Wangfujing Dajie is also great for grazing, and you can watch heavy, northern-style wheat noodles being made by hand as you eat.

The Great Wall is easy to get to from Beijing. Badaling to the north-west and Mutianyu to the north both have renovated parts of the wall that you can walk along for a few kilometres. Mutianyu has a cable car that zips you up to where the wall runs along the peaks of steep mountains and offers more panoramic views than Badaling. One summer, when travelling with Jason and a few other friends, we stayed at the Red Capital Ranch, a small eco-lodge at Yanxi, which is an ideal spot for exploring the wall and the Manchurian foothills. This part of the wall is in disrepair but can still be climbed – even though parts of it are very steep and can be pretty hard going, especially in the humid air. We started our climb early in the morning and ascended for a couple of hours, watching more and more Ming dynasty guard towers stretch enticingly into the distance. It's hard to believe the wall was built so long ago and we could only marvel at the magnitude of such an undertaking. Coming down is harder and more slippery than climbing up, and definitely not for the faint-hearted.

EATING IN BEIJING

SOURCE
14 Banchang Hutong, Kuan Jie, Dongcheng, Beijing
Tel +86 10 6400 3736
Some of the best food in town, with fabulous Sichuan food offered as a set menu. A revelation!

LI QUN
11 Beixiangfeng Hutong, Zengyi Road, Beijing
Tel +86 10 6705 5578
One of the oldest and best Peking Duck restaurants in town, located south-east of Tiananmen Square, in a tangle of alleyways that date back to the Ming dynasty. It's worth booking ahead.

Back on solid ground, lunch never looked so good! The village farms produce excellent honey, walnuts, chestnuts, almonds and root vegetables, and trout is fished from the river. These fresh ingredients were put together to create the healthy dishes served at the Ranch. Two stand-out salads I remember were yin yang salad (white and black fungus mixed with rice vinegar and sesame dressing) and another made with wild willow leaves tossed with tiny, freshly picked white almonds. The trout was simply grilled over a charcoal brazier and served with a salad of fresh bamboo shoots, chilli and vinegar. Perfect.

As a contrast, another time we drove out to Badaling in the depths of winter, to the most-visited part of the Great Wall – even with the icy winds and snow, there were plenty of tourists to dodge. We stopped off for lunch at the stunning Commune by The Great Wall near Shuiguan village, a private collection of twelve contemporary design houses (which are available as accommodation) – each the project of a prominent Asian architect. This exquisite place was masterminded by award-winning (Venice Biennale 2002) and dynamic property developer Zhang Xin; we were left speechless by her vision and its beauty.

The industrial city of Xi'an in the province of Shaanxi is not much to look at – the modern city was obviously built at a time when utilitarian Soviet-style design was the order of the day. About an hour out of town, though, is where thousands of Qin dynasty Terracotta Warriors stand guard in their excavated burial chambers – a spectacle that's well worth seeing. After we'd visited the warriors, Clarence (our guide) took us for lunch at one of his favourite haunts in Lintong, a town midway between Xi'an and the tombs. The food was fantastic: three types of dumpling (pork, spinach and mushroom); dry-fried green beans laced with sliced chilli and Sichuan peppercorns; thick Shandong noodles in a spicy meat broth; a clay pot of mutton; and fried rice with egg and sausage. Keen to walk off the excesses of lunch, we visited another nearby village, where cave houses have been carved into the mountainside near working coal mines. We were invited into one cave house and talked to a woman who was making a huge tray of vegetable dumplings, with her ancient mother at a bench behind her, rolling out the thin sheets of dough. She folded each sheet in half and pressed the edges together with three fingers to make indentations that resembled the notches in bamboo. Apparently, the dumplings would be boiled later and added to soup.

We returned to Xi'an and walked through the night markets in the Muslim Quarter, near the West Gate of the city wall. The side streets are lined with food stalls and we suddenly felt as if we were in a Moroccan medina. The Uyghurs are the minority Muslims in these parts, descendents of the invading Mongols during the times of Genghis Khan, and their presence is well represented in the food. We started with some lamb kebabs, choosing from the wide range on offer – squid, lamb with its fat, kidneys and thin beef slices (well, I think it was beef, but the Uyghurs are also known to use dog, donkey, ox, turtle – and fatty pork). There were bowls of turnip cubes fried with garlic and soy, which were clearly a popular choice; loads of people were perched on stools gobbling them down. As we stood around eating, we watched a couple of boys scraping lumps of dough with knives, making thick Shandong noodles that fell straight into the simmering mutton stock to cook. Many of the stalls were grilling freshwater crayfish – just like Australian yabbies – over charcoal.

Hanging like an earring from the Chinese mainland, the small island of Hong Kong is a cultural kaleidoscope and delivers slick style by the bucket load. Part of the city of the same name lies on Hong Kong island; the rest is

SLEEPING AND EATING AT THE GREAT WALL

RED CAPITAL RANCH

28 Xiaguandi Village, Yanxi Township, Huairou District, Beijing
Tel +86 10 8401 8886
www.redcapitalclub.com.cn/ranch.html
A sister property to Beijing's Red Capital Residence, this eco-tourism resort has a tranquil setting alongside an unrenovated section of the Great Wall. Its restaurant serves deliciously simple, locally sourced food – the vegetables dishes are particularly good.

COMMUNE BY THE GREAT WALL

Exit at Shuiguan, Badaling Highway, Beijing
Tel +86 10 8118 1888
www.communebythegreatwall.com/en
This prestigious property of 12 villas is a masterpiece of design. The Courtyard Restaurant's menu features authentic Chinese regional dishes.

on Kowloon, on the mainland that stretches to the New Territories and the southern province of Guangdong. The place is positively buzzing, challenging Shanghai for being the most gastronomically focused Chinese city. Hong Kong's restaurants showcase the finest of Cantonese, Chiu Chow, Shanghainese, Sichuan, Yunnanese and Hakka food, as well as international cuisines, and the city celebrates its food excellence with annual gourmet festivals.

The people of Hong Kong have exactly the right attitude towards food: it's so much more than mere sustenance. Wander along the back alleys of Wan Chai off Queens Road or off Lockhart Road a block from Wan Chai station and you'll see what I mean. There's the legendary joint that sells roast goose, soya goose and every other bit of the goose, including its intestines and webs. Barbeque pork is one of the city's essential tastes, especially when it's served with green onions, ginger and sesame sauce. You'll also find excellent dumplings, won tons and soups. Markets are dotted across the city and are an essential part of daily life. There's Sheung Wan market, Causeway Bay market (for seafood and poultry), Mong Kok flower market in Kowloon and many, many more. Temple Street night market, off Nathan Road near the Tin Hau Temple, is a tad touristy these days – a jumble of clothes, souvenirs, pirated CDs and fake watches. If you do find yourself there for any reason, stop off for a soul-warming hot pot at one of the hawker stalls at the northern end of the market.

The making of noodles is considered an art form here and the masters twist and throw their dough with aplomb. La Mien are hand-pulled noodles made from wheat flour that are stretched and pulled until they magically form a network of noodle strands. All types of noodles are appreciated here, and every place will serve one type or another. If you've never tried it, look out for XO sauce, a condiment specific to Cantonese food. It's made from finely chopped chillies and garlic cooked to a paste with shredded dried scallop (conpoy) and Yunnan ham – it's utterly addictive, and essential when eating dim sum.

Perhaps Hong Kong's greatest contribution to world food is dim sum or yum cha, a meal that consists of delectable snacks. Dim sum literally translates as 'touch the heart lightly', and taking dim sum is a daily ritual

EATING IN HONG KONG

TUNG'S KITCHEN
32 Lock Road, Tsim Sha Tsui, Kowloon, Hong Kong
A very local 'hole in wall' place that specialises in Chiu Chow food.

LIN HEUNG TEA HOUSE
160 Wellington Street, Central, Hong Kong
Tel +852 2544 4556
Can't go wrong here – a classic old dim sum house full of locals.

TAI HING ROAST GROUP
G/F, Shop 1–3, Cigna Tower, 470–484 Jaffe Road, Causeway Bay, Hong Kong
Tel +852 2577 7038
www.taihingroastgroup.com.hk
Classic Cantonese roast duck.

YUNYAN SZECHUAN RESTAURANT
4F Miramar Shopping Centre, 132–134 Nathan Road, Tsim Sha Tsui, Kowloon, Hong Kong
Tel +852 2375 0800
Order the sugared beef, spicy hot braised prawns and a fiery chicken noodle soup – great robust flavours that pack a punch.

HAN LOK YUEN
16–17 Hung Shing Yeh, Lamma Island, Hong Kong
Tel +852 2982 0680
Walk up the hill when you get off the ferry and look out for this humble courtyard in front of a house with soy-braised pigeons pegged on a clothesline, waiting to be roasted. It's a no-nonsense affair but this is where you come to eat the best pigeon. Start with a delicious sang choi bao while you wait. They stop serving when they run out of pigeons.

STAYING IN HONG KONG

THE PENINSULA
Salisbury Road, Kowloon, Hong Kong
Tel +852 2920 2888
www.peninsula.com
One of the world's grand hotels. Grab a room overlooking the spectacular harbour and have a drink at Philippe Starck's signature Felix Bar on the 28th floor before heading out to mingle with the locals and discover some brilliant street food.

GRAND HYATT
1 Harbour Road, Hong Kong
Tel +852 2588 1234
www.hongkong.hyatt.com
The best place to stay on the island – the pool terrace overlooking the harbour is a perfect afternoon retreat from the madness of the streets. The rooms are generous, as is the service that comes with the club rooms.

right across Hong Kong and in every city of the world where Cantonese people have settled. The array of dim sum is staggering and you choose by visual appeal and sometimes by aroma. I love it for this very reason – there is no menu and, because the plates are small, you can try so many different flavours. The ones I always look out for include cheung fen (rice noodle rolls stuffed with prawns, pork or mushrooms, then steamed and dressed with soy sauce and sesame oil); wu gok (deep-fried taro pastries with a sweet pork or chicken filling); cha xiu bao (steamed barbeque pork buns); har gau (steamed prawn dumplings with translucent wheat-starch pastry); fu pei gun (crisp bean curd rolls); and xiu mai (steamed dumplings with a pork, prawn and water chestnut stuffing). The list goes on and there always seems to be different interpretations at each place – the trick is finding one that does all your favourites! Jasmine or oolong tea is served with the food, and when your pot is empty, you simply remove the lid and rest it on the handle – a sign for a passing waiter to replenish with hot water. It is one of the most affordable feasts imaginable.

There is so much to China – so much to see, explore and experience. Next on my to-do list is a visit to Chengdu, capital of Sichuan province in the west, and Yunnan in the south-west. I want to taste some of my favourite food at its source and breathe in the aroma of Sichuan peppercorns drying in the sun. London-based food writer Fuchsia Dunlop, renowned for her knowledge of the fiery cuisines of Sichuan and Hunan, once gave me a big bag of the freshest Sichuan peppercorns I had ever seen; every time I opened the jar, the air became heavy with their spicy fragrance and my cooking had that extra magical kick.

SHORT AND LONG DUCK SOUP

This easy-to-make soup is inspired by the hundreds of shopfronts with their bronzed and lacquered roast ducks on display in the window. Roast ducks have become something of a national symbol for China throughout the world. Every self-respecting city has similar shops and this certainly takes the hard work out of cooking – just zip down to your local barbeque shop and take it from there.

120 g egg noodles, cooked
2 green onions, finely sliced on the diagonal
1 teaspoon sesame oil

DUCK SOUP
1 Chinese roast duck
6 green onion tops, chopped
6 slices ginger
4 dried shiitake mushrooms
1.6 litres White Chicken Stock (see Essentials)
75 ml light soy sauce
1 teaspoon white peppercorns, cracked

WON TONS
1 teaspoon vegetable oil
2 teaspoons minced ginger
2 green onions, finely sliced
100 g fresh shiitake mushroom caps, finely sliced
2 teaspoons finely sliced chives
¼ teaspoon freshly ground white pepper
20 ml oyster sauce
16 won ton wrappers
rice flour, for dusting

To make the soup, remove the meat and crisp skin from the duck, and discard any fat.

Cut the leg and thigh meat into fine dice and set aside for the won ton stuffing. Cut the breast fillets into thin slices.

Place the duck carcass and bones in a large stockpot with the remaining soup ingredients and bring to the boil. Reduce the heat and simmer gently for 1 hour, skimming the surface occasionally to remove any sediment and fat.

Remove from the heat and pass through a fine mesh sieve, then a double layer of muslin to remove all sediment traces. Discard the solids. Bring the soup back to simmering point, taste and adjust the seasoning if necessary.

To make the won tons, heat the oil in a frying pan and gently fry the ginger, green onion and mushrooms until softened. Remove from the heat and allow to cool.

Mix the chopped duck meat with the mushroom mixture and chives, and season with pepper and oyster sauce.

Lay the won ton wrappers on a bench, a few at a time (keep the rest covered as you work). Put a teaspoon of the filling into the centre of each wrapper, brush the edges with water so they stick, then fold over to form a triangle. Fold the pointed edges in and stick together to make little tortellini-shaped won tons. Sit the prepared won tons on a flat tray dusted with rice flour until ready to cook.

Bring a large saucepan of water to the boil, then reduce the heat slightly. Add the won tons and cook for 2 minutes until soft and heated through. Remove from the water with a mesh spoon or spider and transfer directly into serving bowls.

Add the cooked noodles to the bowls with the sliced duck breast, then ladle on the hot soup and swirl with a chopstick. Add a few green onion slices and a few drops of sesame oil and serve immediately.

SERVES 4

CHICKEN PEARL BALLS

These dim sum-style snacks make a great party bite or canape. I like to serve them with a spicy plum sauce that I make by the litre when blood plums are in season toward the end of summer. It stores well in the refrigerator for use throughout the year.

1 cup white sticky rice
750 g minced chicken
1 egg, beaten
2 teaspoons light soy sauce
2 teaspoons fish sauce
1 teaspoon sea salt
1 tablespoon cornflour
1 tablespoon minced ginger
10 fresh shiitake mushrooms, stems discarded, caps finely diced and softened in a little oil with minced garlic
12 fresh water chestnuts, finely diced
½ cup coriander leaves, chopped
3 green onions, finely sliced

SPICED BLOOD PLUM SAUCE
250 ml Sugar Syrup (see Essentials)
8 blood plums, quartered
180 ml fish sauce
5 star anise, broken
1 cinnamon stick
1 teaspoon cracked Sichuan peppercorns
50 ml fresh lemon juice, strained
30 ml rice vinegar

To make the sauce, heat the sugar syrup in a saucepan to boiling point, then add the plums, fish sauce and spices. Cook over moderate heat for about 20 minutes until it has reduced slightly. Remove from the heat, add the lemon juice and vinegar and pass through a fine mesh sieve, discarding the solids. Keep the sauce refrigerated in sealed jars until ready to use.

Soak the rice in plenty of cold water for 6 hours, then strain and lay on a flat tray lined with a tea towel to dry out.

Work the chicken and remaining ingredients together in a bowl to thoroughly combine, slapping the mix against the sides of the bowl to help tenderise the meat and make it more succulent. With wet hands, roll the mixture into balls (about a flat tablespoon for each).

Roll the balls in the softened rice grains, pressing firmly as you go, to coat the balls properly.

Line a steamer tray with baking paper and place the chicken balls on the paper. Cover and steam for 25 minutes until cooked and the rice has puffed up.

Heat the sauce in a saucepan until warmed through and serve with the pearl balls.

SERVES 8–10 AS A CANAPE

SWEET AND SOUR CHICKEN WITH PERSIMMON SALAD

This salad is one of my dependable backups that I throw together when cooking at home. In true Chinese tradition, it pays respect to premium-quality ingredients and its flavours are clean and light. If persimmons are not in season, use cape gooseberries or even avocado.

500 ml White Chicken Stock (see Essentials)
200 ml light soy sauce
2 tablespoons Shaoxing rice wine
2 tablespoons fish sauce
1 green onion, sliced
4 slices ginger
1 red chilli, sliced
2 free-range, organic chicken breasts

SWEET AND SOUR CHILLI DRESSING
75 ml vegetable oil
2 cloves garlic, sliced
2 red bird's-eye chillies, sliced
2 dried small chillies, crushed
60 ml light soy sauce
100 ml cider vinegar
150 ml Sugar Syrup (see Essentials)
40 ml Sweet Chilli Sauce (see Essentials)
2 teaspoons Chilli Jam (see Essentials)

SALAD
1 persimmon, sliced lengthways
80 g bean sprouts
16 snowpeas (mange-tout), blanched
4 green onions, finely sliced
1 long red chilli, finely sliced
½ small cucumber, sliced
½ cup Asian or Thai basil leaves, torn
100 g small tatsoi or rocket leaves
2 tablespoons Fried Shallot Slices (see Essentials)

To make the dressing, heat the oil with the garlic, chilli and dried chilli over gentle heat. Add the soy sauce, vinegar and sugar syrup and simmer gently for 10 minutes. Remove from the heat and strain, discarding the solids. Stir in the sweet chilli sauce and chilli jam.

To cook the chicken, put all the ingredients except the chicken in a saucepan and bring to the boil.

Add the chicken, simmer for 2 minutes then turn off the heat, cover and leave for 45 minutes. During this time the chicken will cook and remain tender. Remove the chicken and discard the broth. Shred the chicken into thick strips.

To make the salad, mix the ingredients (except the fried shallot slices) together in a bowl and add the chicken and enough dressing to wet the salad. Mix thoroughly with your hands, then arrange the salad on serving plates. Sprinkle with fried shallot slices.

SERVES 4

PRAWN, TOFU AND EGGPLANT FRITTERS

Inspired by dim sum snacks where bean curd or eggplant is stuffed with prawn paste, I adapted the idea to make these delicious sandwiches. They can also be made as bite-size canapes – just cut out smaller rounds from the eggplant.

2 × 200 g eggplants (aubergines)
beaten egg, for dipping
vegetable oil, for deep-frying
1 punnet coriander cress, snipped

PRAWN PASTE
40 ml vegetable oil
6 cloves garlic, minced
3 green bird's-eye chillies, minced
1 tablespoon coriander roots, minced
2 teaspoons freshly ground white pepper
50 ml fish sauce
6 green onions, sliced into fine rounds
3 tablespoons coriander leaves, finely shredded
500 g raw prawn meat, diced
200 g bean curd, drained

To make the prawn paste, heat the oil in a wok and fry the garlic, chilli, coriander root and pepper for about 30 seconds until fragrant. Add the fish sauce and toss over heat for a few seconds to combine. Remove from the heat and cool, then stir in the sliced green onion and shredded coriander. Blend the prawn meat and bean curd to a paste in a food processor. Add the spice base and blend until smooth.

Cut the eggplant into 1 cm thick disks crossways, then cut out small rounds using a 4 cm pastry cutter (you will need two rounds for each fritter). Discard the scraps.

Sandwich two eggplant slices with the prawn paste, smooth the edges with a palette knife, then dip in the beaten egg.

Heat the oil in a wok or deep-fryer to 180°C and deep-fry the stuffed eggplants for 4 minutes until crisp and golden. Serve immediately, topped with a few sprigs of coriander cress.

SERVES 8

CLAY-POT CHICKEN RICE

This is one of those one-pot numbers that is hassle free and can be put together in no time at all. It's a great standby during winter when the warming flavours nourish and comfort.

2 chicken breasts, cut into cubes
2 cups jasmine rice, washed
750 ml White Chicken Stock (see Essentials)
1 Chinese sausage (lap cheung), sliced
8 fresh shiitake mushrooms, sliced
1 tablespoon minced ginger
2 green onions, finely sliced
4 tablespoons chopped coriander leaves

CHICKEN MARINADE
40 ml sunflower oil
60 ml oyster sauce
40 ml light soy sauce
20 ml dark soy sauce
20 ml Shaoxing rice wine
1 teaspoon sesame oil
1 teaspoon chilli oil
2 teaspoons castor sugar
½ teaspoon freshly ground white pepper
1 tablespoon cornflour
40 ml XO Sauce (see Essentials)

Combine the marinade ingredients and pour over the chicken meat, mixing well with your hands to ensure the meat is well covered.

Put the rice in a clay pot with the chicken stock, cover and cook over low heat for 20 minutes.

Spread the marinated chicken, sausage, mushroom slices and minced ginger over the top of the rice. Cover and cook for a further 12–15 minutes until the rice and chicken are cooked.

Remove from the heat, taste and adjust the seasoning if necessary – it may require a pinch of sea salt. Sprinkle the green onion slices and coriander over the top and serve.

SERVES 4

STIR-FRIED HONEY SESAME BEEF

This became one of our 'star' bar bites at the London restaurant, a firm favourite with the drinkers and bar diners. Instead of serving it with rice, we added slippery rice noodles with the beef as it was frying, so you have that option as well.

4 cloves garlic, minced
40 ml light soy sauce
20 ml fish sauce
1 teaspoon sesame oil
2 tablespoons light honey
1 teaspoon freshly ground black pepper
3 red bird's-eye chillies, minced
40 ml vegetable oil
500 g beef tenderloin fillet, thinly sliced
120 g green beans, cut into 2 cm lengths and blanched
2 teaspoons white sesame seeds, lightly roasted
2 handfuls watercress sprigs
1 bunch garlic chives, cut into 5 cm lengths

In a bowl, mix together the garlic, soy sauce, fish sauce, sesame oil, honey, pepper and chilli with half the vegetable oil. Add the beef slices, mix well and leave to marinate for 1 hour.

Heat a large wok, add half the remaining oil then throw in half the beef and marinade with half the beans and toss over a high heat so that the beef sears and cooks quickly (use chopsticks to keep the beef strips separated). Remove from the wok and repeat with the remaining beef and beans – if you cook it in one go, the beef stews and loses its desired texture.

Sprinkle the sesame seeds, watercress and chives over the beef and serve with steamed rice, or spoon into small iceberg lettuce cups in the style of sang choi bau.

SERVES 4

< CLAY-POT CHICKEN RICE

BANG BANG CHICKEN WITH SHANGHAI NOODLES

You just have to love a dish with a name like this! Originally from Sichuan, it is served as one of several cold dishes, a traditional start to any Sichuanese meal. It also pops up on London's chop house and pub bistro menus, where it has transmogrified into cold meat with a satay-style peanut sauce. Some versions serve the chicken with bean thread noodles but I have chosen to use the thicker, worm-like Shanghai noodles. Use chicken thigh fillet as the darker meat holds its own with the full-flavoured sauce.

500 g chicken thigh fillets
1.5 litres White Chicken Stock (see Essentials)
2 teaspoons white sesame seeds, roasted
2 teaspoons sesame oil
200 g cooked Shanghai noodles
2 small cucumbers, peeled and sliced into ribbons lengthways
4 green onions, cut into fine slivers
1 long red chilli, seeded and finely sliced lengthways
½ cup coriander leaves
1 cup watercress sprigs

SESAME SAUCE
40 ml vegetable oil
½ teaspoon Sichuan peppercorns
3 tablespoons Chinese sesame paste
1 tablespoon hot bean paste
2 teaspoons Chinese hot chilli sauce
1 teaspoon sesame oil
2 cloves garlic, peeled
1 teaspoon chopped ginger
20 ml light soy sauce
40 ml Chinese black vinegar
20 ml Shaoxing rice wine
75 ml White Chicken Stock (see Essentials)
1 tablespoon castor sugar

To cook the chicken, heat the stock in a saucepan to boiling point, add the chicken, cover with a lid and remove from the stovetop. Leave the chicken to cook slowly in the hot stock until the stock has cooled. Remove the chicken from the cooled stock and shred the meat with your fingers. Toss with the sesame seeds and sesame oil to coat.

To make the sesame sauce, heat the vegetable oil in a pan and fry the peppercorns until fragrant.

Remove from the heat and allow to cool. Remove the fried peppercorns from the oil and grind to a powder. Reserve the oil.

Place the remaining sauce ingredients in a food processor and blend to make a smooth paste. Add the cooled oil and ground pepper, and pulse until combined. Set aside until ready to serve.

Cook the noodles in a saucepan of boiling water for 2 minutes or until softened. Drain, refresh under cold running water and drain again.

Toss the chicken with enough sauce to coat, then toss through the noodles and the remaining salad ingredients, adding enough sesame sauce to coat the salad. Arrange the salad in bowls in a loose pile to show its various textures, and serve with extra sauce in a small bowl to the side.

SERVES 4

SPICE-ROASTED SQUAB WITH TURNIP CAKE

Each component in this dish can be cooked and served individually – they are complete in themselves. However, my penchant for combining different elements to create a harmony of complex flavours and textures saw this dish evolve into something quite detailed, yet elegantly simple on the plate. Don't confuse Chinese turnips with daikon, which has the wrong texture for this recipe. Chinese turnips have a similar shape to daikon but with a firmer texture, a blush of pale green on its skin near the top and a noticeable pungent aroma. They can be elusive so if you can't find them, the small purple-skinned, white-fleshed sweet potato work extremely well and are always available from Asian food stores.

2 litres Chinese Master Stock (see Essentials)
4 squabs
vegetable oil, for deep-frying
1 teaspoon Sichuan Spice Salt (see Essentials)
Tempura Batter (see Essentials)
4 squab livers, trimmed

STEAMED TURNIP CAKE
20 g dried prawns
2 dried shiitake mushrooms
500 g Chinese white turnips, peeled and grated
20 ml vegetable oil
100 g Chinese sausages (lap cheung), steamed whole for 10 minutes, then diced
2 green onions, finely sliced
½ long red chilli, finely sliced
2 teaspoons brown sugar
2 teaspoons Shaoxing rice wine
1 teaspoon sea salt
½ teaspoon freshly ground white pepper
150 g rice flour
1 tablespoon chopped coriander leaves
1 tablespoon white sesame seeds, roasted
200 ml White Chicken Stock (see Essentials)
vegetable oil, extra, for frying

STAR ANISE BROTH
500 ml Game Stock (see Essentials)
1 star anise, cracked into small pieces
1 teaspoon dried bonito flakes
2 green onions, sliced
3 slices ginger
2 dried shiitake mushrooms
1 small piece cassia bark
1 teaspoon finely grated orange zest
50 ml light soy sauce
30 ml Shaoxing rice wine
40 ml mirin
120 ml Sweet-and-sour Pickle (see Essentials)
20 ml Sugar Syrup (see Essentials)
few drops of sesame oil

SQUAB AND CABBAGE DUMPLINGS
80 g Soy-braised Pork (see Essentials), chopped into fine dice
2 Chinese cabbage stalks (white part), finely diced
1 tablespoon Garlic Pepper Paste (see Essentials)
20 ml fish sauce
1 tablespoon shredded Asian or Thai basil leaves
4 large Chinese cabbage (wombok) leaves (green part only), softened in boiling water >>

<< To make the turnip cake, oil a 12 cm square tin and line with baking paper. Soak the dried prawns in boiling water for 45 minutes, then drain and chop finely. Do the same for the dried mushrooms, removing the stems before chopping. Reserve 50 ml of the mushroom water. Mix the chopped prawns and mushrooms together.

At the same time, put the grated turnip in a bowl, cover with boiling water and soak for 15 minutes. Drain in a colander then squeeze out the excess water until dry.

Heat a wok, add the oil and fry the diced sausage for a minute. Add the prawn and mushroom mix and fry for another minute until fragrant. Stir in the green onion, chilli, sugar, Shaoxing wine, salt and pepper, then add the grated turnip and toss to combine. Stir through the rice flour, coriander and sesame seeds.

Remove from the heat and pour in the hot stock and reserved mushroom water. Stir to combine – the mixture should be quite firm and hold together. Add a little more water if too stiff or a little more rice flour if too sloppy to get the right consistency. Transfer the mixture to the tin and press so it is of uniform height and density (it should be no more than 3 cm high otherwise the cooking time will be affected).

Place the tin on a tray in a bamboo steamer basket, cover and steam over simmering water for 1½ hours until firm. Remove from the heat and allow the cake to cool in the tin. Place in the refrigerator for 5 hours before serving.

When ready to serve, turn the cake slab out onto a board and cut into four 5 cm squares.

Heat some oil in a pan and fry the cakes for 2 minutes until crisp and golden, then flip over and cook the other side for 1 minute.

To make the broth, put all the ingredients in a large saucepan and bring slowly to a simmer. Cook gently for 45 minutes – do not allow to boil. Strain through a fine mesh sieve and discard the solids. Reheat gently when ready to serve.

To prepare the squabs, heat the master stock in a large saucepan and when it reaches simmering point, add the squabs. Turn off the heat and leave the squabs in the hot stock for 5 minutes.

Remove and drain on paper towel. Reserve the stock for later use.

Cut the leg and thigh joints from each carcass, then debone and finely dice. Set the squab carcasses (with breast fillets attached) aside until ready to serve.

To make the squab and cabbage dumplings, mix the diced squab legs, pork and cabbage stalks with the paste, fish sauce and basil leaves until thoroughly combined.

Lay the cabbage leaves on a bench and spoon the squab stuffing onto the centre of each leaf. Roll up, folding in the sides to secure, making small, uniform parcels that are similar in shape to the turnip cakes. Lay the dumplings in a single layer on a plate, seam-side down, and steam for 4 minutes when ready to serve.

Heat the oil in deep-fryer or wok to 180°C and fry the squabs for 5 minutes until crisp, giving the skin a lacquered appearance. Drain on paper towel and rest for 3 minutes before carving.

Carve the breast fillets from each carcass, slice each fillet in half crossways and season with Sichuan spice salt. Season the tempura batter with Sichuan spice salt, then coat the squab livers in the batter and fry in hot oil for 2 minutes until crisp. Drain on paper towel.

To assemble, sit a fried turnip cake in the centre of each plate and top with a steamed cabbage dumpling. Spoon on the star anise broth. Arrange the squab breast slices on the dumpling, sit the tempura liver on top and serve.

SERVES 4 (OR 8 AS A SMALLER TASTE)

PORK RICE PORRIDGE

Jook is a traditional Chinese breakfast dish, hearty and comforting. It's the Chinese equivalent of Scottish-style porridge, but with a more savoury note. I worked the idea into a more substantial offering when I was matching Asian food flavours and dishes to a Rymill MC2, a Coonawarra red wine that's made in the style of Tuscan Chianti by its winemaker John Innes. The creamy silky consistency, succulent pork shreds, the hint of heat with the chilli oil, the smokiness from the Chinese ham (or black bacon) and the astringency of pickled carrots were picked up beautifully by the wine. An optional extra would be the addition of finely diced 100-year-old egg (which can be purchased from any Chinese food store).

200 g medium-grain rice, washed in cold water and drained
500 g pork belly, cut into 4 large chunks
50 g Chinese black bacon, finely sliced
2 litres cold water
sea salt and freshly ground white pepper
1 tablespoon finely sliced ginger
20 ml chilli oil
2 teaspoons sesame oil
50 ml light soy sauce
2 green onions, sliced
2 iceberg lettuce leaves, finely shredded
2 tablespoons salted roasted peanuts, chopped
2 tablespoons coriander leaves
2 teaspoons XO Sauce (see Essentials)

Preheat the oven to 160°C. Combine the rice, pork, bacon and water in a large ovenproof pan and bring slowly to the boil, skimming occasionally. Reduce the heat to a gentle simmer and cover. Transfer to the oven and simmer gently for 2 hours, stirring occasionally to prevent sticking, until the rice grains have virtually dissolved and the pork is tender.

Remove from the oven and take out the pork. Discard the skin and finely shred the meat. Return the pork to the rice with salt and pepper to taste and half the ginger, then simmer on the stovetop for 10 minutes. Stir in the chilli oil, sesame oil and soy sauce, taste and adjust seasoning if necessary.

Ladle into deep bowls. Sit the remaining ingredients on top in the centre, adding the XO sauce last, and serve.

SERVES 4

BREASTS, LEGS AND PINK BITS

This always brings a few smirks when it's written on a menu – it sounds so much more seductive than 'three ways with duck'! I first introduced this for a Moet et Chandon champagne dinner at Pearl Restaurant in Melbourne with chef owner Geoff Lindsay. The idea is quite simple: I prepare the different parts of the duck in their own manner and then create a layered effect when constructing on the plate, hiding the pink livers or foie gras between the slices of tea-smoked breast and duck-neck sausage (made from leg meat).

1.8 kg Aylesbury or Barbary duck
Sichuan Spice Salt (see Essentials)
Tea-smoking Mix (see Essentials)
vegetable oil, for deep-frying
2 teaspoons shaved palm sugar
20 ml coconut cream
2 teaspoons fish sauce
2 teaspoons Tamarind Liquid (see Essentials)
small pinch of chilli powder
120 g foie gras, cut into 4 even slices

DUCK-NECK SAUSAGE
20 ml vegetable oil
1 teaspoon sesame oil
1 tablespoon minced brown onion
2 teaspoons minced garlic
1 teaspoon minced ginger
1 small red chilli, minced
¼ teaspoon Sichuan peppercorns, roasted and ground
½ teaspoon fennel seeds, roasted and ground
½ teaspoon cumin seeds, roasted and ground
2 tablespoons finely diced fennel
2 tablespoons finely shredded cloud-ear fungus
1 teaspoon chopped thyme
4 fresh water chestnuts, blanched and finely diced
leg and thigh meat from the duck, minced
50 g pork fat, coarsely minced (ask your butcher to do this for you)
1 teaspoon sea salt
½ teaspoon freshly ground black pepper
600 ml White Chicken Stock (see Essentials)

SPICED ORANGE SAUCE
2 teaspoons vegetable oil
½ teaspoon sesame oil
300 g chicken giblets
1 tablespoon Chilli Turmeric Paste (see Essentials)
1 teaspoon minced Seville orange zest, blanched
4 cloves garlic, sliced
1 small brown onion, finely chopped
2 red bird's-eye chillies, minced
1 teaspoon minced ginger
100 ml Tamarind Liquid (see Essentials)
250 ml Seville orange juice (simmered until reduced to 125 ml)
50 ml soy sauce
50 ml fish sauce
50 ml Shaoxing rice wine
100 ml tawny port, flamed
1 litre Duck Stock (see Essentials)
60 g palm sugar, shaved

SPICED EGGPLANT
2 × 200 g eggplants (aubergines)
vegetable oil, for deep-frying
1 teaspoon chilli oil
1 teaspoon minced garlic
½ teaspoon minced red chilli
1 teaspoon minced ginger
2 red shallots, finely sliced
2 tablespoons salted yellow beans
35 g yellow rock sugar, crushed
20 ml light soy sauce
20 ml dark soy sauce
20 ml Shaoxing rice wine
40 ml rice vinegar
2 teaspoons fish sauce
½ teaspoon Sichuan peppercorns, roasted and ground
2 green onions, finely sliced
60 g bean sprouts, trimmed

To prepare the duck, remove the breast fillets from the duck, trim where necessary and season lightly with Sichuan spice salt. Set aside for 30 minutes. Preheat the oven to 180°C.

Remove the leg and thigh joints, then take the meat from the bone. Mince the leg and thigh meat.

Cut the neck from the duck and remove its centre so you are left with the skin, cleaning the inside to remove fat and sinew.

Place the carcass, neck off-cuts and bones in a baking dish and roast for 40 minutes until brown. Make a duck stock with the roasted bones (see Essentials).

To make the duck-neck sausage, heat both the oils in a frying pan and saute the onion, garlic, ginger and chilli until softened and slightly coloured. Stir in the ground spices until fragrant, then add the fennel, fungus, thyme and water chestnuts and stir to combine. Tip the mixture into a bowl and allow to cool.

Add the minced duck meat and pork fat to the cooled mixture and combine thoroughly. Season with salt and pepper. Secure the duck neck at one end with kitchen twine. Spoon the duck mixture into a piping bag fitted with a wide nozzle and pipe the mix into the neck skin until three-quarters full, taking care to apply even, steady pressure. Leave a little space for the mixture to expand during cooking, then tie the open end with twine.

Bring the chicken stock to a simmer in a saucepan and add the sausage. Reduce the heat and simmer gently for 15 minutes, then turn the sausage over with a slotted spoon and cook for another 15 minutes. Do not let the stock boil during cooking or the sausage may split. Remove the sausage from the stock and drain on paper towel for 30 minutes.

To make the sauce, heat both oils in a large saucepan over moderate heat and fry the giblets until coloured. Add the chilli tumeric paste, orange zest, garlic, onion, chilli and ginger and cook until softened and fragrant.

Add the remaining ingredients and bring to the boil, then reduce the heat and simmer gently for 1 hour. Pass through a fine mesh sieve and discard the solids. Cool, preferably refrigerated overnight, skimming off any residual oil or sediment. When ready to serve, reheat to simmering point, taste and adjust the seasoning if necessary.

To prepare the eggplant, cut them into thick slices then into batons. Heat some vegetable oil in a wok to 180°C, add the eggplant batons in small batches and deep-fry for 4–5 minutes until browned. Remove with a slotted spoon and drain on paper towel. Set the oil aside for cooking the duck breasts.

Heat the chilli oil and 1 tablespoon of the vegetable oil in a pan and fry the garlic, chilli, ginger and shallots for 1 minute until fragrant. Add the yellow beans, rock sugar, both soy sauces, Shaoxing wine and vinegar and boil for a couple of minutes until the sugar has dissolved into the sauce.

Add the fish sauce, taste and adjust the seasoning if necessary. Stir in the fried eggplant pieces and cook over moderate heat for 1 minute so that the eggplant absorbs the flavours. Remove from the heat, season with the Sichuan pepper and stir in the green onions and bean sprouts.

To tea-smoke the duck breasts, lay the duck breasts, skin-side down, on baking paper inside a steamer tray and cover with a tightly fitting lid. Make sure the paper doesn't cover all the holes in the steamer as the smoke needs to have access.

Line a wok with foil and sit over a high heat. Add the tea smoking mix and when it starts to smoke, sit the steamer tray over the wok and smoke for 8 minutes. Open the lid and flip the breasts over, then replace the lid and smoke for another 3–5 minutes, until the breasts are just cooked and still rare in the centre. Set aside for 10 minutes. Preheat the oven to 200°C. >>

<< When ready to serve, heat a cast-iron frying pan over moderate heat, brush the sausage with a little vegetable oil and fry for 3 minutes. Turn the sausage over and transfer the pan to the oven for 5 minutes. Turn the sausage again and cook for another 3 minutes until crisp and golden. Remove from the pan and drain on paper towel. Slice the sausage into four even disks.

While the sausage is cooking, heat the oil in a deep-fryer or wok to 180°C and fry the duck breasts for 4 minutes until golden. Drain on paper towel, then slice crossways into thin slices and season with a little extra Sichuan spice salt.

Melt the palm sugar into the coconut cream, add the fish sauce, tamarind and chilli and stir for about 3 minutes until caramelised. Reduce the heat to low, add the foie gras slices and simmer for 1 minute. Flip the slices over, take the pan off the heat and allow the foie gras to sit for 30 seconds.

To serve, arrange the eggplant in the centre of the plate and add a ladle of spiced orange sauce.

Sit the slice of duck-neck sausage in the centre of the eggplant, then lay the caramelised foie gras on top. Fan the slices of tea-smoked duck breast across the top of the foie gras and serve immediately.

SERVES 4 (OR 8 AS A SMALLER TASTE)

BREASTS, LEGS AND PINK BITS
(see page 50) >

CELEBRATION ROAST DUCK

For the Chinese, the number eight signifies good luck and prosperity. In China this stuffing is known as 'eight jewel' or 'eight treasure' stuffing, a Hunanese specialty. With its glistening soy-lacquered skin, this is one of the most festive duck dishes imaginable. Unless you are confident enough to tunnel-bone the duck yourself, ask your butcher to do it for you. It's a vital part of the recipe – essentially, you are making a really big sausage with the duck as the outer casing.

2 teaspoons minced fresh ginger
20 ml malt vinegar
25 ml Shaoxing rice wine
2 kg whole duck, cleaned and deboned (tunnel-boned)
60 ml dark soy sauce

EIGHT JEWEL STUFFING
200 g raw prawn meat, chopped
20 ml Ginger Juice (see Essentials)
1 teaspoon Shaoxing rice wine
15 ml fish sauce
1 teaspoon sesame oil
1 tablespoon castor sugar
1 teaspoon light soy sauce
1 teaspoon Chinese black vinegar
2 teaspoons oyster sauce
1 teaspoon freshly ground white pepper
40 ml vegetable oil
2 teaspoons finely shredded ginger
1 cup white sticky rice, soaked in cold water for 2 hours
½ cup black sticky rice, soaked in cold water for 2 hours
500 ml White Chicken Stock (see Essentials)
16 fresh water chestnuts, peeled and diced
10 fresh shiitake mushrooms, stems discarded, caps finely sliced
10 green onions, finely sliced
3 tablespoons bamboo shoots, diced
1 cup cooked lotus seeds
3 teaspoons minced garlic
2 teaspoons sesame oil, extra
2 teaspoons dark soy sauce
2 teaspoons light soy sauce, extra
2 teaspoons castor sugar, extra
1 teaspoon Chinese Five-spice Powder (see Essentials)

To prepare the stuffing, combine the chopped prawn meat, ginger juice, Shaoxing wine, fish sauce, sesame oil, sugar, soy sauce, vinegar, oyster sauce and white pepper. Use your hands to mix thoroughly, then marinate for 30 minutes.

Heat the vegetable oil in a wok and toss in the ginger. As soon as it becomes fragrant, add the prawn mix and fry over high heat, tossing to prevent it sticking or burning. Remove from the heat as soon as the prawn mix changes colour, then spread it out on a flat tray to cool.

To cook the rice, wash it under cold running water for about 10 minutes until the water runs clear, then strain. Place the washed rice in a large bowl and stir in the stock. Sit the bowl on the tray of a bamboo steamer and cover with a lid. Steam over boiling water for 40 minutes until the rice is cooked and liquid has been absorbed. Allow to cool completely.

In a large bowl, mix together the cooled prawn mix and steamed rice with the remaining stuffing ingredients until combined.

To prepare the duck, preheat the oven to 200°C. Mix the ginger, vinegar and Shaoxing wine together in a bowl. Rub the duck inside and out with the mixture. Tie kitchen twine around the neck to secure, then spoon the stuffing into the duck's cavity through the open tail end. Use skewers to close the tail end so the stuffing remains inside and intact, making sure the duck is pressed back into its regular shape (this is exactly the same method as for making a ballotine). Rub the dark soy sauce liberally over the duck skin to completely cover.

Put a water bath at the bottom of the oven. Lay the duck on a wire rack over a baking dish on the rack above the water bath and roast the duck for 40 minutes. Turn over and roast for another 30–40 minutes until the duck turns a rich brown colour. Test the thigh with a skewer and remove the duck from the oven when the juices run clear. Allow the duck to rest for 15 minutes.

Slice the duck into thick slices crossways to serve. The flavours are balanced and complete, needing no further adornment.

SERVES 6

FIRECRACKER CHICKEN

I always thought I had quite a heavy hand when it came to using the fragrant and fiery Sichuan peppercorns – until I tasted a red-hot mouth-numbing chicken dish in Lintong, in Shaanxi province. I asked our guide Clarence to give me the lowdown on how it was made: the chicken was cooked with masses of whole Sichuan peppercorns and whole small dried chillies which set our tastebuds on fire, but it quickly became addictive as we worked our way to the bottom of the plate.

750 g chicken thigh fillets, cut into 3 cm chunks
40 ml vegetable oil
4 small red chillies, sliced
1 red capsicum (pepper), cut into 2 cm dice
6 green onions, cut into 2 cm lengths
1 cup coriander leaves

MARINADE
20 ml Shaoxing rice wine
20 ml light soy sauce
2 teaspoons dark soy sauce
1 teaspoon sea salt
1 teaspoon freshly ground white pepper
1 teaspoon ground Sichuan peppercorns
1 tablespoon potato flour

GARLIC CHILLI SAUCE
60 ml White Chicken Stock (see Essentials)
20 ml light soy sauce
20 ml dark soy sauce
1 teaspoon dried chilli flakes
1 teaspoon chilli oil
1 teaspoon sesame oil
2 teaspoons rice vinegar
1 teaspoon Shaoxing rice wine
2 teaspoons castor sugar
1 tablespoon Roasted Garlic Paste (see Essentials)
1 tablespoon minced fresh ginger
1 tablespoon Chilli Jam (see Essentials)
1 teaspoon Sichuan peppercorns, roasted and ground

To prepare the chicken, mix the marinade ingredients in a bowl, add the chicken and toss to coat. Leave to marinate for 30 minutes.

To make the sauce, heat the chicken stock to simmering point, then add the remaining ingredients (except the ground Sichuan pepper) and stir to combine. Simmer for 10 minutes then remove from the heat and add the pepper. Set aside until ready to use.

Heat a wok over a high heat, add the oil and stir-fry the chicken for 7–8 minutes, tossing the wok to ensure even cooking. Add the chilli slices and diced capsicum and cook for another minute, just until the capsicum softens. Add the garlic chilli sauce and when simmering, toss through the green onion sticks and coriander. Serve immediately.

SERVES 6

MANDARIN AND BLACK PEPPER MOUSSE WITH STRAWBERRIES

This is one of my favourite desserts – the lingering gentle heat of pepper offers a surprise element that works like magic with the strawberries. In London, we used the Mara des Bois strawberries when they were in season towards the end of summer. To my mind, they are a strawberry that has no equal – red and juicy right the way through. When I make this, I set each element in layers so they are all tasted together. It also means that serving couldn't be simpler, as all the work has been done during the preparation.

8 strawberries, finely sliced

STRAWBERRY JELLY
1 kg ripe strawberries
50 g castor sugar
6 g gelatine leaves, softened in cold water

BLACK PEPPER MOUSSE
500 ml double cream
170 ml milk
½ teaspoon black peppercorns, cracked
100 g castor sugar
6 g gelatine leaves, softened in cold water
¾ teaspoon freshly ground black pepper, sieved

MANDARIN JELLY
170 ml mandarin juice, strained
170 ml Sugar Syrup (see Essentials)
6 g gelatine leaves, softened in cold water

MANDARIN CREAM
500 ml double cream
170 ml milk
zest of 2 mandarins (zest directly into the saucepan with the cream to capture the essential oil)
100 g castor sugar
6 g gelatine leaves, softened in cold water

STRAWBERRY SORBET
100 g castor sugar
100 g glucose, softened
500 ml strawberry puree, strained >>

<< To make the strawberry jelly, cut the strawberries in half and sprinkle with sugar. Cover and leave in a bowl for 2 hours until they become very juicy. Stand the bowl with the juice and strawberries over a pan of simmering water and cook over very slow heat – the slower the better – for 1 hour. Put the strawberries and juice in triple-layer muslin, tie to secure and hang over a bowl in the refrigerator overnight. Do not squeeze, just allow the juices to drip out very slowly.

Heat 340 ml of the strawberry juice over low heat until warm, then stir in the softened gelatine leaves. Allow to cool completely then, using half the jelly, pour a thin layer (6 mm) into the bottom of serving glasses or bowls. Refrigerate for 1 hour until set. Reserve the other half of the jelly for the final layer.

To make the black pepper mousse, heat the cream, milk, peppercorns and sugar to simmering point. Stir in the softened gelatine and stir until dissolved. Pass through a fine mesh sieve, then stir in the sieved ground pepper. Allow to cool slightly, then pour the cream into the serving glasses or bowls. Refrigerate for 2 hours until set.

To make the mandarin jelly, heat the juice and sugar syrup together in a pan to simmering point, then stir in the softened gelatine until dissolved. Strain and allow to cool completely, then pour over the black pepper cream. Refrigerate until set.

To make the mandarin cream, heat the cream, milk, zest and sugar in a saucepan over gentle heat until simmering. Stir in the softened gelatine until dissolved then pass through a fine mesh sieve. Discard the zest. Allow the cream to cool completely then pour over the mandarin jelly layer. Return to the refrigerator to set for 2 hours.

Arrange strawberry slices in a circle in the centre of each cream, sprinkle with the tiniest amount of ground pepper, then pour on a little of the reserved strawberry jelly, just enough for the strawberries to stick to the cream. Set for 30 minutes then pour on the rest of the jelly and refrigerate until ready to serve.

To make the strawberry sorbet, stir the sugar and softened glucose into the strawberry puree until dissolved. Churn in an ice-cream machine until firm then transfer to an airtight container and place in the freezer.

To serve, place a perfect quenelle of sorbet in the centre of each assembled dessert (on top of the jelly layer) and serve immediately.

SERVES 4

MANDARIN AND BLACK PEPPER MOUSSE
WITH STRAWBERRIES (see page 57) >

LIQUORICE ALLSORTS

Inspired by chequerboard ice cream – the seminal dessert created by noted Australian chef Phillip Searle in the early eighties – I have expanded on those flavours and constructed the ice-cream and sorbet layers in a different manner. I like to draw on popular iconic names or brands for dessert ideas, often transporting the diner back to early taste memories, while transforming an idea to give it a grown-up appearance. These fruit flavours work beautifully as a finale to assertive Chinese food flavours.

liquorice essence

PINEAPPLE SORBET
50 g castor sugar
50 g glucose, softened
500 ml strained pineapple puree

KIWI FRUIT SORBET
500 ml strained kiwi fruit puree
50 g castor sugar
50 g glucose, softened

PASSIONFRUIT SORBET
50 g castor sugar
50 g glucose, softened
500 ml strained passionfruit juice

STAR ANISE ICE CREAM
250 ml milk
2 star anise, crushed slightly
3 large egg yolks
75 g castor sugar
250 ml pouring (35%) cream

To make the pineapple sorbet, whisk the sugar and softened glucose into the puree until dissolved and combined. Churn in an ice-cream machine until firm. Spoon into a small half-round mould – mine is 7 cm wide, 5 cm deep and 34 cm long – lined with baking paper to make a 1 cm layer. Freeze for 30 minutes, then paint the surface with liquorice essence. Return to the freezer.

To make the kiwi fruit sorbet, whisk the sugar and softened glucose into the puree until dissolved and combined. Churn in an ice-cream machine until firm. Spoon onto the pineapple layer, freeze for 30 minutes, then paint the surface with liquorice essence. Return to the freezer.

To make the passionfruit sorbet, whisk the sugar and softened glucose into the juice until dissolved and combined. Churn in an ice-cream machine until firm. Spoon onto the kiwi fruit layer, freeze for 30 minutes, then paint the surface with liquorice essence. Return to the freezer.

To make the star anise ice cream, bring the milk and star anise to a simmer in a saucepan over very low heat. The slower the infusion, the better the flavour.

Whisk the egg yolks and sugar in a bowl until pale and creamy, then whisk in the hot milk mixture.

Stand the bowl over a pan of gently simmering water and cook, stirring, until the mixture reaches a custard consistency and coats the back of a spoon. Strain the custard through a fine mesh sieve into a clean bowl and discard the star anise. Allow to cool. Stir the cream into the cooled custard, then churn in an ice-cream machine until firm.

Line a rectangular terrine mould with baking paper – mine is 9 cm wide, 8 cm deep and 34 cm long – and spoon enough ice cream into the base to make a 1 cm thick layer. (Make sure you have enough left over to make a border around the sorbet later.) Freeze for 30 minutes.

Turn the sorbet log out from its mould onto a board lined with baking paper and remove the paper lining stuck to the curved side of the sorbet. Paint the curved surface with liquorice essence and freeze for 15 minutes until the liquorice paint has set onto the sorbet.

Sit the frozen sorbet log on top of the bottom ice-cream layer, flat-side down. Fill in the sides and cover the top with a 1 cm layer of star anise ice cream (you want the ice cream to form the same size border around the sorbet centre). Cover and freeze overnight to set.

To serve, dip the mould in hot water for 20 seconds then upturn the mould onto a board. Lift off the rectangular mould and remove the baking-paper lining. Cut into 2 cm thick slices crossways and smooth the cut surface with a hot, wet knife. Lay each ice-cream slice on a cold plate and serve immediately.

SERVES 10

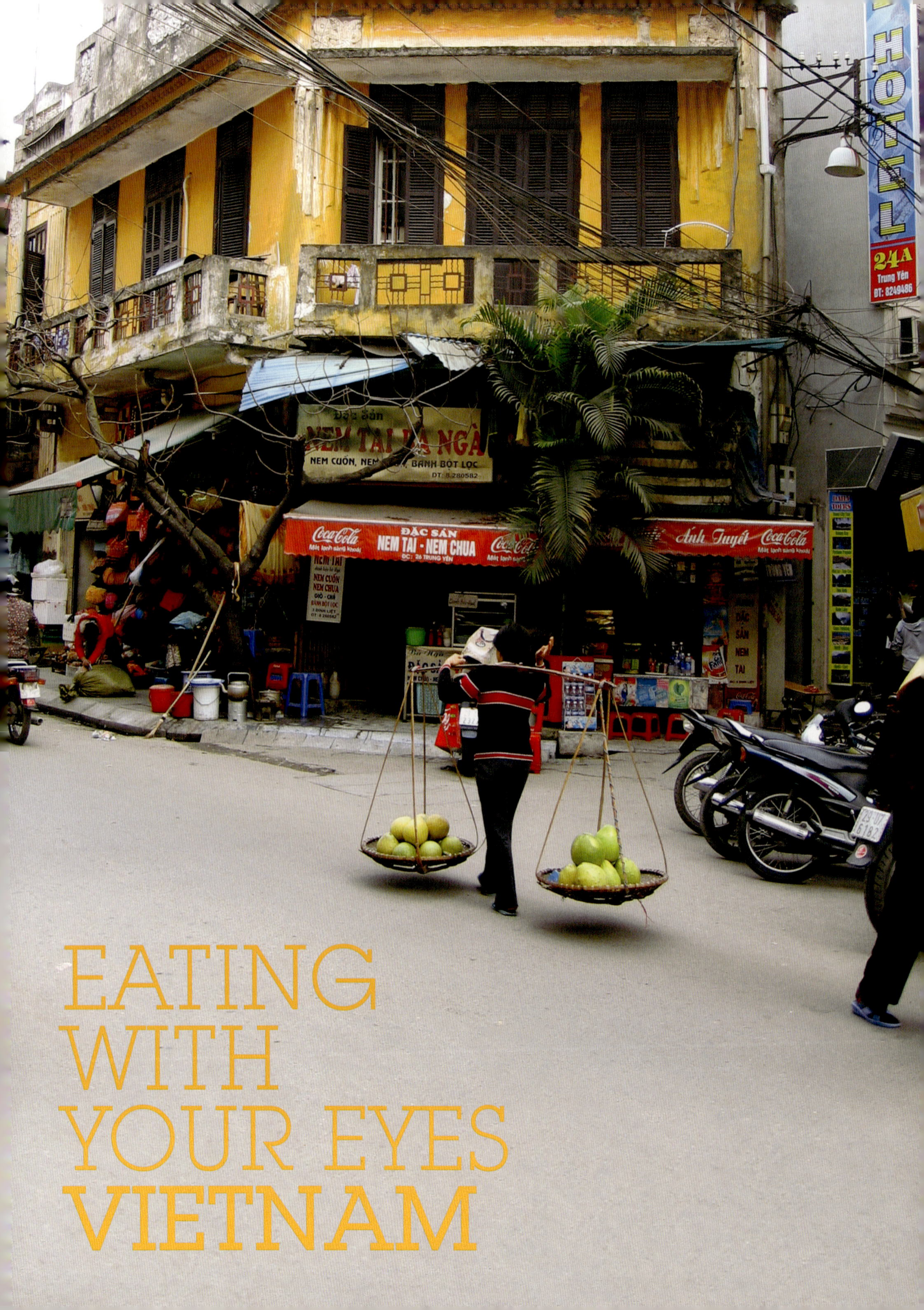

EATING WITH YOUR EYES VIETNAM

Good morning Vietnam! T-shirts and souvenirs echo the famous movie line, and the welcome is genuine wherever you are.

Vietnam has three main regions – the north, the centre and the south – each with a distinctive food tradition. Northern food has close links to China but has definite Vietnamese overtones – there is the lingering fragrance of star anise, ginger and cassia, with the flavours saltier and more simple, the seasoning reliant on black pepper and, surprisingly, dill. The food of central Vietnam reflects its imperial past, when cooking reached a high degree of sophistication. The former imperial city of Hue is renowned for its sweet rice cakes, pork sausages and liberal use of shrimp paste and chilli, and for incorporating Western vegetables (grown in the cooler mountain regions) into its repertoire. With its tropical climate, and influenced by neighbouring Thai and Khmer cultures, the south uses more spice, sugar and leafy greens. A mixture of ground chilli, salt and sugar is sold as a seasoning for freshly cut pineapple, awakening the taste buds first thing in the morning. Everywhere, flavours are lively, diverse, balanced and light.

The rice noodles and pancakes so characteristic of Vietnamese food come in various guises. Besides pho, the ubiquitous rice noodle soup, there are glossy and voluptuous banh trang, fresh rice noodle sheets that look more like silken cloth, which are brought in to the cities daily from villages on the outskirts, where they are laboriously made from scratch. The sheets are used to make fresh rice paper rolls, as well as nem ran, the fried rice-paper rolls of Hanoi (known as cha gio in Saigon). The tissue-thin sheets are made pliable by being wrapped in banana leaf and then left for half an hour before rolling. I particularly love crispy rice pancakes, and you'll find different versions of these all over the country. In Hanoi banh cang are flat pancakes cooked on little clay plates over charcoal, painted with egg yolk then filled with sauteed prawn and green onions when crisp. Then there's the classic banh xeo of the south – the name derived from the sizzling sound made when the batter hits the hot pan. They are crunchy, rich and spicy all at the same time, and totally addictive. The most delicious version we found was at Saigon's Quan An Ngon restaurant. Banh khoai are the 'happy pancakes' of Hue, with textures that are crisp, chewy and crunchy at the same time. Banh cuon are sticky rice pancakes (think noodle sheets) stuffed with mushrooms, then rolled and steamed – not dissimilar to Chinese cheung fen.

The Vietnamese eat small amounts of food throughout the day, almost like a continual grazing – definitely my kind of eating. People shop daily for their food with a rigorous insistence on freshness and quality, and the produce markets have vibrant and tantalising displays. Vietnam is a food-lover's paradise, with a rich and diverse culinary culture that is immediately captivating and seductive. Influenced by both Confucian and Buddhist philosophies, life in Vietnam is defined by decorum, and the art of eating is held in high esteem. Food is seen as a great civilising force, with preparations signifying the harmony of heaven and earth, the yin and yang. Underpinning every dish is the balance of flavours and textures. With their strong Chinese and more recent French heritage, the Vietnamese have borrowed methods and ingredients while maintaining their unique and subtle approach to food and cooking. Perhaps it also says something about how central food is to Vietnamese culture that their revered leader Ho Chi Minh trained as a chef in Europe – a disciple of Escoffier, no less – before coordinating a 30-year war and then ruling the country.

Just a few words of caution. Too often restaurant kitchens will allow the indiscriminate and prolific use of MSG (bot ngot), so it pays to be vigilant on this matter when ordering. Many tables serve pepper and MSG in small bowls as seasoning that can easily be mistaken for salt, and there are big bags of the stuff for sale at the markets. Some crafty cooks will automatically add it to food, their palates deadened long ago by its extreme effects. But it's not all gloom and doom – we found a refreshing and growing trend in more enlightened restaurants and shops, where particular mention was made of its absence from their food.

Essentially an agrarian country, Vietnam has a unique and rich civilisation and enviable natural beauty. Travelling the length of the coastline as it snakes its way down the Indochina peninsula from the southern border of China to the Mekong Delta, you'll see a patchwork of verdant rice paddies, spectacular mountains, busy port towns and endless streams of conical-hatted locals going about their daily business. The dignity and refinement of the Vietnamese people is enchanting – throughout all the invasions and occupations, their nation has preserved the heart of its culture, while adapting well to outside influences. The best-known cities lie at opposite ends of the country, with Hanoi in the north and equatorial Ho Chi Minh City to the south (although 30 years after the Communist takeover, the locals still call it Saigon).

The different perspectives presented by each city offer a remarkable insight into the soul of this country.

Proudly traditional, Hanoi is a city built around several lakes and the Red River. Wide, tree-lined boulevards reflect its French colonial heritage – belle epoque beauty with a more languid pace and charm. This is the best place to experience traditional Vietnamese life. The laid-back provincial atmosphere has changed little even though the city has spread its wings to absorb some of the smaller villages on its outskirts. Being here always makes me think of the images captured so perfectly in the classic movie *Indochine*. While the socialist legacy and transition to a more open economy with enormous growth in the private enterprise sector has seen the country develop rapidly over the past decade or so, this is probably more obvious in Saigon than Hanoi.

I first visited Hanoi on a gourmet culinary tour with Melbourne-based chef and food historian Tony Tan, a most genial and knowledgeable host. Since then, I have travelled the length of the country, gaining more and more appreciation for this special place. Taking a stroll around the old town through the maze of its 36 narrow uneven streets named after their specific guild or craft (hardware, lanterns, silverware etc) is a must – especially along Pho Gia Ngu, a long narrow street packed with a staggering array of food stalls and fresh produce vendors. A few small blocks away is the Dong Xuan market on Hang Chieu Street. The back section is like an undercover supermarket with masses of dried and pickled foods, and the sidewalk is stacked with wicker baskets of dried bamboo shoots, water chestnuts and sour plums. Around the corner is one of the city's oldest street cafes, Cha Ca La Vong, which is famous for its fried fish with herbs and noodles – an essential Vietnamese experience. Sitting comfortably in the middle of this are neat pyramid piles of crusty baguettes, testament to how the Vietnamese have adopted and adapted foreign elements to suit their tastes.

Hanoi is defined by its most famous dish – pho. To me, it is the perfect embodiment of Vietnam in a bowl, and this specialty of the north has spread its magic across the country. Pho is an utterly restorative and seductive dish, though trying to reach the bottom of the bowl can be a task of endurance. Finding the perfect pho became an ongoing quest: we started each time with a flavoursome clear broth, the foundation for the lingering flavour, then added fresh rice noodles and shredded meat (raw beef, cooked brisket or shin or tendons, or shreds of cooked chicken). The condiments are equally important and served separately for each person to add as little or as much as they like – bean sprouts, fresh chilli, lime juice, pepper, chilli sauce, fish sauce and herbs. In Hanoi, black pepper is obligatory. Many pho cooks guard their recipes jealously and each time I slurp my way through a bowl, I notice subtle differences and nuances of flavour. It really comes down to the stock, and pho stocks have been a great source of inspiration in my cooking. Every time we visit Hanoi, we head out to different pho shops for our breakfast noodles, feeding a growing addiction. One of my favourites is Mai Anh, just off Pho Hue in the Hai Ba Trung district, a busy cafe that specialises in chicken pho. Hanoi also has its own version of hot and sour soup (canh chua ca), and I found the subtle differences in flavour from the Thai, Lao and Cambodian versions to be quite a revelation. One morning we even tasted cho (dog meat), sliced from the smoked and roasted carcass, and just so you know, it's like a cross between pork and beef. Back on more familiar territory, we discovered that nom soai (green mango salad with tiny river prawns) makes the perfect lunch on a hot day.

Early one morning, we took a ride on a cyclo (a motorbike with a two-wheeled passenger compartment) to Hanoi's Cho 19–12 (December 19 market), to buy produce for our cooking class back at the hotel. This market is a labyrinth, very clean and fast-moving, with vendors squatting on low stools among a wonderland of aromas, textures and

STAYING IN HANOI

SOFITEL METROPOLE HOTEL
15 Ngo Quyen, Hoan Kiem, Hanoi
Tel +84 4 826 6919
www.sofitel.com
The most central location in the city; the rooms in the old wing are the way to go to get a real sense of this historic French colonial hotel. The chefs here host a cooking school and visits to the produce markets.

MOON RIVER RETREAT
Ngoc Thuy Village, Gia Lam, Hanoi
Tel +84 4 90 450 9045
If you're looking for an escape from the centre of the city, this small boutique property on the Red River is the place for you. It's a sister property to Wild Rice Restaurant (see opposite) so the food is fab.

colours. Shopkeepers fuss over their produce with an eye to detail and perfect hygiene, and tables are piled high with fresh herbs and salad greens, many of which are unique to Vietnam. Baskets and sacks of white, black, chalky, glutinous and young green rice are crammed along the narrow aisles with trays of hen, duck and quail eggs, fresh seafood, and live chickens and ducks. There are big bowls of freshwater pond snails with their glistening black shells, brightly coloured conches, slippery eels, stingrays, a diverse array of fish, crabs and prawns, and women skinning cuttlefish and chopping the heads off live frogs. Along the aisle a bit, we feel the silky texture of arrowroot and tapioca flour, both used as natural thickeners. The French have left their mark in more ways than the obvious baguette; what you might consider distinctly European is right at home here with the local food. Dill, cornichons, pickled vegetables, pickled limes and lemon balm (used with kang kung greens) are as common as roasted sesame oil, lemongrass, ginger and fresh turmeric. We bought some small sweet pineapples, banana blossoms and green star fruit – carambola – to use in salads; an amazing array of vegetables and leafy greens to stir-fry with garlic; dill, purple perilla leaves, sweet marjoram and lemon leaves for wrapping chicken pieces to be grilled over charcoal; and tamarind for clay-pot cooking.

Our dinners in Hanoi usually included a lau (hot pot) of some sort, cooked in turban-shaped clay vessels with fitted lids. My favourites were ga caramen voi xot gung (caramel ginger chicken) and bo kho (a spicy beef stew with lemongrass and green chillies). I asked where I could buy some of the cooking vessels to take home and Van, one of the chefs from the Metropole, kindly took me on a cyclo to Hang Mam (Coffin Street). It was a wonderful insight into local life; women carrying a mobile kitchen suspended from wooden yokes across their shoulders would stop in people's doorways and put together a simple noodle dish. So inventive and considerate: the ultimate in home delivery. Back at the Metropole, the women chefs made us thit lon nuong ong tre (pork shoulder marinated with ginger, herbs and caramelised fish sauce cooked over coals in a bamboo tube); ca qua hap voi bia va rau gia vi (steamed snake-head fish with beer and herbs); and ga nuong la chanh (grilled chicken skewers with lemon leaves).

Smack bang on the central coast, almost 700 kilometres south of Hanoi, Hue is the former imperial capital, where the feasts once cooked for the emperors consisted of hundreds of dishes prepared in a manner that set them apart from regular fare. This detailed, complex and stylised food lies at the centre of Vietnamese culinary history. It was not uncommon for more than 50 dishes to be served at any one time and if there was a special occasion, the feast might have comprised up to 200 different dishes. Even today, a typical Hue menu would include a dozen or more small dishes placed on the table together, a symbolic gesture toward the city's royal heritage. Unfortunately, Hue is no longer the best place to come to experience imperial food; it is much better represented in the restaurants of Hoi An and Saigon.

EATING IN HANOI

WILD RICE
6 Ngo Thi Nahm Street, Hanoi
Tel +84 4 943 8896
Contemporary Vietnamese-style food – delicious tastes.

EMPEROR
18B Le Thanh Tong Street, Hanoi
Tel +84 4 826 8801
Authentic food served in a beautifully restored villa.

CHA CA LA VONG
14 Cha Ca Street, Old Quarter, Hanoi
Tel +84 4 825 3929
Turmeric-marinated fish cooked at your table and served with rice noodles and herbs.

HOA SUA
28A Ha Hoi, Hoan Kiem, Hanoi
Tel +84 4 942 4448
www.hoasuaschool.com
A school established to help street kids and orphans become skilled in the hospitality trade. There's a restaurant, patisserie and bakery here, with tables set out in the garden.

QUAY THUC PHAM CONG NGHE
71 Hang Bo Street, Old Quarter, Hanoi
Small shopfront making banh cuon (steamed rice rolls with various fillings). Fab and cheap.

I even found the early morning Dong Ba market along the river bank unimpressive compared to other Vietnamese markets I have visited.

Heading south, Hoi An is an easy three-hour drive from Hue down the famous Highway One. Hoi An is adorable and stylish, a perfect miniature of the heart and soul of colonial Vietnam; it feels as if you've walked into a 1950s time capsule. Unlike Hue, it managed to escape the brutality of the American War (as it is known in Vietnam) and has been declared a World Heritage site, with its charming old wooden houses and shopfronts preserved as tangible reminders of its Chinese, Japanese and French heritage. We stayed at one of the beachfront hotels a few kilometres from the old town and drove in each day to wander around the narrow streets, the perfect way to experience Hoi An. After engaging in some extremely enjoyable retail therapy, we found an endless choice of cute little cafes and bars that front the river. Our favourite was the Mango Room, with its Latino bright colours, groovy staff, snappy menu and terrific fruity cocktails. Each night we ate exceptional food, finding authentic flavours that had not been dumbed down. We shared a heavenly meal at Brothers Cafe, a glamorous and stylish house on the Thu Bon River, set among perfectly landscaped gardens. They served us tom rang me (prawns in tamarind sauce); the most delicious eggplant smoked over coals and tossed with chilli, garlic and coriander; ca ba trau nuong gung (grilled red snapper with ginger); and muc nuong sa (grilled squid with lemongrass and beef slices wrapped in betel leaves and grilled).

It was in Hoi An that we finally managed to find chao tom (prawn paste grilled on sugar cane sticks), a classic of Hue's imperial cooking. Just as addictive are banh bao banh ngt – rice-flour dumplings shaped like delicate white rose cakes, stuffed with minced prawn and vegetables, steamed and covered with fried garlic and shallot slices. I could easily down a plate of these every day. Cha gio are light and crisp Vietnamese fried spring rolls, wrapped in gossamer-thin rice paper sheets and stuffed with pork and crab. Dried squid is a delicacy here – there are packets of it everywhere hanging above shop counters, at street stalls and in the markets. The prized specialty of Hoi An, served by the street vendors in front of the market on Tran Phu Street is cao lau, a bowl of thick chewy rice noodles – reputedly made by the same family for generations – with bean sprouts, crisp rice crackers (banh da), mint and sliced pork seasoned with fish sauce, sesame oil, soy sauce and lime. Bun bo Hue is a spicy beef noodle soup with fat udon-style rice noodles, served with a heap of chilli. And goi du chi (the Vietnamese version of green papaya salad) is every bit as delicious as the Thai one. I always look out for the young green sticky rice grains (com dep) – the sweet and nutty grains mark the start of the new season's rice. On our last visit we were there at just the right time, so I brought some home to use in desserts; the delicate taste and texture is perfect for adding to custards or creme caramels.

As you travel further south, the food becomes noticeably hotter. Spices are used more generously, curries are aromatic, and coconut milk and sugar cane are de rigueur. Vietnamese five-spice mix is an aromatic blend of ginger, turmeric, anise seeds, cloves and cinnamon, and evokes the flavours of China and India. Some 400 kilometres down the coast from Hoi An, the picturesque southern town of Nha Trang is nestled beside mountains that plunge dramatically into the sea. This vibrant coastal town has perhaps the best food market in Vietnam, and the plethora of seafood is unparalleled. Cho Dam market reflects a thriving community, with seafood merchants selling everything from giant tuna and tiny silver fish to skeins of dried squid; vendors with their live poultry

STAYING IN AND AROUND HOI AN

LIFE RESORT HOI AN
1 Pham Hong Thai Street, Hoi An
Tel +84 510 914 555
www.life-resorts.com
A great central riverside location in the old town (near the market) with great food.

NAM HAI RESORT
Hamlet 1, Dien Duong Village, Dien Ban, Quang Nam
Tel +84 510 940 000
www.ghmhotels.com
Deluxe living comes to the coast – a sophisticated beachside retreat with easy access to the centre of Hoi An.

EATING IN HOI AN

BROTHERS CAFE
27 Phan Boi Chau Street, Hoi An
Tel +84 510 914 150
By far the best place to eat in this town – ask for an outside table overlooking the river. Their menu is utterly delicious, full of delightful and interesting tastes.

in basket cages; noodle knockers; women sitting on outstretched mats with fruit, vegetables and eggs laid out on display; and other women cooking all manner of edible treats ready to be consumed on the spot or taken home for dinner.

Nha Trang is a hedonist's playground: the beaches are perfect scallop-shaped bays of clean white sand and coral, and the river is a mass of blue and red fishing boats that become a flotilla at sea. We stayed in a two-storey bamboo house by the beach, and it was the most magical place to wake each morning, waves gently lapping at the shore. For breakfast we would devour several banh xeo cooked right there on the spot, the crisp rice pancakes stuffed with bean sprouts, shrimp, shredded pork, green onions and Asian basil then rolled with butter lettuce leaves, perilla and mint leaves, followed by the obligatory bowl of pho. And for a memorable evening, you can't beat a barbecued seafood feast on the beach.

Inland from Nha Trang, in the southern central highlands, the hill station of Dalat enjoys a cooler temperate climate. Favoured by the French in colonial times – there's even a miniature Eiffel Tower in the centre of town – some of the old French colonial villas are still used as weekend retreats for well-heeled Saigon residents as an escape from the humid heat of their city. Dalat considers itself a bit of an artists' hangout and many locals paint excellent reproductions of European masters, as well as their own work. The southern diet owes much to the climate of Dalat and its produce, and the markets offer an amazing array of produce not seen elsewhere in the country. Tiny wild strawberries jostle for space next to watermelons, avocados, asparagus, beetroot, mulberries, apples, Nashi pears and peaches. Bunches of tuberoses and myriad other flowers from the vendors just outside the market fill the air with heady fragrance. Other stalls are loaded with sugary confections, lollies and candied fruits, piles of dried shrimps of varying size and colour, and gaudy coloured bottles of snake wine – drunk as a mark of virility. It was here I first saw and tasted ca cuon, a dark green liquid milked from the wings of a beetle that lives in the rice fields. A drop can dramatically change the flavour of food, and its aroma is potent, even when it is stored in a glass jar with tight-fitting lid. It may sound alarming, but really it's no worse than cochineal, another ingredient used to flavour and colour food that is derived from the secretions of a beetle.

STAYING AROUND NHA TRANG

SIX SENSES HIDEAWAY
Ninh Van Bay, Ninh Hoa, Khanh Hoa
Tel +84 58 524 268
www.sixsenses.com
This hidden paradise is a 20-minute boat ride offshore from Nha Trang along the far-flung peninsula of Ninh Van Bay. Its expansive pavilions offer total privacy, and the pampering begins the minute you arrive.

Back on the coast, midway between Nha Trang and Saigon, Phan Thiet is the home of fish sauce, which is made from the liquid expelled after fish have been salted and fermented in barrels. Although it is produced all along the coast of Vietnam, not all sauces are created equal, and the taste differs significantly according to regional differences and the length of the ageing process. Fish sauce is graded like extra virgin olive oil: the best grade will have nhi attached to the label and is used for making nuoc cham, a dipping sauce of lime, vinegar, sugar, fish sauce, chilli and garlic that is a mandatory inclusion on any Vietnamese table; lesser grades are suitable for cooking. The most famous brand, Phu Quoc, is made with bonito or tuna and has a discernible pungency and strong flavour. The fish sauce of Nha Trang is sweeter, quite ambrosial and is perfect to use as a condiment or dipping sauce.

Yang to Hanoi's yin, Saigon is much busier and more urban, a city with an entirely different atmosphere and a commercial imperative, which has a direct effect on the personality of the place. The roads are a cacophony of noise, and pushbikes and motor scooters often have perilously high loads as they weave their way through the traffic. It takes nerves of steel to master your first crossing. We watched how the locals do it (always a good idea) and then followed them as they walked across, keeping a steady pace and never ever stopping. Miraculously, the bikes, cyclos and cars weaved around them, anticipating their path and judging their speed. It is vital to leave the weaving to the traffic – hesitating only mucks up the system. Trust me, it does work!

If Hanoi embodies French colonial style, then Saigon counters with its intact 1960s architecture, and the imposing presence of the Reunification Palace at the top end of the main boulevard. Saigon conjures up an exotic past, albeit one torn asunder by war. The street kids will try to sell anything from chewing gum to war memorabilia, and many brandish copies of Graham Greene's *The Quiet*

American, which was largely set in Saigon during the last days of colonial rule. We did a bar hop one night that took in all the author's favourite haunts still standing around Dong Khoi and the Opera House, from camp-as-Christmas drinks on the rooftop of the Rex and Majestic hotels to the dimly lit faded glory of the garden bars at the Grand and Continental hotels. These days there are plenty of sophisticated bars that would fit comfortably in any modern city. We tested the barman's skills and cocktail menu at Samsara, then moved onto Q Bar and Temple Bar, both of which have decent menus to snack from.

Saigon dishes are complex: the spices reflect a distant Khmer and Indian association and there is a wider repertoire due to the availability of an enviable choice of ingredients and fresh produce. Nourishing soups on offer down this way are sup bi (a ginger and pumpkin number) and canh chua tom (yet another version of Asian hot and sour soup – this one made with a light shrimp stock). For a dazzling display of versatility try bo bay moan – beef prepared seven ways, each served in a separate dish so that the flavours remain distinct and intact. I love this; its progression of flavours and textures reminds me of the Japanese aesthetic. Thoroughly enamoured with pho, we maintained our habit of heading out for breakfast noodles, keen to taste southern interpretations of this classic dish. There are pho kitchens wherever you look, but Pasteur Street in District 1, not far from City Hall, has long been regarded as the place to go.

Good food is everywhere in Vietnam: on the streets, in the markets, in the cafes and restaurants. This is one place where it's almost impossible to go wrong and I wouldn't hesitate to eat food from any of these sources as everything tastes so alive and fresh. Since emerging from brutal imperial rule, decades of war and repression, then years of forced diplomatic and economic isolation, Vietnam has emerged as one of the world's most exuberant and exciting destinations, particularly with regard to its food. The essential elements of taste – hot, sour, salty and sweet – are strong reminders of its culinary heritage and create the starting point for every dish. I am constantly inspired by the enormous repertoire built around rice, vegetables, poultry and seafood, all of which are plentiful and inexpensive, and the relatively recent addition of meat – used cleverly but sparingly. I admire Vietnam for its tenacity, determination and courage, and I love the honour its people confer on their cuisine. No matter how humble it may be, food is sustenance for the soul and holds a revered place in everyday life.

STAYING IN SAIGON (HO CHI MINH CITY)

MAJESTIC HOTEL
1 Dong Khoi Street, District 1, Ho Chi Minh City
Tel +84 8 829 5517
One of the golden oldies overlooking the Saigon River, this place has a great location – right in the thick of things.

EATING IN SAIGON

QUAN AN NGON
138 Nam Ky Khoi Nghia, District 1, Ho Chi Minh City
Tel +84 8 829 9449
Open kitchens, with sections for each style of dish, set up in a courtyard surrounding a big house, and indoor tables as well. Loud and constantly busy, this place is packed with locals.

HOI AN RESTAURANT
11 Le Thanh Ton Street, District 1, Ho Chi Minh City
Tel +84 8 823 7694
Yummy food, showcasing imperial Hue cooking.

PHO HOA
260C Pasteur Street, District 1 (near the river), Ho Chi Minh City
Tel +84 8 829 7943
Vietnamese noodle restaurant that's considered the most famous pho house in town.

ANH THU
49 Dinh Cong Trang, District 1, Ho Chi Minh City
Tel +84 8 825 1658
Specialises in banh xeo rice pancakes – a must to try during your stay.

DEEP-FRIED SCALLOP ROLLS

These little parcels conceal hidden treasures bursting with flavour. In London, I used the Scottish diver scallops, which are much larger than the ones we grow in Australia, so make sure you get the largest scallops possible because you want to experience their texture as much as their taste. I serve these with fresh lettuce and herb leaves, which are used to wrap each roll before you consume it. Perfect party food.

20 jumbo scallops or 40 smaller scallops, cleaned
40 g cooked pork, steamed or roasted
40 g raw prawn meat, minced
½ teaspoon Chilli Jam (see Essentials)
2 teaspoons finely minced cloud-ear fungus
1 tablespoon fish sauce
½ teaspoon freshly ground white pepper
1 tablespoon finely chopped coriander leaves
20 large English spinach leaves, blanched
20 rice paper wrappers
vegetable oil, for deep-frying

FOR SERVING
butter lettuce leaves
mint leaves
perilla leaves
Nuoc Cham (see Essentials)

Slice each scallop in half crossways (if the scallops are small, use two scallops for each roll).

Puree the pork in a food processor to make a paste. Transfer to a bowl. Add the minced prawn, chilli jam, cloud-ear fungus, fish sauce, pepper and coriander and mix until combined.

Spoon a little of the pork mixture onto half of the cut scallops then press the remaining scallops on top to make little sandwich disks.

To wrap each scallop, lay a blanched spinach leaf on the bench and place a stuffed scallop at one end. Roll over, then fold in the edges and roll up to secure.

Soften each rice paper wrapper in hot water for 10 seconds, then lay on a clean cloth to remove any excess moisture. Wrap each scallop parcel in the rice paper so they resemble small spring rolls.

Heat the oil in a deep-fryer or heavy-based saucepan to 180°C, add a few scallop rolls at a time, and cook for 5 minutes until crisp and golden. Drain on paper towel and arrange on a large plate with the lettuce, mint and perilla leaves and nuoc cham.

SERVES 4–6

LOBSTER LOLLIPOPS

Encapsulating the quintessential tastes of Vietnam, these lollipops became a popular snack on our London bar menu. The idea of the savoury lollipop can be credited to Spanish chef Ferran Adria at the start of the millennium, and it has since become a popular item on several Australian menus. The lobster meat can be replaced with other shellfish, such as prawn, marron, yabby or scampi tails. Choose whichever dipping sauce you prefer, whether it be a classic nuoc cham, a fiery nahm jim or a sweet chilli sauce.

250 g raw lobster tail meat, finely chopped
2 tablespoons chopped coriander leaves
2 small green chillies, minced
1 teaspoon minced ginger
½ teaspoon freshly ground white pepper
2 teaspoons fish sauce
vegetable oil, for deep-frying
2 tablespoons rice flour
3 small dried chillies, finely sliced
1 teaspoon finely grated makrut lime zest
1 cup Tempura Batter (see Essentials), seasoned with salt and pepper

Mix the chopped lobster with the coriander, chilli, ginger, pepper and fish sauce and slap the mixture against the sides of the bowl until it thickens and becomes stickier. Roll the mix into small balls.

Heat the oil in a wok or large saucepan to 180°C.

Roll the lobster balls in rice flour to lightly coat.

Stir the dried chilli and lime zest through the tempura batter, then dip the lobster balls in the batter to coat. Deep-fry in the hot oil, several at a time, for 3 minutes then drain on paper towel. Repeat with the remaining balls.

Arrange the balls on a plate and insert a small bamboo cocktail skewer (or cocktail stick) into each one. Serve immediately.

SERVES 6

< LOBSTER LOLLIPOPS

GINGER SALMON TARTARE

Although not a traditional dish, this fish tartare was inspired by my first visit to Vietnam in the late 1990s. It draws on traditional flavours and because of its freshness and lightness, it always reminds me of Vietnam – no matter where I happen to be.

120 g sashimi-grade salmon, finely diced
2 teaspoons chopped chives
2 teaspoons minced Pickled Ginger (see Essentials)
1 teaspoon black sesame seeds
1 small cucumber, sliced into fine rounds
2 tablespoons diced Pickled Vegetables (see Essentials)
2 tablespoons mashed avocado (seasoned with salt, pepper, chilli powder and lemon juice)
1 tablespoon salmon roe

GINGER VINAIGRETTE
20 ml fresh lime juice, strained
20 ml Ginger Juice (see Essentials)
¼ teaspoon Tabasco sauce
100 ml fruity extra virgin olive oil
½ teaspoon sea salt
½ teaspoon freshly ground black pepper

To make the vinaigrette, whisk the ingredients together in a bowl until emulsified.

Mix the salmon, chives, pickled ginger and sesame seeds together in a bowl. Add enough vinaigrette to wet the mixture and stir well.

When you're ready to serve, arrange the cucumber rounds in the centre of a plate and sit a 4 or 5 cm ring mould on top. Add the pickled vegetables then the mashed avocado and press into the mould to give a good shape. Spoon the salmon tartare on top and smooth the top surface. Press firmly.

Remove the ring mould, spoon a quenelle of salmon roe on top and serve.

SERVES 4

BANANA FLOWER AND FISH SALAD

This is a variation on a salad we were shown by the chefs at the Metropole Cooking School in Hanoi. I have chosen to use fish instead of the usual roasted pork or chicken meat, but it's also terrific with cooked crab meat or small prawns. If you can't get mackerel, any other oily fish like bonito or albacore tuna would be fine to use. The trick with preparing banana blossoms is to make sure you only use the softer inner layers and that you discard any immature bananas that grow between the leaves as they are quite bitter and soapy to taste. Using a sharp cleaver or a mandoline slicer is the best way of shaving the blossom finely enough.

200 g fresh banana blossom
20 ml fresh lemon juice, strained
4 × 80 g pieces mackerel fillet, skin removed
1 teaspoon sesame oil
1 teaspoon chilli oil
2 teaspoons sea salt
1 green star fruit, sliced
120 g bean sprouts, trimmed
80 g snowpea (mange-tout) shoots, trimmed
1 long red chilli, finely sliced
1 cup Vietnamese mint leaves, torn
½ cup coriander leaves, shredded
50 ml fresh lime juice, strained
30 ml fish sauce
50 ml Sugar Syrup (see Essentials)
1 teaspoon freshly ground black pepper
2 tablespoons peanuts, roasted and chopped
2 tablespoons white sesame seeds, lightly roasted

To prepare the banana blossom, remove the outer layers from the blossom and reserve 4 for serving the salad. Shave the inner layers finely crossways. Cover the shards with cold water mixed with the lemon juice and soak for 30 minutes. Refresh under cold running water when ready to use.

To cook the fish, mix the sesame and chilli oil together and rub over the fish pieces. Lay the fish on a flat baking tray, sprinkle with the sea salt and cook under a hot grill (or over hot coals, if possible) for 7–8 minutes until the fish is just cooked. Remove from the heat and leave until cool enough to handle.

To make the salad, mix the drained banana-blossom shavings in a bowl with the star fruit, bean sprouts, snowpea shoots, chilli, mint and coriander. Mix the lime juice, fish sauce, sugar syrup and pepper together and toss through the salad to moisten.

Flake the fish into chunks and add to the salad with the roasted peanuts and sesame seeds.

Pile the salad into the reserved banana-blossom petals to serve.

SERVES 4

FIVE-SPICE TOFU, BAMBOO AND WATER CHESTNUT SALAD

I created this salad as one of the tastes on our restaurant's vegetarian menu – it's a great interplay between crunchy and silky soft textures. Make it when fresh water chestnuts are in season to get the best results. If they are unavailable, yam bean can be used instead as it has a similar texture and delicate taste.

2 teaspoons Vietnamese Five-spice Mix (see Essentials)
1 teaspoon sea salt
100 g pressed tofu, cut into thin slices
40 ml vegetable oil
2 tablespoons Pickled Cucumber (see Essentials)
1 tablespoon Pickled Carrot Strips (see Essentials)
4 large cloud-ear fungus, shredded
4 tablespoons finely sliced bamboo shoots
1 coconut palm heart, finely sliced
1 long red chilli, finely sliced
8 fresh water chestnuts, sliced into fine rounds
4 green onions, finely sliced on the diagonal
4 tablespoons coriander leaves
4 tablespoons shredded Asian or Thai basil leaves
4 tablespoons shredded Vietnamese mint leaves
4 Chinese cabbage (wombok) leaves, shredded
3 teaspoons white sesame seeds, roasted

BLACK VINEGAR DRESSING
50 ml light soy sauce
50 ml Chinese black vinegar
1 teaspoon sesame oil
½ teaspoon chilli oil
25 ml sunflower oil

Mix the five-spice mix with the salt, then use half the mixture to dust the pressed tofu. Heat the oil in a frying pan and fry the tofu for a couple of minutes until crisp. Drain on paper towel.

Place the spiced tofu and all the remaining salad ingredients (except the sesame seeds) in a bowl and gently mix together.

To make the dressing, mix all the ingredients together, then toss through the salad.

Pile the salad onto serving plates and sprinkle with the sesame seeds and remaining spice salt.

SERVES 4

CHICKEN BROTH WITH CABBAGE DUMPLINGS

I first had the idea for this dish in Hanoi, where pieces of grilled pork were rolled in softened cabbage leaves and served in a simple broth. It became a starting point that developed into this more complex creation with a broth inspired by the classic breakfast pho.

200 g chicken breast fillet, grilled and finely diced
25 ml fish sauce
15 ml fresh lime juice, strained
1 teaspoon freshly ground black pepper
1 teaspoon minced ginger
3 tablespoons finely diced cloud-ear fungus
2 small green chillies, minced
1 small carrot, finely shredded
2 tablespoons shredded coriander leaves
2 tablespoons shredded Vietnamese mint leaves
2 green onions, finely sliced
8 Chinese cabbage (wombok) leaves (stems removed), blanched
8 chives, blanched
100 g bean sprouts, trimmed
4 red bird's-eye chillies, finely sliced
1 tablespoon chopped garlic chives
1 punnet coriander cress, snipped
2 tablespoons Fried Shallot Slices (see Essentials)
2 tablespoons roasted peanuts, crushed

CHICKEN BROTH
2 chicken leg and thigh portions, each cut into 4 pieces
2 quails, chopped
300 g pork knuckles, chopped (ask your butcher to do this for you)
2.5 litres White Chicken Stock (see Essentials)
1 teaspoon white peppercorns, cracked
3 pieces dried tangerine peel
1 teaspoon orange zest
2 star anise
1 tablespoon chopped ginger
2 teaspoons chopped galangal
2 green onions, chopped
250 ml fresh carrot juice
40 ml fish sauce
1 teaspoon freshly ground white pepper
2 teaspoons fresh lime juice, strained

To make the broth, blanch the chicken, quail and pork in boiling water for 2 minutes, then rinse under cold water. Place in a large saucepan with the stock, cracked pepper, peel, zest, star anise, ginger, galangal and green onions. Simmer gently for 2 hours, skimming the surface occasionally.

Stir the carrot juice into the broth and simmer gently for a further 15 minutes, then pass the broth through a fine mesh sieve. Discard the solids, and season with fish sauce and ground white pepper. When ready to serve the soup, stir in the lime juice at the last minute.

To make the dumplings, season the diced chicken with fish sauce, lime juice and pepper. Mix in the ginger, cloud ear fungus, chilli, carrot, coriander, mint and green onion and stir until well combined.

Lay the blanched cabbage leaves on the bench and add some of the chicken mixture to each. Roll over, then fold in the edges and roll up into small firm parcels. Wrap each parcel with a chive length and tie to secure.

Poach the chicken parcels in simmering water for 2 minutes until warmed through, then transfer to serving bowls, allowing two dumplings per serve.

Add the bean sprouts, chilli, garlic chives and cress to each bowl then ladle on the hot broth.

Sprinkle with fried shallot slices and crushed peanuts to serve.

SERVES 4

FRAGRANT BEEF NOODLE SOUP

I have long been a huge fan of pho – the fragrant soup of Vietnam that feeds its people from sunrise throughout the day. I am constantly inspired by the soups on offer from the most humble of kitchens and roadside vendors. You will find these anywhere in the world where the Vietnamese have settled, a signature of their community.

80 ml hoisin sauce
2 teaspoons sweet soy sauce (kecap manis)
20 ml fish sauce
500 g fresh rice noodles
100 g bean sprouts, trimmed
4 red bird's-eye chillies, finely sliced
4 tablespoons coriander leaves
2 tablespoons Vietnamese mint leaves
160 g beef strip loin fillet, fat removed, finely sliced
40 ml fresh lime juice, strained
1 teaspoon freshly ground black pepper

BEEF BROTH
2 kg veal bones
100 ml Shaoxing rice wine
40 ml vegetable oil
1 brown onion, chopped
3 cloves garlic, chopped
2 teaspoons chopped ginger
1 long red chilli, sliced
1 carrot, chopped
1 leek, sliced
handful of green onion tops, sliced
1 × 400 g tin chopped tomatoes
handful of parsley stalks, chopped
1 teaspoon black peppercorns
2 stalks lemongrass, chopped
6 makrut lime leaves, sliced
2 pieces cassia bark

Preheat the oven to 220°C. To make the broth, roast the bones for 45 minutes or until browned. Drain off the excess fat and deglaze the pan with the rice wine.

In a large stockpot, heat the oil and brown the onion, garlic, ginger, chilli, carrot and leek slices.

When beginning to colour, stir in the remaining ingredients. Add the browned bones and juices and cover with cold water. Bring to the boil, then reduce the heat so that it gently simmers for 2 hours.

Skim the surface regularly with a mesh spoon to maintain the clarity of the stock.

Remove from the heat and pass the stock through a conical sieve first and then through either a very fine mesh sieve or several layers of muslin cloth (Chux superwipes or J-cloths are also good for this). Allow the stock to settle completely and continue to skim the surface, removing any fat particles and sediment. Ideally, the stock is best left overnight to become completely cold so that any sediment that will cloud the broth can be removed.

To finish the soup, reheat 2 litres of the broth to simmering point (reserve the rest for later use) and whisk in the hoisin and sweet soy sauces. Season with fish sauce, then taste and adjust if necessary.

Blanch the rice noodles in boiling water for 2 minutes, strain and divide among soup bowls. Add the bean sprouts, chilli, coriander and mint.

Ladle the broth over the noodles and sit the beef slices on top. Add the lime juice and pepper and stir the beef into the broth with chopsticks so that it remains very tender. Serve immediately.

SERVES 8

CHICKEN AND SCALLOP CONSOMME

Inspired by Vietnamese pho, this elegant consomme is a full-bodied broth made in the classic Chinese style where the stock is clarified through heat control and ginger (rather than using egg white), with the wonderful combination of poultry and seafood – a common feature in Asian cooking.

2 fresh snow (white) fungus, torn into small petals
2 tablespoons finely chopped garlic chives
1 punnet micro watercress, snipped

CHICKEN AND SCALLOP CONSOMME
2 litres White Chicken Stock (see Essentials)
1 free-range chicken breast, skin on
2 dried scallops, shredded
2 teaspoons dried Chinese anchovies
2 cloves garlic, sliced
1 teaspoon minced ginger
½ teaspoon freshly ground white peppercorns
4 green onions, cut into 1 cm lengths
2 dried shiitake mushrooms
65 ml Shaoxing rice wine
50 ml fish sauce
2 coriander roots, minced

SCALLOP WON TONS
1 teaspoon oyster sauce
½ teaspoon soy sauce
2 pinches Sichuan Spice Salt (see Essentials)
8 scallops
1 cloud-ear fungus, finely chopped
16 won ton wrappers, cut into 8 cm rounds using a pastry cutter
egg white, for brushing

To make the consomme, put all the ingredients in a stockpot and bring very slowly to a mere simmer. Do not boil or the broth will become cloudy. Cook gently for 20 minutes, then remove the chicken with a slotted spoon. When cool enough to handle, shred the meat while still warm. Discard the skin and set the meat aside.

Strain the broth through a muslin-lined sieve or a jelly bag to eliminate all sediment. Discard the solids. Taste and adjust the seasoning, then skim the surface if necessary.

To make the won tons, mix the oyster sauce, soy sauce and Sichuan spice salt, then brush over the scallops. Put a few dice of cloud-ear fungus in the centre of eight won ton wrappers. Sit the scallops on top and brush the edges of the wrapper with egg white. Cover with the remaining wrappers and press the edges to seal, ensuring there are no air pockets. The won tons should look like little round pillows.

Reheat the broth in a clean saucepan. Divide the chicken and snow fungus petals among bowls.

Bring a saucepan of water to the boil and cook the won tons in simmering water for 2 minutes.

Place two won tons in each bowl, then carefully ladle in the hot broth. Sprinkle the garlic chives and watercress across the surface and serve immediately.

SERVES 4

TONGUE IN CHEEK

This deliciously complex soup with its many components made its debut on one of our London tasting menus. A dish that evolved over time, it's basically the result of my desire to achieve refined elegance with the lesser cuts of meat – oxtail, tongue, marrow and cheek. I love the playfulness of its name, which creates an aura of mystery and anticipation.

1 calf's tongue, blanched
White Chicken Stock (see Essentials), to cover
100 g bone marrow (extracted from bones), soaked in cold water for 1 hour
80 g bean sprouts
1 tablespoon shredded mint leaves
1 tablespoon small Vietnamese mint leaves
2 tablespoons shredded cloud-ear fungus
½ long red chilli, finely sliced
1 tablespoon chopped chives
25 ml fresh lime juice, strained

OXTAIL CONSOMME
1 teaspoon Sichuan peppercorns
2 litres Oxtail Stock (see Essentials), refrigerated overnight to settle
3 green onions, sliced
4 slices ginger
1 stalk lemongrass, sliced
1 long red chilli, split lengthways
5 makrut lime leaves, shredded
1 star anise, cracked
2 pieces cassia bark
40 ml fish sauce

DUMPLING DOUGH
125 g wheat starch
10 g cornflour
150 ml boiling water
5 g lard

BEEF CHEEK STUFFING
20 ml vegetable oil
2 red shallots, minced
2 cloves garlic, minced
1 coriander root, minced
120 g slow-braised beef cheeks, finely chopped
2 teaspoons shredded mint leaves
½ teaspoon freshly ground black pepper
¼ teaspoon Sichuan Spice Salt (see Essentials)

To make the consomme, dry-roast the Sichuan peppercorns over gentle heat until fragrant, then grind them. Put the remaining consomme ingredients in a stockpot and bring to a simmer over very gentle heat – do not boil or the consomme will become cloudy. Simmer for 1 hour, then carefully strain through a muslin-lined sieve or a jelly bag to ensure the consomme is clear and free of sediment.

To cook the tongue, put the tongue in a large saucepan and cover with stock. Bring to simmering point, then cover and simmer gently over low heat for 3 hours until tender. Remove the tongue from the stock and allow to cool.

Peel the tongue and cut the meat into fine julienne strips, so it resembles fine noodles. You will need 1 tablespoon for each serve, so reserve the rest for another use (it is great in salads or sandwiches).

To make the dumpling dough, mix the wheat starch and cornflour in a bowl, then stir in the boiling water with a chopstick until combined. Cover the dough with a cloth and rest for 5 minutes. Knead in the lard, then rest again for 30 minutes.

Meanwhile, make the stuffing. Heat the oil in a frying pan and saute the shallots, garlic and coriander root until fragrant. Remove from the heat and stir in the finely chopped meat, mint and seasonings. Allow to cool.

To make the dumplings, roll the dough into a long sausage shape and cut into 24 pieces. Rub your bench and rolling pin with a little extra lard to keep the dough moist. Roll each piece of dough into a thin, flat round and cut with a 5 cm round pastry cutter.

Spoon 1 teaspoon of the stuffing into the centre of each round and fold in half, pressing the edges to seal. Sit the dumplings on baking paper, then steam in a large bamboo steamer basket, with plenty of room between them, for 15 minutes until the pastry is translucent.

Cut the bone marrow into 2 cm rounds. Poach in 100 ml of the oxtail consomme for 1 minute until softened. Put the steamed dumplings into bowls with the sliced tongue. Add the bean sprouts, shredded mint, Vietnamese mint leaves, cloud-ear fungus and sliced chilli, then ladle in the hot consomme. Float the bone marrow slices and chives on top, add a splash of lime juice and serve immediately.

SERVES 4

STEAMED PRAWN RICE NOODLE ROLLS

After watching industrious people making noodles in villages on the outskirts of Hanoi, I have incorporated the silken sheets of rice noodles into my ever-expanding repertoire. It is essential to buy fresh noodle sheets to make these rolls so they won't crack. If they have been refrigerated, they will not be suitable. Asian and Chinese food stores sell them and they are usually found on the shelves near the front door, at room temperature – they are made and delivered fresh each day.

500 g fresh rice noodle sheets (banh pho)
1 small carrot, cut into fine julienne strips
1 small cucumber, cut into fine julienne strips
2 tablespoons small coriander leaves
2 tablespoons Fried Shallot Slices (see Essentials)

PALM SUGAR CHILLI SAUCE
100 g palm sugar, shaved
150 ml water
120 ml fish sauce
30 ml coconut vinegar
50 ml fresh lime juice, strained
2 small green chillies, minced
1 clove garlic, minced

PRAWN STUFFING
20 ml vegetable oil
3 teaspoons minced garlic
3 teaspoons finely minced coriander root
4 green onions, finely sliced
½ teaspoon freshly ground white pepper
25 ml fish sauce
2 tablespoons coriander leaves, chopped
1 teaspoon sesame oil
400 g raw prawn meat, roughly chopped

To make the sauce, heat the palm sugar and water in a saucepan until the sugar has dissolved. Remove from the heat and cool, then mix with the remaining ingredients. Taste and adjust the seasoning if necessary.

To make the prawn stuffing, heat the oil in a frying pan and gently fry the garlic and coriander root for about 40 seconds until aromatic. Remove from the heat, add the green onion, pepper, fish sauce and chopped coriander leaves. Mix the sesame oil into the prawn meat, add the garlic seasoning and mix well.

Working on a lightly oiled bench, cut the noodle sheets into 12 rectangular lengths about 7 cm × 14 cm. This will allow for three rolls per serve. Reserve any extra noodle sheets for later use.

Spoon a heaped tablespoon of the prawn mixture onto each wrapper at the base of the shorter side and roll over lengthways to seal. Rest the rolls, seam-side down, on an oiled plate or tray in a single layer. Steam for 8 minutes or until the prawn stuffing is cooked – you may need to do this in batches.

Remove from the heat and use a flat spatula to transfer the rolls to a serving plate. For each serve, put two rolls next to each other in the centre of the plate, then lay the third on top in the centre of the two bottom rolls, making a pyramid shape. Arrange the carrot and cucumber slices across the centre of the rolls and sprinkle with the coriander leaves and fried shallot slices. Serve with the palm sugar chilli sauce.

SERVES 4

BRAISED PORK WITH EGGS AND YOUNG COCONUT

The juice that comes from young green coconuts is particularly delicious when used as a braising liquid or added to a sauce or salad dressing. It works just as well with desserts, and I often use it to make jelly. I first tasted a dish similar to this in a Saigon restaurant years ago, and I remembering taking notes at the time so I could recapture the flavour combination when I got back to my own kitchen. I try to use the meat from a suckling pig for the very best result.

400 g pork shoulder, sliced crossways into 5 cm pieces
75 g castor sugar
25 ml fish sauce
25 ml light soy sauce
1 teaspoon freshly ground white pepper
200 ml White Chicken Stock (see Essentials)
500 ml young coconut juice
40 ml fish sauce, extra
4 large eggs, hard-boiled and cut in half lengthways
60 g young coconut flesh, finely shredded
2 tablespoons small oyster mushrooms, softened in a little oil with minced garlic
2 tablespoons Asian lemon basil leaves, torn

Marinate the pork with the sugar, fish sauce, soy sauce and pepper for 1 hour in a clay pot. Put the pot over a gentle heat, add the chicken stock and half the coconut juice, then cover with a lid and slowly braise for 2 hours until the pork caramelises.

Add the remaining juice and the extra fish sauce and cook for another 30 minutes until the pork is very tender. Add the eggs, shredded coconut and oyster mushrooms and leave on the heat for 3 minutes until heated through. Stir in the lemon basil leaves and serve with steamed jasmine rice.

SERVES 4

CUSTARD APPLE ICE CREAM WITH HONEYCOMB

Make this velvet smoothie of an ice cream during winter when custard apples are in season. I fold in honeycomb chunks after it has churned for textural contrast, and it can also be served with pancakes or waffles.

600 g custard apple puree
300 g castor sugar
8 egg yolks, beaten
60 ml fresh lemon juice, strained
2 tablespoons minced candied (sweet preserved) ginger
600 ml pouring (35%) cream
120 g Honeycomb (see Essentials)

To make the ice cream, mix the custard apple and sugar in a bowl and heat over a pan of simmering water until the sugar has dissolved.

Lightly whisk the egg yolks into the custard apple and continue to cook over the simmering water until it reaches a custard consistency. Stir in the lemon juice, ginger and cream, then remove from the heat and allow to cool completely.

Churn in an ice-cream machine until firm.

Fold the honeycomb through the ice cream, then transfer to a plastic container, cover and freeze for 3 hours before serving.

SERVES 6–8

BLEEDING HEARTS

This moulded ice cream has blood plum sorbet as its heart, which is enveloped in coconut ice cream. It is prepared in individual moulds so its blood-red heart remains hidden, giving an element of surprise. In the restaurant, I have served it as a Valentine's Day dessert for lovers, creating a sense of playfulness.

4 blood plums, peeled and sliced into thin rounds
4 tablespoons Blood Plum Sauce (see Essentials)
1 tablespoon shredded fresh coconut

COCONUT ICE CREAM
750 ml pouring (35%) cream
500 ml milk
75 g fresh coconut, shredded
50 g coconut palm sugar (gula melaka), shaved
150 g castor sugar
12 large egg yolks

BLOOD PLUM SORBET
500 ml strained blood plum puree
100 g castor sugar
100 g glucose, softened
20 ml fresh lemon juice, strained

To make the coconut ice cream, infuse the cream, milk, shredded coconut and coconut sugar in a saucepan over very low heat until simmering point is reached. Remove from the heat and leave to infuse for 30 minutes. Reheat gently when ready to add to the eggs.

Whisk the egg yolks in a bowl until pale and frothy, then whisk in the hot cream mixture. Stand the bowl over a pan of simmering water and cook, stirring, until the mixture reaches a custard consistency and coats the back of a spoon. Pass the custard through a fine mesh sieve into a bowl and discard the solids. Allow to cool, then churn in an ice-cream machine until firm.

Spoon the ice cream into the moulds until they are two-thirds full. Freeze for 2 hours.

To make the blood plum sorbet, mix the ingredients together in a bowl, stirring until the sugar has dissolved. Churn in an ice-cream machine until firm enough to mould.

Scoop the centre from the frozen coconut ice cream in the moulds using a melon baller or parisienne cutter. Scoop the plum sorbet into balls the same size and drop into the centre of each mould. Fill the mould with the remaining coconut ice cream and return to the freezer. Freeze for 5–6 hours or overnight.

To serve, arrange the blood plum slices in a circle in the centre of serving plates for the moulded ice cream to sit on, with the plum slices just visible, like a collar. Add a spoonful of plum sauce.

To turn out the ice creams, dip each mould in hot water for 15–20 seconds to loosen, then turn the ice cream out onto the plates, smoothing the edges with a palette knife. Sit a few coconut shreds on top and serve immediately.

SERVES 4

MANGO AND PASSIONFRUIT TRIFLE

One of my classic desserts and a tribute to my favourite fruit: passionfruit. In creating this recipe, I reinterpreted the idea of the trifle by taking its components and giving them a fresh face with a tropical twist. I like to use dome moulds but you could just as easily assemble each layer in a glass or dish – just reverse the order, remembering the jelly layer has to be on the top. I have been quite specific here about the wine to use for the jelly, simply because I have found it is the best match for the other flavours.

1 sheet edible gold leaf
1 large ripe mango, finely sliced
Genoise Cake (see Essentials)
30 ml Sugar Syrup (see Essentials)
30 ml passionfruit juice, strained

WINE JELLY
125 ml Mount Horrocks Cordon Cut Riesling (or similar)
2 g gelatine leaves, softened in cold water

PASSIONFRUIT CARAMEL
150 g castor sugar
30 ml water
125 ml passionfruit juice, strained
3 tablespoons passionfruit pulp

PASSIONFRUIT CREAM
75 ml milk
2 egg yolks
75 g castor sugar
50 ml passionfruit juice, strained
1.5 g gelatine leaves, softened in cold water
125 ml pouring (35%) cream, whipped to soft peaks

To make the jelly, pour the wine into a saucepan and heat to simmering point. Remove the pan from the heat and stir in the softened gelatine. Pour the jelly into dome moulds and refrigerate for 1 hour until set.

When set, stick a few small flecks of gold leaf in the centre of each jelly, then arrange a few slices of mango in a single layer on top.

To make the passionfruit cream, heat the milk in a saucepan to simmering point. Whisk the egg yolks and sugar until pale and creamy. Add the hot milk, place the bowl over a pan of simmering water and stir in the passionfruit juice. Cook to a custard consistency (the mixture should coat the back of a spoon), whisking continuously to increase the volume and give a lighter texture.

Add the softened gelatine and when dissolved, remove from the heat and sit the bowl over a bowl of ice to stop further cooking. Allow the custard to cool then fold in the whipped cream. Spoon the passionfruit cream into the moulds and smooth the top (the moulds should be three-quarters full). Refrigerate for 1 hour until set.

Lay the remaining mango slices over the cream in a single layer to cover.

Cut a sheet of genoise sponge that is 1.5 cm thick, then cut out four disks the same diameter as the base of the moulds.

Mix the sugar syrup and passionfruit juice together in a bowl and soak each genoise disk for 20 seconds in the syrup until moist. Lay the genoise over the mango to seal the mould and press gently to make even. Wrap each mould in plastic film to make it airtight and refrigerate for 2 hours before serving.

To make the passionfruit caramel, heat the sugar and water in saucepan over high heat until it becomes a caramel colour (do not stir). Add the passionfruit juice when it reaches the right colour, reduce the heat and cook for a few minutes until combined. Remove from the heat and allow to cool completely before stirring in the passionfruit pulp.

To turn out, hold the mould in hot water for 20 seconds then turn over and unmould – the trifle should slide out easily onto the plate. Spoon some passionfruit caramel around the base of the trifle and serve.

SERVES 4

CHASING
LARA CROFT
THE TEMPLES
OF ANGKOR

Influenced over the centuries by Indian, Siamese and Javanese kingdoms, the Khmer culture of Cambodia is ancient, intriguing and gracefully elegant, with a heady juxtaposition of Hindu and Buddhist history. Descending from the clouds by plane and taking those first steps on Siem Reap soil, in Cambodia's north-west, I felt the magic and spirituality draw me close. Merely an hour's flight from the mayhem of Bangkok, it was as if I had been transported to another world. I was immediately struck by the friendliness and obvious warmth of the people, which seemed at odds with the brutal events of the country's recent history.

My first visit coincided with the start of the wet season but here, as everywhere, global warming is changing the weather patterns and we were blessed with continual sunshine in mid-July when it is usually monsoonal. The ideal time to visit is from late October to early March – although our next trip was in April, an ideal time to evade heavy rain but not the excessive humidity.

We decided to go to the temples in the relative cool of the early morning and again late in the afternoon, giving us time to surrender to the midday heat. From the air, the terrain hadn't looked as dense or foreboding as I had anticipated, but this perception quickly changed when I saw the enormous trunks and branches of the kapok trees that envelop some of the ancient temples like Ta Prohm (where the popular movie *Lara Croft Tomb Raider* was filmed); only then did I get a real sense of the mighty power and presence of the jungle. When the temples were discovered in the 19th century, after being deserted for 400 years, they were totally entangled in nature's bondage and have since been slowly and painstakingly restored.

Angkor Wat is the most well-known temple in the complex, the jewel in the crown with its exquisite architecture and profoundly spiritual atmosphere, but there are many other temples around Siem Reap and throughout Cambodia – about 250 in all, we were told by our affable young guide Dinar, a proud history graduate who clearly cherishes his Khmer culture. Angkor's beauty and majesty is matched, even surpassed by the magnificence of Bayon, a neighbouring temple built within the ancient walls of royal city Angkor Thom. The entrance is dramatic, a long causeway flanked by imposing stone statues of gods and devils on either side, and the temple itself has 54 towers topped with enormous images of an early king's face carved into the stone on each side. The ancestral presence seems to emanate from the walls and the stone sculptures – the apsaras (celestial nymphs), mythical serpents, garudas and guardian lions all weave their way into the Hindu and Buddhist myths and legends of the place.

It is easy to feel like a stranger here, so foreign is the culture – but it is that very point of difference that is so compelling. We were told by a leading Italian historian, who has spent 12 years translating the Sanskrit scripts on the temple walls, that several temples in the north of the country and nearer the Thai border are still off-limits because of the deadly land mines and unexploded bombs left by the Khmer Rouge. It seemed hard to conceive of such a gruesome past as we walked around the peaceful and contemplative temples – the air thick with incense, the faces smiling and innocent. Having survived these troubled times, Cambodia's heritage is under threat of being obliterated due to the constant theft and plundering of these ancient sites. The original splendour and

STAYING IN SIEM REAP

AMANSARA RESORT
Road to Angkor, Siem Reap
Tel +855 63 760 333
www.amanresorts.com
Even if you're not a guest here you can book for dinner or lunch. Two set menus are offered, both of which change daily: a Khmer menu of six dishes, and a three-course meal of more Western-style home cooking. Wines and cheeses are flown in from Europe – there's even a temperature-controlled cheese room (this is a serious food lover's pit-stop). All other ingredients are sourced locally.

FOREIGN CORRESPONDENTS' CLUB (FCC) ANGKOR
Pokambor Avenue, Siem Reap
Tel +855 63 760 280
www.fcccambodia.com
Ideal riverfront location in an old colonial building, including sunset drinks and assorted Asian-style bar snacks in the upstairs bar. Hotel rooms are stylish yet completely affordable.

brilliance of the temples can only be imagined: gold and bronze have been stripped away, marble removed, and precious stones pilfered.

Every day we spent in Cambodia, we took our stomachs and taste buds on a journey of discovery. Thanks to our friend Toby (who manages the Amansara Resort) we were given a first-hand glimpse into Khmer life, eating only local foods prepared according to simple recipes that have been verbally passed down through generations of women. A typical Khmer meal includes a variety of dishes – generally a salad, curry, stir-fry, soup and a vegetable dish – all put on the table at the same time and served with steamed rice. There are almost no books that detail Cambodia's culinary history so it is vitally important that their traditions be observed and recorded, a project I hope to be involved with in the future.

There are two produce markets in Siem Reap: the main Psar Leu, a huge wholesale market that stretches along National Highway 6 just beyond the river; and Psar Chas, a smaller local market in the old town, abuzz with energy and mayhem, so typical of this part of the world. Early morning is the best time to visit. To get energised, we would start with a bowl of om bok – rice flakes that have been pounded and flattened and served as cereal with sugar, young coconut juice and tiny sugar bananas. Then on to soak up the familiar aromas of chilli, sour tamarind, fermented fish paste, raw meat, fragrant lemongrass and limes, salted fish, and pungent fruits and vegetables. Bargaining is the order of the day and is taken in goodwill. You might only be haggling over a few cents – so play the game, but don't be mean-spirited – remember, for many people, the markets are their livelihood.

One day I cooked lunch for the chefs of the hotel where I was staying, as a gesture of thanks for allowing me to observe them at work. Sharing information is one of the great things about kitchen camaraderie. After I'd prepared a salad of chilli coconut chicken and stir-fried beef noodles, they all concluded that I cooked like a Thai – very hot and spicy (between the giggles and asking for more!). They claimed their palates were attuned to less chilli and relied on a more simple fragrance. To return the favour, they cooked the most magnificent dinner for us to celebrate my partner Margie's birthday, after she received a birthday blessing from a local monk. The meal included these wonderful dishes – each mouthful was as delicious as the next: minced pork and eggplant salad; stir-fried squid and green onion; stir-fried water spinach and garlic; sour fish soup; chicken and pumpkin curry; and rice flour dumplings with coconut cream.

We often ventured around town on bicycles, the typical mode of transport and a welcome echo of the past. Vespas and motor scooters are becoming more and more popular with many workers, while cars are still the domain of the rich, the governing or the visiting. My favourite way to get around has to be the charming and comfortable remorks, which are the cutest motorbikes with hooded carriages towed behind, perfect for two or three people to cruise around and take in the sights at a leisurely pace.

A wonderful way to enjoy the sunset is to have drinks at the outdoor garden bar of the Foreign Correspondents' Club (originally the local police station), which overlooks the river. It's a great way to unwind after a day of trekking around the temples, instilling a sense of grandeur and decadence. For a taste of the local action, head for Khmer Kitchen, a modest cafe in the centre of town that offers authentic dishes such as fried rice noodles with vegetables and chicken; a gently spicy fish salad; another salad of pork, long beans and coconut cream; ginger fried pork; minced pork stir-fried with chilli and basil; and fish or chicken cooked with pumpkin, garlic, egg and green onions. Washed down with a few glasses of local beer, the flavours are refreshing and clean.

A distinctive ingredient in Khmer cuisine is the black pepper sourced from Kampot in southern Cambodia.

EATING IN SIEM REAP

KHMER KITCHEN
The Passage, behind Bar Street, Siem Reap
Tel +855 63 964 154
Very local no-frills cafe with a fabulous menu of distinct, tingling flavours – a definite must when visiting.

MERIC
Hotel de la Paix, Sivatha Boulevard, Siem Reap
Tel +855 63 966 000
The chefs at this community-focused restaurant also work with underprivileged Cambodian kids and students. The Khmer tasting menu is an enlightening experience.

It has a lovely pungent fragrance and fruity citrus taste, quite distinct from Indian or Indonesian pepper, and was a revered export to France during their colonial rule. I just love its taste, and buy a bag of peppercorns from the airport every time I leave. A recent addition to the restaurant scene in Siem Reap is the opening of Meric, named in honour of the pepper, where the chefs reproduce traditional recipes to foster a growing awareness of Khmer culture and heritage – a brilliant initiative. Another uniquely Khmer flavour is an aromatic curry spice blend that combines ground ginger, coriander, pepper, nutmeg, cinnamon, turmeric, lemongrass, lime leaf and chilli. Cooked with coconut milk and crushed shallots, it makes a delicious sauce for meat or chicken, a bit like a mellow version of a Thai yellow curry.

Having an outdoor dinner at the remote and rarely visited Banteay Samre temple beyond the East Baray (a now-dry reservoir to the east of Angkor Thom) was one of the most unforgettable experiences of my life. Complete with traditional Apsara dancers who appeared to emerge from their stone images along the temple walls, seducing us with their beauty, we were left speechless with awe. A near full moon illuminated the temple in the midst of the jungle, soft candles flickered, and out of sight Khmer cooks created a heavenly feast for us over charcoal braziers. We were amazed at the way they cooked beef skewers with lemongrass and garlic to perfection with only a candle to work by. We felt like the original royalty who used to live and worship amongst these stone walls. Words cannot express how much I treasure the memory of that evening.

Earlier that day, we had left Siem Reap at sunrise and driven for 2 hours out to Phnom Kulen (Lychee Mountain), past scenes of village life unfolding into another day. We stopped along the way at a street lined with stalls selling basketware, to watch women serving bowls of nom banh chok for breakfast – thin rice noodles and slivers of freshwater fish in a green coconut soup flavoured with turmeric and ginger, topped with fresh herbs and greens. It reminded me of Vietnamese pho and Thai kanom jin, other firm favourites of mine for kick-starting the day. Ascending the dirt road up the mountain, little did we realise that we were amongst the few fortunate foreigners who had ever ventured this far into the jungle on this mountain plateau. Our guide Sokon had extensive knowledge of this region, having worked in these remote parts on the production of a local film only a few years before. We drove until the road ended in a village, then negotiated with locals to ride pillion on their bikes so we could explore deeper into the jungle. What an adventure! We came across lost sacred Hindu and Buddhist monuments covered in moss, were blessed by monks and taken into caves to meditate with them. Along the way we stopped off at a few mountain villages, where we were offered just-picked lychees by subsistence farmers, intrigued and wide-eyed at our presence. We felt like pioneers who had arrived at one of the untouched and undiscovered corners of the globe, difficult to comprehend in an age when most of the world seems so accessible. On our descent, we stopped by the rapids on the river for a picnic lunch under a canopy of trees. We had arranged to meet chefs from our hotel there, and more delicious Khmer flavours greeted us: the most delicious chicken and pomelo salad; a sour spicy soup (not unlike a Thai tom yam) with river prawns, tomato and lemongrass; and skewers of bar fish grilled over a charcoal brazier with lime and chilli. It was an idyllic repast.

Siem Reap is one of those places that leaves its mark on your soul. I know I will return to experience again its beguiling beauty, its serene and graceful people and its delicious food. On my next visit, I plan to take a boat down the Mekong River, starting in northern Laos near the Thai border and drifting through the heartland of Cambodia for a healthy dose of Khmer culture on the way to the Mekong's sprawling delta in Vietnam. I can't wait.

CLEAR FISH BROTH WITH NOODLES

This type of soup is an essential part of a Khmer meal, light and refreshing with clean, uncomplicated flavours. Any type of white fish can be used, from sand or red-spot whiting fillets to larger, fleshier deep-sea fish, even river fish – the choice is yours.

240 g fish fillets, skin removed
200 g thin rice noodles (rice sticks), cooked
8 Roasted Cherry Tomatoes (see Essentials)
4 stalks long-leaf (saw-tooth) coriander, shredded
2 green onions, finely sliced on the diagonal

FISH BROTH
1 litre Fish Stock (see Essentials)
50 ml Ginger Juice (see Essentials)
3 tomatoes, chopped
½ stalk lemongrass, chopped
25 ml light soy sauce
25 ml fish sauce
25 ml Sugar Syrup (see Essentials)
½ teaspoon freshly ground white pepper
25 ml fresh lime juice, strained

To make the broth, heat the stock, ginger juice, tomatoes, lemongrass and soy sauce in a saucepan and simmer gently – do not boil – for 30 minutes to allow the flavours to infuse. Add the fish sauce, sugar syrup and pepper and cook for another 5 minutes.

Remove from the heat and pass through a fine mesh sieve. Discard the solids and stir in the lime juice. Taste and adjust the seasoning if necessary.

Cut the fish into 2 cm chunks. Bring the soup back to simmering point, add the fish and cook gently for 3 minutes.

Divide the noodles among serving bowls, then ladle the soup and fish over the top. Add the roasted tomatoes, coriander and green onion and serve.

SERVES 4

COCONUT CRAB SOUP

I love the gentle clean flavours of this soup and I make it when fresh blue swimmer or spanner crabs are at their peak, to make the most of their inherent sweetness. It's very straightforward and rewarding to make.

300 g flaked cooked fresh crabmeat
2 makrut lime leaves, finely shredded
2 red bird's-eye chillies, finely sliced
2 tablespoons coriander leaves
2 tablespoons Fried Shallot Slices (see Essentials)

COCONUT SOUP
750 ml coconut milk
2 teaspoons minced galangal
1 teaspoon minced ginger
2 red bird's-eye chillies, minced
2 coriander roots, minced
5 red shallots, sliced lengthways
4 makrut lime leaves, shredded
1 stalk lemongrass, finely chopped
finely grated zest of 1 makrut lime
750 ml Light Crab Stock (see Essentials), made from the shells
75 ml fish sauce
50 ml fresh lime juice, strained

To make the soup, bring the coconut milk to the boil in a large saucepan and boil for a few minutes. Add the galangal, ginger, chilli, coriander, shallots, lime leaves, lemongrass and lime zest and simmer for a few minutes. Stir in the stock and fish sauce and simmer gently for 15 minutes. Pass the soup through a fine mesh strainer, discard the solids then add the lime juice.

Taste and adjust the seasoning if necessary.

Divide the crabmeat, shredded lime leaves, chilli and coriander leaves among serving bowls or cups, then ladle on the hot soup. Sprinkle some fried shallot slices over the top and serve.

SERVES 4

BLACK PEPPER CHICKEN TEA

The secret to this dish lies in starting with the most superior chicken stock possible, one that has been prepared consomme-style – clear with a pronounced chicken flavour. The 'tea' idea came about because the way the dish looked in a bowl reminded me of a brewed tea, and I played with the idea further by smoking the chicken over tea leaves. Serving it in tea cups gives it a whimsical note.

1 chicken breast fillet, steamed
½ punnet enoki mushrooms, stalks trimmed
2 tablespoons finely chopped chives
2 tablespoons coriander leaves
1 punnet micro watercress, snipped

CHICKEN TEA
1 head garlic
25 ml vegetable oil
1 brown onion, chopped
1 long red chilli, sliced
1 teaspoon chopped ginger
½ teaspoon black peppercorns, freshly ground
1 teaspoon Sichuan peppercorns, freshly ground
50 ml Shaoxing rice wine
3 makrut lime leaves, shredded
3 green onions, chopped
2 litres Brown Chicken Stock (see Essentials)
50 ml light soy sauce
30 ml fish sauce
25 ml fresh lime juice, strained
2 teaspoons freshly ground black pepper

To make the chicken tea, preheat the oven to 180°C. Wrap the garlic in foil and roast for 30 minutes or until soft. Remove from the oven and slice in half.

Heat the oil in a large heavy-based saucepan and fry the onion, chilli and ginger until softened and beginning to colour. Add the ground peppers, then deglaze the pan with the rice wine. Remove the pan from the heat when the wine comes to a boil.

Add the roasted garlic, lime leaves, green onions, chicken stock and soy sauce to the pan and slowly bring to a boil over gentle heat. Reduce the heat and simmer for 1 hour, skimming the surface regularly with a mesh spoon – do not boil or the consomme (tea) will become cloudy.

Strain the consomme through a muslin-lined sieve or a jelly bag to ensure the stock is clear and free of sediment, pressing firmly to extract as much liquid as possible. Discard the solids and allow to cool, then cover and refrigerate.

Remove any residual fat from the cooled consomme, then strain into a clean saucepan, avoiding any sediment. Bring to a simmer, then add the fish sauce, lime juice and black pepper and cook for 2 minutes. Taste and adjust the seasoning if necessary.

To serve, shred the chicken meat with your fingers into thin threads and divide among serving cups. Add the enoki, chives, coriander and watercress. Ladle in the hot consomme and swirl with a chopstick to combine. Serve immediately.

SERVES 8–10

PORK AND EGGPLANT SALAD

I try and always use the long green Asian eggplants for this dish. Harder to find than regular purple eggplant, they have a thin skin and creamy texture with no bitter aftertaste – perfect for this preparation. They taste wonderful when they have been blistered over hot coals, taking on a delicious smoky character. This is a Khmer take on the perfect synergy between pork and eggplant, and makes an ideal accompaniment to several other dishes served together.

6 long green Asian eggplants (aubergines)
40 ml vegetable oil
6 cloves garlic, minced
125 g minced pork
40 ml oyster sauce
20 ml fish sauce
1 tablespoon shaved palm sugar
1 teaspoon freshly ground black pepper
2 tablespoons Asian or Thai basil leaves, torn
6 green onions, finely sliced

Grill the eggplants whole until the skin blisters, then remove and leave until cool enough to handle.

Remove the burnt skins and wipe the eggplant with paper towel to clean – don't rinse as this will dilute the flavour. Chop the eggplants into 3 cm lengths.

Heat the oil in a frying pan and cook the garlic until softened. Add the pork and cook until it begins to change colour. Season with the oyster and fish sauces, palm sugar and black pepper and toss to combine thoroughly. Mix in the torn basil and green onions.

Arrange the eggplant slices on a serving plate, spoon the pork mixture over the top and serve.

SERVES 4

SMOKED TROUT, ROE AND POMELO SALAD

In Cambodia the fish used for this salad would be the river catfish, which has its own distinctive flavour. I have chosen the milder-tasting rainbow trout, a freshwater or river fish we have easy access to in Australia. You can buy the fish already smoked from your fishmonger. Another suitable alternative would be Victorian smoked eel, available from fish markets or better fishmongers.

1 smoked rainbow trout
4 tablespoons freshwater salmon roe
1 pomelo, peeled and broken into small segments
2 teaspoons dried prawns, soaked then pounded
2 cloves garlic, finely sliced
40 g roasted cashews, chopped
2 tablespoons shredded fresh coconut, lightly roasted
1 tablespoon shredded mint leaves
4 makrut lime leaves, finely shredded
2 tablespoons Fried Shallot Slices (see Essentials)
2 tablespoons castor sugar
20 ml fish sauce
20 ml fresh lime juice, strained

Remove the skin and bones from the smoked trout, flake the meat and place in a large bowl.

Add the remaining ingredients and toss thoroughly to combine. Taste and adjust the seasoning if necessary. Arrange on individual plates and serve.

SERVES 4

SEARED BEEF WITH KHMER CURRY SAUCE

During our time in Cambodia we often ate curries for dinner, and found Khmer curries to be quite mild and aromatic when compared with those of their neighbours. I found a Khmer curry powder mix on one visit that travelled home with me. Rather than the traditional curry where the meat is cooked in the gravy sauce, I have given it the Western treatment and seared the beef separately then doused it with the curry sauce as I assemble it on the plate. If you want to vary the vegetable accompaniment, you could serve the beef with a potato gratin, steamed broccolini or jasmine rice cooked in coconut milk.

60 ml vegetable oil
300 g sweet potato, chopped into large chunks
sea salt and freshly ground black pepper
40 ml Ginger Juice (see Essentials)
500 g beef scotch fillet, cut into 4 equal portions
2 tablespoons Asian or Thai basil leaves

KHMER CURRY POWDER
1 tablespoon ground dried galangal
2 teaspoons ground turmeric
1 tablespoon ground coriander
1 tablespoon ground star anise
2 teaspoons dried lime-leaf powder
2 teaspoons ground cassia
2 teaspoons dried lemongrass powder
1 teaspoon ground chilli

CURRY SAUCE
500 ml coconut cream
250 ml Beef Stock (see Essentials)
60 g palm sugar
200 ml coconut milk
50 ml fish sauce

To make the Khmer curry powder, mix all the ingredients together until combined. Store in an airtight container until ready to use.

To make the curry sauce, bring the coconut cream to boiling point in a saucepan. In a bowl, mix 4 tablespoons of the curry powder with just enough water to make a thick paste. Add the curry paste to the coconut cream and simmer gently for 5 minutes so the flavours infuse. Add the stock and palm sugar and cook over a low heat for 15 minutes until the sauce has reduced slightly. Stir in the coconut milk and bring to boil, then add the fish sauce and cook for another 10 minutes. Taste and adjust the seasoning if necessary.

To cook the sweet potato, preheat the oven to 185°C. Rub a roasting pan with 2 tablespoons of vegetable oil and add the sweet potato chunks. Season lightly with salt and pepper, then cover the pan with foil and roast for 40 minutes until tender. Remove from the oven and leave to cool for 10 minutes. Increase the oven temperature to 200°C.

Blend the sweet potato with the ginger juice in a food processor until smooth. Taste and adjust the seasoning if necessary.

To cook the beef, rub a little of the remaining curry powder onto each piece of beef then season lightly with salt and pepper. Heat a cast-iron frying pan, add the remaining oil and sear the beef for 3 minutes.

Turn the beef over and fry for another 2 minutes. Set aside to rest for 5 minutes to allow the juices to settle.

When ready to serve, heat the beef in the oven for 1 minute, then cut each piece crossways into four or five slices.

Spoon the roasted sweet potato puree onto the centre of serving plates and arrange the beef slices on top. Spoon on the curry sauce, garnish with basil leaves and serve.

SERVES 4

CRISPY RICE CAKES WITH CHILLI PORK SAUCE

This is a great way to use up leftover rice, a common practice in Cambodia and Thailand. The cooked rice is dried out, pressed into flat cakes and deep-fried until crisp. Making the rice cakes bite-size makes them easier to eat. The rich pork sauce is used for dipping and makes a great snack with drinks or as a shared start to a meal.

3 cups cooked jasmine rice, spread out to dry on a tray overnight
vegetable oil, for deep-frying

CHILLI PORK SAUCE
20 ml vegetable oil
120 g minced pork
3 small dried chillies, soaked in hot water until softened, then finely chopped
5 cloves garlic, minced
3 small red chillies, minced
5 red shallots, minced
1 teaspoon freshly ground black pepper
150 ml coconut cream
100 ml coconut milk
3 tablespoons shaved palm sugar
25 ml fish sauce
20 ml fresh lime juice, strained
2 makrut lime leaves, finely shredded
75 g roasted cashews, ground
½ punnet micro watercress, snipped

To prepare the rice cakes, mould the dried rice into small rounds and flatten, using about a tablespoon of rice for each cake. Heat the oil in a deep-fryer or large saucepan to 180°C and deep-fry the cakes a few at a time until crisp and golden. Drain on paper towel and continue until all the cakes are fried.

To make the chilli pork sauce, heat the oil in a wok and stir-fry the pork and chopped dried chilli over high heat, stirring so it doesn't clump together. Add the garlic, chilli and shallots and cook for 2–3 minutes until the pork is brown. Add the pepper, coconut cream and milk and bring to simmering point, then stir in the sugar and fish sauce and cook for another 3 minutes until the sugar has dissolved. Stir in the lime juice and shredded lime leaf.

Taste and the adjust seasoning if necessary, then add the cashews and remove from the heat. Toss through the snipped watercress. Serve the pork sauce in a bowl with the rice cakes on the side.

SERVES 6–8

PALM SUGAR FISH WITH GREEN MANGO

This is my interpretation of a classic dish we ate at Khmer Kitchen and Amansara – it's finger-licking good with fresh clean flavours. Any large white fish fillets are suitable, such as bar cod, blue eye, jewfish, trevally, sea bass, barramundi, red emperor or snapper.

500 g thick white fish fillet, skin removed
80 g rice flour
2 teaspoons sea salt
2 teaspoons freshly ground black pepper
vegetable oil, for deep-frying, plus extra for pan-frying
4 cloves garlic, finely sliced
3 small green chillies, finely sliced
2 tablespoons salted dried radish, rinsed in cold water
200 g palm sugar, shaved
80 ml fish sauce
3 small tomatoes, peeled then pureed
2 green mangoes, peeled and finely shredded
12 cherry tomatoes, halved
50 g bean sprouts, trimmed
3 tablespoons Asian or Thai basil leaves, torn
2 tablespoons shredded long-leaf (saw-tooth) coriander

Cut the fish into 2 cm chunks and dust with rice flour, salt and half the pepper.

Heat the oil in a wok to 180°C and deep-fry the fish chunks in small batches for 3 minutes until golden. Remove and drain on paper towel.

Heat 2 tablespoons of oil in a frying pan and cook the garlic and chilli until fragrant. Add the dried radish strips and fry for another minute. Remove from the heat and add to the cooked fish.

Combine the palm sugar and fish sauce in a saucepan and cook until it becomes a rich caramel colour (add a little water if necessary), then add the tomato puree and stir to combine. Simmer for a few minutes, then season with the remaining pepper and add the fish. Toss to coat evenly and simmer gently for a few minutes to heat through.

Remove from the heat, toss through the remaining ingredients and serve.

SERVES 4

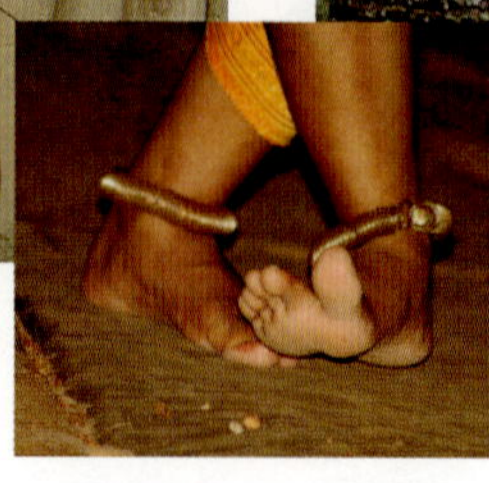

STEAMED CHICKEN AND CUCUMBER SALAD

Honest, clean and uncomplicated flavours like this underpin much of the street food of Cambodia, and a salad like this one would not be out of place at a Khmer dinner, served with a range of other complementary dishes.

2 organic chicken breasts
½ teaspoon sea salt
½ teaspoon freshly ground white pepper
20 ml light soy sauce

CUCUMBER SALAD
1 cucumber, peeled and seeded
1 tablespoon palm sugar
40 ml rice vinegar
20 ml fish sauce
20 ml fresh lime juice, strained
20 ml mandarin juice
2 red shallots, finely sliced
1 long red chilli, finely sliced
50 g roasted cashews, chopped
2 tablespoons chopped coriander leaves
1 tablespoon shredded mint leaves
1 tablespoon Fried Shallot Slices (see Essentials)

Season the chicken breasts with salt, pepper and soy sauce and lay on a flat plate. Place in a bamboo steamer basket over simmering water and cook, covered, for 25 minutes or until tender. Shred the meat into thin lengths using your fingers, going with the grain of the meat.

To make the salad, dice the cucumber into 1 cm cubes. Dissolve the palm sugar into the vinegar in a saucepan over gentle heat, then remove from the heat and stir in the fish sauce and lime and mandarin juices. Taste and adjust the seasoning and balance of flavours if necessary.

Mix the dressing into the diced cucumber, leave for 2 minutes then add the shallots, chilli, cashews and herbs. Toss to combine. Add the shredded chicken and combine, then arrange on plates and sprinkle with fried shallots to serve.

SERVES 4

WHITE PEACHES WITH LYCHEE GINGER SYRUP

This syrup can be made ahead and stored in the refrigerator until ready to use. It's a great standby to have on hand and gives a flavour boost to any tropical fruit.

6 white peaches
pulp from 2 passionfruit
16 lychees, cut in half and seeded
2 teaspoons candied (sweet preserved) ginger, finely sliced

LYCHEE GINGER SYRUP
100 g palm sugar, shaved
6 makrut lime leaves, torn
5 cm stalk lemongrass, coarsely chopped
2 tablespoons sliced young ginger
750 ml Sugar Syrup (see Essentials)
50 ml Stone's green ginger wine
60 ml fresh lime juice, strained
60 ml lychee liqueur

To make the syrup, heat the palm sugar, lime leaves, lemongrass, ginger and sugar syrup in a large saucepan until boiling. Add the ginger wine, then reduce the heat and simmer gently for 15 minutes to allow the flavours to infuse. Stir in the lime juice and lychee liqueur.

Add the peaches to the syrup and simmer for 15 minutes until softened, stirring often so the peaches cook evenly in the syrup.

Remove the peaches and when cool enough to handle, peel the skins and discard. Cut the peaches in half and remove the stones. Strain the syrup through a fine mesh sieve and leave to cool.

Mix the peaches with the other fruits and the candied ginger in a bowl and pour on the cooled syrup. Leave for 5 minutes before serving.

SERVES 4

WHITE PEACHES WITH LYCHEE GINGER SYRUP >

COCONUT TAPIOCA CREAM WITH SUGAR BANANAS

Tapioca and rice play an integral part in the Khmer repertoire, and this traditional dessert fits the 'comfort food' category perfectly. The tiny sugar bananas that are so prevalent in Asia are necessary for this dish to succeed – it just doesn't taste the same with larger or floury bananas. I have added the coconut wafers to add a crunchy texture to the dessert. You could also use coconut macaroons.

6 small sugar bananas
50 g unsalted butter
30 g brown sugar
40 ml coconut cream, warmed

COCONUT WAFERS
50 g unsalted butter
50 g castor sugar
2 egg whites
50 g plain flour
1 tablespoon shredded fresh coconut

TAPIOCA CREAM
750 ml water
150 g tapioca pearls
250 ml coconut milk
½ teaspoon sea salt
75 g castor sugar
4 tablespoons shredded fresh coconut

To make the coconut wafers, cream the butter and sugar in an electric mixer until pale and creamy – this will take up to 10 minutes. Fold the unbeaten egg whites into the mixture, a little at a time.

Add the flour and work until the dough becomes smooth and pliable. (If you are making the mixture ahead of time, this is the point to refrigerate it in an airtight container. Let it come back to room temperature before working with it.)

Butter and flour a 30 cm × 24 cm baking tray. With a palette knife, spread a thin layer of the wafer mixture onto the tray, then sprinkle with the shredded coconut. Put the tray in the refrigerator for about 1 hour until the mixture becomes firm. This prevents the biscuits from fracturing during cooking.

Preheat the oven to 160°C. Bake the chilled wafer mixture for 4 minutes, then remove from the oven. The mixture should be just set but not cooked or coloured. Using a sharp knife and a round pastry cutter, quickly cut biscuits to your desired shape and size, then remove the unwanted mixture and return the tray to the oven for 3 minutes. The biscuits should now be cooked and pale golden brown. Slide the biscuits onto a wire rack to set, cool completely, then store in an airtight container until ready to use.

To make the tapioca cream, bring the water to the boil in a saucepan and add the tapioca. Cook over moderate heat for about 15 minutes or until transparent and softened, whisking constantly. Add the coconut milk, salt and sugar and stir to dissolve. Bring to the boil, then reduce the heat and simmer for 5 minutes. Add the shredded coconut and simmer for another 5 minutes, then remove from the heat.

Spoon the tapioca cream into serving glasses, bowls or dariole moulds and refrigerate for 2 hours until set. If you choose to mould the tapioca, turn it out from the mould onto a plate and proceed from there.

To prepare the bananas, peel and cut into 2 cm round slices. Heat the butter in a frying pan, add the sugar and when dissolved, add the bananas and toss over heat until glazed and softened.

Spoon the warmed coconut cream over the tapioca, then arrange the bananas on top and serve with a coconut wafer.

SERVES 4

CARAMEL AND GINGER CHOCOLATE ICE CREAM

I have layered these two ice-cream flavours in a tin, but you could just as easily store the churned ice creams in separate airtight containers in the freezer and use an ice-cream scoop to serve.

120 g Ginger Snap Wafers (see page 204), crushed

CARAMEL ICE CREAM
100 g castor sugar
25 ml water
250 ml pouring (35%) cream
125 ml milk
3 egg yolks
30 g castor sugar, extra

GINGER CHOCOLATE ICE CREAM
500 ml milk
1 tablespoon minced ginger
6 egg yolks
200 g castor sugar
300 g dark couverture chocolate, chopped into small pieces and melted
500 ml pouring (35%) cream
2 tablespoons minced candied (sweet preserved) ginger

Line an 8 cm × 24 cm rectangular tin with baking paper, with the edges overhanging for manoeuvrability. Sprinkle a third of the crushed biscuit to cover the base. Set aside.

To make the caramel ice cream, cook the sugar and water in a saucepan over high heat, without stirring, until it turns to caramel.

While this is cooking, make the custard base. Heat the cream and milk in another saucepan. Whisk the egg yolks and extra sugar together until pale and creamy, then stir in the hot cream.

As soon as the caramel is ready, add 2 tablespoons of the custard base to the caramel, then pour the caramel back into the remaining custard and cook in a bowl over a pan of simmering water until it thickens and reaches custard consistency. Remove from the heat and allow to cool completely.

Churn the custard in an ice-cream machine until thick, then spoon into the lined tin until half full. Smooth the surface and freeze while you make the next layer.

To make the ginger chocolate ice cream, heat the milk and minced ginger in a saucepan until simmering. Whisk the eggs and sugar in a bowl, then add the hot milk and melted chocolate and cook over a pan of simmering water until it reaches custard consistency. Pass the custard through a fine mesh sieve and discard the solids.

Allow to cool for 20 minutes, then stir in the cream. Cool completely then churn in an ice-cream machine until firm. Add the candied ginger to the mix for the last 5 minutes of churning.

Sprinkle half of the remaining crushed biscuit over the caramel ice cream in the tin, then spoon the chocolate ice cream on top until the tin is full. Smooth the surface and sprinkle the remaining biscuit crunch on top. Freeze for another 4 hours until firm.

To serve, dip the tin in hot water for 20 seconds, turn the tin upside down and use the overhanging paper to pull the ice cream from the tin onto a board. Cut the ice cream into 3 cm thick slices using a hot sharp knife.

SERVES 10

STUPAS AND SAFFRON ROBES
LUANG PRABANG

Laos is a recent discovery for me. I was inspired to travel here after reading Alan Davidson's acclaimed culinary stories of his time spent in Laos as British ambassador; he later published the only written record of royal Lao cuisine from notes given to him by the king's chef. Natacha Du Pont De Bie's *Ant Egg Soup*, about her adventures as a food tourist in Laos, also struck a chord. I could certainly identify with her insistence on discovering the true essence of the country through its food – from chicken laap and sour bamboo fish soup to the local specialty of Paradise Chicken and, of course, ant eggs. I would stop short at drinking turkey or snake blood, though; there are some tastes I would prefer to leave to the imagination!

'Sabaidee' will be the first word you hear on arrival – welcome to Laos! As the small propeller plane descended through the mountains where teak forests, palm and coconut trees reached up to salute us, and gilded stupas poked through the fringes of the trees, we were greeted by the breathtaking beauty of Luang Prabang. Sandwiched between the mighty Mekong and Khan rivers, the enchanting ancient city of Luang Prabang proved to be a revelation. Once the royal capital of Laos, this is a place lost in time, a living museum of enormous beauty with its blend of East–West colonial charm, ornate temples, and graceful but crumbling French mansions. The pace of life continues to revolve around the lives of the saffron-robed Buddhist monks who tread the streets, and this leisurely atmosphere makes Luang Prabang immediately appealing and beguiling.

Staying in Luang Prabang gives you the chance to take part in the time-honoured ritual of Tak Bat – offering sticky rice to the hundreds of monks who emerge at dawn to walk single file through the streets collecting alms. As the sun slowly rises over the sleepy streets, the monks make a dramatic spectacle in their distinctive saffron robes. Within half an hour they have disappeared again, melting back into the various temple complexes, but we see them again later in the day, swimming in the river, chanting in the temples or relaxing as the sun starts to set. It is astonishing to think this practice has been a part of everyday life since the 7th century.

The former Royal Palace, now a museum, sits majestically in the centre of town, and the golden stupas of the temples can be seen on nearly every street. The muted tones of the houses and buildings give the place a distinctive colonial grace. Inspired by the beauty and serenity of this town, and with the imagery and tastes alive in my mind, I sat on the front terrace of our hotel one morning after breakfast to write these words, the air a smoky haze from the back-burning in the mountains before the summer monsoonal rains.

Like other former royal or imperial cities of the region – Thailand's Ayutthaya, Vietnam's Hue, Cambodia's Angkor and China's Lijiang – Luang Prabang is a World Heritage site, one that partly owes its well-preserved monuments and streetscapes to the fact that the capital was moved south to Vientiane in the 16th century. The city was also spared the ravages of war – unlike other parts of the country, which suffer the legacy of American bombs dropped for almost a decade as part of the Secret War waged against North Vietnamese troops on the Ho Chi Minh Trail. Laos has the dubious distinction of being the most bombed country in the world, and the amount of unexploded ordnance serves as a savage reminder of the stupidity of war. More recently, it appears that communist rule has done much to protect this unique and remote society by effectively isolating it from the outside world until the late 1980s. I only hope the march of progress doesn't destroy the natural charm and ambience of this languid town, or begin to erode the preservation measures that have been put in place.

I couldn't help thinking of the senseless war that had been inflicted on the Lao people as we puttered up the Mekong from Luang Prabang in a long-tail boat on our way to visit the sacred and revered caves at Pak Ou, where thousands of Buddha images keep watch in twin caves high above the limestone cliffs. Passing the villagers as they went about their daily lives by the river – fishing, panning for minerals, farming their crops on the banks and scouring the rocks for edible moss – we tried to imagine what they must have thought as they were relentlessly battered by bombs falling from the sky. Hmong people and about 60 other ethnic groups live further upstream and in the mountains, and still seem to be virtually untouched by the modern world.

SHOPPING IN LUANG PRABANG

THE BLUE HOUSE
Sakkarine Road (main street)
Tel +856 71 252 383
Authentic Lao handicrafts.

Resplendent in ornamental headwear and brightly coloured clothes, some come to sell their produce or wares at the town markets.

I have heard many times that Lao food is like Thai food on steroids, which is understandable, given that the Isaan people who inhabit north-east Thailand and southern Laos share a common heritage and similar culinary habits. The morning street market that stretches along Souvanabanlang Road, on the Mekong side of town, is inspirational and fascinating. It reveals the ingenuity of the locals, who eat anything and everything that lives or grows in the surrounding jungle and mountains. Their repertoire consists of what is immediate, so many of the ingredients are wild as opposed to farmed. I watched as women sliced open long rattan branches to sell their soft white centres, bundled together – a vegetable with an astringent taste and a texture like palm heart but firmer. As we strolled through the market we saw all sorts of weird and wonderful things on display – vegetables, jungle greens, wild birds, frogs, tadpoles, lizards, wild deer, small fish splayed on bamboo sticks and grilled until crisp, and pork and buffalo (the staple meats) in abundance. If you have culinary daring, this is the place to come to taste pickled scorpions, flying foxes, tree monkeys, lizards and wild birds from the jungle, termite eggs, snakes, moles and badgers. Though I didn't see any water beetles (cockroaches) for sale – as described by Natacha in her book – there were plenty of snails, periwinkles and other wriggly creatures from the rivers, along with the blackened carcasses of smoked water rats. Like the Chinese, the Lao apparently consider anything with legs – except a table – fair game.

Each morning we sat on low rickety stools as an old woman made us yaw dip, breakfast rolls of triangular sheets of fresh rice paper filled with shredded vegetables and herbs. She made a dipping sauce from ingredients lined up in bowls: salt, sugar, crushed peanuts, chilli paste, rice vinegar and fish sauce. She also had bowls of chopped raw liver and other unidentifiable offal and animal bits to be used in fillings, but we graciously declined these offerings. The laap salads became firm favourites, especially the ones made just with vegetables and leafy greens, sometimes with a few bits of chopped tofu or minced chicken added – such clean and distinct flavours, brimming with freshness. Equally appealing were the boulangeries (bakeries), a reminder of Laos's colonial past. Freshly baked baguettes were served each day for breakfast at our hotel with premium-strength Lao coffee and fresh fruit – a perfect start to the day.

At the market and elsewhere we noticed ceramic jars of padek, a condiment used liberally in much of the food. More pungent than fish sauce and with little chunks of pickled fish in it, along with broken rice husks, most households make their own. Some can be so strong they nearly blow your head off when the lid is removed – powerful stuff indeed, but the potent fermented aroma does subside somewhat during cooking.

Luang Prabang is renowned for local delicacies not found elsewhere in Laos, which is not surprising given its royal heritage. Small birds, such as quail, pigeon or waterfowl, might be braised with cabbage or leafy greens; common meats include wild deer and the densely textured buffalo; chicken and duck appear in all manner of guises; wild greens and leafy vegetables like mountain watercress, ferns, river moss and other pungent leaves are a signature; and yam beans, radishes, tiny sweet potatoes, snake beans, cucumbers and various types of eggplants and gourds provide a crunchy texture.

Sticky rice is served with everything and is eaten with your fingers. You take a portion of rice from the steaming basket, hold it in one hand and take small amounts from

STAYING IN LUANG PRABANG

THE APSARA
Ban Wat Sene, Kingkitsarath Road
Tel +856 71 254 670
www.theapsara.com
Modestly priced but stylish guesthouse facing the Khan River with super-friendly staff, wonderful breakfasts and a delicious menu. Sunset cocktails in the bar became a mandatory nightly event for us.

THREE NAGAS
Ban Wat Nong, Sakkarine Road
Tel +856 71 253 888
www.alilahotels.com/3nagas
Gorgeous small hotel in the centre of the city with wonderful attention to detail and the most authentic Lao food. Make sure you have dinner at their restaurant (Three Nagas Lao), which serves refined and elegant royal Lao cooking.

it to roll into a small ball and dip into jeow (relishes). We quickly learnt it is considered bad manners to leave grains of rice in communal dishes, so the type of rice and the rolling action is all important. A couple of quick lessons and we were there, all looking the part and showing off our manual dexterity. The custom is to serve the rice with grilled or steamed foods using lots of vegetables, herbs and leafy greens with relatively simple flavours. The rice steamer is a conical bamboo basket that sits in a funnel-shaped pot with boiling water, so the grains steam and become sticky as they soften and cook. Impressed, we all left with extra bags full of these wonderful steamers.

We ate an unforgettable lunch at a newly opened cafe, Tamarind, opposite Wat Nong in the historic quarter. Steamed sticky rice was served in individual little bamboo baskets and we deftly rolled it into small balls in the palms of our hands, which we then dipped into various jeow. We devoured the jeow bong (a far superior version to others we tasted – without the rubbery buffalo hide that is commonly used), and were enamoured of the gorgeous smokiness of jeow mak keua (eggplant) and the fresh pungency of the coriander jeow pak hom. We worked our way through the menu and found another favourite: khai pene – crisp dried sheets of leafy river greens that have been dried and pressed into sheets with sesame, garlic and tomato. It is similar in appearance and taste to laver or toasted nori seaweed, but with more flavour. We shared a communal plate of sai oua (the local pork sausage) and sinh savanh (thin sheets of air-dried buffalo). We loved the miang (betel-leaf parcels) filled with boiled apple eggplant made into a paste with sticky rice flour and sugar. Or lam was a delicious experience, a stew of buffalo meat, eggplant and a bitter spicy root vegetable that has no equivalent. I love it when I discover another dimension of flavour, another way of expanding my repertoire with familiar and new ingredients. It was a wonderful introduction to Laos, and Luang Prabang in particular. We kicked ourselves that we were not there on Friday when they cook pun pa, a traditional Lao feast of fish barbequed in banana leaves with lemongrass and herbs, served with noodles, herbs and dipping sauce – and that in itself is reason to return.

I had a memorable birthday dinner at Three Nagas Restaurant, with food from their traditional Lao menu – not their French or Falang (foreigner) menu. The menu is divided into sections so a dish from each comprises a typical Lao dinner, structured to create harmony and balance with flavours and textures. There's phan (wrapped food); laap (minced salads that can use either raw or cooked protein); oua (stuffed vegetables); ping (grilled food); kranab (ingredients wrapped with fresh herbs and grilled in banana leaf); mok (wrapped in banana leaf and steamed); pon (simmered with herbs and fermented fish); oor (stews); kroua (sauteed meats); trod (fried food); nung (steamed); supp (boiled); and keng (soups), all served with jeow and sticky rice. Of these, the stand outs were a minced chicken salad fragrant with lemongrass, mint and lime; the specialty pork sausage of Luang Prabang with a slightly sour tamarind flavour; buffalo cooked with garlic to a meltingly tender texture; fish steamed with coconut in banana leaf, which had an ethereal texture and zesty citrus flavour; and I would walk over hot coals to eat more of the minced pork stewed with fermented fish and lemongrass, a symphony of long-lasting flavours on the palate.

Trying to work our way through the myriad and diverse foods available, our visit became something of a food frenzy, all of it lip-smackingly good. Relying on local advice, we went to the end of Kingkitsarath Road on the Khan River side of town, to the front terrace of someone's house for dinner one night, with the express purpose of

EATING IN LUANG PRABANG

TAMARIND

Kounsoa Road, opposite Wat Nong
Tel +856 20 777 0484
This place is owned by a Melbourne woman, Caroline Gaylord, and her Lao boyfriend, Joy. They make the most fabulous sampling plates and fresh juices and are well informed and enthusiastic about their town. The jeow bong is divine and you can even get it to take away. Lunch only, closed Sundays.

TUM TUM CHENG COOKING SCHOOL

Nok Khao Leum Khon Arts House
29/2 Sakkarine Road, opposite Wat Khily
Tel +856 71 252 019
www.tumtumcheng.com
One-day classes that start at the market: learn to cook a few local dishes with the young team, then eat them for lunch afterwards.

tasting phet (duck). This family cooks for anyone prepared to pay a nominal fee for basic home cooking. The Lao eat early so we arrived just before 6 p.m., but already the keng sam phet (sour spicy duck soup) and op phet (oven-baked duck stew) were finished. We settled on a few plates of ping phet (duck pieces threaded onto bamboo skewers and cooked over hot coals), served with a fiery chilli dipping sauce. We washed it down with a glass or two of Lao beer and watched a thunderstorm roll over, intensifying the smells of the jungle. It was perfect.

We left with a deep fondness for this place and vowed to return, moved by its ease and immediate comfort. This land had woven its magic spell over me and I was utterly charmed by the gentle ritual of daily life, the food, majestic temples and stunning landscapes coloured with the fleeting saffron robes of the monks. The mango and frangipani trees at our beach house remind me of Laos, and the flavours of Lao food have woven their way into my cooking, giving it an added and distinctive dimension and my pantry a few of its essential ingredients.

GINGER SQUID SALAD

This salad was inspired by the produce I saw at the Lao markets. It's so easy to make and is perfect when you want to start a meal with light, clean flavours. I use squid in my version, instead of small river fish.

600 g small squid
8 Asian or Thai basil leaves, shredded
8 purple perilla leaves, shredded
2 tablespoons shredded mint leaves
100 g bean sprouts, trimmed
2 tablespoons salted cashews, chopped
4 tablespoons Fried Shallot Slices (see Essentials)
8 won ton wrappers, cut into thin strips and deep-fried until crisp

GINGER DRESSING
1 clove garlic, minced
1 tablespoon castor sugar
20 ml fresh lime juice, strained
40 ml fish sauce
40 ml rice vinegar
2 tablespoons sliced ginger
2 red bird's-eye chillies, sliced
4 red shallots, finely sliced

To make the dressing, mix the garlic, sugar, lime juice, fish sauce and rice vinegar together in a bowl and stir until the sugar has dissolved. Pound the ginger and chilli in a mortar and pestle to make a paste then stir into the dressing with the sliced shallots.

Clean the squid and rinse the tubes and cleaned tentacles under cold running water. Split each tube open, flatten out onto a board and slice into thin strips lengthways. Drop the squid strips into a saucepan of boiling water and cook for 20 seconds. Strain through a sieve.

Toss the hot squid through the ginger dressing until thoroughly coated and leave to marinate for 2 minutes. Stir in the shredded herbs and bean sprouts.

Spoon the salad into bowls and sprinkle the cashews and fried shallot slices over the top. Crunch the fried won ton strips over the salad and serve.

SERVES 4

CRAB AND GREEN PAPAYA SALAD

You can cook the crabs yourself for this salad and pick the meat from the shells or alternatively, buy the ready-picked crabmeat from the fish market or reputable fishmongers. In Laos, they use the tiny river crabs, eaten whole, which we saw everywhere but were warned against – even our iron guts would have suffered as a result.

30 ml fresh lime juice, strained
2 teaspoons Tamarind Liquid (see Essentials)
20 ml Sugar Syrup (see Essentials)
20 ml fish sauce
250 g green papaya, finely shredded
400 g fresh cooked crabmeat
1 tablespoon dried prawns, ground to a floss in a spice grinder
6 cherry tomatoes, quartered
1 tablespoon red shallot slices
2 red bird's-eye chillies, finely sliced
1 tablespoon shredded Asian or Thai basil leaves
2 tablespoons raw peanuts, lightly roasted and roughly chopped

Mix the lime juice, tamarind liquid, sugar syrup and fish sauce together in a bowl, then add the green papaya and crabmeat. Leave to marinate for 5 minutes.

Add the remaining ingredients and toss thoroughly to combine. Arrange on plates and serve immediately.

SERVES 4

SPICY CHICKEN SALAD

This is my interpretation of the fresh and flavour-packed traditional laap, one of the most common Lao salads, and a close relative of the Thai larb or larp. The salad can be served in the traditional manner, piled inside crisp iceberg lettuce cups (like Chinese sang choi bao) or just piled into serving bowls. For a picnic or lunchbox, iceberg leaves can be wilted then stuffed with salad and rolled into neat parcels for transporting.

400 g organic chicken thigh fillets, cut into quarters
40 ml vegetable oil
½ teaspoon chilli powder
½ teaspoon freshly ground black pepper
2 tablespoons shredded long-leaf (saw-tooth) coriander
4 apple eggplants (aubergines), finely sliced
2 small red chillies, finely sliced
1 teaspoon minced galangal
1 teaspoon minced lemongrass
25 ml fish sauce
25 ml fresh lime juice, strained
2 Chinese cabbage (wombok) leaves, finely shredded
2 iceberg lettuce leaves, finely shredded
2 tablespoons shredded mint leaves
1 tablespoon white sticky rice, roasted and ground, plus extra to serve

In a bowl, mix the chicken with the oil, chilli powder and pepper. Cook over coals or under a hot grill for 5–6 minutes until cooked. Mince the meat using a sharp knife or cleaver (do not blend as this ruins the texture).

In a bowl, mix the finely minced chicken with the coriander, eggplant, chilli, galangal and lemongrass, then moisten with the fish sauce and lime juice. Leave for 2 minutes to marinate slightly.

Stir in the shredded cabbage and lettuce leaves, mint and roasted rice powder. Spoon the chicken salad into serving bowls and dust with a little extra roasted and ground rice, and serve.

SERVES 4

SPICY CHICKEN SALAD >

CARAMEL PORK SALAD

Caramel sauce is one of those essential South-east Asian preparations that is used in myriad ways, particularly with meat and fish. Pork prepared in this manner is often referred to as paddy-field pork, as it's a staple dish for farmers and those who till the rice paddy fields. It can be served with steamed rice, hard-boiled eggs or tossed through the raw salad ingredients as I have done here. The pork can be replaced with chicken thigh meat if you prefer.

125 g palm sugar
75 ml water
100 ml fish sauce
3 red shallots, finely diced
1 teaspoon minced lemongrass (use a Microplane)
2 small red chillies, finely sliced
1 teaspoon freshly ground black pepper
50 ml rice vinegar
400 g pork loin
2 cloves garlic, finely sliced
8 hard-boiled quail eggs, halved
8 wing beans, sliced
80 g bean sprouts, trimmed
½ yam bean, peeled and finely shredded
½ green mango, finely shredded
3 green onions, finely sliced
6 flowering garlic chives, cut into 3 cm lengths
40 g mizuna leaves

To make a caramel sauce, heat the palm sugar with the water in a saucepan over moderate heat until it starts to caramelise. Add the fish sauce and cook until combined and smooth. Add the shallots, lemongrass, chilli and pepper and cook for another few minutes. Add the rice vinegar and bring back to simmering point.

Cut the pork into very thin strips and add to the sauce with the garlic. Toss over the heat to coat the meat, then reduce the heat to low and simmer gently for 15 minutes for the pork to caramelise in the sauce. Add a little extra water if the caramel becomes too thick or sticky.

Toss the remaining ingredients in a bowl until combined. Arrange the salad on plates, pile the caramel pork and its sauce on top and serve.

SERVES 4

HOT AND SOUR FISH NOODLE SOUP WITH BAMBOO SHOOTS

Light and refreshing, the flavours in this dish are quite punchy and require a careful hand to get it just right. Too much sourness and the balance is thrown out of whack. The soup can be made ahead of time and refrigerated, then finished with the fresh juices and seasoning at the last minute to keep the flavours vibrant.

50 ml fresh lime juice, strained
50 ml fish sauce
1 tablespoon castor sugar
300 g white fish fillet, finely sliced
120 g cellophane (glass) noodles, soaked in boiling water until softened
2 cloves pickled garlic, finely sliced
6 makrut lime leaves, finely shredded
2 red shallots, finely sliced
1 punnet enoki mushrooms, stalks trimmed
4 tablespoons shredded Pickled Bamboo Shoots (see Essentials)

HOT AND SOUR SOUP
2 litres Fish Stock (see Essentials)
4 dried shiitake mushrooms, broken into pieces
2 stalks lemongrass, smashed
2 tomatoes, chopped
2 pieces dried tangerine peel
2 small red chillies, minced
40 ml fermented fish sauce (padek)
60 ml Tamarind Liquid (see Essentials)
2 teaspoons minced galangal
4 green onions, chopped
30 ml fresh pineapple juice
25 ml fresh lime juice, strained
½ teaspoon freshly ground black pepper

To make the soup, put the fish stock in a large saucepan and add the dried mushrooms, lemongrass, tomatoes, tangerine peel, chilli, fish sauce, tamarind, galangal and green onions. Bring to simmering point over low heat and simmer gently for 30 minutes, skimming the surface occasionally.

Pass through a fine mesh sieve and discard the solids. Reheat the soup and add the pineapple and lime juices and pepper. Taste and adjust the seasoning if necessary.

To prepare the fish, mix the lime juice, fish sauce and sugar in bowl and pour over the fish slices.

Leave to pickle for 1 hour.

To serve, divide the softened noodles evenly among soup bowls, then add the pickled fish and remaining ingredients. Ladle the hot soup over the top and serve.

SERVES 6

DUCK EGG AND HERB SALAD

Taking my lead from khai tom na som, an egg dish we tasted one morning at the markets, I have used duck eggs which give a richer flavour. Chicken eggs can just as easily be used, just reduce the cooking time for the egg. Jeow bong is an essential condiment served with everything in Laos – I prefer the version without the chunks of dried buffalo in it as I find them too chewy and stringy without improving the inherent flavour of the chilli paste.

2 teaspoons shaved palm sugar
40 ml Tamarind Liquid (see Essentials)
20 ml fish sauce
4 duck eggs

JEOW BONG
6 red shallots
2 heads garlic
12 dried small chillies, roasted and broken into small pieces
2 teaspoons chopped coriander roots
2 teaspoons chopped galangal
2 teaspoons sea salt
20 ml fish sauce

HERB SALAD
4 leaves long-leaf (saw-tooth) coriander, shredded
1 tablespoon coriander leaves
1 tablespoon small mint leaves
1 tablespoon finely sliced chives
3 green onions, finely sliced
1 tablespoon Asian or Thai lemon basil leaves, torn
1 tablespoon pickled young tamarind leaves
1 punnet onion cress (rock chives), snipped
1 punnet mizuna cress, snipped

To make the jeow bong, roast the unpeeled shallots and garlic over hot coals or in a dry cast-iron frying pan until blackened. Remove from the heat. Peel and pound the softened shallots and garlic in a mortar and pestle with the roasted chilli, coriander, galangal and salt to make a smooth paste.

Stir in the fish sauce and if the mixture is too dry, add a little hot water. Taste and adjust the seasoning if necessary.

To make a dressing, heat the palm sugar and tamarind together over gentle heat until the sugar has dissolved. Remove from the heat and stir in the fish sauce.

Crack the eggs, one at a time, into a saucepan of gently boiling water (taking care not to break the yolks) and coddle for 4 minutes in just-simmering water. Remove with a slotted spoon and drain on paper towel. Alternatively, you can boil the eggs in their shells for 4 minutes, then peel.

To make the salad, toss all the ingredients together in a bowl and add just enough dressing to moisten, without the leaves becoming soggy.

Divide the salad among four bowls, sit an egg on top, then add a little jeow bong. Drizzle some dressing around and serve with extra jeow bong on the side.

SERVES 4

PUMPKIN AND DUCK EGG CURRY WITH ROASTED PEANUTS

Eggs play an integral role in daily food preparations in Laos as meat is more expensive and therefore is used prudently. I use salted duck eggs for this as they add a greater depth of flavour. They can be bought ready-salted from any Chinese or Asian food store. This rich curry should satisfy vegetarians and meat eaters alike with its earthy flavours.

200 ml coconut cream
600 ml Vegetable Stock (see Essentials) or water
4 makrut lime leaves
1 stalk lemongrass, sliced
50 ml light soy sauce
400 g butternut pumpkin, peeled and cut into 3 cm cubes, roasted
½ daikon radish, peeled and sliced into thick rounds, steamed
4 salted duck eggs, steamed for 30 minutes, shelled and quartered
1 cup Asian or Thai basil leaves
6 makrut lime leaves, extra, finely shredded
2 long red chillies, sliced into rounds
50 g roasted peanuts, chopped

CURRY PASTE
6 small dried chillies, crushed
6 golden shallots, chopped
10 cloves garlic
2 tablespoons chopped coriander roots
2 stalks lemongrass, chopped
2 tablespoons chopped galangal
1 tablespoon kapi (Thai shrimp paste)
100 g roasted peanuts
¼ teaspoon grated nutmeg
1 tablespoon sea salt

To make the curry paste, pound the ingredients together in a mortar and pestle until it forms a smooth paste. You need 5 generous tablespoons of paste for this recipe; store the remainder in an airtight container in the refrigerator for later use.

To make the curry, heat the coconut cream in a saucepan over high heat until it cracks (splits). Reduce the heat to moderate, stir in the curry paste and cook for 10 minutes. Add the stock, whole lime leaves and lemongrass, bring to boil and simmer for 20 minutes. Season with soy sauce, taste and adjust if necessary.

Add the roasted pumpkin, steamed radish and duck eggs and simmer gently for 10 minutes until heated through.

Stir in the basil leaves, shredded lime leaves, chilli slices and roasted peanuts. Serve with steamed sticky rice and Chilli Jam or Sambal Bajak (see Essentials).

SERVES 4–6 AS PART OF A SHARED TABLE

STEAMED FISH SANDWICH

This recipe is inspired by the traditional Lao kanab pa fak, and I have given it some structure by creating a sandwich effect and steaming it as opposed to the traditional grilling method. The dressing gives the fish an extra flavour boost. You can use various white fish for this sandwich – if blue eye is not available, use trumpeter, hapuku or snapper.

5 × 100 g portions blue eye fillet, cut from the middle of the fish, skin removed
½ teaspoon sea salt
¼ teaspoon freshly ground black pepper
2 small green chillies
1 stalk lemongrass, shredded using a Microplane
4 red shallots, peeled
2 teaspoons minced ginger
1 teaspoon minced makrut lime leaf
100 g fatty pork shoulder, minced
2 tablespoons shredded coriander leaves
2 teaspoons minced dill
20 ml fish sauce
4 banana leaves, for wrapping
1 punnet coriander cress, snipped
2 makrut lime leaves, extra, finely shredded
2 tablespoons dried Chinese anchovies, deep-fried until crisp

COCONUT LIME DRESSING
125 ml coconut milk
30 ml coconut vinegar
50 ml fresh lime juice, strained
20 ml Ginger Juice (see Essentials)
30 ml fish sauce
25 ml Sugar Syrup (see Essentials)
1 small green chilli, minced

To prepare the fish, cut four of the fish portions in half though the centre to make eight even-sized rectangular pieces. Season with salt and pepper. Chop the remaining piece into a fine mince.

Pound the chilli, lemongrass, shallots, ginger and minced lime leaf in a mortar and pestle until it forms a smooth paste.

In a bowl, mix together the minced pork and fish, shredded coriander, dill, lemongrass paste and fish sauce until thoroughly combined.

Lay four fish rectangles on separate banana leaves then spoon the pork and fish mixture onto the fish. Cover with the remaining pieces of fish to make a sandwich, smoothing the edges so they are even. Wrap each sandwich with the banana leaf to make a parcel and secure with toothpicks.

Place the fish parcels in a single layer in a bamboo steamer basket, cover with a lid and steam over gently boiling water for 12–15 minutes until cooked through.

To make the dressing, place all the ingredients in a bowl and whisk until thoroughly combined.

Unwrap the fish, discarding the banana leaves, and transfer the fish sandwiches to serving plates. Stir the snipped coriander cress into the dressing, then spoon over the fish. Sprinkle with the shredded lime leaf and fried anchovies and serve.

SERVES 4

BARBEQUED DUCK WITH MUSHROOMS

This number is a more elaborate version of the ping phet (grilled duck) we had one night, cooked over coals in a rudimentary barbeque vessel on our host's front verandah. Rather then cut the duck into pieces to cook, I have left it whole so the meat is more tender and pink. I have tossed the barbequed duck through a tangy mushroom stir-fry to give added complexity, though it could just as easily be served with stir-fried noodles, added to a vegetable salad or served simply with your preferred condiment or vegetable pickle.

2 kg Aylesbury or Barbary duck, cleaned
1 tablespoon jasmine tea leaves
2 star anise
1 piece cassia bark
2 pieces dried tangerine peel
300 ml boiling water
75 ml honey
4 slices ginger
1 teaspoon sea salt
tops of 6 green onions, finely sliced on the diagonal

MUSHROOM STIR-FRY
40 ml sunflower oil
2 cloves garlic, minced
2 teaspoons minced ginger
2 green onions, finely sliced
8 fresh shiitake mushrooms, stems discarded and caps halved
8 small oyster mushrooms, trimmed
8 nameko or chestnut mushrooms, trimmed
½ punnet enoki mushrooms, trimmed
25 ml light soy sauce
20 ml oyster sauce
1 bunch chives, cut into 1 cm lengths

Cut the duck down its backbone and press down on the duck to flatten it out. Dry with paper towel.

Make a brew with the tea leaves, spices, tangerine peel and boiling water and leave to infuse for 10 minutes. Strain and allow the tea to cool, then stir in the honey and ginger. Pour the cooled tea over the duck and leave to marinate overnight.

Remove the duck from the marinade and pour the strained marinade into a saucepan. Bring to boiling point and cook until reduced by half. Set aside.

Grill the duck, skin-side down, over hot coals in a kettle barbeque, basting every few minutes.

Turn the duck after 15 minutes, cover with a lid and cook for another 20 minutes or until the duck is cooked but still slightly pink in the centre. Rest for 10–15 minutes.

Slice the meat from the carcass, then slice the breast and thigh fillets into 2 cm thick slices and season with salt.

To prepare the mushroom stir-fry, heat the oil in a wok over a high heat and fry the garlic and ginger for 30 seconds until fragrant. Add the green onions and mushrooms and toss for about 2 minutes until wilted. Add the soy and oyster sauces and 2 tablespoons of the reduced duck marinade and cook briefly, long enough for the sauce to coat the mushrooms. Remove from the heat and stir in the chives.

Arrange the mushrooms in the centre of serving plates and lay the duck slices on top. Drizzle a little extra sauce over the duck and scatter with the green onion slices.

SERVES 6

WOK-SEARED VENISON WITH LEMONGRASS AND MINT

A very straightforward preparation, this requires minimal last-minute cooking once all the components have been prepared. The weight and density of the venison meat offers a lovely rich texture and balance to the other flavours. It can be expanded with noodles or served with sticky rice as part of a shared table if you prefer.

50 ml vegetable oil
1 teaspoon sesame oil
400 g venison loin, cut into 2 cm strips
150 ml Sweet Tamarind Dressing (see Essentials)
1 long green chilli, finely sliced
1 carrot, cut into julienne strips
1 long cucumber, shaved lengthways into ribbons with a peeler
4 green onions, cut into 1 cm lengths
4 tablespoons mint leaves, torn
60 g small tatsoi leaves
2 tablespoons raw peanuts, roasted and lightly crushed

LEMONGRASS PASTE
1 stalk lemongrass, shredded using a Microplane
2 small green chillies
2 red shallots, peeled
2 cloves garlic, chopped
2 coriander roots, chopped
1 teaspoon minced galangal
2 makrut lime leaves, shredded
½ teaspoon black peppercorns
2 teaspoons fresh green peppercorns
2 teaspoons castor sugar
40 ml fish sauce

To make the lemongrass paste, pound the lemongrass, chillies, shallots, garlic, coriander roots, galangal, lime leaves and peppercorns in a mortar and pestle to make a paste. Add the sugar and fish sauce and pound until the paste becomes smoother.

To cook the venison, mix the lemongrass paste with the oils, add the venison strips, coat well and marinate for 30 minutes.

Heat a wok over high heat, add the venison and its marinade and cook for 2 minutes, tossing continuously so the paste doesn't burn. Add the tamarind dressing, chilli, carrot, cucumber and green onions and toss to combine.

Add the mint and tatsoi leaves, toss once so the leaves do not overcook, then pile onto serving plates and sprinkle with the roasted peanuts.

SERVES 4

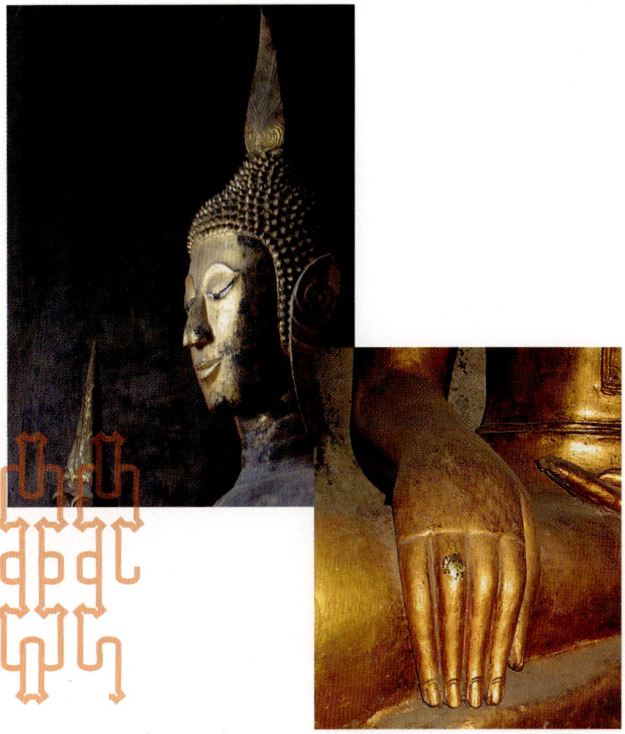

COCONUT RICE PUDDING WITH PAPAYA AND LIME

Once again, the common link is the combination of coconut and lime, this time using the texture of rice to carry them. I would serve this in elegant glasses or bowls to give the rice a defined shape. To offer contrast to the richness of the creamed rice, I use the small red papayas from north Queensland for their taste and texture, which are conveniently available throughout the year.

160 g short-grain rice
500 ml coconut milk
200 ml milk
100 g castor sugar
finely grated zest of 2 limes
½ teaspoon vanilla bean paste
250 ml double cream
20 ml fresh lime juice, strained
1 small red papaya, peeled and cut into 1 cm cubes
80 ml Lime Syrup (see Essentials)

Wash the rice under cold running water, then place in a saucepan with the coconut milk, milk, sugar, lime zest and vanilla bean paste. Cook over moderate heat to simmering point, stirring occasionally.

When simmering, cover with a lid and reduce the heat to low. Cook for 40 minutes or until the rice is soft and has absorbed the liquid. Remove from the heat and leave for 10 minutes, then stir in the cream and half the lime juice. Spoon into serving bowls.

Spoon the remaining lime juice over the papaya cubes, then stack on top of the rice and drizzle with lime syrup.

SERVES 4

LIME TAPIOCA AND COCONUT CREAM

This elegant interpretation of familiar Asian flavours is at once ethereal and light with a mellow richness.

2 tablespoons finely shredded young coconut
2 mangosteens, peeled and segmented

COCONUT JELLY
180 ml young coconut juice
2 g gelatine leaves, softened in cold water

LIME TAPIOCA
40 g tapioca pearls
2 small egg yolks
40 g castor sugar
½ teaspoon finely grated makrut lime zest
25 ml fresh lime juice, strained
2 teaspoons makrut lime juice
50 g unsalted butter, chopped
2 g gelatine leaves, softened in cold water

COCONUT CREAM
110 ml milk
85 g grated fresh coconut, roasted
2 teaspoons lychee liqueur
50 ml coconut cream
3 small egg yolks
15 g castor sugar
3 g gelatine leaves, softened in cold water
190 ml pouring (35%) cream

LYCHEE SORBET
40 g glucose
40 g castor sugar
250 ml Boiron lychee puree

To make the jelly, heat the coconut water to simmering point, then stir in the softened gelatine. Pass through a fine mesh sieve and leave to cool. Spoon the jelly into four 180 ml dariole moulds to make a 6 mm layer in each one. When set, cover the jelly layer with a few coconut shreds.

To make the lime tapioca, pour the tapioca pearls straight into a saucepan of boiling water. Whisk and cook over moderately high heat for 10 minutes until softened, then rinse under cold running water. Whisk the egg yolks and sugar until pale and creamy, then sit the bowl over a pan of simmering water and whisk in the zest and both lime juices. Continue to whisk to increase the volume, then slowly add the cold butter piece by piece, making sure each piece is incorporated before adding the next. Add the softened gelatine with the last piece of butter, remove the bowl from the heat and sit over a bowl of iced water to stop further cooking. Stir in the soft tapioca pearls and allow to cool completely.

Spoon the lime tapioca curd into the dariole moulds then refrigerate for an hour until set.

To make the coconut cream, heat the milk with the roasted coconut over low heat to simmering point. Remove from the heat and stir in the liqueur and coconut cream. Whisk the egg yolks and sugar in a bowl until pale and creamy. Gently whisk in the hot milk then sit the bowl over a pan of simmering water and continue to cook until thickened to a custard consistency. Stir in the softened gelatine and remove from the heat. Pass the custard through a fine mesh sieve and discard the solids. Allow to cool completely.

Whisk the cream until thickened to the same volume as the custard, then gently fold it through the custard. Spoon the coconut cream into the moulds to fill, then refrigerate for 3 hours until set.

To make the lychee sorbet, heat the glucose in a bowl over a pan of simmering water until softened to a pouring consistency. Whisk the sugar into the lychee puree then add the softened glucose and stir until combined. Churn the sorbet in an ice-cream machine until firm. Transfer to an airtight container and store in the freezer until ready to serve.

To serve, unmould the creams by dipping the moulds in hot water for 20 seconds, then turn out onto plates. Arrange the mangosteen segments and a small quenelle of lychee sorbet on top of the jelly, then finish with any remaining coconut shreds.

SERVES 4

FROM BUDDHA WITH LOVE THAILAND

If you love food, this is definitely the country to visit as it is celebrated in the daily ritual of life. No wonder Thailand is called the Land of the Smiling Faces – good food makes for happy people! I am always struck by the colours and textures on the plate, the intoxicating aromas, the beauty and exotic elegance of every morsel. As is common throughout Asia, there is an absolute insistence on freshness, and the adoption of some of the Thai practices in Australia has made us more aware and better cooks, I think, giving us a more articulate culinary language.

Thailand differs from its other Asian neighbours in that it has never been subjected to European colonisation – a legacy of the mighty power of the Kingdom of Siam – which may account for its more fiery flavours, never tempered by foreign palates. However, its food does reflect a combination of indigenous and imported techniques, borrowed from places such as India, Burma, Laos and China. Rice is the centrepiece of every meal and the accompanying dishes are meant to be enjoyed with rice rather than served in sequence. Whether it is steamed jasmine rice or the sticky rice of the north, Thais revere rice in much the same way as Westerners do decent bread. When eating, remember to put rice on your plate first to show respect for its importance. Rice also has great significance in spiritual life: it is central to daily offerings at the spirit shrines and temples, and monks hold the grains to be symbolic of the Buddha.

There is nothing quite like stumbling into the bustling urban jungle that is Bangkok – the air thick with humidity, petrol, and the mingled scents of jasmine, frangipani, durian and coconut. The ornate temples (wats) are majestic, dotted around the city and along the riverfront, making the skyline unequivocally Thai. Much has changed since the days when the roads were ruled by tuk-tuks – those three-wheel motorbikes with covered carts attached and the noisiest engines in the universe. There are still a few lurking about and we take a hair-raising ride in one every time we visit, for the sheer fun of it (and the adrenaline rush), but similar thrills can be had by jumping on the back of a motorbike. These motorbike taxis gather at most street corners, are easily recognised by their brightly coloured vests, and will take you wherever you want to go in no time at all for very little money. It feels really liberating to jump on, as the locals do, and place implicit trust in an unfamiliar rider as he negotiates the onslaught of traffic. Of course, there are also car taxis with air-conditioning if you want less thrills and spills, but somehow that seems too slow and sanitised for the chaos that is Bangkok.

This is a city that eats non-stop so the food action is as incessant as the traffic; the whole city is like one enormous cafe. The Thais eat little and often rather than sticking to three meals a day – so much healthier and infinitely more interesting for the palate. The flavours of sweet, salty, sour, bitter and hot are perfectly balanced with enticing aromas and creamy, crisp, slippery, soft and crunchy textures. Every bite is a revelation, and it was here that the limitless possibilities of taste first became apparent to me. Life in Bangkok is a perpetual feast and the day generally starts with a bowl of noodles from a street cart at dawn. The vendors go home as soon as they sell out, and the trick is knowing when each one is set up, so you can grab the food while it is still warm and time has not diminished its freshness and flavour.

I have done a couple of stints in Bangkok as a guest chef in residence: once at the Shangri La Hotel on the Chao Phraya River, and more recently at the elegant Sukhothai Hotel on Sathorn Road. Those working visits gave me a more intimate understanding of this dynamic city's food culture, as I would venture out to local places to eat khao dtang nar dtang (crispy rice cakes with a rich pork and prawn coconut sauce), khao mun gai (chicken rice) or really terrific pad thai noodles.

STAYING IN BANGKOK

THE SUKHOTHAI
13/3 South Sathorn Road, Bangkok
Tel +66 2 344 8888
www.sukhothai.com
Like a tranquil oasis in the midst of urban mayhem, this hotel has been my Bangkok retreat for many years now. The gardens and pool are the best.

LUXX
6/11 Decho Road (between Silom and Surawong roads), Bangrak, Bangkok
Tel +66 2 635 8800
www.staywithluxx.com
Totally affordable, stylish boutique hotel in the centre of town, close to the Chong Nonsi SkyTrain station for extra convenience.

I love exploring the different districts that make up the city: Yaowarat (Chinatown), with its winding lanes and wholesale market along Sampeng Lane; Phahurat (Little India), where you can find authentic roti, made on the spot at Roti Mataba; and Banglamphu, with the magnificent Golden Mount at its centre. This was formerly the highest point in Bangkok, but has long since been eclipsed by the city's skyscrapers. I have been to a couple of bars around here and let me tell you, looking out onto the Golden Mount makes for a great nightcap, even with the incessant blowing of car horns.

One of my favourite haunts is Pak Khlong Talat, the oldest market in town, alongside the Chao Phraya River just south of Wat Pho. Every day there is a dazzling array of fresh produce on display here: endless bowls of curry pastes and sauce concoctions; dried fish; shrimp paste; fruit and vegetables so fresh they seem to leap out of their bamboo baskets; and the mingling aromas of turmeric, green peppercorns, galangal and chillies. With no comparable market in Australia, I miss being able to cook with furry golden eggplants (perfect in salads), long green Thai eggplants, ginger blossoms, coconut palm hearts, som saa limes, white turmeric, untreated tamarind and palm sugar, and hand-made fish sauce, to name but a few. At night, the market transforms itself into a giant flower market, where you can grab some delicious noodles for supper while you load up with fresh flowers. Teenagers hover around the edges with their ghetto blasters and music, giving it a nightclub feel. I used to love coming here after working a dinner shift and soaking up the atmosphere. If it's really late and you find yourself hungry when the bars and clubs close at 2 a.m., head straight to Soi 38 in the Sukhumvit area, where there's another lively late-night market.

Another fabulous market is Or Tor Kor – just take the subway train to Kamphaeng Phet and you're right there. It's jam-packed with the most delicious things to eat and is a great place to stock up on essentials. Everything is sold in little plastic bags inflated and cleverly tied with rubber bands to seal in the treasures, and the produce is spanking fresh. It is impossible for me to be reserved when shopping here – I want it all. The roast pork is so

STREET EATS IN BANGKOK

Street food is everywhere in Thailand, and the choice is enviable. Never be afraid to try anything – hygiene standards are extremely high, and the turnover is fast as lightning.

The strip near the Four Seasons Hotel on Ratchadamri Road becomes an impromptu dining room at certain times of the day, with small trucks serving straight out of the side to hungry diners. Later in the day it has the usual array of snacks.

Behind Lang Suan and Sarasin is a small neighbourhood that serves the office workers from the area – the sois (lanes) are so small that at lunchtime a motorcycle can only *just* squeeze past.

At certain times of the day, the side streets of Chinatown at Yaowarat Road and around the main train station become littered with tin tables and chairs serving up everything from duck, pork and seafood to noodles and rice.

Soi Polo Fried Chicken
137/1–2 Soi Polo, off Withayu, Lumphini
Tel +66 2 655 8489
This is the definitive fried chicken shop, definitely the best in town. The chicken is smothered in fried garlic slices and is absolutely divine.

Pak Khlong Talat
Food market in the old town, near Pinkalo Bridge (old bridge) on Phra Athit Road
Dive into the back areas and find great stalls with loads of food choices.

Ban Klang Nam
3792/106 Rama III Road, Soi 14, Khlong Toey
Tel +66 2 292 1075
Down a small lane near the river – lots of seafood, and the chilli squid is great.

Withayu and Ploenchit roads
This main intersection has lots of food stalls and great variety – popular with the locals.

Tha Tien Pier
On the riverside near the Grand Palace
Frenetic activity, with many pavement vendors to choose from, selling everything from fried fish cakes to sour curries and noodles.

Soi Lang Suan
This is where you will find all the transient 'garage' noodle shops – yum!

Rut & Lek
Yaowarat Road, corner of Soi Texas
Sidewalk tables with fab seafood.

mouthwatering that it's hard to stop. Just across the road is the Chatuchak weekend market, a Bangkok institution that stretches for a few blocks and sells everything imaginable. If you're game, buy a bag of crunchy fried bugs, though actually you'll taste little more than the sweet chilli syrup they were dunked in after cooking. On our first visit to Bangkok, Margie and I bought our first-ever chunk of durian at this market and jumped in a taxi back to the hotel. Halfway there, the driver insisted we dump our fruit as its smell was so overwhelming (imagine a ripe blue cheese that has been left in the sun). Cut durian is now banned on public transport.

Our friends David and Peter live near Lumphini Park, a garden oasis in the centre of town, and this is where we often stay when visiting. The area has its fair share of colour and action, and the Suan Lum Night Bazaar is directly opposite, bringing with it the dull roar of a noisy crowd. Weekend stalls in the park offer anything and everything, including snake blood and bile, which is considered a health tonic – I figure I am healthy enough, so I generally avoid that one!

One evening our good friend Tanongsak took us to a shopfront on Rama IV Road that specialises in goose. We sat roadside on little plastic stools and ate every bit of the bird: soup, stir-fried giblets, braised liver, webs in a sour tangy sauce, roast breast with crispy skin, and all sorts of unidentifiable bits. I admire such a single-minded approach; to have a place that focuses on just one ingredient is quite something – and it's crammed full, all the time. In search of the best sweet shops in town, we crossed the river and visited Kanom Dessert Shop in Thonburi and bought boxes of weird and wonderful things to have back at the hotel with our pot of afternoon tea. Some tastes are a heady blend of salty, sour and sweet – totally out there in terms of the flavour spectrum as we know it – but we found that fried shallots, peanuts, sesame, tangy tamarind and dried prawns are not out of place in sugary confections.

EATING IN BANGKOK

CAFE DE LAOS
16 Soi 19, Silom Road, Trok Wet, Bangkok
Tel +66 2 635 2338
Lovely Isaan food of northern Thailand and Laos (some fiery tastes here!) served in a colonial wooden house.

Many visitors have left their mark on Bangkok, perhaps none more so than Jim Thompson, a former US military intelligence officer who revived the Thai silk industry. The teak houses built on land he bought alongside a khlong (canal) near Rama I Road, with lush tropical gardens and water ponds, are a living and working museum to his memory and his excellent taste and style. The peace and tranquillity of this place also offers welcome respite from this frenetic urban jungle, as does a river trip or khlong tour. Ferries will take you upstream past the Royal Barges near the Grand Palace – with their ornately carved figureheads, they look truly spectacular when they glide up and down the river in procession. Look out too for the hotel boats moored in front of the Oriental, Shangri La and Peninsula hotels, which shuttle back and forth across the river. If you're up for a bit of fun, go to the Memorial Bridge and barter with a long-tail boat owner for a private charter and scoot noisily around the city's khlongs for an hour or two. This is the best way to get up close to the traditional wooden Thai houses (ban song) built on stilts over the water, and to explore the maze of khlongs that are the city's lifeblood. Be prepared to get slightly wet as the water sprays up when other boats pass, though. The khlongs are a flurry of activity that starts just before dawn with the floating markets. These mobile shops are long wooden canoes filled with food and fresh produce; some are floating cafes that sell ready-made noodles, soups, salads and curries, a common sight in South-east Asian countries.

If you want to get out of town for the day or overnight, head north to the original Siamese capital, Ayutthaya. There are lovely restored rice barges available for private charter from Bangkok, a more tranquil option than the noisy drone of the long-tail boats. One year Margie and I had a memorable oriental-style Christmas here with friends, gliding on the river in a hired wooden boat with a captain to drive us. We stopped off at riverside food vendors to snack on tod mon pla (fish cakes), sai grop (smoked pork sausage), khao man gai (poached chicken and rice with cucumber), pad thai noodles, som dtam (green papaya salad), soy-braised eggs and fried rice with crabmeat, all washed down with a glass or two of the champagne we'd brought with us. We even managed to find room for a seafood feast for dinner – pure heaven.

I well remember our first visit to northern Thailand, back in the 1980s. We arrived in Chiang Mai, the ancient capital of the Kingdom of Lanna, at sunset after a gruelling eight-hour bus ride from Bangkok and went straight out to find some local food. We ventured into a humble shopfront because it was full of locals, and they politely gave us menus – written only in Thai. We laughed, as did they, and then we just looked at what was on the other tables and pointed at whatever took our fancy. Everything was delicious and so bloody hot; little bird's-eye chillies were laced through every dish. I also noticed the flavours seemed sharper and more astringent than those of the south, with more obvious use of tamarind and lime, and less coconut cream or milk.

We ate a lot of catfish, the local river fish that can grow to be quite enormous, and I loved the use of pork in many of the dishes. Then there were the sausages: some more fermented than others, quite piquant and sour-tasting. The plethora of noodle dishes was a bit of an eye-opener and we made sure we tried different versions each day. One local favourite is khao soi, flat ribbon noodles swimming in a spicy chicken or beef curry sauce, a typical Muslim dish that can be found at any one of the many noodle stalls and cafes scattered around Chiang Mai.

On a more recent visit we followed the advice of Thai food aficionado David Thompson (by then a firm friend) and went to Larp Dip for lunch, a humble street-front cafe just inside the main western gate of the Old City. It would be easy to walk straight past if you didn't know its hidden secrets – and it has no sign, so ask for directions locally. With nothing written in English, I lifted the lids on the row of pots that lined the table and ordered several dishes to share at one of the plastic-covered tables at the back of the shop. The catfish larp (salad) was a stand-out, as was a minced beef dish that had been cooked with chilli, tamarind and grachai (a ginger-like rhizome) until it resembled a thick, dark mass – nothing to look at but utterly delicious, with flavours that burst on the palate. Like many local places, they open early and close when they run out of food – usually by mid-afternoon – so lunch is the only way to go.

If you are game to join thousands of backpackers at the Night Bazaar, head straight to either Anusarn or Kalare markets, both enclaves of hawker stalls clustered around a central square. For daytime browsing, go to the Lam Yai markets behind the flower stalls that front the Ping River, off Wichayanon Road. You'll find an amazing array of fresh produce as well as little bowls and plates of ready-made food. Next to that, the Warorat Market, which sells clothing, crafts and local produce by day, and flowers by night, is also worth a visit.

Chiang Mai is a showcase for its traditional Lanna heritage, enhanced by majestic natural beauty. The visual appeal of the wooden temples and their golden stupa spires embody classic Thai design. This is also the home of traditional handicrafts, with workshops producing silverware, ceramics, silks and woodwork. Many of these are on the main roads out of town and you can go in to see the work in progress first hand. Don't expect a bargain, though. The scene has recently undergone something of a renaissance, as this vibrant artistic community rediscovers and celebrates its rich cultural history. Known for its flourishing youth culture, Chiang Mai is also where the gorgeous young things strut their stuff. When the Songkran water festival (Thai New Year) gears up every April, it's impossible to stay dry: the streets turn into a huge party and water is thrown on everyone and everything.

EATING IN CHIANG MAI

THE HOUSE
199 Moonmuang Road, Chiang Mai
Tel +66 53 419 011
Fab setting and ambience in a lovely wooden villa. Quite decent martinis if the mood takes you.

PALAAD TAWANRON
100 Huay Kaew Road, Suthep, Chiang Mai
Tel +66 53 216 576
Great local pit-stop. Grab an outdoor table, check out what the locals are eating – and copy!

KHUN MOR'S THAI NOODLES
10/1 Nimanhaemin Soi 17, Chiang Mai
Tel +66 53 226 378
Street stall with brilliant noodle dishes.

STAYING IN CHIANG MAI

CHEDI CHIANG MAI
123 Charoenprathet Road, Chiang Mai
Tel +66 53 253 333
www.ghmhotels.com
Breathtakingly beautiful, the former British Embassy has been transformed into one of the most glamorous hotels in Asia. Dinner in the garden overlooking the Mae Ping River is pretty damn fine too.

Chiang Mai's most sacred site is the 16th-century Buddhist temple complex of Wat Phrathat, with its giant stairway flanked by balustrades in the form of nagas (mythical sea creatures). Located near the summit of a hill overlooking the city, a drive up the steep, winding road provides welcome relief from the searing heat of the plains. The atmosphere at the temple is pretty laid back – it's a pleasure to sit and talk with the monks, and the small admission fee goes towards providing education for poor students from the remote villages in the surrounding hills.

Chiang Mai makes an excellent base for exploring northern Thailand's beautiful countryside. On our first visit, we drove north to the Golden Triangle, deep in the mountains to the west of Chiang Rai – the far north's main town and another one-time capital of the Lanna Kingdom – to visit small villages surrounded by their tea (formerly opium) plantations. We couldn't resist stopping to taste the local food on the way; there are some terrific street vendors and cafes on Highway 118 en route to Chiang Rai, particularly the noodle shops. We made it to Mae Sai, had tea at a small Hmong village (where our guide came from), then followed the Burmese border through the mountains. We stopped for lunch at Sop Ruak, in the heart of the Golden Triangle, where we stood on the banks of the Mekong and looked across to Laos. The food in these parts is Isaan and is characterised by a preference for strong, rich flavours, a liberal use of palm sugar and kapi (Thai shrimp paste) and a diversity of ingredients. This is the home of nam prik (Thai spicy relish) and its myriad permutations. We saw makeshift stalls by the roadside selling earthenware jars of home-made fermented fish and raw fish sauces, some with pungent aromas that nearly blew our heads off. I also spotted some pickled vegetables in glass jars and saw bamboo mats covered with tamarind pulp being dried in the sun. We had a deliciously hot som dtam, pounded in a deep wooden mortar and pestle right there on the spot. A plate of gai yang (grilled chicken) followed, served with sticky rice.

For more than twenty years, my travels have been punctuated with annual visits to Phuket, an enchanted island in the glittering Andaman Sea, and a hedonist's playground if you know where to look and what to avoid. Phuket remains my preferred place to lounge poolside or beachside with a book and emerge revitalised and refreshed. The sea is a perfect aquamarine fringed by powdery-fine white sand, colourful bursts of bougainvillea are everywhere, and the air is heady with the lingering fragrance of frangipani. Even the rainy season, when the seas swell and the sky is a uniform grey, brings with it healing solitude and repose. For several years, our friends Peter and David had a luxurious and secluded beachfront villa at Layan Beach in Phuket, tucked away from the tourist crowds. As regular visitors, we have fond memories of lazing on sunbeds by the pool, reading books, chatting and cooking. The villa girls looked after us beautifully and cooked some memorable meals: our favourites included grilled fish and seafood with various dipping sauces; a fragrant seafood soup with a light coconut broth; a super-rich massaman chicken curry; popiah sot (fresh spring rolls) with vegetables or prawns and shredded chicken; a healthy salad of greens, herbs and aromatics that we dubbed Jurassic salad for its inclusion of tightly furled, fossil-like fern tips; and a terrific southern-style som dtam.

The food in the south shows Chinese, Malay and Indian influences – most obviously in the richly flavoured Muslim massaman curry, with its liberal use of Indian spices. Local breakfasts include kanom jin (fermented rice noodles) served with kangkung (water spinach) leaves and fish cooked in curry sauce with cucumber, green beans and bean sprouts. Another traditional breakfast dish is kao yam, cooked rice dried overnight then mixed with shallots, roasted coconut, dried chilli, dried prawns, lime leaves and bean sprouts, seasoned with a dressing based on fish sauce or lime juice and tossed like a salad. Look out too for stalls by the roadside and in markets selling black sticky rice steamed in banana leaves with coconut

STAYING ON PHUKET

CHEDI PHUKET
118 Moo 3, Choeng Talay, Pansea Beach
Tel +66 76 236 550
www.chedi-phuket.com
Fabulous beachfront bungalows on a private beach shared with Amanpuri Resort next door. Close to Surin and other local villages.

ANDAMAN WHITE BEACH RESORT
28/8 Moo 4, Tambon Sakoo, Amphur Thalang, Nai Thon Beach
Tel +66 76 316 300
www.andamanwhitebeach.com
An affordable place in a fantastic location on a quiet private beach on the north-west Andaman coast, far removed from the busy tourist strips further south.

EATING ON PHUKET

KA JOK SEE
26 Thanon Takua Pa, Phuket Town
Tel + 66 76 217 903
Lek, the owner, is legendary in Phuket for his music (he spins the discs at the restaurant). In this lovely old-style Chinese shophouse crowded with memorabilia, waiters often dress up and do drag shows during dinner. The appetisers are the way to go here, with more interesting and balanced flavours – the XO chicken is to die for, cooked in a palm sugar and chilli sauce made with Johnnie Walker whisky.

RAAN JEE NGUAT
Thanon Dibuk, corner of Thanon Satul, Phuket Town
Come here in the morning after a visit to the market – you'll find very good kanom jin (fermented rice noodles).

TRISARA
60/1 Moo 6, Srisoonthorn Road, Cherngtalay, Nai Thon Beach
Tel +66 76 310 100
www.trisara.com
The waterfront restaurant at this resort offers some of the most authentic and delicious Thai food on the island – assiduously spiced, with balanced flavours that are refreshingly honest. The cocktails are just as inviting, so make a day of it and stay for a sunset drink after a long, leisurely lunch.

cream and dried prawns – a great snack at any time of day. Phuket Town has a bustling market, restaurants geared to locals rather than tourists, and streets lined with traditional Chinese shophouses. During the annual vegetarian festival, the streets are festooned with yellow banners, and special meals are prepared, including smoked or fried tofu with cabbage, white cabbage stewed in broth with shiitake mushrooms, and black sesame seed sweets in syrup.

Phuket also makes a good base for exploring this stunning stretch of coastline. The nine Similan Islands, 60 kilometres offshore, boast snow-white beaches and vast boulders that shield underwater grottoes where hairy crabs and spiny lobsters live in rock crevices. To the south, the spectacular limestone stacks and caves of Phangnga Bay make for breathtaking scenery, and it's worth taking a trip on a boat or kayak to explore the hongs (lakes inside caves open to the sea) and to glide past stilt villages where the pungent aroma of fermenting fish sauce and kapi hangs in the air.

Thailand is full of intoxicating contradictions. The grace and beauty of this country, as reflected in its dazzling architecture, the monks in their saffron robes, and the hushed and contemplative atmosphere of the temples, is juxtaposed with bustling cities, traffic smog and increasing Westernisation. What I love most about Thailand is the meticulous attention to detail that is in evidence on every street corner everyday, the frenetic energy that drives the street vendors selling every type of food imaginable, and the sheer vitality of life on the street. My dear friend and comrade David Thompson waxes lyrical about the awesome beauty of the north-east of the country, and has discovered many hidden treasures there, from locally made fish sauces to sensational noodles. Through his enthusiasm and love for his adopted country, I am drawn back to Thailand time and time again, always discovering something new. There's no two ways about it, I am utterly captivated by its edgy excitement, ongoing enlightenment and endless delicious tastes.

DEEP-FRIED QUAIL EGGS WITH CARAMELISED COCONUT SALAD

This was an extremely popular dish on our vegetarian tasting menu in London, drawing its inspiration from the familiar flavours and textures of Thailand. Chicken eggs can be used instead (in which case, allow only one per serve) but I prefer the delicacy of the smaller quail eggs. Have everything ready to go before you fry the quail eggs as they need to be served as soon as they are cooked.

8 quail eggs
4 small dried chillies, roasted and ground
1 tablespoon sea salt
200 g rice flour
vegetable oil, for deep-frying
8 betel leaves
1 teaspoon Chilli Jam (see Essentials)
2 tablespoons Fried Shallot Slices (see Essentials)

CARAMELISED COCONUT
1 coconut
50 g palm sugar, shaved
40 ml fish sauce
120 ml coconut cream
1 tablespoon Tamarind Liquid (see Essentials)
small pinch of hot chilli powder (ideally the Thai one called Blue Tongue)

COCONUT CHILLI SAUCE
250 ml coconut milk
30 g palm sugar, shaved
30 ml fish sauce
½ teaspoon makrut lime zest, minced
2 teaspoons Chilli Jam (see Essentials)
20 ml fresh lime juice, strained

SALAD
1 coconut palm heart, finely sliced
2 tablespoons shredded young coconut flesh
½ pomelo, peeled and segmented
4 wing beans, finely sliced
1 tablespoon shredded Asian or Thai basil leaves
4 long-leaf (saw-tooth) coriander, shredded
2 green onions, finely sliced
4 makrut lime leaves, finely shredded
3 small red chillies, finely sliced
1 cup picked watercress leaves

To prepare the caramelised coconut, crack the coconut in half, and reserve the coconut juice for another use. Shred the coconut flesh with a zester to get long threads.

Heat the remaining ingredients in a saucepan to boiling point. Add the coconut shreds, reduce to a simmer and allow the coconut to caramelise in the sauce (the coconut will absorb most of the sauce during this process). Set aside to cool.

To make the coconut chilli sauce, heat the coconut milk, palm sugar, fish sauce, lime zest and chilli jam in a saucepan to boiling point, then simmer for 10 minutes to allow the flavours to infuse. Remove from the heat and pass through a fine mesh sieve, discarding the solids. Stir in the lime juice and reheat gently when ready to serve.

To make the salad, mix all ingredients together in a bowl with 4 tablespoons of the caramelised coconut threads. Reserve the rest for another use.

To cook the eggs, break each egg into a small cup or dish. Mix the ground chilli, salt and rice flour together in a bowl.

Heat the oil in a wok or deep-fryer to 180°C, and drop the eggs into the hot oil, one at a time, splashing with a spoon to keep them separate and in shape.

Fry for 1 minute then remove from the oil with a slotted spoon and drain on paper towel. Sprinkle with the chilli salt mix to lightly coat and season.

Toss the salad with the warmed coconut chilli sauce until combined. Set two betel leaves on each plate and pile the salad on top. Lay two fried quail eggs on each salad, add a little chilli jam and scatter with the fried shallot slices.

SERVES 4

SALTED SALMON, ROE AND POMELO BETEL LEAVES

We often made these as bite-size canapes at the restaurant, in the style of the classic Thai miang (betel-leaf parcels). Planning ahead for this dish is of paramount importance but once the main components are prepared, the last-minute cooking and assembly is a walk in the park. It is a particularly convenient and thrifty way of using up the offcuts of fish, such as the belly strip or tail ends that may have been left from another dish.

4 × 100 g thick slices salmon fillet, cut from the middle of the fish
1 tablespoon castor sugar
1 teaspoon freshly ground white pepper
100 ml light soy sauce
vegetable oil, for deep-frying
4 large betel leaves
2 tablespoons Fried Shallot Slices (see Essentials)
2 tablespoons tiny dried Chinese anchovies, deep-fried until crisp

SWEET CHILLI PICKLE
1 teaspoon chopped galangal
1 small green chilli
1 clove garlic
1 teaspoon chopped coriander roots
15 g palm sugar
15 ml fish sauce
50 ml fresh lime juice, strained
80 ml Sweet-and-sour Pickle (see Essentials)

SALAD
4 tablespoons salmon roe
2 tablespoons Fish Crackling (see Essentials), broken into small pieces
3 pomelo segments, broken into small pieces
6 makrut lime leaves, finely shredded
2 tablespoons shredded fresh coconut
2 tablespoons red shallot slices
2 teaspoons small red chilli, sliced into fine rounds
3 tablespoons shredded mint leaves
3 tablespoons shredded Asian or Thai basil leaves
2 tablespoons shredded coriander leaves
1 punnet celery cress, snipped

To prepare the salmon, mix the sugar and pepper into the soy sauce and pour over the fish in a baking dish. Cover and marinate at room temperature for 2 hours.

Remove the fish from its soy bath, lay on a wire rack and allow to semi-dry for 12 hours or overnight, standing the rack on a shelf above the stove or in another warm place. The fish needs to lose some of its moisture but not cook.

To make the sweet chilli pickle, pound the galangal, chilli, garlic and coriander roots in a mortar and pestle until smooth. Add the sugar and fish sauce, pound to combine, then add the lime juice. Mix with the sweet-and-sour pickle, whisking to combine. Taste, and adjust the balance and seasoning if necessary.

To cook the fish, heat the oil in a wok or deep-fryer to 180°C and fry the fish in batches for 2 minutes until crisp. Remove from the oil and drain on paper towel. Flake the fish into smaller pieces with your fingers.

Mix the salad ingredients together in a bowl, add the fish and enough sweet chilli pickle to wet, and toss to combine.

Lay a betel leaf in the centre of each plate, arrange the salad in a pile on top and drizzle with a little extra dressing if necessary. Scatter with the fried shallot slices and crispy anchovies and serve.

SERVES 8

STEAMED CRAB DUMPLINGS

These soft and luscious dumplings are a triumph of texture and taste. The trick with making the dumpling wrappers is to have everything else ready to go, as they need to be filled and wrapped as soon as they come out of the pan while they are pliable. As each dumpling is made, lay it on its seam on a flat tray lined with plastic film.

rice flour, for dusting
150 ml Ginger Vinaigrette (see Essentials)
1 punnet onion cress (rock chives), snipped

POTATO DUMPLING WRAPPERS
9 egg whites
75 g potato flour
2 teaspoons fish sauce
150 ml water
20 ml vegetable oil

CRAB STUFFING
250 g picked white crabmeat
40 g shredded fresh coconut
3 makrut lime leaves, finely shredded
2 tablespoons finely diced yam bean
2 green onions, finely sliced
2 tablespoons shredded coriander leaves

To make the dumpling wrappers, whisk the egg whites briefly and then add the potato flour, fish sauce and water and whisk to make a smooth batter.

Heat a 15 cm non-stick frying pan over medium heat, brush the pan with a little oil and pour on enough batter to just coat the base of the pan, as if you were making a crepe. When each sheet has set (this takes about 45–60 seconds), carefully remove it from the pan with a spatula and lay it on a flat surface. Cover with a sheet of baking paper then repeat the process until all the mixture has been used. Roll the dumplings within 1 hour of making the wrappers, and do not refrigerate them as the pastry will harden and fracture.

To make the crab stuffing, mix all the ingredients together in a bowl until combined.

Lay the wrappers on a flat work surface dusted lightly with rice flour (this prevents the wrappers sticking; rice flour is best as it contains no gluten). Spoon some crab mix onto one end of the wrapper and roll over. Fold in the sides and roll up to secure, as if you were making a spring roll. As the pastry is so fresh, the edges will seal together automatically when you roll them. Sit the rolled dumplings on their seams until ready to cook.

Place the dumplings in a covered bamboo steamer basket and steam, covered, over gently boiling water for 8 minutes or until heated through.

Transfer the dumplings to plates, drizzle with the ginger vinaigrette and top with the onion cress. Serve immediately.

SERVES 4

CHICKEN AND LOBSTER SALAD, FOIE GRAS AND YOUNG COCONUT

This decadent salad with its soft, luscious textures works perfectly with a vintage rose champagne, for yet another level of luxury.

2 organic chicken breasts, skin on
600 ml White Chicken Stock (see Essentials)
3 slices ginger
400 ml young coconut juice
200 g raw lobster tail, shell removed
100 g foie gras, cut crossways into 4 even slices
1 tablespoon palm sugar
20 ml fish sauce
60 ml coconut cream
2 teaspoons Tamarind Liquid (see Essentials)
a small pinch hot chilli powder (preferably Blue Tongue)
sea salt, to serve

COCONUT GINGER DRESSING
65 ml fresh lime juice, strained
65 ml Ginger Juice (see Essentials)
25 ml rice vinegar
50 ml young coconut juice
few drops of chilli oil
few drops of sesame oil
1 teaspoon Roasted Garlic Paste (see Essentials)
2 teaspoons minced red shallot
1 teaspoon black sesame seeds
25 ml fish sauce
25 ml mirin
40 ml sunflower oil
50 ml fruity extra virgin olive oil
½ teaspoon freshly ground black pepper

COCONUT SALAD
40 g salted jellyfish
90 g young coconut flesh, finely shredded
4 tablespoons Pickled Bamboo Shoots (see Essentials)
4 tablespoons Pickled Carrot Slices (see Essentials)
1 tablespoon Pickled Ginger Slices (see Essentials)
¼ cup finely sliced green onion
2 tablespoons white sesame seeds, roasted
¼ cup coriander leaves
1 punnet rocket cress, snipped
1 punnet mache cress, snipped

To make the coconut ginger dressing, whisk all the ingredients together in a bowl.

To prepare the salad, soak the jellyfish in cold water for 4 hours or until it feels tender, then drain and wash under cold running water for 15 minutes to remove any excess salt. Squeeze dry and slice into fine shreds. Add enough ginger dressing to wet the jellyfish and leave to marinate while you prepare the other ingredients.

To cook the chicken, heat the stock and ginger in a saucepan to boiling point. Add the chicken, reduce the heat to the lowest setting and leave for 5 minutes.

Turn off the heat, cover the pan and leave the chicken in the hot stock for 20–25 minutes or until tender. Remove from the stock and cut the breasts into 2 cm thick slices crossways. Drizzle a tablespoon of the ginger dressing over the chicken to season.

Heat the coconut juice in a saucepan to simmering point. Cut the lobster tail into four medallions and add to the pan. Turn off the heat, cover with a lid and leave to gently cook in the hot liquid for 10 minutes. Remove from the pan and discard the liquid.

To cook the foie gras, heat the palm sugar with the fish sauce to make a caramel, then add the coconut cream, tamarind and chilli powder. Cook for a few minutes until caramelised, then add the foie gras slices and saute gently for 1–2 minutes only, just enough to soften and coat with the coconut caramel. Remove from the pan immediately.

To complete the salad, combine the prepared jellyfish with the remaining salad ingredients and toss together.

Make a stack with alternate layers of chicken and lobster interwoven with salad and extra coconut ginger dressing as you go. Sit the foie gras on top, sprinkle with sea salt, drizzle with a little dressing and serve.

SERVES 4

CHILLI CARAMEL CHICKEN WITH HOT AND SOUR SALAD

I have vivid memories of a fabulous chicken dish that tasted something like this at Ka Jok See Restaurant in Phuket Town. Lek, the owner, reckons the secret to the sauce is the addition of his preferred tipple: blue-label Johnnie Walker single-malt whisky. Whatever, it is finger-licking good – and not a colonel in sight!

40 ml sunflower oil
1 teaspoon sea salt
½ teaspoon freshly ground black pepper
½ teaspoon ground chilli
2 chicken breasts, skin on
120 g bean sprouts, trimmed
2 tablespoons Fried Shallot Slices (see Essentials)
2 tablespoons Asian or Thai basil leaves, deep-fried

CHILLI CARAMEL
100 ml Tamarind Liquid (see Essentials)
200 g palm sugar
150 ml Scotch whisky
4 cloves garlic, minced
4 small red chillies, minced
zest of 2 limes, minced using a Microplane
75 ml fish sauce
12 small dried chillies, deep-fried
25 ml fresh lime juice, strained

HOT AND SOUR SALAD
40 ml fresh lime juice, strained
½ teaspoon chilli oil
few drops of sesame oil
25 ml fish sauce
25 ml Tamarind Liquid (see Essentials)
15 ml Sugar Syrup (see Essentials)
½ cup loosely packed coriander leaves
½ cup small Vietnamese mint leaves
2 tablespoons small Asian or Thai basil leaves
4 wing beans, finely sliced
1 small fennel bulb, shaved into fine rounds
2 green onions, sliced diagonally
1 teaspoon finely shredded fresh ginger
2 green bird's-eye chillies, sliced into fine rounds
1 long green chilli, sliced into fine lengths
2 red shallots, finely sliced
4 Chinese cabbage (wombok) leaves, shredded
100 g bean sprouts, trimmed

Preheat the oven to 200°C. Season the sunflower oil with salt, pepper and ground chilli, then rub the spiced oil all over the chicken breasts. Place the chicken on a baking tray, skin-side up, and roast for 15 minutes. Turn over and roast for another 10 minutes or until the chicken is tender and golden. Cut the chicken into 4 cm chunks.

To make the chilli caramel, combine the tamarind, palm sugar and half the whisky in a saucepan and bring to the boil. Add the garlic, chilli and lime zest and simmer for 10 minutes or until it starts to caramelise. Add the fish sauce and fried dried chillies and simmer for another 10 minutes, until it has reduced by one-third. Add the remaining whisky and when it simmers, stir in the lime juice and remove from the heat. The sauce should have the consistency and colour of honey.

Add the chicken chunks to the sauce and simmer for 5 minutes, then toss in the bean sprouts.

To make the salad, mix the lime juice, chilli oil, sesame oil, fish sauce, tamarind and sugar syrup in a bowl until combined. Toss the salad ingredients together in a bowl with the hot and sour dressing, then arrange on plates.

Add the caramelised chicken, scatter with the fried shallot slices and basil leaves and serve immediately.

SERVES 4

PEPPER BEEF AND PINEAPPLE SALAD

This dish immediately transports me back to Thailand and to the street vendors where I buy my neua sawan, or 'heavenly beef'. Its marinade is a classic Thai paste that is also used for stir-fries. When we used to prepare the beef like this in the restaurant, it was hard work keeping everyone's hands off it, the flavour and texture are so incredibly addictive. If you don't have time to dry the beef beforehand, you can always season it with the same paste and quickly stir-fry it instead.

200 g fresh pineapple, finely diced
½ long red chilli, sliced into fine rounds
2 red shallots, finely sliced
1 tablespoon finely shredded fresh ginger
4 makrut lime leaves, finely shredded
½ small cucumber, finely sliced
2 tablespoons mint leaves, shredded
2 tablespoons Asian or Thai basil leaves, torn
1 punnet tatsoi cress, snipped
2 tablespoons long-grain rice, roasted and coarsely ground
4 large betel leaves
4 tablespoons Fried Shallot Slices (see Essentials)

PEPPER BEEF
4 coriander roots, chopped
1 tablespoon chopped garlic
1 teaspoon white peppercorns
1 teaspoon fresh green peppercorns
1 teaspoon sea salt
3 teaspoons castor sugar
20 ml oyster sauce
20 ml light soy sauce
50 ml vegetable oil
600 g blade or skirt (or onglet) beef, sliced into thin strips

TAMARIND CHILLI DRESSING
½ teaspoon chopped galangal
1 small red chilli
1 small clove garlic
2 coriander roots
15 ml fish sauce
2 teaspoons palm sugar
40 ml fresh lime juice, strained
40 ml Tamarind Liquid (see Essentials)
20 ml Sugar Syrup (see Essentials)
60 ml fresh pineapple juice
1 teaspoon Ginger Juice (see Essentials)
1 teaspoon sesame oil

To prepare the beef, make a paste with the coriander roots, garlic, peppercorns and salt in a mortar and pestle. Continue to work the paste with the sugar, oyster and soy sauces until well blended. Stir in the oil. Transfer to a bowl, add the beef strips and rub the paste into the meat. Lay the meat in a single layer on a flat tray and leave to marinate for 3 hours.

To make the tamarind chilli dressing, pound the galangal, chilli, garlic and coriander roots in a mortar and pestle until smooth. Add the fish sauce and sugar and pound to combine. Stir in the lime juice. Whisk the remaining ingredients into the chilli paste and set aside until ready to serve.

To make the salad, place the pineapple, chilli, shallots, ginger, shredded lime, cucumber, mint, basil and tatsoi cress in a bowl and mix well. Add enough tamarind dressing to moisten and toss to combine.

To cook the beef, heat a wok and stir-fry the beef with its marinade in batches for 2 minutes until crisp. Drain on paper towel. Add the fried beef strips with half the roasted rice to the salad and toss to combine. Add a little extra dressing if necessary.

To serve, place the betel leaves on serving plates and arrange the salad on top. Dust with the remaining roasted rice and sprinkle with fried shallots.

SERVES 4–6

LEMONGRASS CHICKEN NOODLE SOUP

Dtom kha gai (chicken and coconut soup) was one of the first flavour combinations I fell in love with eons ago on the first of my many visits to Thailand. I have since adapted the fragrance and balance of flavours of this classic to suit my own style of cooking.

1 litre coconut milk
zest of 1 makrut lime, minced
1 litre White Chicken Stock (see Essentials)
80 ml fish sauce
4 chicken thighs fillets, cut in half
160 g dried somen noodles
75 ml fresh lime juice, strained
1 small red chilli, finely sliced
1 teaspoon minced galangal
2 teaspoons finely shredded ginger
4 makrut lime leaves, finely shredded
2 tablespoons Thai or holy basil leaves
3 tablespoons coriander leaves

CHILLI PASTE
6 slices galangal
3 slices ginger
6 coriander roots
6 red shallots
6 red bird's-eye chillies
8 makrut lime leaves
2 stalks lemongrass

To make the chilli paste, finely chop the galangal, ginger, coriander roots, shallots, chillies, lime leaves and lemongrass and mix together.

Bring the coconut milk to the boil in a large saucepan and boil for a few minutes until it splits. Stir in the chopped aromatics and lime zest then return to the boil.

Add the stock and fish sauce, return to the boil once more then reduce to simmering point. Add the chicken thigh fillets and simmer gently over the lowest heat for 15 minutes until the chicken is tender.

Remove the chicken carefully with a slotted spoon and set aside until cool enough to handle. Shred the meat into small lengths.

Cook the somen noodles in a saucepan of boiling water for about 2 minutes until soft. Drain and divide among serving bowls, then add the shredded chicken.

Strain the soup through a fine mesh sieve, discarding the solids, then return to the rinsed-out pan, bring back to the boil and add the lime juice. Taste and adjust if necessary.

Ladle the soup over the chicken and noodles, and garnish with the sliced chilli, galangal, ginger, shredded lime leaves, basil and coriander.

SERVES 4

SWEET AND SOUR CHILLI LOBSTER

In Phuket, they sell and serve their colourful native lobsters fished from the Andaman Sea, and this is my interpretation of the popular southern-style 'Three flavour sauce' – the very first taste memory I have of Thailand. I call this the holy trinity of flavours, combining the heat of chilli with the sweetness of palm sugar and the sourness of tamarind – a perfect combination for the lobster meat.

3 tablespoons rice flour
1 teaspoon chilli powder
2 teaspoons sea salt
1 teaspoon freshly ground white pepper
600 g raw lobster tail meat (from 1.2 kg whole lobster), cut into large chunks or medallions
vegetable oil, for deep-frying
20 ml fresh lime juice, strained
2 cabbage leaves, shredded
4 makrut lime leaves, finely shredded
1 long red chilli, finely sliced
½ cup Asian or Thai basil leaves, deep-fried

SWEET AND SOUR SAUCE
2 red shallots, chopped
1 teaspoon chopped garlic
1 teaspoon chopped ginger
1 teaspoon chopped coriander roots
1 small red chilli, chopped
20 ml vegetable oil
60 g palm sugar, shaved
50 ml Tamarind Liquid (see Essentials)
25 ml fish sauce
20 ml Thai sweet plum sauce

To make the sauce, blend the shallots, garlic, ginger, coriander root and chilli with the oil in a food processor or mortar and pestle until it forms a smooth paste.

Heat a wok over high heat, add the paste and cook, stirring continuously, for about 4 minutes until it begins to colour and become fragrant. Add the palm sugar, tamarind and fish sauce and simmer for 5 minutes. Add the sweet plum sauce, then take the wok off the heat.

To cook the lobster, mix the rice flour with the chilli, salt and pepper to make a crust. Add the lobster and toss to lightly coat. Discard any excess.

Heat the oil in a wok or deep-fryer to 180°C and fry the lobster chunks a few at a time for 3 minutes until just cooked and crisp. Drain on paper towel. Add the lobster to the hot sauce and toss in the wok to thoroughly coat with the sauce, then add the lime juice.

Lay the shredded cabbage leaves on a plate and spoon the lobster and sauce on top. Scatter with shredded lime leaf, chilli slices and fried basil leaves and serve.

SERVES 6

GARLIC PEPPER CHICKEN

These are delicious chicken nuggets given a Thai makeover and are quite addictive. They were on our dim sum-style bar menu in London – a perfect accompaniment to any number of Asian-inspired cocktails.

500 g chicken thigh fillets
1 litre Chinese Master Stock (see Essentials)
1 tablespoon Sichuan Spice Salt (see Essentials)
2 tablespoons rice flour
vegetable oil, for deep-frying
80 g baby spinach leaves, stems removed
4 tablespoons coriander leaves
4 green onions, sliced on the diagonal

GARLIC LEMON DRESSING
4 cloves garlic
1 tablespoon chopped coriander roots
2 teaspoons freshly ground white peppercorns
1 teaspoon fresh green peppercorns
60 ml fresh lemon juice, strained
30 ml fish sauce

To make the dressing, pound the ingredients together in a mortar and pestle until smooth.

Cut the chicken into 5 cm chunks, so the meat retains some texture after its double cooking. Heat the master stock to boiling point, add the chicken and turn off the heat. Leave for 25 minutes, then remove the chicken from the stock and drain on paper towel. Mix half the Sichuan spice salt with the rice flour and toss the chicken through the mix to coat.

Heat the oil in a wok or deep-fryer to 180°C and fry the chicken in small batches for 3 minutes until crisp. Drain on paper towel.

Season with the remaining Sichuan spice salt and toss with the spinach leaves, coriander and dressing. Garnish with green onion and serve.

SERVES 6–8

BLACK PEPPER SOFT-SHELL CRAB WITH FRIED RICE

Try to find the soft-shell crabs farmed in southern Queensland by Watermark when you prepare this. These crabs have been bred ethically and with a keen eye to sustainability – more than can be said for most of the imported product, and they are also of far superior quality. The gentle heat of the pepper and green chilli make a great contrast to luscious sweet crabmeat and the voluptuous rice completes the dish. Fried rice is the comfort food of Asia, incredibly versatile and best made in small batches. This is also a great accompaniment to grilled or barbequed fish or caramelised pork if you can't get hold of any soft-shell crabs. You'll get the best results with rice that was cooked the day before as it has had a chance to lose some of its moisture, making it crisp when fried.

4 soft-shell crabs
2 tablespoons plain flour
2 tablespoons rice flour
2 teaspoons sea salt
2 teaspoons freshly ground black pepper
½ teaspoon ground chilli
2 egg whites, lightly beaten
vegetable oil, for deep-frying

FRIED RICE
40 ml vegetable oil
2 teaspoons minced garlic
1 tablespoon minced white onion
1 large egg
1 cup steamed jasmine rice, spread out to dry on a tray overnight
1 teaspoon light soy sauce
1 teaspoon oyster sauce
½ teaspoon castor sugar
2 tablespoons finely sliced green onions
2 tablespoons soy bean sprouts, trimmed
80 g cooked spanner crabmeat
1 tablespoon chopped coriander leaves
2 teaspoons fresh lime juice, strained

GREEN CHILLI DIPPING SAUCE
2 cloves garlic
2 green bird's-eye chillies
25 ml Sugar Syrup (see Essentials)
50 ml fresh lime juice, strained
40 ml fish sauce
1 teaspoon chopped coriander root

To make the dipping sauce, pound the garlic and chilli in a mortar and pestle, gradually working in the sugar syrup, lime juice and fish sauce until the flavours are balanced. Stir in the coriander root.

To prepare the crabs, peel the top shell from back to front and pull off the filters (dead man's fingers) and discard, being careful not to lose the crab tomalley (roe). Snip the crab in half down the centre with scissors.

To prepare the rice, heat a wok over high heat, add the oil and fry the garlic and white onion until softened. Crack the egg, add to the hot oil and allow the whites to firm before scrambling with a chopstick. Stir in the rice, spreading it around the wok, and reduce the heat to low. Season with the soy and oyster sauces and the sugar, tossing to combine.

Add the green onion, soy bean sprouts and crab and cook for 2 minutes, tossing until heated through. Toss in the coriander and lime juice and remove from the heat.

Mix together the flours, salt, pepper and chilli. Immerse the crab pieces in egg white to coat, then roll in the seasoned flour, shaking off the excess.

Heat the oil in a wok or saucepan to 180°C and deep-fry the crab pieces, a few at a time to maintain the oil temperature, for 2 minutes until crisp and cooked. Remove from the oil with a slotted spoon and drain on paper towel.

Pile the fried rice in small mounds on serving plates and lay the fried soft-shell crab on top. Serve with the green chilli dipping sauce.

SERVES 4

SPICY PORK BALLS WITH CHILLI LEMONGRASS SAUCE

This recipe gives a whole new meaning to the concept of 'rissoles'. It's quite a rich dish, so I tend to serve it in small quantities or as part of a shared table.

4 tablespoons pea eggplants (aubergines)
4 makrut lime leaves, finely shredded
2 teaspoons finely sliced pickled grachai
1 long red chilli, finely sliced
24 fried Asian or Thai basil leaves

SPICY PORK BALLS
400 g minced pork
2 tablespoons Chilli Lemongrass Paste (see Essentials)
2 teaspoons sea salt
4 cloves garlic, minced
2 teaspoons minced galangal
6 makrut lime leaves, minced
2 tablespoons shredded Asian or Thai basil leaves

CHILLI LEMONGRASS SAUCE
400 ml coconut cream
4 tablespoons Chilli Lemongrass Paste (see Essentials)
30 g palm sugar, shaved
30 ml fish sauce
250 ml White Chicken Stock (see Essentials)
50 ml Tamarind Liquid (see Essentials)

To make the pork balls, mix the ingredients together in a bowl, then slap the mixture repeatedly against the sides of the bowl. This softens the meat, breaking down any texture and gives a melt-in-the-mouth feel when cooked. Roll the mixture into small balls, place on a flat tray, then cover and refrigerate for 1 hour.

To make the sauce, heat the coconut cream in a saucepan over high heat until it cracks (splits), then stir in the chilli lemongrass paste and cook for a couple of minutes until combined. Add the palm sugar and fish sauce and simmer gently for 2 minutes until slightly thickened. Stir in the stock and tamarind liquid and simmer for another 5 minutes.

Add the pork balls to the sauce and gently poach for 15 minutes, turning every now and then, until cooked.

Add the pea eggplant and cook for 3–4 minutes. Add the shredded lime leaf, grachai and chilli slices and top with the fried basil leaves. Serve with steamed jasmine rice.

SERVES 4

TAMARIND CHICKEN WITH GRILLED EGGPLANT

I love the combination of coconut and tamarind. The flavours offer such contrast and this chicken dish is an old stalwart from our early restaurant days in Sydney. The long green eggplants are far superior in flavour but if you can't find them, use the long Japanese purple eggplant – just be aware that its flesh won't be as creamy. Cooking them whole over hot coals gives a delicious smoky flavour that is hard to emulate with electricity. I always fire up the barbeque when I cook eggplant like this – the end result is worth the effort.

500 g chicken thigh fillets
vegetable oil, for deep-frying
1 punnet coriander cress, snipped
2 tablespoons Fried Shallot Slices (see Essentials)

TAMARIND MARINADE
250 ml Tamarind Liquid (see Essentials)
20 ml fish sauce
40 g coconut palm sugar (gula melaka), shaved
1 teaspoon freshly ground black pepper
20 ml light soy sauce
500 ml White Chicken Stock (see Essentials)

TAMARIND COCONUT SAUCE
2 teaspoons kapi (Thai shrimp paste)
1 brown onion, chopped
3 cloves garlic, chopped
4 red bird's-eye chillies, chopped
1 stalk lemongrass, finely sliced
3 coriander roots, chopped
2 teaspoons minced ginger
40 ml vegetable oil
1 teaspoon sesame oil
375 ml Tamarind Liquid (see Essentials)
400 ml coconut milk
1 litre White Chicken Stock (see Essentials)
25 g palm sugar, shaved
25 ml fish sauce

GRILLED EGGPLANT
4 long green eggplants (aubergines)
40 ml fresh lime juice, strained
25 ml fish sauce
15 ml Tamarind Liquid (see Essentials)
2 teaspoons castor sugar
¼ teaspoon roasted chilli powder (preferably Blue Tongue)
2 tablespoons shredded mint leaves
2 red shallots, finely sliced

To make the marinade, bring all the ingredients to the boil in a stockpot. Simmer for 10 minutes, then add the chicken pieces and remove from the heat. Cover and allow the chicken to cool in the marinade for 45 minutes.

Remove the chicken with a slotted spoon and rest on paper towel. When cool, cut each thigh fillet into three even-sized pieces.

To make the sauce, dry-roast the kapi in a frying pan over gentle heat until fragrant. Place the kapi, onion, garlic, chilli, lemongrass, coriander root, ginger and half the vegetable oil in a food processor and blend to a smooth paste.

Heat the sesame oil and remaining vegetable oil in a large saucepan over moderate heat and fry the paste for about 5 minutes until fragrant and softened, stirring regularly to prevent sticking.

Add the tamarind liquid, coconut milk and stock and bring to the boil. Boil over moderate heat for 45 minutes or until reduced by half. Add the palm sugar and fish sauce and simmer for 10 minutes. Taste, and adjust the seasoning if necessary. Strain through a fine mesh sieve and discard the solids. Cool. Remove any residual oil, and reheat gently when ready to serve.

To prepare the eggplant, grill over hot coals or direct flame until charred and softened. Stand in a colander for 15 minutes until cool enough to handle. Peel off the blistered skin and break the eggplant into thick lengths. Mix the remaining ingredients in a bowl, add the eggplant and leave to marinate while the chicken is cooking.

To cook the chicken, heat the vegetable oil in a wok to 180°C and deep-fry the chicken pieces for 3 minutes until crisp and golden. Remove from the oil with a slotted spoon and drain on paper towel.

Arrange the eggplant on serving plates, sit the chicken on top and spoon the sauce around. Scatter the coriander cress and fried shallots over the top and serve immediately.

SERVES 4

TROPICAL PARADISE ICE-CREAM SLICE

This recipe is based on the refreshing fruit flavours of the tropics. The flavours are constructed in a mould in several layers and frozen, then unmoulded onto a flat board and sliced to serve – too easy. In restaurant life, I construct ice creams and sorbets using various shaped moulds to create unique and interesting patterns, as in the photo here. At home, however, you'll still get a stunning result by simply making layers of a uniform width in your chosen mould. It's best to line the mould first with baking paper, leaving the ends overlapping to give leverage when removing the finished ice cream from its mould.

MANGO SORBET
150 g glucose
500 ml mango puree
15 ml fresh lime juice, strained

STRAWBERRY GUAVA ICE CREAM
250 ml strawberry guava puree
125 ml strawberry puree
25 ml fresh lemon juice, strained
270 g castor sugar
375 ml pouring (35%) cream

MAKRUT LIME SORBET
375 ml Sugar Syrup (see Essentials)
zest of 3 makrut limes
3 makrut lime leaves, crushed
150 ml water
juice of 3 makrut limes

PASSIONFRUIT ICE CREAM
5 egg yolks
150 g castor sugar
190 ml passionfruit juice, strained
375 ml pouring (35%) cream

To make the mango sorbet, heat the glucose in a bowl over simmering water until softened, then stir through the mango puree with the lime juice. Churn in an ice-cream machine until firm, then spoon into a large rectangular mould lined with baking paper. Freeze until firm.

To make the strawberry guava ice cream, stir all the ingredients together in a bowl, then churn in an ice-cream machine until firm. Spoon on top of the frozen mango to make a second layer, smooth the surface with a spatula and return to the freezer.

To make the lime sorbet, heat the sugar syrup with the lime zest, crushed leaves and water to simmering point. Remove from the heat and leave for 20 minutes to infuse. Pass through a fine sieve and discard the solids. Stir in the lime juice and when cool, churn in an ice-cream machine until firm. Spoon the mixture on top of the strawberry layer, smooth the surface with a spatula and return to the freezer.

To make the passionfruit ice cream, whisk the egg yolks and sugar until pale and creamy. Whisk in the passionfruit juice. Heat 200 ml of the cream to simmering point, then pour over the egg mix, whisking to combine.

Sit the bowl over a pan of simmering water and cook to a custard consistency. Remove from the heat and pass through a fine sieve. Allow to cool then stir in the remaining cream. Churn in an ice-cream machine until just firm and spoon over the lime sorbet layer, smoothing the surface.

The mould should now be full. Cover the surface with baking paper, return to the freezer and leave overnight to set.

To unmould, run some very hot water over the base of the mould; this will loosen the ice cream and allow it to slip out easily. Turn the mould upside down and let the ice cream slip out onto a flat board. Return the ice cream on its board to the freezer for 5 minutes so the softened edges firm up again.

To serve, cut 2 cm thick slices using a hot sharp knife. Lay each slice flat on a cold plate and serve immediately. Cover the remaining ice cream with baking paper and return to the freezer.

SERVES 10–12

PANDANUS AND MAKRUT LIME CREAM WITH LEMONGRASS JELLY AND LYCHEES

I like to use traditional Asian ingredients and fruits blended with western techniques of preparation to create desserts that fit within the flavour spectrum of Asia, yet don't have their quirkiness. The textures are luscious and velvety soft, and the flavours are refreshing on the palate. If lychees are not in season, use longans, mangosteen or ripe mango instead.

20 ml coconut cream
12 lychees, peeled and halved, seeds removed
12 longans, peeled and halved, seeds removed
2 makrut lime leaves, finely shredded

MAKRUT LIME CREAM
400 ml pouring (35%) cream
200 ml milk
5 cm piece fresh pandanus leaf
3 makrut lime leaves, minced
minced zest from 1 makrut lime
80 g castor sugar
4 g gelatine leaves, softened in cold water
25 ml lychee liqueur
1 teaspoon makrut lime juice

LEMONGRASS JELLY
90 ml Sugar Syrup (see Essentials)
25 ml lychee liqueur
65 ml water
¼ stalk lemongrass, minced using a Microplane
5 cm piece fresh pandanus leaf
2 g gelatine leaves, softened in cold water

To make the lime cream, heat the cream, milk, pandanus leaf, lime leaves, zest and sugar in a saucepan over gentle heat to simmering point, giving it time to slowly infuse. Stir in the softened gelatine leaves until dissolved. Remove from the heat, add the liqueur and lime juice and pass through a fine mesh sieve, discarding the solids.

Pour the cream mixture into small ramekin dishes or serving glasses and refrigerate for about 2 hours until cold and firm.

To make the lemongrass jelly, heat the sugar syrup, liqueur, water, lemongrass and pandanus leaf in a saucepan over gentle heat and simmer for 5 minutes. Add the softened gelatine and stir until dissolved. Remove from the heat and pass through a fine mesh sieve, discarding the solids. Allow to cool completely but not set.

Spoon the cooled jelly onto the lime cream and refrigerate until firm.

To serve, spoon a little coconut cream into the centre of each jelly, arrange the lychees and longans on top, stacked in the centre of the jelly, and add a few fine shreds of lime leaf.

SERVES 4

JASMINE BLOSSOM JELLIES

Inspired by the 'perfume water' of Thailand, these jellies are perfect when made as a small taste to serve after dinner with green tea. Light and delicate, they have a flavour burst that captures the heady aroma of fresh jasmine blossom – the definitive scent of Bangkok. Flecks of gold leaf give them an even greater opulence. To make the jasmine-scented sugar syrup, soak fresh-cut jasmine blossoms in the sugar syrup for 3–4 days in the refrigerator. Strain the flowers from the sugar before proceeding with the recipe. I use small pyramid-shaped fleximats when I make these jellies.

150 ml fresh coconut juice
105 ml Sugar Syrup (see Essentials), infused with fresh jasmine blossom
5 g gelatine leaves, softened in cold water
1 sheet edible gold leaf

To make the jellies, heat the coconut juice and sugar syrup to simmering point, then stir in the softened gelatine. Remove from the heat and pass through a fine mesh sieve.

Allow to cool completely, then stir in tiny flecks of gold leaf.

Pour into small fleximat moulds or sake cups and set in the refrigerator until firm. Turn out of the moulds when ready to serve.

SERVES 4–6

MELTING POT MALAYSIA

The hybrid culture and cuisine of Malaysia has always fascinated me. It's a real melting pot of indigenous Malay, Indian and Chinese philosophy and practice, an early example of the true essence of fusion. Penang is a curious mix of bustling port, heritage city and inviting food frontier. The core of the city, Georgetown is awash with street vendors selling everything from snacks to noodle soups and curries, and is considered Malaysia's capital for street food. Alongside pockets of Indian and Malay traders, it has a thriving Chinatown. A stroll along any of the twisting streets that run off the main thoroughfare Jalan Penang will take you past Chinese shophouses, the odd temple or mosque, fresh vegetable markets and colourful stalls. The smoke from the charcoal pits and the constant clatter of mahjong tiles only adds to the atmosphere.

I have wonderful memories of Penang, particularly cruising along Gurney Drive after sunset to pick out new things to taste from the rows of food carts. Everything is cooked on the spot in makeshift conditions as you order it; everyone can choose exactly what they want from what they see, or each choose a favourite dish and share it all – such an exciting way to have dinner, like a huge picnic under the stars. Sugarcane juice is extracted from fresh stalks in manually operated presses by the side of the road, and is a perfect foil for the fiery spices and chilli dishes. Much of the food served at hawker stalls is kampong (village) cooking, such as chicken or pork satay with peanut sauce that is sometimes laced with grated pineapple; paper-wrapped chicken; nasi goreng (fried rice) with little chunks of omelette, tiny prawns and garlic chives tossed through; or fresh and crunchy vegetable rojak salad. I will never forget my first taste of popiah, thin crepe-like pastry wrappers rolled to order with just the right amount of chilli paste to get the palate excited. Other hawker gathering places include the Esplanade, along the waterfront, for seafood; and Swatow Lane, behind the Sheraton Hotel, which specialises in Indian (banana leaf rice and mee rebus) and halal food (mee goreng, popiah and gado gado).

This is a place where you experience first-hand how food reflects ethnic diversity: Muslim Malays cook beef and lamb; the Indian Hindus use mutton; the Chinese do great things with pork and duck; and they all champion chicken, fish and loads of vegetables. I am a big fan of Indian-style roti canai, wafer-thin sheets of bread cooked on the griddle and served with a spicy mutton or chicken curry. One morning I felt brave enough to try nasi lemak for breakfast: coconut rice with ikan bilis (dried anchovies fried until crisp), beef rendang and roasted peanuts. I have never looked back, and could now eat this any time of the day. Another well-known hawker dish is char kway teow – rice noodles tossed with Chinese sausage, prawns (or beef) and flavoured with chilli and soy sauce, with a lingering smoky flavour from 'the breath of the wok'. The laksa here is known as penang laksa or assam laksa and is made with tamarind water rather than coconut milk, resulting in a flavour that is sour, tangy and fiery hot. This is also the place to get the best fried carrot cake (char koay kark) – a mysterious name since it's made with white radish – and mee rebus, thick Hokkien noodles smothered in a rich curry sauce with sweet potato, egg and sprouts. One of my all-time favourite rice-noodle dishes is cheung fen, where silky noodle sheets are filled with any manner of stuffings, then rolled and steamed. It's also worth trying the chilli-hot fish-head soup or curry with a splash of kalamansi, a small sour lime. I could go on and on, the repertoire is so vast and seductive.

One evening, we went to the summit of Penang Hill by cable car to indulge in our first steamboat dinner. The Bellevue Hotel has fabulous views of the city below and is surrounded by lush gardens filled with enormous hanging heliconias and frangipani. Steamboat is basically an Asian take on fondue – with so much more flavour. The round vessel of the steamboat sits over charcoal and

STAYING IN PENANG

EASTERN & ORIENTAL HOTEL
10 Lebuh Farquhar, Georgetown, Penang
Tel +60 4 222 2000
www.e-o-hotel.com
One of the grand dames among Asian hotels has had a recent and much-needed facelift. Ask for a room that faces the sea.

CHEONG FATT TZE MANSION
14 Lebuh Leith, Georgetown, Penang
Tel +60 4 262 0006
www.cheongfatttzemansion.com
A glamorous and authentic homestay with great individuality and personality, smack bang in the heart of Georgetown.

is filled with a light broth, perfumed with dried shiitake mushrooms, ginger and green onions. Each person is given chopsticks and a small wire-mesh ladle for transferring the cooked food to their own rice bowl. A selection of raw or marinated ingredients (we had prawns, chicken and beef strips) is placed in the middle of the table so that each person can cook their own feast. Condiments include pickled ginger, soy and chilli sauces and freshly picked herbs – such a fun and interactive way to eat.

It's worth taking a peek beyond the city centre and exploring the rest of Penang Island, where spice plantations are set amongst the thick green jungle canopy. It is fascinating to watch nutmeg being harvested: the pale, pulpy fruit is peeled back to reveal the red arils of mace that close around the nutmeg pod like a perfect lace glove; the mace is laid on woven bamboo mats to dry in the sun, while the nutmeg pods are stored whole for later use. Look out for farms growing huge clove trees, as well as forests of cinnamon and rubber trees.

By contrast, Kuala Lumpur, midway between Penang and the Singapore border, is a modern, affluent metropolis with an exotic mix of East and West. The original houses, with their ornately carved tiled roofs, are fast disappearing, giving way to the mega-scale developments that dominate the centre of town. Chinatown has been reduced to a couple of streets with a crammed and boisterous night market around Jalan Petaling. The colonial splendour of the Sultan Abdul Samad Supreme Court and central railway station reside majestically next to the Golden Triangle business district, a forest of high-rise glitz including the postmodern Petronas Twin Towers, for a time the tallest buildings in the world. It's quite something to ride the elevators to the top and check out the view, or walk along the platform that connects the two towers. The elevated monorail runs above the busy streets and flyovers keep sprouting to accommodate the congestion of the rapidly growing volume of traffic.

I have visited the city for leisure several times and also for work, as a guest chef in residence for an 'Absolutely Australian' food and wine promotion in 2000. One sure-fire way to get to the heart of any city is to hang out with the locals, and I was fortunate enough to explore the street food, bars and cafes of KL with those in the know – the local chefs, who took great pride in their culture and cuisine. We went to late-night bars in Bangsar, lining our stomachs first with a quick supper from the vendors at the Telawi Tiga Food Centre, where I have been known to devour a huge plate of curry puffs. Later we savoured the atmosphere at the Chow Kit night markets. The hawker food here is sensational, with enough different types of noodle dishes to put me in a state of blissful indecision. The atmosphere is electric, heady with the scent of spices and all manner of things being cooked. Chinatown is the place to go for a fix of char kway teow or a comfort plate of Hainanese chicken rice. If I'm there during the day, I zip into Yook Woo Hin for some of my favourite dim sum snacks; the steamed radish cake with chilli is a stand-out.

One morning we drove to the limestone caves at Batu village, now part of the suburban sprawl of the city. We climbed the 300-odd stairs to see the Hindu shrine deep inside the cave, along with hundreds of monkeys, then descended to ground level, anxious to find some breakfast. We found it at the cafe across the road in the form of Indian-style rumali (handkerchief bread), which is like a transparent crepe. A thin batter is poured onto a large flat hotplate and cooked briefly until set, filled with a potato curry, then folded and wrapped – like a handkerchief. Such a perfect start to the day.

EATING IN PENANG

KEDAI KOPI & MAKANAN LOW ENG HOO
84 Lorong Selamat, Georgetown, Penang
Small local cafe open for lunch only. Order the popiah and char kway teow.

KELAWEI CURRY FISH HEAD
43 Jalan Kelawei, Georgetown, Penang
Tel +60 4 226 4573
This place offers the Malay specialty of extra-hot fish-head curry. Go foraging for the sweet flesh of the fish cheeks and tender meat of the head. Any leftover gravy is divine spooned into rice.

LAKSA BALIK PULAU
Balik Pulau Market, Penang
A fab laksa stall – for lunch only.

STAYING IN KUALA LUMPUR

HOTEL MAYA
138 Jalan Ampang, Kuala Lumpur
Tel +60 3 2711 8866
www.hotelmaya.com.my
Right in the heart of the city, this affordable gem feels modern and urban – a refreshing change from the chain-hotel mentality.

Further south, on the west coast, lies the old colonial city of Melaka, birthplace of Nonya cuisine. The Chinese in this region are called Straits Chinese, Peranakan or Baba-Nonya (the men are called 'Baba' and the women 'Nonya'), and their distinctive food takes its name from these women, who pass on their knowledge to the next generation. Sadly, Melaka's valuable Nonya gastronomic heritage is in danger of being lost as younger generations become more interested in Western-style food. The keepers of this important history are growing old and it would be a great shame to see it disappear altogether.

Right from the start, Nonya food has been a major influence on the way I cook, and I have great respect for its rich and unique heritage – a hybrid of Chinese, Portuguese, Dutch, Indian, Arabic and English traditions. This cultural overlay has shaped Melaka, making for one hell of an interesting mix, almost like an Asian version of Creole. The culture remains a medley of Muslim, Taoist, Hindu and Christian cultures, as a walk down the aptly named Temple Street quickly demonstrates: Hindu and Chinese temples jostle for space with mosques and churches. Old Melaka is charming, a small enclave of crumbling Dutch and Portuguese churches mixed in with Chinese merchant houses. The compact streets and narrow laneways of shophouses are charming reminders of a bygone era, when land taxes were determined by the width of street frontage, so the houses were built narrow but very, very long.

Jonker Street (or Jalan Hang Jebat) is one of the main thoroughfares in Melaka, and is a haven for antique collectors and bargain hunters. It is so popular it quicky becomes clogged with vehicle and foot traffic, even more so after 7 p.m., when the street takes on a market atmosphere. There are plenty of cafes and eating houses in the area, as well as rows of hawker stalls along Jalan Merdeka, which was originally the waterfront (much of Melaka has been constructed on reclaimed land). Typical Nonya dishes on offer here include chicken rice balls; bak kut teh (pork ribs tea), ribs and organ meats in a pork broth: popiah, soft hand-made spring roll wrappers with a vegetable and chilli stuffing; mee goreng, Indian-inspired egg noodles tossed in a fiery chilli sauce; otak otak, fish pounded into a paste with spices and steamed in bamboo or banana leaf; orh jian, stir-fried oyster omelette with a chilli dipping sauce; and laksa lemak, the famous spicy coconut soup made with noodles, chicken balls and seafood.

Many shops and cafes sell cendol – pandan-flavoured jelly balls in coconut milk sweetened with jaggery or gula melaka (a coconut-flavoured palm sugar). Cendol can also be made with red beans and sago pearls. Another sweet treat is black rice cooked with coconut cream and palm sugar, which is often served with small sweet bananas. The Indonesian and Dutch influence is best displayed in desserts and baking: melt-in-the-mouth flaky pastries feature prominently, as do tropical fruits such as pineapple, mango and durian. I still remember enjoying

EATING IN KUALA LUMPUR

COCHINE
64 Jalan Doraisamy, Kuala Lumpur
Tel +60 3 2697 1180
A menu of Asian favourites with a drop-dead gorgeous Buddha Bar, or recline on the opium beds in the basement bar.

KL STREET FOOD: PETALING JAYA
Not too far from the centre of town (about a 20-minute drive) is the area of Petaling Jaya, an enclave of industry, business and universities that's well worth a visit for its diverse array of street food. There's all manner of noodle and dumpling dishes: big steaming bowls of won ton soup, excellent chilli crab, laksa, murtabak (a sort of filled crepe), beef rendang and otak otak (a spiced fish paste steamed in a banana leaf packet, then grilled over hot coals). Wander around the streets and lanes and let your senses guide you – here are just a few to get you started.

Restoran Fatty Crab
2 Jalan SS24/13, Petaling Jaya
Turn up and queue – chilli crab and hot-and-sour crab are the pick of the bunch.

Restoran Mee Yoke Lim
Cheow Yang area
Great prawn and seafood lobak (radish cake).

SS4C Night Market
For the definitive laksa assam.

Gerai Mang Kee
This place does bloody good ginger duck.

a local interpretation of mango cream, mousse-like in its lightness and laced with pomelo segments. The gentle acidity of the fruit balanced the richness of the cream perfectly. Look out too for a slightly sweet tea made with Chinese red dates – it's a perfect match for the food.

Largely a home-based cuisine, Nonya food is quite time-consuming to prepare. Rempah form the basis of many dishes: these pounded spices and herb pastes become fragrant when fried, releasing their essential oils to perfume and flavour the food. The 'many hands' approach to cooking developed in the homes of the wealthy, who could afford the ingredients and labour to prepare the complex dishes. Flavours range from sweet and sour (jaggery and tamarind) to hot and creamy (chilli and coconut milk), with a prolific use of aromatic herbs. Complexity is built by layering flavours and textures. Inspired by its history of integration and fusion, and drawn to its ingenuity, this is one of the first cuisines I looked to when developing my own personal style, and I continue to incorporate Nonya techniques and philosophy into my repertoire.

EATING IN MELAKA

NANCY'S KITCHEN
15 Jalan Hang Lekir, Melaka
Tel +60 6 283 6099
Follow the advice of local foodie Su-Lyn Tan: sit at a courtyard table and go for favourites like sayur lodeh (vegetables in spicy coconut sauce), ayam buah keluak (chicken slow-cooked with black nuts) and itek tim (duck and vegetable soup).

HOE KEE
4 Jalan Hang Jebat (Jonker Street), Melaka
Stop off for the best chicken rice balls – a Nonya specialty.

STAYING IN MELAKA

THE BABA HOUSE
125 Jalan Tun Tan Cheng Lock, Melaka
Tel +60 6 281 1216
Modest guesthouse in a restored shophouse with classic Peranakan features, centrally located in the old quarter.

CRAB POPIAH

With its origins in Nonya cooking, popiah is the Malay equivalent of the Vietnamese fresh spring roll or the Chinese bao bing. These fresh, uncooked spring rolls are made with tissue-thin wrappers filled with vegetables or fish and seasoned with chilli. I first became addicted to them when I lived in Adelaide, where one of the hawker-style food stalls at the Central Market makes them to order. Popiah are best eaten fresh and at room temperature – something seems to be lost when they are refrigerated. The wrappers are very easy to make, but you can use Vietnamese rice-paper wrappers instead if you don't have time (soften them first in warm water to make them pliable before filling).

150 g cooked crabmeat
2 teaspoons Sambal Bajak (see Essentials)
2 teaspoons salted yellow beans, mashed
4 snowpeas (mange-tout), finely sliced lengthways
1 small cucumber, peeled, seeded and cut into fine julienne strips
40 g bean sprouts, picked
2 Chinese cabbage (wombok) leaves, shredded
12 Asian or Thai basil leaves, shredded
1 teaspoon fish sauce
10 butter lettuce leaves, halved lengthways
3 tablespoons Fried Shallot Slices (see Essentials)

POPIAH WRAPPERS
180 g fine rice flour
25 g superfine cake flour
½ teaspoon sea salt
4 large eggs
1 teaspoon vegetable oil
500 ml warm water
vegetable oil, extra, for pan-frying

To make the wrappers, combine the flours and salt in a bowl. Beat the eggs in another bowl and add the oil and water. Blend the wet and dry ingredients in a food processor to form a batter, then refrigerate for 1 hour.

To cook the wrappers, heat a non-stick frying pan and brush with the minimum amount of oil possible, then pour in a little batter and swirl to coat the base. The procedure is the same as when making crepes – it is important to keep the batter as fine and even as possible. Do not flip the wrapper; instead, turn out onto a plate when set.

Stack the popiah on top of each other, covering them with a cloth until you have finished cooking. You should have 18 wrappers in all.

Combine the crabmeat, sambal bajak, mashed yellow beans, snowpeas, cucumber, bean sprouts, cabbage leaves, basil leaves and fish sauce and heat gently in a frying pan until warmed through.

Arrange the wrappers on a bench. Sit a piece of lettuce on each, spoon in some of the crabmeat filling, then sprinkle with fried shallots. Wrap up each popiah as you would a spring roll, folding in the edges as you go. Serve immediately.

SERVES 6

STEAMED PRAWN CRUMPET

This recipe is really a tribute to the infinite talent and creative vision of Phillip Searle, the owner-chef of Oasis Seros (now at Vulcans in the Blue Mountains), who employed me when I moved to Sydney in 1988. With Phillip as a mentor, I discovered a real melting pot of flavours and techniques.

1 punnet onion cress (rock chives), snipped

PRAWN MOUSSE
300 g raw prawn meat, chopped
1 egg white
½ teaspoon sea salt
½ teaspoon freshly ground white pepper
1 teaspoon fresh lemon juice, strained
125 ml pouring (35%) cream

SPICED PRAWN SAUCE
400 ml Prawn Stock (see Essentials)
2 teaspoons Sambal Bajak (see Essentials)
200 ml pouring (35%) cream
2 teaspoons fresh lime juice, strained
sea salt and freshly ground white pepper

CRUMPET BATTER
140 g plain flour
½ teaspoon sea salt
50 ml milk
50 ml water
30 g fresh yeast
½ teaspoon castor sugar
2 large eggs, beaten
¼ teaspoon sesame oil
½ teaspoon extra virgin olive oil

To make the mousse, chill the food processor bowl for 20 minutes then blend the prawn meat, egg white, salt, pepper and lemon juice until smooth, being careful not to overwork – it is important that the mixture remain very cold. Add the cream and blend until just incorporated. Cover and refrigerate until ready to use.

To make the sauce, bring the prawn stock to the boil and cook until reduced by half (to give you 200 ml). Stir in the sambal bajak and cream and simmer for 10 minutes. Add the lime juice and season to taste with salt and pepper. Reheat gently when ready to serve.

To make the crumpets, mix the flour and salt in the bowl of an electric mixer. Heat the milk and water to blood temperature then add the yeast and sugar and leave to dissolve for 5 minutes. Using a dough hook attachment, add the beaten egg to the flour and beat on medium speed. When incorporated, add the warm milk mixture and oils and continue to beat for another 5 minutes.

Cover the bowl with plastic film and a tea towel and leave in a warm place for 50–60 minutes until the batter doubles in volume. Large airy bubbles will appear on the surface.

Heat an 18 cm round non-stick pan, add a ladleful of batter to cover the base of the pan and cook over low heat until small bubbles appear on the surface. Put the pan under a hot grill for 20 seconds to cook the top surface, then remove the crumpet from the pan. Cover with a dry tea towel and repeat with the remaining batter to make three crumpets in all.

While the crumpets are still warm and pliable, spread each one with prawn mousse to make a 2 cm thick layer. Roll the crumpet up like a jam roll, seam-side down.

Line a steamer tray with baking paper and lay the filled crumpets on top, close to each other in a single layer. Cover and steam over gently boiling water for 40 minutes. Remove the crumpets from the tray and lay on a dry tea towel for a few minutes.

To serve, spoon the sauce into bowl plates. Cut each crumpet in half, and then in half again. Lay two slices on each plate and top with onion cress to serve.

SERVES 6

SOY-BRAISED PORK, EGGPLANT AND SOBA NOODLE SALAD

An idyllic blend of delicious textures and great flavour, this salad is easy to whip together if you have any soy-braised pork left over, crying out to be used. It makes a great lunchtime treat.

100 g organic soba noodles
olive oil and sesame oil, to prevent sticking
vegetable oil, for deep-frying
300 g eggplant (aubergine), cut into batons
300 g Soy-braised Pork (see Essentials), cut into 2 cm cubes
2 teaspoons Sichuan Spice Salt (see Essentials)
2 green onions, finely sliced on the diagonal
2 sticks celery, finely sliced crossways
1 cup watercress sprigs
1 punnet celery cress, snipped
4 tablespoons coriander leaves
1 tablespoon white sesame seeds, roasted
2 tablespoons Fried Garlic Slices (see Essentials)

SESAME MISO DRESSING
75 ml Soy Pork Jelly (see Essentials)
25 ml light soy sauce
1 teaspoon sesame oil
25 ml Chinese black vinegar
½ teaspoon chilli oil
30 g shiro (white) miso paste
25 ml mirin
25 ml rice vinegar
½ teaspoon freshly ground black pepper
100 ml sunflower oil

Cook the noodles in boiling salted water for 2 minutes. Drain and refresh under cold running water to stop the cooking. Drain again and toss through a little olive oil and a dash of sesame oil to prevent sticking.

To make the sesame miso dressing, heat the pork jelly in a small pan until melted. Allow to cool then whisk with all the remaining dressing ingredients in a bowl until emulsified.

Heat the vegetable oil in a large saucepan or wok to 180°C and deep-fry the eggplant batons in small batches for 4–5 minutes until golden. Drain on paper towel.

Fry the pork cubes in the hot oil for 3 minutes until crisp then drain on paper towel and season with the spice salt.

Mix the fried eggplant and pork with the noodles, green onions, celery, watercress, celery cress and coriander. Add the dressing and toss to thoroughly combine.

Arrange the salad on plates, sprinkle with roasted sesame seeds and fried garlic and serve.

SERVES 4

CHICKEN SOUP WITH PORK WON TONS

Soups like this are timeless and universally adored, a perfect meal in itself or as part of a shared table. I am a huge fan of the Asian practice of mixing different proteins together, whether it be seafood and meat, or in this case, chicken and pork. A few of the old remaining shophouses in Kuala Lumpur's Chinatown still make this type of soup every day, always one of my first stops when I visit.

1.6 kg organic chicken
4 litres water
2 onions, finely sliced
1 tablespoon sliced ginger
2 sticks cinnamon
6 green cardamom pods, cracked open
3 star anise
1 tablespoon jaggery
1 teaspoon sea salt
40 ml Vietnamese fish sauce
20 ml fresh lime juice, strained
2 green onions, finely sliced
200 g bean sprouts, trimmed
1 small red chilli, minced
1 tablespoon Vietnamese mint (laksa) leaves, shredded
2 tablespoons coriander leaves

PORK WON TONS
160 g minced pork
50 g water chestnuts, blanched and finely diced
1 teaspoon minced ginger
1 tablespoon finely diced cloud-ear fungus
1 teaspoon freshly ground black pepper
2 green onions, finely sliced
50 ml light soy sauce
30 ml Shaoxing rice wine
20 ml fish sauce
1 teaspoon sesame oil
24 won ton wrappers
rice flour, for dusting

To make the soup, rinse the chicken, splay the legs open for even cooking and place in a large saucepan. Cover with the water and bring to the boil, skimming the surface when necessary. Just as it starts to simmer, add the onion, ginger, spices, jaggery and salt.

Reduce the heat and simmer gently for 35 minutes. Remove the chicken from the pan and set aside until cool enough to handle. Strain the stock through a fine mesh sieve.

Reheat the stock with the fish sauce. When simmering, add the lime juice, taste and adjust the seasonings if necessary. Shred the chicken meat and set aside.

To make the won tons, slap the pork mince against the sides of a bowl to soften. Mix the pork with the water chestnuts, ginger, fungus, pepper, green onion, soy sauce, Shaoxing wine, fish sauce and sesame oil, working thoroughly to combine.

Place a teaspoon of the pork mix in the centre of each won ton wrapper and brush the edges with a little water. Fold the wrapper in half then bring the two pointed corners together and press firmly (in the same style as tortellini). Lay the won tons on a flat tray dusted with rice flour to prevent sticking.

Bring a saucepan of water to the boil, add the won tons and cook for 5 minutes. Remove with a slotted spoon and divide among soup bowls.

Add the shredded chicken meat, scatter with the green onion, bean sprouts, chilli, mint and coriander leaves, and ladle on the hot soup.

SERVES 4

HOT AND SOUR PRAWN SOUP

The vibrant flavours of this soup pack a punch yet remain refined and elegant. I love the interplay of the hot and sour elements with the sweetness of the prawns and tomatoes.

30 ml vegetable oil
1 stalk lemongrass, finely sliced
4 red bird's-eye chillies
3 makrut lime leaves, shredded
2 teaspoons minced galangal
2 teaspoons minced ginger
5 cloves garlic, minced
3 red shallots, sliced
2 coriander roots, chopped
1 tablespoon chopped mint leaves
2 litres Prawn Stock (see Essentials)
75 ml fish sauce
85 ml fresh lime juice, strained
12 large raw king or tiger prawns, shelled and deveined
12 cherry tomatoes, blanched and peeled
4 makrut lime leaves, finely shredded
1 long red chilli, cut into fine julienne strips

Heat the oil in large pan and fry the lemongrass, chillies, lime leaves, galangal, ginger, garlic, shallots, coriander roots and mint leaves until fragrant. Add the stock and bring to a simmer over gentle heat, then simmer for 1 hour.

Strain through a fine mesh sieve, discarding solids. Return the soup to the rinsed-out pan and stir in the fish sauce and lime juice while the soup is still very hot. Taste and adjust seasoning if necessary.

Add the prawns and simmer gently for 3 minutes, until just cooked.

Lift prawns from pot with a slotted spoon and divide between soup bowls, along with the peeled tomatoes. Sprinkle with lime leaf and chilli, then ladle in the hot soup over and serve.

SERVES 4–6

SAMBAL FISH AND COCONUT RICE CAKE

This recipe is based on the traditional nasi lemak, a one-dish meal that can be found everywhere in Malaysia, from street vendors to elaborate festive tables. I have taken a more structured approach for assembling this dish, moulding the fish, eggs and rice to give a defined and elegant shape.

4 salted duck eggs, steamed for 30 minutes and shelled
40 g dried Chinese anchovies, deep-fried until crisp
2 tablespoons roasted peanuts
½ teaspoon Chilli Salt Crust (see Essentials)
1 small cucumber, sliced and cut into thin julienne strips
1 punnet coriander cress, snipped
2 tablespoons Fried Shallot Slices (see Essentials)

PEANUT SAUCE
25 ml peanut oil
2 tablespoons Laksa Paste (see Essentials)
150 ml coconut cream
100 ml Tamarind Liquid (see Essentials)
60 ml White Chicken Stock (see Essentials)
150 g roasted peanuts, crushed
30 g jaggery
1 teaspoon sea salt

COCONUT RICE
300 g jasmine rice
1 teaspoon sea salt
5 cm length fresh pandanus leaf
300 ml coconut milk
200 ml water

SAMBAL FISH
600 g fish fillets, skin and bones removed
2 tablespoons Sambal Bajak (see Essentials)
4 tablespoons shredded fresh coconut
½ teaspoon sea salt
½ teaspoon freshly ground black pepper
40 ml fresh lime juice, strained

To make the peanut sauce, heat the oil and fry the laksa paste until fragrant. Add the coconut cream and bring to simmering point, stirring occasionally. Add the tamarind liquid, stock, crushed peanuts, jaggery and salt and simmer for 10 minutes. Taste and adjust the seasoning if necessary.

To make the coconut rice, wash the rice thoroughly a few times in cold water. Put the rice, salt, pandanus leaf, coconut milk and water in a saucepan and stir well. Cover and bring to the boil over moderate heat. Stir to prevent sticking, then reduce the heat and simmer for 15 minutes until the liquid has been absorbed by the rice, and the grains are soft but not broken. Remove the pandanus leaf.

Pack the coconut rice into medium-size Chinese-style soup bowls until just over half full, press down firmly to compact the rice and smooth the surface.

Cut the steamed eggs into thin slices crossways and arrange on the rice in one layer.

To make the sambal fish, cut the fish fillets into narrow 6 cm lengths and mix with the sambal bajak, coconut, salt, pepper and lime juice. Arrange the sambal fish over the eggs and press to make even.

Cover with plastic film, then cover and cook in a bamboo steamer for 12 minutes until the fish is cooked. Remove from the heat and discard the plastic film.

To serve, spoon the peanut sauce onto plates, then carefully turn the fish and rice out from its mould (upside down) on top of the sauce.

Toss the fried anchovies and peanuts through the chilli salt crust to lightly dust and season. Mix with the cucumber strips, coriander cress and fried shallots and arrange on top of the rice.

SERVES 8

BAKED LEMONGRASS FISH WITH CORIANDER NOODLES

This is a wonderfully reliable lunch dish that I often make at the beach house because the fish parcels can just as easily be cooked on the barbeque hotplate outside. I sometimes serve the noodles as a salad so there's no pressure to have everything hot and ready at the same time.

4 × 150 g thick white fish fillets (such as snapper, blue eye or barramundi), skin on
1 punnet coriander cress, snipped
2 makrut lime leaves, finely shredded

LEMONGRASS PASTE
6 makrut lime leaves, shredded
1 stalk lemongrass, minced using a Microplane
2 cloves garlic, finely sliced
2 long red chillies, finely sliced
1 tablespoon minced ginger
½ cup coriander leaves, stalks and roots, finely chopped
finely grated zest and juice of 2 limes
80 ml sunflower oil
40 ml light soy sauce

CORIANDER NOODLES
200 g fresh egg noodles
20 ml sunflower oil
1 teaspoon chilli oil
2 zucchini (courgettes), cut into thin julienne strips
60 g bean sprouts, trimmed
3 green onions, finely sliced on the diagonal
60 ml fish stock
2 teaspoons fish sauce
2 teaspoons Tamarind Liquid (see Essentials)
2 teaspoons fresh lime juice, strained
2 tablespoons Coriander Pesto (see Essentials)
2 tablespoons coriander leaves
40 g tatsoi leaves

To make the lemongrass paste, pound the aromatics in a mortar and pestle to make a paste. Add the lime juice, oil and soy sauce, taste and adjust the seasoning if necessary.

Score the skin surface of the fish. Rub the paste into the fish and leave for 30 minutes.

Preheat the oven to 220°C. Take four large squares of foil and sit a square of baking paper on top of each one. Lay the fish and its marinade, skin-side up, in the centre of the baking paper, then fold over, folding in both sides to secure. Make sure the parcels are a little loose around the fish for cooking – you don't want them too tight. Lay the fish parcels on a flat tray and bake for about 12 minutes (depending on the type of fish), then remove from the oven and leave the parcels for another 2 minutes before opening.

To prepare the noodles, cook the noodles in boiling water for 2–3 minutes until softened. Strain.

Heat both oils in a wok and toss the zucchini, sprouts and green onion for a minute until wilted.

Add the hot noodles and toss to combine.

Mix the fish stock, fish sauce, tamarind liquid and lime juice together and add to the wok.

Simmer for 1 minute then stir in the coriander pesto, coriander and tatsoi leaves.

Remove from the heat and pile the noodles onto plates. Sit the baked fish on top with some of its lemongrass marinade and garnish with cress and shredded lime leaf. Serve immediately.

SERVES 4

SPICED DUCK AND GREEN BEAN SAMBAL

These are some of my favourite flavours – rich, spicy and intense. Nonya cooking features a stunning array of spice pastes (rempahs) and sambals, which also form the foundations of much of my cooking. The preparation can be time-consuming but the results are never less than spectacular.

250 g green beans, tailed
vegetable oil, for deep-frying
3 cloves garlic, minced
2 teaspoons minced ginger
1 small green chilli, minced
2 teaspoons fish sauce
1 teaspoon castor sugar
1 teaspoon sweet soy sauce (kecap manis)
2 teaspoons Chinese black vinegar
2 teaspoons salted yellow beans
1 tablespoon Sambal Bajak (see Essentials)
4 green onions, finely sliced
1 teaspoon Sichuan Spice Salt (see Essentials)
1 punnet celery cress, snipped

SPICED DUCK
1.7 kg Aylesbury or Barbary duck
2 teaspoons Sichuan Spice Salt (see Essentials)
1 teaspoon Chinese Five-spice Powder (see Essentials)
4 slices ginger
2 green onions, chopped
vegetable oil, for deep-frying

To prepare the duck, remove the wings, neck and tail end, then wipe the duck dry inside and out with paper towel. Mix the Sichuan spice salt and five-spice powder and rub into the skin and cavity of the duck. Place on a tray lined with a dry tea towel, then cover with another tea towel and refrigerate for 12 hours to cure.

Put the duck, breast-side down, in a large bowl and add the ginger and green onion. Cover the duck with baking paper, then seal the bowl with foil. Steam in a large bamboo or metal steamer for 90 minutes, turning the duck every 30 minutes to ensure even cooking. Insert a skewer into the thigh – if the juices run pale pink, the duck is ready.

Remove the duck from the bowl and discard the green onion and ginger. Strain the accumulated cooking juices through a fine mesh sieve into a jug and refrigerate until set to a jelly. Remove the fat layer and discard. Set aside the duck jelly for the bean sauce.

Deep-fry the beans in hot oil for 2 minutes, then drain on paper towel.

Heat a wok over high heat, add 1 tablespoon of the hot oil and fry the garlic, ginger and chilli for 20 seconds until fragrant. Add the fish sauce, sugar, soy sauce, black vinegar, salted yellow beans and sambal bajak and stir to combine. Add the reserved duck jelly, then taste and adjust the seasoning if necessary.

Add the fried beans and toss over heat for 2 minutes until the beans are cooked and coated with the sambal sauce. Stir in the green onion and transfer to serving plates.

To fry the duck, heat vegetable oil in a deep-fryer or large saucepan to 180°C and fry the duck for 4 minutes until crisp, keeping it submerged with tongs. Drain on paper towel. Remove the breast and leg meat and slice (discard the carcass).

Arrange the sliced duck on top of the bean mixture, sprinkle with Sichuan spice salt, scatter with celery cress and serve.

SERVES 4

GINGER CHICKEN RICE

I gave humble Hainanese chicken rice a facelift for an exclusive dinner to launch the 1999 Moet et Chandon rose champagne in Australia in 2005. There are several elements to the dish, some of which can be prepared beforehand to make your life easier for when it comes to serving.

½ teaspoon ground ginger
1 teaspoon Sichuan Spice Salt (see Essentials)
2 chicken breast fillets, skin on
vegetable oil, for deep-frying
20 ml XO Sauce (see Essentials)
2 tablespoons finely shredded ginger, deep-fried until crisp
2 green onion tops, finely sliced on the diagonal
½ punnet coriander cress, snipped

CHICKEN BROTH
500 g chicken giblets
50 ml Shaoxing rice wine
40 ml vegetable oil
1 small brown onion, diced
4 cloves garlic
1 tablespoon chopped ginger
4 coriander roots, chopped
1 litre White Chicken Stock (see Essentials)
2 teaspoons white peppercorns, cracked
100 ml light soy sauce
50 ml fish sauce
125 ml Soy Pork Jelly (see Essentials)
4 chicken feet, blanched

CHICKEN RICE
1 cup jasmine rice, washed
750 ml White Chicken Stock (see Essentials)
sea salt and freshly ground white pepper
2 green onion tops, finely sliced

GINGER GARLIC RELISH
40 g young ginger, peeled and chopped
3 cloves garlic
3 green onions, sliced
1 cup (loosely packed) coriander leaves
25 ml vegetable oil
30 ml light soy sauce >>

<< To make the broth, preheat the oven to 220°C and lightly oil a roasting pan. Lay the giblets in the pan and roast for 30 minutes or until browned and crisp. Remove from the oven and pour off any fat. Place the tray over moderate heat and deglaze with the Shaoxing wine.

Heat the oil in a large saucepan and fry the onion for a couple of minutes until softened, then add the garlic, ginger and coriander root and cook for 3 minutes. Add the giblets and pan juices and fry over moderate heat until browned.

Add the stock, white pepper, soy sauce, fish sauce and pork jelly and bring to simmering point. Add the blanched chicken feet and cook over gentle heat for 90 minutes, without allowing to boil – the surface should maintain a steady and gentle ripple effect. Skim occasionally with a mesh spoon.

Strain the broth through a fine mesh sieve, reserving the feet, and leave the broth to cool and settle. Skim the surface, and taste and adjust the seasoning if necessary. Reheat when ready to serve.

When the chicken feet are cool enough to handle, split each one lengthways down the centre of the underside, splitting the surface just enough to carefully pull out all the bones, leaving the shape pretty much intact. I use a small curved paring knife to do this. Lay the boned feet on a wire rack, cover and leave to dry out overnight. They should lose much of their moisture during this time and take on the appearance of parchment paper.

To prepare the rice, put the rice and chicken stock in a large saucepan and bring to the boil. When it starts to boil, stir the rice then cover with a lid and reduce the heat to its lowest setting. Leave until the stock has been absorbed and the rice is cooked. Season with salt and pepper to taste and stir in the sliced green onion tops.

Spoon the rice into individual round moulds (that are more shallow than deep) until full, then press the surface to compress the rice slightly. (If you do this in advance, steam the rice moulds in a bamboo or metal steamer for a few minutes to warm through when ready to serve.)

To prepare the relish, blend the ginger, garlic, green onion and coriander in a food processor until smooth, then pour in the oil and soy sauce and pulse until combined. Set aside until ready to serve. Don't make this too far ahead as it relies on its fresh pungency for the best result.

To cook the chicken, mix the ground ginger and Sichuan spice salt. Season the chicken with the spice mix then lay the fillets on top of each other at opposite ends (the thin end over the thick end, with the skin on the outside) so they are of even width. Lay the chicken at one end of a large sheet of plastic film and roll over at least 10 times then tie both ends in knots to firmly secure.

Gently poach the chicken in a pan of water held at 80°C for 30 minutes, rolling occasionally to ensure even cooking. Remove from the water and allow to rest for 5 minutes. Remove the plastic wrapping and slice the chicken roll into 4 thick slices crossways.

Heat the oil in a wok or large saucepan to 180°C and deep-fry the chicken feet for 5 minutes until crisp and golden (warning: they have a tendency to splutter in the hot oil, so stand back). Drain on paper towel and sprinkle with a little extra Sichuan spice salt.

To serve, turn the rice out from their moulds into the centre of serving plates and top with a dollop of ginger garlic relish. Sit a crispy fried chicken foot on top, and ladle some of the hot chicken broth around the rice to make a small puddle. Sit the chicken slices on top then spoon over a little XO sauce and garnish with the fried ginger threads, green onion and coriander cress. Serve immediately.

SERVES 4

CLAY-POT LAMB AND POTATO CURRY

This is an adaptation of rendang, a classic Malay curry where the meat is slow-cooked in spice paste and coconut, absorbing the liquid as it cooks, rendering the meat soft and succulent and packed with flavour. We used to make this for staff lunch and it tastes even better when made the day before. The curry cooks quite differently in a clay pot, so if you are using a regular saucepan or flameproof dish you will need to adjust the heat and cooking time. Clay pots need to be soaked in water for an hour before use so the unglazed clay doesn't crack; after that they can stand over a direct flame without a problem.

1 kg lamb shoulder or leg, cubed
2 teaspoons ground turmeric
1 teaspoon freshly ground black pepper
2 tablespoons coriander seeds, roasted and ground
2 teaspoons cumin seeds, roasted and ground
10 dried chillies, roasted and ground
10 cloves garlic, chopped
2 tablespoons chopped ginger
20 fresh curry leaves
4 tablespoons ghee
2 brown onions, finely sliced
250 ml Brown Chicken Stock (see Essentials)
800 ml coconut milk
250 g potatoes, quartered
1 stick cinnamon
5 cardamom pods, cracked
1 teaspoon fennel seeds, roasted
125 ml Tamarind Liquid (see Essentials)
sea salt and freshly ground black pepper

Rub the lamb cubes with turmeric and pepper.

Blend together the ground coriander, cumin, chilli, garlic, ginger and half the curry leaves in a food processor to make a paste.

Heat the ghee in a 3 litre clay pot and fry the onion over moderate heat until soft. Add the paste and cook for a few minutes until aromatic. Add the lamb and toss well to coat with the paste. Stir in the stock and 600 ml of the coconut milk and bring to the boil. Add the potatoes, reduce the heat and simmer gently, covered with a lid.

When the liquid has reduced and been absorbed by the meat and potatoes, add the cinnamon stick, cardamom, roasted fennel and remaining coconut milk. Cook over gentle heat for 1 hour and when the meat is tender, stir in the tamarind liquid and season with salt and pepper to taste.

Fry the remaining curry leaves until crisp and throw into the curry when ready to serve. Serve with steamed rice or coconut rice (see page 170).

SERVES 6–8 AS PART OF A SHARED TABLE

COCONUT MOUSSE AND LYCHEES

This dessert made its debut in London and quickly became the one that everyone seemed to lust after. Appearances can be deceiving – the virginal white-on-white layers set in elegant glassware create an image of purity and simplicity. The transparent, tissue-thin cigar wafers are filled with the sorbet at the very last minute then rested on top of the fruit for serving. Use the most glamorous glasses you can find as the dessert relies on its visual appeal as much as taste to achieve the overall *wow* factor.

8 lychees, peeled and halved
60 g young coconut flesh, cut into thin strips

CIGAR WAFERS
225 g fondant
150 g glucose
20 g butter
1 vanilla bean, scraped
20 g flaked almonds, lightly roasted

COCONUT MOUSSE
500 ml pouring (35%) cream
170 ml milk
85 g shredded fresh coconut, lightly roasted
100 g castor sugar
6 g gelatine leaves, softened in cold water

COCONUT JELLY
425 ml young coconut juice
5 g gelatine leaves, softened in cold water

COCONUT LYCHEE SORBET
400 ml Boiron coconut puree
100 ml Boiron lychee puree
25 g castor sugar
100 g glucose, softened

To make the cigar wafers, preheat the oven to 140°C and line a flat baking tray with baking paper. Combine the fondant, glucose, butter and vanilla seeds in a saucepan and cook over moderate heat to 135°C, using a sugar thermometer to check the temperature. Remove from the heat and add the roasted almonds.

Pour the mix onto a silicone mat (silpat) and leave to cool and harden. Break into pieces and grind to a fine powder in a blender or food processor.

Cut out a 5 cm × 10 cm template from cardboard or thick plastic. Dust the wafer powder onto the baking tray using the template (you need to make eight wafers). Bake for 5–6 minutes or until set – the wafers should not develop any colour as they are meant to be transparent. Wrap each wafer around a narrow cigar-shaped cylinder tube while hot, then leave to cool and set into the desired shape. Store in an airtight container between sheets of baking paper until required – take care as they are very fragile.

To make the coconut mousse, put the cream, milk, coconut and sugar in a saucepan and infuse for 30 minutes over gentle heat. Stir in the softened gelatine, then remove from the heat. Pass through a fine mesh sieve, half-fill the glasses and refrigerate until set.

To make the coconut jelly, heat the coconut juice until warm, then stir in the gelatine. Allow to cool completely, then pour gently onto the set mousse to make a 1 cm layer. Refrigerate for 2 hours before serving.

To make the coconut lychee sorbet, stir both the purees with the sugar and softened glucose until dissolved and combined. Churn in an ice-cream machine until firm then freeze in an airtight container until ready to serve.

To serve, mix the lychees and coconut strips together, then arrange in a small pile on top of the jelly in the centre of each glass. Spoon the sorbet into a piping bag with a small round nozzle and pipe it into the cigar wafers from both ends until full. Sit two cigar wafers across the fruit, resting against one edge of the glass, and serve immediately.

SERVES 4

PANDANUS CREAM, SWEET COCONUT RICE AND ROASTED SESAME

Quintessential Asian dessert flavours given a Western twist – a folly of mine. The heady perfume of pandanus leaf works its magic with the creamy textures, and the roasted sesame gives a nutty roundness to it all.

1 mango, sliced
40 ml coconut cream
1 tablespoon white sesame seeds, roasted

ROASTED SESAME WAFERS
50 g unsalted butter
45 g glucose
90 g castor sugar
25 g white sesame seeds
45 g plain flour

PANDANUS CREAM
2 pandanus leaves
250 ml milk
500 ml pouring (35%) cream
100 g castor sugar
5 g gelatine leaves, softened in cold water

SWEET COCONUT RICE
1 cup white sticky rice, soaked overnight in cold water
1 pandanus leaf
250 ml coconut cream
200 g castor sugar
1 teaspoon salt

To make the wafers, melt the butter and glucose in a bowl over a simmering water bath. Mix the sugar, sesame seeds and flour in another bowl, then pour in the melted butter and glucose and stir to combine. Allow to cool before proceeding. (Refrigerate the mixture in an airtight container at this stage if making it ahead of time.)

Preheat the oven to 180°C and line two baking trays with baking paper. Roll the mixture into small balls, using a teaspoonful for each. Cook two wafers at a time on the baking tray, well spaced, for 5 minutes or until caramel-coloured. Remove the tray from the oven, then allow the biscuits to cool for 15–20 seconds. While warm and pliable, cut each biscuit into rounds using a 4 cm pastry cutter. Allow the biscuits to cool and firm on the tray, then transfer them to an airtight container until ready to use. Repeat the process until you have the number of wafers you need.

To make the pandanus cream, chop the pandanus leaves and pulse briefly in a blender with the milk (this extracts maximum flavour). Combine the pandanus milk, cream and sugar in a saucepan, stir and bring to simmering point over very low heat, allowing maximum infusion time. When it simmers, add the softened gelatine leaves, then pour through a fine mesh sieve. Discard the solids. Pour the cream into serving bowls or glasses until half-full and refrigerate for 3–4 hours until set.

To make the coconut rice, drain and rinse the rice under cold running water. Line a steamer tray with a double layer of muslin, sit the pandanus leaf on the muslin and pile the rice over the top. Cover and steam the rice for 20 minutes until softened. Remove the pandanus leaf.

Heat the coconut cream with the sugar and salt and stir until dissolved. Add the cooked rice to the hot coconut cream and stir until the rice absorbs the cream. Cover and leave for 30 minutes or more, until just warm (if it's too hot, it will melt the pandanus cream when added).

To serve, arrange the mango slices on top of the pandanus cream in a single layer. Spoon some coconut rice on top (shape into quenelles with large spoons if you like). Pour a little coconut cream over the rice and sprinkle with sesame seeds. Stand a roasted sesame wafer against the side of the rice and serve.

SERVES 4

DEEP SLURP THERAPY SINGAPORE

I always think of Singapore as a user-friendly introduction to the steamy and sensual Asian aesthetic. Getting off the plane and driving through the heavy traffic with the window down sends you immediately into sensory overload; the air is always thick with humidity and the intense perfume of tropical flowers and fruit. Singapore has changed dramatically since my first visit three decades ago; many of the old shophouses have been replaced by burgeoning modern development, and inevitably elements of the local heritage and colonial romance have gone. However, in recent years the buildings that remain have undergone careful restoration in an attempt to recapture some of the city's history. Further afield, some of the distinctive black and white mansions stand strong, reminiscent of a bygone era.

I love to walk through the beautiful botanical gardens in the early morning or at sunset, enjoying the gorgeous orchids. As the gardens overlook the city, you also get a feel for the architectural – not to mention spiritual – diversity of the place: the Hokkien Chinese Thian Hock Keng Temple, the Indian Sri Mariamman Temple, the Taoist Wak Hai Cheng Bio Temple, the Thai Buddhist Muni Buddha Gaya Temple and the golden-domed Sultan Mosque are all situated in the Chinatown precinct around South Bridge Road, in close proximity to each other. Along the Singapore River, the revitalised waterfront areas have breathed new life into the city. Restaurants, bars, cafes and hotels vie for key positions along Boat, Robertson and Clarke quays, making this a great place to go at night – you'll find whatever action suits your style.

Having absorbed culinary influences from its Chinese, Malay, Indian, Indonesian and Peranakan population, Singapore takes the business of eating very seriously and food is a national obsession. Singaporean cuisine is seriously sophisticated, and the wine culture is unexpected and surprising – some of the best private wine cellars anywhere in the world can be found here. I have many treasured memories of accompanying Iggy Chan, a well-known local restaurateur and bon vivant, tasting anything and everything. He had access to some of the most remarkable wines on the island, and every moment we spent together seemed to involve a delicious morsel or a glass of something amazing – restorative therapy.

Another intriguing restaurant worthy of a visit is the Chinese Imperial Herbal Restaurant. It's extraordinary – a resident herbalist advises you about the best concoction to eat to improve your health; a soup or health tonic is then prepared and served to you. The concept is based on the Confucian tenet that 'you are what you eat'. A word of warning: expect anything. You are quite likely to encounter scorpions, wolfberries, deer penis, lingzhi fungus or black ants in your dish.

The local enthusiasm for food is reflected in the number of places to eat, and the diversity of what is on offer: Nonya laksa, Hainanese chicken rice, char kway teow, Indian roti prata, Malay rendang, Chinese pork rib soup – you name it! One of my favourites is chee pow kai (deep-fried paper chicken), where chunks of chicken are marinated in Chinese five-spice powder with Shaoxing rice wine and sesame oil, then wrapped in baking paper and deep-fried in hot oil. Union Farm Eating House makes the most divine version of this. But in my opinion, there is one dish that stands head and shoulders above the rest: the sensational black pepper crab, a local specialty that is available everywhere, from the simplest of street stalls to the best of restaurants. I love this even more than Singapore's other signature dish – chilli crab – and that's saying something. Eating these heavenly dishes is a tactile affair requiring

STAYING IN SINGAPORE

FOUR SEASONS HOTEL
190 Orchard Boulevard
Tel +65 6734 1110
www.fourseasons.com
Attention to detail, great service and a terrific central location still outshine other new kids on the block, where quirky design can override substance. The rooftop pool is a haven – absolutely the best place to escape from the humidity, heat and frenzied shopping.

THE INN ON TEMPLE STREET
36 Temple Street, Chinatown
Tel +65 6221 5333
www.theinn.com.sg
A converted shophouse in the heart of old Chinatown with many hawker centres close by.

hands and bibs, so I prefer to have it in a modest place rather than anywhere posh or fancy. I need to focus on the food rather than worrying about making a mess!

I once read that Singapore has long been regarded as the culinary bazaar of the East, and the sheer diversity of the street food certainly supports that sentiment. I find myself drawn back here time and time again for dishes such as sambal stingray (skate wing) steamed in banana leaf; vegetable rojak salad (where the vegetables can be raw or deep-fried and served with a spicy dipping sauce and a cucumber salsa); hai shen (sea cucumber); ducks' feet; fish-head curry; and Hokkien fried noodles with the obligatory freshly squeezed sugarcane juice. Similarities with Malay food are immediately apparent.

A blend of Malay and Chinese influences, Peranakan or Nonya culture has been championed in Singapore, and Nonya food is thriving in the multi-layered cuisine of this tiny island state. Without doubt, the best laksa I have ever had was cooked by one of the city's most celebrated home cooks, Melina Yung, and was served as part of a sumptuous feast. I made it my business to try a range of laksas at hawker stalls and to my mind, the best one was from the Redhill Hawker Centre, a neighbourhood joint attached to a market. If you're heading that way, it's just up the road from Tiong Bahru – another great local food centre that is tucked away for the locals and those in the know. For more Nonya cooking, head to the Katong district. At True Blue, a Nonya restaurant opposite the Katong Mall, I was completely won over by ayam buah keluak, a delicious dish of chicken marinated with Indonesian black nuts and slow-cooked in a clay pot.

The fresh produce markets remain one of the few links with the city's lively street culture of days gone by. Wet markets (so named because the concrete floors are easily hosed down after a day's trade) bring the city to life every morning, and I have spent many happy hours trawling through different markets buying daily supplies. It's a great way to learn about new and interesting ingredients – the vendors are so generous and proud when interest is shown in what they are selling. The earthiness and hospitable spirit of these places says far more about the essence of Singapore than any glitzy shopping mall, and there are so many of them. Try the wet markets on Chinatown's New Bridge Road; the Zhujiao Centre on Serangoon Road for Indian produce; Rasool Shop on Buffalo Road for spices; and for Malay and Nonya produce, zip over to the Geylang Serai market.

EATING IN SINGAPORE

IGGY'S
The Regent Hotel, Level 3, 1 Cuscaden Road
Tel +65 6732 2234
www.iggys.com.sg
The best tasting menu in town – sit at the small intimate counter and watch the kitchen magic. Iggy's wine knowledge and delight in gauging the experience will keep you captivated.

THREE KOMALA VILAS
Upper Dickson Road
Tel +65 6297 2234
and
76–78 Serangoon Road
Tel +65 6293 6980
For the best South Indian thali – perfect for breakfast and brunch.

UNION FARM EATING HOUSE
435A Clementi Road
Tel +65 6466 2776
Humble, hawker-style food.

CHINESE IMPERIAL HERBAL RESTAURANT
Metropole Hotel, 41 Seah Street (behind Raffles Hotel)
Tel +65 6337 0491
Herbal remedies combined with culinary treats to offer an unparalleled experience, including a physician on hand to give health advice before ordering – be brave!

SIN HUAT SEAFOOD
659–661 Geylang Lorong 35 (corner of Geylang Road)
Tel +65 6744 9755
This long-time favourite is fantastic for genuine seafood classics (including *the* best black pepper crab), which you enjoy sitting by the roadside. Choose from live seafood tanks.

TRUE BLUE CUISINE
Level 2, 117 East Coast Road, Katong
Tel +65 6440 0449
The place to sample Nonya classics, including the distinctive ayam buah keluak (chicken slow-cooked with black nuts).

During one visit to Singapore, I was lucky enough to be taken to a traditional Malay wedding at one of the government housing estates near Changi. These marathons run over three days, with people coming and going all the time. It was a riotous affair, warm and hospitable, with hundreds of people making the most of the festivities. Home-made Malay food was presented buffet-style, with a fish curry and rice as the centrepiece. Sweetened coconut rice had been wrapped in small parcels as a parting gift to guests. The whole experience was delightful and I felt honoured to be included.

If you happen to be in Singapore around August, try to catch the Autumn Moon Festival, a time to worship the moon and its powers. The streets are awash with coloured paper lanterns and everybody seems to be making or eating mooncakes – rich egg pastry stuffed with bean paste, duck egg yolks and lotus seeds. The beginning of the durian season is also celebrated with a festival, and the pungent aroma can be detected at every turn. Some restaurants even offer a durian tasting menu. With the mix of so many religious groups, there is always something going on in Singapore. The calendar is punctuated with festivals and it is always fun to coordinate a visit with any one of them. Start with the food, and you won't put a foot wrong. Just follow your nose.

HAWKER FOOD CENTRES

The best way to sample a range of local food in Singapore is by visiting any of the hawker food centres that are dotted around the city. Each stall operates as a small family enterprise and specialises in one particular dish, which is freshly prepared to order. You will experience flavours that are easy to fall in love with.

Lau Pa Sat – at the junction of Boon Tat Street and Robinson Road

Tiong Bahru Market – take the MRT underground rail to Tiong Bahru

Redhill Hawker Centre – the next MRT stop after Tiong Bahru

Newton Food Centre (Newton Circus) – the oyster omelettes are worth discovering, and the freshly squeezed sugarcane juice is perfect with the spicy flavours

Maxwell Road Food Centre – at South Bridge

Commonwealth Avenue Food Centre (also known as Margaret Drive Centre) – good chicken rice

Victoria Street Food Centre – near the Allson Hotel

Koh Fong Food stalls – just up the road from Victoria Street

Long House Hawker Centre (Upper Thompson Road) – great noodle soups

COCONUT PRAWN SOUP

I have long been a fan of laksa, a rich soup made famous by the Nonya cooking of Singapore and Malaysia, and this recipe has been a part of my repertoire ever since I first tasted it, even though I tweak it every now and then for a subtle difference. To make it vegetarian-friendly, replace the prawn stock with a spiced vegetable stock and double the amount of bean curd.

3 tablespoon Laksa Paste (see Essentials)
1 tablespoon Chilli Jam (see Essentials)
500 ml coconut milk
750 ml Prawn Stock (see Essentials)
25 ml fresh lime juice, strained
30 ml fish sauce
12 raw king prawns, shelled, deveined and butterflied open
400 g fresh rice noodle sheets, cut into strips
4 bean curd squares, cut into quarters and deep-fried until crisp
100 g bean sprouts, trimmed
2 tablespoons Fried Shallot Slices (see Essentials)
2 small red chillies, finely sliced
2 tablespoons coriander leaves
2 tablespoons Vietnamese mint (laksa) leaves

Combine the laksa paste, chilli jam and coconut milk in a large saucepan over gentle heat until it bubbles, and simmer for 10 minutes, allowing the flavours to infuse. Add the prawn stock and bring to the boil, then reduce the heat and simmer for a further 15 minutes. Season with the lime juice and fish sauce, taste and adjust if necessary. Pass through a fine mesh sieve and discard the solids.

Return the soup to the saucepan and bring back to simmering point. Add the prawn tails and cook over gentle heat for 2 minutes until the prawns are translucent. Add the rice noodles to soften and warm through.

Spoon the noodles, prawns and fried bean curd into deep soup bowls and ladle on the soup. Add the bean sprouts, fried shallot slices, chilli slices, coriander and mint leaves.

SERVES 4

CHILLI EGGPLANT SAMBAL

Watch out for this – it's highly addictive! To make it even more lush, I sometimes add some leftover Soy-braised Pork (see Essentials), which I mince then add to the sambal when serving.

6 small purple eggplants (aubergines), ends trimmed
vegetable oil, for deep-frying
2 green onions, finely sliced
2 tablespoons coriander leaves

CHILLI SAMBAL
8 dried small chillies, soaked in hot water for 30 minutes
20 long red chillies, chopped
5 cloves garlic, chopped
6 red shallots, chopped
125 ml sunflower oil
2 tablespoons dried prawns, ground to a floss in a spice grinder
2 tomatoes, pulped to a puree
100 ml fresh lime juice, strained
1 tablespoon castor sugar
20 ml fish sauce

To make the sambal, chop the softened dried chillies and pound with the fresh chillies, garlic, shallots and 1 tablespoon of the oil in a mortar and pestle until it forms a paste. Stir in the dried prawn floss.

Heat the remaining oil in a frying pan and fry the paste over moderate heat for about 3 minutes until it becomes fragrant. Add the tomato pulp and cook for 10 minutes until the sambal thickens. Season to taste with the lime juice, sugar and fish sauce.

Cut the eggplants in half lengthways or into thick diagonal slices if larger. Heat the oil in a wok to 180°C and deep-fry the eggplants in batches until softened and browned. Drain on paper towel.

Lay the eggplant on serving plates, spoon the chilli sambal over the top and scatter with the green onion and coriander.

SERVES 4

LOBSTER TARO PASTRIES

Woo gok are my all-time-favourite dim sum or yum cha pastries. They always remind me of Phillip Searle, as they were one of the first things I learnt to make when I started working for him at Oasis Seros. They need to be made the same day as you are serving them – the pastry suffers if it has been anywhere near a refrigerator, so give yourself plenty of time when you decide to give these gorgeous mouthfuls a go. The lobster stuffing can be prepared ahead of time, if that's any help!

rice flour, for dusting
vegetable oil, for deep-frying

LOBSTER STUFFING
1 teaspoon sea salt
1 teaspoon castor sugar
2 teaspoons light soy sauce
1 teaspoon sesame oil
2 teaspoons oyster sauce
1 teaspoon Shaoxing rice wine
½ teaspoon freshly ground white pepper
100 g lobster meat, minced with a cleaver
100 g lean pork, coarsely minced
4 dried shiitake mushrooms, soaked until soft, stems discarded, caps finely chopped
2 green onions, finely sliced

TARO PASTRY
500 g taro root, peeled
⅓ cup wheat starch
130 ml boiling water
1 teaspoon sea salt
1 teaspoon Chinese Five-spice Powder (see Essentials)
3 tablespoons lard

To make the lobster stuffing, combine all the ingredients and work with your hands until thoroughly mixed together. Heat the oil in a wok and fry the filling over high heat for a minute, tossing to cook evenly, just until the meat changes colour. Transfer to a large tray, allow to cool, then chill for 2 hours before using.

To make the taro pastry, cut the peeled taro into big chunks. Sit on a flat plate or tray and steam in a covered bamboo steamer basket for about 1 hour until soft. Mash the soft taro in a large bowl while still warm.

Mix the wheat starch and water to make paste, add to the taro and mix until combined and smooth. Add the salt, five-spice and lard and knead well to combine. The dough should be soft and pliable. Cover the dough with a cloth while you proceed to roll and assemble the pastries.

To make each pastry, break off a small amount of dough, roll to make a round thin disk then flatten slightly with the palm of your hand. Put a small spoonful of lobster filling in the centre with the edges lifted, like a small well. Press the edges together and smooth out, to make an oval-shaped pastry with a flat bottom. Discard any excess pastry.

Line a tray with baking paper and dust with rice flour to prevent sticking. Sit the pastries in a single layer on the tray.

Heat the oil in a deep-fryer or wok to 180°C, add a few pastries at a time and fry for 5 minutes until crisp and flaky. Drain on paper towel and serve with a hot chilli sauce.

SERVES 4–6

POACHED CHICKEN WITH SPICED TURMERIC LEMONGRASS BROTH

Another variation on the winning combination of turmeric and lemongrass – great flavour partners, and the pickled mushrooms provide an added depth of texture. I created this particular dish for a special-event dinner in Sydney a few years ago, with a respectful salute to the flavours of Singapore and South-east Asia.

2 organic chicken breast fillets
200 g English spinach leaves, blanched
80 g bean sprouts, trimmed
1 cucumber, peeled and shaved into long thin ribbons (use a peeler)
2 tablespoons Pickled Shiitake Mushrooms (see Essentials)
2 tablespoons coriander leaves
2 tablespoons Fried Shallot Slices (see Essentials)

TURMERIC LEMONGRASS BROTH
20 ml vegetable oil
3 cloves garlic, sliced
1 tablespoon minced ginger
2 red bird's-eye chillies
1 stalk lemongrass, finely sliced
4 tablespoons Laksa Paste (see Essentials)
1 tablespoon sliced fresh turmeric
1.5 litres White Chicken Stock (see Essentials)
300 ml Tamarind Liquid (see Essentials)
100 ml light soy sauce
75 ml Sugar Syrup (see Essentials)
30 ml fresh lemon juice, strained
1 teaspoon freshly ground white pepper

CHICKEN STUFFING
50 ml vegetable oil
3 cloves garlic, minced
4 coriander roots, minced
2 green bird's-eye chillies, minced
1 teaspoon freshly ground white pepper
50 g Chinese black bacon, finely diced
200 g chicken thigh meat, minced
3 green onions, finely sliced
20 ml fish sauce
2 tablespoons chopped coriander leaves
4 tablespoons Pickled Shiitake Mushrooms (see Essentials)

GINGER GARLIC RELISH
75 g fresh ginger, chopped
6 cloves garlic, sliced
12 green onions, sliced
1 cup coriander leaves
50 ml vegetable oil
50 ml light soy sauce

To make the turmeric broth, heat the oil in a stockpot and fry the garlic, ginger, chillies and lemongrass until fragrant. Add the laksa paste and fry over moderate heat until aromatic and slightly coloured. Stir in the fresh turmeric. Pour in the stock, tamarind liquid, soy sauce, sugar syrup and lemon juice and bring to the boil. Reduce the heat and simmer gently for 10 minutes.

Strain through a fine mesh sieve and discard the solids. Reheat the broth in a clean pot and stir in the pepper before serving. Taste and adjust the seasoning if necessary.

To prepare the chicken stuffing, heat the oil in a frying pan and fry the garlic, coriander root, chilli and white pepper for a few seconds until fragrant. Add the diced black bacon and fry until softened.

Add the chicken thigh mince and fry until coloured, then stir in the green onions. Season with fish sauce to taste and stir in the coriander leaves and pickled shiitake. Allow to cool completely.

To stuff the chicken, butterfly open the chicken breast fillets, spoon the stuffing into the centre, then roll up to enclose, making a sausage shape. Wrap in plastic film (or cryovac, if possible) and tie to secure. Poach the chicken parcels in a pan of gently simmering water held at 65°C for 35–40 minutes until cooked – do not allow the water to boil or the meat will toughen. Remove from the water and leave to rest for 5 minutes before taking off the plastic wrapper.

To make the ginger garlic relish, blend the ginger, garlic, green onion and coriander in a processor, then slowly pour in the vegetable oil and soy sauce until emulsified. Store in the refrigerator until ready to serve.

To serve, steam the spinach and place in the centre of four deep plates or bowls. Sit the bean sprouts, cucumber ribbons and a spoonful of pickled shiitake mushroom slices on top of the spinach, then add a teaspoon of ginger garlic relish. Cut each chicken sausage into 4 slices and arrange two slices over the vegetables on each plate. Ladle the hot broth around the chicken, sprinkle with coriander leaves and fried shallot slices and serve immediately.

SERVES 4

BLACK PEPPER SNOW CRAB SALAD

I have reworked the flavours of Singapore's most famous crab dish into an elegant salad, offering all the flavour without the mess of dealing with crab shells at the table. The snow crabs from Tasmania are simply the best, having the most succulent and perfectly textured sweet meat, so look out for their satiny white shells in the tanks at the fish markets. If unavailable, other crabs such as blue swimmer, spanner or mud crab can be used instead.

1 × 600 g Tasmanian snow crab, snap-chilled for 1 hour in the freezer
12 small oyster mushrooms
1 inner stick celery, finely sliced
40 g green beans, blanched then finely sliced on the diagonal
1 small cucumber, peeled, seeded and finely sliced
2 green onions, finely sliced
2 tablespoons shredded mint leaves
1 cup small watercress leaves
1 punnet tatsoi cress, snipped
1 punnet celery cress, snipped

BLACK PEPPER DRESSING
2 small red chillies
3 coriander roots
3 cloves garlic
2 teaspoons chopped young ginger
40 ml sunflower oil
20 ml oyster sauce
2 tablespoons light soy sauce
2 teaspoons dark soy sauce
2 teaspoons castor sugar
100 ml White Chicken Stock (see Essentials)
3 teaspoons black peppercorns, crushed in a mortar and pestle
60 ml Chilli Caramel (see Essentials)

Place the crab in a large saucepan and half-cover with cold water. Put the pan over high heat, cover with a lid and bring to the boil. Cook the crab for 6 minutes then remove from the pan and plunge into icy cold water to stop the cooking. Crack the shell, remove the meat and set aside. Discard the shell.

To make the dressing, pound the chillies, coriander roots, garlic and ginger in a mortar and pestle to make a paste. Heat the oil in a wok and when smoking, add the paste and fry for a minute until fragrant. Add the oyster sauce, both soy sauces and sugar, cook for a minute until combined and bubbling, then add the stock and crushed peppercorns and cook for another minute. Remove from the heat and stir in the chill caramel. Set aside to cool.

Heat 3 tablespoons of the black pepper dressing in a pan and quickly fry the oyster mushrooms for a minute, just until they have softened. Remove from the heat and allow to cool.

To make the salad, mix the celery, bean slices, cucumber, green onion, mint, watercress and tatsoi cress with the cooled mushrooms and add a little black pepper sauce. Make a nest of salad on each serving plate, top with crab meat and drizzle with the black pepper. Scatter the celery cress leaves over the top and serve.

SERVES 4

PORK, SQUID AND CASHEW SALAD

This staple of my restaurant repertoire has wonderfully diverse textures punctuated with aromatic zesty flavours that seem to bring everyone to their knees when they taste it – always a good sign! Anybody who appreciates the supreme qualities of the pig will love this salad.

vegetable oil, for deep-frying
200 g Soy-braised Pork (see Essentials), cut into 3 cm cubes
1 teaspoon Sichuan Spice Salt (see Essentials)
120 g squid tubes, cut into thick strips and finely scored
2 tablespoons Black Pepper Salt Crust (see Essentials)
4 large betel leaves

RED CHILLI DRESSING
2 coriander roots
1 small clove garlic
2 small red bird's-eye chillies
25 g castor sugar
minced zest of ½ lime
50 ml fresh lime juice, strained
2 teaspoons fish sauce
75 ml Chilli Caramel (see Essentials)

PINK GRAPEFRUIT AND CASHEW SALAD
2 tablespoons cucumber julienne strips
8 pink grapefruit segments, diced
1 red shallot, finely sliced
1 teaspoon finely shredded young ginger
½ long red chilli, sliced into fine rounds
½ green mango, finely shredded
1 apple eggplant (aubergine), cut in half then finely sliced
3 makrut lime leaves, finely shredded
2 tablespoons coriander leaves
2 tablespoons Vietnamese mint (laksa) leaves, shredded
2 tablespoons mint leaves, finely shredded
2 tablespoons cashews, boiled and deep-fried until golden
1 tablespoon Fried Shallot Slices (see Essentials)
1 tablespoon Fried Garlic Slices (see Essentials)
1 iceberg lettuce leaf, finely shredded
2 small betel leaves, shredded

To make the red chilli dressing, pound the coriander root, garlic and chillies in a mortar and pestle until smashed and smooth. Add the sugar and pound, then add the lime zest, juice and fish sauce.

Taste and adjust if necessary, then stir in the chilli caramel.

Heat the vegetable oil to 180°C and deep-fry the pork cubes for 1 minute until crisp. Remove from the heat and toss with the Sichuan spice salt.

Toss the squid strips in the black pepper crust and deep-fry for 30–40 seconds until crisp. Drain on paper towel.

To make the salad, combine all the ingredients in a bowl with the crisp pork and squid. Add enough red chilli dressing to wet and toss with your hands to combine.

Sit a betel leaf in the centre of each plate and carefully arrange the salad in a neat stack on top.

SERVES 4

SHAOXING CHICKEN AND PICKLED CARROT

I will always remember going to Melbourne's Flower Drum restaurant and having my first bite of Drunken Pigeon, a dish this salad honours. Slices of chicken sitting unadorned on a plate belied the depth of flavour and the silken texture of the meat. Start this in the morning to have it ready for dinner that night. Best results are achieved when the meat has returned to room temperature so the flavours are not masked by the cold – allow at least an hour for this.

600 ml White Chicken Stock (see Essentials)
75 ml light soy sauce
60 ml Shaoxing rice wine
2 green onions, chopped
6 slices ginger
2 chicken breasts, on the bone
1 teaspoon white peppercorns, cracked
1 punnet coriander cress, snipped
2 tablespoons chopped chives
4 tablespoons Pickled Carrot Strips (see Essentials)
1 bunch flowering garlic chives, trimmed

SHAOXING MARINADE
500 ml White Chicken Stock (see Essentials)
2 green onions, chopped
1 tablespoon diced ginger
3 teaspoons castor sugar
1 star anise, broken into pieces
1 stick cinnamon
1 bay leaf
1 tablespoon sea salt flakes
175 ml Shaoxing rice wine

Make the marinade first so it cools before the chicken is added to it. Put all the marinade ingredients except the Shaoxing wine in a saucepan, bring to the boil and simmer gently for 5 minutes. Allow to cool for 10 minutes, strain and discard the solids. Stir in the Shaoxing wine and leave to cool at room temperature.

Bring the stock, soy sauce, Shaoxing wine, green onion and ginger to simmering point in a saucepan. Add the chicken breasts and make sure they are submerged in the stock. Stir in the pepper, then reduce the heat to the lowest setting and gently poach the chicken for 10 minutes. Turn off the heat and leave the chicken in the stock for another 10 minutes.

Remove the chicken breasts from the stock and immerse in a bowl of ice to cool immediately and stop any further cooking. Remove the bones from the meat.

Add the chicken breasts to the Shaoxing marinade and marinate in the refrigerator for 4 hours.

To serve, allow the chicken to return to room temperature, then remove it from the marinade, cut each fillet into thick slices and arrange the slices on plates. Mix the coriander cress and chives into the carrots, twirl the julienne strips into a small nest and arrange on top of the chicken. Sit a few strands of garlic chives across the carrot, drizzle with a little remaining marinade and serve.

SERVES 4

SLOW-ROASTED DUCK WITH SPINACH AND BEAN SPROUTS

Nonya heritage has made a huge impact on the culinary practices of Singapore and dishes such as this one, underpinned with the complex flavours of a rempah or spice paste, have become something of a benchmark of mine. It's also a foolproof way of preparing duck, given its slow cooking method.

1.8 kg Aylesbury or Barbary duck, cleaned
3 fresh banana leaves, washed
150 ml coconut cream
150 ml Duck Stock or Brown Chicken Stock (see Essentials)
1 tablespoon shaved palm sugar
20 ml fish sauce
2 teaspoons fresh lime juice, strained
120 g bean sprouts, trimmed
½ green mango, finely shredded
16 cape gooseberries, cut in half
8 slices young ginger, finely shredded
2 tablespoons shredded Asian or Thai basil leaves
2 small red chillies, finely sliced
6 red shallots, finely sliced
60 g baby spinach leaves, washed, stalks removed

SPICE PASTE
3 red shallots
3 cloves garlic
2 teaspoons minced ginger
1 teaspoon minced galangal
1 teaspoon minced turmeric
½ stalk lemongrass, minced using a Microplane
3 red bird's-eye chillies, chopped
3 candlenuts
2 teaspoons belacan (Malaysian shrimp paste), dry-roasted
1 teaspoon coriander seeds, roasted and ground
1 teaspoon cumin seeds, roasted and ground
1 clove
1 teaspoon ground cinnamon
½ teaspoon ground cardamom
⅛ teaspoon freshly grated nutmeg
½ teaspoon ground turmeric
½ teaspoon freshly ground white pepper
60 ml vegetable oil

To make the spice paste, blend all the ingredients together in a food processor until it forms a smooth paste.

Preheat the oven to 200°C. Spread half the spice paste over the skin and internal cavity of the duck. Wrap the duck in banana leaves, place in a baking tray and cover the tray with foil. Bake over a water bath on a lower rack for 1 hour 40 minutes. Remove the duck from the oven and discard the banana leaves.

When the duck is cool enough to handle, remove the breasts and leg meat from the carcass and shred the meat. Discard the carcass.

Heat the remaining spice paste with the coconut cream and stock in a saucepan until it reaches boiling point. Add the palm sugar and fish sauce and simmer for 10 minutes, then pass through a fine mesh sieve. Discard the solids.

Add the lime juice and shredded duck meat to the hot sauce and set aside while you prepare the salad.

In a bowl, mix together the bean sprouts, shredded green mango, cape gooseberries, ginger, basil, chilli and shallots. Remove the duck meat from the sauce and add to the salad ingredients.

Wilt the spinach leaves in the sauce for a few seconds only, then add the spinach and the sauce to the salad. Mix thoroughly and pile the warm salad onto serving plates.

SERVES 4

STEAMED MURRAY COD AND SCALLOP MOUSSE WITH SPICED COCONUT SAUCE

Another play on the sandwich idea to yield soft and silky textures combined with a little fieriness in the fragrant sauce. Snapper, bar cod, silver perch or sea bass can be used instead of the Murray cod.

4 × 150 g Murray cod fillets, skin on, bones removed
8 queen scallops, cleaned
2 teaspoons vegetable oil
sea salt and freshly ground black pepper
1 tablespoon snipped coriander cress

SCALLOP MOUSSE
150 g fish trimmings (from the Murray cod)
60 g scallop meat
30 g scallop roe
1 egg
60 ml double cream
sea salt and freshly ground white pepper
2 teaspoons chopped coriander leaves

PASTE
1 clove garlic
25 g minced ginger
4 coriander roots
2 teaspoons fish sauce
¼ teaspoon sea salt
½ teaspoon freshly ground white pepper

SPICED COCONUT SAUCE
250 ml coconut cream
60 g Chilli Lemongrass Paste (see Essentials)
120 g palm sugar, shaved
250 ml coconut milk
125 ml White Chicken Stock (see Essentials)
2 makrut lime leaves, chopped
1 stalk lemongrass, chopped
25 ml fish sauce
2 teaspoons fresh lime juice, strained

To prepare the fish, cut the tail and belly pieces off each fillet, then cut each fillet in half so you have eight uniform squares. Remove the skin from the off-cuts.

To make the mousse, dice the fish off-cuts, scallops and roe then refrigerate for 30 minutes. Blend the diced fish with the egg until smooth, then fold in the cream. The mousse should be reasonably stiff. Season with salt and pepper and refrigerate for another 30 minutes.

To make the paste, pound the garlic, ginger, coriander root and fish sauce in a mortar and pestle until smooth, then season with salt and pepper. Mix the paste into the scallop mousse and fold in the chopped coriander.

Lay four fish slices on a bench, skin-side down, and spread the scallop mousse on top, making a 3 cm thick layer. Smooth the edges with a small palette knife. Cover with the remaining fish pieces, skin-side up, and press gently to sandwich together. Refrigerate for 30 minutes so the fish becomes quite firm again.

To make the coconut sauce, heat the coconut cream in a heavy-based pan until it cracks (splits), then add the chilli paste. Cook carefully for 6 minutes (don't stir too much) and let the mixture crack. Stir in the palm sugar. Add the coconut milk and simmer for 3–4 minutes, then add the stock, lime leaves, lemongrass and fish sauce and cook for a further 5 minutes. When ready to serve, stir in the lime juice to taste.

To cook the fish, lay each fish sandwich on a small sheet of baking paper, then sit in a steamer tray. Cover and steam over gently simmering water for 15 minutes or until the fish and mousse are cooked.

Coat the scallops with the oil and lightly season with salt and pepper. Heat a small frying pan and sear the scallops for 2 minutes, turning once. Remove from the heat.

Gently remove the fish sandwich from the tray and paper using a right-angle slide and place on serving plates. Ladle the spiced coconut sauce around and float the scallops in the sauce at the side of the fish. Arrange a few sprigs of the coriander cress on top of the fish and serve immediately.

SERVES 4

FRAGRANT PORK RIB SOUP

A restorative broth that reflects careful slow cooking punctuated with the freshness of chopped herbs and the lingering heat of chilli. This is one of my favourite late-night snacks after working a restaurant dinner service.

600 g pork spare ribs (on the bone), cut into 5 cm chunks
2 litres White Pork Stock (see Essentials)
4 cloves garlic, crushed
2 teaspoons chopped galangal
3 pieces dried liquorice root
2 sticks cinnamon
2 dried small chillies, broken into small pieces
2 star anise
1 teaspoon whole white peppercorns, cracked
1 teaspoon whole black peppercorns, cracked
3 teaspoons sea salt
2 teaspoons castor sugar
20 ml dark soy sauce
4 small red chillies, finely sliced
3 tablespoons shredded coriander leaves
2 tablespoons Vietnamese mint (laksa) leaves, torn
8 garlic chives, finely sliced
2 tablespoons Fried Shallot Slices (see Essentials)

Put the pork rib chunks into a large saucepan and cover with cold water. Bring slowly to the boil, skimming any rising sediment from the surface. Once they come to boil, remove the pork chunks from the pan with a slotted spoon and rinse under cold running water.

Put the blanched pork pieces in a clean large saucepan with the stock, garlic, galangal and spices. Bring slowly to the boil and simmer gently for 1 hour, skimming the surface regularly. Remove the pan from the heat, take out the pork pieces then pass the soup through a fine mesh sieve. Discard the solids. Allow the soup to cool and settle and remove any fat or oil that rises to the surface.

Return the soup to the heat and when simmering, season with salt, sugar and soy sauce. Taste and adjust if necessary.

Remove the pork meat from the bones and slice finely, discarding the bones and skin. Divide among serving bowls, add the chilli, chopped herbs and shallot slices, then ladle on the hot soup.

SERVES 6

LIQUORICE AND STAR ANISE CREAM WITH SPICED PINEAPPLE

This luscious dessert epitomises the distinctive tangy flavours of Asia, with each layer a textural contrast. There are several stages to its assembly, and you need to work in the order of the layers to achieve the desired result.

SPICED PINEAPPLE
50 g ghee
600 g fresh pineapple, diced
1 vanilla bean, split
2 star anise
40 ml dark rum
2 tablespoons brown sugar
2 tablespoons honey

PINEAPPLE JELLY
170 ml reserved pineapple cooking syrup
40 ml water
3 g gelatine leaves, softened in cold water
½ gold leaf

STAR ANISE CREAM
120 ml milk
2 g crushed star anise
2 egg yolks
75 g castor sugar
2 g gelatine leaves, softened in cold water
125 ml pouring (35%) cream, whipped

LIQUORICE CREAM
120 ml milk
2 egg yolks
60 g castor sugar
2 teaspoons liquorice paste
2 g gelatine leaves, softened in cold water
125 ml pouring (35%) cream, whipped

CANDIED GINGER WAFERS
2 teaspoons minced candied (sweet preserved) ginger
2 tablespoons Glass Wafer Mix (see Essentials) >>

<< To prepare the spiced pineapple, melt the ghee in a frying pan over moderate heat and cook the pineapple, vanilla bean and star anise until slightly caramelised. Stir in the rum, sugar and honey and cook for another 5 minutes. Remove the pan from the heat and discard the vanilla bean and star anise.

Strain the pineapple and allow to cool. Reserve the cooking syrup and allow to cool completely, then remove the layer of fat – it will cloud the syrup if left.

To make the pineapple jelly, heat the pineapple cooking syrup and water to simmering point then add the softened gelatine and stir until dissolved. Pass through a fine sieve and allow to cool completely.

To make the star anise cream, heat the milk and star anise in a saucepan over low heat until simmering. Whisk the egg yolks and sugar until pale and creamy, then pour in the hot milk. Set the bowl over a pan of simmering water and continue to whisk until it reaches a custard consistency and coats the back of a spoon. Continual whisking will give a lighter, more voluminous result. Add the softened gelatine and whisk until dissolved.

Remove from the heat and pass through a fine mesh sieve. Stand the cream in a bowl over a bowl of ice to prevent further cooking and to cool it down quickly. When cool, fold in the whipped cream.

To make the liquorice cream, heat the milk in a saucepan over low heat until simmering. Whisk the egg yolks and sugar until pale and creamy, add the liquorice paste and whisk until combined. Pour in the hot milk and whisk. Set the bowl over a pan of simmering water and continue to whisk until it reaches a custard consistency and coats the back of a spoon. Add the softened gelatine and whisk until dissolved.

Remove from the heat and pass through a fine mesh sieve. Stand the cream in a bowl over a bowl of ice to prevent further cooking and to cool it down quickly. When cool, fold in the whipped cream.

LIQUORICE AND STAR ANISE CREAM
< WITH SPICED PINEAPPLE (see page 201)

To assemble the dessert into individual glasses or bowls, start with the star anise cream. Fill the glasses until just over one-third full, then leave to set in the refrigerator for 2 hours. Spoon on a 1 cm layer of spiced pineapple. Spoon in the liquorice cream until the glasses are just over two-thirds full, then set in the refrigerator for 2 hours.

Mix a few specks of gold leaf through the cooled jelly and gently spoon over the liquorice cream to make a 5 mm layer. Refrigerate for another 2 hours before serving.

To make the ginger wafers, preheat the oven to 180°C and line a flat baking tray with baking paper or a silicone mat. Mix the candied ginger through the wafer mix until combined.

For each wafer, take ½ teaspoon of wafer mix, roll into a short length and lay on the tray. Arrange two on the tray at a time. Bake for 5 minutes until golden – the wafers will spread when heated, so make sure there is plenty of space between them so they do not join on the tray.

Remove the tray from the oven and press another sheet of baking paper on top. Run a flat-bottomed glass over the wafers to flatten and make them completely smooth with no air holes.

Carefully peel off the top layer of paper, then gently lift the wafers from the bottom sheet of paper and cool on a wire rack for 3 minutes. Repeat the process twice to make six wafers, reserving the rest of the mix for a later use. Store in an airtight container with small pieces of baking paper between each wafer to prevent them sticking together.

To serve, lay a ginger wafer across the top of the glass, or stick one end in the dessert so it stands upright.

SERVES 6

STAR ANISE GINGER CREAMS

I love it when desserts combine the elements of silky, rich textures and pungent spiciness, both of which are intrinsic to the broader Asian repertoire. This dessert again draws on the magical pairing of star anise and ginger, but this time the cream is baked in the oven in the style of a classic French creme caramel.

200 g castor sugar
40 ml water
200 ml pouring (35%) cream
100 ml milk
30 ml Stone's green ginger wine
2 star anise, broken into small pieces
1 tablespoon minced ginger
1 egg
4 egg yolks
50 g castor sugar, extra

GINGER SNAP WAFERS
150 g unsalted butter
60 g brown sugar
125 g castor sugar
1 large egg yolk
30 ml molasses
250 g plain flour
½ teaspoon bicarbonate of soda
¼ teaspoon salt
1 tablespoon ground espresso coffee
2 teaspoons ground ginger
1 teaspoon ground cinnamon
½ teaspoon ground cloves
½ teaspoon ground allspice
castor sugar, extra, for dusting

STAR ANISE PEARS
400 ml Sugar Syrup (see Essentials)
4 slices ginger
2 star anise, broken
50 ml Poire William liqueur
2 pears, peeled

To make the ginger snap wafers, cream the butter and both sugars together until light and fluffy. Stir in the egg yolk and molasses.

Sift the flour, soda, salt, coffee and spices into another bowl, then stir in the butter mix until combined. Refrigerate for 30–45 minutes to allow the dough to become firm and workable. Roll the chilled dough into small round logs about 2–3 cm in diameter, and wrap in plastic film.

Refrigerate again for another hour (you can also keep the dough like this in the freezer until ready to use). Preheat the oven to 170°C and line a flat baking tray with baking paper.

Unwrap the dough and slice into 5 mm rounds. Lay the wafer slices on the tray and bake for 15 minutes. Leave the wafers on the tray to cool then transfer to a wire rack and dust with the extra castor sugar. They become firm with a 'snap' texture when they are totally cold. Store in an airtight container until ready to serve.

To make the ginger creams, reduce the oven temperature to 150°C. Make a caramel by boiling the castor sugar and water over high heat without stirring. Pour the hot caramel into four 150 ml dariole moulds, working quickly as the caramel will continue to cook and will darken. Tilt the moulds to ensure they are evenly lined with caramel, then discard any excess and allow the caramel to cool.

Bring the cream, milk, green ginger wine, star anise and fresh ginger to simmering point in a saucepan over gentle heat. Whisk the egg, egg yolks and extra sugar in a bowl until just incorporated, then gently whisk in the hot cream mixture. Pass the custard through a fine mesh sieve into a jug, then fill the prepared moulds. Remove any surface bubbles using a teaspoon.

Place the moulds in a water bath (the water should come two-thirds of the way up the sides of the moulds) and bake for 35–40 minutes. Keep an eye on them to ensure even cooking. Remove the water bath from the oven and take the creams out of the water. Allow them to cool, then refrigerate for at least 3 hours before serving.

To poach the pears, put the sugar syrup, fresh ginger, star anise and liqueur in a wide-based stainless steel saucepan and bring to the boil. Simmer for 15 minutes to intensify the flavour and reduce the liquid slightly.

Peel, halve and core the pears and lay them gently in the poaching liquid. Press baking paper down on the pears to keep them submerged (this ensures even cooking and avoids discoloration), then simmer gently for about 20 minutes until cooked and softened.

Remove the pears from the poaching liquid, slice them in half again and set aside. Reduce the poaching liquid over moderate heat until it reaches the consistency of syrup, then pass it through a fine mesh sieve and discard the solids. Allow the syrup to cool, then pour it over the poached pear and keep cool until ready to serve.

To serve, cut the pears into thin slices and arrange in a circle in the centre of each plate. Dip the baked cream moulds into hot water to loosen then invert and let the creams slide out gently on top of the sliced pear. Drizzle with a little star anise syrup and serve with a ginger snap wafer.

SERVES 4

AMONGST GODS AND DEMONS BALI

Known as the 'Island of the Gods', Bali is a tiny speck in the Indonesian archipelago that stretches across the Java Sea. Because of its proximity to the equator, there are only two seasons: the hot and rainy season from October to March and the slightly cooler dry season for the other half of the year. Unlike the rest of Indonesia, where the vast majority of people are Muslim, the Balinese adhere to a life of Hindu ritual and devotion. There are frequent blessings to keep the demons away, and great importance is placed on maintaining happiness, good luck and prosperity. With all this goodwill buzzing around, and the cultural significance attached to food, I guess it was inevitable that I would grow to love this place.

We first visited Bali in the early 1990s, when Genevieve Harris (Margie's sister) worked as executive chef at the Amankila resort on the east coast. To reach Candidasa, we drove east through Gianyar and Klungkung, then on past Jukung beach with its black sands. At Amankila, our villa was surrounded by breadfruit and jackfruit trees laden with heavy fruit; white bougainvillea in elegantly proportioned ceramic pots adorned the terraces and vases of tuberoses were on every table, creating a visual feast and the most intoxicating aroma, particularly at night.

Our introduction to the specifics of Balinese food was a delicious feast laid on for Margie's birthday, comprising a traditional megibung (shared plate) feast from the Karangasem region of Bali. This became one of Genevieve's signatures during her time in Bali, generously offered on any occasion that was cause for celebration. The food is served all at once, placed around a tall cone of turmeric rice (nasi kuning) that holds centre stage on the table, with its peak often wrapped in edible silver leaf. We still have the intricate place cards from that dinner, etched by hand onto gold paper by one of her artistic staff – just one of our many treasured mementos. The feast included acar (pickled vegetables), ikan bilis (deep-fried peanuts and small dried fish), sayur urap (vegetable salad with coconut dressing), pelecing kangkung (stir-fried water spinach), tempe goreng manis (deep-fried tempeh with chilli and sweet sauce), ayam goreng (deep-fried chicken), sate babi/ayam/sapi (pork/chicken/beef satay with peanut sauce), rendang daging (dry beef coconut curry), krupuk udang (prawn crackers) and sambal belacan (sambal made with fresh chillies, shallots, garlic and shrimp paste).

Rice is central to any meal or feast. Dewi Sri, the rice goddess, personifies the life force of the country and is the most worshipped deity. Life is ruled by the rice harvest, and ritual offerings are an inescapable part of the daily routine. The Balinese always seem to be celebrating some festival or another, and witnessing the happy atmosphere of a temple festival gave us a better appreciation of the important role that food plays. Women walk gracefully down the road with baskets of food piled high on their heads – an amazing and colourful sight – and the ceremonial feasts and festivals often bring the community together around a roasted suckling pig (babi guling). The impromptu style of the Padang (Sumatran) food served in the villages and eating houses reminds me of Spanish tapas, except that the dishes are always served with rice. We would choose small plates of the various things on offer: sambals or chilli paste condiments; melt-in-the-mouth chicken or pork satays; and a wide variety of vegetables and leafy greens, many of them gathered from the wild.

Every morning Genevieve would go to the markets for supplies, and it was a treat to accompany her. While many of the same ingredients are readily available throughout Asia, it is how they are used that defines the regional Balinese tradition. She bought coconut milk made that morning, and explained that the milk must be bought fresh as it ferments quickly. Many homes don't have adequate refrigeration so most of the cooking is done by the middle of the day, and the cooled food is eaten for dinner. Fried tempeh (fermented bean curd cake) is a staple, and small amounts of meat, poultry or fish are eaten with rice. Duck and pork are the preferred meats; in fact, a pig can secure enough income for retirement when it is sold – an interesting take on the superannuation payout! The juice squeezed from grated fresh turmeric is added during cooking to flavour and colour rice and sauces, pandanus leaves are cooked with rice to perfume it and there's an abundance of lemongrass, galangal and lemon basil. Root vegetables, such as cassava, taro and potato, are common, and coconut is a favourite, whether it be the milk, juice from the young coconut or the grated flesh. Less orthodox ingredients can also include dragonflies, flying foxes, crickets and larvae but I don't think I have knowingly tasted these. I'm not keen to, either . . .

Seafood is not as plentiful as you would imagine, given that Bali is an island and surrounded by sea. The Balinese are not renowned fishermen; to them, the sea is considered dangerous and impure – unlike the mountains, which are worshipped. Farmed prawns are big business, so there are plenty on hand. Otherwise, the most widely available fish is tenggiri, similar to Spanish mackerel and absolutely the best on offer. When tuna does make an appearance, it is the white albacore variety.

The markets are where you discover the essential difference between Bali and the rest of Indonesia, as revealed in the subtle nuances and personality of its food. While Denpasar, Bali's capital, has a thriving daily produce market in the centre of town, I find the lively atmosphere of the night market at Gianyar, a town known for its temples and gamelan dancers, much more appealing. It also happens to have the best roast pig on the island – now that's a bonus! On the east coast, the smaller market at Klungkung is definitely worth a visit in the early morning: be tempted by nasi campur (rice served with fried chicken, chilli sambal, vegetable salad, omelette roll, crispy dried anchovies and salted peanuts).

When exploring the east coast of the island, you can't escape the powerful presence of Mount Agung, a massive volcano revered by the Balinese. It last erupted in 1963, sending seething streams of black lava down to the sea. If you possibly can, treat yourself to a helicopter ride around its peak at sunrise – it's a magical experience of colour and light, which makes it easier to appreciate the significance of this place in Balinese cosmology. At its base, we visited the stunning water gardens and temples of Tirtagangga, then drove past the terraced rice fields that hug the mountainside, creating a vibrant green tapestry. The nearby village of Manggis is known for black magic, while nearby Tenganan has a unique religious heritage and the Aga people who live here regard themselves as divinely blessed. Visiting this traditional village, we felt as if we had stepped back in time. We bought several woven black baskets and a few metres of precious hand-woven geringsing cloth to take home. The cloth is said to possess magical powers of protection, which are invoked by the local people when they drape the fabric around the stone statues that are everywhere in Bali, as well as being relied on to ward off everyday misfortune.

To me, Bali is the ideal place to recuperate from the hectic and demanding rigours of kitchen life. On subsequent visits, we have stayed at Jimbaran Bay in the island's south. We would often drive to Seminyak for breakfast at one of the laid-back beach clubs or go later in the day to watch the sunset as we worked our way through the cocktail list. The southern tip of Bukit Peninsula also has a lot to offer. On this part of the island it almost seems as if the whole world is sleeping, such is the tranquillity and peace that emanates from it. Perched on steep cliffs facing the wild sea below is Uluwatu Temple, one of the oldest temples in Bali. It's a brilliant place to sit and watch the sunset – just don't take any food with you, or you'll get no peace from the hordes of menacing monkeys that inhabit the temple. They'll nick your sunglasses too if you're not careful!

Centrally located Ubud, in the island's interior, is like another world. It's quite a bohemian place with many expats who have been seduced by the rich culture and lush surroundings. One shining example is Casa Luna – a cooking school and restaurant run by ex-Melbournite Janet de Neefe who married a local lad and now spends her time opening people's eyes to the wonders of Balinese cooking. While you're here, look out for a couple of great little places in the backstreets if roast pig (babi

SLEEPING AND EATING ON THE BALINESE COAST

THE BALÉ
Jalan Raya Nusa Dua Selatan, Nusa Dua Beach
Tel +62 361 775 111
www.thebale.com
Luxurious private pavilions that offer the perfect retreat, yet are close enough to other places of interest when you feel the need to leave the compound.

OBEROI BALI
Jalan Laksmana, Seminyak Beach, Denpasar
Tel +62 361 730 361
www.oberoibali.com
Luxury private villas nestled between rice fields and the beach.

KU DE TA
Jalan Laksmana 9, Petitinget (near Seminyak)
Tel +62 361 736 969
www.kudeta.net
Ocean-front location that sets a stylish standard – modern Western food, wonderful all-day breakfasts, and the sunset cocktails are not to be missed.

guling) is your thing – just follow your nose as the smoky aroma of burning charcoal fills the air around sunset. We sometimes stay in this area to take a break from the beach; the mountain air and the lively arts scene make a refreshing change. Each village around Ubud is known for a specific artisan craft, whether it be basket weaving, wood carving, stone carving, kite making, slate, ceramics, masks or silverware. One of the better known areas is Monkey Forest Road, just out of Ubud, which is home to dozens of craft shops hawking their wares, with a temple at the end of the road that's full of monkeys. What is it with temples and monkeys?

Wherever you are in Bali, you will hear the distinctive sound of gamelan music with its haunting notes that drift across the sky, particularly at sunset. It's almost as if the instruments are channelling the spirits, and it's hard not to get caught up in the mysticism of it all. I will always think of Bali as an island of tranquillity, festivity – and all-day snacking! The heady perfume of the tuberoses is a constant, fragrant symbol of the island. We always seem to leave with a suitcase full of treasures in an attempt to create our own little piece of Bali paradise at home. We don't have nearly enough yet.

SLEEPING AND EATING IN UBUD

COMO SHAMBHALA ESTATE
Begawan Giri (near Ubud)
Tel +62 361 978 888
www.comoshambhala.bz
For when you want over-the-top luxury accommodation to share with a few friends. The property is about a 25-minute drive from Ubud and is simply divine.

WARWICK IBAH LUXURY VILLAS
Campuhan, Ubud
Tel +62 361 974 466
www.ibahbali.com
Atmospheric villas set in gorgeous gardens.

CASA LUNA
Jalan Raya, Ubud (just down from the village market)
Tel +62 361 973 282
www.casalunabali.com
Janet de Neefe's renowned cooking school and restaurant showcases the best that Bali has to offer. Enjoy easygoing and relaxed service.

BEBEK BENGIL
Padang Tegal, West Ubud
Tel +62 361 975 489
Located near the Ubud Palace, this place specialises in duck. The salad with smoked duck (bebek betutu) is good, but my favourite is the crispy fried duck. Sit in one of the garden pagodas.

CHICKEN SOUP WITH MUNG BEAN NOODLES

This nourishing and restorative soup was inspired by the Indonesian soto, a clear meat broth flavoured with aromatics and spices that vary according to the region and the cook making it. Chickens roam freely in Bali and while they may appear scrawny, their flavour is second to none. I have included eggs as a play on the chicken and the egg relationship and how one can't exist without the other.

1 tablespoon chopped ginger
2 teaspoons chopped galangal
3 cloves garlic, chopped
4 red shallots, chopped
3 small green chillies, chopped
1 teaspoon coriander seeds, roasted and ground
½ teaspoon cumin seeds, roasted and ground
1 teaspoon freshly ground black pepper
2 litres White Chicken Stock (see Essentials)
3 makrut lime leaves
½ stalk lemongrass, chopped
4 organic chicken thighs, on the bone
50 ml fish sauce
40 ml vegetable oil
50 ml Tamarind Liquid (see Essentials)
30 g palm sugar, shaved
80 g cellophane (glass) noodles, soaked in hot water and cut into 10 cm lengths
2 fresh cloud-ear fungus, finely shredded
4 hard-boiled eggs, sliced
½ small cucumber, peeled and shaved into fine ribbons
4 sticks Asian celery, finely sliced
4 green onions, finely sliced
4 tablespoons shredded ginger, deep-fried until crisp
2 tablespoons Fried Shallot Slices (see Essentials)

To make the soup, pound the ginger, galangal, garlic, shallots, chilli, ground coriander, cumin and pepper in a mortar and pestle to make a paste.

Pour the chicken stock into a large saucepan and bring to the boil over moderate heat. When it starts to simmer, add the spice paste, lime leaves and lemongrass and simmer gently for 15 minutes for the flavours to infuse. Add the chicken thigh fillets and simmer gently for 4 minutes. Turn off the heat, cover the pan and leave for 30 minutes until the chicken is tender.

Remove the chicken from the soup and when cool enough to handle, remove the bones and shred the meat. Strain the soup through a fine mesh sieve, discard the solids and add the fish sauce. Taste and adjust the seasoning if necessary.

Heat the oil in a wok, add the shredded chicken, tamarind liquid and palm sugar and toss over heat for about 3 minutes until the sugar has dissolved and caramelised.

Divide the chicken among soup bowls, add the softened noodles, cloud-ear fungus, sliced egg, cucumber, celery and green onion. Ladle on the hot soup, swirl with a chopstick and serve immediately. Garnish with the deep-fried ginger and fried shallot slices.

SERVES 6

SPICED BONITO AND GREEN MANGO SALAD

The fresh flavours and textures in this salad harmonise so perfectly and bounce off each other, making it delightful to eat. If I was cooking this in Bali, I would use tenggiri (a local fish of the mackerel family), but you can really use any mackerel, tuna or even yellowtail with equal success – just make sure you buy the freshest fish available to you at the time.

2 teaspoons sea salt
1 teaspoon ground turmeric
½ teaspoon ground chilli
1 teaspoon ground coriander
1 teaspoon mild curry powder
½ teaspoon freshly ground black pepper
60 ml vegetable oil
500 g bonito fillet (sashimi-grade), skin removed, cut into 4 rectangular logs

GREEN MANGO SALAD
30 ml fresh lime juice, strained
2 teaspoons Tamarind Liquid (see Essentials)
20 ml Sugar Syrup (see Essentials)
20 ml fish sauce
250 g green mango, finely shredded
80 g bean sprouts, trimmed
1 tablespoon dried prawns, ground to a floss in a spice grinder
8 cherry tomatoes, quartered
3 red shallots, finely sliced
2 red bird's-eye chillies, finely sliced
1 tablespoon shredded Asian or Thai basil leaves
2 tablespoons raw peanuts, roasted and chopped

To make the green mango salad, mix the lime juice, tamarind liquid, sugar syrup and fish sauce together. Combine the remaining salad ingredients in a bowl, keeping aside 2 teaspoons of the chopped peanuts, and toss with half the dressing. Allow to marinate while you prepare the fish.

To prepare the bonito, mix the salt and spices with the oil and roll the fish logs through the spiced oil to thoroughly coat.

Heat a frying pan over high heat and sear the bonito for 1 minute on each side (the fish should remain quite rare in the centre). Remove from the heat and cut into slices crossways.

Add the seared bonito to the mango salad and toss to combine.

Pile the salad onto plates, spoon the remaining dressing over the top and sprinkle with the reserved peanuts.

SERVES 4

STIR-FRIED CHILLI PRAWNS WITH WATER SPINACH AND GREEN BEANS

I make this when I want something quite simple to serve with steamed rice for a casual lunch. It takes no time to cook and rewards with its lingering flavour. Water spinach is a staple leafy green in Bali and is also known as water convolvulus, kangkung or swamp cabbage. It shrinks within seconds of being heated, so requires minimal cooking, and quickly takes on the flavours it is cooked with.

60 ml vegetable oil
4 red shallots, sliced
3 cloves garlic, minced
2 small red chillies, minced
400 g small raw prawns, shelled and deveined
1 tablespoon Sambal Bajak (see Essentials)
160 g green beans, sliced in half and blanched
200 g water spinach, washed and cut into 10 cm lengths
40 ml light soy sauce
2 tablespoons Fried Garlic Slices (see Essentials)

Heat the oil in a large wok, fry the shallots until softened then add the garlic and chilli and fry for another 30 seconds.

Add the prawn meat and sambal bajak and toss over heat to coat the prawns with the paste. Add the beans and toss over heat for a minute before adding the water spinach and soy sauce. Cook for 30–40 seconds until wilted.

Sprinkle the fried garlic slices over the top and serve with steamed rice.

SERVES 4

FRAGRANT BEEF AND BLACK MUSHROOMS

A dry stir-fried dish that takes no time at all once the basic preparation has been done. The flavours are robust and linger on the palate. Any red meat can be prepared like this – I have used venison and lamb with equal success. The rich red meat of wild hare is also terrific if you happen to come across any.

6 dried shiitake mushrooms, soaked in hot water for 40 minutes
6 red shallots
4 cloves garlic
1 tablespoon minced lemongrass
2 tablespoons Black Pepper Stir-fry Paste (see Essentials)
60 ml dark soy sauce
1 tablespoon brown sugar
500 g beef sirloin fillet, cut into thin strips
40 ml vegetable oil
2 teaspoons fish sauce
8 garlic chives, cut into 2 cm lengths
1 punnet shimeji mushrooms, trimmed

Remove the stalks from the mushrooms and cut the caps into thin slices.

Pound the shallots and garlic in a mortar and pestle to make a paste, then place in a bowl with the lemongrass, black pepper paste, soy sauce and sugar and mix until combined. Add the beef strips and mix thoroughly until the beef is well coated. Leave to marinate at room temperature for 1 hour.

Heat the oil in a large wok, add the beef and its marinade and cook over high heat for 1 minute, tossing to cook evenly. Add the mushroom slices and cook for another minute until the beef is tender. Stir in the fish sauce, garlic chives and shimeji mushrooms. Taste and adjust the seasoning if necessary.

Serve with steamed rice and a chilli condiment of your choice.

SERVES 4

GENEVIEVE'S SLOW-ROASTED DUCK SALAD

The origins of this melt-in-the-mouth duck dish, bebek betutu, date back to ancient Balinese times. Margie's sister Genevieve made it for us when we visited her while she was working in Bali, and I will always associate it with her.

1.8 kg Pekin, Aylesbury or Barbary duck, wing tips and excess fat removed
2 large hard-boiled eggs, shelled
4 pieces fresh banana leaf
410 ml coconut milk
175 ml Ginger Juice (see Essentials)
fish sauce, to taste
4 snake beans
30 g bean sprouts, trimmed
2 long red chillies, finely sliced
4 makrut lime leaves, finely sliced
1 tablespoon freshly grated coconut
2 tablespoons Fried Shallot Slices (see Essentials)

MARINADE PASTE
4 cloves garlic
6 red shallots
2 long red chillies, roughly chopped
2.5 cm piece ginger, roughly chopped
1 cm piece turmeric, roughly chopped
4 cm piece galangal, roughly chopped
20 ml vegetable oil

STUFFING
2 stalks lemongrass, minced
8 celery leaves, shredded
20 ml sweet soy sauce (kecap manis)
40 ml oyster sauce
sea salt and freshly ground black pepper

To make the marinade paste, place the garlic, shallots, chilli, ginger, turmeric, galangal and vegetable oil in a food processor or blender and process to a rough paste.

Rub the inside and outside of the duck with three-quarters of the marinade paste.

To make the stuffing, combine the lemongrass, celery leaves, soy and oyster sauces, salt and pepper in a bowl, add the remaining marinade paste and mix together. Stuff the duck with the eggs and the stuffing.

Wrap the duck in the banana leaves, then in foil, and refrigerate for 6 hours or overnight.

Preheat the oven to 160°C. Place the duck in a roasting pan and cook for 4 hours or until the meat is tender. Remove from the oven and set aside to cool.

When cool enough to handle, unwrap the duck, remove the meat and shred it with your fingers. Discard the skin but retain the bones. Remove the stuffing and eggs from the duck's cavity, cut the eggs into quarters and set aside.

Place the stuffing in a saucepan with the duck bones, coconut milk and ginger juice. Cover and infuse over a very low heat for 1 hour. Strain through a fine mesh sieve, discard the solids and retain the liquid, which will be used as a dressing. Taste and adjust the seasoning with fish sauce if necessary.

Cut the snake beans into 5 cm lengths and blanch in boiling water. Drain and refresh in cold water. Blanch the bean sprouts, drain and refresh in cold water.

Place the egg pieces, snake beans, bean sprouts, duck meat, chilli, lime leaves and grated coconut in a large bowl. Ladle on just enough dressing to coat the salad and toss well to combine.

To serve, place some salad on each plate, distributing the egg quarters evenly, and ladle on a little extra dressing. Sprinkle with the deep-fried shallot slices and serve.

SERVES 4

DEEP-FRIED WHITEBAIT WITH CHILLI TAMARIND SALAD

Rojak has become something of a staple in the Balinese repertoire and I particularly love the interplay between the heat and tartness of the dressing and the acidity of the fruit. Try and use fruit that is slightly under-ripe, for both flavour and texture. It can be eaten just as a snack or served with any fried fish or meat, such as the whitebait I have suggested here – my take on the popular ikan bilis.

4 tablespoons diced pineapple
½ mango, cut into large dice
¼ papaya, cut into large dice
4 pomelo segments, cut in half
2 rose apples, coarsely diced
½ cucumber, peeled and seeds removed, then coarsely diced
½ yam bean, peeled and diced
vegetable oil, for deep-frying
250 g whitebait
2 egg whites, lightly beaten
125 g Chilli Salt Crust (see Essentials)

CHILLI TAMARIND DRESSING
2 small red chillies, chopped
1 teaspoon sea salt
½ teaspoon belacan (Malaysian shrimp paste), dry-roasted
75 g palm sugar, shaved
50 ml Tamarind Liquid (see Essentials)
20 ml fresh lime juice, strained

To make the dressing, pound the chillies, salt and belacan in a mortar and pestle. Add the palm sugar and tamarind and pound until combined. Add the lime juice, taste and adjust the balance if necessary.

Combine the diced fruit, cucumber and yam bean, add the dressing and toss to combine.

Heat the oil in a large wok or deep-fryer to 180°C. Toss the whitebait through the beaten egg white then toss through the chilli salt crust, shaking off any excess. Fry the fish in small batches (to maintain oil temperature) for 2 minutes until crisp. Drain on paper towel and repeat with the remaining whitebait.

Place the chilli tamarind salad in a bowl and arrange the crispy fish on top. Serve immediately.

SERVES 4

SPICED MASALA BEEF WITH PARSNIP

This is the rock-star version of steak and mash. I created the recipe in honour of Marita, a friend who loves a good steak and often cooks one for me too.

75 ml coconut cream
2 tablespoons tomato puree
1 tablespoon shaved palm sugar
20 ml fish sauce
750 ml Beef Stock (see Essentials)
500 g beef tenderloin fillet, cut into 4 thick medallions

SPICE PASTE
75 ml vegetable oil
2 teaspoons belacan (Malaysian shrimp paste), dry-roasted
2 teaspoons dried prawns, ground to a floss in a spice grinder
1 teaspoon Sichuan peppercorns, roasted and ground
1 teaspoon cumin seeds, roasted and ground
2 teaspoons coriander seeds, roasted and ground
1 teaspoon ground turmeric
pinch of freshly grated nutmeg
½ teaspoon ground cinnamon
1 teaspoon freshly ground black pepper
25 ml sesame oil
1 brown onion, diced
4 cloves garlic, chopped
1 tablespoon chopped ginger
2 teaspoons chopped galangal
5 small red chillies, chopped
2 tablespoons minced lemongrass
2 teaspoons chopped turmeric
4 coriander roots, chopped
2 salam leaves, torn
2 makrut lime leaves, chopped
4 candlenuts

ROASTED PARSNIP MASH
40 g unsalted butter, diced
250 g parsnips, chopped into 3 cm chunks
2 teaspoons sea salt
1 teaspoon freshly ground white pepper
½ teaspoon mild curry powder
50 ml thick (45%) cream

To make the paste, blend half the oil with all the ingredients in a food processor to make a smooth paste. Heat the remaining oil in a heavy-based pan, add the paste and cook for 5–6 minutes until fragrant, stirring constantly to prevent sticking. Remove half the paste and set aside to cool.

Add the coconut cream and tomato puree to the remaining paste in the pan and simmer for 10 minutes until thickened. Add the palm sugar, fish sauce and stock and simmer for 45 minutes.

Pass the sauce through a fine mesh sieve, discard the solids, then taste and adjust the seasoning if necessary.

Cover the beef medallions with the cooled spice paste until thoroughly coated and leave to marinate for 1 hour.

To make the parsnip mash, preheat the oven to 180°C. Grease a baking dish with a little of the butter, then place the chopped parsnips and diced butter in the dish. Stir the salt, pepper and curry powder through the cream and mix into the parsnips. Cover the dish with foil and bake for 45 minutes or until soft. Remove from the oven and blend in a food processor until smooth. Taste and adjust the seasoning if necessary.

Heat a flat grill plate and cook the beef medallions for 5 minutes then flip over and cook for another 3 minutes. Set aside to rest for 8 minutes, allowing the juices to settle.

To serve, make a mound of parsnip mash on the centre of plates and spoon the masala sauce around. Cut each beef medallion into 4 slices across the grain, arrange on top of the mash and serve.

SERVES 4

FIVE-SPICE ROASTED SUCKLING PIG WITH STEAMED GARLIC EGGPLANT

To make this, you will need to order your pig from your butcher a few days in advance; while you're at it, ask your butcher to split the pig in half for you. Any leftovers can be sliced and used in salads or stir-fries, and the crispy ears should be fought over! I love to serve it with this luscious steamed garlic eggplant as the tangy flavours contrast so brilliantly with the roasted pork meat, but you could also have it with a refreshing hot and sour salad (see page 140). Make this for your next family celebratory feast.

½ cup sea salt, plus extra to serve
6 kg suckling pig, split in half lengthways
80 ml vegetable oil
60 ml sweet soy sauce (kecap manis)
2 tablespoons Chinese Five-spice Powder (see Essentials)

STEAMED GARLIC EGGPLANT
6 × 250 g eggplants (aubergines), cut into large chunks or lengths and deep-fried
6 tablespoons Fried Garlic Slices (see Essentials)
60 ml light soy sauce
60 ml oyster sauce
200 ml tomato puree
3 tablespoons castor sugar
1 tablespoon Chilli Jam (see Essentials)
30 ml sesame oil
3 teaspoons chilli oil
150 g baby spinach leaves
36 Roasted Cherry Tomatoes (see Essentials)
1 teaspoon freshly ground white pepper
6 green onions, finely sliced on the diagonal
1 cup coriander leaves

Rub half the salt onto the skin of the pig and leave for 30 minutes until moist.

Preheat the oven to 200°C and lightly oil a baking tray. Combine the oil, sweet soy, five-spice powder and remaining salt and massage over the pig. Lay the pig halves in the baking tray, skin-side up, and roast on the bottom rack of the oven for 2½–3 hours until crisp and golden. Test with a skewer and when the juices run clear, the meat is cooked. Remove from the oven and rest for 15 minutes before slicing.

To prepare the eggplant, lay the fried eggplant on a flat plate and sprinkle with half the fried garlic slices. Cover and steam in a bamboo steamer for 10 minutes until soft.

Combine the soy and oyster sauces, tomato puree, sugar, chilli jam and sesame and chilli oils in a saucepan and heat just to simmering point. Stir in the spinach leaves and roasted tomatoes, then pour the sauce over the steamed eggplant, mixing gently.

Sprinkle with white pepper and finish with the green onion slivers, coriander and remaining fried garlic.

Slice the pig into 2 cm thick slices, sprinkle with a little extra sea salt and serve with the steamed garlic eggplant.

SERVES 12

TAMARIND FISH CURRY WITH PINEAPPLE SAMBAL

I sometimes serve this curry with steamed jasmine rice that has loads of finely shredded fresh herbs added to it. The best leaves to use are turmeric, Vietnamese mint, Asian or lemon basil, coriander and makrut lime. I also add fine shreds of torch ginger or pink ginger blossom when I can get hold of them. The rice complements the tangy flavours of the curry sauce perfectly and the pineapple sambal balances the sourness of the tamarind.

60 ml vegetable oil
2 tablespoons Laksa Paste (see Essentials)
2 teaspoons minced galangal
1 teaspoon minced turmeric
2 small red chillies, minced
120 ml Tamarind Liquid (see Essentials)
300 ml fish stock
75 ml coconut cream
40 ml fish sauce
1 tablespoon shaved palm sugar
4 × 150 g thick fish fillets (jewfish, snapper or blue eye), cut from the middle of the fish
20 ml fresh lime juice, strained
2 tablespoons shredded Vietnamese mint leaves
3 makrut lime leaves, finely shredded

PINEAPPLE SAMBAL
1 small cucumber
1 cup finely diced fresh pineapple
2 small red chillies, minced
3 red shallots, finely sliced
2 teaspoons fish sauce
1 tablespoon castor sugar
40 ml fresh lime juice, strained

To make the sambal, peel the cucumber, cut in half lengthways and scrap out the seeds. Cut the cucumber into thin slices on the diagonal and mix with the remaining ingredients. Set aside.

To make the curry sauce, heat the oil in a wide-based pan and fry the laksa paste, galangal, turmeric and chilli until fragrant. Add the tamarind liquid and stock and simmer for 10 minutes. Stir in the coconut cream, fish sauce and palm sugar until dissolved. Taste the sauce and adjust the seasoning and balance if necessary.

Add the fish to the pan and spoon the sauce over it, then reduce the heat to low and simmer gently for 10 minutes or until the fish is just cooked. Stir in the lime juice, shredded mint and lime leaves and serve with rice and the pineapple sambal.

SERVES 4

TURMERIC RICE AND CHICKEN OMELETTE ROLLS

The idea for these elaborate rolls comes from a traditional Javanese dish that is eaten to break a fast, one that incorporates the elements of nasi kuning (turmeric rice), omelette strips and chilli. I love discovering the various sambals and condiments that often accompany rice dishes in Bali – it's a great way to take your palate on a gastronomic adventure when travelling.

20 ml Turmeric Water (see Essentials)
1 teaspoon sea salt
½ teaspoon freshly ground white pepper
300 g chicken tenderloin fillets
20 ml sunflower oil
24 lemon basil leaves
4 tablespoons salted peanuts, with skins
2 tablespoons dried Chinese anchovies, deep-fried
2 tablespoons Sambal Bajak (see Essentials)
2 teaspoons Tamarind Liquid (see Essentials)
2 tablespoons Fried Shallot Slices (see Essentials)

COCONUT SAUCE
20 ml vegetable oil
2 tablespoons Laksa Paste (see Essentials)
1 tablespoon minced lemongrass
1 small red chilli, chopped
2 makrut lime leaves, chopped
150 ml coconut cream
40 ml Tamarind Liquid (see Essentials)
200 ml Fish Stock (see Essentials)
20 ml fish sauce
1 teaspoon fresh lime juice, strained

TURMERIC RICE
125 ml White Chicken Stock (see Essentials)
1 tablespoon ground turmeric
1 cup jasmine rice, washed
2 slices fresh turmeric
1 slice galangal
1 makrut lime leaf
½ stalk lemongrass, cut into 4 lengths on the diagonal
3 teaspoons sea salt
375 ml coconut milk

OMELETTE
6 eggs, lightly beaten
2 teaspoons light soy sauce
few drops of sesame oil
1 teaspoon freshly ground black pepper >>

<< To make the coconut sauce, heat the oil in a pan and fry the laksa paste, lemongrass, chilli and lime leaves for about 5 minutes, or until fragrant. Add the coconut cream and bring to simmering point. Cook over gentle heat for 5 minutes, then add the tamarind and stock. Simmer for 20 minutes, then add the fish sauce and lime juice. Taste and adjust the seasoning if necessary. Remove from the heat and strain the sauce through a fine mesh sieve or muslin. Discard the solids. The sauce can be made ahead of time and gently reheated when ready to serve.

To cook the rice, bring the stock to a simmer and infuse with the ground turmeric. Combine the rice, fresh turmeric, galangal slice, lime leaf, lemongrass and salt in a saucepan. Stir the coconut milk and turmeric chicken stock into the rice mixture. Cover with a lid and bring to the boil over moderate heat, then reduce the heat to low and cook for 15 minutes until the rice has absorbed all the liquid, stirring occasionally to prevent sticking. Remove the whole spices and lemongrass chunks, and taste and adjust the seasoning if necessary. Spread onto a flat tray and allow to cool.

To cook the chicken, mix the turmeric water, salt and pepper. Add the tenderloin fillets and roll in the mixture to coat and season the meat. Heat the oil in a non-stick pan and fry the chicken fillets on both sides until just cooked. Drain on paper towel. Shred the chicken into small pieces.

To make the omelettes, season the beaten egg with the soy sauce, sesame oil and pepper. Cook the omelettes, one at a time, in a non-stick pan over moderate heat, so the egg sets but doesn't colour too much. Stack the omelettes on top of each other and cover with a tea towel as you work. You need to make three omelettes per serve (twelve in total).

To make the rolls, lay each omelette on a work surface and spoon some rice into a neat pile at the end of the omelette closest to you. Sit a few pieces of shredded chicken on top, then add a couple of torn basil leaves. Fold the omelette over, then fold in both sides and roll up to secure – in much the same manner as you would with a spring roll.

Lay the omelette rolls, seam-side down, on a flat plate and steam in a bamboo steamer for 4–5 minutes, until warmed through.

Mix the salted peanuts and fried anchovies with the sambal and tamarind, stirring to combine.

To serve, cut the omelette rolls in half crossways. Spoon some coconut sauce onto plates then stand omelette rolls upright in the centre. Garnish with the crunchy peanut sambal and sprinkle the fried shallots over the top. Serve immediately.

SERVES 4

BLACK RICE PUDDING

This is one of those dishes that works just as well for breakfast with fruit as it does as a dinner dessert. I particularly like it with custard apple segments that have been gently poached in coconut milk.

250 g black sticky rice
500 ml water
½ pandanus leaf, split along its middle rib and tied in a loose knot
125 g palm sugar
175 ml water, extra
400 ml coconut milk
80 ml coconut cream

Rinse the rice under cold running water, place in a saucepan with the water and the pandanus leaf and bring to the boil. Reduce the heat and simmer for about 10 minutes until the rice has absorbed the water. Remove from the heat, cover and leave the rice to steam for about 10 minutes or until cooked. Remove the pandanus leaf.

Place the palm sugar and extra water in a saucepan, bring to the boil and stir until the palm sugar has dissolved. Remove from the heat, then add the palm sugar syrup to the rice, a little at a time, until it is sweet enough (to taste). Reserve a little of the syrup for serving.

To serve, place the black rice mixture in a wide-based saucepan, add the coconut milk and remaining palm sugar syrup and heat gently until the rice is warmed through. Serve in a glass bowl with the coconut cream poured over the top.

SERVES 8

COCONUT AND PALM SUGAR PANCAKES

Coconut and palm sugar are constants in Asian desserts and manage to press all the right buttons for many when it comes to sweet indulgence. This is another of Genevieve's recipes, and she gave me a brass pan to cook these pancakes as a farewell gift after our first visit – it reminds me of Bali every time I use it. This recipe makes 16–20 small pancakes, plenty for sharing.

250 g plain flour
2 eggs
pinch of sea salt
400 ml coconut milk
350 ml water
50 g melted butter, for pan-frying

FILLING
100 g palm sugar
200 ml water
1 pandanus leaf, split along its middle rib and tied in a loose knot
300 g freshly grated coconut
120 ml coconut milk

Sift the flour into a bowl. In a separate bowl, combine the eggs, salt and coconut milk. Pour the egg mixture into the flour, whisking to a smooth batter, then add the water to thin to a pouring consistency. Strain the batter through a fine mesh sieve and set aside for several hours before use.

Place a small non-stick frying pan over moderate heat and add a little melted butter. Pour in a thin stream of batter, swirling to cover the pan, and cook for 1–2 minutes or until set. Turn the pancake out of the pan. Repeat with the remaining batter to make 16–20 pancakes. Cover with a tea towel or cloth while you make the filling.

To make the filling, put the palm sugar, water and pandanus leaf in a saucepan over moderate heat and simmer until the sugar has dissolved. Remove the pan from the heat and pass the syrup through a fine mesh sieve. Discard the pandanus leaf. Place the coconut in a bowl, add the syrup and coconut milk and mix to combine. If the mixture is too runny, add a little extra freshly grated coconut.

To fill the pancakes, place a sausage-shaped spoonful of filling on one end of each pancake. Roll up, tucking in the ends as you go, in the same way as you would with a spring roll. Lay the filled pancakes on plates and serve immediately.

SERVES 4–6

BOLLYWOOD MASALA NORTHERN AND CENTRAL INDIA

Long before visiting India, I was aware that its food repertoire consisted of more than the ubiquitous tandoori, vindaloo, dal, naan and samosas, all of which have been adapted to suit the Western palate (indeed, chicken tikka was invented in the UK!). What really opened my eyes, though, was experiencing first-hand the incredible diversity and ingenuity of Indian people across this vast nation. The country comprises a gastronomic tapestry that is complex, varied and ancient, underpinned by the masterful use of spices. Modern Indian cooking has its roots firmly planted in Ayurvedic practice, where food is revered as a most precious resource, promoting life, health and longevity.

In India, food preparation is bound up in spirituality, and this needs to be understood to fully appreciate the subtle nuances. Food embodies happiness, joy and pleasure, and every morsel seems to hold some magical meaning, in stark contrast to our modern ways. In a similar fashion to the Chinese philosophy of yin and yang, Indians classify foods according to their energetic qualities, and stress the importance of maintaining a balance between them. This helps to explain the way flavours and textures are married together. I admire the astute use of spices in Indian cooking; more than simply enhancing the flavour of a dish, spices act as cooling agents for the body, helping to combat heat and humidity. Since the Spanish and Portuguese introduced the chilli to India towards the end of the 15th century, it has become an indispensable ingredient and is woven into so many preparations. The chillies of Kashmir differ from those of the south. The northern ones are long and slender, and are usually dried before using; the ones from Gujarat are small and round, similar to the cascabel or pipian.

Across India, ingredients are chosen for their compatibility with the weather of the region. In the north, where it's cold and dry, almonds, cinnamon and root vegetables are commonly used, and breads are a staple with every meal. The breads of the desert regions are more dense and heavy than elsewhere. They are cooked on a flat, iron tawa hotplate and the rest of the food is cooked in a brass, copper or steel kadhi (which looks like a deeper, more rounded wok); the cooking fuel is charcoal, as wood and small branches are plentiful and cheap. In the south, where it is steamy hot and wet, cooling agents like tamarind, mint, coconut and cardamom are the go, with steamed rice replacing the heavier breads. Dal and pickles are served everywhere, and the type of dal will vary according to region. In the north and west, the black urad lentils, green haria lentils and red kidney beans are used, while in the south the softer and smaller yellow toor lentils are the norm. Desserts tend to be staggeringly sweet: my all-time favourite is gulab jamun, little balls of besan (chickpea flour) and milk dough fried then soaked in a rosewater-scented syrup and dusted with pistachios.

This is a land of contradictions and contrasts, of beauty and despair, of wealth and poverty – India has it all in unequal measure. It's the colours that draw you in: the saris and turbans are like electric splashes of light against a dun, earthy background. If you have ever seen a Bollywood film, you can begin to imagine the drama of everyday life here. The cities are large, sprawling and massively overcrowded; squalor competes with incredible luxury, but there is a strong sense of acceptance, with all walks of life mingling together on the streets. It's impossible not to be inspired and moved by the grace and friendliness of the people, and their gentle ways are most disarming. I relish the chaos, but if you're spending any length of time here it does pay to learn the value of patience; there is absolutely nothing to be gained by getting annoyed or indignant. That doesn't mean you can't be assertive – it's all about the subtlety of the delivery.

Talking of chaos, how can I possibly describe the madness and mayhem of Indian traffic? The lines on the road that constitute lanes or pedestrian crossings are hardly ever heeded, just fanciful white markings. Buses and trucks will drive straight at you down the wrong side of the road and swerve at the very last second, somehow finding space to fit back into the flow of the traffic. Time and again we have seen unimaginable feats of driving and the traffic police just shrug their shoulders. I would never for one minute consider getting behind the wheel of a car here. Thank God India has not succumbed to road rage – I can't imagine what it would do to the mortality rate. Oblivious to the craziness, people walk and work on the side of the road – as do the cows, who amble around bringing traffic to a halt. On road trips, we generally take breaks at dhabas (roadside stops full of truck drivers); trust me, these are the best places for tea, snacks and relatively clean toilets. Train travel offers unexpected sights such as the black-bum salute, especially if you pass by a village or town soon after sunrise when public ablutions are being performed. Only the cow is held sacred here – nothing else!

Modern India is one of the most diverse countries in the world, and despite its long history of invasion and occupation it has always maintained its own identity, using foreign influences to its advantage. This is most evident in the food, with its breathtaking array of regional flavours and cooking styles. The family is the fabric of Indian life, and offering hospitality is considered an honour for any host. Traditionally, home cooking is cherished above all other food, which explains the relative dearth of privately owned and operated restaurants. This is starting to change, though, with the increasing number of tourists and the burgeoning middle class, and eating out is becoming more commonplace in the bigger cities.

The street food capital of India is Mumbai, the Indian name for Bombay, even though most of the locals still refer to it by its English name. This vibrant city is jam-packed, with a population so dense it feels hard to breathe at times – a little unnerving, but exciting nonetheless. Mumbai has a serious passion for food; north merges with south, and every region is represented at its street stalls and restaurants. It's fascinating to wander around, tasting delicious tiffin snacks such as pani puri – small puri (puffed rice balls or flakes) with spicy chickpeas spooned into the hollow and dressed with tamarind yoghurt and mint. Equally more-ish are bhel puri – a snack of potato and peas dressed in tamarind with crispy puri scattered over the top. I also love the piquancy of chat masala (broken puris mixed with steamed potato chunks and tossed with chat masala spice mix) or bhaji – vegetable fritters in a besan and turmeric batter.

Mumbai's tiffin wallahs are an urban marvel. Every day they deliver home-cooked lunches in dabbas (round, three-tiered metal containers) to millions of workers. Chai wallahs act as a mobile tea service; glasses of milky tea are served from a central point on the street, then carried on trays or little baskets to shop owners, passers-by, people waiting at train stations – anyone who wants it – and all for a pittance.

When it's time to eat, jump into the heart of the action and visit the noisy and frenetic Crawford Market or have lunch at one of the few local eating houses. If you order a thali platter, start from the left and work your way around, mixing little bits with a morsel of rice from the mound in the centre each time, using only your right hand like a spoon to scoop the food – and turn to see hundreds of eyes fixed on you, seeing if you can do it like a local.

Other favourite regional specialties include tamatar palak bhaat (a rice pilaf with diced tomato and spinach); kohlapuri murg (a fiery chicken dish cooked with red chilli, ginger and white poppy seeds); pattagobhi nariyal (shredded cabbage tossed with mustard seeds, curry leaves and grated coconut); fulvar ola watana ana batatya chi bhaji (a lovely mix of peas, cauliflower and potatoes tossed with spices and shredded coconut); samosa pastries; and the luscious sweet threads of syrupy jalebi (fried batter curls soaked in saffron-coloured syrup).

SLEEPING AND EATING IN MUMBAI

TAJ MAHAL PALACE AND TOWER
Apollo Bunder, Mumbai
Tel +91 22 6665 3366
www.tajhotels.com
This grand wedding cake of a hotel has an ideal location, next to the Gate of India facing the Arabian Sea.

TRISHNA
Sai Baba Marg, next to Commerce House, Kala Ghoda, Mumbai
Tel: +91 22 2270 3213
This restaurant near the Taj Mahal Palace and Tower offers seafood – try the tandoori crab, jassi prawns and toor dal.

SWATI SNACKS
248 Kerai Estate, Tardeo Road, Mumbai
Tel: +91 22 5660 8405
Fab snacks and small tastes – my favourite is the deep-fried bathura bread with chickpea curry.

BACHU NI VAADI
Sayeed Sheekh Kabab Center (Shop 7), Bachi Vaadi, RS Nimkar Marg, Mumbai
Tel: +91 22 5529 0646
For some of the best sheekh kebabs in town.

THACKERS CLUB
31 Dadi Seth's Road, 11 Kalbadevi Road (opposite GT High School), Mumbai
Tel: +91 22 2206 9916
Don't be put off by the down-at-heel surroundings – this place has great food, home-cooked Gujarati-style. It is best at lunch, when it's always full of local businessmen.

SAVORAM BHARAN
This chain serving decent, reliable food seems to pop up in every Indian city. I always opt for the thali (a platter of dishes served in individual bowls) – eating with your right hand is de rigueur here.

The Parsi people have a strong presence in Mumbai and their repertoire adds a further dimension to the city's food. The Parsis are Zoroastrians who arrived in India as refugees more than eleven centuries ago, to escape religious persecution in Persia. Considered excellent gourmands, the Parsis have a distinctive cooking style, seamlessly blending Indian and Western influences with their Arabic heritage. Different again from the Moghul cooking of the Arabs who settled in northern India, Parsi cuisine favours spices, dried fruits, nuts, eggs, chutneys and coconut – a liberal use of pomegranate, tamarind and lime creates sauces that are sharp and rich simultaneously. Parsis love a banquet, and the procession of dishes can be quite remarkable.

When exploring the city, it's worth checking out the Portuguese vernacular houses and villas in the heritage Khotachiwadi area of Mumbai. Another must-see is Chowpatty, Mumbai's most famous beach. Join the queue at the Great Pani Puri Seller, one of the many food carts on the beach, or kick back at one of the new modern bars that face the beach and enjoy the sunset. The scene is remarkably different to Western beach culture. For one thing, everyone is totally covered – it's a sea of saris, scarves, kaftans and kurtas (long kaftan-style shirts). And no one swims! The experience is purely social: family groups and friends meet to share chai and snacks and exchange news.

The Portuguese colonial influence is also apparent in India's smallest state of Goa, on the west coast to the south of Mumbai. Goa joined India a decade or so after independence and even today is seemingly cocooned from the rest of the country by its uniqueness. It is renowned for its sandy beaches and bohemian lifestyle, but perhaps its greatest point of difference is its food, which celebrates its Portuguese heritage, as seen in vindaloo, a spicy Goan rendition of pork cooked in wine (vinh) or vinegar and garlic (d'alho). The land is fertile so crops are abundant, the ocean provides a wealth of seafood, the curries are rich and pork is prominent. The old town of Panjim has a colonial atmosphere, with a unique blend of Christian baroque and Hindu architecture. On our first visit to Goa, we stayed at Cabo de Rama, on the coast to the south – wonderful for barefoot beach living. The cooks made us a great beach barbeque one night, with lobsters bathed in green masala paste and coconut; fish baked whole in banana leaves with a mild chilli paste; and a fantastic chicken xacuti (chicken pieces braised in a rich sauce made from roasted spices). For dessert we ate bathique, a cake made with semolina, eggs and coconut, and dodol, made from coconut cream cooked to a paste with jaggery and rice flour. Like everywhere in India's south, desserts are achingly sweet, and sugar is used liberally as a foil to the rich spiciness of the food.

One year, I was lucky enough to be in India during Diwali (the Festival of Lights), which usually falls in October or November and is the most celebrated festival on the Indian calendar. This is when Hindus pray to Lakshmi, the goddess of prosperity. Special sweet rice cookies are made for the occasion, and every house, shop and hotel hangs out lights, paper lanterns and flickering candles – we even saw candles floating on leaves down the river, a magical sight. Then comes the noise! For three nights, everyone goes berserk and lets off firecrackers down the street; it's like a carnivale-style street party. There was nothing else for it but to go buy some firecrackers ourselves – those small Tom Thumb ones I remember from childhood when it was still legal to buy them. We got right into the spirit of things and had a great time throwing them down from our hotel balcony.

First impressions of New Delhi, India's capital city, can be deceiving. On the surface, with its expansive boulevards, beautiful British Raj-style edifices, dramatic Lutyens architecture and manicured gardens, there certainly seems to be a sense of calm and order. But cross into Shahjahanabad or Old Delhi, past the architectural marvel that is the Jama Masjid mosque and the imposing walls of the Red Fort, or take a rickshaw ride through the market area of Chandni Chowk, for quite a different story. Suddenly everything is chaotic. Women in brilliantly coloured saris seem to float through the crowds, boys and men push their trolleys through the mayhem, and cows amble amidst the rickshaws, bikes, cars, trucks and bullock carts laden with goods. The narrow lanes and congested streets around Chandni Chowk can be a one-stop shopping adventure if you have nerves of steel and the patience of a saint; even the most simple purchase involves some serious negotiation, but it's all part of the fascination and fun. It can be quite a challenge to navigate your way around – I find walking with a local guide helps. Right in the heart of the bazaar is Karim's, one of Delhi's oldest restaurants and a great place to eat with the locals. I don't consider the street food culture to be nearly as mesmerising as that of Mumbai, but Delhi does offer a dazzling array of regional dishes in many of its finer restaurants, making it a great place to travel vicariously through your tastebuds if you don't have time to visit each region.

Heading east from Delhi, we took the Shatabdi Express train to Lucknow, in the state of Uttar Pradesh. It was such a relaxing way to travel, passing through the open plains and crossing the Ganges River, to a city that reflects the glory days of the Nawabi era, from the late 18th to mid-19th centuries. When the Moghuls arrived in northern India around the 16th century, they brought with them a rich gastronomic culture that blended perfectly with the Indian style. The powerful nawabs (Muslim noblemen), who thrived under Moghul reign, had refined tastes and encouraged the palace cooks to be creative and to constantly expand their repertoire – it must have been a mighty display of one-upmanship. It was the royal chefs of the Moghul courts who invented the tandoor oven, and introduced the rich pilafs, kormas, biryanis and kulfi ice-cream confections to the culinary arts. I have always found this period of history fascinating, so a visit to Lucknow had long been on my agenda.

On arrival, Lucknow seemed rather untamed and wild, especially after the relative calm of Delhi. A sea of faces greeted us as we emerged from the train, and the platform was packed with sleeping bodies, and chai wallahs and porters vying for space and attention. Lucknow was left with an impressive architectural legacy by its ruling nawabs, the faded grandeur of the past evident in its rich tapestries, graceful pillars and intricate decorations.

The most spectacular monument is the Great Imambara, a truly amazing sight – massive in scale and richly decorated. We climbed the stairs and followed a maze of hidden passages so we could stand on the rooftop of this majestic building and take in the views across the city. Unfortunately, a protest prevented us from walking through the Chowk bazaar (the Muslim population was enraged by George Bush's visit), so we missed out on seeing the vark shops where varkwallahs make thin sheets of silver and gold leaf by hand, and the ittar vendors with their scented oils. We did manage to check out the chikan shops in the Aminabad bazaar where the prized silk-embroidered cotton cloth is sold and, needless to say, we couldn't resist buying some.

SLEEPING AND EATING IN DELHI

IMPERIAL HOTEL
Janpath, New Delhi
Tel +91 11 2334 1234
www.theimperialindia.com
This decadent Victorian colonial hotel has been given a modern facelift. It is packed with character and style, and is worth the splurge when staying in Delhi.

BUKHARA
Diplomatic Enclave, Sadar Patel Marg, New Delhi
Tel +91 11 2611 2233
This hotel restaurant serves regional specialties from Kashmir and Punjab – the grilled meats and breads are irresistible.

DUM PHUKT
Diplomatic Enclave, Sadar Patel Marg, New Delhi
Tel +91 11 2611 2233
This place showcases food cooked in the dum phukt manner (steamed in earthenware pots sealed with a rope of dough). The pot sits over a bed of coals or a pan of boiling water and hot coals are placed on the lid so heat penetrates the dish from top and bottom for slow, even cooking, retaining all the natural aromas and flavours. Stand-out dishes include dum ki khumb (mushrooms slow-cooked in a ginger and fennel gravy), koh-e-avadh (rogan josh-style lamb shanks with cardamom, saffron and bone marrow) and jhinga dum sunahari (king prawns simmered in a turmeric, garlic and coconut sauce).

KARIM'S
Near Jama Masjid, Old Delhi
Tel +91 11 2326 9880
Several hundred years old, this local workers' cafe in the alleyways of Chandni Chowk specialises in kebabs, including lamb chops or paneer (curd cheese) rubbed with spice and cooked over coals, grilled meats and offal. The menu is authentic: mutton (goat or kid meat in our lingo) or lamb feature heavily; raan (roasted leg of lamb); khmer (a mild curry of lamb mince); and mangodi (fried balls of mung bean paste, a specialty of the house). There is also a brain curry but I haven't ventured that far yet.

BANGLA SWEET HOUSE
115 Bangla Sahib Marg New, New Delhi
Tel +91 11 2336 3780
Terrific pastries and Indian sweets – the jalebi are made to order, which is magical.

YAMU'S PANCHAYAT PAAN PARLOUR
92 NDMC Market, Connaught Place, New Delhi
Tel +91 11 2341 4644
An extensive menu of hand-rolled paan (betel-leaf parcels filled with aromatics reputed to aid digestion), to take away.

We had dinner one evening at the haveli (nobleman's home) of the royal descendents, Nawab Mir Jafah Abdullah and his cousin Nawab Masood Abdullah. We watched one of the cooks as she prepared lamb kebabs over hot coals on the rooftop, marinated with papaya seeds to tenderise the meat, and seasoned with black pepper and cardamom. In the dining room, we sat cross-legged on the floor around a large embroidered mat that had been set with a lavish feast of biryani chicken, a rice pilaf, three different lamb dishes, a couple of salads and an endless supply of handkerchief-thin rumali bread.

Our lunches were more simple affairs and mostly based around seasonal vegetables: bhindi nazakat, okra dry-fried with cumin and amchur (green mango powder); baingan ka salan, baby eggplants grilled and coated with a sesame and peanut sauce; lahori aloo, a typical spicy potato preparation of the north; and ashafi kebabs, spicy little paneer patties stuffed with peas and fried in ghee. This is also the home of the Moghul dish of makhani murgh or butter chicken – and paan, betel-nut leaves rolled with rose-petal jam, coconut, fennel, betel nuts, silver leaf, cardamom seeds and any number of other things, which is lauded for its medicinal and digestive properties. The latter is definitely an acquired taste, and one I haven't acquired.

Another railway adventure took us on the overnight train from Lucknow to Agra, the home of the incomparable Taj Mahal. We were in hysterics most of the way: with six people to a compartment – well, there were no doors, just a through passageway – it felt like a throwback to our backpacker days. Although the beds were hard and narrow, sheets and pillows were supplied, and we had a fun night, helped along with generous swigs of wine. We arrived in Agra at dawn, and as we passed the outlying villages it looked as if the entire world was seeing to their morning ablutions. Agra is considered the gateway to Rajasthan and was once the heart of the Moghul Empire. Most people come here to stand in awe before the grandiose work left by Shah Jahan: the Taj Mahal is the world's most famous monument to love, built for his favourite wife, Mumtaz Mahal. Completed in 1648, it has stood the test of time and still takes my breath away every time. It is magical at sunrise, with the pale pink glow of the rising sun against the beautiful white marble tiles. Sunset is pretty incredible as well. The story goes that Shah Jahan intended to build a replica in black marble for himself to stand alongside his wife's mausoleum, but fate stepped in and it never became a reality. In a cruel irony, he died imprisoned by his treacherous son in the nearby Agra Fort overlooking the Taj Mahal.

Perhaps the most dazzling state of all is Rajasthan, ablaze with colour everywhere you look. Escaping to the relative peace and quiet of the desert provides welcome relief from the polluted and crowded cities, and shows yet another side of this varied land. The landscape is dotted with historic forts, many of which have been converted into luxury accommodation, set against the dramatic backdrop of the Aravali Mountains. A heady mix of Indian and Moghul heritage, Rajasthan moves at its own pace; camels, elephants and plodding cows vie for space on the roads. This is where India's precious gems are mined, and the women wear the most vividly coloured saris adorned with stunning jewellery. The air is thick with the pervasive aromas of cinnamon, mustard, saffron and turmeric, and when asked, the inquisitive locals are more than generous when it comes to sharing their recipes and food knowledge. Like many cuisines, Rajasthani food has been influenced by the availability of local ingredients. Because water is scarce, milk, buttermilk and curd are used quite liberally. Dried lentils, indigenous ker sangri (small and narrow desert beans), millet grain, corn and other cereals replace leafy greens, and local spices include mustard, turmeric, fenugreek and coriander. The pungent leaves of the fenugreek plant (methi) are also used and are particularly good when mixed with fenugreek seeds, spinach and tomato.

EATING IN LUCKNOW

OUDHYANA
Taj Residency Hotel, Gomtinagar, Lucknow
Tel: +91 522 239 3939
Sumptuous Moghul cooking, with elaborate biryanis and kebabs.

ARYAN RESTAURANT
90 Mahatma Gandhi Marg (opposite Raj Bhawan), Lucknow
Tel: +91 522 223 0499
Best for lunch – ignore the rest of the menu and opt for the vegetable dishes. The vegetable koftas, methi paneer (fenugreek leaves cooked with curd cheese) and mushroom masala are delicious.

The ancient walled cities of Jaipur, Jodhpur and Udaipur are defined by colour – pink, blue and ivory, respectively. These are places that remain etched in your memory forever, and it's possible to enjoy their opulence, even on a modest budget. We allowed ourselves to wallow in the richness of Rajasthan's palace hotels, moving from one gorgeous palace to the next, trying to imagine life during the Raj – a lovely indulgence. On the road between Jaipur and Delhi, near Shahjahanpur, Neemrana is a beautifully restored 15th-century fort palace that sits majestically on a hill, overlooking the village after which it was named. While we were staying there, we rode to our chosen picnic site on camels and shared a memorable meal of various salads based on vegetables and pulses in the fields beyond the village. On our walk back to the fort, we stumbled across a massive underground stepwell that went down several storeys. Fascinated, we explored its layers of rooms for passing traders and separate sleeping quarters for the camels and other animals. Such a discovery seemed quite amazing to us all, and rounded off a perfect day.

Considered the gateway to Rajasthan, Jaipur is the largest of the state's fortified cities, and is awash with pink, the hue of the locally mined rock used in its buildings. The museums of the City Palace display the opulence of palace life and are definitely worth a look. The men of Jaipur stand out with their coloured turbans and twirled moustaches – which they turn into an art form – and the women often veil their faces with their neon-coloured saris, and their arms and ankles are adorned with silver jewellery. The bazaars, shops and markets offer a hard-to-beat shopping experience, and it is nigh on impossible to leave empty-handed. The vegetable vendors display their colourful and diverse produce so invitingly; it is a joy to see everything so sparkling fresh and clean. Wherever you look, business is brisk, the turnover fast. A side-trip to explore the magnificent Amber Fort, 11 kilometres north of the city, is essential. If you are keen to ride up the hill on an elephant, get there early in the morning and be prepared for a long wait; otherwise ride up on the back of a jeep.

On one occasion a group of us were in Jaipur during Holi, the Festival of Colour. There was much exuberant throwing of coloured powders, to rejoice in the arrival of spring and the abundance it brings. Of course, we seized the opportunity to take part in the boisterous street party – the locals seemed to take extra delight in drowning visitors in colour, so we all looked like a mad batik by the end of the day! Special sweets are made at this time of year: we tried some fudge-like barfis and some gooey jalebis. That night there was a feast at our hotel in the desert. We tasted Kashmiri morel mushrooms braised in a spicy sauce, and perfectly textured besan dumplings poached in a spicy curd gravy. We watched as the cooks effortlessly displayed the art of making naan in a tandoor oven – a few of us had a go but couldn't match their deft touch. Margie and I had brought bindis for everyone to wear; a few of the women were brave enough to wear colourful saris, and a couple of the men came with Raj-style turbans and flowing kurtas. It was a lively evening that carried on into the wee hours.

Udaipur is a small city of palaces, lakes, chhatris (dome-shaped pavilions) and gardens that gives you a little breather from the usual crush; an ivory glow emanates from the buildings of pale sandstone and white marble, quarried and polished at nearby towns. Entering Lal Ghat, the city's oldest bazaar, is like opening Pandora's box – so many treasures to collect or admire. A sunset gondola ride around Lake Pichola is a wonderful way to enjoy the spectacular beauty of this city, or drive up to the abandoned Monsoon Palace on the hill facing the city for another visual treat. The surprise finale was sunset cocktails on the terrace of Fateh Prakesh (Crystal Palace), hosted by the reigning Maharana, Arvind Singh Mewar. Needless to say, the experience had us enthralled for hours.

One of the finest fort-palace hotels is near Udaipur. For me, Devi Garh is unrivalled for its sophistication and character, steeped in Indian tradition but with a refreshingly contemporary ambience. The food is produced with the same level of attention to detail. One night we feasted on fiery hot Kashmiri food, served on antique silver thali dishes. Chef Vimal prepared an extraordinary menu of ledur (lamb cooked with fennel and milk); charwan (goat's liver roasted with ginger and tomatoes); hadder nadur (wild mushrooms and tiny lotus stems in a pungent sauce with fresh coriander); monj haakh (baby turnips and their leaves braised with

EATING IN JAIPUR

LAXMI MISTHAN BHANDAR
MB Hotel, Johri Bazaar, Jaipur
Tel: +91 141 256 5844
Surrounded by the market shops in the main street, this restaurant has been operating for more than 250 years. The thali is sensational – a must for lunch.

Kashmiri red chilli); chaaman methi (curd cheese stewed with fenugreek leaves and spices); long grains of basmati rice studded with cashews, dried apple and pomegranate; and we had yet another version of paratha, this time warqui, which reminded me of crisp disks of puff pastry. The whole meal was an elaborate assembly of tastes and textures.

If you have time, a worthwhile detour on the way to Jodhpur is a visit to Ranakpur, about 100 kilometres north of Udaipur, to see one of the most extraordinary Jain temples in India. The thousands of carved marble pillars and intricate domes and towers will blow you away. The Jain religion prescribes a strict vegetarian diet, excluding anything that could cause harm to any form of life. Nothing can be killed for food, and this may include onions, garlic and root vegetables. Adherents also practise fasting on holy days and abstinence during the monsoon season, when dietary prohibitions may extend to greens of any plant, chickpeas or honey. In addition, no eating is permitted after dark in case an insect is inadvertently harmed. Jainism is certainly not an easy way of life, but is one you can't help admiring.

Sitting at the edge of the Thar Desert that stretches west to Jaisalmer and into Pakistan, the medieval city of Jodhpur is tinged with indigo blue, the colour of the wash traditionally used on the buildings of the old city. Looming above it is the imposing Meherangarh Fort. Jodhpur is at its most beguiling just before sunset. On a recent visit, we stayed a couple of hours' drive outside the city at Chhatra Sagar, the former hunting preserve of the Nimaj estate. Overlooking a vast reservoir lake to the Aravali Mountains, this luxury tented camp is an oasis of calm and tranquillity, and a shining example of environmentally conscious accommodation. The air is sweetly scented

PALACE HOTELS AND LODGES OF RAJASTHAN

NEEMRANA FORT PALACE
Village Neemrana, District Alwar, Rajasthan
(120 kilometres south of Delhi, on the main road to Jaipur)
Tel +91 149 424 6006
www.neemranahotels.com
This lavishly renovated fort oozes grace and style, and brims with personality. Make time for a stopover here when travelling between Delhi and Jaipur – it's an easy place to spend a few days. Taking tea on the rooftop terrace in the late afternoon sun is particularly enjoyable.

RAMBAGH PALACE
Bhawani Singh Road, Jaipur, Rajasthan
Tel +91 141 221 1919
www.tajhotels.com
A sanctuary in the heart of the city – lunch on the terrace overlooking the gardens is pretty fab.

SAMODE PALACE
Samode District, Jaipur, Rajasthan
(about 40 kilometres north-west of Jaipur)
Tel +91 142 324 0014
www.samode.com
A beautiful Moghul palace that is truly majestic – one of the best in India and definitely worth a detour.

DEVI GARH
Delwara, NH-8, near Eklingji, Nathdwara, District Rajsamand, Rajasthan
(28 kilometres north-east of Udaipur)
Tel +91 295 328 9211
www.deviresorts.com
Fabulous hilltop fort restored with contemporary style and amazing attention to detail – perhaps the most glamorous hotel in India. The food is equally splendid, especially the gulab jamun, which I order wherever I go to see who makes the best version; highest marks to date go to the chefs here.

TAJ LAKE PALACE HOTEL
Post Box No. 5, Lake Pichola, Udaipur, Rajasthan
Tel +91 294 242 8800
www.tajhotels.com
Renowned hotel that encapsulates the romance of Udaipur and Rajasthan. When the lake is full after the monsoon rains, it resembles a floating palace. The food at the Neel Kamal Restaurant is a showcase of Indian regional food: order the rogan josh (lamb curry) and fish podina (fish with mint and yoghurt sauce) – both are divine.

CHHATRA SAGAR
P.O. Nimaj, District Pali, Rajasthan
(about 100 kilometres east of Jodhpur)
Tel +91 941 412 3118
www.chhatrasagar.com
This luxury tented campsite is centred around a former hunting lodge and overlooks a massive bird sanctuary. It also boasts eco-friendly, sustainable farming practices and the most sublime cooking.

ROHET GARH
P.O. Rohet, District Pali, Rajasthan
(about 40 kilometres south of Jodhpur)
Tel +91 293 626 8231
www.rohetgarh.com
Luxury lakeside heritage hotel and wilderness camp.

by flowering trees and shrubs, peacocks strut their stuff and pelicans and geese float on the lake. Hosts Harsh, Raj and their families are there to pamper and spoil, and the exquisite food prepared in the family kitchen by Harsh's wife, Shrimidhi, is made using organic produce from neighouring farms. Sundowner drinks are served around a blazing bonfire and fresh corn pappads are cooked directly over a charcoal brazier until crisp, without the need for any oil. Dinner is served by candlelight. Shrimidhi invited us into her kitchen late one afternoon to show us a few of the recipes we had tasted the night before – everyone clamoured for the eggplant cooked in tamarind. Questions fired from every corner were graciously handled by Shrimidhi, and we were all impressed by the way she managed to cook in her high-quality pure-silk sari without getting a single mark or splatter on it.

When we set off the next day, Chhatra Sagar packed a wonderful picnic lunch for us. On a rocky outcrop by the roadside, we found a fabulous neem tree to sit under and settled down on mats. Plates and bowls were made from the dried leaves of the Flame of the Forest tree – disposable and eco-friendly, and fingers did the work of cutlery. Each person was given their own tiffin, with layers comprising nepali aloo (potatoes with roasted sesame and coriander); panchkutta (a local caravan recipe consisting of dried fruits and beans from trees that grow on the property); the definite favourite, dokhamchur (a fabulous spicy chutney of dried mango pieces and raisins); and a fragrant dry curry of young goat meat, eaten with parathas. We finished with crisp and delicious til papadi (sweet pappadam disks of sesame and pistachio pressed into sugar). Curious truck drivers stopped to see what this bunch of Westerners were up to, and donkeys sauntered over to eat the leftovers. Beats sitting at a roadhouse any day, though we all hoped the passing traffic missed what I dubbed our 'white-bum salute' . . .

As much as India is a visual feast, it is also a gastronomical feast and my first taste started a life-long love affair. It's quite a balancing act to fit in all the historical and cultural attractions with non-stop eating – I mean, everything is there to be sampled and who can say no? I have a direct and emotional response to Indian cuisine, and its principles have woven their way into my work in the most positive and enlightening manner. I can't imagine being creative in the kitchen without using ingredients from my Indian pantry.

KASHMIRI TOMATO SALAD

My thanks to Vimal, the chef at Devi Garh, near Udaipur, for sharing this recipe with me. I love his cooking, his astute and confident hand with spicing and the delicious flavour combinations he produces, often reflecting his Kashmiri heritage. This salad makes a great addition to a thali plate, where many small tastes are put together. It is equally delicious served simply with some grilled fish.

60 ml vegetable oil
1 teaspoon mustard oil
1 teaspoon brown mustard seeds
2 teaspoons nigella seeds
1 tablespoon finely shredded ginger
2 small green chillies, minced
1 teaspoon castor sugar
1 teaspoon ground turmeric
½ teaspoon ground chilli
6 ripe tomatoes, cut into eighths – do not peel
1 teaspoon sea salt

Heat both the oils in a frying pan and temper the mustard and nigella seeds until they begin to pop. Add the ginger, green chilli and sugar and fry for about 30 seconds until softened.

Stir in the ground turmeric, chilli and tomatoes and cook for 5 minutes, just enough to soften without the tomato breaking down. Remove from the heat and allow to stand for 15 minutes until the juices emerge.

Season with salt to taste and serve warm.

SERVES 4

TAMARIND EGGPLANT

Shrimidhi, at Chhatra Sagar lodge, near Jodhpur, is perhaps the finest cook in Rajasthan, in my book anyway. As part of our arrival dinner, she served this to-die-for eggplant dish – everyone was in raptures. Well and truly hooked, we watched her make it the next day in her kitchen, and ate it again and again . . .

vegetable oil, for deep-frying
1.2 kg small purple eggplants (aubergines), cut in half lengthways
8 cloves garlic, minced
3 small red onions, finely diced
175 g brown sugar
400 ml thick Tamarind Liquid (see Essentials)
1 teaspoon ground cumin
2 teaspoons sea salt
½ cup chopped coriander leaves

Heat the oil in a wok or large saucepan to 180°C, add a few eggplant slices at a time and deep-fry for 4–5 minutes until golden. Remove from the oil and drain on paper towel. Repeat with the remaining eggplant pieces.

Heat 100 ml of the oil in a frying pan over moderate heat and fry the garlic and onion until beginning to colour. Add the sugar, tamarind, cumin and salt and simmer gently for 5 minutes.

Taste and adjust the seasoning if necessary – the sweet, sour and salty flavours should be equally balanced.

Add the eggplant, stir to coat thoroughly and simmer for 3–4 minutes. Remove from the heat and scatter with the chopped coriander to serve.

SERVES 6

RAJASTHANI SPICED GREEN TOMATOES

We were shown how to prepare this simple vegetable dish at Rohet Garh many years ago by the matriarch of the household and it has become a regular feature of my Indian-inspired dinners. Make sure you buy firm, green and totally unripe tomatoes to get the right texture and flavour.

75 ml vegetable oil
1 teaspoon cumin seeds
½ teaspoon brown mustard seeds
600 g green tomatoes, blanched and peeled, then cut into thick rounds
2 teaspoons sea salt
1 teaspoon ground turmeric
1 teaspoon chilli powder
50 g castor sugar

Heat the oil in a saucepan, add the cumin and mustard seeds and fry for 30 seconds until fragrant.

Add the tomato rounds and cook over medium heat, stirring occasionally, for 5 minutes or until the tomatoes are soft but still holding their shape.

Add the salt, turmeric and chilli powder and toss to combine, then add the sugar and 100 ml water and cook for 10 minutes until the water has evaporated.

Taste and adjust the seasoning if necessary. Serve warm.

SERVES 6

CABBAGE AND COCONUT SALAD

This is a typical dry vegetable salad (thoran) from Rajasthan, which we had for lunch one day at Chhatra Sagar. The textures are so crisp and fresh, the spicing is subtle yet apparent, and it makes a refreshing change from the usual array of cooked dishes.

60 ml vegetable oil
1 tablespoon brown mustard seeds
20 fresh curry leaves
1 tablespoon finely shredded ginger
10 Savoy cabbage leaves, finely shredded
½ cup shredded fresh coconut
2 teaspoons sea salt
4 tablespoons coriander leaves, chopped

Heat the oil in a frying pan and temper the mustard seeds and curry leaves together until they begin to pop. Add the ginger and stir in the shredded cabbage until it is well coated with the spices.

Toss over heat for about a minute until it wilts, then remove from the heat.

Add the coconut, salt and coriander leaves and serve.

SERVES 6

BHINDI MASALA (see page 240); RAJASTHANI SPICED GREEN TOMATOES; CABBAGE AND COCONUT SALAD >

BHINDI MASALA

Bhindi is Hindi for okra, which in India is picked young and small before it develops that slimy quality. You could also substitute small eggplant for the okra – just cut it into chunks and deep-fry before adding to the mix. Any vegetable preparation like this that is quite dry (not swimming in sauce) is an ideal accompaniment to dal. Of course, dal can be served alone or with any number of Indian dishes, but here I have chosen to celebrate the prominence of vegetables on the Indian table.

500 g small okra, washed
50 ml vegetable oil
1 teaspoon mustard oil
1 teaspoon brown mustard seeds
12 fresh curry leaves
1 small red onion, finely diced
1 teaspoon ground cumin
1 teaspoon ground coriander
2 teaspoons garam masala
1 teaspoon ground turmeric
4 cloves garlic, minced
3 small green chillies, sliced
1 teaspoon sea salt
1 tablespoon chopped coriander leaves

Trim the tops off the okra and cut into 6 mm slices.

Heat both the oils in a wide pan or wok and fry the mustard seeds until they start to pop. Add the curry leaves and fry for about 30 seconds until crisp. Add the onion and saute over moderate heat until it begins to colour, stirring constantly.

Stir in the spices and cook for a minute until fragrant. Add the sliced okra, garlic and chilli and saute gently for 10 minutes until the okra is soft. The sauce should be quite dry and thick, coating the okra. Season with salt, taste and adjust if necessary. Stir in the chopped coriander just before serving.

SERVES 6

LAMB AND EGGPLANT YOGHURT SALAD

A great flavour-packed summer salad inspired by Indian flavours. The spiced yoghurt seasons and tenderises the meat as it cooks and the yoghurt dressing offers a change from the regular salad vinaigrette. Try wrapping the salad in hot naan or roti bread for a quick and delicious lunchtime sandwich.

300 g lamb backstrap fillet, trimmed
1 small cucumber, peeled
16 cherry tomatoes, halved
1 tablespoon shredded ginger
2 golden shallots, finely sliced
2 small Japanese eggplants (aubergines), cut into 1 cm slices and deep-fried
125 g thick plain yoghurt
2 teaspoons Spiced Eggplant Pickle (see Essentials)
1 teaspoon sea salt
50 ml fresh lemon juice, strained
2 tablespoons shredded mint leaves
2 tablespoons shredded coriander leaves
1 punnet mache cress, snipped

SPICED YOGHURT MARINADE
1 teaspoon coriander seeds
1 teaspoon cumin seeds
1 teaspoon brown mustard seeds
1 teaspoon garam masala
1 teaspoon ground turmeric
1 teaspoon nigella seeds
2 teaspoons sea salt
1 teaspoon freshly ground black pepper
60 g thick plain yoghurt
2 cloves garlic, minced
1 teaspoon minced ginger

To make the yoghurt marinade, dry-roast the coriander, cumin and mustard seeds in a pan over low heat until fragrant. Allow to cool. Grind in a spice grinder or mortar and pestle then mix with the remaining marinade ingredients.

Cut the lamb into four even pieces across the fillet and add to the marinade, tossing to combine. Leave to marinate for 30 minutes at room temperature.

Cook the lamb in a frying pan or on a flat grill plate over medium–high heat for 2–3 minutes each side. Allow the meat to rest for 5 minutes.

Cut the cucumber in half lengthways, scoop out the seeds and cut into thin slices diagonally. Place in a bowl with the tomatoes, ginger, shallots and fried eggplant and toss to combine.

Mix the yoghurt with the spiced eggplant pickle, salt and lemon juice, stirring to combine.

Cut the lamb across the fillet into thin slices, and add to the salad with the shredded herbs and mache cress. Toss gently and arrange on plates. Drizzle the yoghurt dressing over the top and serve.

SERVES 4

CURRY FISH SALAD

I have used the flavour spectrum of India to make this refreshing salad that relies as much on texture as it does flavour. Puffed rice is one of the ingredients in bhel puri, the ubiquitous savoury tiffin snack found on every street corner in Mumbai. If you can get hold of any puri crisps (from an Indian restaurant or grocer), add them to the salad for extra crunch. The dressing can be made ahead of time and kept refrigerated.

1 teaspoon ground turmeric
1 teaspoon sea salt
½ teaspoon freshly ground black pepper
40 ml vegetable oil
300 g salmon or ocean trout fillets, skin removed
2 tablespoons fresh curry leaves, deep-fried until crisp

CURRY DRESSING
40 ml fresh lime juice, strained
25 ml coconut vinegar
25 ml fish sauce
25 ml Sugar Syrup (see Essentials)
1 clove garlic, minced
1 teaspoon ground ginger
1 teaspoon mild curry powder
1 teaspoon Chilli Jam (see Essentials)
½ teaspoon freshly ground black pepper
1 teaspoon sesame oil
175 ml sunflower oil

SALAD
1 small cucumber, peeled and shaved into fine ribbons
1 stick celery, finely sliced
½ red onion, finely sliced
80 g puffed rice
1 punnet coriander cress, snipped
1 punnet celery cress, snipped
1 tablespoon shredded mint leaves
40 g baby spinach leaves

To make the curry dressing, put all the ingredients in a bowl and mix with a stick blender or whisk until emulsified.

Mix the turmeric, salt and pepper into the oil, then rub over the fish to season. Lay the fish on a flat baking tray and cook under a hot grill for 6 minutes, turning once (the fish should remain rosy in the centre). Remove from the heat and allow to cool for a few minutes while you prepare the salad.

Mix the salad ingredients together in a bowl. Flake the fish into small pieces and add to the salad greens with enough dressing to moisten. Toss to combine, then pile onto plates, sprinkle with the fried curry leaves and serve.

SERVES 4

SPICED CHICKPEA AND SPINACH SOUP

One of the essential pulses of the Indian pantry, chickpeas are used in myriad preparations, from everyday dishes to celebratory feasts. For the best texture, buy dried chickpeas and soak and cook them yourself – the ones in tins tend to be overcooked and too soft, in my opinion. In India, I have cooked this with fresh fenugreek leaves (methi), but sadly these are not available here, so I have used spinach leaves instead.

200 g dried chickpeas, soaked in cold water overnight
2 tablespoons ghee
1 brown onion, finely diced
2 small red chillies, minced
2 cloves garlic, minced
1 teaspoon minced fresh turmeric
2 teaspoons brown mustard seeds
1 teaspoon fenugreek seeds
1 teaspoon ground turmeric
2 teaspoons fresh curry leaves
500 ml coconut milk
300 ml White Chicken Stock or Vegetable Stock (see Essentials)
3 teaspoons sea salt
20 ml fresh lime juice, strained
3 tomatoes, peeled, seeded and finely diced
12 green beans, cut crossways into 5 mm slices
120 g baby spinach leaves, roughly chopped
20 ml Mint Yoghurt Sauce (see Essentials)
2 teaspoons fresh curry leaves, deep-fried until crisp

TURMERIC SPINACH FRITTERS
50 g chickpea flour
50 g plain flour
1 teaspoon ground turmeric
1 teaspoon ground cumin
1 teaspoon sea salt
50 ml water
vegetable oil, for deep-frying
16 small spinach leaves

Put the chickpeas in a large saucepan and cover with cold water. Bring to boil and cook over moderate heat for 1 hour or until softened, skimming the surface occasionally. Check the water level as the peas cook and top up if necessary. Drain and set aside.

Heat the ghee in a large saucepan and fry the onion, chilli, garlic and fresh turmeric until softened.

Add the spices and curry leaves and cook for 2 minutes until fragrant. Stir in the coconut milk, bring to the boil, then simmer for 5 minutes. Add the stock and simmer for another 20 minutes, then stir in the cooked chickpeas. Season with salt and lime juice.

To make the spinach fritters, combine the flours, spices, salt and water in a bowl to make a thin batter.

Heat the oil in a wok or large saucepan to 180°C and dip the spinach leaves, one at a time, in the batter to lightly coat. Fry in the hot oil for 2 minutes until golden and crisp. Remove and drain on paper towel

Stir the tomato, beans and spinach into the soup and cook for 2 minutes until the spinach has wilted. Ladle into bowls, add a dollop of yoghurt sauce and sprinkle with fried curry leaves. Sit the turmeric spinach fritters on top and serve immediately.

SERVES 4

SPICED PEA PASTRIES WITH CORIANDER YOGHURT SAUCE

A salute to the wonderful tiffin snacks of Mumbai, one of the most delightful and informal ways of eating in that vast city. These samosa pastries are perfect to serve with pre-dinner drinks as a party snack or as a palate teaser before dinner.

30 g ghee
200 g waxy potatoes, cut into small dice and parboiled
1 teaspoon minced garlic
1 teaspoon minced ginger
2 small green chillies, minced
125 g shelled fresh peas, blanched
2 teaspoons Chat Masala (see Essentials)
2 tablespoons chopped coriander leaves
1 teaspoon sea salt
½ teaspoon freshly ground black pepper
vegetable oil, for deep-frying

CORIANDER YOGHURT SAUCE
2 tablespoons chopped coriander leaves
1 tablespoon chopped spearmint leaves
1 small green chilli, sliced
1 red shallot, chopped
1 teaspoon minced ginger
1 teaspoon sea salt
1 teaspoon fresh lime juice, strained
150 g plain thick yoghurt

SAMOSA PASTRY
200 g plain flour
50 g chickpea flour
1 teaspoon sea salt
100 g ghee, melted
75 ml warm water

To make the yoghurt sauce, blend all the ingredients except the yoghurt to a paste in a food processor. Add the yoghurt and pulse until the mixture comes together. Do not overwork or the yoghurt will split and thin the sauce. Refrigerate until ready to serve.

To make the pastry, blend all the ingredients in a food processor until the dough forms a ball.

Wrap in plastic film and rest at room temperature for 2 hours.

To make the filling, melt the ghee and saute the potato, garlic, ginger and chilli until softened and fragrant. Add the peas and toss until combined. Remove from the heat and stir in the chat masala, chopped coriander and salt and pepper. Allow to cool completely.

Roll the pastry into a long sausage. Cut into 18 pieces, then roll the pieces out thinly into rounds. Spoon the filling into the centre of each round, then fold in half and then in half again to make a triangle, pressing the edges together firmly with your fingertips to seal.

Heat the oil in a deep-fryer or wok to 180°C and fry the pastries a few at a time for 5 minutes until golden and crisp. Keep them submerged in the hot oil with a slotted spoon to ensure even cooking. Drain on paper towel, and repeat with the remaining pastries. Serve with the coriander yoghurt sauce.

SERVES 6

MASALA PRAWNS WITH LEMON AND PINE NUT RICE

The rice pilaf or pulao is an ideal partner for fried or grilled fish and shellfish. I have tasted similar pilafs at many restaurants in Mumbai and Delhi, where cashews or almonds are sometimes used instead of pine nuts. When preparing this, I suggest you marinate the prawns first, then start the rice and while it's cooking in the oven, fry the prawns so that they are both ready at the same time.

12 large raw tiger prawns, shelled and deveined
1 teaspoon ground chilli
1 teaspoon ground turmeric
4 cloves garlic, minced
1 teaspoon sea salt
2 tablespoons ghee
4 golden shallots, minced
1 tablespoon fresh curry leaves
2 tomatoes, peeled and chopped
1 teaspoon finely grated lemongrass (use a Microplane)
1 teaspoon ground coriander
½ teaspoon ground cumin
20 ml fresh lemon juice, strained

LEMON PINE NUT PILAF
50 g ghee
1 tablespoon brown mustard seeds
12 fresh curry leaves
2 teaspoons nigella seeds
4 cloves garlic, minced
1 large red chilli, minced
½ teaspoon ground cardamom
1 teaspoon finely grated lemon zest
250 g basmati rice, soaked in cold water for 30 minutes then drained
750 ml White Chicken Stock (see Essentials)
40 ml fresh lemon juice, strained
3 teaspoons sea salt
4 tablespoons roasted pine nuts
2 tablespoons shredded mint leaves

Mix the prawns with the ground chilli, turmeric, garlic and salt and marinate for 10 minutes.

Heat the ghee in a frying pan, fry the shallots until softened then add the curry leaves and fry for another 2 minutes. Add the tomato, lemongrass, ground coriander and cumin and cook until the liquid evaporates and the mixture appears quite dry. Add the prawns and marinade and saute until the prawns change colour, tossing over heat to combine. Stir in the lemon juice, then taste and adjust the seasoning if necessary.

To prepare the pilaf, preheat the oven to 150°C. Heat the ghee in a wide-based ovenproof pan and fry the mustard seeds until they start popping. Add the curry leaves and nigella seeds and fry for another 20 seconds. Stir in the garlic and chilli, then add the cardamom and lemon zest and fry for a few seconds longer. Add the soaked rice and stir to coat with the spices.

Pour in the hot chicken stock, cover the pan and transfer to the oven. Cook for 20 minutes until the rice is tender and all the liquid has been absorbed. Remove from the oven and stir in the lemon juice, salt, pine nuts and mint. Taste and adjust the seasoning if necessary.

Spoon the rice pilaf onto plates and arrange the prawns on top to serve.

SERVES 6

BAKED FISH WITH CASHEW MASALA

Another one of my favourite fish preparations, with gentle fragrant flavours. Any deep-sea firm-fleshed fish is suitable for this recipe – try jewfish, kingfish, trevally or trumpeter fillets.

4 tomatoes, peeled
20 ml Spiced Tomato Chilli Pickle (see Essentials)
2 teaspoons sea salt
1 tablespoon castor sugar
100 ml vegetable oil
2 teaspoons coriander seeds, roasted and ground
2 teaspoons cumin seeds, roasted and ground
500 ml Fish Stock (see Essentials)
125 g thick plain yoghurt
1 tablespoon chickpea flour
30 ml fresh lime juice, strained
60 ml pouring (35%) cream
4 × 150 g jewfish fillets, cut from the middle of the fish
20 ml mustard oil
2 tablespoons chopped coriander leaves
1 long green chilli, finely sliced

CUCUMBER SALAD (KACHUMBER)
1 small cucumber, peeled, seeded and diced
1 small red onion, finely diced
3 tomatoes, peeled, seeded and finely diced
2 tablespoons chopped coriander leaves
2 tablespoons fresh lemon juice, strained
1 teaspoon sea salt
½ teaspoon Kashmiri chilli powder

CASHEW MASALA
1 tablespoon brown mustard seeds
1 teaspoon ground turmeric
1 teaspoon chilli powder
60 g freshly grated coconut
1 tablespoon minced ginger
4 cloves garlic, chopped
3 small green chillies, chopped
2 brown onions, chopped
2 tablespoons raw cashews, soaked and chopped
20 ml mustard oil

To make the cucumber salad, mix the ingredients together in a bowl until combined.

To make the cashew masala, place all the ingredients in a food processor and blend to make a smooth paste.

Mash the tomatoes and cook in a pan with the tomato chilli pickle until reduced by half, then add the salt and sugar.

Heat the vegetable oil in a wide-based pan and fry the ground and roasted coriander and cumin for 30 seconds until fragrant. Add the cashew paste to the pan and fry over moderate heat for about 5 minutes until aromatic and starting to colour. Add the reduced tomato and the stock and simmer for 10 minutes.

Mix the yoghurt with the chickpea flour then add to the sauce with the lime juice and cream and cook, stirring, over low heat for 5 minutes.

To cook the fish, preheat the oven to 200°C. Brush the skin with mustard oil and sprinkle with a little sea salt. Heat a heavy-based pan and lay the fish in the pan, skin-side down. Fry for 3 minutes, then turn the fish over, put the pan in the oven and bake for 3 minutes until the fish is half cooked.

Pour the mustard cashew sauce over the fish and bake for another 4–5 minutes, depending on the thickness of the fish. Remove from the oven and leave for 2 minutes for the juices to settle.

To serve, lay the fish on a serving plate. Stir the chopped coriander and green chilli slices into sauce and spoon over the fish.

Serve with steamed basmati rice and the cucumber salad.

SERVES 4

GARAM MASALA BAKED GOAT

I have tasted many different curries during my travels through Rajasthan, most using kid or goat meat – which, curiously, is referred to as lamb or mutton, respectively. I have used tender milk-fed goat (kid) meat here but you can also make it with milk-fed spring lamb if you prefer. Based on the mild korma curries of Lucknow, this is more aromatic than hot-spicy and is a great introduction to the world of curry for timid eaters. One of our friends, Mark, is one of the best home cooks I know, and he makes brilliant curries so it feels only right that this curry be dedicated to him and his finely tuned palate.

100 g ghee
2 brown onions, finely diced
50 g blanched almonds
½ teaspoon ground mace
½ teaspoon ground cloves
2 teaspoons freshly ground black pepper
¼ teaspoon ground green cardamom
4 small green chillies, finely sliced
4 cloves garlic, minced
1 tablespoon minced ginger
2 fresh bay leaves
2 teaspoons coriander seeds, roasted and ground
2 teaspoons garam masala
3 teaspoons sea salt
2 teaspoons Kashmiri chilli powder
1.25 kg kid goat leg, on the bone
75 g thick plain yoghurt
1 tablespoon chickpea flour
1 litre White Chicken Stock (see Essentials)
25 ml fresh lime juice, strained
2 tablespoons Fried Shallot Slices (see Essentials)
2 tablespoons almond flakes, roasted

Heat the ghee in a wide-based ovenproof pan and fry the onions until coloured. Remove from the oil. Fry the almonds until golden, then remove from the oil and drain on paper towel. Allow to cool, then blend the onions and almonds with the ground mace, cloves, pepper and cardamom in a food processor until pureed.

Saute the chilli, garlic, ginger and bay leaves in the same oil until softened.

Preheat the oven to 160°C. Mix the ground coriander, garam masala, salt and chilli powder together and rub over the leg meat. Add the spice-crusted leg to the pan and fry for 5 minutes, then turn over and fry the other side for a further 5 minutes.

Mix the yoghurt with the chickpea flour, then stir into the pan until it has been absorbed by the pan juices. Stir the spiced onion puree into the pan and fry for another 2 minutes.

Add the stock and cover with foil. Transfer to the oven and cook for 1 hour 30 minutes until the meat is tender. Remove the goat leg from the sauce and carve into slices off the bone.

Add the lime juice to the sauce, taste and adjust the seasoning if necessary.

Arrange the meat slices on plates, spoon the sauce over the top and scatter with the fried shallot slices and toasted almonds.

SERVES 4

ROSE SYRUP DUMPLINGS

Gulab jamun is one of the definitive desserts of India, one I order whenever I can as part of my eternal search for the best version. These fried dumplings are soaked in a spicy syrup for extra decadence. They are best eaten as soon as they are made, just like you would in India, where they are sold in sweet shops and at roadside stalls near any of the markets. The edible silver leaf adds an extra element of luxury – perfect for a celebration.

40 g self-raising flour
1 tablespoon fine semolina
100 g milk powder
½ teaspoon ground cardamom
30 g ground almonds
30 g ground pistachios
125 ml milk, warmed
75 g ghee, melted
vegetable oil, for deep-frying
2 tablespoons pomegranate seeds
2 tablespoons chopped pistachios
1 sheet edible silver leaf

ROSE SYRUP
500 g castor sugar
325 ml water
5 green cardamom pods, split open
few drops of rosewater

Sift the flour, semolina, milk powder and cardamom into a bowl. Mix in the ground almonds and pistachios. Mix the warm milk and ghee together, pour onto the flour and gradually incorporate the dry ingredients until a smooth dough forms. Cover the bowl with cloth or plastic film and leave to rest for 30 minutes.

With wet hands, roll the dough into 20 small balls. Heat the oil to 170°C and deep-fry the balls, a few at a time, for about 3 minutes until golden brown. Remove with a slotted spoon and drain on paper towel.

To make the syrup, combine all the ingredients in a large saucepan and bring to boiling point, stirring occasionally. Simmer for 5 minutes, then add the fried balls and simmer gently for another 10 minutes so they absorb the syrup.

Stir in the pomegranate seeds and serve the dumplings while they are still warm, sprinkled with chopped pistachios. Cut the silver leaf into small pieces and stick to the dumplings.

SERVES 4

SPICE ODYSSEY
SRI LANKA AND SOUTHERN INDIA

This exotic part of the world conjures up images of impossibly lush tropical jungles, enchanting beauty and heady aromas of spice. Think beaches fringed with swaying coconut palms, fertile tea, spice and rubber plantations, tropical fruit orchards, smiling faces and a landscape dotted with shrines and temples. Both Sri Lanka and southern India embrace the rich heritage of Buddhist, Hindu, Christian and Muslim influences, adding layers of complexity to their food, architecture and social order.

The south of India has long been important to spice traders, and the port towns have always played a key role in the spice routes. Cardamom is indigenous to both Sri Lanka and southern India, and is traded with the rest of the world. Over 90 per cent of the world's supply of cinnamon is produced in Sri Lanka, and it is regarded as the finest quality. Fresh green peppercorns, black pepper, small fiery green chillies, nutmeg, cloves, turmeric and tender young rhizomes of ginger make their presence felt in just about every recipe, but it is how these spices are blended that gives each dish its particular flavour profile. To capture the authentic tastes of this region, my pantry essentials include a liberal quantity of coconut (cream, milk, vinegar and oil), fresh curry leaves, ginger, tamarind, cashew nuts, pepper and various aromatic spices, small green chillies, limes, split black gram (urad dal) and rice.

Like a perfect teardrop earring, Sri Lanka hangs off the south-eastern tip of India. Surrounded by protective coral reefs, the island is framed by steamy coastal plains that contrast with the cool, misty air in the central highlands. During its English colonial days, Sri Lanka was known as Ceylon, a name that is forever immortalised in its tea. Compared to the frenzy of India, the atmosphere on the island is relaxed, despite its population of over 20 million inhabitants (in an area roughly the same as that of Tasmania or Ireland). This is a credit to the people, especially when you consider the turmoil of civil war that has raged for more than 20 years; in addition, Sri Lanka is still recovering from the 2004 tsunami, which devastated the island and its population. The stories are heart-wrenching, the distress still palpable. Wreckage of buildings and boats stand as chilling reminders of the ocean's power, but reconstruction is underway everywhere you look. Life goes on.

The island's interior holds some of the greatest Buddhist sites in the world. At Polonnaruwa there's an enormous reclining Buddha, and in Kandy there's the Temple of the Tooth, which houses the relic of Buddha's tooth, an object of veneration for the world's Buddhists. White-clad pilgrims flow into the temple each day to the beat of ancient drums; frangipani, the temple flowers, are floating in bowls of water everywhere; and the skyline is dotted with white dagobas and hilltop shrines.

The chaotic metropolis of Colombo, Sri Lanka's capital city, is an absorbing introduction to the island's peoples and cultures. The Tamils in the north of the island share their culture and cuisine with the Tamil population of the Indian state of Tamil Nadu, just across the Palk Strait, with an extensive range of vegetarian dishes, rasams (light peppery broths) and the liberal use of curd. Their culture and language are quite distinct from those of the dominant Sinhalese. Beyond the city, many Tamils, from South India as well as Sri Lanka, are employed as labourers to pick tea in the highland plantations. The quintessential Sinhalese dish is rice and curry, but these humble words belie a complexity of preparation, and the reality is often a miniature banquet of contrasting flavours and textures. The curry spectrum includes white, red and black. In the white version, the spices are poached in coconut milk; these mildly flavoured curries are often served at breakfast with string hoppers (steamed noodle 'nests'). Red curries use lots of dried red chilli or paprika for colour and flavour, but it is the black curries that are the definitive Sri Lankan curries – the spices are roasted to a deep coffee brown, resulting in a rich and complex flavour.

The city itself is a mish-mash of colonial architecture, grand houses and ugly, featureless modern design. Traffic manoeuvres are somewhat reminiscent of dodgem cars – a thrill a minute and often just as hair-raising. Jerome (our driver) enthusiastically described the custom of 'short eats', the Sri Lankan equivalent of food on the go. This can mean just about anything: vadai (spicy lentil doughnuts), roti, egg rolls, hoppers (coconut-infused crepes), pakoras (vegetable fritters) or many other savoury treats available from roadside vendors, humble shopfronts and street markets. We tried some delicious chickpeas, cooked in a large iron pan with chilli and garlic then wrapped in a cone of newspaper. A lunchtime favourite is lampries (or lamprais): steamed rice wrapped in a banana-leaf parcel with an assortment of goodies such as chicken or fishball curry, boiled egg, a pickle, sambol and vegetables, then baked – it's a complete meal in a packet.

At Pettah, Colombo's main market, we watched as the spice traders ground whole spices in a rough stone ulundu (a flat grinding stone with a thick, round pestle like a short rolling pin), although many home cooks seem to buy their spices whole and grind them as they need them. The narrow lanes and streets of this part of the city play host to the hustle and bustle of thriving commerce, and scenes of daily life.

In January 2007, I was invited to participate in the inaugural Galle Literary Festival. I stayed at Lunuganga, Geoffrey Bawa's residence near Bentota, which is on the coast between Colombo and Galle. Bawa, who died in 2003, was Sri Lanka's most influential and prolific architect. His works are renowned for the harmonious way they relate to their natural surroundings, whether they be houses, hotels or public buildings. It was in this illustrious setting that I cooked lunch for the festival's authors and guests, who sat at a long table on one of the dramatic garden terraces. At daybreak on the morning of the lunch, I headed to the fish market at Beruwala, a little further up the coast, together with the resident manager, Charles, and head chef Samandha. Spoilt for choice, I settled on paraw and seer fish and a bucketful of king prawns, so fresh they were still jumping. Apparently this is where the Arab traders first arrived centuries ago, and fishing boats have filled the small harbour ever since. It's a hive of early-morning activity and I soon came to receive as much attention as the fish from the inquisitive locals.

Another day the house cooks at Lunuganga prepared a special menu featuring the regional food of nearby Dedduwa village, served with fluffy basmati rice and the nutty small grains of red rice (or country rice), cultivated in nearby Ulpotha. Small bowls passed clockwise around the table were brimming with a fiery red curry of fish; chilli-pungent tiny river prawns; curries made with beetroot and starchy white yams; an eggplant moju, stir-fried with capsicum and onion; paripu, the Sri Lankan equivalent of dal; sambols made with banana blossom, onion, coconut, carrots and bitter gourd; tempered red and green wing beans; mallums, or mallungs – wild leafy greens that looked like sea kale, plucked from the lake at the bottom of the garden; and kutumurunga, a type of fern, wilted quickly over heat and seasoned.

Other feasts we enjoyed featured curries made with the seeds and flesh from jackfruit, curries of potato, gotu kola (a pungent green leafy shrub) and pineapple; tempered greens – tender pumpkin tendrils, pea sprouts and kangkung (water spinach); and a rich dessert of wattalappam – a baked egg custard of Malay origin, sweetened with hakuru (the local palm sugar) or kittul (treacle from the kittul palm).

Madhur Jaffrey was also a house guest at Lunuganga during our time there and we had many a conversation about food, travel and writing during our visit. We continued these animated conversations on the drive from Bentota to the southern port city of Galle; I don't think I could ever tire of listening to her astute observations and storytelling, bringing taste memories alive. Madhur prepared a delicious dinner at Amangalla, a boutique hotel set in a beautifully restored colonial building at the heart of the World Heritage-listed Galle Fort. Her Muslim-style Gujarati baked lamb shami kebabs tasted just as she described them in *Climbing the Mango Tree*, her book of reminiscences about growing up in India. The Gujarati mango soup (of Hindu origin) was a puree of just-ripe fruit thickened with chickpea flour and buffalo curd, seasoned with mustard, ginger and curry leaf – an absolute revelation to me.

Galle has a history of colonial rule, firstly by the Portuguese, then the Dutch (who built the ramparts in the 17th century), and finally the British, who stayed until Independence in 1948. In his 1900 Sri Lankan travelogue, *Golden Tips*, Henry Cave writes that 'the interest of the place is not confined to the mere loveliness of its scenery. Galle is by far the most venerable emporium of foreign trade now existing in the universe; it was the resort of merchant ships at the earliest dawn of commerce, and

SLEEPING AND EATING IN COLOMBO

PARK STREET HOTEL
20 Park Street, Colombo
Tel +94 11 243 9977
www.taruvillas.com
Small contemporary boutique hotel that's an oasis in the heart of the city, with attentive and friendly service.

GALLERY CAFE
2 Alfred House Road (off Alfred House Gardens), Colombo
Tel +94 11 258 2162
Well-executed food with fresh and lively flavours, and great cocktails, all served in a wonderfully serene setting.

it is destined to be the centre to which will hereafter converge all the rays of navigation, intersecting the Indian Ocean and connecting the races of Europe and Asia.' Galle was known to the Eastern world for its commercial importance a thousand years before it came to the attention of the Europeans, and the resulting racial mix makes for interesting people-watching and lends quite a bohemian air to the place. The Burghers are descendants of the early Dutch traders and English colonialists who intermarried with the Sinhalese and Tamils and made Sri Lanka their home. The Chettiar traders from the Indian state of Tamil Nadu, a relatively short distance away, also make regular visits for trade, promenading the streets decked out in their opulent jewellery. There's a pleasing aesthetic to the houses and villas in Galle – with internal courtyards, lush tropical gardens, wide covered verandahs and generously proportioned balconies. At the markets here and at Tangalle (further along the coast), we found konda kavum – traditional Sinhalese sweetmeats made with rice flour and treacle and fried in oil until crisp.

About half an hour's drive east of Galle lies Thalpe, where Margie and I stayed in one of the most beautiful beach villas we have ever come across. Sitting just above the waves that break over the coral, stilt fishermen perched on their ingenious stick contraptions right in front of us, with unbaited lines dangling in the water to catch small fish for supper. At sunset, local lads emerged to surf the waves. We befriended a couple of them, Indika and Iskole, and spent several days scooting around in their tuk-tuk down narrow country lanes to nearby inland villages. The temperature increased the minute we left the ocean and its cooling breezes. The boys took us to a lobster farm, right on the main road where cement tanks were brimming with lobsters hand-caught from the rocky crevices at the beach by plucky young divers. We bought one for dinner that night, and Leela, the house cook, grilled it over charcoal and tossed the meat through salad greens with a curry dressing that I helped to make. At Koggala Lagoon, we strolled through spice gardens where Ayurvedic remedies are made and sold. Further inland, the head gardener at our villa's sister property of Illuketia, walked us around his garden, proudly showing us how he had transformed the jungle into a tropical garden full of ginger blossom, heliconias and lotus-filled ponds, plus organically grown vegetables and herbs. We also visited the majestic Yatagala Buddhist Temple near Unawatuna on the day of the full moon – an auspicious time for

STAYING ON SRI LANKA'S SOUTH-WEST COAST

AMANGALLA
Galle Fort, Galle
Tel +94 91 223 3388
www.amanresorts.com
Resort hotel in the centre of Galle Fort.

THE FORT PRINTERS
39 Pedlar Street, Galle Fort, Galle
Tel +94 91 224 7977
www.thefortprinters.com
Wonderful historic place with lovely Sri Lankan and Mediterranean-inspired food. There are five generous suites in this small boutique property.

GALLE FORT HOTEL
28 Church Street, Galle Fort, Galle
Tel +94 91 223 2870
www.galleforthotel.com
Lovingly restored with sophisticated style by two ex-Sydney boys. Chris cooks a delicious set menu of Asian-style food for dinner each night.

APA VILLA THALPE
78 M.S. Matara Road, Thalpe
Tel +94 91 228 3320
www.villa-srilanka.com
The epitome of laid-back barefoot elegance, this is my favourite beach property in Sri Lanka. During your stay, take a side-trip to Illuketia, a plantation house 20 minutes inland, where you can arrange to have lunch on the terrace before returning to the coast.

LUNUGANGA
Dedduwa Lake, Bentota
Tel +94 91 438 0275
www.lunuganga.net
Geoffrey Bawa's former residence, with five guest rooms – the garden studio is my favourite. Lunuganga operates as an artists' retreat for six months of the year, so check before booking. The house cooks produce some very fine food, especially the vegetable dishes.

THE RIVER HOUSE (BALAPITIYA) AND TAPROBANA (BENTOTA)
Tel +94 11 576 9500
www.taruvillas.com
These exceptional properties complement each other perfectly – one is beachside, the other riverside. Chef Ruwan manages the menus for both and cooks excellent local specialties.

Buddhists, when thousands walk from the surrounding villages to pray at sunset as the moon rises in the sky.

Driving east along the south coast, we passed through many more villages that bore the scars of the tsunami. The roads became quieter the further east we travelled, and the scenery became more and more rural; indeed, our surroundings suddenly started to feel rather remote. We spent a few idyllic days at Nakulugamuwa Beach, near Tangalle. The skyline was fringed with massive coconut palms and the sound of the gentle surf rolling in was like soothing white noise: I couldn't have felt more relaxed.

Heading back along the south-west coastal road, we broke our journey at the River House, near Balapitiya. This gorgeous place overlooks the Madhu Ganga, an estuary peppered with thirty islands that are home to exotic bird life, Buddhist temples, fish farms, villages and cinnamon plantations. We watched cinnamon farmers strip the bark from the trees, in a few deft movements producing long curls or quills, which are then dried on racks hanging from the roof above. Nothing from the cinnamon tree is wasted – pencils and key rings are made from the fragrant wood chips. We explored the estuary at daybreak one morning in a small motor boat, moved by the serenity of the scene.

From there, Margie and I flew up to the mountains in a float plane, eliminating nine hours of bone-crunching road travel up twisting, narrow roads. We landed on the lake at Nurawa Eliya, a former English colonial hill station in the heart of tea country. The air was cool and intoxicatingly fresh; at sunrise and sunset there was a fine mist over the valleys and mountains, and the landscape was dotted with manicured English gardens. We drove past enormous waterfalls and tea factories through the small towns of Hatton and Dikoya to reach Norwood Estate, a former tea-planter's bungalow where we were to stay. The house is perched high above Castlereagh Reservoir with vistas of towering mountains and unrivalled beauty all around it, making our journey worthwhile. We walked through a couple of the tea estates before breakfast, stopping to talk with some Tamil women on the way, who couldn't resist dressing Margie in their headwear and basket for a photo, obviously finding the whole business highly amusing.

Given our surroundings, it seemed natural to adopt the practice of taking tea. Guided by descriptions from Milroy, the tea sommelier for Dilmah Estate, who compares the flavour notes to those of wine, we tried various single-estate teas. I bought a tin of the light Ran Watte Estate tea to take home; grown at 1740 metres above sea level, its delicacy is likened to champagne. I also took a shine to the rich and golden Uda Warre Somerset Estate tea, with its spicy orange flavour. We almost felt we were drinking the very essence of Sri Lanka – a fitting gesture of farewell before heading to southern India.

Southern India is dramatically different from the northern part of the country, in all aspects – cultures, languages, customs, architecture and food. Southern food is wet, rich and spicy with a prolific use of grains, lentils and legumes, curd cheese, vegetables and tamarind. Thalis are a feature, like a personal buffet – either served modestly on banana leaves or on large silver plates with the components in small dishes or cups, while the rice takes centre stage. Fruits are plentiful and varied in the south. Bananas are a staple throughout the year, and the breakfast plate often includes guava, pineapple and pawpaw, cut into pieces and sprinkled with a mix of salt and dried chilli.

My introduction to southern India came in 1996, with the role of guest chef in residence at the Taj Coromandel Hotel in Chennai (Madras), the capital city of Tamil Nadu, as part of a cultural exchange program set up by the Australian Department of Foreign Affairs. Having worked for renowned Australian chef Phillip Searle – a devotee of all things Indian – I jumped at the chance. Four Australian chefs were chosen to represent the best of Australian gastronomy in four different Indian cities. While I was in Chennai doing my thing, Phillip was in Delhi, David Thompson was in Mumbai (Bombay) and Tony Bilson was in Kolkata (Calcutta). Our culinary

STAYING IN SRI LANKA'S TEA COUNTRY

TEA TRAILS
Tel +94 11 230 3888 (office); +94 51 492 0400 (Norwood bungalow)
www.teatrails.com
Bungalows set across a swathe of mountainside in the heart of Tea Country, each with its own character. The pick of the group is Norwood – dramatic scenery, generous-sized rooms, fabulous gardens and a swimming pool. It makes a good base if you want to scale the heights of nearby Adam's Peak, the island's highest and most sacred mountain.

creations were supported by contingents representing the arts, music and dance. Margie accompanied me on this trip and we were fortunate enough to see the Bangarra Dance Company for the first time, in a local theatre in Chennai. We sat amongst a sea of smartly dressed Indians who got right into the performance, the Dreamtime stories and captivating music – it was as fascinating to watch the audience as it was the dancers.

Arriving in the hotel's kitchens that first day was something of a shock – for them as much as me. I walked into the large main kitchen to find at least 50 chefs: all Indian, all male and all in their crisp whites, with tall hats and moustaches neatly in place (facial hair is cultivated as a sign of manliness in India). I asked for directions to the local fish and vegetable markets, so I could see the produce on offer before finalising my menu. It was politely suggested that this was not recommended for someone like me – being white, female and an important visitor – but I was insistent, so our small party of a couple of the head chefs, the bookkeeper and the manager set off to explore.

Immediately I felt in my element. The vegetable markets were fabulous; lots of the produce was locally grown, with more trucked down from the temperate mountain regions near Bangalore and Mysore. The variety was simply astounding, and I was excited to see the drumstick vegetable for the first time. The freshness of the spices bowled me over – I could smell the spice shops long before I reached their doors. The fish markets, however, proved more confronting: the fish were just kept on the ground, with the vendors squatting nearby, running wet sand over them to keep them moist. We found a man who would supply me with certain fish each day, coming straight to the restaurant as soon as his boat landed at the beach. The bartering took place between the fisherman and the hotel bookkeeper (hence his presence on all outings), a deal was struck and hands were shaken – a pretty straightforward system really.

Home cooking is revered in this part of the world. Having said that, there is a thriving demand for street food, selling snacks for locals to eat on their way to and from work, and throughout the day. Keen to taste this food for myself, I often ventured out with a few of the chefs during the kitchen's break between lunch and dinner service. They were eager to show me around and we would jump on the back of a motorbike, swerving wildly to get through the traffic congestion. We'd stop off at one of the few local canteen-style cafes, always packed with locals, and order a thali. My eyes were opened to the regional differences of southern food, tasting sweet pak (a specialty of Mysore), the spicy heat of the kosambri salads of Karnataka, and the Brahmin specialties of Tamil Nadu. Each state has its own interpretation of the dosa (a thin crepe made with fermented rice flour and dal); some are even made with millet.

The chefs showed me how they made yoghurt curd each morning and the various bread doughs that were pounded and stretched and rolled into parathas, naan and roti. I watched as they soaked lentils for the various dals that were on the menu, and picked up a few tips about preparing masala pastes – those that we often associate with curry. The term curry was actually introduced during the days of the British Raj; it originally derived from the Tamil word 'kari', meaning spicy or peppery, but has since become synonymous with any spicy gravy or sauce.

One Sunday, Margie and I hired a car and driver and headed 58 kilometres south of Chennai to visit the ancient and crumbling Hindu shore temples at Mamallapuram, a village where generations of stone carvers have created an impressive array of cave temples and sculptures. Inland lie several other major temple attractions, including the sprawling Vishnu temple just north of Trichy (Tiruchirapelli), where we witnessed the grisly exorcism of a young girl, and the most revered Shiva temple in India at Madurai. You could spend your life visiting temples in India but after seeing those three, I decided I'd done the best of them and returned my focus to food, a source of great spiritual pleasure for me.

Tamil Nadu is where you will find the most highly developed vegetarian cuisine of the Brahmins, and also the spiciest – from the Chettiars in the southern part of the state. I'd always wanted to make the pilgrimage to Karaikudi in the Chettiar heartland, and now I had my chance. Chettinad food is markedly different from the more subtle flavours of Tamil Nadu's Brahmin cuisine, which actually seems mild by comparison. Spicy and aromatic, Chettinad food has a vast repertoire of delicious vegetable, legume, dried fish and meat preparations, including tiny lamb meatballs in spicy gravy, quails cooked with black pepper, a lovely tangy eggplant number that we ate one night at the Bangala homestay, tomato or curd rice, spicy pineapple rasam, and various kootu (milder dishes made with lentils and/or vegetables) and poriyals (dry curries).

If I were to come back to this earth as an Indian, I think I would want to live in Kerala, on the Malabar Coast. This part of India is like no other, with a unique heady sensuality. The lush green jungle is thick with coconut palms, banana, jackfruit, cashew and betel-nut trees, and spice, tea and rubber plantations. Long associated with the spice trade, Kerala is fragrant with black pepper, cardamom, turmeric and ginger; it is also known for Ayurvedic medicinal practice, and devotees come from around the world to experience its healing powers. In this ancient system of healthcare, spices and herbs play an integral part in the daily diet and natural remedies. The food here is all about coconut. Whether it's the cream, milk, oil, vinegar or the water from this most versatile fruit, it finds its way into everything. Even the sap is tapped into clay pots tied to the tree – this ferments to make the mildly alcoholic toddy, which of course we tried one evening after watching the toddy tapper climb the tree to collect the sap.

In Alappuzha (Alleppey), we boarded a kettu vallom, a converted rice barge built of bamboo thatch, teakwood and coir, equipped with all the comforts of home, including air-conditioning. Comfortably installed, we cruised along the backwaters – a maze of waterways, canals and lakes that eventually empty into the Arabian Sea. I wrote these words floating along with travelling companions Jan and Lyndie, eating our way through an endless array of delicious food cooked by Sabu, our on-board Keralan chef.

On arrival we were greeted with a typical banana-leaf lunch, which is small spoonfuls of various dishes arranged around a central mound of steamed Keralan rice (its grains much plumper and shorter than the northern basmati), set out on a just-picked banana leaf. We were given hot mango achar (pickle); crisp banana chips; thoran (a dry vegetable dish); avial (made with drumstick vegetable cooked in turmeric water); pachadi (a wicked beetroot and yoghurt relish); meen varathathu (seer fish fried with turmeric and ginger paste); a fish mooli with chillies, ginger and lime; and a few other things – all with coconut, of course. Sambar (lentil and vegetable stew) was spooned over the rice to moisten it, and little mounds of salt were provided for seasoning. Something sweet is always offered, and one specialty served in honour of guests is payasam, a coconut milk concoction with tiny threads of rice vermicelli, sultanas and cashews, scented with cardamom.

Every morning, we tucked into delicious masala omelettes with just enough chilli to wake up the tastebuds, then soothed the heat with fruit salad. Seeing ducks everywhere on the waterways, I requested duck for dinner one evening. Sabu baked it Varutha Tharavukari-style (in coconut oil with a spicy masala paste). Of course there were several other dishes to accompany the duck: mahzkkupuratty (small okra sliced and tossed in a little coconut oil with grated coconut, mustard seeds, ginger, garlic, curry leaves and green chilli), a thoran of shredded snake beans, a spicy dal, chapati and steamed rice. Getting about on these waterways was a relaxing, yet fascinating way to travel – ploughing through the floating water hyacinths, watching ferries glide past full of school kids on their way home for lunch (all waving), field labourers stopping for chai and sweets at one of the waterside vendors, or women in brightly coloured saris slapping their washing against the rocks at the water's edge. The rhythm of daily life seemed so gentle; everyone we passed had a huge smile on their face, and the children were simply adorable. I felt like I never wanted to leave.

SLEEPING AND EATING IN TAMIL NADU

TAJ CONNEMARA
Binny Road, Chennai, Tamil Nadu
Tel +91 44 6600 0000
www.tajhotels.com
Old-world charm set in lovely gardens – a tranquil base to have while staying in Chennai.

DAKSHIN
Park Sheraton Hotel
TTK Road, Chennai, Tamil Nadu
Tel +91 44 2499 4101
A stand-out restaurant with a menu showcasing authentic food from all four southern states. We put ourselves in the hands of chef Praveen Anand and were rewarded with brilliant food, displaying distinct and complex flavours – one of the most memorable dinners of our trip.

THE BANGALA
Karaikudi, Tamil Nadu
Tel +91 45 6522 0221
www.thebangala.com
In heartland of the Chettinad region, this generously proportioned heritage bungalow is family operated, and the home cooking shared around the large family table is delicious.

Heading inland, our driver, Babu, took us through the dramatic and fragrant Cardamom Hills, part of the larger Western Ghats mountain range that divides the southern tip into east and west. Staying at Shalimar Spice Garden, in the Periyar region, we were treated to a Syrian Christian feast. Ulathiya irachi (translated boringly into English as 'beef fry') was totally delectable: beef pieces dry-fried with coconut, curry leaves, spices and black pepper. So many tastes became utterly addictive – and after a week of sensuous eating, we found it increasingly hard to choose a favourite.

Wandering through a large spice plantation at nearby Kumily soon after sunrise, we tasted green cardamom ready to be picked, the fresh fruit so pungent and zesty. There were acres of pepper vines and vanilla vines winding their way up support trees that bore rose apple, clove, allspice and nutmeg. We stocked up on fresh spices at Lord's, a terrific spice market on the main street; their pungent aroma reminds me of this place every time I open the packet. We also drove past many plantations of cashew trees, with their beautiful red, bell-shaped flowers – the entire west coast of India has cashew trees in abundance and the nuts appear in many different guises in the food.

Back on the coast, the historic port city of Kochi (Cochin) straddles islands and promontories, and is divided into three parts: Ernakulum is the new town; Fort Cochin is the old town, its streets shaded by canopies of banyan and tamarind trees; and Willingdon Island lies between the two. We based ourselves in Fort Cochin, to be close to the water's edge and all the activity of car and people ferries ploughing their way to and from the nearby islands. Breakfast is hard to beat in these parts, so our days started with plates of idli (steamed rice cakes), iddiappam (steamed rice-noodle cakes), vadai (fried spongy dumplings to die for) and dosa (savoury crepes). Thanks to Mini, a local Keralan with a passion for food, we experienced an amazing array of dishes in a short amount of time through her astute guidance. Our extravagant eating marathon included soft and fluffy red rice; achappam (crisp wafers like pappadams that are flavoured with black sesame and cumin, and served with chutneys and pickles); various gourds (bitter, ribbed, smooth, snake and bottled, used in salads and curries); rasam (peppery broth); puri (puffed rice); appam (spongy rice pancakes served with wet curries); avial (assorted vegetables steamed in turmeric water then shredded and mixed with yoghurt, fresh coconut and chilli); vegetable poriyals and kootu, and sweet payasam desserts. Confirming my

SLEEPING AND EATING IN KERALA

SHALIMAR SPICE GARDEN
Murikkady P.O., Kumily, Idukki, Kerala
Tel +91 486 922 2132
www.shalimarkerala.net
Gorgeous property set in acres of spice gardens high in the Cardamom Hills, surrounded by tropical jungle. The house cooking includes Syrian Christian specialties. There are loads of spice gardens within easy walking distance, or stay for a couple of days and explore the nearby Periyar wildlife sanctuary.

MALABAR HOUSE
1/268–1/269 Parade Road, Fort Cochin, Kerala
Tel +91 484 221 6666
www.malabarhouse.com
Gorgeous boutique hotel with a relaxed beach-house ambience – the downstairs rooms have private courtyards. The restaurant, Malabar Junction, serves a fabulous seafood thali.

BRUNTON BOATYARD
Calvetty Road, Fort Cochin, Kerala
Tel +91 484 221 5461
www.cghearth.com/brunton_boatyard
Breezy whitewashed rooms with balconies. The rooftop terrace after sunset is the best – it overlooks the busy port for the car ferry that transports people and cars across to nearby islands.

BADETTU RESTAURANT
Sarovaram Hotel, NH-47 Kochi Bypass, Maradu P.O., Ernakulam, Kochi, Kerala
Tel +91 484 230 5519
Terrific Kerala-style vegetarian thalis, with several spicy curries to choose from, and the breakfasts are fab. Make like a local and eat with your hands.

AYISHA MANZIL
Court Road, Tellicherry, Kerala
Tel +91 490 234 1590
This part of Kerala is worth every bit of the journey – there's plenty to see and do around town and the beaches are pristine. Stay at this stylish heritage guesthouse surrounded by coconut and tamarind trees; Faiza's food is sensational.

undying love for eggplant, one dish that stood out was small eggplants smoked whole over coals, then peeled and mashed with garlic, ginger, onions, ground chilli and just enough coconut oil to moisten. Scrumptious!

A 30-minute flight from Kochi to Calicut takes you to the heart of northern Kerala. This is a Muslim area, and brightly decorated mosques sit comfortably beside temples and churches. We drove north from the airport for two hours through an endless stream of busy towns and villages before arriving at Ayisha Manzil, a generously proportioned 19th-century heritage bungalow in Tellicherry that has been in the Moosa family for more than 100 years. The house was filled with the heady aroma of spice, and every morning we awoke to the smell of deep-fried bathura bread and mutta sirka (ground rice and egg dumplings, served with home-made cardamom syrup). After the first bite, we declared their name should be 'heavenly'. I'd made the detour to this area with the express purpose of discovering the culinary secrets of the Moplahs, descendents of early Muslim Arab merchants. Our dinners at Ayisha Manzil were sumptuous affairs, and we sat out under the stars in the balmy night air after watching dramatic sunsets over the Arabian Sea while Faiza Moosa presided over the kitchen. Every dish showcased an array of spices and aromatics where the flavours were simultaneously many and one, a sign of a sure hand from a confident cook.

The bustling city of Tellicherry (or Thalassery, to give its Indian name) has been the epicentre of the spice trade for centuries and traces its history back to Phoenician and Roman times, with a more recent colonial past of French and British settlement. The fish markets are truly inspiring, an unusual thing to be able to say in India. We stood on the beach one morning and watched as the fishing boats unloaded baskets of mussels collected from the small rocky islands a few hundred metres offshore, while other boats had nets full of sparkling sardines. Faiza later cooked the mussels with a masala-style spice paste that had everyone at the dinner table drooling.

The Kerala region is socially diverse, with Hindu, Catholic, Syrian Christian, Jewish and Muslim cultures all co-existing side by side with no real evidence of tension. The rich heritage of these various traditions results in an interesting and tolerant community. This is a state that was the first in the world to freely elect a communist government, and has the highest literacy rate and lowest birth rate in India. There is a distinct air of prosperity and well-being: the houses are larger than elsewhere in India or Sri Lanka and are well maintained, everyone seems content, and the melodic Malayalam language is like music. I cherish the time spent here; its progressive spirit utterly restores my faith in human nature.

The myriad flavours of Sri Lanka and southern India resonate in my cooking and will continue to be a source of inspiration. Experiencing this unique cuisine first hand has left an indelible mark on my mind and my work.

BAKED MASALA MARRON

In Kerala there are jumbo shrimps that weigh about 350 g each, fished from the Arabian Sea and similar to our native freshwater marron, but any similar shellfish can be used for this recipe (lobster, crayfish, yabbies or even fleshy white fish) – just adjust the cooking time according to the size. Spiced coconut gravies such as this are called mollee in Kerala, and are a particular favourite with fish and seafood, making good use of the local star ingredients: coconut, pepper and cardamom.

8 × 300 g live marron (put in the freezer for 20 minutes before cooking)
2 teaspoons fresh lime juice, strained
2 tablespoons coriander leaves
1 small green star fruit, finely sliced crossways
40 ml sunflower oil
1 tablespoon fresh curry leaves
1 teaspoon brown mustard seeds
1 large clove garlic, finely sliced

MASALA SAUCE
1 brown onion, finely diced
3 cloves garlic, chopped
1 teaspoon minced fresh turmeric
1 teaspoon minced ginger
2 small green chillies, minced
30 g ghee
1 teaspoon cumin seeds, roasted and ground
½ teaspoon nigella seeds
½ teaspoon ground turmeric
½ teaspoon ground cardamom
2 teaspoons sea salt
1 teaspoon freshly ground black pepper
3 ripe tomatoes, peeled and diced
225 ml coconut cream

To make the sauce, blend the onion, garlic, fresh turmeric, ginger and chilli in a food processor to make a paste. Heat the ghee in a pan and fry the paste for about 3 minutes until fragrant, then stir in the ground spices, salt and pepper and cook for 2 minutes. Add the diced tomatoes and simmer for 3 minutes then add the coconut cream. Bring to boil, then reduce the heat and simmer gently for 10 minutes. Taste and adjust the seasoning if necessary.

Plunge the marron into cold water in a large saucepan, cover with a lid and bring to simmering point. Take them out of the water as soon as it starts to simmer and remove the tails from their shells.

Remove the intestinal tracts from each marron tail. Cut each tail into three thick medallions, add to the sauce with the large claw meat and simmer over gentle heat for 4 minutes or until just cooked.

Stir in the lime juice, coriander and star fruit slices and remove from the heat.

Heat the sunflower oil in a small frying pan and fry the curry leaves, mustard seeds and garlic slices until crisp. Pour the tempered oil over the marron and serve with steamed rice or rumali roti (handkerchief bread).

SERVES 4

SPICED WATERMELON, SQUID AND MINT SALAD

This has the spice elements of a curry, lightened up and transformed into a salad. The vibrant flavours come alive with the sweetness of the watermelon and the cooling mint – a perfect foil for the squid.

20 ml vegetable oil
½ teaspoon cumin seeds
2 teaspoons minced garlic
1 red bird's-eye chilli, minced
2 teaspoons ground chilli
½ teaspoon ground coriander
½ teaspoon ground turmeric
150 g small squid tubes, cleaned, cut in half and scored
200 g watermelon, seeds removed and cut into 2 cm dice
50 ml watermelon juice
40 ml fresh lime juice, strained
50 ml Sugar Syrup (see Essentials)
40 ml fish sauce
4 tablespoons mint leaves, roughly chopped
2 tablespoons finely sliced red shallots
2 tablespoons Fried Shallot Slices (see Essentials)

Heat a large pan or wok over moderate heat, add the oil and fry the cumin seeds for 30 seconds until fragrant. Add the garlic and minced chilli and cook until softened, then stir in the ground chilli, coriander and turmeric.

Increase the heat to high, throw in the squid and toss for a few minutes until it starts to curl, then add the diced watermelon and cook for about 30 seconds until warmed through.

Mix the watermelon and lime juices with the sugar syrup and fish sauce. Taste and adjust if necessary. Pour into the pan and toss through to coat the squid. Remove from the heat and add the mint and red shallot slices.

Arrange the salad on plates, sprinkle the fried shallot slices over the top and serve.

SERVES 4

OYSTER, CUCUMBER AND YOGHURT SALAD

The oysters give this refined take on the traditional Indian raita an added dimension of texture as well as the fresh flavour of the sea, and the richer yoghurt made with buffalo milk adds an ethereal quality. Light and smooth, this salad is perfect for summer as a new way of serving oysters – or raita, for that matter.

250 g buffalo yoghurt, hung in muslin overnight to thicken
1 tablespoon chopped dill
½ teaspoon minced ginger
1 teaspoon minced red shallot
2 teaspoons sea salt
½ teaspoon freshly ground white pepper
40 ml fresh lime juice, strained
1 teaspoon nigella seeds
2 tablespoons finely diced cucumber
12 Pacific oysters, freshly shucked
2 green onions, finely sliced
1 punnet mustard cress, snipped
1 cucumber, peeled and shaved into fine ribbons
20 ml Cucumber Juice (see Essentials)

Place the yoghurt, dill, ginger, shallot, salt, pepper and half the lime juice in a bowl and mix until combined. Stir in the nigella seeds and half the diced cucumber.

Mix the oysters and their juices with the green onion, mustard cress and remaining cucumber dice and lime juice in a bowl.

Arrange the cucumber ribbons in each bowl and spoon some of the yoghurt mix on top. Sit the oyster salad on top, spoon the cucumber juice around and serve.

SERVES 4

STIR-FRIED CURRY MUD CRAB

Crab is a favourite on the Sri Lankan table and their crabs are very similar to our mud crabs from the Northern Territory and Queensland. Buy them live and kill them humanely. (I find the best way is to put them in the freezer for 1 hour before immersing them in cold water and bringing the water to simmering point. Remove the crabs from the water and proceed with the recipe.) This curry is great to have at home where there are no inhibitions about getting into a mess – just don the bib and dive in.

2 × 1 kg live mud crabs
4 cloves garlic
½ teaspoon sea salt
2 small red chillies
1 tablespoon chopped ginger
40 ml vegetable oil
40 ml fish sauce
20 ml Tamarind Liquid (see Essentials)
2 teaspoons castor sugar
1 egg, beaten
125 ml coconut milk
4 sticks Asian celery, cut into 1 cm lengths
2 green onions, cut into 1 cm lengths
2 red shallots, finely sliced
4 tablespoons chopped coriander leaves

SRI LANKAN CURRY POWDER
2 tablespoons cumin seeds
4 tablespoons coriander seeds
2 teaspoons fennel seeds
1 teaspoon fenugreek seeds
1 teaspoon ground turmeric
1 teaspoon ground chilli
1 teaspoon ground ginger
1 teaspoon garlic powder
4 fresh curry leaves, ground
1 teaspoon ground cinnamon
1 teaspoon garam masala
2 teaspoons dried lime-leaf powder
½ teaspoon dried lemongrass powder
¼ teaspoon ground nutmeg
½ teaspoon ground cardamom
1 teaspoon paprika
½ teaspoon ground clove

To make the curry powder, roast the cumin, coriander, fennel and fenugreek seeds separately over low heat until dark brown. Allow each to cool before grinding together to a powder. Mix with the remaining ingredients until combined.

To clean the crabs, remove their carapaces and dead man's fingers, reserving the mustard or roe for later. Wash the crabs and cut them into quarters, keeping their large front pincers separate. Crack these slightly to split the shells to ensure even cooking and easy access when eating.

Pound the garlic, salt, chilli and ginger in a mortar and pestle to make a paste. Heat a wok, add the oil and fry the garlic paste for a minute until it starts to colour. Add 4 tablespoons of the prepared curry powder and toss over heat for about 2 minutes until fragrant.

Add the fish sauce, tamarind and sugar, then stir in the egg and cook for 30 seconds (just until the egg white starts to change colour) then add the reserved crab mustard. Add the crab pieces and the coconut milk, then reduce the heat to low and simmer for 6 minutes until the crab is cooked, stirring occasionally to make sure it is evenly coated. The curry should be quite dry, with most of the curry paste attaching itself to the crab shells and meat.

Add the celery, green onion and shallots and toss to combine. Pile onto plates and sprinkle with the chopped coriander to serve.

SERVES 4

CHETTINAD CHILLI CHICKEN

Ever since I first tasted Chettinad cooking in Chennai more than a decade ago, I have been fascinated by its culinary traditions and its links with the spice traders since the 16th century. A more recent visit to the Chettinad region in and around Karaikudi to further experience what is considered the hottest and spiciest food in India left me completely enamoured of its complex layering of flavours.

75 g ghee
2 brown onions, diced
1 tablespoon minced ginger
5 cloves garlic, minced
3 small red chillies, minced
20 fresh curry leaves
1 star anise
2 teaspoons ground chilli
3 tablespoons Red Masala Paste (see Essentials)
2 tablespoons shredded fresh coconut
4 chicken thighs, on the bone
3 tomatoes, peeled and chopped
200 ml White Chicken Stock (see Essentials)
1 tablespoon sea salt
20 ml fresh lime juice, strained
1 cup coriander leaves

Heat the ghee in a wide-based pan, fry the onions until softened then add the ginger, garlic and chilli. Add the curry leaves and stir until they become crisp, then add the star anise, ground chilli, red masala paste and coconut, stirring to combine.

Add the chicken and saute in the paste for 10 minutes, turning once to make sure the cutlets are evenly coated. Add the tomato and cook for 5 minutes, then stir in the stock. Reduce the heat to low, cover and simmer for 25 minutes or until the chicken is tender. Season with salt and lime juice, then taste and adjust if necessary.

Remove the chicken with a slotted spoon and take out the bones. Cut each thigh in half and return the meat to the sauce. Scatter the coriander leaves over the top and serve with steamed rice.

SERVES 4

EGGPLANT AND CHERRY TOMATO MASALA

This spicy vegetable stew is served over fluffy idli (steamed rice cakes) with a fresh coconut chutney. It pays homage to the vegetarian cooking of India's southern states, where each component is characteristically flavoured with tempered spices.

40 ml vegetable oil
1 teaspoon mustard seeds
10 fresh curry leaves
2 teaspoons urad dal (black gram)
2 brown onions, finely sliced
2 teaspoons sea salt
1 tablespoon tomato paste
½ teaspoon chilli powder
½ teaspoon ground fennel
½ teaspoon ground coriander
1 teaspoon ground turmeric
250 ml Tamarind Liquid (see Essentials)
400 g eggplants (aubergines), cut into wedges and deep-fried
250 g cherry tomatoes, halved
coriander leaves, to serve

COCONUT CHUTNEY
30 g ghee
1 tablespoon fresh curry leaves
½ teaspoon brown mustard seeds
½ teaspoon nigella seeds
80 g grated fresh coconut
1 small green chilli, minced
1 tablespoon chopped coriander leaves
20 ml Tamarind Liquid (see Essentials)
20 ml fresh lime juice, strained
1 teaspoon castor sugar
1 teaspoon sea salt
½ teaspoon freshly ground black pepper

STEAMED RICE CAKES
100 g split urad dal (black gram)
60 g rice flour
¼ teaspoon Kashmiri chilli powder
½ teaspoon brown mustard seeds
1 teaspoon sea salt
vegetable oil, for brushing

To make the chutney, heat the ghee in a frying pan and fry the curry leaves, mustard and nigella seeds until they pop and crisp. Remove from the heat and set aside. Blend the coconut, chilli, coriander, tamarind, lime juice, sugar, salt and pepper with a stick blender or small food processor until smooth. Add the fried spices and mix to combine.

To make the steamed rice cakes, rinse the split urad dal then soak it in cold water for 6 hours or overnight. Drain the dal, then blend in a food processor with 100 ml water to form a smooth paste.

Mix the rice flour, chilli, mustard seeds and salt in a bowl then stir in enough water to make a thick batter. Stir the dal paste into the batter, cover bowl with a damp tea towel and leave for 8 hours or until the batter has doubled in volume and the surface has bubbled.

Brush 12 idli moulds (or small cupcake or muffin moulds) with vegetable oil and fill with batter. Steam, covered, over simmering water for 15 minutes until firm and puffed.

Remove from the steamer and allow to cool for a couple of minutes before removing the cakes from their moulds. Serve hot. They can be reheated gently in the steamer when ready to serve.

To make the masala, heat the oil in a pan, add the mustard seeds, and as they begin to pop, add the curry leaves and urad dal. Cook, stirring, for a few minutes until the dal is golden, then add the onion and a little salt and cook, stirring occasionally, until the onions are brown. Remove half the onions and keep to one side.

To the remaining onions in the pan, add the tomato paste, chilli powder, ground fennel, coriander and turmeric and mix well. Add the tamarind liquid, bring to the boil and simmer for 10 minutes. Add the fried eggplant, cherry tomatoes and reserved onions. Bring back to the boil and simmer gently for 4 minutes. Check the seasoning and add the remaining salt if necessary.

Spoon into serving bowls and garnish with coriander leaves. Serve with the steamed rice cakes and coconut chutney.

SERVES 4

SABU'S KERALA DUCK

Sabu was the cook on our rice barge when we cruised the backwaters of Kerala, in an area known as Kuttanad. I made a special request for duck one day and he cooked it in his home style, typically Malayalam, with lingering spicy flavours. It's a taste memory that has stayed with me ever since. This is his version of Keralan Kuttanad duck. Thank you, Sabu!

80 ml coconut oil
4 duck marylands (leg and thigh portions), cut into chunks
1 tablespoon finely chopped ginger
12 cloves garlic, crushed
20 small red shallots, chopped
4 small green chillies, sliced
1 tablespoon shredded fresh turmeric
1 tablespoon ground coriander
2 teaspoons freshly ground black pepper
1 tablespoon ground turmeric
400 g tin peeled tomatoes, roughly chopped
400 ml coconut milk
55 g raw cashews, soaked for 30 minutes then drained
2 teaspoons ground cumin
1 tablespoon sea salt
100 ml coconut cream
3 tablespoons coriander leaves

Heat the coconut oil and fry the duck pieces until browned. Remove from the pan, then add the ginger and garlic and fry until just beginning to colour. Add the shallots and fry until softened then toss in the chilli. Stir in the spices and cook for a minute until aromatic. Add the tomatoes and their juices and the coconut milk and bring to simmering point. Add the duck pieces, cover with a lid and braise slowly over gentle heat for about an hour until the duck is softened and cooked. Check occasionally, and if it looks a little dry add a splash of water.

Blend or pound the soaked cashews to make a paste. Add the cashew paste and cumin to the pan and cook for 5 minutes. Season to taste with salt and when ready to serve, remove from the heat and stir in the coconut cream and coriander leaves. Serve with steamed rice.

SERVES 4

TEA-BRAISED CHICKEN WITH TAMARIND MUSHROOMS

I love the flavour that the tea imparts into the chicken when prepared this way. It's terrific shredded into a salad or added to an aromatic broth or soup, like black pepper chicken tea (see page 94). When I first started preparing this dish, I used Karaikkuai tea with its rich, fruity aromatics and lingering sweetness. For a more smoky flavour, I would use Lapsang Souchong. After visiting the highland tea plantations of Sri Lanka and tasting the warmth and spiciness of cinnamon tea, I converted to using that when poaching chicken in this manner. The flavours pay homage to the two main products of Sri Lanka – tea and cinnamon – and the tamarind sambol became one of my addictions while I was there, an essential and versatile condiment. I consider it a gift from the Tamils.

1.8 kg organic chicken
2 tablespoons ghee
2 cloves garlic, minced
2 teaspoons finely shredded ginger
2 red shallots, finely sliced
2 tablespoons fresh cloud-ear fungus, torn into bite-size pieces
8 straw mushrooms, sliced lengthways
8 chestnut mushrooms, stalks trimmed and cut in half
½ punnet enoki mushrooms, stalks trimmed
120 ml Tamarind Dressing (see Essentials)
¼ bunch water spinach

TEA STOCK
¼ cup Dilmah cinnamon tea leaves
1 piece dried tangerine peel
1 star anise
½ teaspoon Sichuan peppercorns
5 cm cinnamon stick, broken in half
3 litres White Chicken Stock (see Essentials)
40 ml light soy sauce
20 ml Shaoxing rice wine
40 ml mirin

TAMARIND COCONUT SAMBOL
3 tablespoons shredded fresh coconut
4 fresh curry leaves
1 teaspoon minced ginger
1 small green chilli, sliced
1 small clove garlic, chopped
pinch of ground turmeric
¼ teaspoon sea salt
65 ml Tamarind Liquid (see Essentials)

To make the tea stock, combine all the ingredients in a large saucepan, bring slowly to the boil and simmer gently for 10 minutes. Add the chicken and weigh it down with a plate or lid so it stays submerged in the stock. Cook for 5 minutes on the lowest setting then turn off the heat and leave the chicken to 'cook' in the hot stock for 1 hour until tender.

Remove the chicken from the stock and brush off any tea leaves that have attached themselves to the skin. Allow to cool for 10 minutes. Joint the bird, remove the meat from the bones and cut into fine slices. Discard the skin and bones.

To prepare the sambol, put all the ingredients except the tamarind liquid in a food processor and blend briefly, just until combined. With the motor running, pour in the tamarind liquid, stopping as soon as the sambol is mixed.

Heat a wok, add the ghee and saute the garlic, ginger and shallots until softened and beginning to colour. Add the cloud-ear fungus and mushrooms and toss over heat for 2 minutes until wilted. Add the tamarind dressing and water spinach leaves and cook for a minute until the leaves have wilted.

Remove from the heat and mix the mushrooms with half the sambol, tossing to combine. Spoon onto plates, arrange the chicken slices on top and finish with a small dollop of sambol. Serve immediately.

SERVES 4

TWICE-COOKED MASALA BEEF

This is my adapted version of a Syrian Christian dish we tasted at a few places throughout Kerala. Ulathiya irachi translates to the dull-sounding name of 'beef fry' – tragic for a dish that is anything but. It gets even better after a couple of days and reheats quite easily. Rather than using a pressure cooker in the traditional manner, I steam the beef first with the spices so it remains more succulent. I know the coconut oil is an extravagance but it really adds to the depth of flavour, so splurge just this once! I have added soft rice noodles and crunchy green beans to round out the meal.

6 cloves garlic, minced
1 tablespoon minced ginger
4 golden shallots, finely diced
3 small green chillies, minced
3 teaspoons sea salt
50 ml coconut cream
500 g beef sirloin, cut into 2 cm strips
50 ml coconut oil
2 spring onion bulbs, finely sliced lengthways
2 tablespoons fresh curry leaves
1 cup shredded fresh coconut
100 g green beans, finely sliced and blanched
160 g fresh rice noodles, softened in boiling water

MASALA SPICE MIX
½ teaspoon fennel seeds
1 star anise
2 cloves
2 teaspoons ground chilli
1 teaspoon ground turmeric
1 tablespoon ground coriander
1 teaspoon ground cinnamon

To make the masala spice mix, grind the fennel seeds, star anise and cloves together, then mix with the remaining spices.

Combine the spice mix with the garlic, ginger, shallots, chilli, salt and coconut cream in a wide bowl. Add the beef and mix until thoroughly coated. Cover and marinate for 20 minutes then place the bowl in a bamboo steamer and steam for 45 minutes.

Remove from the heat, transfer the beef to a wire rack over a tray and allow to cool and dry out for 1 hour at room temperature.

Heat the oil in a wok and fry the spring onion strips for 5–6 minutes until they begin to colour. Add the curry leaves and when they begin to crisp, add the beef and cook over medium heat for 2–3 minutes, tossing the wok to prevent the beef sticking or burning. Add the shredded coconut, beans and noodles and toss gently to combine.

Taste and adjust the seasoning if necessary (you may need a little extra salt), then toss to combine, remove from the heat and serve piled in bowls.

SERVES 4

FRIED TURMERIC FISH WITH BEETROOT YOGHURT RELISH

A vegetable relish has many guises in Kerala and I fell in love with this beetroot version when it was served to us on the houseboat for lunch one day. Having eaten many different versions of pachadi I had to declare this one the best, and it goes particularly well with fish. Use swordfish steaks if you can get any – they work brilliantly when cooked in this manner – otherwise buy thick cutlets of any white fish such as kingfish, sea bass or hapuku.

½ teaspoon ground chilli
1 teaspoon ground turmeric
1 teaspoon freshly ground black pepper
1 tablespoon minced ginger
3 cloves garlic, minced
2 teaspoons minced fresh turmeric
2 teaspoons sea salt
1 tablespoon coconut vinegar
4 × 150 g thick swordfish steaks, cut from the middle of the fish
60 ml vegetable oil
1 punnet swiss chard cress, snipped
1 punnet mustard cress, snipped
2 tablespoons fresh curry leaves, deep-fried until crisp

BEETROOT YOGHURT RELISH
40 ml vegetable oil
1 teaspoon brown mustard seeds
12 fresh curry leaves
400 g beetroots, peeled and sliced into fine julienne strips
3 cloves garlic, minced
2 teaspoons minced ginger
4 red shallots, finely diced
40 ml water
2 teaspoons mustard powder
3 teaspoons sea salt
400 g thick plain (sheep's milk) yoghurt

To make the relish, heat the oil in a pan, add the mustard seeds and as they begin to pop, add the curry leaves and fry for a few seconds. Add the beetroot, garlic, ginger and shallots to the pan and saute for a minute. Pour in the water and cook until the water has been absorbed and the beetroot is soft. Stir in the mustard powder and salt, then remove from the heat and allow to cool. When ready to serve, stir the yoghurt into the cooled beetroot. Taste and adjust the seasoning if necessary.

Combine the ground spices with the ginger, garlic, turmeric, salt and vinegar. Add the fish steaks to the paste, toss until coated then cover and marinate for 20 minutes.

Heat a frying pan over moderate heat, add the oil and fry the fish with its paste for 5 minutes. Flip over and fry the other side for 4 minutes or until cooked, depending on the thickness of the fish. Make sure the heat is not too high or the paste will burn.

Spoon the beetroot relish onto plates, combine the snipped cress leaves and scatter over the relish. Lay the fish on top, season with a little extra sea salt and garnish with fried curry leaves to serve.

SERVES 4

FAIZA'S FISH BIRYANI

Faiza Moosa, one of Kerala's foremost home cooks, led a hands-on workshop in her kitchen one day and this is one of the dishes we prepared for dinner while staying at Ayisha Manzil in Tellicherry – it is typical of the Moplati cuisine of this region.

5 teaspoons ground chilli
1 teaspoon ground turmeric
1 tablespoon sea salt
500 g kingfish, hapuku, bass grouper or hake fillet, cut into 1 cm chunks
125 g ghee
5 green cardamom pods, cracked
5 cloves
2 cinnamon sticks
4 brown onions, finely sliced
1 tablespoon minced ginger
2 cloves garlic, minced
8 small green chillies, minced
1 tablespoon ground coriander
150 ml Fish Stock (see Essentials)
30 ml fresh lime juice, strained
2 tablespoons shredded coriander leaves
1 tablespoon shredded mint leaves
2 tomatoes, peeled, seeded and diced
500 g medium-grain rice, washed until the water runs clear
750 ml boiling water
4 tablespoons Fried Onion Slices (see Essentials)
¼ teaspoon saffron powder
20 ml rosewater
2 tablespoons coriander leaves, extra

FAIZA'S GARAM MASALA
1 teaspoon ground cumin
1 teaspoon ground caraway
1 teaspoon ground mace
1 teaspoon grated nutmeg
1 teaspoon ground allspice
1 teaspoon ground cinnamon
1 teaspoon ground cardamom
1 teaspoon ground cloves

To make the garam masala, mix the spices together until combined and store in an airtight jar.

To prepare the fish, combine half the ground chilli, half the turmeric and half the salt with enough water to make a paste. Add the fish and rub to coat the surfaces. Leave to marinate for 20 minutes. Heat 1 tablespoon ghee in a frying pan and fry the fish for 2 minutes each side, until browned.

In an ovenproof pan (with a lid and handles), heat half the remaining ghee and fry two of the cardamom pods, two cloves, one cinnamon stick and the sliced onion until softened. Add the ginger, garlic and green chilli and saute for 5 minutes. Add the ground coriander, fish stock and remaining ground chilli and turmeric and simmer over moderate heat for 5 minutes.

Add the fried fish, lime juice, shredded coriander, mint leaves, diced tomato and 1 teaspoon of the garam masala. Simmer over gentle heat for a few more minutes until the sauce thickens.

In another pan, heat the remaining ghee, add the remaining cardamom, cloves and cinnamon and stir until fragrant. Add the washed rice and fry for 4 minutes until the grains are coated with ghee. Add the boiling water and the remaining salt and cook for about 15 minutes until the water has been absorbed and the rice is cooked.

Preheat the oven to 150°C. Add 1 teaspoon of the garam masala to the fried onion slices and spread a quarter of these evenly over the top of the fish masala. Mix the saffron into the rosewater.

Spread half the rice on top of the fish masala and sprinkle with saffron rosewater and some more fried onions. Spread the remaining rice on top, sprinkle with more rosewater and half the remaining fried onions. Cover the pan and seal the lid (traditionally done using a basic bread dough made with flour and water) and bake in the oven for 10 minutes.

To serve, spoon the rice onto a large serving plate and lay the fish on top. Garnish with the remaining fried onion slices and scatter with the coriander leaves.

SERVES 8

GRILLED FISH WITH SPICED VEGETABLE MASALA

Inspired by Tamil flavours, this dish is quite straightforward to prepare. I made it for the participants at the inaugural International Writers Festival hosted in Galle in January 2007. Apart from speaking about my spice travels and writing, I was given the once-in-a-lifetime opportunity to cook in the gardens of Lunuganga, Geoffrey Bawa's former residence in Bentota. This vegetable masala was one of several dishes I prepared that day, emulating the Sri Lankan moju. I use fillets from smaller fish – like flathead, spot whiting, garfish, orange roughy, perch or John Dory – for their more delicate texture.

2 tablespoons ghee
1 small green chilli, minced
2 teaspoons curry powder
½ teaspoon sea salt
½ teaspoon freshly ground black pepper
4 × 120 g fish fillets
2 teaspoons chopped coriander leaves
1 teaspoon chopped mint

VEGETABLE MASALA
150 g pumpkin, cut into 1 cm dice
vegetable oil, for drizzling, deep-frying and pan-frying
sea salt and freshly ground black pepper
12 cherry tomatoes, halved
200 g eggplant (aubergine), cut into 1 cm dice
1 small red onion, finely diced
3 cloves garlic, minced
1 teaspoon minced ginger
1 teaspoon curry powder
1 zucchini (courgette), cut into 1 cm dice
1 red capsicum (pepper), roasted and cut into 1 cm dice
20 ml fresh lemon juice, strained
2 tablespoons chopped coriander leaves
2 tablespoons hot mango chutney

Preheat the oven to 175°C. To prepare the vegetable masala, toss the diced pumpkin with 2 tablespoons vegetable oil. Transfer to a baking tray and season lightly with salt and pepper. Bake for 20 minutes until soft. Set aside.

Lay the cherry tomato halves on a baking tray, drizzle lightly with 2 teaspoons of oil and season with salt and pepper. Roast in the oven for 15 minutes until soft and starting to caramelise.

Set aside. The tomatoes and pumpkin can both be cooked at the same time.

Heat the oil in a deep-fryer or large saucepan and fry the diced eggplant in small batches until golden. Drain on paper towel.

Heat 3 tablespoons vegetable oil in a frying pan and saute the onion until softened, then add the garlic and ginger. Saute for another 3–4 minutes until starting to colour. Add the curry powder and stir until combined. Add the diced zucchini and cook over gentle heat for about 5 minutes, until the zucchini is soft.

In a large bowl, mix together the zucchini, eggplant, pumpkin, tomatoes and capsicum. Add the lemon juice, chopped coriander and mango chutney and toss gently to combine.

To cook the fish, melt the ghee in a frying pan and add the chilli as it starts to sizzle. Stir in the curry powder, salt and pepper. Add the fish fillets and fry over moderate heat for 2–3 minutes, then flip over and fry the other side for 2 minutes. Add the chopped coriander and mint and swirl the pan to coat the fish.

Spoon the vegetable masala onto plates, arrange the fish on top and drizzle with the pan juices.

SERVES 4

SPICED RICE PUDDING WITH GRILLED APRICOTS

The comfort factor of creamed rice is found in many different cuisines; this one honours the Indian kheer. Many south Indian desserts begin with rice, vermicelli or tapioca (as in the classic payasam) cooked with milk and spices. If apricots are not in season then use mango or papaya as the fruit component, but don't cook them. I like to use fresh tangy curd made with buffalo milk as the extra richness works brilliantly with the rice.

6 apricots, cut in half and stones removed
2 tablespoons brown sugar
2 tablespoons fresh buffalo curd or thick plain yoghurt

CINNAMON WAFERS
50 g unsalted butter
45 ml glucose
90 g castor sugar
45 g plain flour
1 teaspoon ground cinnamon

RICE PUDDING
40 g unsalted butter
2 cups short-grain rice, soaked in cold water for 30 minutes, washed and drained
2 litres milk
2 vanilla beans, split lengthways
300 g castor sugar
125 ml pouring (35%) cream
½ teaspoon ground mace
40 ml Lime Syrup (see Essentials)

To make the wafers, melt the butter and glucose in a bowl over a pan of simmering water. Mix the sugar, flour and cinnamon in a separate bowl, then pour in the melted butter and glucose and stir to incorporate. Allow to cool completely.

Preheat the oven to 180°C and line two baking trays with baking paper. Roll the mixture into small balls, using a teaspoonful for each. Place two balls at a time on the baking tray, well spaced, and bake for 5 minutes or until caramel-coloured. Remove the tray from the oven and allow the biscuits to cool for 15–20 seconds.

While still warm and pliable, cut each wafer into a round using a pastry cutter. Allow the wafers to cool and firm on the tray, then transfer them to an airtight container until ready to use. Repeat the process until you have four wafers.

To make the rice pudding, melt the butter in a frying pan and fry the rice briefly until well coated in the butter. Add the milk, vanilla and sugar and cook over low heat until the rice absorbs the liquid. Stir in the cream and mace, and discard the vanilla beans. Spoon into serving glasses or bowls, then spoon on the lime syrup.

Lay the apricots, cut-side up, on a baking tray and sprinkle liberally with sugar. Cook under a hot grill until the sugar has caramelised and the apricots have softened.

Arrange three apricot halves over each serving of rice, add buffalo curd and sit a wafer across the top. Serve while the rice and fruit are warm.

SERVES 4

BANANA PANCAKES WITH COCONUT SORBET AND JAGGERY CARAMEL

I am a sucker for a decent pancake, and Sri Lanka and south India deliver by the spadeful with their myriad dosas – savoury and sweet. I make these pancakes like little pikelets so I can stack them before adding the coconut sorbet and caramel. There is not much that does not include some type of coconut product from these parts. We travelled through Kerala during peak banana season, so it was impossible to avoid them as well. We tasted several different varieties, from the tiny sugar bananas full of juicy sweetness, to deep yellow and red-skinned ones with a firmer flesh, each with specific uses in cooking. I try to find these at home as they are far superior to the floury flavourless ones often available in our market.

2 tablespoons shredded fresh coconut

COCONUT SORBET
600 ml coconut milk
150 ml water
100 g castor sugar
25 g glucose
150 ml Boiron coconut puree
20 ml fresh lime juice, strained

JAGGERY CARAMEL
160 g jaggery, shaved
40 ml water
150 ml coconut cream
40 g unsalted butter
2 teaspoons fresh lime juice, strained

BANANA PANCAKES
100 g rice flour
60 g plain flour
½ teaspoon baking powder
½ teaspoon salt
150 g sugar bananas, mashed
25 g castor sugar
30 g ghee, melted
½ teaspoon ground cardamom
60 ml water
vegetable oil, for brushing

To make the coconut sorbet, bring the coconut milk and water to simmering point in a pan. Add the sugar and glucose and stir until dissolved. Remove from the heat and stir in the coconut puree and lime juice. Churn in an ice-cream machine until firm, and freeze until ready to serve.

To make the caramel, heat the jaggery and water in a pan until caramelised, then add the coconut cream and cook over gentle heat until thickened. Add the butter and stir until combined. Remove from the heat and stir in the lime juice. Set aside until ready to serve.

To make the pancakes, sift both the flours, the baking powder and salt into a bowl. Mix the mashed bananas with the sugar, ghee and cardamom, then stir into the flour. Add the water and mix until it forms a batter (add a little more water if the batter is too thick).

Heat a non-stick frying pan and brush with oil. Drop spoonfuls of batter into the pan to make 6 cm rounds, pressing the centres slightly to flatten so the pancakes are not too thick and cook evenly. Cook over moderate heat for 4–5 minutes until brown, then flip over and cook the other side for 3 minutes until cooked through.

Remove the pancakes from the pan, stack on top of each other and cover with a cloth. Repeat the process until all the pancakes are made (I allow three per serve).

Pile three pancakes on top of each other, layering with shredded coconut and a little caramel sauce as you go. Scoop the coconut sorbet into a ball and sit on top of the pancake stack, spoon a little caramel sauce around the stack and serve immediately.

SERVES 4

WATERMELON SHERBET

This refreshing sherbet is fabulous to have on hand during summer as a light dessert or a zingy addition to a vodka cocktail. As a dessert, I like to serve it in glasses with mangosteen segments, champagne melon and watermelon balls.

1.1 litres fresh watermelon juice (blended from chopped fruit)
50 ml fresh lime juice, strained
50 ml Caribbean golden rum
250 ml Sugar Syrup (see Essentials)

Mix the ingredients together in a bowl until combined. Pour into a shallow tray and freeze for 6 hours or overnight. Don't let it sit in the freezer for too long or it will become too icy.

To serve, flake the sherbet with a fork into serving glasses or over fresh melon balls.

SERVES 6–8

ROASTED COCONUT CARAMEL WITH PAPAYA

After tasting different versions of the Sri Lankan classic, wattalappam, I reworked the rich coconut and caramel flavours into this elegant dessert. In keeping with tradition, treacle made from the kittul palm is ideal to splash over before serving but if you cannot find it, use another treacle product or even a little maple syrup.

1 papaya
2 teaspoons fresh lime juice, strained
2 limes
2 tablespoons treacle
2 tablespoons shredded fresh coconut

COCONUT CARAMELS
250 g castor sugar
50 ml water
320 ml pouring (35%) cream
25 g shredded fresh coconut, roasted
45 g coconut palm sugar, shaved
1 whole egg
4 egg yolks
60 ml coconut liqueur

To make the coconut caramels, preheat the oven to 145°C (not fan-forced). Bring the sugar and water to boiling point in a saucepan and cook over high heat, without stirring, until it turns a caramel colour. Pour the hot caramel into six 150 ml dariole moulds, swirling each one so that the entire inside surface is coated with a thin layer of caramel. Pour out the excess.

Heat the cream, roasted coconut and coconut sugar and simmer, stirring, over gentle heat until the sugar has dissolved. Place the egg and yolks in a bowl and whisk until pale, then stir in the coconut liqueur. Slowly pour in the hot cream, stirring to combine. Pass the custard through a fine mesh sieve into a jug, then pour the hot custard into the caramel-lined moulds until full.

Stand the custards in a baking dish, then pour enough boiling water into the dish to come two-thirds up the sides of the moulds. Place the dish in the oven and cook the custards for 45 minutes or until just set. Turn the dish around halfway through cooking to ensure an even result. Remove the cooked caramel creams from the water bath and allow to cool. Refrigerate for 4 hours before serving.

Peel the papaya, slice into fine rounds and remove the seeds. For each serve, lay a couple of slices of papaya on top of each other in the centre of a plate and drizzle with lime juice. Fill in the centre hole with smaller pieces of papaya to make an even surface. Peel and segment the limes.

Dip the caramel custard moulds into hot water to loosen then turn out each custard so it sits on top of the papaya, pouring any excess caramel around. Spoon a little treacle over each custard and surround with lime segments. Top with shredded coconut and serve.

SERVES 6

HOT TAMALES **MEXICO**

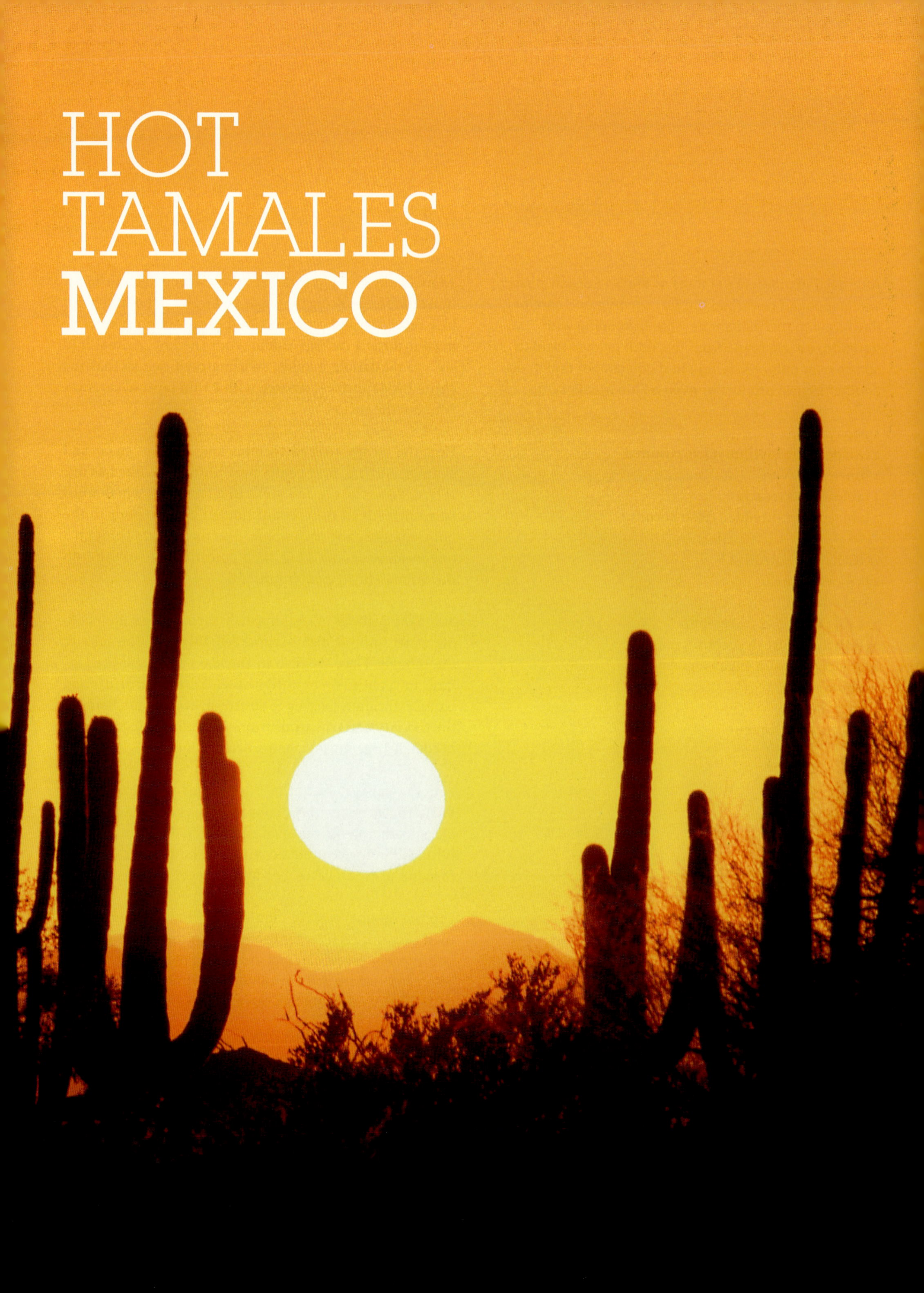

The inspiration to visit Mexico came from our dear friend Barbara Alexander, who used to work with us in the early days of Paramount and is now the director of the Napa Valley Cooking School in California. We stayed with Barbie, her husband Adam (also a chef) and their divine little girl Ava in the summer of 2005, when they had recently returned from a working visit to Ensenada on the Baja Peninsula, and we feasted on fish tacos and ceviche (citrus-marinated seafood). Meeting Luis, one of Barbie's Mexican students, sealed our decision to visit, and we jetted off to Mexico that Christmas. The minute we got off the plane in Puerto Vallarta, on Mexico's Pacific Coast, we felt a welcome surge of warm, tropical air scented with jasmine and frangipani. The landscape of banana and coconut trees and the easy-going atmosphere reminded me of Asia in many ways, and I felt instantly at home.

As with any resort town that relies on the tourist dollar for its income, Puerto Vallarta has the good, the bad and the just plain ugly. Our driver took us past the Hotel Zone, as it is known: hideous rows of condominiums and hotels completely lacking in style, to be avoided at all costs. Things improved when we drove through the charming Viejo Vallarta (old town), with its cobblestone streets, and got better still when we arrived at the quieter southern side of town.

We had booked a private casa (house) that was nestled into the hillside at Alta Vista, overlooking Playa de los Muertos, and received a warm welcome from Susan, the owner. Our little patch of paradise was constructed in the style of a palapa, a pitch-roofed pavilion made of beams lashed together with rope and thatched with thick layers of palm fronds, perfect for the tropical climate. We had so much space to luxuriate in, plus a deck for being lounge lizards, a plunge pool to cool down in and the best view imaginable. The balmy air was heaven – even in winter the temperature remains around 25°C – and we instantly knew we had made the right decision in coming. The stress of the long journey evaporated and we headed out to do some exploring.

We couldn't wait to experience Christmas Mexican-style, without the usual constraints of tradition and family expectations. We had been told of a street where people gather to celebrate on Christmas Eve. When we found the street, we were soon encouraged to join in the ritual of hitting brightly coloured pinatas with a long stick. Made from papier mache moulded into hollow birds or animals, the pinatas are full of candy. When it came to the adults' turn, they were blindfolded. Of course, Margie and I had a go and laughed hysterically as we waved the stick around in the air, making absolute idiots of ourselves and getting completely covered in kids, their hands everywhere as the bloody thing finally broke open and spilled its load of candy. I love celebratory gatherings like these that bring communities together. In Mexico, each region has its own traditions: the southern city of Oaxaca celebrates la noche de rababos (the night of the radishes), two days before Christmas, when people gather to carve large radishes which are then judged in the main square.

The south-side area of Puerto Vallarta, which incorporates Malecon, Olas Altas, Alta Vista and Playa de los Muertos, feels a bit like Sydney's Oxford Street goes to the beach, with its recognised gay beach in front of Calle Malecon. The long boardwalk along the shoreline offers a veritable feast for the eyes and we felt right at home promenading up and down each day. Playa de los Muertos has a bustling, international atmosphere and locals mingle with travellers from just about everywhere. The town beaches are not renowned for super-clean water, though, and we found that the best places for swimming were a little out of the town. Day boats depart from the town pier and can drop you off at Yelapa, on the southern end of Banderas Bay, a peaceful fishing village that can only be reached by boat. We were advised to take basic supplies with us as the only food available at the beach is mediocre and tourist-orientated, but the water was pristine and clear and fantastic for swimming. We bought bags of totopos (corn chips) to go with some guacamole I had made, spiked with diced tomatillo, coriander and green serrano chilli. I love the tangy flavour and crisp texture of green tomatillos – they look like little green tomatoes but grow like cape gooseberries, with papery caps that cover the fruit. Who needs to eat much during a day at the beach anyway?

The other option is to hire a jeep or scooter and head north about 50 kilometres along the coast to the Punta de Mita peninsula, where Banderas Bay meets the Pacific Ocean (I suggest you avert your eyes as you pass through the seriously ugly condo time-share development of Nuevo Vallarta). Either stop off at some of the secluded beaches along the way or venture a little further north to the small village of Sayulita, popular with surfies and full of rustic charm. The coastal road south to Manzanillo follows the rugged Costa Alegre, with exclusive, eco-friendly resorts that provide total privacy and tranquillity. This is Mexico unspoilt!

One day, Susan arranged a private charter of a small boat and we ventured out in search of humpback whales – our guide was a local boy who had been brought up by these waters, with the whales as playmates. The whales come in close to shore during their mating season in winter, and God was on our side that day: a large pod of whales breached, twisted and back-flipped no more than 20 metres from our boat, with several baby whales mimicking the adults. They put on the best show I have ever seen, and we all sat there transfixed by their immense beauty and grace.

Puerto Vallarta is in the state of Jalisco, the home of tequila, so it seemed only natural that we try some at its source. Not a difficult task, since tequila is as common as water in these parts – every bar, cafe and restaurant serves it. Produced from the blue agave plant, the sap of which is distilled and aged to produce different grades of tequila. The most common is blanco, white tequila bottled straight from the distillery without any barrel age, and this is generally used for mixed drinks and cocktails. Reposado is golden and has been aged for three to twelve months in oak barrels before being bottled. Smooth and mellow, with a richer and more pronounced flavour, it can be drunk neat with a squeeze of lime and salt as a chaser, or used to make a classic margarita. Anejo (meaning aged) is blanco that has been left to age in barrels for anything from one to ten years; this deep amber liquor should only ever be served neat. Its refinement and complexity of flavour are reminiscent of a fine single malt. It soon became obvious that I would have to buy some to take home, especially when I discovered there are many premium brands that don't get sold outside the country – these are definitely the ones to look out for. No matter where I am at the time, a shot of tequila always takes me straight back to that day.

Flying into Mexico City, perched 5000 metres above sea level between the Pacific and Gulf coasts, was a startling contrast to the laid-back beach scene. The city is pulsating, dynamic and cosmopolitan in everything, particularly

SLEEPING AND EATING IN PUERTO VALLARTA

CASA DE LOS ARCOS
Calle las Hortencias 168, Colonia Alta Vista, Puerto Vallarta
Tel +52 322 222 5990
www.casadelosarcos.com
A gorgeous private property on the mountainside overlooking the ocean with various spaces for rent – all are generous in size, with kitchen and living areas. Susan (the owner) is most helpful, with impressive local knowledge.

CASA VENTANA
Puerto Vallarta
www.casaventana.com
A spacious private villa in the Alta Vista district with fabulous outdoor decks overlooking the town and beach below.

CAFE EL REPOLLO ROJO (THE RED CABBAGE)
Calle Rivera del Rio 204, Puerto Vallarta
Tel +52 332 223 0411
This out-of-the-way gem celebrates Mexico's unique culinary heritage, including Frida Kahlo's fiesta menus, in an eclectic and authentically Mexican style – all colour and madness. Chiles en nogada is a signature dish: large fresh poblano chillies are roasted then stuffed with spiced ground pork and vegetables before being covered with a creamy walnut sauce and served cold. Owner Lola Bravo works the room, all four foot nothing of her! This is a cash-only place.

CAFE DE OLLA
Calle Basillo Badillo 168 A (at Olas Altas), Puerto Vallarta
Tel +52 332 223 1626
Terrific local food served in a simple, rustic style, with no hint of sanitised Tex-Mex. Salsa music adds to the lively atmosphere. No bookings or credit cards – just turn up and wait for a table.

LA PALAPA
Calle Pulpito 103 (at the Emperador Hotel), Playa de los Muertos, Puerto Vallarta
Tel +52 332 222 5225
Right on the beachfront, the tropical, laid-back ambience and friendly service here make for a relaxing experience. We came here daily for our hit of espresso, and again at sunset for a margarita. For dinner there are candlelit tables set in the sand. One word of advice: stick with a light salad – the servings are huge!

VISTA GRILL
Pulpito 377, Colonia, Alta Vista, Puerto Vallarta
Tel +52 332 222 3570
www.vistagrill.com
One evening we had dinner on the outdoor terrace at Vista Grill, and enjoyed unparalleled views of the city and coastline. Seafood plays a starring role on the menu, and I was particularly inspired by a crab and cucumber cannelloni.

its mix of people. Some of the characters on the street reminded us of the fabled Zorro adventures, or the Mexican Wild West, with cowboys strutting about in their large sombreros, colourful ponchos and moustaches to match. On the down side, the city has some of the most shocking air pollution in the world – air as thick as fog blankets the city – and some of the outskirts are notorious for their impoverished living conditions.

To get an overview of this sprawling metropolis, Margie and I jumped on the open-roofed, double-decker Touribus that takes nearly four hours to complete its circuit, weaving its way through the inner zones of the city, taking in all the important sites in the historic centre and following part of Avenida Insurgentes – at 42 kilometres, the longest street in the world. After that, we felt more confident about walking around, even braving the subway metro the next day. Directions are very easy to follow and it saves the hassle of sitting in heavy traffic, especially in the congested streets around the historic centre and Zocalo, the great square that was the heart of the ancient city. We also found it quite easy to hail the local taxis (green and white VW beetles), and met so many characters along the way. The taxi drivers were highly amusing; we communicated in very broken Spanglish and spent much of our journeys laughing. One 80-year-old driver sat almost sideways in his seat, eyeballing other drivers if they got too close while he swerved all over the place and drove at breakneck speed in second gear all the way. Lucky we're not easily scared!

We stuck to the inner-city districts, where prominent landmarks helped us to navigate; beyond that, endless look-alike suburbs stretched into the distance. A walk along fashionable Michoacan Avenue took us past small neighbourhood bistros, local bars and cafes, gelato bars and some interesting design shops, on the way to the food vendors at nearby Chapultepec Park. We also explored the Zona Rosa (pink zone, so named for its liberal attitude and international ambience) and Polanco, the gentrified establishment quarter, full of five-star hotels, designer-label shops and expensive restaurants. We found the southern districts of Coyoacan and San Angel very appealing – true local neighbourhoods with no tourist hotels.

The artistic life of the city has been heavily influenced by the talent of Frida Kahlo and the public murals of Diego Rivera, with whom she shared a tumultuous relationship. I had seen an exhibition of Kahlo's work at the Tate Modern in London, and been mesmerised by her spectacular self-portraits and their depiction of such raw beauty and intense emotion. I felt the connection again when we visited the Casa Azul or blue house (now a museum) in Coyoacan, where she spent much of her life, and was utterly captivated by the blaze of colour and the strength of her presence. I was even more impressed when I found out that she applied the same exacting attention to detail when it came to food. Proudly Mexican, she hosted lavish feasts in her house; the daily ritual of the table was a constant celebration. Many of her recipes have been recorded and published, providing a terrific insight into the culinary psyche of the country, as seen through the eyes of this unique woman. Interestingly, most of the chefs in Mexico seem to be women, which is a cause for celebration in itself when too many people still consider women to be cooks and men professional chefs.

Exploring further afield, an hour's drive north of the city took us to the pre-Colombian ruins of Teotihuacan, where we were taken aback by the scale of the temple pyramids. The Pyramid of the Sun is as large as those in Egypt, but is built quite differently, ascending in stepped stages. We climbed the Pyramid of the Moon and were rewarded with the most beautiful view of this ancient city that was once home to nearly 200,000 people.

Back in town, we took advantage of the capital city's array of restaurants that specialise in regional cooking, sampling dishes from the European-influenced cuisine of the Yucatan Peninsula; the state of Veracruz, on the Gulf of Mexico and famous for its seafood; and the earthy cuisine of Oaxaca, with its rich mole sauces.

Part of the aim of our visit had been to experience and taste the real heart of Mexican regional cooking, to come to the birthplace of the chilli and worship its diversity. As Lola Bravo, owner of Puerto Vallarta's Cafe el Repollo Rojo, explains: 'Mexico was not an unsophisticated culture

STAYING IN MEXICO CITY

CONDESA HOTEL
Avenida Veracruz 102 (at Parque Espana),
Colonia Condesa, Mexico City
Tel +52 55 5241 2600
www.condesadf.com
A hip hotel in one of the coolest districts of the city, with terrific restaurants, cafes and bars within easy walking distance.

which the Europeans needed to civilise when they arrived in the early 1500s. The Mayan civilisation at its peak had been highly developed, as was the empire of the Aztecs when the Spanish first encountered it. Music, theatre, commerce, art and religion were well advanced in these cultures. Not the least of those elements was their food. The imperial Aztec table was characterised by advanced preparation techniques and a sophisticated blending of ingredients resulting in imaginative dishes . . . While corn, beans and chillies have continued to be fundamental foods, the rich native heritage and external influences have also been vastly elaborated upon with unique Mexican style and flavour, evolving into a most distinctive gastronomic tradition.'

Mexican street food all seems to start with the soft tortilla, which is made with cornmeal or wheat flour, depending on the region, and then stuffed with roasted pork, chicken or fried fish, vegetables, fried onion and salsa. I decided the best thing to do was to eat my way through the entire repertoire to experience the subtleties of each of these flatbreads. We watched tortillas being made at one of the tortillerias in Mexico City, and the result was not unlike a soft pancake. Quesadillas are flour tortillas that are folded in half, filled with any number of things (not just cheese), then fried. The ones we tasted were filled with minced fish, pork or zucchini blossom; only once did we have them with the local panela cheese, made from goat's milk. Taquitos are soft tortillas wrapped around chunks of grilled chicken (we certainly ate our fair share of those!). Enchiladas are soft tortillas stuffed with minced meat or cheese which are rolled cannelloni-style, then smothered with a red or green chilli salsa and baked in the oven. Tacos are soft tortillas that have been filled and rolled, then grilled or fried on a flat grill – a popular snack food, these are available at the taquerias you find on just about every street corner. Gorditas are tortillas that had been fried then filled with pork and sausage and topped with cheese and shredded lettuce – they look more like the tacos we are familiar with in the West. And a dorado is a stuffed, deep-fried taco, while tostadas are flat deep-fried tortillas topped with salsa or fried minced meat. Empanadas are pastry turnovers stuffed with savoury meat or diced vegetables; they are then either baked or fried and can vary in size from small ravioli-style to large family-sized gallega. Tamales are another key element of Mexico's cuisine: masa (cornmeal dough) is moulded around a filling of chicken, meat, fish or cheese then wrapped in fresh corn husks or banana leaves before being steamed, roasted or fried. Although the outsized sheets of chicharrones (fried pig skin) looked amazing hanging in bags from the vendors' carts, my favourite street snack was a bag of hot churros coated in cinnamon sugar.

Mexicans love a fiesta, and the food is as essential to these events as the people and the music. A typical home-style banquet would start with botanas (snacks), followed by totopos (fried tortilla pieces, or corn chips) with a salsa

EATING IN MEXICO CITY

LOS ALMENDROS
Campos Eliseos 164, Colonia Polanco, Mexico City
Tel +52 55 5531 6646
This restaurant specialises in the regional food of the Yucatan Peninsula. The waiters are charming, helpful and knowledgeable.

LOS GIRASOLES
Plaza Manuel Tolsa (next to the National Art Museum), Calle Tacuba 8, Mexico City
Tel +52 55 5510 0630
True to its name, the restaurant building is painted with sunflowers – you can't miss it. The menu showcases regional specialties, a great way to sample all of Mexico in one place. They also use some indigenous ingredients from pre-Hispanic times, such as ant roe, maguey worms from the cactus plant, grasshoppers (usually fried until crisp and served with lime and dried chilli powder), and the variety of mole sauces that originate from Oaxaca.

AGUILA Y SOL
Avenida Moliere 42, Colonia Polanco, Mexico City
Tel +52 55 5281 8354
Well-known chef Marta Ortiz creates magic with her traditional food given a modern twist – Nuevo Cocina Mexican. Each dish is small, refined and delicate. Start with agua de Jamaica, a drink made with dried hibiscus petals.

CAFE DE TACUBA
Calle Tacuba 28 (at Allende), Colonia Centro, Mexico City
Tel +52 55 5518 4950
You can't book here, so just turn up to this age-old institution in the downtown area – a converted convent – and put your name on the list (the wait is never very long). The menu features well-known local favourites, including authentic tamales, and the room is stunning. The waiters' outfits are a particular treat and will take you back in time.

or two, and spiced peanuts. Antojitos (entrees) are always centred around loads of fresh tortillas in myriad forms. There seems to be a never-ending supply of the dishes as the table is always replenished. The main dish might be roast pork or whole fish skewered on long sticks, grilled over charcoal and served with lime.

It was fascinating to discover just how complex, subtle, refined and imaginative real Mexican food is – nothing like the inept imitations and bastardised Tex-Mex dished up in restaurants around the world. Originating from the imperial tables of the Aztec kings, mole is the national dish. Markets and shops display colourful mole pastes shaped into mounds in large enamel bowls, and they are sold by weight. The pastes range from fairly simple through to complex blends that can have up to a hundred ingredients, a great example of the fusion of native Indian and introduced Spanish ingredients. The moles of Oaxaca are spectacular, from negro (black) – so dark and rich on the palate – to lighter green and yellow versions. My favourite is puebla (or poblano), where bitter chocolate is added to a chilli paste made with spices, sesame seeds and mild poblano chillies, with some versions adding almonds.

Chillies are perhaps Mexico's defining ingredient and there are up to a hundred varieties available. The chillies of Mexico and South America are prized for their flavour rather than their heat, and regional dishes and salsas often call for specific chillies (or chiles, in American-speak) because their flavour and level of heat are instrumental in achieving the desired result. At the markets, chillies are sold according to their grade. The hottest is the small bell-shaped habanero from Yucatan – used sparingly, this type of chilli is superb with seafood, has a distinct fruitiness and gives a great kick to anything pickled or spiced. At the other end of the scale, the mild poblanos are large, fleshy and green and are used for stuffing (chillies rellenos). The mild, long, fleshy red or green Anaheims are great finely sliced and added to salads, as are serranos, which are similar to Asian bird's-eye chillies. I love using tabasco chillies, named after the southern Mexican state of Tabasco (although the sauce of the same name is produced in Louisiana). About the same size as serrano chillies, they can be yellow, orange or red, and have a more intense heat. Just to complicate things, dried chillies are known by different names: jalapenos become chipotles when smoked and dried; ancho and mulato are both dried versions of the poblano; and pasados are New Mexico or Anaheim red chillies that have been roasted and dried, giving them a sweet, liquorice-like flavour. Dried cascabels are round and rattle when shaken.

I returned home with bags of dried mora rojo, another dried jalapeno similar to the chipotle. Their soft flesh, smoky flavour and gentle heat are wonderful with oven-dried tomatoes and root vegetables. And I grabbed a bag of pasilla, the dried chilaca chilli, also known as chilli negro because of its black colour. It's essential in mole preparations, but I have also used it in chilli pastes, and ground it after roasting to stir through sauces to lend an elusive quality to the flavour. I also bought some Brazilian malagueta, which look the same as Thai bird's-eye chillies, with the same small bullet shape, and with an equally intense searing heat – fantastic in a tomato sauce.

Annatto seeds are crushed to make achiote paste, which gives a lovely red colour to sauces; mixed with chilli, it becomes recado, a spicy Yucatan marinade. I was equally intrigued by romeritos, a stringy-looking green vegetable that tasted like spinach – a centrepiece on the Christmas table, we had it cooked with potato and garlic, and also with sliced nopales (cactus pads) that tasted rather like asparagus.

Given Mexico's extensive coastline, fringing the Pacific Ocean and the Gulf of Mexico, a vast range of seafood is available: everything from swordfish and marlin to snook, tuna and shrimps, red snapper and striped sea bass. I loved the small freshwater shrimps called barbon, great as ceviche, and the even smaller saltwater shrimps known as camarones. Simply cooked, with heaps of minced garlic and chilli and a squeeze of lime, these became my holiday version of garlic prawns. Another discovery was agua de Jamaica, a refreshing drink made by infusing water with dried Jamaica flowers – also known as roselle, these are a species of hibiscus. I took a large bag home to experiment with, using them in sweet syrups to serve with sliced fruit during summer; I also ground the dried blossoms with garlic and oil to make a deliciously different salad dressing.

There is much to learn (and taste) to fully appreciate this amazing culture. Like any cuisine of note, the astute use of chilli as a spicy flavouring is of paramount importance when cooking. Mexican cuisine is a blend of indigenous Indian, Mayan and Spanish dishes; influenced by its close neighbours, it has distinct regional variations. The food today offers multi-faceted flavours and textures that have been inherited from the imperial Aztec table, where the sophistication and abundance of dishes rivalled what was offered to the Chinese emperors at a similar point in history. Here is a country that has shared so many of its indigenous ingredients with the world: tomatoes, tomatillos, corn, avocados, jicama, chillies; pinto, lima, kidney and black beans; vanilla, allspice and the all-important cacao beans that would become the basis for chocolate production. This changed the face of European culinary tradition forever and, with the spread of trade, influenced Asia as well. In return, Mexican cuisine absorbed ingredients from Europe and Asia, such as garlic, pomegranates, sugar cane, ginger, bananas and coconuts.

During our short visit we discovered just how ingenious and inventive the Mexicans are, and found ourselves drawn to their warm and inviting spirit. We'll definitely be back; there's so much still to do. I need to visit Oaxaca to taste all seven versions of mole, and to find out more about the acceptance of muxe (men who dress and behave as women) as a third gender among the Zapotec, the indigenous people of that state. I want to sample the abundant seafood and delicious ceviche of Veracruz, and to experience its Caribbean style. On the Baja Peninsula, Ensenada is on my list, for authentic fish tacos and to sample the local wines, reputedly the best in Mexico. And who could resist the lure of Acapulco, a place to laze in the sun and remember the Hollywood of the past? Then there's the Yucatan Peninsula, with its Mayan ruins, where I could try authentic recado and eat yet more tamales. The Yucatan is also home to the habanero, the hottest chilli of the lot – a large, thriving habanero plant in my garden at home serves as a constant reminder of what I love about Mexico. As famed Mexican author Laura Esquivel writes, 'chilli runs in our veins'. Maybe that's the attraction? Or perhaps I just want to have another bash at the pinatas with the kids.

CHICKEN LIME SOUP

This broth is a classic of the Yucatan Peninsula, which juts out into the Caribbean Sea and is home to the hotter-than-hot habanero chilli. The soup is so clean in taste, while the vegetables and silken chicken offer textural contrast. It is traditionally served with totopos (natural flavoured corn chips) broken over the top of the soup, and is surprisingly refreshing in warmer weather.

1 cup fresh corn kernels (from 2 corn cobs)
1 habanero chilli, finely sliced
1 stick celery, finely sliced
2 tablespoons chopped chives
3 tablespoons shredded coriander leaves
2 tablespoons diced red capsicum (pepper)
2 tablespoons diced yellow capsicum (pepper)
2 tablespoons finely diced cucumber

SOUP
2 litres White Chicken Stock (see Essentials)
5 tomatoes, roasted
1 head garlic, roasted
2 coriander roots, chopped
2 habanero chillies, sliced
5 slices ginger
2 green onions, sliced
2 sticks celery
½ small fennel bulb
2 teaspoons black peppercorns
2 fresh bay leaves
500 g organic chicken thigh fillets
100 ml fresh lime juice, strained
1 tablespoon sea salt
1 teaspoon freshly ground black pepper

To make the soup, pour the stock into a large saucepan and add the tomatoes, garlic, coriander root, chilli, ginger, green onion, celery, fennel bulb, peppercorns and bay leaves. Bring slowly to boil over low heat, allowing the flavours to infuse.

When simmering, add the chicken thigh fillets and leave over very low heat for 5 minutes, then turn off the heat and allow the chicken to slowly cook in the stock for another 20 minutes. Remove the chicken from the stock and set aside until cool enough to handle.

Return the stock to the boil, then reduce the heat and simmer for 15 minutes. Pass through a fine mesh sieve, discard the solids and season the soup with lime juice, salt and pepper to taste, making sure the flavours are balanced.

Shred the chicken meat with your fingers and divide among serving bowls. Add the remaining raw ingredients to the bowls, then ladle on the hot soup to serve.

SERVES 4

PICKLED COCONUT PRAWN COCKTAIL

I first made this cocktail for a lunch I cooked at Palm Cove in northern Queensland to showcase the quintessential tropical flavours of coconut, lime and chilli. I also wanted to pay tribute to the Latin American art of ceviche (pickling raw seafood in a slightly acidic marinade before serving). I prefer the soft-textured flesh of the tropical banana prawns for this cocktail, but red-claw yabbies, marron or pearl perch fillet could also be used.

1 kg raw banana or tiger prawns, shelled and deveined
125 ml coconut milk
25 ml coconut vinegar
50 ml fresh lime juice, strained
½ green jalapeno chilli, sliced
2 teaspoons sea salt
1 teaspoon castor sugar
1 teaspoon chopped ginger
3 red shallots, finely diced
10 yellow pear (or grape) tomatoes, sliced
3 tablespoons coriander leaves, chopped

Cut the prawn meat into thin slices on the diagonal.

Puree the coconut milk, vinegar, lime juice, chilli, salt, sugar and ginger in a blender. Pour the coconut mix over the prawn meat in a bowl and stir to combine. Sit the bowl over another bowl of ice and allow to pickle for 2 hours before serving.

To serve, stir the shallots, tomato slices and coriander through the prawns and serve in chilled coupe glasses.

SERVES 4

SCALLOP CEVICHE WITH RUBY GRAPEFRUIT

I had a similar dish to this for Christmas dinner in Puerto Vallarta, made with Chilean sea bass. I have used large, fleshy scallops instead, as their briny iodine flavour harmonises beautifully with the citrus flavours and fresh herbs. It is possible to use Spanish Iberian jamon in place of the prosciutto if you wish – it will add a slightly sweeter flavour.

1 ruby grapefruit, peeled, sliced into segments, then cut into small dice
50 ml fresh lime juice, strained
1 teaspoon fleur de sel or other sea salt
50 ml fresh ruby grapefruit juice
30 ml mandarin or tangelo juice
2 teaspoons mirin
2 tablespoons mint leaves, shredded
1 small green chilli, minced
2 red shallots, finely diced
2 tablespoons chopped chives
16 large scallops, cleaned and sliced into thin rounds
1 punnet celery cress, snipped
4 thin slices prosciutto, grilled until crisp and crumbled

Mix the diced grapefruit with the lime juice, salt, fruit juices, mirin, mint, chilli, shallots and chives until combined. Add the scallops and leave to marinate in the dressing for 15 minutes.

Arrange the ceviche in small bowls and pour the remaining marinade over the top. Sprinkle with the celery cress and prosciutto crumbs and serve.

SERVES 4

SCALLOP CEVICHE WITH RUBY GRAPEFRUIT >

WHITING, AVOCADO, CORN AND TOMATILLO SALAD

Here's a salad that incorporates ingredients native to Mexico – corn, avocado, chilli and tomatillo. It's a glorified fish sandwich that uses the flatbread in a slightly different way. You could also leave the tortillas soft (just warmed) and wrap the fish and salsa inside, in the traditional style of a tortilla sandwich. If you are lucky enough to have fresh tomatillos, boil them for 2 minutes beforehand to soften them and bring out their flavour. Tinned tomatillos have already been cooked.

4 × 15 cm soft tortillas
40 ml olive oil, plus extra to serve
1 teaspoon sea salt
½ teaspoon freshly ground black pepper
¼ teaspoon ground chilli
200 g King George whiting fillets, cut into 5 cm strips
4 tomatillos, sliced
1 punnet coriander cress, snipped
1 punnet micro watercress, snipped

CORN CREAM
150 g fresh corn kernels (from 1 cob)
25 g unsalted butter
1 teaspoon sea salt
½ teaspoon freshly ground white pepper
2 teaspoons pouring (35%) cream

AVOCADO SALSA
1 avocado, diced
1 tablespoon finely diced red onion
1 tablespoon chopped coriander leaves
1 small red chilli, minced
30 ml fresh lime juice, strained
2 tablespoons diced tomato
4 tablespoons cooked corn kernels
few drops of Tabasco sauce
2 teaspoons extra virgin olive oil
1 small clove garlic, crushed
½ teaspoon sea salt
¼ teaspoon freshly ground black pepper

To make the corn cream, cook the corn kernels in boiling water for 2 minutes until softened. Strain and blend with the butter, salt and pepper until smooth, then stir in the cream. Pass the corn cream through a sieve to make a smooth sauce. Set aside.

To make the avocado salsa, mix all the ingredients together in a bowl.

Preheat the oven to 150°C. Brush the tortillas with a little olive oil and toast in the oven until crisp.

Combine the remaining oil with the salt, pepper and chilli and brush over the fish. Lay the fish on a baking tray, skin-side up, and cook under a hot grill for 4 minutes, just until the fish changes colour.

To assemble, smear the corn cream onto the tortilla crisps and make a stack, layering the tortilla with fish, tomatillo slices, avocado salsa and cress, finishing with avocado salsa and cress. Drizzle a little extra virgin olive oil over the top and serve.

SERVES 4

GOAT'S CHEESE, ASPARAGUS AND MOREL GRATIN

In Australia, we have access to some wonderful cheeses made with goat's milk, particularly the Woodside artisanal cheeses crafted by Kris Lloyd in South Australia. This dish works brilliantly with her soft and creamy Virgo goat's cheese, which is lightly bloomed to give subtle vanilla and almond flavours. This simple gratin captures the essence of Mexico, and I have added a sprinkling of crispy pork rind crumbs to honour a classic Mexican snack – chicharrones – which are sold in bags at street vendors everywhere. I like to use the crunchy crackling from home-cooked roast pork, but you can also buy a chunk of roast pork from Chinese barbeque shops and use the crisp skin for this (saving the meat for another dish). If you are fortunate enough to have access to fresh morel mushrooms, by all means use them.

50 ml olive oil
1 white onion, finely diced
5 cloves garlic, finely sliced
1 green jalapeno chilli, finely diced
1 teaspoon chopped thyme
20 g dried whole morel mushrooms, soaked in warm water until softened
2 tablespoons creme fraiche
1 bunch green asparagus, cut into 3 cm lengths, blanched
1 teaspoon sea salt
1 teaspoon freshly ground black pepper
120 g fresh goat's cheese, broken into small chunks
1 tablespoon shredded coriander leaves
2 tablespoons crispy pork crackling crumbs

Heat the oil in a frying pan and saute the onion, garlic and chilli until softened. Add the chopped thyme and cook for another minute until fragrant.

Squeeze the softened morel mushrooms and reserve 100 ml of the mushroom water.

Add the mushrooms to the onion mix and stir over moderate heat for 3 minutes. Add the reserved mushroom water and simmer for 2 minutes. Stir in the creme fraiche, then remove the pan from the heat and add the blanched asparagus. Season with salt and pepper.

Spoon the mushroom mix into small gratin dishes and add goat's cheese to each one, mixing in lightly with your fingers. Bake the gratins under a hot grill for 3 minutes, then remove from the heat – the cheese should be warmed but not melted. Sprinkle the shredded coriander and crisp pork crumbs over the top and serve immediately.

SERVES 4

FISH AND AVOCADO TACOS

These tacos hail from the coastal town of Ensenada, in Baja California, but were first cooked for us in the Napa Valley by our friends Barbie and Adam, who had just returned from a working visit to Mexico. I think you will agree they taste infinitely better than what passes for tacos in many parts of the world. This is a great dish to serve with family or friends as it demands an interactive approach at the table, with everyone getting involved and making their own as they go.

12 soft corn tortillas
200 g sour cream
2 limes, cut into quarters

AVOCADO SALSA
2 avocados
2 teaspoons finely diced red onion
1 green serrano chilli, minced
1 teaspoon Tabasco sauce
60 ml fresh lime juice, strained
2 teaspoons sea salt
1 tablespoon diced tomato

GREEN CHILLI SALSA
2 green habanero chillies
½ green capsicum (pepper), chopped
2 cloves garlic
8 cooked tomatillos, with 75 ml of their juices
25 ml fresh lime juice, strained
2 teaspoons sea salt
½ cup coriander leaves

SALSA ROSA
5 tomatoes, roasted and peeled
4 cloves garlic, roasted and peeled (roast with the tomatoes)
1 raw clove garlic
1 small white onion, diced
3 chipotle chillies, soaked in warm water to soften
2 teaspoons sea salt
2 tablespoons chopped coriander leaves

SALAD
12 small cos lettuce leaves, finely shredded
4 tablespoons coriander leaves, shredded
2 vine-ripened tomatoes, peeled, seeded and diced
½ small cucumber, finely sliced
½ red onion, finely sliced
½ jicama, finely shredded
2 teaspoons fresh lime juice, strained

FISH
40 ml olive oil
2 teaspoons sea salt
2 teaspoons freshly ground black pepper
1 teaspoon allspice
1 teaspoon chillli powder
800 g sea bream (or similar) fillets, skin on

To make the avocado salsa, mash or pulse-blend the avocado with the onion, chilli, Tabasco, lime juice and sea salt. Stir in the diced tomato. Taste and adjust the seasoning if necessary.

To make the green chilli salsa, place all the ingredients in a blender or food processor and process until combined.

To make the salsa rosa, place all the ingredients in a blender or food processor and process until smooth. Taste and adjust the seasoning if necessary.

To make the salad, combine all the ingredients together in a bowl and dress with just enough green chilli salsa to moisten.

To cook the fish, combine the oil, salt, pepper, allspice and chilli powder. Cut each fish fillet into 8 cm lengths and toss the fish through the spiced oil. Place the fish on a hot grill plate, skin-side down, and cook for 2 minutes. Turn over and cook the other side for 2 minutes, then remove carefully from the grill.

Heat the tortillas briefly over a hot grill plate and serve warm.

To serve, place each component in the centre of the table and invite your guests to assemble their own tacos. To do this, take one warm tortilla and add some of the salad along the centre, followed by a dollop of avocado salsa and some green chilli salsa. Top with a couple of pieces of crisp fish, some sour cream (optional), and finish with the salsa rosa. Fold the taco into a roll to secure and eat!

The limes are served in case you want to add an extra squeeze of juice to your taco. If you find the green chilli salsa too hot, go easy and just use the milder salsa rosa.

SERVES 4

ZUCCHINI BLOSSOMS WITH POLENTA

Rather than the heaviness of a cornmeal quesadilla (in which the blossoms are traditionally cooked), I have combined the essential elements in a lighter manner with a modern twist. Perfect for summer eating, this dish can be served as a starter or as an accompaniment to grilled fish.

50 ml olive oil
3 cloves garlic, minced
2 golden shallots, finely diced
1 long red chilli, finely sliced
4 tablespoons corn kernels, blanched
200 g green zucchini (courgettes), cut into fine julienne strips
2 tablespoons coarse polenta
20 zucchini (courgette) blossoms, split in half lengthways
2 tablespoons diced tomato
20 ml fresh lemon juice, strained
1 tablespoon shredded parsley leaves
1 teaspoon sea salt
½ teaspoon freshly ground black pepper

Heat the oil in a frying pan and saute the garlic, shallot and chilli for about 2 minutes until softened.

Add the corn and cook for another minute until heated through.

Toss the zucchini strips through the polenta until coated then add to the pan and toss over heat to combine with the other ingredients. Add the blossoms, tomato and lemon juice and cook over moderate heat until softened. Stir in the parsley, season with salt and pepper and spoon onto plates to serve.

SERVES 4

FISH STEW WITH TOMATOES AND GREEN OLIVES

I made this based on the memory of a terrific fish stew we had in Mexico City – the dish is typical of Veracruz, a city on the Gulf Coast south of Mexico City, where seafood features prominently. While large sea bass was used there, I have opted for the meaty jewfish, which responds beautifully to braising in the tomato sauce. Mahi mahi, hapuku or groper make excellent substitutes, so go with the freshest fish you find. Imported from Spain, Navarrico natural tomatoes are peeled organic tomatoes vacuum-sealed in jars. If unavailable, use any good-quality organic tinned tomatoes.

4 × 150 g thick jewfish fillets, cut from the middle of the fish
30 ml fresh lime juice, strained
2 teaspoons sea salt
60 ml olive oil
1 red onion, finely diced
5 cloves garlic, minced
2 green jalapeno chillies, finely sliced
1 tablespoon achiote paste
660 g jar Navarrico natural tomatoes
125 g manzanillo (large green) olives
2 tablespoons small salted capers, rinsed and drained
2 teaspoons chopped oregano
2 sprigs thyme
2 fresh bay leaves
1 stick cinnamon
3 cloves
400 ml Fish Stock (see Essentials)
20 ml Worcestershire sauce
2 teaspoons sea salt, extra
1 teaspoon freshly ground black pepper
4 tablespoons shredded parsley leaves
2 tablespoons shredded coriander leaves

Marinate the fish in the lime juice and sea salt for about 30 minutes.

Meanwhile, heat the oil in a large frying pan and saute the onion for 5 minutes until softened. Add the garlic and chilli and cook for another minute, then stir in the achiote paste and cook for 5 minutes. Add the tomatoes and their juices, and mash with a fork to break down. Cover and cook over gentle heat for 15 minutes, so it just simmers.

Stir in the olives, capers, oregano, thyme, bay leaves, cinnamon, cloves, stock and Worcestershire sauce, then cover and cook for 10 minutes. Season with salt and pepper, taste and adjust if necessary.

Add the marinated fish to the sauce and simmer gently, covered, for 10–12 minutes until the fish is just cooked. Make sure there is enough liquid to cover the fish so that it stews. Remove from the heat, sprinkle with the parsley and coriander and serve with steamed rice or sourdough bread.

SERVES 4

TURKEY SCHNITZEL WITH BEETROOT, JICAMA AND ORANGE SALAD

Turkey is considered an everyday meat in Mexico, as well as taking centre stage for celebrations. The beetroot salad is a festive specialty, called Christmas Salad. We had it at a couple of different restaurants over the Christmas season and I was intrigued by the combination. In Australia, the best time to make it is during autumn when the baby beets are at their peak and readily available. Larger beets, which have a longer season, can be prepared in the same manner, but will need a longer cooking time of 1–1½ hours.

400 g turkey breast
1 teaspoon sea salt
1 teaspoon freshly ground black pepper
40 g coarse polenta
40 ml sunflower oil
40 ml fresh lemon juice, strained
1 punnet swiss chard cress, snipped

BEETROOT SALAD
1 bunch baby red beetroot
1 bunch baby golden beetroot
50 ml red wine vinegar
2 teaspoons honey
½ teaspoon sea salt
½ teaspoon freshly ground black pepper
100 ml extra virgin olive oil
½ small jicama, peeled and cut into fine julienne strips
½ small red onion, finely sliced
2 oranges, peeled and segmented
40 g tiny beetroot leaves
2 tablespoons pomegranate seeds
2 tablespoons seedless raisins

To prepare the beetroot salad, preheat the oven to 175°C. Combine the red and golden beetroots in a baking dish with a splash of oil and bake for about 25 minutes until softened. Remove the skins and tops while still warm and slice into rounds.

To make the dressing, whisk the vinegar, honey, salt, pepper and olive oil together until emulsified. Mix the beetroot slices with the jicama strips, onion, orange segments, beetroot leaves, pomegranate seeds and raisins, and toss through the dressing.

Cut the turkey breast into four slices, then open out each slice and flatten with a meat mallet until it is 1 cm thick (escalope style).

Combine the salt, pepper and polenta and dust the schnitzels until coated. Heat the oil in a frying pan and fry the schnitzels for 3 minutes, then flip over and cook the other side for 2–3 minutes until the crust is crisp and the meat is tender.

Lay the turkey schnitzels in the centre of each plate, drizzle with lemon juice and arrange the beetroot salad in the centre of each schnitzel. Sprinkle with the snipped cress and drizzle with a little extra dressing. Serve immediately.

SERVES 4

MANGO MARGARITA PARFAIT

Inspired by the classic cocktail of Mexico, this frozen dessert is a parfait, which is more dense than an ice cream because it's not churned before freezing. Serve with a shot of really decent reposado (aged) tequila, the same as the one you add to the parfait.

4 egg yolks
75 ml water
225 g castor sugar
2 egg whites
pinch of salt
600 ml mango puree, strained
50 ml fresh lime juice, strained
60 ml reposado tequila

Line a 30 cm × 9 cm × 9 cm rectangular or triangular tin with baking paper. Whisk the egg yolks, water and 100 g of the sugar in a bowl until pale and creamy. Sit the bowl over a pan of simmering water and continue to whisk as the mixture cooks to a very thick custard consistency – it should be stiff enough to hold its own weight. Remove from the heat and continue to whisk the mixture with beaters until cool. It should be light and fluffy at this stage.

Using electric beaters, whisk the egg whites with the salt and 1 tablespoon of the sugar until soft peaks form. With the motor running, gradually add the remaining sugar and whisk until stiff, glossy and smooth.

Fold the egg white mixture into the custard base, then whisk in the mango puree, lime juice and tequila until combined, keeping the mixture light and airy. Pour the mix into the lined tin until full, then freeze for 6 hours or overnight until firm.

To serve, lift the parfait log from its mould and cut into 3 cm thick slices. Serve with sugar wafers or tuile biscuits.

SERVES 10

CHILLI CHOCOLATE CREAM HEARTS

I devised this variation on the classic coeur a la creme, adding chocolate infused with the gentle smoky heat of chipotle chilli as a tribute to the spiciness of the movie *Chocolat*. You need to have small porcelain heart-shaped moulds to make this dessert – the small holes in the moulds allow the excess moisture to drip out during setting. Raspberries, baked quince or spiced cherries can be used instead of the strawberries if you wish.

100 g creme fraiche
100 g cream cheese, softened
100 g dark couverture chocolate, melted
3 teaspoons ground chipotle chilli
75 g castor sugar
100 ml thick (45%) cream
100 g thick plain yoghurt
4 large strawberries
20 ml Strawberry Sauce (see Essentials)

Blend the creme fraiche, cream cheese, cooled chocolate, chilli and sugar in the cold bowl of a food processor until smooth. Scrape the sides with a plastic spatula to keep the mixture evenly distributed.

Add the cream and yoghurt and blend briefly to incorporate – do not overwork or the mixture will split.

Line ceramic heart moulds with squares of double-layered wet muslin and carefully spoon in the cream mixture until the moulds are full and the surface is even. Sit the heart moulds on a flat tray, cover with plastic film and leave to set in the refrigerator for at least 8 hours before serving.

To serve, lift the cream hearts out of their moulds by pulling the muslin and turn each heart onto a plate. Slice each strawberry into thin rounds and arrange on the plate above the heart. Drizzle with strawberry sauce and serve.

SERVES 4

CHILLI CHOCOLATE CREAM HEARTS >

CHURROS WITH CARAMELISED VANILLA CREAMS

The Mexicans are very fond of caramel and it is a prominent feature in many of their desserts. Churros are popular Spanish deep-fried pastries, like doughnut sticks, that are usually served for breakfast. I love them in desserts as much as I do first thing in the morning, and they are great when dunked into the vanilla cream – a seriously yummy combination.

75 g unsalted butter
250 ml water
½ teaspoon sea salt
100 g castor sugar
150 g plain flour, sifted twice
1 large egg
vegetable oil, for deep-frying
2 teaspoons ground cinnamon

VANILLA CREAMS
275 g castor sugar
25 ml water
350 ml pouring (35%) cream
180 ml milk
1 vanilla bean, split lengthways
4 egg yolks
2 eggs

CARAMEL SAUCE
60 g castor sugar
30 g glucose
2 teaspoons water
10 g unsalted butter
60 ml thick (45%) cream

To make the vanilla creams, preheat the oven to 145°C. Heat 200 g of the sugar and the water in a saucepan over high heat until it turns a caramel colour. Pour the hot caramel into six 150 ml dariole moulds and swirl them around (using tongs) to coat the inside surface of the moulds. Set aside.

Heat the cream, milk and vanilla bean in a saucepan over gentle heat until simmering. Lightly whisk the yolks and whole eggs with the remaining 75 g sugar – don't aerate too much. Slowly whisk in the hot vanilla cream and stir until combined.

Pour through a fine mesh sieve and discard the vanilla bean. Press firmly to extract as much liquid and tiny vanilla seeds as possible. Fill the caramel-lined moulds with the hot custard.

Stand the moulds in a baking dish and pour in enough boiling water to come three-quarters of the way up the sides of the moulds. Cook, uncovered, in the oven for 50 minutes or until just set. Remove from the water bath, leave to cool and then refrigerate for 4–5 hours before serving.

To make the caramel sauce, heat the sugar, glucose and water and cook over high heat until it turns a caramel colour. Remove from the heat and whisk in the butter and then the cream until smooth. Allow the caramel to cool before serving.

To make the churros, heat the butter, water, salt and 1 tablespoon of the sugar in a saucepan to boiling point. Reduce the heat and gradually add the flour, whisking continuously. Continue to whisk over gentle heat for another minute or two until the flour has cooked.

Tip the hot mix into the bowl of an electric mixer with a paddle attachment. Beat the dough on low speed for 30 seconds, to cool and aerate it slightly. Add the egg and continue to mix until the dough becomes elastic and shiny. Leave to cool slightly for 15 minutes, then spoon the dough into a piping bag with a small star-tipped nozzle.

Heat the oil in deep-fryer or large saucepan to 180°C. Mix the cinnamon and remaining sugar in a bowl until combined.

Pipe the dough into 5 cm lengths directly into the hot oil, a few at a time. Fry for 4 minutes, turning with a spoon so the churros cook evenly in the oil. Drain on paper towel then roll in the cinnamon sugar until coated. Repeat with the remaining dough.

To serve, dip the vanilla cream moulds in hot water to soften the caramel then turn out onto plates. Spoon caramel sauce over the top and serve with the hot churros.

SERVES 6

CONSTANT CRAVING
CENTRAL SPAIN AND THE BASQUE COUNTRY

It is simply impossible not to fall in love with this country, and I seem to have gathered so many stories about Spain that I can't help but devote several chapters to them. From my very first visit, my passion for this seductive country proved all-consuming. I find the frenetic energy of its people mesmerising, the diversity of its landscapes simply awesome, and the regional character of the food mind-boggling. Wherever you go, the social fabric revolves around food and wine – from the constant grazing at tascas (tapas bars), to the home-cooked feasts with family and friends, and the elegant offerings at the showcase restaurants. It seems that every single person in this country lives, breathes and talks food. Having grown up in suburban Australia, which was devoid of such a depth of cultural or culinary inheritance at the time, I find it all incredibly alluring. I am always brought to life by a glass of rosado in a local tasca, hanging out with my dear Spanish friends Eduardo and Augustin, who now live in Madrid. I thrive on Eduardo's love of food and all things Spanish.

As I become more familiar with its people, customs and regions, Spain seems to me like a flower bud that blossoms in the sun, opening up to reveal its inner beauty and complexities. Part of Spain's raw appeal is that its ostracisation during the repressive political reign of Franco preserved its distinct culture. At the same time, the regional traditions of its cuisine were kept intact and have since exploded onto the world stage with a creative zeal that has seen their best chefs become the world's culinary leaders. This is a country hungry for excellence.

Wedged between the Atlantic Ocean and Mediterranean Sea, Spain is defined by its regions. In response to the harshness of Franco's regime, the regions have clung to their autonomy, thus retaining their inherent character. Each region is divided into several provinces, which also have unique identities, creating the most amazing tapestry of diversity. In every city you'll find a thriving food market overflowing with divine fresh produce: the famous La Boqueria in Barcelona; the central markets of Valencia and Sevilla; the Maravillas (walnuts) market in Madrid that is now filled with ingredients from South America and Asia; and the La Bretxa in San Sebastian. Even the smallest towns have weekly markets. There is strong support for local ingredients and a celebration of seasonal produce. The largest meal of the day is taken at lunchtime, with lighter snacks or tapas eaten later in the evening as people wind down from the day's work. It's a great eating model – so much healthier and better for digestion than our tendency to have the largest meal at night. Spaniards thrive on interaction, especially when it comes to eating and drinking. Talk to the locals wherever you are, follow them to their preferred tascas, squeeze in amongst them at the bar (they are always busy) and point at whatever takes your fancy. Be brave; you'll soon find the language barrier becomes virtually irrelevant. It's an addictive and nourishing way to live.

Madrid is a wild city, overflowing with superb examples of Castillan architecture and grandiose style. This is a real nocturnal oasis, replete with flamenco clubs, supper and dancing shows. The spirit of this city is reflected in the films of Almodovar, which so perfectly capture the emotional essence of its people and culture. The city has undergone something of a reinvention over the past decade, emerging from its former dowager status to become a culinary epicentre with a nightlife that has reached legendary status. I love walking around Chueca, the old quarter off Gran Via – it has a distinctly bohemian atmosphere and, with a substantial gay community, celebrates alternative lifestyles. Many nooks and crannies are home to terrific tascas and wine bars, and I find that with every visit there is always something new to taste and discover. Madrid sits atop a flat plain high above sea level in the country's arid interior and is best avoided during the sweltering heat of summer. Many of the locals relocate to the mountains or the coast at this time.

If I do find myself there over summer, I head about an hour north to the Somosierra mountains, where Eduardo and Augustin have built a country house in Los Cortos, fronting onto a large forest of poplars, beech and oak trees. Every time I visit, they take me to their local village, Duruelo, for lunch at Los Arcos restaurant, a casa de comidas (working-class restaurant) full of the local workers in from the fields. We always go with the express purpose of eating the very best suckling lamb in the country. The taste and texture is extraordinary – melt-in-the-mouth tender and voluptuous. On one occasion, we went for a short drive after lunch to the fortified Roman town of Sepulveda, complete with a castle, an 11th-century cathedral and gorgeous ochre houses dotted along the steep hills. We sat in the town square sipping wine and coffee while admiring our surroundings. Eduardo and Augustin know an ideal spot for foraging for wild mushrooms at the top of the mountains above Rianza, a 20-minute drive from their house. We collected a kilo of ceps and I cooked them that evening with garlic and herbs, to accompany toast spread with a pate of red partridge

EATING IN SEGOVIA

MESON DE CANDIDO
Plaza del Azoguejo 5, Segovia
Tel +34 921 425 911
www.mesondecandido.es
This is pig heaven, serving up the best suckling pig in Spain. Book in advance – people drive from Madrid just for lunch.

LOS ARCOS HORNO DE ASAR
Duruelo, Segovia Province
Tel +34 921 545 063
This humble place that serves the local farm-workers does the best suckling lamb – order it the day before. About a 70-minute drive north of Madrid, Duruelo is a tiny village, so once you've found it, you cannot miss the eating house.

we had bought earlier that day from another village – a perfect supper.

The province of Segovia, north-west of Madrid, has a beguiling beauty. On a recent visit, we strolled through the narrow cobblestone lanes of Pedraza, the most complete walled medieval town in Spain, before driving a little further to explore the gardens of the former royal summer palace in La Granja, designed in the same classical style as Versailles. Not far away is Segovia, the main city of the province. This is the place to go for the very best roast suckling pig (cochinillo), cooked in earthenware cazuelas placed in wood-fired ovens (asadors). The secret lies in the age of the pigs (less than 25 days), the small amount of water poured into the cazuela while roasting which creates steam to tenderise the meat and keep it moist, and the garlic that is added to the hot fat towards the end of cooking. Another contender for the best pig award can be had at Meson de Candido, near the massive arches of the Roman aqueduct. The taste sensation is as sublime as the suckling lamb – I would be hard-pressed to choose which is better. If you are a pig lover like myself, take the time to visit these places – it's worth every minute, and mouthful! Just remember to book and order in advance. To walk it off, promenade with the locals through the streets down to the Alcazar, stopping for an espresso at any one of the cafes that line Plaza Mayor.

Another day's adventure took us further afield, to some of the wine regions of Castilla y Leon. We drove first to the Rueda wine region, where we walked through the underground cellars of the Grupo Yllera winery and attended a tasting of verdejo, the region's DO (Denominacion de Origen) white wine, and one of my favourites. It was close enough to Ribera del Duero to warrant a detour to taste the elegant and rich tempranillo wines of this prestigious region. We drank both over lunch, then bought more to enjoy back at the house at a more leisurely pace. While in Castilla y Leon, we visited Salamanca, which is definitely one of the most beautiful cities in Spain. As I walked around with Augustin, Eduardo and his sister Ana, the streets are alive with frenetic activity and, as this is their hometown, I was treated to all the inside information. I got to taste hornazo, a local delicacy – a pie of rich short pastry filled with chorizo, hard-boiled eggs, morcilla and game sausage. One slice is extremely filling: energy food for the rest of the day.

On a winter-time visit, we took a day-trip to Toledo, about 70 kilometres south of Madrid; the sun was out and the air was warm and fragrant. The city has historically been associated with ironwork: swords and weapons have long been forged there. The shops and antique stores are full of them. The best way to take in the sights is to park outside the Old City walls, up on the hill near the Parador de Toledo, and have a glass of wine with a slice of warm tortilla as you take in your surroundings. When you're ready, walk over the drawbridge into the city and stroll around the maze of narrow cobblestone streets and laneways. There are many tascas in the old quarter, and local specialties include venison and rabbit. After sampling a few delicious plates of tapas, we bought little Magdalena cakes from the nuns at the Real Monasterio de Santa Ursula. Because the nuns prefer to remain hidden from view, we called our order through a curtained window then a box of goodies was passed through. Quite an intriguing experience, and I must say the cakes were eaten in minutes.

My second visit to Spain was in the late 1990s. I went with a small group of Australian chefs and wine writers on a gastronomy tour hosted by Eduardo, who was working at the Spanish Commercial Office in Sydney at the time. The schedule was punishing but we did have a lot of ground to cover, and so much to taste and drink. We started on the east coast, in Valencia, the home of paella, with a swim in the warm Mediterranean waters – heavenly after the long flight from Sydney. As soon as we caught our collective breaths, we started working our way through the entire range of Spanish wine varietals and eating plates of chipirones a la plancha (tiny squid cooked whole on the charcoal grill), followed by a terrific paella with rabbit and fish at a modest place in Sueca, a small village about 20 kilometres south of town that's well known for its seafood. Our journey took us up the coast to Catalonia (see page 339) and then cross-country to the Basque region.

Everywhere we went, we observed a largely agrarian culture in operation: agricultural co-operatives that protected the rights and produce of the land owners, and produce markets that made us green with envy. Some artisanal food factories even boasted a complete hands-on approach, providing vital human contact with a food source – a rarity in today's automated world. The same commitment to quality was evident in all areas of food production: fruit orchards, olive oil, pimiento harvesting, rice, ham, wine and cheese, to name a few. We discovered a staggering array of cured meats and sausages, and drank so many wines we kept finding new favourites: tempranillo of the Ribera del Duero region and albarino from Rias Baixas in Galicia were particularly good.

On the way to San Sebastian, we stopped for lunch with some of the local cheesemakers at a modest country inn, Venta Udabe, in Valle de Basaburua, 28 kilometres north-west of Pamplona. The woman who owns it cooked us a divine lunch of chistorra (spicy pork sausages), hongos belza (Basque black mushrooms), and a yummy ajoarriero (Navarrese piquillo peppers stuffed with salt cod and braised in a tomato sauce). We also tasted some of the best cheeses I have ever come across: the firm textured, nutty Manchego; the wild blue Cabrales; the soft, creamy Torta del Casar; peppery Mahon from the Balearic Islands; Ibores (a goat's milk cheese from Extremadura); the locally made, cured and slightly smoky Idiazabal; and the gorgeously smooth, grassy-tasting Tetilla (formed in the shape of a breast) – all made with raw milk, which makes a huge difference to the flavour. Then we managed to get totally drunk on the local brew, Pacharan, made from anise and sloe berries.

Arriving in San Sebastian (properly known as Donostia-San Sebastian) in the late afternoon was like entering a film set – the scene before us was simply breathtaking. The capital of the Basque region, San Sebastian is its heartbeat, and the people are staunchly proud of their

SLEEPING AND EATING IN AND AROUND MADRID

In addition to the places listed below, there are three fabulous Madrid tapas bars along Cava Baja, near Plaza Mayor: Casa Lucas (number 30), Hijos de Lucio (number 35) and Taberna Tempranillo (number 38).

HOTEL URBAN
Carrera de San Jerónimo, Madrid (near the Prado Museum, not far from Plaza de Santa Ana)
Tel +34 91 787 7770
www.derbyhotels.es
Designer addition to the Madrid hotel landscape, with stylish bedrooms, breakfast served until 1 p.m., and a fab glass rooftop terrace bar – the tapas snacks are pretty yummy.

XENTES RESTAURANT
Calle Humilladero 13, Madrid
Tel +34 91 366 4266
For great seafood specialties from Galicia – make sure you order the Arroz Caldoso (lobster rice).

LA PANINOTECA D'E
Velazquez 32 (near Calle Goya), Madrid
Tel +34 91 426 3816
One of my favourite places for lunch: the best sandwiches in the world and a decent list of sherries.

LA BROCHE
Hotel Miguel Angel
Calle Miguel Angel 29, Chamberi, Madrid
Tel +34 91 339 3437
Chef Sergi Arola crafts the most creative food in town, with well-considered flavours.

LA VENENCIA
Calle de Echegaray 7, Madrid
Tel +34 91 429 7313
Near Plaza de Santa Ana, this fab tapas bar has the best five sherries on offer, and that's all they serve to drink! A classic of the city.

EL BOCAITO
Libertad 6, Chueca, Madrid
Tel +34 91 523 1219
One of my favourite tapas bars in Madrid.

PARADOR DE TOLEDO
Cerro del Emperador, s/n 45002, Toledo
(about 70 kilometres south of Madrid)
Tel +34 925 221 850
www.parador.es
A great place for a drink, with panoramic views across Toledo.

EATING IN NAVARRA

VENTA UDABE
Valle de Basaburua, 31869 Udabe-Basabu, Navarra
Tel +34 948 503 105
www.hotelventaudabe.com
Beautifully rustic country inn between Pamplona and San Sebastian, serving regional specialties.

unique heritage and exquisitely fussy about their food. This small but affluent city sits like a string of pearls on the perfect scallop-shaped Bay de la Concha, on the wild and often windswept Atlantic coastline. This place just screams food. It's gastronomic heaven, with the highest concentration of tascas and Michelin-starred restaurants in all of Spain. There's the wonderful La Bretxa produce market in the centre of town and the Txoko Sociedades Gastronomicas – a network of cooking clubs that give men the opportunity to cook (never from a book), eat, drink, talk about food and sing. This type of club is unique to the region, an organic communal activity that transcends class barriers, but excludes women. We were actually invited to have lunch at the club, and for once they made special provision for women to enter their inner sanctum so we could all experience their generous and warm hospitality. I recall the food being quite rustic, as you would expect, and needless to say, the wine flowed freely.

The Basques revere food with a religious fervour. Here, tapas are called pintxos, and many places specialise in just one thing; we found the best approach was to follow the crowd, taste the house specialty, then move on. The custom is to choose what you want from the selection on display (or from a blackboard list of small plates cooked to order). It's up to you to keep tabs on what you've eaten, so just let the barman know when you've finished, then pay him. Honesty and trust are the order of the day – such a civilised and welcoming system. Memorable tastes included sweet and rich morcilla (black sausage); roasted pimientos stuffed with salt-cod paste; boquerones (white anchovy fillets pickled in vinegar then packed in olive oil and served neat); small, rounded green chillies deep-fried whole that were mild yet full of flavour; luxurious ham from acorn-fed Iberian black pigs (thankfully now available in Australia); a luscious eggy tortilla laced with wild mushrooms; and mussels cooked with red chilli and a splash of olive oil.

A great way to appreciate this special place is to stroll around the shoreline and amble through the narrow streets and plazas. The locals are always up for a good chat and aren't shy about sharing their political views, regardless of language barriers. It felt like we had entered one enormous street party, the atmosphere was so alive and electric. We had to ask ourselves: when do these people ever sleep?

EATING PINTXOS IN SAN SEBASTIAN

ALONA-BERRI
Calle Birmingham 24, San Sebastian
Tel +34 943 290 818
www.alonaberri.com
Go there for pigeon, quail and game.

GANDARIAS
Calle 31 de Agosto 25, San Sebastian
Tel +34 943 428 106
Perhaps the best selection of pintxos in town (all cooked to order) and excellent wines by the glass.

BAR AMBROSIO
Plaza de la Constitucion 13, San Sebastian
Tel +34 943 428 104
Best charcuterie and Jabugo ham.

BAR LA CEPA
Calle 31 de Agosto 9, San Sebastian
Tel +34 943 426 394
This is ham heaven!

GANBARA
Calle de San Jeronimo 21, San Sebastian
Tel +34 943 422 575
This place specialises in wild mushrooms, so expect a wonderful variety of mushroom dishes.

BAR BERGARA
Calle General Artetxe 8, San Sebastian
Tel +34 943 275 026
Wild mushrooms and lobster, and a brilliant wine list too.

BAR TXEPETXA
Calle Pescadería 5, San Sebastian
Tel +34 943 342 277
Anchovy specialties, prepared dozens of ways – my all-time favourite.

For the final leg of the gastronomy tour, we drove along the coast from San Sebastian to Bilbao and stopped off at Ondarroa, a small fishing village, to visit the renowned Ortiz fish-canning factory. Every process is performed by hand and their produce is second to none. The hand-filleted anchovies, cooked tuna in a jar, boquerones, piquillo peppers and sardines are all exceptional. Frank Gehry's architectural masterpiece, the Guggenheim Bilbao, has made famous a Basque town previously known only for its steel and fishing industries. The city has been rejuvenated by the museum and other noted architecture, attracting many visitors. The beauty and external structure of the museum can keep you captivated for hours, and that's before you even begin to think about the artwork inside. I love the complexity of this building – it inspires me to dream up food equivalents of its spirit, in the same way as the works of Dali and Gaudi do. We took the underground (designed by contemporary English architect Norman Foster) to the old town, Casco Viejo, a neighbourhood that overflows with character. We walked into the main square, Plaza Nueva, which is full of cafes, bars, wandering minstrels, and people having a good time wherever you look. When our thoughts turned to food, we were spoilt for choice – and soon realised it is pretty hard to eat badly in this town.

More recently, I drove with Eduardo through the Sierra Morena mountains that separate Andalucia and Extremadura, heading west towards the Portuguese border. Our mission: Aracena and Jabugo, two small towns dedicated to the curing of jamon from the sweet meat of the Iberian black pig – Spain's national treasure. The two premium hams of Spain are Jabugo from the Huelva region (considered ever-so-slightly sweeter by connoisseurs) and Guijuelo from Salamanca, further north. This territory is pig central (or ham headquarters, as I dubbed it). The landscape is mountainous, lush and dotted with piggeries, with acres of cork and acorn trees where the pigs roam and feed. The curing houses are perfectly located and well ventilated in these high climes, where the air is just the right temperature to cure the hams without allowing them to spoil. It feels quite remote, and very rural. To cap off our visit, we took a detour to check out the ancient Roman ruins at Merida, and just happened to stumble on a terrific gourmet shop right opposite where we parked the car – as you do. The shop specialises in produce of the Extremadura region, so of course we sat down with a glass of wine and tasted more ham and the local Torta del Casar cheese, which you eat by cutting the top off and scooping it out with a spoon – absolutely divine.

I always keep some of the essential tastes of Spain in my pantry, including a couple of different virgin olive oil varietals, assorted regional olives, a selection of sherries (chilled manzanilla is so perfect for summer), a couple of farmhouse cheeses (the ones that we are allowed to import), roasted pimientos from Navarra, boquerones, and Ortiz hand-packed anchovy fillets. Until recently it was simply impossible to get hold of bona fide jamon or other pork products (such as morcilla or salchichon sausages) or raw-milk cheeses in Australia because of our strict import laws, but thankfully this has begun to change recently, to the benefit of our food culture here. There have

SLEEPING AND EATING IN BILBAO

ITURRIENEA OSTATUA
Santa Maria 14, Casco Viejo, Bilbao
Tel +34 944 161 500
Charming small pensione in the old town.

XUKELA
Calle del Perro 2, Bilbao
Tel +34 944 415 9772
All the classic Basque tastes here, including various types of fish with mayonnaise.

VICTOR MONTES
Plaza Nueva 8, Casco Viejo, Bilbao
Tel +34 944 157 067
The plaza in the old town is full of bars and cafes, and this one has terrific food.

CAFE BAR BILBAO
Plaza Nueva 6, Casco Viejo, Bilbao
Tel +34 944 151 671
Whether it's an espresso or a glass of wine, this place oozes atmosphere and local colour.

CAFE IRUNA
Jardines de Albia 5, Bilbao
Tel +34 944 237 021
Go for fab tapas, ham and local red wines. The tortilla is particularly good.

long been locally made versions of hams and sausages, but they lack the depth of flavour of the Spanish classics. This is not such a bad thing – there's something very special about having to travel to find and taste something unique at its source. These days, just about everything is available everywhere and it can all become depressingly homogenous and uniform.

My travels through Spain are far from complete. For starters, I long to visit Asturias and Galicia, on the north-west tip of the peninsula, to taste the amazing array of seafood at its source, and to see Cabrales, the region's unique blue cheese, being made. And I might just run with the bulls one day in Pamplona as well – who knows? What I do know is that I will keep returning to experience the abundance of flavours that are on offer. Hasta luego!

GREEN GAZPACHO WITH CRAB

After the London restaurant closed, Jessica and Kylie went to live and work in Alicante. When I went to visit them in summer, Jess made this delicious soup for dinner one night – her inventive adaptation of the classic red version. I have added fresh-picked crabmeat for further luscious coolness. Use whatever fresh crabmeat you can get your hands on: blue swimmer, mud, spanner, snow or king crab.

250 g picked crabmeat
1 teaspoon shredded mint leaves
½ teaspoon green Tabasco sauce
½ teaspoon freshly ground black pepper
40 ml extra virgin olive oil
3 slices Iberian ham, cut into fine julienne strips

GAZPACHO
500 g cucumber, chopped
400 ml Tomato Water (see Essentials)
50 g white onion, chopped
25 g celery, chopped
1 small green chilli, chopped
70 g green capsicum (pepper), chopped
20 ml sherry vinegar
30 ml (peppery) extra virgin olive oil
2 kiwi fruit, chopped
1 tablespoon chopped coriander leaves
1 tablespoon mint leaves
2 tablespoons crushed ice
1 teaspoon sea salt
½ teaspoon freshly ground white pepper

To make the gazpacho, mix all the ingredients together in a blender until very smooth. Taste and adjust the seasoning if necessary, then ladle into bowls or glasses.

Mix the crabmeat with the mint, green Tabasco, pepper and oil and spoon on top of the soup.

Cook the ham strips in a hot pan or under a hot grill until crisp, then sprinkle over the crab. Serve immediately.

SERVES 6

SCALLOP CEVICHE, FENNEL CREAM AND CUCUMBER JELLY

I created this dish for my 'Seduced by Spain' guest-chef dinners at Sydney's Coast restaurant in late 2001. In it I use flavours and ingredients found in Spain but give them a bit of a twist by layering the flavours with different textures, working from a more Japanese-style aesthetic.

120 g scallop meat, finely diced
2 teaspoons chopped chives
1 teaspoon minced Pickled Ginger (see Essentials)
80 ml Ginger Vinaigrette (see Essentials)
2 teaspoons Sterling caviar

CUCUMBER JELLY
250 ml Cucumber Juice (see Essentials)
50 ml verjuice
5 g gelatine leaves, softened in cold water
1 stick celery

FENNEL CREAM
2 shallots, chopped
15 ml extra virgin olive oil
150 g fennel, finely chopped
150 ml White Chicken Stock (see Essentials)
150 ml pouring (35%) cream
4 g gelatine leaves, softened in cold water
sea salt and freshly ground black pepper
1 tablespoon chopped fennel tops

To make the cucumber jelly, heat the cucumber juice and verjuice in a saucepan until hot but not simmering – just warm enough to dissolve the gelatine. Stir in the gelatine until dissolved, then pass through a fine mesh sieve.

Pour the jelly into the bases of serving vessels (glasses or small dishes) and refrigerate for 1 hour or until set. Cut the celery into fine slices and arrange in a single layer on top of the jelly.

To make the fennel cream, sweat the shallots in the olive oil until softened but not coloured. Add the fennel, cover and cook over gentle heat for about 10 minutes until soft. Pour in the stock and cook over high heat until reduced by half.

Add the cream and boil over moderate heat for 10 minutes to reduce further. Remove from the heat, blend and then pass through a fine sieve. The liquid should measure 300 ml – if not, top up with extra cream.

Add the softened gelatine leaves, stir to combine and strain again. Season to taste with salt and pepper and allow to cool completely. Stir in the chopped fennel tops.

Spoon the cooled cream into the dishes on top of the cucumber jelly and celery and refrigerate for 1 hour until firm.

To prepare the ceviche, mix the diced scallop meat, chives and ginger together in a bowl. Add two-thirds of the ginger vinaigrette and stir to combine. Leave for 5 minutes for the scallops to gently pickle.

When ready to serve, spoon the remaining ginger dressing on top of the fennel cream, pile the ceviche mix onto the fennel cream and top with caviar.

SERVES 6

SCALLOPS WITH BLACK SAUSAGE AND APPLE

A visit to any Spanish market will reveal an astonishing array of morcilla, a sweet-tasting sausage made with pig's blood, suet and spices. In Australia, these sausages are readily available at food stores that specialise in Spanish produce. The flavour and texture go particularly well with shellfish.

2 morcilla, sliced into 12 rounds
12 Toffee Apple Slices (see Essentials), mashed to a puree
12 scallops, cleaned
2 teaspoons olive oil
sea salt and freshly ground black pepper
2 red radishes, cut into fine julienne strips
4 slices green apple, cut into fine julienne strips
½ punnet radish cress, snipped
½ punnet celery cress, snipped

SHERRY SAUCE
60 ml Pedro Ximenez sherry
30 ml fig vinegar
2 red shallots, finely sliced
2 cloves garlic, finely sliced
80 ml White Chicken Stock (see Essentials)
75 g unsalted butter, diced
½ teaspoon sea salt
½ teaspoon freshly ground black pepper

To prepare the sherry sauce, combine the sherry, vinegar, shallots and garlic in a saucepan and bring to the boil. Boil until the liquid has reduced by two-thirds, then add the stock and continue to boil until reduced by half. You should have about 60 ml liquid remaining. Strain through fine mesh sieve and discard the solids.

When you are ready to serve, heat the liquid in clean pan and when it starts to boil, whisk in the cold butter, a piece at a time. As soon as the last piece has been added, remove the sauce from the heat and season with salt and pepper. Do not return to the heat as the sauce will split.

Grill the sausage slices until crisp, turning over to cook both sides.

Warm the toffee apple puree in a steamer for 3 minutes.

Brush the scallops with the olive oil and lightly season with salt and pepper. Heat a frying pan, sear the scallops for 2 minutes then toss through the hot sherry sauce until coated.

Spoon the apple puree in the centre of each plate and sit a slice of grilled sausage on top. Drizzle with the sherry sauce. Mix the radish and apple strips with the cress leaves and arrange on the sausage, then top with a scallop. Serve immediately.

SERVES 4

CHILLI SQUID WITH CHORIZO AND WHITE BEANS

If you can find tiny squid (known as chipperones in Spain), use them whole – they are sensational. You will probably have to do some searching around, as they are usually thrown back to sea because of their size. I have managed to get them on the Costa Centrale (as we euphemistically call the area north of Sydney where our beach house is) straight from a fisherman who thought I was bonkers for wanting to cook 'bait'. But there you go – it is possible if you are persistent enough. Cuttlefish also work really well here.

400 g squid tubes, cleaned
1 tablespoon rice flour
1 teaspoon cornflour
1 teaspoon sea salt
½ teaspoon freshly ground black pepper
3 small dried chillies, roasted and ground
50 ml extra virgin olive oil
2 cloves garlic, minced
2 chorizo sausages, sliced into 2 cm rounds
400 g cooked cannellini beans
2 tablespoons chopped roasted pimiento (piquillo pepper)
75 ml White Chicken Stock (see Essentials)
1 teaspoon Spanish smoked paprika
25 ml fresh lemon juice, strained
1 punnet Roasted Cherry Tomatoes (see Essentials)
vegetable oil, for deep-frying
large handful of wild rocket leaves
2 tablespoons snipped basil cress
2 tablespoons Alioli (see Essentials)

Slice the squid lengthways into thin strips. Mix together the rice flour, cornflour, salt, pepper and chilli and coat the squid with the mixture. Pass through a sieve to remove any excess flour.

Heat the extra virgin olive oil in a frying pan and gently saute the garlic and chorizo slices until beginning to crisp. Add the beans, pimientos, stock, paprika and lemon juice and simmer gently for a few minutes until the beans are hot. Add the roasted tomatoes. Taste and adjust the seasoning if necessary.

To cook the squid, heat the vegetable oil in a deep-fryer or deep saucepan to 180°C and fry the squid strips in small batches for 30 seconds until crisp. Drain on paper towel. Repeat with the remaining squid.

Stir the rocket leaves and basil cress into the bean mixture until just wilted, then spoon the beans and chorizo onto serving plates and add a dollop of alioli. Top with the fried chilli squid and serve immediately.

SERVES 4

LOBSTER RICE

I fell in love with the first spoonful of this rustic rice dish that Eduardo and Augustin introduced me to. It is made in the style of paella but with more stock added at the end so the rice is sloppy and soup-like and the grains are beginning to break. The magical flavour comes from the rich lobster stock.

2 × 800 g live lobsters (put in the freezer for 1 hour before cooking)
3 tomatoes, halved
2 litres Fish Stock (see Essentials)
20 ml olive oil
1 small red onion, finely diced
2 cloves garlic, minced
1 red capsicum (pepper), seeded and diced
1 small red chilli, minced
½ teaspoon saffron threads
2 teaspoons tomato puree
2 teaspoons sea salt
1 teaspoon freshly ground black pepper
250 g Calasparra or Bomba short-grain rice
1 punnet basil cress, snipped

SAFFRON CREAM
½ teaspoon saffron threads
100 ml pouring (35%) cream

Preheat the oven to 160°C. Put the lobsters in a large saucepan and half-cover with cold water. Cover and bring to the boil, then reduce the heat and cook for 2 minutes. Remove the lobsters from the saucepan and extract the tail and claw meat. Chop the meat into chunks and set aside.

To make a lobster stock, put the lobster head and shells in a baking dish with the tomatoes and roast in the oven for 15 minutes. Transfer the roasted shells and tomatoes to a large saucepan and cover with the fish stock. Bring to the boil, then reduce the heat and simmer gently for 45 minutes. Pass through a fine mesh sieve and discard the solids. Reserve 100 ml for the saffron cream.

To make the saffron cream, combine the saffron, reserved stock and cream in a saucepan and simmer over gentle heat for a few minutes until infused. Set aside.

Preheat the oven to 180°C. Heat the oil in a wide-based pan and fry the onion, garlic, capsicum and chilli until softened. Add the saffron, tomato puree, salt and pepper and then stir in the rice until the grains are coated. Add 1 litre of the lobster stock and bring to simmering point. Transfer the pan to the oven and bake for 18 minutes. Add another 500 ml stock and cook for another 5 minutes. Remove from the oven and stir in the lobster meat, basil cress and saffron cream. Taste and adjust the seasoning if necessary.

The rice should be quite soupy and sloppy with liquid, rather than dry, so add a little extra stock if need be. Serve with chunks of crusty bread.

SERVES 4

SQUID WITH BLACK RICE

This is how I remember the look and taste of a dish I ate at Ama Lur Restaurant when staying in Ibiza one Christmas. I was impressed by their modern interpretation of the Spanish classic (arroz negro), which I originally learnt to cook from my dear friend Eduardo. Here, the rice remains virginal white with the squid cooked into it toward the end. It is then moulded and turned out into a deep plate in a pool of black ink sauce which stains the rice black as you start to eat.

400 g small squid tubes, cleaned
40 ml extra virgin olive oil
tentacles from 4 squid
sea salt and freshly ground black pepper
1 tablespoon shredded parsley leaves
4 teaspoons Alioli (see Essentials)
1 tablespoon parsley leaves, deep-fried until crisp

BLACK INK SAUCE
50 ml extra virgin olive oil
1 red onion, chopped
6 cloves garlic, chopped
2 small red chillies, sliced
4 roasted tomatoes, smashed
2 tablespoons parsley leaves, chopped
½ teaspoon Spanish sweet paprika
200 ml Fish Stock (see Essentials)
200 ml Prawn Stock (see Essentials)
75 ml squid ink
50 ml pouring (35%) cream
1 teaspoon sea salt
1 teaspoon freshly ground black pepper
25 ml fresh lemon juice, strained

RICE
75 ml olive oil
1 white onion, minced
6 cloves garlic, minced
½ teaspoon ground chilli
500 g Calasparra or Bomba short-grain rice
1.5 litres Fish Stock (see Essentials), at simmering point
2 teaspoons sea salt
1 teaspoon freshly ground white pepper

Slice the squid tubes open to flatten out, then cut four of the tubes into thin strips lengthways. Cut the remaining tubes into small dice.

To make the black ink sauce, heat the oil in a pan and saute the onion, garlic and chilli until softened and beginning to colour. Add the roasted tomatoes and their juice, parsley, paprika and both the stocks and bring to the boil. Simmer for 10 minutes, then whisk in the squid ink and simmer for a further 5 minutes. Stir in the cream and season to taste with salt and pepper. Pass through a fine mesh sieve and discard the solids. When ready to serve, reheat the sauce and add the lemon juice.

To cook the rice, heat the oil in a paella pan or frying pan and saute the onion, garlic and ground chilli over low heat for about 4 minutes until softened and fragrant. Stir in the rice until the grains are properly coated. Pour in the hot fish stock and bring to a simmer over medium–high heat. Reduce the heat and cook gently for 10 minutes without stirring until the rice is nearly cooked but there is still a small amount of liquid visible.

Stir the diced squid into the rice and simmer gently for 4–5 minutes. By this time the rice should have absorbed all the liquid and the squid should be cooked. Season with salt and pepper, taste and adjust if necessary. Remove from the heat and spoon the cooked rice into small round bowls (like Chinese rice bowls) rubbed with olive oil. Press down to make firm.

Heat a frying pan and add the olive oil, reserved squid strips and tentacles. Toss over heat for a minute, just until the squid curls and cooks. Season with salt and pepper to taste. Add the shredded parsley and toss through, then remove from the heat immediately.

To serve, turn the moulded squid rice out onto serving plates and spoon the black ink sauce carefully around its base. Spoon the alioli over the rice, sit the squid tentacle and strips on top and scatter with the fried parsley.

SERVES 4

PARTRIDGE ESCABECHE

Escabeche is a Castillan specialty where fish or poultry is spiced, fried and then pickled. Not only does it preserve, it has the added advantage of making food taste even better. I have used the red and grey species of partridge that are available during the autumn months in England. They are available in Australia, but may be harder to source, so you could easily substitute poussin, squab, quail, guinea fowl or pheasant – just alter the cooking times accordingly. Use a really good quality vinegar for this as its taste will carry through. I use the Spanish Forum cabernet vinegar or the French Banyuls.

1 teaspoon sea salt
½ teaspoon freshly ground white pepper
½ teaspoon ground allspice
½ teaspoon ground chilli
200 ml extra virgin olive oil
2 grey partridges, cleaned
3 golden shallots, quartered
4 cloves garlic, cut in half
½ fennel bulb, sliced
250 ml White Chicken Stock (see Essentials)
250 ml red wine vinegar
2 fresh bay leaves
3 sprigs thyme
4 cloves
1 teaspoon white peppercorns, cracked
1 stick cinnamon
2 teaspoons Roasted Garlic Paste (see Essentials)
1 teaspoon Harissa (see Essentials)
12 baby carrots, peeled, cut into thirds on the diagonal
3 teaspoons honey
2 tablespoons chopped chives
1 punnet mizuna cress, snipped

Mix the salt, pepper, allspice and chilli in a bowl with 40 ml of the olive oil. Rub the spiced oil liberally over the partridge skin.

Heat a braising pan and saute the partridges on all sides for about 5 minutes until browned. Remove the birds from the pan, then add the shallots, garlic and fennel and saute until softened. Add the stock, vinegar, bay leaves, thyme, cloves, peppercorns and cinnamon and bring to simmering point. Add the birds, cover the pan and turn off the heat.

Let the birds cool completely in the stock then refrigerate overnight. When ready to serve, remove the birds from the stock and slice the breast and leg meat off the bone (discard the bones). Pass the stock through a fine mesh sieve and set aside. Discard the solids.

Heat 100 ml of the strained pickling stock with the garlic paste and harissa until simmering, then remove from the heat. Taste and adjust the seasoning if necessary. Add the sliced meat to the sauce and leave to stand while the carrots cook.

To prepare the carrots, bring some of the pickling stock to the boil in a saucepan and add the carrots and honey. Cook for 3 minutes until the carrots are tender but not too soft, then remove from the stock and season with salt and pepper.

Toss the chives and mizuna cress through the carrots and arrange the partridge meat on top. Add a little extra harissa sauce if necessary and serve.

SERVES 4

CHORIZO AND POTATO TORTILLA

This tortilla first appeared on the 'Seduced by Spain' menu I presented at Sydney's Coast restaurant in 2001.

150 g chorizo sausage, finely sliced
olive oil, for pan-frying
2 large eggs
250 ml pouring (35%) cream
2 teaspoons sea salt
1 teaspoon freshly ground black pepper
500 g waxy potatoes, sliced into thin rounds
20 g unsalted butter

Preheat the oven to 175°C and oil a gratin dish or clay cazuela dish.

Heat a frying pan and fry the sausage slices in a little oil for about 2 minutes each side until slightly coloured. Remove from the pan and cool on a wire rack. Discard the oil.

Whisk together the eggs, cream, salt and pepper.

Cover the base of the prepared dish with an overlapping layer of potato slices then brush with the egg mix. Scatter a few sausage slices across the surface then repeat the layers of potato and egg mix. Continue until all the potato and sausage slices are used, finishing with a potato layer. Pour any remaining egg mix over the top, and dot the butter across the surface.

Cover the dish with a sheet of baking paper then foil. Stand another fitted dish inside it to weigh it down and keep the tortilla pressed and uniform. Bake for 25 minutes until nearly cooked. It should be soft but not sloppy (check with a skewer).

For the last 10 minutes of cooking, remove the foil and weight, increase the heat to 200°C and bake until the surface forms a glazed crust. Remove from the oven and allow to cool for a few minutes before slicing into 6 cm squares to serve.

SERVES 8

KYLIE'S TORTILLA

Tortilla is a Spanish staple, served in every tapas bar from breakfast right through the day. Try a slice of warm tortilla one morning with a glass of sherry and a few slices of ham, and suddenly you'll feel like you're in Spain. During her time there, Kylie mastered the art of the perfect tortilla. This is her recipe.

125 ml olive oil
1 small onion, finely diced
2 large potatoes, sliced
3 eggs
1 teaspoon sea salt
½ teaspoon freshly ground black pepper
½ teaspoon ground chilli

Heat the oil in a cast-iron frying pan and fry the onion until softened. Add the potato slices and fry for a few minutes until softened. Remove the potatoes and onion from the pan and discard any excess oil.

Lightly beat the eggs in a bowl with the salt, pepper and chilli.

Put the potatoes and onion back in the pan and pour the beaten egg over the top. Cook over moderate heat until the eggs have just set. Leave to sit in the pan for 5 minutes before turning out.

Turn the tortilla out of the pan onto a board or plate and cut into slices to serve.

SERVES 4

LOVE SHACK PAELLA – SAFFRON PRAWN

We have a tradition at our beach house (aka The Love Shack) of long Sunday lunches a few times a year when we want to catch up with some dear friends. As there is always a large gaggle of them, we cook up a huge paella. I have two versions depending on who's coming – a seafood-based one for those who shun meat, and one with chicken and chorizo for those who don't eat seafood. Margie makes the salads beforehand and then it just all goes on the table with a stack of bread – definitely the easiest way of cooking for large numbers.

1 litre Fish Stock or Light Crab Stock (see Essentials)
100 ml extra virgin olive oil
1 small brown onion, diced
3 cloves garlic, minced
5 ripe tomatoes, peeled, seeded and chopped
1 teaspoon saffron threads
200 ml Spanish roasted tomato sauce (Navarrico brand, or similar)
300 g Calasparra or Bomba short-grain rice
18 large raw prawns, shelled and deveined
6 scallops
2 teaspoons sea salt
1 teaspoon freshly ground black pepper
250 g squid tubes, cleaned, sliced and scored
500 g black mussels, cooked and removed from the shells
3 tablespoons parsley leaves, shredded
60 ml fresh lemon juice, strained
4 tablespoons Alioli (see Essentials)

Heat the stock in a large saucepan to simmering point.

Heat the oil in a paella pan and fry the onion for about 2 minutes until softened.

Add the garlic and fry for another minute, stirring constantly. Add the tomato, saffron and tomato sauce to make a sofrito and cook for about 5 minutes until thickened. Stir in the rice and coat with the tomato mix.

Pour in three-quarters of the hot stock and cook over high heat for 10 minutes. Don't stir as you want the paella to develop a crust. Add the remaining stock with the prawns and scallops. Season with salt and pepper. Cook over medium heat for 3 minutes then add the squid pieces and mussels. Stir once.

Cook for another 3–4 minutes until the seafood is just cooked through and all the liquid has been absorbed. Allow to stand for 5–10 minutes before serving. Taste and adjust the seasoning if necessary, then stir in the shredded parsley and lemon juice.

Serve with alioli and crusty bread.

SERVES 6

HAVING MY WAY WITH A SUCKLING PIG

This requires you to start with the smallest suckling pig you can get hold of and use all its parts, with nothing going to waste. In Spain we could source pigs as small as 3 kg but it's more common to find them around the 6–8 kg weight in Australia. When you are dealing with the belly, keep the ribs and reserve to make barbequed spare ribs. This preparation will be enough for a feast, so invite plenty of friends around and treat them to all the delicacies. The terrine can be served as a starter and the belly is more substantial. Both work brilliantly with the cabbage and ginger salad, a perfect foil for the rich meat.

2 belly sides from a whole 6 kg suckling pig
1 tablespoon sea salt
160 ml extra virgin olive oil

PIG'S HEAD TERRINE
head and trotters from the suckling pig
2 tablespoons sea salt
1 carrot, diced
1 onion, diced
1 stick celery, sliced
1 long red chilli, sliced
1 head garlic, cut in half crossways
1 tablespoon chopped ginger
2 stalks parsley
2 teaspoons black peppercorns
1 bay leaf
1 teaspoon fennel seeds
3 g gelatine leaves, softened in cold water

CABBAGE AND APPLE SALAD
¼ red cabbage
2 green apples
25 ml fresh lemon juice, strained
4 slices pancetta, cut into fine julienne strips
1 bunch chives, cut into 3 cm lengths
4 red shallots, finely sliced
120 ml Sweet Ginger Dressing (see Essentials)

To prepare the pig, remove the head and trotters and set aside. Bone out the legs and shoulders and reserve the meat for another use, leaving the skin intact. (I would roast the leg meat with five spice, Chinese-style, and use the shoulder in a slow braise. Otherwise mince the meat to add to stuffings or dumplings.)

Cut the two belly sections into even square pieces, approximately 12 cm × 20 cm. Rub salt and oil into the belly pieces then seal each piece in a cryovac bag or a double layer of zip-lock plastic bags, adding any extra oil before sealing.

Heat a large pan of water to 85°C – use a cooking thermometer to check the temperature. Add the bags of pork belly and cook at a constant 85°C for 6½ hours. Remove the bags from the hot water and plunge into a large bowl of iced water to stop the cooking immediately. Lay on a flat tray and refrigerate overnight.

When ready to serve, reheat the parcels in 65°C water for 10 minutes. Drain and remove the pig from the plastic bags.

Heat 20 ml of the oil on a flat grill or cast-iron pan over moderate heat, add the pig, skin-side down, and weigh down with another heavy pan so the meat holds its shape. Fry for about 6 minutes until golden, without allowing it to burn. Cut each piece into four portions and serve with the cabbage and apple salad.

To prepare the pig's head terrine, put the head with its ears in a saucepan with the trotters and the remaining ingredients except the gelatine, and cover with cold water. Bring slowly to simmering point and simmer gently for 2 hours, skimming occasionally to remove any rising sediment. Remove the head and trotters from the pan with a slotted spoon, then strain the stock through a filter or jelly bag. Discard the solids.

Reheat 300 ml of the stock to simmering point, season with extra salt and pepper to taste and stir in the softened gelatine. Allow to cool slightly while you prepare the meat. >>

<< Carefully remove the skin and shred it, then remove the meat from the cheeks and head. Keep the snout and chop it into small pieces. Discard the bones and eyes. Extract the brain and tongue, keeping them whole, then slice into small pieces. Cut the ears into fine shreds. Mix the chopped and shredded meats together.

Line a terrine mould (I use a triangular one) with baking paper. Pack the mould with the meat and pour on the jellied stock. Cover and refrigerate overnight until set.

To serve, turn the terrine from its mould onto a board and allow the terrine to sit at room temperature for 45 minutes. Slice the terrine into portions and serve with the cabbage and ginger salad.

To prepare the salad, shred the cabbage leaves very finely with a sharp mandoline. Cut the apple into fine julienne strips and toss with the lemon juice to prevent browning. Saute the pancetta strips until crisp, then drain on paper towel. Mix together the cabbage, chives, shallots, apple and crisp pancetta. Add enough dressing to moisten and toss with your fingers.

SERVES 10–12

APPLES AND CURD

A light and cleansing dessert starring fromage blanc, a fresh curd cheese that is common throughout Europe. In Australia, a couple of excellent ones are made in Victoria by Richard Thomas (which can be eaten directly from its tub with a spoon) and Meredith Dairy. It's a perfect partner for the toffee apples and the fresh acidity of the green apple snow.

300 g fromage blanc
100 ml pouring (35%) cream
16 Toffee Apple Slices (see Essentials)

MOSCATEL JELLY
150 ml moscatel sherry
60 ml Sugar Syrup (see Essentials)
3 g gelatine leaves, softened in cold water

GREEN APPLE SNOW
550 g small granny smith apples, washed
160 ml Sugar Syrup (see Essentials)

Whisk the fromage blanc and cream together until just firm and aerated. Press the curd cream into serving glasses and smooth the surface. Refrigerate for 2 hours.

To make the jelly, heat the moscatel and sugar syrup in a saucepan to simmering point. Stir in the softened gelatine until dissolved. Remove from the heat and allow to cool completely.

To make the apple snow, chill an ice-cream machine. Cut the apples in half and remove the core, leaving the skin on. Juice the apples and mix the juice with the sugar syrup. Pour straight into the ice-cream machine and churn until firm. Transfer to the freezer until ready to serve.

Cut each toffee apple slice in half lengthways and arrange in a single layer over the curd cream to cover.

Spoon the cooled jelly on top, enough to cover the apple layer, and refrigerate for about 2 hours until set.

Sit a quenelle or rounded scoop of green apple snow in the centre of the jelly and serve.

SERVES 4

ALMOND NOUGAT ICE CREAM WITH PRALINE

Some of the best nougat (or torrone) is made in Alicante, packets of which always return with me to Sydney after each visit. You can make your own nougat for this ice cream if you feel so inclined, otherwise buy a reputable brand and chop it into small chunks.

400 ml milk
100 ml latte di mandorla
½ vanilla bean, split lengthways
4 egg yolks
120 g castor sugar
500 ml pouring (35%) cream
100 g almond nougat, chopped into small pieces
1 cup Almond Praline (see Essentials)

To make the ice cream, heat the milk, latte di mandorla and vanilla bean in a saucepan to simmering point over gentle heat.

Whisk the egg yolks and sugar in a bowl for about 10 minutes until pale and creamy. Pour on the hot milk and whisk to combine. Sit the bowl over a pan of simmering water and cook, stirring, until the mixture reaches a custard consistency and coats the back of a spoon. Pass through a fine mesh sieve and discard the vanilla bean. Stir the cream into the custard base and leave to cool completely.

Churn the mixture in an ice-cream machine until firm and holding its shape. Scoop into a bowl and stir in the nougat pieces.

Line a rectangular terrine tin with baking paper. Pour one-third of the ice cream into the tin and sprinkle the surface with praline. Freeze for 20 minutes to allow it to firm slightly. Repeat twice so you have three layers of ice cream and praline, reserving some of the praline for later. Freeze for 5 hours or overnight.

To serve, turn the ice cream out of its mould onto a board and roll the sides in the reserved praline to coat. Cut into 3 cm thick slices using a hot wet knife and lay on cold plates to serve.

SERVES 8

ALMOND NOUGAT ICE CREAM WITH PRALINE >

FINDING NIRVANA CATALONIA

I have travelled through Catalonia many times now, and always start in its dynamic capital, Barcelona. This is a city that fills me with excitement and inspiration. Every corner seems to offer another surprise: the medieval streets, the modernist architecture, the inviting aromas of food in the air, the street theatre, the urban parks – Barcelona has it all.

Our first visit to Barcelona coincided with Margie's 40th birthday. We were keen to celebrate the passing of such a momentous year somewhere new to us, and were attracted to the elaborate architecture of Antoni Gaudi and the artistic brilliance of Salvador Dali and other surrealist artists, not to mention the food and wine. As it turned out, there was a rally for peace in the city on the day of her birthday, with more than a million people taking to the streets to protest a Basque separatist bombing. The streets were awash with white as doves were released into the air. We watched for a while from the vantage point of our hotel rooftop deck, then left for dinner at C'al Isidre, soon realising that we were travelling in the same direction as the protesters. There was absolutely no hope of a taxi, so we joined the crowds for a couple of kilometres, unwittingly discovering the warren of back streets in the Barri Xines red-light district, to the west of the Ramblas (the grand street that is the city's most famous landmark), as we walked. I remember thinking what a nice gesture it was on the part of the Spanish to turn out in such numbers for Margie's birthday! When we finally got to C'al Isidre, we had the most delicious dinner, trying out new wines and some extraordinary dishes made with wild mushrooms, the house specialty. We would soon discover that Catalan cooking owes much to the region's pervasive Roman and Moorish heritage.

Our next priority was to explore the brilliant architectural creations of Gaudi, starting with Casa Mila and Casa Batllo. Both are private residences, and we wondered what it must be like living there, with people constantly gawking at the peculiar silhouettes of the buildings and pondering their effect on the streetscape. Further downtown, just off the Ramblas, is another Gaudi-designed private mansion: the Palau Guell. The exterior is perhaps less striking, but the interior is mesmerising. To complete the Gaudi experience, we took a local bus to some of his larger public works that lie north-west of the city centre: the inventive Parc Guell and the knockout La Sagrada Familia cathedral, which was incomplete at the time of his death and is only now nearing completion. The rich and diverse images I took away with me would have a seminal influence on my work, inspiring me to think about how I could incorporate those shapes and designs into food, particularly desserts, which offer more scope for whimsy and fantasy.

Gaudi's work displays an excitement and lateral vision that forces you to think outside the square, as do the designs of architects Josep Puig i Cadafalch and Domenech i Montaner, Gaudi's contemporaries in the modernista movement that changed the face of the city in the early 20th century. Anyone remotely interested in architecture should visit the Mies van der Rohe Pavilion, in the Montjuic area of the city. Designed as the German National Pavilion for the International Exhibition (Expo) in 1929, it has an interesting history and is a testament to the timelessness and perfect elegance of minimalist design. The nearby complex of museums and gardens are also worth a look while you're in this beautiful and cultural part of the city.

Venturing out of the city, we took a 1-hour train trip to Montserrat, which certainly lives up to its name (serrated mountain) – the jagged grey rocks loomed over us with an almost ghostly appearance. A steep cable-car ride to the summit brings you to a monastery with a basilica housing La Moreneta, the Black Madonna. That first visit sure left its mark – a fabulous fortnight that started a life-long love affair with this brilliant country.

STAYING IN BARCELONA

HOTEL OMM
Calle Rossello 265, Eixample, Barcelona
Tel +34 934 454 000
www.hotelomm.es
A beacon of contemporary design and style close to the heart of Barcelona, with the famous Roca brothers managing the hotel's uber-cool Moo Restaurant.

CASA CAMPER
Carrer Elisabets 11, El Raval, Barcelona
Tel +34 933 426 280
www.casacamper.com
Small boutique hotel that makes you feel like a local. Owned by the same people who gave us the funky Camper shoes, this affordable hotel is a welcome addition to the scene.

The food of Barcelona is shaped by El Mercat de Sant Josep (or La Boqueria, as it is better known), the oldest and most famous market in the city. It is an incredible spectacle, whetting your appetite with its colours, aromas and flavours. It was here that I first saw and tasted razor clams, percebes (gooseneck barnacles), espardenyas (sea cucumbers) and galeras (mantis shrimp) – and encountered the 85-year-old woman in charge of the tuna counter. With her peroxide bouffant hair and deft skill with a very large knife, she alone would make the trip worthwhile. The variety of mushrooms defies description, with a few shops devoted exclusively to wild species, and there are several stand-up bars and chiringuitos (stands) where you can sample just about anything.

I always start my visit with breakfast at Bar Pinotxo, just inside the main entrance: cortado (coffee), xuxo (a wicked Catalan pastry) and freshly squeezed orange juice. This wonderful bar has been here forever and is part of the fabric of the market, as is its charming host, Juanito. And I never leave the market without buying a few pastries at Escriba, at the east side of the main entrance.

Although La Boqueria is the most well known, there are several other markets dotted across town. About 15 minutes' walk away is the much smaller Mercat de Sant Antoni, with equally wonderful produce. The Mercat de la Concepcio, in the Eixample area, is a great one to visit too, with its food and stunning flowers – and the countless bars and cafes that surround it.

Another area that is terrific for exploring (and eating) is Barceloneta, along the waterfront. Recently rejuvenated, it's full of seafood bars and cafes – some better than others – and it is easy to while away the time here, enjoying a long, casual lunch under an umbrella. One summer, our friends Jane and Jon, who had just flown in from Ireland, took us down to a little seafront taberna, Casa Costa Cal Pinxo, and we ate the most wonderful zarzuela (seafood stew) and escalivada (roasted vegetable salad). Afterwards, we wandered through the narrow streets, finishing up on the rooftop terrace of our hotel, where we celebrated the sunset with a bottle of cava.

The tascas of Barcelona are like the heartbeat of the city. Some are gastronomic, while others are more social; some

EATING IN BARCELONA

C'AL ISIDRE
Carrer de les Flors 12, Barcelona
Tel +34 934 411 139
A city institution, this restaurant serves traditional Catalan cuisine with a French twist in a room full of Spanish surrealist artworks.

SANTA MARIA
Comerç 17, Born-Ribera, Barcelona
Tel +34 933 151 227
Warm and inviting, owner/chef Paco Guzman makes contemporary minimalist tapa tastes. Hang out with the cool locals here.

XOCOA
Carrer Petritxol 11, Barcelona
Tel +34 933 011 197
www.xocoa-bcn.com
A premium chocolate boutique that specialises in all things chocolate.

CACAO SAMPAKA
Carrer Consell de Cent 292, Barcelona
Tel +34 932 720 833
www.cacaosampaka.com
Chocolate desserts are a gastronomic staple here, and there's also plenty of other treats.

ESCRIBA PATISSERIE
La Rambla de les Flores 83 (just past the Boqueria market entrance), Barcelona
Tel +34 933 016 027
For the most sublime pastries and cakes in town – this is one of the iconic food shops of Barcelona.

CAL PEP
Plaça de les Olles 8, Born-Ribera, Barcelona
Tel +34 933 107 961
Considered by gourmands around the world – and the locals – as the best tapas bar in Barcelona. Every taste is pure gold and you can't go wrong under their guidance.

BAR PINOTXO
Boqueria market (just inside the main entrance), Barcelona
This tapas bar is always dependable – ask for the daily specials. Go early to grab a wicked xuxo pastry before they disappear.

are sleek and modern, while others feel like they have been there forever, ancient and well worn. This is where you will also find some of the hippest cocktail and wine bars. I always find a new spot to add to my growing list.

So much about Barcelona reminds me of Sydney: the same openness and raunchiness, that 'city by the sea' feeling, the art, culture, bars and clubs, the overall sophistication – a total nirvana. The warmth of the people puts you immediately at ease, and Margie and I treasure the lasting friendships we have made here.

In 2001 I was offered the opportunity to spend a couple of weeks on the Costa Brava, in the kitchens of the iconic El Bulli restaurant with chef and owner Ferran Adria. We had just closed our Sydney restaurant Paramount, so it didn't take me long to pack my bags and knives and get on the next plane. This was at the time when molecular gastronomy (the application of science to culinary practices) was exploding onto the world stage, and here I was, working smack bang in the middle of all the excitement. The premise behind it all is the creation of textural fantasies from ingredients while maintaining the integrity of their flavour; textures are transformed or manipulated to take new forms and shapes, to add an element of excitement and mystery. Nothing is as it seems. Every menu at El Bulli consists of 30-odd miniature tastes, each with a distinct and substantial flavour, designed for maximum impact. Behind the scenes, the staff debate how best to present each taste, resulting in a culinary experience that is witty, intriguing and surprising. Margie and I had dinner there before I began work, which allowed me to see not only the preparation, but also how it all came together at the table – something most of El Bulli's 40 chefs were not fortunate enough to experience.

Ferran Adria is well known for his resolute stance on food: 'Cultured and modern cuisine is not for ruminants, it's for trained gourmands who seek intellectual stimulation. Food and wine can only expand if chefs are prepared to change their way of thinking.' His oeuvre has been captured in three hefty volumes that allow you to explore and research further, but I love his single-mindedness and his determination to always stay one step ahead. Each year he releases his new work to all the chefs in Spain, so they may share his expertise and feel encouraged to incorporate these techniques into their own repertoires. The restaurant is closed from November to March, and the small permanent brigade of kitchen staff relocates to El Taller, the Bulli workshop-laboratory in the centre of Barcelona, where the alchemy and experimentation occurs. I spent a day there with Ferran and a couple of the other chefs, and what a day it was. I learnt how to make trufa carbonara, pumpkin and mandarin ravioli, liquid ravioli, and maki of white asparagus and ruby grapefruit; how to foam (which I don't bother with); how to treat vegetables or raw seafood like tissue-thin pastry sheets; how to set water to make fine sheets used to suspend caviar; how to encase a raw quail-egg yolk in gold leaf to make croquant; how to make parradillas (vegetable jellies that can be heated without melting and have a smoky barbeque flavour); how to create myriad wafers and biscuits for savoury and dessert fantasies (something I love); how to make puffed rice that tasted like paella; how to make chicken feet crackling (brilliant); how to construct the scientific-looking prawn pipette; and how to use a Pacojet machine to change textures. I could go on. My summation of that time is that I witnessed a chef who was not confined by the boundaries of Spanish cuisine, yet showed deference to local product, custom and ideology – a celebration of his roots.

El Bulli Restaurant is located on the relatively quiet beach of Cala Montjoi, halfway between Cadaques and Roses along the dramatic coastline of the Costa Brava. During my time there, I stayed at a beachfront hotel in Roses, 30 minutes' drive away, but prior to that, Margie and I had spent several days at the beautiful seaside town of Cadaques, at the northern end of the Costa Brava. The surrounding hills are stone terraced, a legacy of the ancient Romans, and everywhere there are prickly pears and fig, olive and bay trees; rosemary and wild fennel grow by the side of the road, and lavender and lemon verbena scent the air. The scenery is dramatic, with high cliffs that have sheer drops to the ocean, and a rugged, deeply indented coastline of headlands and small sandy bays. One day, we walked the few kilometres to nearby Port Lligat to visit Dali's quirky and ever-so-slightly-surreal summer house, which remains a shrine to his memory. We walked around the gardens (and yes, we saw the famous phallus-shaped swimming pool), then ventured inside the house, which is kitted out with totally whacko furniture. Two single beds are set up high like thrones with gaudy red robes and gold tassels – from here, Dali and his wife and muse, Gala, would hold court.

With Figueres (Dali's home town and the place where he is buried, as well as the site of the Museu Dali) a 30-minute drive inland from Cadaques, this whole area has come to be associated with the surrealist movement in Spain.

We began to fondly imagine certain surrealist aspects to the people, as we watched them promenade in the afternoons: a large proportion of the local men sported Daliesque moustaches, nautical stripey shirts were much in evidence, and the scene became almost theatrical at times. Apparently, there is a wind called the Tramontana that blows down to the coast from the Pyrenees. Legend holds that it can make people either geniuses or crazed; evidently, the wind blows through their heads and transforms them, one way or the other. At any rate, the passing parade was wonderful to observe from one of the beachside open-air bars.

Of course, we also sampled as much of the local cuisine as we possibly could: lovely fish soups with stock made from the rock scorpion fish of Roses; suquet de peix, a Catalan fish stew cooked in a clay cazuela; garlic prawns; and grilled gilt-head bream and red mullet (salmonetes). My favourite was definitely the lenguado (small sole cooked whole over charcoal) – try it at La Rafas, a modest local taberna in Roses. Somehow we always finished off with crema catalana – similar to the French creme brulee, this Spanish favourite originated here, as its name suggests.

During a gastronomy tour of regional Spain with a small group of Australian chefs and wine writers (see page 314), we travelled the well-worn roads of Catalonia, following the Mediterranean coastline and driving north through the small town of Tortosa on the Ebro River, where the landmark castle has been converted into a parador. Along the way, we checked out the rice fields of the Ebro Delta and the olive-oil production facility at Reus (near the fortified city of Tarragona), where we sat at the table of a most generous man, Bill Devin, who manages the Unio Agraria Co-operative that produces the fruity Siurana extra virgin olive oil. In what became a defining moment of our journey, he cleverly demonstrated the essence of hospitality and palate seduction with his beautiful oils. He also passed on his recipe for romesco sauce, one that I have modified over time, but I think of him and that day every time I make it. I am also a fan of other small boutique producers in this region, including the premium Eduard

SLEEPING AND EATING ON THE CATALAN COAST

HOTEL BLAUMAR
Carrer Massa d'Or 21, Cadaques
Tel +34 972 159 020
www.hotelblaumar.com
With a quiet location on a hill overlooking the bay, a laid-back ambience and friendly staff, staying at this hotel is like staying at a friend's beach house.

SANT PAU
Calle Nou 10, Sant Pol de Mar
Tel +34 937 600 662
www.ruscalleda.com
Star chef Carme Ruscalleda cooks brilliant food at her restaurant on the coast, about a 45-minute drive north of Barcelona. Her food is a studied approach to textures and flavour profiles, including an innovative cheese micro-menu that pairs cheese with contrasting tastes.

EL RACO DE CAN FABES
Carrer Sant Joan 6, Sant Celoni
Tel +34 938 672 851
www.canfabes.com
Just inland from the coast, a 45-minute drive north from Barcelona, this Michelin three-starred restaurant has one of the best menus in Spain. I can still recall an amazing dish of foie gras caramelised with figs and Pedro Ximenez sherry, and the scallops served with a delicate fennel mousse. Chef/owner Santi Santamaria has now added a few luxury suites, making this an ideal base for exploring the region.

EL BULLI
Cala Montjoi, Roses
Tel +34 972 150 457
www.elbulli.com
Little more needs to be said about this Spanish institution. Long considered at the forefront of world-class dining, El Bulli is prized for its revolutionary food and chef Ferran Adria's unique vision. It is only open for 6 months each year, from April through to September; bookings open in February for each season and the place is completely booked out within days – good luck!

LA RAFAS
Calle San Sebastia 56 (across from Snack-Mar), Roses
Tel +34 972 254 003
A tiny local restaurant in the back streets of town (ask locally for exact directions), offering the best seafood on the Costa Brava, so simple and delicious. This place feels completely unpretentious – like being in a modest home.

Pons from L'Albages, near Lleida – which, like Siurana from Reus, is available in Australia. Many Spanish oil producers specify the olive varieties used to make their oil, and most Catalan producers prefer the arbequina, a small oval-shaped olive with a low flesh-to-stone ratio. This makes its oil highly acidic, with the tastes of apples and tropical fruits – because of the inherent freshness of its flavour profile, it is best consumed as soon after pressing as possible.

Another time I visited the Borges factory at Tarrega, an hour's drive to the west of Barcelona. It is a massive commercial operation – an important stop, as I was intent on comparing the quality of the oils produced by large and small operations. A smaller factory on the property manufactures the aromatic and flavoured oils designed for Borges by chef Ferran Adria. Our host Manuel (of course!) took us through an olive-oil tasting – an interesting experience straight after breakfast. Later that day, we drove further west to the small town of Borges Blanques, where the olive oil museum is situated. This is a fascinating place to visit and, in its garden, has one of the oldest olive trees in Spain, which is several hundred years old.

The impact of Catalonia on the world of food has been dramatic. A fierce independent spirit shines through the people, and their pride in their culture, language and food is palpable. Collectively, the tascas of Barcelona play a pivotal role in the thriving food culture of the city – and everywhere in Spain, for that matter. In Australia, we are beginning to adopt elements of the Spanish way, as part of a shift towards less formal dining. Serving small tastes across the counter, in the same manner as tapas, makes eating much more sociable and enjoyable; it encourages a certain freedom, in that you can jump from one place to the next, tasting little morsels as you go. We can learn a great deal from the Spanish model, and so much of it is appropriate for the Australian lifestyle. Having said that, we are severely hamstrung by protectionist licensing laws, and until our laws allow greater flexibility, we will not be able to fully embrace the Spanish philosophy, which represents an entirely different way of thinking about food. Our loss, I think.

BILL'S ROMESCO SAUCE

In the spirit of the occasion, I am passing on a morsel of Bill Devin's wisdom and giving you his recipe for that famous Catalan sauce. It is perfect for the Australian climate and has a multitude of uses: serve it with grilled or barbequed fish, chilled shellfish and seafood, chicken or lamb, roasted Mediterranean vegetables, as a dressing for bitter greens or as a salsa for crusty bread. It will keep in the refrigerator for two weeks, but is at its best freshly made and still slightly warm.

15 ripe tomatoes, top core removed
2 heads garlic, tops sliced off
olive oil, for roasting
250 g blanched almonds
250 g hazelnuts
2 long red chillies, roasted, skins and seeds removed
3 cloves garlic, minced
275 ml Siurana extra virgin olive oil (or other fruity, non-bitter oil)
75 ml red wine vinegar
sea salt and freshly ground black pepper

Preheat the oven to 180°C. Place the tomatoes and garlic heads in a roasting pan, fill the tomato cores with olive oil and drizzle oil over the garlic heads as well. Roast for 1½ hours until well baked and slightly caramelised.

Roast the almonds and hazelnuts in a pan over gentle heat until slightly coloured. Take care not to burn the nuts or they will give off a bitter taste.

Remove the skins from the roasted tomatoes and garlic and discard. Place the tomatoes and garlic in a food processor with the nuts, roasted chillies, minced fresh garlic and pulse until coarsely ground.

With the motor running, slowly add the Siurana olive oil, as if you were making a mayonnaise. Add the red wine vinegar in small amounts, stopping the processor to taste and test the texture. It is necessary to do this as vinegars vary in strength and acidity. Add salt and pepper to taste and serve.

SERVES 12

ROMESCO TOMATOES WITH YABBIES

Now that you have mastered the romesco sauce, it's time to put it to good use. Scampi or small river prawns can be used in place of the yabbies if you have trouble sourcing these freshwater babies.

4 ripe medium-size tomatoes
200 ml Romesco Sauce (see left)
200 ml extra virgin olive oil
4 cloves garlic
1 small red chilli, split lengthways
2 sprigs thyme
16 raw yabby tails, shelled and deveined
½ teaspoon sea salt
¼ teaspoon freshly ground black pepper
20 g hazelnuts, roasted and chopped

Preheat the oven to 100°C. Blanch the tomatoes in boiling water for 10 seconds then peel. Cut off the tops and scoop out the seeds, taking care not to break the outer wall. Fill the tomato shells with romesco sauce, reserving 80 ml for later.

Pour the olive oil into a small baking dish (so tomatoes fit snugly together) and add the garlic, chilli and thyme. Sit the tomatoes in the oil – it should come two-thirds of the way up the sides of the tomatoes. Bake for 1 hour until the tomatoes soften and become confit-like. Using a slotted spoon or spatula, carefully remove the tomatoes from the oil without breaking.

Pour 40 ml of the tomato oil into a pan (reserve the rest for another use) and when it starts to sizzle, saute the yabby tails for 2 minutes until just cooked. Remove from the pan and season with salt and pepper.

Strain the reserved romesco sauce through a fine mesh sieve, discarding the solids, and heat in a pan until warmed through. Place spoonfuls of romesco sauce onto a plate and sit the tomatoes on top. Arrange the yabby tails on the tomatoes and sprinkle with the chopped hazelnuts. Serve immediately.

SERVES 4

TUNA WITH CRAB AND ROASTED CAPSICUM AND CAPER SALSA

This recipe offers an alternative way of serving tuna sashimi: the fish is sliced into thin rectangular lengths, stuffed before rolling, then cut in half in the manner of Japanese maki sushi. This dish first appeared on our Paramount menus in the late 1990s, and is a terrific example of how Spanish flavours and Japanese technique can be fused together to create intriguing combinations.

250 g sashimi-grade bluefin or yellowfin tuna
1 tablespoon Alioli (see Essentials)
2 teaspoons freshwater salmon roe

ROASTED CAPSICUM AND CAPER SALSA
1 red capsicum (pepper)
1 yellow capsicum (pepper)
2 long red chillies
1 tablespoon small salted capers, rinsed
2 golden shallots, finely diced
3 tablespoons parsley leaves, finely shredded
½ teaspoon sea salt
¼ teaspoon freshly ground black pepper
¼ teaspoon Spanish sweet paprika
50 ml extra virgin olive oil

CRAB FILLING
125 g picked crabmeat (blue swimmer or spanner)
1 teaspoon finely diced preserved lemon rind
2 teaspoons finely diced fennel bulb
2 teaspoons Alioli (see Essentials)
1 teaspoon chopped chives
1 teaspoon shredded parsley leaves
¼ teaspoon sea salt
¼ teaspoon freshly ground white pepper

To make the salsa, roast the capsicums and chillies over a direct flame until the skins have blistered. Transfer to a plastic bag and leave them to steam for 5 minutes. Take them out of the bag and peel off the skins. Cut into coarse 5 mm dice and place in a bowl. Stir in the capers, shallots and parsley, season with salt, pepper and paprika and dress with oil. Set aside at room temperature until ready to serve.

To make the crab filling, combine all the ingredients in a bowl.

Cut the tuna into 5 mm thick rectangular slices that are 9 cm × 6 cm, to make four portions. Lay the fish slices on a board with their narrowest end nearest you. Spoon the crab filling onto one end and roll up. Rest on the seam until ready to serve.

To serve, smear each plate with alioli in the centre and spoon some of the salsa on top (reserve the rest for another use). Slice each tuna roll in half across the centre and stand the two rolls next to each other on top of the salsa with the filling facing upwards. Spoon a little salmon roe into the centre of each roll and serve.

SERVES 4

GARLIC MUSSEL SOUP

This soup is inspired by suquet – a garlicky potato-based Catalan seafood broth or stew first introduced to me by Sarah, a Spanish woman living in Sydney. She told me about several tabernas in Cadaques and Roses where I could taste this regional classic, and I have some great taste memories to draw on. Make a full-flavoured fish stock with whole small rock cod before you start, as this underpins the final result.

1.5 kg mussels, scrubbed
60 ml olive oil
1 brown onion, diced
4 large cloves garlic, chopped
2 small red chillies, chopped
½ teaspoon ground fennel seeds
1 stick celery, sliced
2 tablespoons diced fennel bulb
1 carrot, diced
3 potatoes, diced
4 roasted tomatoes, chopped
100 ml white wine
½ teaspoon saffron threads
400 ml Fish Stock (see Essentials)
400 ml Prawn Stock (see Essentials)
30 ml fresh lemon juice, strained
2 teaspoons sea salt
1 teaspoon freshly ground black pepper
2 tablespoons shredded parsley leaves

To prepare the mussels, heat a wide-based pan and add enough mussels to cover the base of the pan. Cover and steam for about 2–3 minutes, allowing the mussels to open. Remove the mussels and plunge into iced water to stop the cooking. Remove the mussels from their shells, snip off the beards and set aside. Repeat the process until all the mussels have been removed from their shells.

To make the soup, heat the oil in a large saucepan, fry the onion until softened, then add the garlic, chilli and ground fennel and cook for about 3 minutes until softened. Add the celery, fennel, carrot, potato and tomato and cook for a couple of minutes. Add the wine and saffron and simmer for 3 minutes, until the wine has reduced slightly. Add the fish and prawn stocks and bring to the boil.

Reduce the heat and simmer for 35–40 minutes until the potato is soft.

Pass the soup through a mouli or push through a coarse sieve (do not blend in a processor as it will make the potatoes gluey). Season to taste with lemon juice, salt and pepper.

To serve, toss the mussels with the parsley, divide among serving bowls and ladle the soup over the top.

SERVES 4

ESCALIVADA WITH SMOKED OCEAN TROUT

Taking my inspiration from escalivada (a classic Catalan grilled vegetable salad), I have used the same elements and combined them with raw or smoked fish. In particular, I love to use the flavoursome Woodbridge smoked ocean trout from Tasmania. The fish are sourced from the pristine waters of Macquarie Harbour and smoked over cuttings from the apple trees on the Woodbridge property. The smoky flavours meld perfectly in this delicious combination.

120 ml Romesco Sauce (see page 344)
200 g smoked ocean trout fillet, finely sliced
½ teaspoon sea salt
¼ teaspoon freshly ground black pepper
3 tablespoons salmon roe

ESCALIVADA SALAD
1 eggplant (aubergine)
1 red capsicum (pepper)
1 yellow capsicum (pepper)
1 fennel bulb
1 red onion
olive oil, for roasting
2 ripe tomatoes
1 tablespoon shredded parsley leaves
8 anchovy fillets, chopped
2 tablespoons Anchovy Mayonnaise (see Essentials)

To make the escalivada salad, roast the eggplant and capsicums until the skins are blackened. Transfer to a plastic bag and leave them to steam for 5 minutes, then remove the skins and seeds and cut into thin strips.

Preheat the oven to 180°C. Slice the fennel and onion, toss with a little olive oil and roast for about 15 minutes until caramelised. Remove from the oven and reduce the temperature to 160°C.

Cut the tomatoes in half lengthways, drizzle with a little olive oil and slow-roast in the oven for about 25 minutes until caramelised. Remove the skins and seeds and slice into strips.

Mix the roasted vegetables together with the parsley and chopped anchovy fillets and bind with the anchovy mayonnaise.

Heat the romesco sauce and pass through a fine mesh sieve, discarding the solids.

Brush four 150 ml dariole moulds with olive oil. Season the ocean trout with salt and pepper, line the moulds with the fish slices, overlapping slightly. Fill the moulds with the warm roasted vegetable salad. Fold the fish slices over to seal the moulds and press.

Spoon the romesco sauce onto plates. Upturn the moulds immediately onto the plates (as the vegetables are still warm and will cook the fish otherwise). Spoon the salmon roe over the fish and serve.

SERVES 4

SAFFRON FISH STEW

I still remember the first time I tasted zarzuela (a Catalan fish stew) at one of the waterfront tabernas in Barceloneta, and I get a real kick out of emulating its flavours in this dish. Typically Mediterranean, it is a close relative of the French and Italian fish stews that use very similar ingredients.

100 ml olive oil
1 brown onion, sliced
6 cloves garlic, minced
1 fennel bulb, sliced
1 teaspoon fennel seeds, roasted and ground
200 ml Tomato Pasta Sauce (see Essentials)
1 teaspoon saffron threads
75 ml white wine
600 g large white fish fillets (such as blue eye, snapper, jewfish, deep-sea perch or monkfish)
finely grated zest and juice of 1 lemon
2 tablespoons pitted black olives
3 roasted pimientos (piquillo peppers), sliced
1 small fennel bulb, extra, shaved
1 punnet Roasted Cherry Tomatoes (see Essentials)
2 teaspoons sea salt
2 teaspoons freshly ground black pepper
1 cup torn basil leaves
2 tablespoons Saffron Alioli (see Essentials)

Preheat the oven to 170°C. Heat the oil in a large ovenproof pan and saute the onion, garlic and fennel until slightly coloured. Add the ground fennel and stir to combine. Stir in the pasta sauce, saffron and white wine and bring to the boil. Reduce the heat and simmer gently for 10 minutes.

Cut the fish into large chunks and add to the sauce with the lemon zest and juice, olives, roasted pimiento, shaved fennel and roasted tomatoes. Season with salt and pepper. Cover with foil (or a lid) and bake in the oven for 12 minutes.

Remove from the heat and stir in the basil leaves. Taste and adjust the seasoning if necessary, then swirl the saffron alioli through the sauce. Serve with crusty bread or roasted potatoes.

SERVES 4

BARBEQUED OCTOPUS WITH ROASTED GARLIC, TOMATO AND PIMIENTO SALAD

This makes a fabulous starter or summer lunch dish. It's worth using unbeaten baby octopus, which are readily available from fish markets and good fishmongers these days. They have a soft texture because they haven't been tumbled through a mixer and cook very quickly on the barbeque or grill plate.

400 g baby octopus, heads removed
50 ml olive oil
sea salt and freshly ground black pepper
6 roma tomatoes
2 small red onions, peeled
8 cloves garlic, peeled
120 g roasted pimientos (piquillo peppers), cut into strips
80 g wild rocket leaves
2 tablespoons Alioli (see Essentials)

DRESSING
40 ml aged balsamic vinegar
120 ml extra virgin olive oil
½ teaspoon sea salt
½ teaspoon freshly ground black pepper

Preheat the oven to 200°C. Toss the octopus in a bowl with 30 ml of the olive oil and season to taste with salt and pepper.

Cut the tomatoes in half lengthways, brush with oil and roast in the oven for about 20 minutes until softened and slightly caramelised.

Slice the onions into eighths lengthways and lay on a baking tray with the whole garlic cloves, drizzle with the remaining olive oil and roast in the oven for about 15 minutes until soft and coloured.

Combine the roasted onion and garlic, roasted tomatoes and pimiento strips in a bowl.

Cook the octopus over a hot chargrill or barbeque briefly for 4–5 minutes until tender and changed to a pink colour.

To make the dressing, place the vinegar, extra virgin olive oil, salt and pepper in a bowl and whisk until combined. Add the dressing to the salad ingredients with the cooked octopus and rocket leaves. Toss to combine.

Arrange the salad on serving plates and drizzle the alioli over the top.

SERVES 4

CHICKEN SAUSAGE ROLL WITH CAULIFLOWER AND PISTACHIO

The detailed preparation for this whimsical play on the iconic 'sausage roll' is rewarded by its elegant appearance and divine taste – all those wonderful flavours captured within its skin. Most of the work can be done beforehand, to the point where you bake the chicken roll, making it an ideal dish to serve when you want the *wow* factor without being absent from the table for too long. The cauliflower couscous pays homage to Ferran Adria's brilliance, a reminder of one of the first tasks I performed when I spent a short time in his kitchen.

1 x 1.8 kg organic chicken
50 ml olive oil
4 cloves garlic, minced
3 shallots, finely diced
100 g speck, diced
2 teaspoons sea salt
1 teaspoon freshly ground white pepper
½ teaspoon ground cinnamon
½ teaspoon ground ginger
1 teaspoon cumin
150 g veal sweetbreads, blanched and peeled
2 egg whites
1 tablespoon chopped oregano
1 tablespoon chopped parsley leaves
40 g shelled pistachios, roughly chopped
½ batch Creme Fraiche Pastry (see Essentials), rolled out into 2 rectangular sheets
1 egg yolk
¼ cauliflower
2 slices Iberian ham, cut into fine julienne strips
30 g shelled pistachios, extra, finely chopped
sea salt and freshly ground black pepper

PX SAUCE
2 litres White Chicken Stock (see Essentials)
120 ml Pedro Ximenez sherry
30 ml fish sauce
1 teaspoon freshly ground black pepper

GREEN SAUCE
5 cloves garlic, chopped
1 teaspoon sea salt
½ teaspoon cumin seeds, roasted and ground
2 cups coriander leaves, tightly packed
½ cup parsley leaves
250 ml extra virgin olive oil
½ teaspoon freshly ground black pepper
2 teaspoons sherry vinegar

Preheat the oven to 180°C. Snip the wings off the chicken and set aside. Split the chicken down the backbone and carefully remove the skin in one piece. Remove the two leg and thigh joints from the carcass, then carve off the two breast fillets. Remove the leg and thigh meat from the bones. Put the chicken carcass, bones and wings in a baking tray and roast for 25 minutes until browned.

To start the PX sauce, add the roasted bones to the chicken stock in a large saucepan and bring to simmering point. Simmer for 1 hour then strain and discard the bones. Return the strained stock to the pan and bring back to simmering point.

Chop the leg meat into a fine mince. Cut the thigh meat into 2 cm cubes. Butterfly open the breast fillets, and cut the chicken skin lengthways into two pieces.

Heat the olive oil in a pan and fry the garlic, shallots and speck until softened and starting to colour. Remove from the pan and leave to cool.

Mix the salt, pepper, cinnamon, ginger and cumin together. Lightly season the diced chicken thigh meat with half the spice mix and fry in the same pan as the garlic mix for about 5–6 minutes until browned. Remove from the pan and allow to cool.

Cut the peeled sweetbreads into 2 cm dice and combine with the chicken thigh pieces. >>

<< Mix the minced chicken leg meat with the egg white, oregano, parsley, cooled garlic mix and 1 teaspoon of the spice mix until combined. Stir in the chopped pistachios and the chicken and sweetbread chunks to make the stuffing.

Stretch each sheet of chicken skin out onto a work surface, with the inside facing up and season with some of the remaining spice mix. Lay a butterflied breast fillet lengthways on each piece of skin, following the same direction as the skin. Season with spice mix.

Spoon the stuffing mix down the centre of each breast fillet then fold over to enclose the stuffing. Wrap the skin over, folding in the edges to completely seal.

Sit the two chicken parcels on a flat tray and refrigerate for 1 hour until the meat becomes firm. Wrap each parcel in a double layer of muslin, with enough length to wrap around the chicken three times. Tie both ends tightly with kitchen twine to secure – the parcels should be sausage-shaped and firmly sealed.

Add the chicken parcels to the simmering stock, making sure they are fully submerged, and cook over the lowest heat for 15 minutes (the surface should not be bubbling). Turn the heat off, cover the pan and leave the chicken to poach in the stock for 45 minutes. Remove the chicken parcels from the stock and allow to cool completely, then refrigerate for 1 hour until cold.

To complete the PX sauce, leave the stock to cool and settle then skim the surface. Bring the stock back to the boil, skim the surface again and continue to boil until the stock has reduced by half. Add the sherry and continue to reduce by a third. Season to taste with fish sauce and freshly ground black pepper.

To make the green sauce, blend the garlic, salt and cumin in a food processor, add the coriander and parsley leaves and pulse until combined. With the motor running, slowly add the oil, a little at time, to make a thick paste. Season to taste with pepper and vinegar.

Preheat the oven to 180°C and line a baking tray with baking paper. Remove the muslin layers from the chicken, then wrap each chicken parcel in a sheet of pastry, trimming the excess from the edges so each parcel resembles a sausage roll. Lay the chicken pastries on the baking tray and brush with egg yolk.

Bake for 25 minutes until the pastry is golden. Cut each chicken pastry into 4 cm thick slices.

While the pastries are baking, shave the cauliflower with a medium-coarse Microplane to make tiny pieces that resemble couscous grains. Blanch the cauliflower in boiling water for 20 seconds, then strain.

Fry the ham strips until crisp, then stir into the cauliflower with the finely chopped pistachios. Season to taste with sea salt and freshly ground black pepper.

To serve, spoon the cauliflower mix into the centre of each bowl plate and ladle around the PX sauce, enough to make a small pool. Spoon a little of the green sauce on top of the cauliflower, then place a slice of the chicken sausage roll on top.

SERVES 6

CHICKEN SAUSAGE ROLL WITH
< CAULIFLOWER AND PISTACHIO (see page 353)

ROASTED POUSSINS WITH CLEMENTINES

On a gastronomy tour of Catalonia with a small group of Australian chefs in 1998, I visited a couple of different clementine farms and co-operatives near Tarragona. It was the first time I had tasted clementines straight from the tree – a mix between a mandarin and an orange, they are deliciously sweet and juicy with a gentle underlying acidity, and are terrific teamed with all types of poultry. Mandarins, tangelos or blood oranges make an acceptable substitute.

4 × 500 g poussins
1 tablespoon coriander leaves
1 tablespoon shredded parsley leaves
2 clementines, seeded and sliced into rounds
3 teaspoons demerara sugar

CLEMENTINE MARINADE
juice and zest of 3 clementines
juice and zest of 2 limes
2 small red chillies
6 cloves garlic, minced
1 teaspoon chopped thyme
1 teaspoon chopped oregano
50 ml balsamic vinegar
120 ml extra virgin olive oil
1 teaspoon sea salt
1 teaspoon freshly ground black pepper

Split the poussins down their backbone and flatten out. Snip off the wing tips.

To make the marinade, blanch the clementine and lime zest in boiling water for 1 minute. Place the zest in a bowl with the remaining marinade ingredients and mix to combine.

Lay the birds in a large baking dish in a single layer, pour on the marinade and rub into the birds. Lay the birds breast-side down and leave to marinate for 2 hours.

Preheat the oven to 200°C. Pour the marinade off the birds and turn them over so they are breast-side up. Roast in the oven for 30 minutes or until cooked and lightly browned. Spoon a little marinade over the birds as they cook to keep them moist.

Pour the remaining marinade into a saucepan and simmer until reduced by half.

Strain and discard the solids, then stir the coriander and parsley leaves into the sauce.

Lay the clementine slices on a flat tray and dust with the sugar. Cook under a hot grill until caramelised.

Arrange the clementine slices in the centre of each plate. Cut the poussins in half, and lay over the clementine slices. Spoon the sauce over the top and serve.

SERVES 4

PORK AND FENNEL SAUSAGES

Sausage making is one of my favourite kitchen rituals. I find it very therapeutic, and the results of my labour seem to weave their way into so many dishes. For instance, these sausages can be grilled then sliced into a tangy fennel and lemon salad, served with spicy lentils, or added to a paella. They are also fabulous simply cooked over hot coals or on the barbeque.

2 teaspoons fennel seeds
1 kg pork shoulder, minced
200 g pork fat, coarsely minced
50 ml vegetable oil
1 brown onion, minced
10 cloves garlic, minced
1 fennel bulb, finely diced
2 long red chillies, minced
1 tablespoon Spanish sweet paprika
1 tablespoon sea salt
2 teaspoons freshly ground black pepper
4 tablespoons shredded parsley leaves
300 g sausage casings, washed
3 litres White Chicken Stock (see Essentials)

Dry-roast the fennel seeds over gentle heat until fragrant. Cool, then grind to a fine powder.

Combine the minced pork with the pork fat in a large bowl, working together with your fingers. Set aside.

Heat the oil in a wide, heavy-based pan over moderate heat and saute the minced onion, garlic, fennel bulb and chilli for about 2 minutes until softened.

Stir in the paprika and ground fennel and cook for a few minutes until fragrant and beginning to colour. Remove from the heat and season with salt and pepper. Allow to cool completely.

Stir the cooled spice mixture and parsley into the minced pork until thoroughly incorporated. Fry a small spoonful of the mixture in oil to test for seasoning. When cooked through, taste and adjust if necessary.

To make the sausages, tie a knot in one end of the sausage casing. Spoon the pork mixture into a piping bag fitted with a wide nozzle and pipe the mix into the casing, taking care to apply even, steady pressure and to leave a little space for the mixture to expand during cooking. Twist the filled casing every 10 cm to give the sausages their shape. Secure the filled and twisted casing with a knot.

Bring the stock to a gentle simmer in a stockpot and poach the sausages in a single layer for 15 minutes. Turn them once for even cooking. Remove from the stock and hang the sausages on a hook over a tray and allow to cool completely.

Place the sausages on a clean tray, then cover and refrigerate until ready to use. They will keep for 2 days in the fridge, or can be frozen for up to a month.

MAKES 1.5 KG

LEMON CREAM, WITH TOFFEE FIGS AND MERINGUE

Figs are synonymous with summer. During the European summer they are prolific and deeply respected, from Spain, London and Greece to Turkey and the Middle East. The combination of ripe, juicy figs and the lemony fromage blanc (a soft white cheese) is a very sensual experience that honours one of the oldest fruit trees in the world. As Stephanie Alexander so eloquently puts it in *The Cook's Companion*, 'eating a fully ripe fig warm from the tree is an emotional experience'.

150 ml Sugar Syrup (see Essentials)
6 thin slices of lemon, blanched
9 figs
1 tablespoon demerara sugar
1 tablespoon Lemon Caramel (see Essentials)
6 cooked Meringue Disks (see Essentials)

LEMON JELLY
90 ml Sugar Syrup (see Essentials)
25 ml limoncello
3 g gelatine leaves, softened in cold water
65 ml fresh lemon juice, strained

LEMON CREAM
100 ml milk
zest of 1 lemon
3 egg yolks
110 g castor sugar
65 ml fresh lemon juice, strained
2 teaspoons limoncello
2.5 g gelatine leaves, softened in cold water
100 ml thick (45%) cream
80 g fromage blanc

To make the lemon jelly, heat the sugar syrup and Limoncello to simmering point. Take off the heat, add the softened gelatine and lemon juice and stir until dissolved. Allow to cool slightly, then pour into six 150 ml dariole moulds to make a 6 mm thick layer. Refrigerate until set.

To confit the lemon slices, heat the sugar syrup to simmering point, add the lemon slices and cook over gentle heat for 30 minutes. Remove the lemon slices from the syrup and lay on a flat plate to cool. When cool, lay a lemon slice over the jelly in each of the moulds.

To make the lemon cream, heat the milk and lemon zest in a pan to simmering point. Whisk the egg yolks and sugar until pale and creamy, then slowly add the lemon juice and Limoncello, whisking to combine. Pour in the hot milk and whisk to combine.

Stand the bowl over a pan of simmering water and cook to a custard consistency, until the mixture coats the back of a spoon. Add the softened gelatine leaves and stir until dissolved. Remove from the heat and pass through a fine mesh sieve into a bowl, discarding the solids.

Stand the bowl over another bowl of ice to prevent further cooking and allow the custard to cool completely. Whip the cream and fromage blanc together until just combined – do not overwork or it will split and become granular. Gently fold the whipped cream through the custard until combined. Spoon the lemon cream into the moulds until full. Smooth the surface and refrigerate for 4 hours until set.

Cut each fig into four slices crossways and lay on a flat tray in a single layer. Sprinkle with demerara sugar and caramelise with a blow torch (or under a hot grill) until golden. Arrange six fig slices in a circle in the centre of each plate and drizzle with lemon caramel.

Sit a meringue disk on top of the figs, so the edges of the figs are still visible from beneath the meringue. Dip the dariole moulds into hot water for 20 seconds to loosen, then turn out and sit the lemon cream on top of the figs.

SERVES 6

ORANGE FANTASY

Oranges in different textures is the best way to describe this offering. Using the same ingredient in different ways allowed me to explore the possibilities and see how they could be translated onto the plate. Even though each component can be served by itself, I like how they come together to create a symphony for the palate. There are seven components: each one is made in miniature (petit-four size), using different orange varieties and assembled on the same plate, resulting in a spectacular visual effect. There is absolutely nothing stopping you from making any one of these recipes and serving them solo, but you may have to adjust the quantities slightly to suit. Warning: this entire presentation is for those adventurous cooks amongst you!

ORANGE CARAMEL CREAM
3 egg yolks
1 large egg
40 g castor sugar
45 ml fresh orange juice, strained
175 ml pouring (35%) cream
2 teaspoons finely grated orange zest
50 ml sauternes

CARAMEL
200 g castor sugar
40 ml water

Preheat the oven to 140°C – do not use fan-force. Make a caramel by boiling the castor sugar and water over high heat without stirring. Pour the hot caramel into four 100 ml moulds, working quickly as the caramel will continue to cook and will darken. Tilt the moulds to ensure they are evenly lined with caramel, then discard any excess and allow the caramel to cool.

Whisk the yolks, egg and sugar together until the sugar has dissolved, then whisk in the orange juice.

Heat the cream with the orange zest in one pan and the sauternes in another pan and bring them both to simmering point.

Stir the sauternes into the egg mix, then add the cream, stirring constantly. Pass the custard through a fine mesh sieve and skim the surface to remove any bubbles. Pour the custard into the toffee-lined moulds.

Stand the custards in a baking dish and pour in enough boiling water to come three-quarters of the way up the sides of the moulds. Bake for 40 minutes, turning the baking dish around after 15–20 minutes to ensure even cooking.

Remove the custards from the water bath and allow to cool. Refrigerate for 4 hours before serving.

ORANGE BLOSSOM JELLY
180 ml Seville orange juice
100 ml Sugar Syrup (see Essentials)
50 ml orange blossom water
5 g gelatine leaves, softened in cold water

Bring the orange juice, sugar syrup and blossom water to the boil in a saucepan.

Stir in the softened gelatine until dissolved, then remove from the heat. Pass through a fine mesh sieve and allow to cool.

Pour the cooled mixture into a fleximat mould set on a flat tray – I use the small pyramid-shaped ones. Refrigerate for about 3 hours, until set.

Pop the jellies from the mould when ready to serve.

CHOCOLATE JAFFA BALLS
zest of 2 oranges
60 ml fresh orange juice, strained
1 clove
3 g cassia bark
½ vanilla bean
60 g glucose
25 g honey
50 ml Mandarin Napoleon liqueur
200 ml creme fraiche, warmed
300 g Valrhona Orange Noir chocolate, chopped and melted
20 ml extra virgin olive oil
½ cup Almond Praline (see Essentials) >>

<< Combine the orange zest, orange juice, clove, cassia bark, vanilla bean, glucose, honey and liqueur in a saucepan and bring to simmering point.

Pass through a fine mesh sieve and add the creme fraiche, melted chocolate and olive oil. Stir to combine then blend with a stick blender or firm whisk to ensure smoothness.

Pour the chocolate ganache into a dish and refrigerate until set and very firm.

Shape into balls using a small parisienne cutter, then roll the chocolate balls in praline and refrigerate again until ready to serve.

ORANGE AND ALMOND WAFERS
100 g egg whites (about 3 or 4 eggs)
90 g castor sugar
90 g plain flour
90 g blanched almonds
30 g candied orange peel, minced

Preheat the oven to 175°C and line a small rectangular cake tin with baking paper.

Whisk the egg whites in an electric mixer until stiff peaks form, then add the sugar in a slow, steady stream, beating continuously. Fold in the flour, nuts and minced orange with a spatula. Spoon the mixture into the prepared tin and bake for 30 minutes.

Remove the loaf carefully from the tin and cool on a wire rack. When cool, wrap it in foil and freeze for about an hour, until firm enough to slice.

Preheat the oven to 75°C. Cut the frozen loaf into paper-thin slices using a very sharp knife, then arrange the slices in a single layer on a baking tray. Transfer to the oven and toast the almond bread for about 15 minutes until crisp and only slightly coloured (you don't need to turn them). Store in an airtight container until ready to serve.

ORANGE OLIVE OIL CAKES
3 large eggs, separated
90 g castor sugar
1 teaspoon minced lemon zest
1 teaspoon minced orange zest
65 ml extra virgin olive oil
60 ml sauternes
80 g plain flour, sifted
pinch of sea salt
1 egg white, extra
¼ teaspoon cream of tartar
icing sugar, for dusting

ORANGE CURD
2 egg yolks
40 g castor sugar
45 ml fresh orange juice, strained
50 g unsalted butter, diced

To make the orange curd, place the egg yolks and sugar in a bowl and whisk until pale and creamy. Add the orange juice and whisk until combined.

Stand the bowl over a pan of simmering water and continue to whisk until the mixture cooks and thickens. Add the butter piece by piece, adding the next piece when the previous one melts into the curd. Remove the bowl from the heat as soon as the last piece of butter is added and stand the bowl over ice to cool immediately and prevent the curd from splitting or overcooking. Refrigerate until ready to serve.

To make the cakes, preheat the oven to 170°C. Whisk the egg yolks with half the sugar until light and thickened. Add the minced citrus zest, then whisk in the olive oil and then the sauternes. Mix the flour with the salt and gently fold into the egg yolk mix until just combined.

Whisk the egg whites with the cream of tartar until soft peaks form. Gradually add the remaining sugar and beat until stiff. Fold gently into the base mixture.

Spoon the batter into small fleximat moulds (or small moulds lined with cupcake papers) set on a flat tray. Bake for 8 minutes, then reduce the oven temperature to 150°C and bake for a further 10 minutes. Turn the oven off, and leave the cakes in the oven for 10 minutes before removing.

Pop the cakes out of their moulds, cut the tops off and hollow out the centres slightly. Spoon the orange curd into the hollow cake centres until full, then replace the cake tops as a lid and dust with icing sugar to serve.

TANGELO AND MINT SALAD
2 tangelos, peeled and cut into segments
2 tablespoons mint leaves, roughly chopped
20 ml tangelo juice
1 teaspoon finely grated orange zest
20 ml Sugar Syrup (see Essentials)

Mix the tangelo segments with the mint leaves.

Combine the juice, zest and sugar syrup in a bowl, then stir into the salad.

BLOOD ORANGE SORBET
250 ml fresh blood orange juice, strained
50 g glucose, softened
50 g castor sugar

Mix the juice with the glucose and sugar and whisk until the sugar dissolves. Pour into the bowl of an ice-cream machine and churn until firm and chilled. Spoon into small dariole moulds and smooth the surface, then cover with plastic film and freeze until ready to serve.

To assemble the orange fantasy, arrange each component separately on a large plate to give a dramatic appearance and serve immediately.

SERVES 6–12

RASPBERRY RIPPLE

Inspired by the deft and exacting craft of the chefs at El Bulli and other Spanish dessert chefs, I developed this idea for the East@West dessert menu, and it achieved something of an iconic status during its time there. The cellophane wafer is so clear that the cream and raspberries appear to be suspended over the plate.

80 ml Raspberry Sauce (see Essentials)
1 punnet raspberries
3 tablespoons Meringue Dots (see Essentials)

CELLOPHANE WAFERS
150 g fondant
100 g glucose

YOGHURT VANILLA CREAM
475 ml pouring (35%) cream
2 vanilla beans, split and scraped
165 g castor sugar
7 g gelatine leaves, softened in cold water
25 ml Frangelico liqueur
315 g thick plain yoghurt

To make the wafers, put the fondant and glucose in a saucepan and heat to 150°C, using a sugar thermometer to gauge the temperature. Pour onto a silpat (silicone mat) and allow to cool. Break the hard mix into small pieces, then blitz to a fine powder in a food processor.

Preheat the oven to 150°C. Lay a silpat on a baking tray and sieve on the wafer powder using a rectangular-shaped template 6 cm × 12 cm to make the desired shape. Transfer to the oven and bake until the mixture has melted and set, but not coloured. Repeat to make six wafers in all.

Working with one wafer at a time, remove and lift carefully off the mat with a palette knife and wrap around either a square or round tube mould, pressing at the join with your fingers until it has set. Store the wafers between tissue paper in an airtight container until ready to serve.

To make the yoghurt vanilla cream, combine the cream, vanilla and sugar in a saucepan and bring to simmering point over gentle heat. Stir in the softened gelatine until dissolved, then add the Frangelico. Pass through a fine mesh sieve and discard the solids. Allow to cool for 5 minutes, then gently whisk in the yoghurt. Refrigerate for about 3 hours until set.

To serve, stand a cellophane wafer on each plate. Spoon the yoghurt vanilla cream into a piping bag with a medium-size round nozzle. Pipe a small amount of vanilla cream into each wafer, swirling a little raspberry sauce through as you go to give a ripple effect, and adding a raspberry and a few meringue dots here and there – for texture and crunch. Continue until the wafer is full.

Sit some raspberries on top and spoon a small puddle of raspberry sauce on the plate around the base of the wafer. Serve immediately.

SERVES 6

LIKE A VIRGIN ANDALUCIA

The expansive region of Andalucia stretches across southern Spain, incorporating the coastal provinces of Huelva, Cadiz, Malaga and Almeria, and spreading inland to Sevilla, Cordoba, Jaen and Granada, where the rolling hills are cloaked with olive trees. The Sierra Nevada mountains offer a dramatic backdrop that separates Granada and Almeria to the east. The peaks remain snow-capped right through summer and there are wonderful forests and national parks to explore. The Moors occupied these lands for 700 years through the Middle Ages, leaving a unique legacy that is reflected in the region's culture, food and architecture. It feels distinctly different from other parts of Spain. The classic Andalucian houses, haciendas and hotels have internal courtyards fragrant with lemon trees and rose bushes (a style that is also found in Morocco, due to its own Moorish history), and the houses are painted white with distinctive yellow and green tiles, a colour scheme that is used throughout the entire region.

I first travelled to the south of Spain in 2001. I had no time constraints, which meant I was free to immerse myself in the Andalucian way of life and pursue some personal research. Margie joined me and we set off to explore Sevilla, Cordoba and Granada. It was the height of summer and the intense heat bounced off the ochre-coloured earth, just like it does in the outback of Australia.

Arriving in Sevilla, we couldn't believe our eyes. What a place! The cobblestone streets of Santa Cruz (the medieval Jewish quarter at the heart of the old city), the gardens full of orange blossom and jasmine, the majestic Giralda tower and cathedral that are the city's main landmarks, and the beautiful Alcazar palace, all conveyed a strong Moorish influence. There is much to see and absorb here – the commercial districts of La Macarena and Centro, as well as the atmospheric alleyways of Santa Cruz and the old port area of El Arenal. One evening we went to watch a bullfight in Maestranza de Sevilla, the most famous bullring in the world, and watched in horror as one of the matadors was severely gored by a dying bull. The smell of blood filled the air. It was an amazing, if shocking, experience to sit amongst the locals who hold this tradition so dear. Afterwards, we crossed the Guadalquivir River to the lively district of Triana, to eat at one of the local tabernas along the water's edge. Crowded tascas (tapas bars) beckoned, so we went and stood with the locals, pointing at what we wanted. On the first night, we were shown to a table in the restaurant area, but quickly realised we were in Siberia and that all the action was happening out front at the bar, so we left and joined the throng. Much more fun.

For our final night in Sevilla, we made the pilgrimage to El Bulli Hotel Hacienda Benazuza, for dinner at La Alqueria, to enhance our appreciation of the magic that Ferran Adria weaves across Spain. The menu features some of the classic El Bulli tastes, and the setting is enchanting: a luxurious hacienda-style house with sumptuous gardens.

In Cordoba, we lingered in the Mezquita (the great mosque in the centre of the old town), as its immense stone walls provided welcome relief from the blazing 40°C heat. Staying in a hotel with a swimming pool also proved to be

SLEEPING AND EATING IN SEVILLA

LAS CASAS DEL REY DE BAEZA
Plaza Jesus de la Redencion 2, Centro, Sevilla
Tel +34 954 561 496
www.hospes.es
Stylish, modern and sexy accommodation.

HACIENDA BENAZUZA
Sanlucar La Mayor, Sevilla
Tel +34 955 703 344
www.elbullihotel.com
About 15 kilometres outside the city, on the main road to Huelva, this Moorish farmhouse is now a fully fledged El Bulli hotel. It also houses La Alqueria restaurant, with its inventive El Bulli menu, for a gastronomic feast – worth a visit even if you are not staying here.

LA BODEGUITA
Calle Hernando Colon 1–3, Santa Cruz, Sevilla
Tel +34 954 564 230
Probably the best tapas in town, especially the eggplant dishes. A tiny space so just turn up and hope for the best.

CASA PLACIDO
Calle Meson del Moro 5, Sevilla
Tel +34 954 563 971
Traditional fino bar with hams hanging from the ceiling – very local and atmospheric.

a very wise decision. We took to seeing the sights in the morning when it was slightly cooler, then swimming in the afternoon before our siesta, emerging at sunset feeling cool and refreshed – a lifestyle we grew increasingly comfortable with. Cordoba moves at a slower pace then Sevilla, and we spent many days exploring the back roads that lead from Cordoba to the east and south, stopping to gaze at the white-washed villages that cling to the hillsides. The landscape was covered by great swathes of olive groves – the main reason for my visit to this region.

Spain is the world's largest producer of olive oil, and around half of all Spanish olive oil is produced in Andalucia. We were invited to spend the day at Nunez de Prado, in Baena, about an hour east of Cordoba. We drove through the olive groves (mostly picual and picudo varieties here, and all are grown organically), tasted the latest release being bottled and had a delicious lunch of local dishes with our charming hosts, Paco and Felipe. I will always remember my first taste of salmorejo, the Andalucian version of gazpacho, made creamy and smooth with olive oil. Another day, we travelled south to Santaella and visited another olive oil cortijo (estate), Barneo. They make their oil using a variety of olives – hojiblanca, ocal, picual and arbequina – so it was interesting to taste and compare the different attributes.

The multitude of olive varieties grown in Spain offer a diverse range of culinary opportunities: for example, arbequina, picual, hojiblanca, lechin, picudo and cornicabra are used to make extra virgin olive oils; while gordal, blanqueta and manzanillo varieties are served as table olives. Each type has its own taste, whether it be savoury, sweet, acidic, astringent or bitter. As I was to learn, terroir (the unique characteristics of the local environment) is also an important factor in determining the flavour of an extra virgin olive oil, just as it is when growing grapes for wine-making. The differences in terrain, climate, rainfall and hours of sunshine result in oils that differ from each other in taste, aroma and colour. Understanding the unique character of each variety of olive allowed me to appreciate its sensory profile and the range of culinary possibilities for the resulting oil. After a month of research, I felt I had achieved my mission, but every time I visit I still feel compelled to dig deeper; there is always something new to learn – and taste!

The Andalucian cooking style incorporates various fish and shellfish which are commonly floured or breaded, then fried in olive oil and served with alioli, a garlic mayonnaise. Table olives often arrive stuffed with almonds, anchovies, lemon or soft cheese; and roasted pimientos and other vegetables are also stuffed before being breaded and fried. Ripe tomatoes are in abundance during the summer months, along with cucumbers, capsicums, zucchini and fennel. We found the best way to get the most out of local produce was to stay with friends; this gave us access to a kitchen so we could shop and cook on a daily basis, feeling eminently more local. The pace was relaxed and comfortable, in marked contrast to the more bustling urban centres of Madrid or Barcelona. In Andalucia, you can take your time to shop, eat, wander aimlessly, catch up with friends, or stop for an espresso or cortado coffee at a local bar along the way.

To complete the holy trinity for this trip, we went to Granada to see the most important monument in Spain: the spectacular Alhambra Palace, the ancient residence of the Moorish monarchs of Granada. We had to get up at some disgusting hour in the morning to queue for tickets (such is its popularity), but this inconvenience was soon forgotten the minute we entered the immense grounds. The palatial rooms with their various chambers, galleries and gardens took our breath away. Back in town, we joined

EATING IN CORDOBA

CASA PEPE DE LA JUDERIA
Calle Romero 1, Cordoba
Tel +34 957 200 744
Some really interesting and innovative tapas are served at this local favourite.

SLEEPING AND EATING IN GRANADA

PARADOR DE GRANADA
Real de la Alhambra s/n, Granada
Tel +34 958 221 440
www.parador.es
A converted monastery set in the magnificent gardens of Alhambra Palace – ask for a room overlooking the Albaicin district. The food here is equally enticing.

LOS DIAMANTES TAPAS BAR
Calle Navas 26, Granada
Tel +34 958 227 070
The best Andalucian-style seafood tapas in town, especially the tiny white (blanco) prawns from Huelva.

the locals on their evening promenade in the Albaicin area, on the hillside opposite the palace, and watched the sun setting over the mountains, before finding a garden terrace to sit and have dinner.

Some years later, keen to explore more of the south, I met up with Jess and Kylie in Alicante, on the Costa Blanca, where they had been living and working since the closure of our London restaurant. After eating our way around Alicante, we traversed the entire southern coastline of Andalucia that summer, driving the length of the Autovia del Mediterraneo. Murcia looked like the largest market garden in the world, with more hothouses than you could ever imagine – a sea of white plastic roofs stretched in every direction. This region is known as the salad bowl of Spain and we could certainly see why. In contrast, the rugged wilderness of Almeria felt almost other-worldly. Then there were the endless high-rise apartments, a real blight on the landscape in some parts. We whizzed past Malaga, tourist capital of the south, and gentrified Marbella, on the Costa del Sol, to the fishing village of Sabinillas, at the western end of the Costa del Sol, to stay with our friends Eduardo and Augustin at their beach apartment. This journey offered yet another perspective of Andalucia: pink- and red-flowered oleander trees lined the roadside, but there was a harshness to the environment in some parts. In summer, the roads are constantly jammed, and there are hordes of people everywhere you look.

EATING IN ALICANTE

MONASTRELL
Calle San Fernando 10, Alicante
Tel +34 965 200 363
www.monastrell.com
Chef/owner Maria Jose San Ramon champions the ground-breaking Spanish culinary style at her fine-dining restaurant, a small and intimate space with contemporary minimalist design features.

TABERNA DEL GORMET
Calle San Fernando 10, Alicante
Tel +34 965 200 363
Casual sister to Monastrell, with reliable favourites – the jamon is delicious and the service friendly.

NOU MANOLIN
Calle Villegas 3, Alicante
Tel +34 965 200 368
This is definitely the best tapas bar in town, with some really interesting selections – just trust the waiter to choose for you. This place is always packed with locals, and is well away from any tourist haunts.

We took it all in our stride – I mean, summer days at the beach do it for me no matter where I am.

After settling in, we decided to take advantage of the fabulous fresh produce sold daily at the market. We found little shops up in the hills that sold the juiciest picked figs, the sweetest-flavoured small black mussels straight from the sea, delicious and briny local olives, and sun-ripened tomatoes. It was pure heaven. The boys always managed to find some interesting local wines for us to taste, so one day just melted into the next.

But drive a few kilometres inland and you'll see an entirely different country, with mountain-top pueblos blancos (white-washed villages) perched high in the Sierra Bermeja. Just a 30-minute drive from the beach, these villages are great for an afternoon escape from the heat. We wound our way up the steep mountains through Casares, negotiating countless hairpin bends along the way, before reaching pristine and elegant Gaucin. Leaving the car squeezed into a tight spot, we walked up the narrow, winding streets with doorways that open right on the cobblestone streets and balconies awash with flowering bougainvillea. When we reached the top, not only was there the ruin of a Moorish castle to climb, but we could also see across the sea to the curved coastline of northern Morocco, the Rock of Gibraltar reduced to a little bump in the foreground. Relishing the edge-of-the-world feel of the place, we lingered into the late afternoon over a few beers and wines before making our descent back to the beach. I felt as if I had found a little piece of paradise up there in the mountains. My only regret was that we ran out of time to explore the inland Moorish frontier town of Ronda, framed by massive gorges. Reputedly, it has the best parador hotel in Spain, along with renowned restaurants and tascas, and anyone who has been there raves about it. I have added it to my 'to do' list, which seems to be growing by the minute.

STAYING IN THE PUEBLOS BLANCOS

HOTEL CASABLANCA
Calle llana 12, Gaucin
Tel +34 952 151 019
www.casablanca-gaucin.com
Drive up into the hills behind Malaga to this beautiful white-washed town perched on top of the mountain looking down to the coast and Gibraltar, and on a clear day, across the strait to Morocco.

After several days of fun in the sun, we headed west toward Cadiz, zipping past Gibraltar and Tarifa. Beyond the mountains near Algeciras, we discovered another world – the unspoilt beauty of the Costa de la Luz, with its small and relatively untouched coastal villages. We stopped to clamber down the cliffs for a swim at Los Canos de la Meca, near the tuna-fishing port of Barbate de Franco, and drove through national parks to reach out-of-the way beaches. Reluctant to leave this tranquil oasis, we also stopped off at El Palmar, a beach Jess and Kylie had discovered the previous winter, when it was totally deserted. Even at the height of summer, it was quiet – and there was a great outdoor beach bar with thatched umbrellas in the garden right opposite the sand dunes that was just perfect after a swim in the ocean. As we got closer to Cadiz, we passed hills dotted with scenic pueblos blancos, which had been fortified in earlier, more turbulent times – hence the 'de la frontera' tag at the end of many placenames in this area. The entire landscape has a distinct Moorish patina but felt remarkably different from the inland towns of Sevilla, Cordoba and Granada.

The thriving port town of Cadiz, situated on a narrow peninsula that juts out into the Atlantic Ocean, is the gateway to the Spanish sherry region and has a proud history of exporting sherry since Roman times. Farmers around the Sierra de Cadiz near Prado del Rey have established a network of eco-friendly farms that use organic methods of cultivation and foster biodiversity, collecting seed crops that can be used across the country, in a brilliant and progressive initiative. I heard a lot of inspiring stories like this while travelling through Spain – confirmation, if any were needed, of the country's ground-breaking role when it comes to food and gastronomy.

However, our prime motivation for this particular adventure was to visit the three towns that comprise the golden triangle of sherry (an anglicised version of the Spanish 'jerez'): Jerez de la Frontera, Sanlucar de Barrameda and El Puerto de Santa Maria. We were all keen to taste sherry in all its guises, and to blow away its out-dated image as a granny pacifier. Ever since cooking a special Spanish Sherry Extravagance dinner to showcase the depth and versatility of Spanish sherry in Sydney in 2003, I had been longing to see this part of the world.

The three towns that comprise the sherry region sit in a neat triangle near the coast to the north of Cadiz, and the surrounding hills and plains are planted with vineyards, each with their own unique character. Instead of olive groves, we saw grapevines stretching into the distance, interspersed with vegetable gardens and fruit orchards. This is where palomino fino (a white grape) reigns supreme; its juice creates the entire range of sherries, from the bone-dry fino to the fragrant oloroso. Most of the bodegas or sherry warehouses are centred around Jerez, where the legendary wines are fermented and bottled, but we made our first stop at the seaside town of El Puerto de Santa Maria, the smallest and least-visited of the three. Fishing boats were in constant motion in and out of the port, and there was an abundance of top-quality seafood. One of the highlights of our stay was a dinner cooked by local chef Fernando Cordoba – I particularly enjoyed the escabeche of monkfish with garlic and salmonetes (red mullet) roasted whole with an eggplant and tomato confit. The tascas and sherry bars here are also justifiably renowned and the beaches are some of the best we'd seen since leaving the Costa de la Luz.

Sanlucar de Barrameda lies about 20 kilometres to the north-west of El Puerto de Santa Maria, on the estuary of the Guadalquivir River. An old Roman town with some flamboyant architecture, it has salty air that permeates the manzanilla sherry produced here – and far too many sand flies at sunset down by the river! The minute we ordered our first glass of manzanilla the little blighters honed in on us, ready for a feast, driving us indoors. Luckily, it was safe to venture outside again a few hours later for an al fresco supper. Both manzanilla and fino sherries are made with a flor – a thick yeast layer that sits over the sherry like a blanket as it ferments and ages in oak barrels for anything up to seven years before being bottled. The unique flavour of manzanilla, with its crisp salty tang that makes it a perfect partner for seafood, comes from the thickness of its flor and the local seaside winds that ventilate the bodegas during the maturation process.
I spent a day with Eduardo, Jess and Kylie in the Barbadillo bodega, hosted by Arne, one of its managers. We discussed the subtle variations between sherries, over a few tastes naturally – and all immediately after our breakfast coffee . . . it was to be a long day. The white palomino grape is a serious work-horse: not only is it the foundation grape for most sherries, but some vintners have also started making table wines with it; the ones we tasted were light, refreshing and easy to quaff. I'd love to return to Sanlucar for the annual manzanilla fiesta in June, which also heralds the start of the flamenco season. Better add that to the list as well!

In the firm belief that we couldn't have enough of a good thing, we carried on to Jerez, the most well known of the sherry towns. With its beautiful boulevards and well-maintained Moorish palatial buildings, Jerez struck us as a diverse and interesting place as we wandered around. Besides its pivotal position in the sherry triangle, it is well known for its large gypsy population, and for being the home of flamenco – and they do like a spot of horse riding too. But we were there for the sherry! We spent a day at the Gonzalez Byass bodega, right next to the imposing Alcazar de Jerez fortress. Eduardo had arranged a private tour of the bodega and a tasting for us, which was a wonderful experience for our minds and our tastebuds. Styles of sherry include the pale, crisp fino; the amber-coloured, nutty amontillado; oloroso, which can be dry or sweet; sweeter moscatel; and the luscious, treacle-like sweetness of Pedro Ximenez (PX, or black sherry). The variation within these styles is extraordinary and it was here that we had the opportunity to parallel taste and consider the entire sherry portfolio. This bodega makes the world-renowned Tio Pepe, possibly the most-consumed of all fino sherries, sold in black bottles for the local market and green bottles for export. I can't remember how many bottles of hard-to-find sherries like Alfonso Oloroso Seco Palomino, 30-year-old Matusalem or Nectar Pedro Ximenez (even more rich and textured than regular PX) I bought for later consumption.

To cap off the experience, we stayed in an adorable parador up in the mountains at Arcos de la Frontera, right next to its 11th-century castle. Some 30 kilometres east of Jerez, this beautiful white-washed village teeters on the edge of huge cliffs, with expansive views that I could never tire of. We celebrated Eduardo's birthday with a dinner of berenjenas arcenses (eggplant cooked with tomato, garlic, spices and oil), the parador's signature dish and typical of the area, and braised pork cheek, served by waiters who looked as if they had just stepped from the pages of a medieval book – frightful uniforms seem to be obligatory for all parador staff. It was an idyllic way to finish our journey of discovery, looking down over the golden triangle of sherry, whose images remain so strongly imprinted in my imagination. A nightcap of moscatel out on the terrace under the stars was the perfect finale and, as we raised our glasses, we saluted Somerset Maugham for his observation that 'sherry is the most civilised of drinks'. He was spot on.

SLEEPING AND EATING IN THE SHERRY REGION

EL FARO DE EL PUERTO
Carretera de Fuentebravia, Puerto de Santa Maria
Tel +34 956 858 003
www.elfarodelpuerto.com
Renowned for the very best seafood in Andalucia, it's worth the detour just to sample the menu of chef Fernando Cordoba.

CASA BIGOTE
Bajo de Guia s/n, Sanlucar de Barrameda
Tel +34 956 362 696
This place in the old fishing quarter along the beachfront has some of the best seafood tapas and a great range of manzanilla sherries; the tortilla with tiny camarones prawns is excellent.

PARADOR DE ARCOS DE LA FRONTERA
Plaza del Cabildo s/n, Arcos de la Frontera
Tel +34 956 700 500
www.parador.es
Situated a half-hour drive east of Jerez, this hotel is the perfect place to stay when visiting the sherry region, with easy driving access to the three main sherry-producing towns.

NEW WORLD GAZPACHO

During our final months at Paramount, we hosted a dinner called Hasta La Vista, inspired by the Spanish surrealists, as one of the participating restaurants in Sydney's Good Food Month 'Hats Off' dinners. I mimicked El Bulli's method of deconstruction and prepared the components separately, giving the traditional soup a totally new look. It's best to make this towards the end of summer when tomatoes are at their peak – ripe, juicy and full of flavour. The marron can be replaced by lobster, scampi or king prawns.

4 kg over-ripe tomatoes
300 g live marron
extra virgin olive oil, for brushing
sea salt
freshly ground white pepper
8 Bread Wafers (see Essentials)
2 teaspoons Alioli (see Essentials)
8 chervil leaves

PICKLED CUCUMBER
60 ml fresh lime juice, strained
20 ml fish sauce
2 teaspoons Sugar Syrup (see Essentials)
1 cucumber, cut into fine julienne strips

STUFFED CHERRY TOMATOES
8 cherry tomatoes, blanched and peeled
1 tablespoon minced marron claw meat
½ teaspoon minced roasted pimiento (piquillo pepper)
½ teaspoon Roasted Garlic Paste (see Essentials)
1 teaspoon finely chopped chives

SALMOREJO SAUCE
100 g sourdough bread, crusts removed
500 g fresh tomatoes, peeled, seeded and chopped
3 cloves garlic, minced
30 ml sherry vinegar
1 teaspoon sea salt
90 ml extra virgin olive oil >>

<< Line a sieve with four layers of muslin cloth and sit the sieve over a deep bowl or bucket. Puree the tomatoes in a blender and spoon carefully onto the muslin. Don't pour the puree in as this will force it through the muslin too quickly – the idea is for the clear water from the tomatoes to slowly drip through the muslin. Cover the surface with plastic film and leave in the refrigerator for 2 days. The tomato water will drip through very slowly and cannot be rushed.

Remove the sieve and reserve the tomato pulp for other use. I usually pass it through a mouli and then cook the smooth puree in some oil over gentle heat until thickened to make tomato puree.

Pour the clear tomato essence into a saucepan and bring slowly to the boil, removing any sediment that may rise to the surface. Simmer over gentle heat for 10 minutes then set aside until ready to serve.

To prepare the marron, place in the freezer for 20 minutes to stun it. Place it in a large saucepan half-submerged in cold water, cover and bring to the boil. When the water boils, reduce the heat to medium and cook for 3 minutes. Remove from the pan and plunge into iced water to stop the cooking.

Remove the claw meat from the shells and reserve for the tomato stuffing. Remove the tails, discarding the shells, and carefully pull out the intestinal tract. Cut the tail meat into eight 1 cm thick medallions. Brush the medallions with olive oil and sprinkle with salt and pepper.

To pickle the cucumber, combine the lime juice, fish sauce and sugar syrup in a bowl, add the cucumber strips and leave for 20 minutes. Strain the cucumber from the pickling liquid when softened.

To prepare the stuffed tomatoes, thinly slice the tops off each peeled tomato and hollow out the centres using a small melon baller or parisienne cutter. Take care not to break or cut the tomato shells – just remove the seeds. In a bowl, mix together the remaining stuffing ingredients, season to taste with salt and pepper and carefully spoon into the tomatoes, leaving some of the stuffing exposed at the top.

To make the salmorejo sauce, soak the bread in cold water for 5 minutes to soften, then squeeze the excess water from the bread. Blend in a food processor with the tomato, garlic, vinegar and salt until smooth. With the motor running, slowly add the oil so the sauce thickens and emulsifies. Taste and adjust the seasoning if necessary.

Sandwich two bread wafers together with a smear of alioli to make four double wafers, then spoon a small dollop of alioli on top and garnish with chervil leaves. Sit a double wafer in the centre of each bowl (I use a classic bouillabaisse bowl).

In each bowl, place six small, evenly spaced blobs of salmorejo sauce in a circle around the wafer. On each blob of sauce sit either a stuffed tomato, marron medallion or little pile of pickled cucumber (about the same size as the tomatoes).

Heat the tomato essence to simmering point, transfer to a serving jug and pour into the bowls at the table.

SERVES 4

PICKLED ANCHOVIES AND SERRANO HAM WITH FENNEL AND AVOCADO SALSA

Several years ago I devised this as a tapas for a Spanish food promotion in Australia, using the classic ingredients of ham and anchovy but trying to combine them in a new and interesting manner. Boquerones are fresh white anchovy fillets that have been pickled in lemon juice and olive oil; imported from Spain, they are readily available from specialist food stores. I use the peppery picual olive oil from Andalucia for this dish.

12 serrano ham slices
24 white anchovy fillets (boquerones)
½ avocado, mashed
2 tablespoons finely diced fennel
3 tablespoons green olive Tapenade (see Essentials)
12 witlof (chicory) leaves
1 tablespoon finely shredded parsley
2 teaspoons extra virgin olive oil

ANCHOVY SAUCE
2 large eggs
3 teaspoons Roasted Garlic Paste (see Essentials)
1 egg yolk
6 Ortiz anchovy fillets, chopped
25 ml sherry vinegar
1 teaspoon fresh lemon juice, strained
300 ml extra virgin olive oil
½ teaspoon sea salt
½ teaspoon freshly ground white pepper

To make the anchovy sauce, boil the eggs for 2 minutes only. Place in a food processor with the garlic paste, egg yolk and anchovy fillets and blend until smooth. Add the sherry vinegar and lemon juice. With the motor running, slowly drizzle in the olive oil until the sauce emulsifies. Season with salt and pepper, taste and adjust if necessary. Keep refrigerated until ready to use.

To make the rolls, lay out the ham slices, then sit two anchovy fillets side by side on top of each ham slice. Combine the avocado, fennel and tapenade, spoon onto the centre of the fish then roll up to secure.

To serve, spoon a little anchovy sauce onto each witlof leaf, then sit a ham roll on top. Sprinkle with parsley and drizzle with a little extra virgin olive oil.

SERVES 4

SEARED SCALLOPS, FOIE GRAS AND ARTICHOKE CREAM

Another original from the Hasta La Vista dinner at Paramount, we called this La Duende (from the inside) – scallops from inside a shell, foie gras from a duck's liver and artichoke hearts from the centre of the plant's flower. This dish went on to feature on many of my later menus. The combination was inspired by my experiences in Spanish restaurants, particularly their inventive approach to ingredient combinations.

8 scallops, trimmed
2 teaspoons extra virgin olive oil
1 tablespoon Truffle Butter (see Essentials)
4 slices foie gras, 1 cm thick × 3 cm diameter (cut with a round pastry cutter)
½ teaspoon sea salt
1 tablespoon chervil leaves
2 tablespoons hazelnuts, roasted and roughly chopped

TRUFFLE HAZELNUT DRESSING
25 ml verjuice
25 ml Forum cabernet vinegar
1 g fresh black truffle, minced
80 ml extra virgin olive oil
25 ml hazelnut oil
1 teaspoon truffle oil
½ teaspoon sea salt
¼ teaspoon freshly ground black pepper

GLOBE ARTICHOKE CREAM
80 g cooked globe artichoke hearts
30 ml extra virgin olive oil
½ teaspoon sea salt
½ teaspoon freshly ground white pepper

GLOBE ARTICHOKE CONFIT
4 globe artichokes, cleaned and trimmed
80 ml extra virgin olive oil
2 teaspoons sea salt

To make the dressing, whisk the ingredients together in a bowl until emulsified.

To make the artichoke cream, puree the artichokes in a blender with the oil, salt and pepper until smooth. Pass through a mouli or fine sieve to make a superfine cream, discarding the solids.

To confit the artichokes, trim the artichoke hearts and cut into 5 mm thick slices lengthways. Place the slices in a cryovac or ziplock bag with the olive oil and the salt and seal. Cook the artichokes in a pan of water held at 65°C for 1 hour (use a thermometer to monitor the temperature). Remove from the bag and cut into fine slices.

Toss the scallops with the oil. Heat a pan over high heat, quickly sear the scallops, then cut each one in half so you have four round slices per serve. Toss the scallops in a bowl with 40 ml of the dressing.

Heat the truffle butter in non-stick pan over moderate heat (be careful not to burn it), fry the foie gras briefly then flip over and fry for another 30 seconds. Remove from the heat and season with sea salt.

To serve, sit the confit artichoke slices on serving plates. Spoon the artichoke cream into the centre, lay four scallop slices in a circle in the middle of the cream, then sit the foie gras on top. Drizzle with a little extra dressing and scatter the chervil leaves and hazelnuts over the top.

SERVES 4

HONEY FIG AND GOAT'S CHEESE SALAD

During a summer retreat when we were staying with Eduardo and Augustin, I made this as a light refreshing starter for dinner – perfect after hours spent lazing in the sun. In Australia, I use the gorgeous hand-made cheese from Indigo's cheese-maker Paula Jenkins or one of the Little Darlings (fresh goat's cheese) from Woodside Cheese. In Europe, I would use a Chabichou or St Maure.

120 g white-mould goat's cheese (Woodside, St Maure or similar)
120 g mache (lamb's lettuce) leaves, washed
8 white figs, cut in half
40 g pine nuts, lightly roasted
2 tablespoons shredded parsley leaves

HONEY DRESSING
50 ml honey
25 ml fresh lemon juice, strained
25 ml aged sherry vinegar
100 ml extra virgin olive oil
½ teaspoon sea salt
½ teaspoon freshly ground black pepper

To make the dressing, place all the ingredients in a glass jar with a lid and shake until emulsified.

Cut the cheese into 12 thin slices using a hot sharp knife.

Arrange the mache leaves on plates and sit the cheese and fig slices on top in alternate layers.

Spoon the dressing over the top to moisten, then sprinkle with the pine nuts and parsley and serve immediately.

SERVES 4

CRAB AND TOMATO SALAD WITH GAZPACHO DRESSING

This recipe features fresh and lively flavours that use the ingredients for gazpacho in quite a different way. The salad relies on all the elements being of premium quality, and it must be served as soon as it's made. Any fresh-picked cooked crabmeat would be suitable, from mud crab to snow or spanner crab – whatever happens to be in season and in peak condition.

400 g picked blue swimmer crabmeat
16 yellow pear tomatoes, halved
16 cherry roma tomatoes, halved
1 small cucumber, sliced and cut into fine julienne strips
½ yellow capsicum (pepper), finely sliced
2 tablespoons chopped chives
1 punnet chervil cress, snipped
1 punnet onion cress (rock chives), snipped

GAZPACHO DRESSING
2 ripe tomatoes, chopped
60 ml Cucumber Juice (see Essentials)
½ red capsicum (pepper), chopped
1 long green chilli, chopped
½ red onion, diced
½ teaspoon Tabasco sauce
1 teaspoon Roasted Garlic Paste (see Essentials)
30 ml Forum cabernet vinegar
120 ml extra virgin olive oil
1 teaspoon sea salt
½ teaspoon freshly ground black pepper

To make the gazpacho dressing, blend the tomatoes, cucumber juice, capsicum, chilli, onion, Tabasco and garlic paste in a food processor until smooth. Pass through a fine mesh sieve and discard the solids. Whisk the vinegar and oil into the puree until combined and season with salt and pepper. Taste and adjust the seasoning if necessary.

Mix the crab with all the salad ingredients and toss through some of the gazpacho dressing.

Arrange the salad on serving plates, spoon a little extra dressing over and serve immediately.

SERVES 4

FUNGUS AND JELLY

This is a folly inspired by the Spanish surrealist masters where layers of different textures are created using mushrooms. I save this dish for special-occasion dinners when I want to combine dramatic effect with earthy pleasures.

100 ml Soy Pork Jelly (see Essentials)
40 ml extra virgin olive oil
1 clove garlic, minced
4 small Swiss brown mushrooms, finely sliced
4 fresh shiitake mushrooms, finely sliced
1 teaspoon sea salt
½ teaspoon freshly ground black pepper
2 tablespoons chopped chives
vegetable oil, for deep-frying
120 g Soy-braised Pork (see Essentials), cut into 1 cm dice
2 teaspoons Sichuan Spice Salt (see Essentials)
½ teaspoon dried porcini powder
½ punnet enoki mushrooms, stalks trimmed
1 cup Tempura Batter (see Essentials)

MUSHROOM CREAM
15 g dried porcini mushroom slices
250 ml pouring (35%) cream
2 small cloves garlic, sliced
4 g gelatine leaves, softened in cold water

Heat the pork jelly until it liquifies then spoon into six 150 ml dariole moulds to make a 5 mm thick layer. Refrigerate for 1 hour until firm.

To make the mushroom cream, soak the dried porcini slices in hot water for 20 minutes until softened. Strain and reserve the mushroom water. Chop the porcini until finely minced and set aside.

Heat the cream, garlic and 175 ml of the reserved mushroom water in a saucepan over gentle heat to simmering point. Add the softened gelatine and stir until dissolved, then pass through a fine mesh sieve, discarding the solids. Allow the cream to cool completely but not set.

While the cream is cooling, heat the olive oil in a frying pan and saute the garlic and sliced mushrooms for about 2 minutes until softened, stirring often. Add the reserved minced porcini and cook for a further 2 minutes. Season with salt and pepper, then remove from the heat and stir in the chives. Cool, then spoon evenly over the jelly to make a second layer in the moulds – it should be about 6 cm thick.

Pour in enough cooled mushroom cream to just cover the mushrooms and refrigerate until this layer starts to firm (this stops the mushrooms from rising through the cream and losing their distinct layer). When this layer starts to set, pour in the remaining cooled mushroom cream to fill the moulds, then refrigerate for 4 hours before serving.

To serve, dip the moulds into hot water then turn out the mushroom creams onto plates. The jelly will now be on top.

Heat the vegetable oil in a saucepan or wok to 180°C and deep-fry the pork cubes for 1 minute until crisp and golden. Drain on paper towel, then season lightly with the combined Sichuan spice salt and dried porcini powder.

Coat the enoki mushrooms lightly with tempura batter, then add spoonfuls of the batter to the hot oil and fry for 30 seconds to make six crisp fritters. Drain on paper towel.

Scatter the fried pork cubes onto the plate around the mushroom cream, place a fried enoki fritter on top of each jelly and serve.

SERVES 6

MUSSELS AND CHORIZO WITH CHICKPEAS

Another summer favourite that is inspired by Andalucia's Moorish heritage. Jess and I cooked this up for an al fresco beachside dinner after spotting a boatload of mussels being dispatched to the fish shop early one morning.

300 g dried chickpeas, soaked overnight
1 kg mussels, scrubbed
250 g cherry tomatoes
200 ml extra virgin olive oil
sea salt and freshly ground black pepper
2 red onions, finely diced
5 cloves garlic, minced
1 tablespoon minced ginger
3 small red chillies, minced
2 teaspoons cumin seeds, roasted and ground
2 spicy chorizo sausages, peeled and diced
3 tomatoes, grated
100 ml white wine
2 green capsicums (peppers), finely diced
75 ml fresh lemon juice, strained
2 teaspoons sea salt, extra
1 teaspoon freshly ground black pepper, extra
100 g spinach leaves, washed and roughly chopped
2 tablespoons basil leaves, chopped
2 tablespoons parsley leaves, chopped

Rinse the chickpeas and place in a saucepan of clean cold water. Bring to the boil, cover with a lid and simmer for about 1 hour or until softened. Remove from the heat, strain and set aside.

To prepare the mussels, place them in a large saucepan, cover with a lid and sit over high heat. Leave for a few minutes and as soon as the mussels open, remove them and plunge into icy cold water to stop the cooking. Remove the mussels from the shell and snip off the beards.

Preheat the oven to 150°C. Place the cherry tomatoes on an oven tray, add 20 ml olive oil to coat and season with salt and pepper. Slow-roast in the oven for 20 minutes until softened and lightly coloured.

Heat 50 ml of the extra virgin olive oil in a wide pan (a paella pan is perfect) and saute the onion, garlic, ginger and chilli for about 2 minutes until softened. Add the cumin and cook for 1 minute until fragrant. Add the diced chorizo and cook until it begins to colour, stirring constantly. Stir in the grated tomatoes and the wine and bring to the boil.

Reduce to a simmer, toss in the cooked chickpeas, diced capsicum, mussels and roasted cherry tomatoes and cook for 5 minutes until heated through and well coated. Stir in the lemon juice, extra salt and pepper and remaining olive oil. Taste and adjust the seasoning if necessary.

Stir in the spinach, basil and parsley leaves and serve immediately.

SERVES 4

TUNA TARTARE WITH GARLIC AND ALMOND CREAM

This garlic cream takes its inspiration from the Andalucian ajo blanco or white gazpacho, a chilled soup that showcases the very best extra virgin olive oil and freshly picked snow-white almonds. We were served this soup many times while travelling through Andalucia, but my favourite version was at a small family-run restaurant on the Triana side of the river in Sevilla, right after we had been to a bullfight at La Maestranza.

250 g sashimi-grade yellowfin or bluefin tuna
25 ml aged sherry vinegar
sea salt and freshly ground black pepper
75 ml extra virgin olive oil
1 tablespoon finely chopped chives
16 seedless green grapes, peeled and halved
4 Bread Wafers (see Essentials)

GARLIC AND ALMOND CREAM
175 g day-old sourdough bread, crusts removed
150 g whole blanched almonds (as fresh as possible)
1 tablespoon Roasted Garlic Paste (see Essentials)
100 ml White Chicken Stock or Vegetable Stock (see Essentials)
125 ml extra virgin olive oil
2 teaspoons sea salt
1 teaspoon freshly ground white pepper
75 ml sherry vinegar

To make the garlic and almond cream, soak the bread in cold water for a few minutes until softened, then squeeze to remove any excess liquid. Blend the bread, almonds and garlic paste in a food processor until combined, then add the stock and blend to a smooth paste. With the motor running, gradually add the oil in a steady stream. Add the salt, pepper and vinegar, pulse to combine then taste and adjust if necessary. The consistency should be quite thick rather than soupy, with reasonable body.

Cut the tuna into fine dice with a knife or cleaver. Mix the vinegar, salt, pepper and oil in a bowl until emulsified, add the diced tuna, chives and grapes and stir to combine.

Spoon the garlic cream into the centre of each bowl, arrange the tuna and grape salad on top in the middle of the cream and rest a crisp bread wafer against the tuna. Serve immediately.

SERVES 4

BRAISED RABBIT WITH BLACK OLIVES AND ORANGES

Olives and oranges capture the essence of Andalucia, and the rabbit is prepared in the classic ballotine method. Clementines or honey murcott mandarins can be substituted for the oranges if they are in season.

1 farmed rabbit
2 teaspoons sea salt
freshly ground black pepper
1 orange, peeled and segmented
1 tablespoon finely diced fennel bulb
8 sun-dried black olives, pitted and quartered
2 tablespoons picked chervil leaves
1 tablespoon snipped chives

OLIVE AND ORANGE STUFFING
40 ml olive oil
1 small brown onion, finely diced
3 cloves garlic, minced
30 g pancetta, cut into thin julienne strips
1 teaspoon ground coriander
½ teaspoon ground cumin
1 teaspoon sea salt
1 teaspoon freshly ground black pepper
125 g coarsely minced pork shoulder
125 g coarsely minced pork fat
2 rabbit livers, minced
1 tablespoon shredded parsley leaves
40 g pine nuts, lightly roasted
50 g pitted small black olives
zest of 1 orange, blanched and minced

ORANGE AND BLACK PEPPER DRESSING
40 ml fresh orange juice, strained
20 ml sherry vinegar
25 ml Pedro Ximenez sherry
¼ teaspoon vanilla bean paste
½ teaspoon sea salt
1 teaspoon freshly ground black pepper
60 ml Colonna Arancia (orange) extra virgin olive oil
65 ml extra virgin olive oil

To bone the rabbit, remove the leg and thigh joints. Remove the livers and clean, then dice finely to add to the stuffing. Carefully remove the carcass from the rabbit, working outwards from its belly, until you have one piece opened out, removing the front leg and shoulder bones last. The breast fillets should still be attached to the skin, so butterfly open. Remove the thigh and leg meat from their bones and lay on the rabbit next to the breast fillets so the entire surface has an even layer of meat covering it. Sprinkle the rabbit meat with salt to season.

To make the stuffing, heat the oil in a pan and saute the onion and garlic until starting to colour, then add the pancetta strips and cook until crisp. Stir in the ground coriander, cumin, salt and pepper, then remove from the heat and allow to cool completely.

In a bowl, mix together the cooled onion mix, pork mince and fat, minced liver, parsley, pine nuts, olives and orange zest and stir thoroughly to combine. Heap the stuffing across the rabbit at the end nearest to you and roll the rabbit over and up to enclose the stuffing. Secure, making a sausage shape.

Wrap the rabbit in several layers of plastic film to completely secure into a neat sausage-shaped parcel, expelling all air before you tie the ends. Rest on a flat tray in the refrigerator for 1 hour before cooking.

To cook the rabbit, poach in a pan of water held at 75°C (use a thermometer to monitor the temperature) for 2 hours, rolling over every 30 minutes so it cooks evenly. Transfer the rabbit to a flat tray or plate and allow to rest for 30 minutes. Unwrap and cut into eight 3 cm thick slices, then season with a little pepper. Arrange a slice on the centre of each plate.

To make the dressing, whisk all the ingredients together until emulsified.

Cut the orange segments into smaller pieces and toss with the fennel and olives. Add the herbs and toss with enough dressing to moisten. Arrange on top of the rabbit and drizzle with a little extra dressing.

SERVES 8

VALDEON AND QUINCE SANDWICH WITH MANCHEGO WAFERS

This is a perfect match for moscatel sherry, with a fantastic synergy between the pungent cheese and the sweet quince. Quince paste and quince syrup are both obtainable from specialist food stores, making light work of this dish.

120 g Valdeon (Spanish blue cheese)
80 g quince paste
40 ml quince syrup

MANCHEGO WAFERS
40 g unsalted butter, melted
2 sheets filo pastry
50 g Manchego cheese, finely grated

To make the Manchego wafers, preheat the oven to 170°C. Line a flat baking tray with baking paper and brush the surface with butter. Lay a sheet of filo on the paper and brush the top surface with butter. Sprinkle with a thin, even layer of grated cheese, lay the second sheet of filo over the cheese and press gently. Brush the top with butter and cover with a sheet of baking paper. Lay another (heavy) baking tray of the same size on top to compress and bake for 10–12 minutes until the pastry is golden.

Take out of the oven, remove the top baking tray then peel off the top sheet of paper. With the cooked pastry sitting on the baking tray, cut the pastry into 5 cm squares using a sharp knife, cutting lengthways then crossways, trimming the edges first. You need to have two squares for each serve. Carefully lift the pastry squares off the tray with a spatula and transfer to a wire rack to cool for 5 minutes. Store in an airtight container between paper until ready to serve.

Slice the blue cheese into four 5 cm squares that are 1 cm thick. Do the same with the quince paste.

To serve, spread the quince syrup onto the centre of each plate. Make a sandwich, starting with a cheese wafer then the blue cheese, then the quince paste, and finishing with a wafer.

SERVES 4

OLIVE OIL AND MUSCATEL ICE CREAM WITH POACHED FIG

As I have said before, olive oil not only adds flavour to desserts, it has the ability to improve texture, giving a beautiful sheen and silkiness to custards and creams. I devised this recipe for the Spanish Trade Commission, for inclusion in one of their recipe books for Spanish olive oil. I have teamed the ice cream with figs, one of my favourite fruits and another star of the Andalucian table.

300 ml Sugar Syrup (see Essentials)
½ teaspoon vanilla bean paste
1 stick cinnamon
25 ml fresh lemon juice, strained
6 large purple figs, peeled
100 ml Lustau moscatel sherry

OLIVE OIL ICE CREAM
150 ml arbequina (fruity) extra virgin olive oil
1 stick cinnamon
½ vanilla bean, split lengthways and scraped
500 ml pouring (35%) cream
3 large egg yolks
150 g castor sugar
20 ml fresh lemon juice, strained
½ teaspoon ground cinnamon
½ cup sun-dried muscatels (seedless), soaked in Lustau moscatel sherry for 1 hour, then drained

To make the ice cream, bring the oil, cinnamon, vanilla bean and half the cream to simmering point in a pan. Remove from the heat before it starts to boil and set aside to infuse.

Beat the egg yolks with the sugar and lemon juice until pale and thick, then fold the spiced cream mixture through the egg. Sit the bowl over a pan of simmering water and continue to whisk until the mixture thickens to a custard consistency and coats the back of a spoon. Remove from the heat and pass the mixture through a fine mesh sieve, discarding the solids. Stir in the remaining cream and cinnamon and allow to cool.

Churn in an ice-cream machine until firm then remove and fold in the soaked muscatels. Pour into your preferred mould and freeze for 2–3 hours before serving.

To prepare the figs, bring the sugar syrup, vanilla, cinnamon and lemon juice to the boil in a saucepan. Simmer for 5 minutes to allow the flavours to infuse then add the figs and simmer gently for 6 minutes or until the figs are tender. Stir every couple of minutes to make sure they cook evenly. Add the sherry, turn off the heat and leave the figs to gently poach in the sherry syrup for 15 minutes.

Remove the figs with a slotted spoon and set aside. Bring the syrup back to the boil and simmer until the liquid has reduced by about a third to a syrup consistency. Allow to cool completely.

To serve, remove the ice cream from its mould and cut into 2 cm thick slices. Sit an ice cream slice on each plate, stand a poached fig on top and spoon on a little of the sherry syrup. Serve immediately.

SERVES 6

GOAT'S CURD AND BLOOD ORANGE CREAM

I love the voluptuous texture of this dessert, with its lovely balance of acidity from the curd and yoghurt cutting through the sweetness. I prefer to use fresh goat's curd from either Woodside in South Australia or Yarra Valley's Richard Thomas because of its superior creaminess. The dessert can be made in one large tin or constructed in smaller ring moulds (that can be easily lifted off), resulting in a stylish offering for each person.

40 ml fresh blood orange juice, strained
60 g castor sugar
3 g gelatine leaves, softened in cold water
20 ml orange blossom water
200 g fresh goat's curd
200 ml thick (45%) cream
1 teaspoon blanched and minced blood orange zest
150 g thick plain yoghurt
50 g amaretti biscuits
50 g plain digestive or granita biscuits
40 g unsalted butter
4 tablespoons Blood Orange Curd (see Essentials)

FRUIT SALAD
1 orange or tangelo, peeled and segmented
1 blood orange, peeled and segmented
6 large strawberries, sliced

Line a triangular or rectangular terrine mould with baking paper.

Heat the orange juice and sugar over gentle heat until the sugar dissolves. Stir in the softened gelatine and remove from the heat. When cool, add the orange blossom water.

Whisk the goat's curd, cream and zest briefly until combined, then add the yoghurt and whisk until just combined. Fold in the cooled orange juice. Pour the mixture into the mould until three-quarters full, smooth the surface and refrigerate for 1 hour.

Crush the amaretti and digestive biscuits to a fine crumb in a food processor then rub in the butter with your fingers until the mixture resembles wet breadcrumbs.

Spoon the biscuit mix over the orange curd until the mould is full, pressing gently to make sure the layer is even throughout. Cover the mould with plastic film and refrigerate for 5 hours or overnight.

To make the fruit salad, mix the orange segments with the strawberry slices.

To serve, unmould the goat's curd cake from the terrine, remove the paper and cut into 3–4 cm thick slices. Spoon a little orange curd onto the centre of each plate, sit the cake slices on top and arrange the fruit salad alongside.

SERVES 6

CHOCOLATE JAFFA TRUFFLE CAKE WITH PX JELLY AND BOOZY CUMQUATS

Pedro Ximenez was invented to go with chocolate, I am absolutely sure of it. There can be no more perfect partnership in the food world than the rich deep complexity of this black sherry and velvety chocolate. The flavours create an incredibly sexy feeling in the mouth – in fact, there have been many who have proclaimed this dessert to be better than sex! It can be made in either one large tin or mould then sliced into portions, or made as smaller individual desserts using round metal collars for moulding.

Chocolate Fudge Cake (see Essentials)
16 Boozy Cumquats (see Essentials), cut in half and seeds removed

DARK CHOCOLATE GANACHE
130 g unsalted butter
1 tablespoon orange zest
1 stick cinnamon, broken
200 g Valrhona Manjari chocolate, coarsely grated
4 eggs
2 egg yolks
40 g castor sugar

MILK CHOCOLATE GANACHE LAYER
130 ml pouring (35%) cream
210 g Valrhona Jivara chocolate, coarsely grated
25 ml Mandarin Napoleon liqueur

PX JELLY
375 ml Pedro Ximenez sherry
4 g gelatine leaves, softened in cold water

Grease and line individual moulds or a 23 cm round springform tin with baking paper, cut to size. Cut a 1 cm thick layer of cake to fit perfectly into the base. Press gently to make sure it reaches the edges and is even across the base.

To make the dark chocolate ganache, melt the butter with the orange zest and cinnamon. Pass through a fine mesh sieve and discard the solids. Melt the chocolate and whisk in the flavoured butter. Whisk the eggs, yolks and sugar together for about 10 minutes until pale and creamy. Fold in the chocolate, then pour into the tin over the cake base and refrigerate for an hour until set.

To make the milk chocolate layer, heat the cream gently then stir in the chocolate with the liqueur until the chocolate is melted and smooth. Allow to cool completely then pour on top of the dark chocolate layer and refrigerate until set.

To prepare the jelly, heat half the sherry to simmering point, add the softened gelatine and stir to dissolve. Remove from the heat, add the remaining sherry and allow to cool completely. Pour the cool jelly over the ganache to make a thin layer and return to the refrigerator. Leave to set for 3 hours until firm.

Unmould the cake and run a hot sharp knife around the edges to ensure they are smooth and even. Arrange the cumquat halves, cut-side down, on top of the cake and serve.

SERVES 8

ROCK THE KASBAH MOROCCO

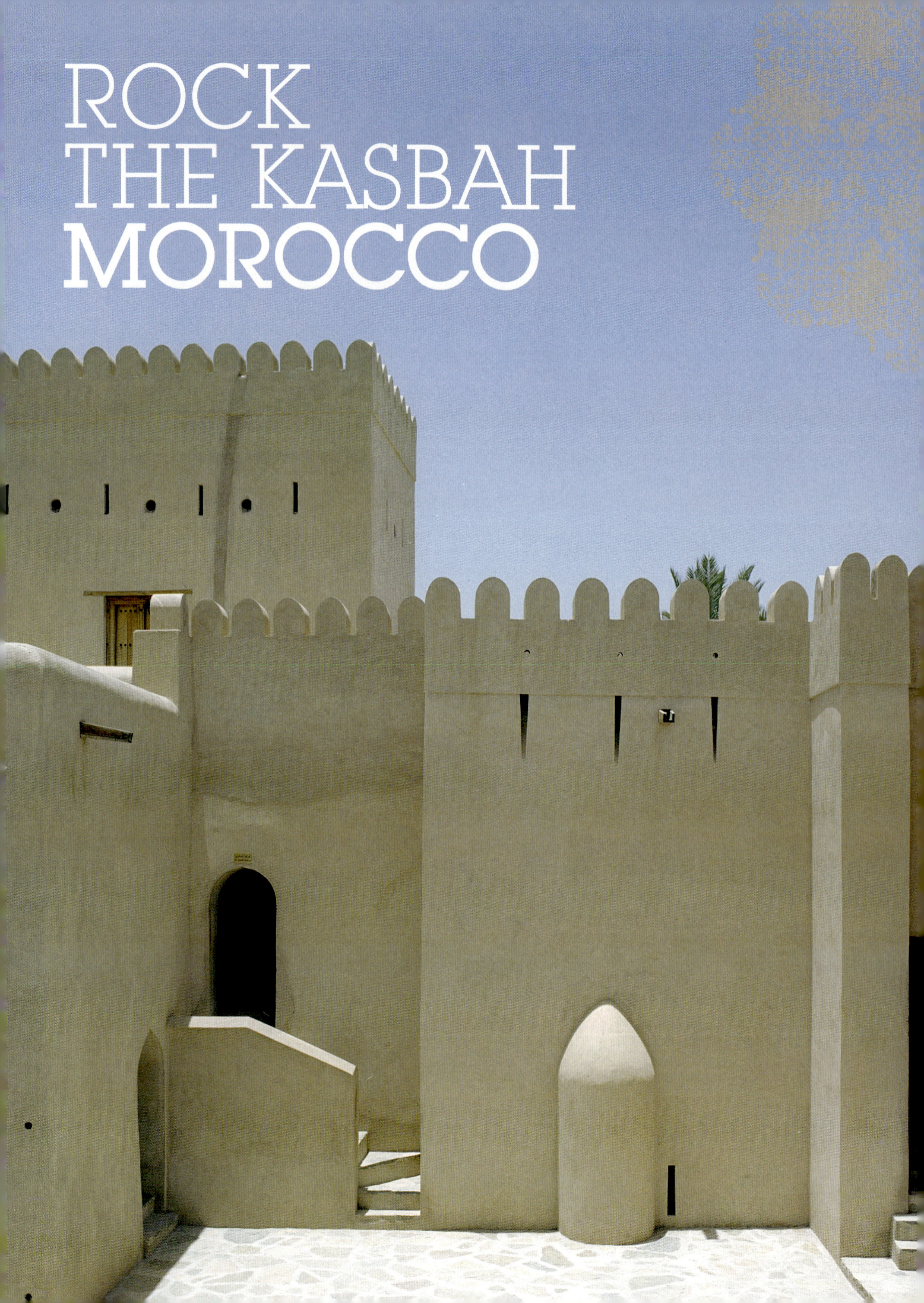

For me, Morocco conjures up the exotic, intriguing and intoxicating – a country that has it all, in spades. With its myriad colours and aromas, its vivid and alluring mix of cultures, faces that tell a thousand stories, architecture, art, music and life, this is a place that engages all the senses. Having inspired writers, artists and film makers for eons, Morocco continues to captivate and, in an age of creeping uniformity, offers diversity and adventure amid landscapes filled with rosemary, citrus, fig, almond and pomegranate trees, lavender and lemon verbena bushes. Its seductive powers draw me back time and again.

Moroccan places are very much defined by colour: the white of Fes, the beige-ochre of Marrakech, the blues of Essaouira and Rabat, the red of Casablanca, the yellow of Tangier. Even the petit-taxis of each city or town are colour-coded accordingly – how cool is that? Each city has its own distinct personality that is strongly reflected in its food and way of life, a sharp contrast to urban centres elsewhere. But everywhere the skyline is dominated by minarets – some ancient, some new – and the call to prayer becomes the gently soothing rhythm of the day. Although growing tourism has made Morocco more prosperous, it has stayed true to its heritage.

When planning a visit, the midsummer heat should be avoided, if at all possible. It gets scorching hot in July and August, and the simplest of tasks become a burden in heat close to 45°C – as it was the very first time I visited, when even the thick walls of the medinas (the old parts of a city) offered little respite. From then on, I have always timed my visits for between September and November, when it is cooler but still pleasantly warm, or late April, before the onset of the summer heat. November in Marrakech is particularly divine, as the roses are in full bloom. It should be called the city of roses – they are everywhere, adding to the pinkness of this desert city, their perfume filling the air as you look across to the majestic, snow-capped Atlas Mountains in the distance.

Together with Marrakech, Meknes and Rabat, Fes is one of Morocco's four imperial cities. Founded by the Arabs and the oldest living city in Morocco, Fes resembles a biblical panorama – it is breathtakingly beautiful, especially when viewed from El Borj, along the crumbling ramparts of the Fes el-Bali (old city) wall at sunset. The pale pink light over the old white limestone buildings is just stunning. Equally captivating is sitting in the sunshine on the private terrace of a riad (a traditional courtyard house), listening to the frenzied morning activity in the medina below over breakfast, having been woken by the call to prayer. The Fassi people are proud of their city, which they consider to be the cultural, artistic and philosophical nexus of the country.

Moroccan medinas are organised around the craft guilds and are full of medieval charm. A riot of colour assaults your vision as you enter a sensory fantasy and the richness of oriental life spills out onto the streets at every corner. The medina at Fes is the largest in the whole of the Maghreb, with half a million people living within its maze of streets, where any connection with the modern world seems very remote. The narrow rookery of lanes allow for foot traffic and donkeys only. Cars are relegated to Fes el-Jdid (the 'new' city, built during the Middle Ages) and beyond – outside the old city walls, where petit-taxis and buses hover by the city gates. The Mellah (Jewish quarter), shops, fondouks (inns), souks (commercial districts) and workshops of the new city have an entirely different atmosphere but are still a seemingly endless source of mystery and surprise.

Navigating the labyrinth of the medina and souks for the first time is a challenging but delightful experience. Caught up in the fast-moving crowds, my way of coping is to give in and just go with the flow, following the narrow lanes and melting into walls as heavily laden donkeys go past while their guides shout out a warning 'balek balek!' (watch out, get out of the way!). Formed in ever-tightening circles spiralling down to its centre, the medina is not easy to get to know. Saida, a local woman who has been my guide on each of my visits, lived in the medina with her family as she grew up, and she told me that as a child she was once lost for two days, confused by the density of so many twisting and turning alleyways and their similar appearance. One of my favourite entrance points is through the Bab Bou Jeloud gate, which leads straight to the food section of the medina. There is a charming cafe right by the gate with a roof terrace upstairs, which is great for a mint tea or espresso before heading into the fray.

The high walls that line the frenetic alleyways and lanes form the outside walls of houses, enclosing another world – one of calm and beauty, with gracious internal courtyards containing a water fountain and maybe a lemon tree or two. This Arab-Andalous style of architecture is prevalent in many buildings, ranging from humble abodes to sophisticated mansions, just as it is in Spanish Andalucia. In some ways, the houses reflect the culture: beauty is often veiled from view, and privacy and discretion are respected. It feels as if this place has existed like this since time immemorial and it is so easy to be charmed by its antiquity – an experience that is not easily forgotten, and one that is renewed with each visit.

The Fes medina is a hive of activity: the communal bread ovens (kanouns); the tanneries near Place as-Seffarine; the Kairaouine mosque and mederesa (university), considered one of the oldest in the world; the women making ouarka (the most ethereal, gossamer-thin pastry sheets) or the richer trrid pastry over hot iron plates; the food market near Bab Semmarine (Gate of Nails), its stalls laden with khli (spiced dried beef preserved in beef fat) or pastries; the date shops and spice traders; the carts with live snails waiting to be plunged into a large pot of peppery broth and consumed as a snack by avid locals; and last but not least, the numerous carpet factories. The trick lies in trying not to buy what you don't really want or need; the vendors are expert in the power of persuasion and many unsuspecting visitors leave with their wallets considerably lighter. A new taste I was introduced to in the herb section of the market was shsheeba, a feathery herb like a cross between fennel and wormwood, which is used to add a smoky liquorice flavour to some soups and tajines.

After sunset, the restaurants come alive to the beat of the Arab-Andalous music, and the air is filled with the exotic aromas of spicy food cooking over charcoal. I have spent many a night at a diffa (feast), enjoying mouth-watering stuffed eggplants; meat tajines with figs or dates and nuts; tangy lemon chicken; thick harira soup; and the iconic b'stilla made with pigeon or quail encased in ouarka. Cous cous, the national staple of semolina grains, is served with every meal. The traditional cous cous with seven vegetables is considered almost sacred, and you will find it on most menus. I also love the peculiar and powerful taste of smen, a type of cultured butter that is aged in earthenware pots, until it smells and tastes like a ripe, salty blue cheese. Since smen is not available outside Morocco, in my recipes I suggest melting some pungent blue cheese (such as gorgonzola or Roquefort) and sea salt into butter to approximate the authentic taste. My breakfast favourite has to be m'samen (Moroccan galettes) – fine sheets of pastry made from a slightly oily elastic dough which are filled with cheese, tomato, egg and herbs, folded into a square like a handkerchief, then cooked to order in smen in an earthenware pan. Absolutely delicious.

Heading west from Fes, you come to the unassuming city of Meknes. Founded by the Berbers (indigenous people of the Maghreb) in the 7th century, it's well worth a visit to take in some extraordinary ancient sites. The massive city gate, Bab el-Mansour, is considered the most beautiful in Morocco, and the royal granaries of Heri es Souani, with their perfectly symmetrical structure, are equally impressive. It's easy to while away a quiet hour or so wandering around Meknes – as this is not the most-visited part of Morocco, it makes for a pleasant change of pace. The road north of the city winds through Moulay Idriss to Volubilis, where the massive and largely intact Roman ruins stand as a testament to an outpost of their far-flung empire. The majesty and beauty of this ancient place is simply breathtaking, and I find that the best way to take it all in is to spread out a picnic lunch alongside one of the stone columns on the hillside.

About an hour's drive further on from Meknes, across the Khemisset plain, lies the royal town of Rabat, the political capital and seat of government. With its coastal setting and laid-back, friendly feel, this compact city is easy

SLEEPING AND EATING IN FES

LA MAISON BLEUE
2 Place de L'Istiqlal, Batha, Fes
Tel +212 35 636 052
www.maisonbleue.com
Thoughtfully restored guesthouse in the heart of the medina. Without a doubt, the best food in Fes, particularly their 'cous cous du 13eme siecle' (cous cous of the 13th century) with roasted ground almonds and cinnamon. The pastilla au lait (almond milk pastry) is unbelievably good.

RIAD MAISON BLEUE
33 Derb el Mitter, Talaa el Kabira, Fes
Tel +212 35 741 873
www.maisonbleue.com
Situated in the medina overlooking the ramparts, this sister establishment to La Maison Bleue is a grand Fassi home of Arab-Andalous style. There's a courtyard pool (essential in summer) and fabulous rooftop terraces for breakfast and private dinners.

to navigate your way around. It also has some low-key sights that are worth a look, including the archaeological museum, the royal palace, the remains of the ancient city at Chella, and the walled Oudayas Kasbah with its beautiful Hispano-Moorish garden.

About an hour's drive south-west along the coast from Rabat lies Casablanca. Of all the Moroccan cities, Casablanca inspires me the least. Established by the French as a bureaucratic and economic headquarters for their protectorate during the first half of the 20th century, the modern city has since become a huge metropolis. Granted, some of the boulevards are quite grand and there is some interesting Art Deco architecture, but it can be a struggle to see beyond the monotonous urban sprawl and the millions who flock here to find their fortune. However, as well as being the country's largest city and main port, Casablanca is the arrival point for most air travellers, so it's difficult to avoid entirely. Many visitors hope to find the romantic place so effectively portrayed in the classic film of the same name, but while Sammy's Bar is a must-visit for nostalgic film buffs, you're unlikely to find any Humphrey Bogart-type characters. If you are here for a day or two, one of the most pleasant things to do is to spend some time wandering along the corniche that borders an uninterrupted sweep of beaches, swimming pools, hotels, cafes and restaurants. Rising into the sky from the shores of the Atlantic Ocean, the massive Hassan II Mosque is the largest in the world after Mecca, and is one of the few mosques in Morocco to allow non-Muslims to enter.

Some of the best food in Casablanca is to be had at cheap local cafes, especially those along Rue Chaoui, opposite the Central Market, where you can feast on roast chicken and kebabs – a humble introduction to the splendours of Moroccan cuisine. The harbourside fish market sells seafood straight off the boats, and a stroll along the pier will reveal the day's catch, often including sardines, rouget and albacore tuna. As with most commercial transactions here, haggling or bartering for an agreed price is all part of the fun.

Then there's the imperial city of Marrakech, about three hours' drive south of Casablanca, with its Berber heritage and a totally different vibe from the almost medieval atmosphere of Fes. In a sense, it is far more international and cosmopolitan, with its wide boulevards, palm trees and carnival atmosphere. Fringed by desert, and with a backdrop of the mighty Atlas Mountains, the excitement and allure of Marrakech is palpable. From its still-intact mud-brick red clay ramparts that stretch around the Old City, turning from dusty pink to deep crimson at sunset, to the more modern French-style boulevards of Gueliz in the new town, I think this city has the most amazing architecture in the country. With so many traditional riads in the medina being restored to make comfortable luxurious houses or small boutique hotels, much foreign and local money has been poured into the beautification of this city, and its civic pride and commitment to preservation is evident as you peek behind the giant doors and high walls. Each year more glamorous riads open their doors to visitors, revealing oases of calm with a palatial blend of Moroccan architecture and contemporary comfort.

Being perched on the edge of the desert, Marrakech has always been an important trading town populated by Berbers, Moroccans and Senegalese, and as a result there are many caravanserai, or resting places on trade routes, still operating in some parts of the medina. Although the Marrakech medina might appear overwhelming at first, I don't find it is as tricky to navigate as the one in Fes – you seem to get your bearings much faster here, despite the endless maze of narrow alleyways that look alarmingly similar at first. The souk comprises a labyrinth of interconnecting markets that unfolds from the main square Djemaa el-Fna in the centre, a wide, open space filled with energy and life. The roads around the edges of the square seethe with people, donkeys and vehicles as they dodge and weave around each other in a maze of frenetic activity and perpetual motion. Smoke rises from the charcoal fires of the food stalls in the centre and the frenzied drumming and wailing can be quiet deafening. The whole experience is a total assault on the senses – in a good way.

STAYING IN RABAT

VILLA MANDARINE
19 Rue Ouled Bousbaa, Souissi, Rabat
Tel +212 37 752 077
www.villamandarine.com
Located in the Embassy district of Rabat, this charming small hotel is only about 10 minutes by taxi from the medina and kasbah, and is set in gardens full of fragrant citrus trees – a peaceful retreat that's definitely worth the 90-minute drive from Casablanca airport if you want a gentle introduction to Morocco.

Daily activity has focused around this square since medieval times, and oral histories have been played-out here for centuries. The storytellers are accomplished, recounting personal stories and legends – which are never finished, so you are lured back to the square the next day. To soak up the hypnotic pace and carnival-like atmosphere of the Djemaa el-Fna, your best bet is to sit at any cafe around the perimeter and watch the passing parade. A most extraordinary array of people and images will be unveiled before you: a giddying display of colour and activity, the source of hours of fascination and spectacle peppered with mystery and menace. There are children turning somersaults, and everywhere people are selling, haggling, performing and cajoling; it's almost impossible not to get sucked into the madness of bartering and consummate salesmanship. I gave in to the henna painters one evening and had my hand decorated with a naive design, only to find that when I washed off the caked-on mud a couple of hours later, as recommended, my hand was covered with a clumsy-looking bright orange

SLEEPING AND EATING IN MARRAKECH

LA MAISON ARABE

1 Derb Assehbe, Bab Doukkala, Marrakech
Tel +212 24 387 010
www.lamaisonarabe.com
This boutique hotel sets the standard for Marrakech, with its wonderful service and generously proportioned rooms and suites, some with private terraces – a real bonus within the medina walls. A shuttle service ferries guests to the hotel's garden property, 10 minutes' drive away, which houses a large swimming pool and a cooking school where guests can discover the magic of Moroccan cooking. Under the watchful eye of Aziza, the head dada (cook), and genial and knowledgeable host Mohammed, traditional dishes are prepared for lunch, which is then eaten at a long table under the massive fig tree in the garden; it's a wonderful way to fall under the spell of this country and its people.

LA SULTANA

403 Rue de la Kasbah, Marrakech
Tel +212 24 388 008
www.lasultanamarrakech.com
This is fantasyland – like staying on the set of *1001 Arabian Nights* – with opulent luxury. A beautiful property within the medina walls right by the Royal Palace, and the roof terrace restaurant serves absolutely delicious Moroccan and French food.

KASBAH TAMADOT

BP 67 Asni, Marrakech
Tel +212 24 368 200
www.virgin.com/kasbah
An easy 50-minute drive from Marrakech, the Moroccan retreat of Sir Richard Branson is the place to come if you want to sleep and dine in pampered luxury. Enjoy utterly delicious Mediterranean-inspired food for lunch on the al fresco terrace, or equally delicious Moroccan food for dinner served by an open fire with candlelight.

RIAD KNIZA

34 Derb L'Hotel, Bab Doukkala, Marrakech
Tel +212 24 376 942
www.riadkniza.com
A large riad lovingly restored by owner Mohammed Bouskri, noted antique dealer and personable host. This place also has the friendliest staff in the city, great food and a divine roof terrace for relaxing and checking out the rooftops of the medina.

LE TOBSIL

22 Derb Abdellah ben Hessaien, Bab Ksour, Marrakech
Tel +212 24 444 052
I love this hidden gem – their chicken tajine with honey and roasted almonds is simply sensational.

RIAD TAMSNA

Riad Zitoun Jdid 23, Derb Zanka Daika, Marrakech
Tel +212 24 385 272
Tucked away down an alleyway south of the main square, this tastefully restored riad serves drinks, lunch and dinner in a cool courtyard or on the rooftop terrace. The Senegalese owner's menu includes classics from his home country, such as poulet yassa, an intensely flavoured ginger and chicken dish, as well as modern Moroccan and international cuisine.

DAR MOHA

81 Rue Dar el Bacha, Marrakech
Tel +212 24 386 400
A most inventive modern take on traditional classics; their degustation menus are the best way to explore the flavours.

BAR L'ESCALE

Rue Mauritania (just off the corner of Boulevard Mohammed V), Gueliz, Marrakech
This favourite local hangout serves simply divine charcoal-grilled chicken – no fuss, no nonsense, just terrific food.

pattern not nearly as glamorous as the intricate design I'd anticipated – and it took over a month to wear off, much to my horror. Needless to say, I was more circumspect the next time I visited the square, and settled for watching the snake charmers instead (from a safe distance!).

If you happen to arrive at the square late in the afternoon, you can watch the vendors setting up rows and rows of outdoor food stalls, the air thick with wafting smoke as the grills are fired up. Each stall specialises in one dish, and the deal is this: you order what you want from each of the stalls that takes your fancy, find a spot at the communal tables nearby and wait for your order to be cooked – so civilised. My favourites are the stalls selling eels, snails and spiced merguez sausages. Eating this way is a feast for the eyes as much as the stomach, and a great way to interact with the locals. There are also some absolutely wonderful restaurants here, by far the best in the country. They mostly serve traditional food banquet-style, often with a modern twist, so make sure you come with a healthy appetite – you will never leave hungry.

Another distinctive sight around the medina are the water-sellers, with their lavishly colourful outfits and hats, carrying water bags and small cups as they dispense water to thirsty shoppers. They'll encourage you to have a souvenir photo taken with them at the square – for a small fee, of course. The drag queens that cavort around the square always attract a big crowd (you can't miss them!), and they are hysterical to watch; just be careful not to get drawn into their web, or you might find yourself dancing with them surrounded by hundreds of onlookers.

For some respite from the chaos, Marrakech's gardens are not to be missed. One of my favourites is the Majorelle Gardens, owned by Yves Saint Laurent and Pierre Berge, where an amazing array of plants, including bamboo, towering palms and cacti, surround a startling cobalt-blue house. It is a tranquil place to come and while away an afternoon. Another is the Menara Garden, an expansive eulogy to water and beauty, with its green tiles that are so characteristic of Islamic design; I had a wonderful picnic lunch there one autumn day with friends. A morning walk through the new town of Gueliz, just beyond the medina walls, takes you along broad avenues past chic shops and art galleries; there is an entirely different feel here, with French-style cafes along the boulevard sidewalks. On the outskirts of the city lies the Palmeraie, with its resorts, private clubs and enormous luxurious villas and mansions, many of them available for rent. Thousands of tall palm trees dominate the horizon, making it a spectacular sight, especially when arriving by road – like an enormous oasis in the desert. Camels are available for a short ride if you're feeling like an adventure on four legs.

Marrakech also offers many cultural sites to explore – from the Saadian Tombs, where over a hundred Saadian princes and their entourages were laid to rest, to the vibrantly coloured Koutoubia Mosque and the Bahia Palace, with its almost kitsch overload of shiny marble, stucco plasterwork cornices and painted ceilings. But my favourite would have to be the Medersa Ben Youssef, a Koranic school of scripture and law that was built in the 14th century and has been beautifully restored to showcase its signature Arab-Andalous architecture, with carved wooden archways and doors, and tranquil patios. I always find it hard to leave this place. Somehow it has a kind of magic to it that makes you want to stay, to discover more of its secrets. Still, there's always next time.

During my many visits, I have developed a strong affinity with Marrakech. One year I visited during Ramadan, which provided a contrasting perspective to the usual frenzied activity. The streets were quiet during the day as people fast from sunrise to sunset, an act of self-discipline and faith that's also intended to foster greater compassion for the poor. That year I was shown around by a pair of charming local guides, Hicham and Mohammed. One evening Hicham took me to his family home, where three generations lived, and I watched as his sisters prepared the food to break the fast, a meal known as Iftar. The fast is usually broken with a glass of sweet milk, some dates, harira soup, ksra (bread) and sweet syrupy chbakiyya pastries; naturally sweet food and drinks are used to sate the appetite and thirst. Proper dinner is not had until much later in the night, usually after midnight, and might include several tajines, cous cous sweetened with dried fruits, and plates of various sweets and pastries like ma'amoul (melt-in-the-mouth biscuits made with dates and pistachios) or sticky honey cakes and fried pastries bathed in scented syrups. To my astonishment, our guides not only lasted all day without even a sip of water, they insisted on talking their way through the day and never showed any sign of flagging, regardless of where we went. Ramadan is not an ideal time to visit, as many places are closed during the day, or empty – and it seemed improper to be sitting, eating or taking tea when no one else was. While spending the day without food was not a drama in the least for me, I did have to drink water and tea ever so discreetly.

At any time of the year, sweets play an integral role in the social life of Morocco. As well as breaking the fast during Ramadan, they are eaten on important occasions, and a box of sweets taken as a gift for the host when visiting a home is considered the correct etiquette. Hence the plethora of shops selling prepared sweets and pastries, including the local specialties of qa'b el ghazal (gazelle horns), ghoriba (rich buttery sesame shortbreads with a whole almond pressed into the centre), m'hanncha (buttery ouarka pastry stuffed with almond paste and flavoured with cinnamon and orange blossom water, then rolled snake-like into a coil and baked) and makroud (semolina and date biscuits).

If you have the time, you should venture out of the cities to discover the Atlas Mountains that lie to the east, and the vastness of the desert beyond. The drive south-east from Marrakech to Ouarzazate is a jaw-dropping ride as you climb over the Tizi n'Tichka pass in the High Atlas Mountains on impossibly narrow roads that seem to be meant only for donkeys. The oasis town of Ouarzazate, orginally built as a French foreign legion outpost, has been transformed by a thriving film industry keen to take advantage of the surrounding desert landscapes. We had such fun riding over the dunes on fat-tyred motorbikes one afternoon, with thrills and squeals all round! This is also the gateway to the Sahara Desert: if a serious nomadic adventure is what you're after, head further afield through the undulating sand dunes and palm groves of the Draa Valley to Zagora, or head along the Dades Valley to the east, which is jam-packed with converted kasbahs that epitomise comfort and effortless glamour.

A highlight of my first visit to this region, in October 2001, was a charming dinner in the desert one night, hosted by some local Berbers. We were just 5 kilometres from town, but sitting under the moonlit sky amass with stars, it felt like the middle of nowhere. A Berber-style campsite, complete with a massive tent and blazing campfires, had been set up, and we were welcomed by tribal elders from a nearby village. In keeping with the tradition of storytelling through music, the men began playing drums and high-pitched ghaita pipes and, out of the darkness, came a chorus of a dozen or more women, dressed in their best Berber outfits – all white and dazzling pinks and reds. Our hosts cooked up a storm: simple, earthy vegetable salads followed by a tajine of lamb and dried fruits with honey and cous cous, then date pastries with mint tea. They even produced a few bottles of local wine. Much as I was swept away by the experience, I couldn't help but reflect on the incongruity of events on the world stage – America had just begun its bombing raids on Afghanistan. We felt privileged to be sharing the moment with our Berber friends, who looked after us with a sincerity that made the aggressive events of the day seem even more appalling. We all remember that night for very different reasons.

The seaside town of Essaouira, a three-hour drive west of Marrakech, is blessed with long sweeping beaches that bear the brunt of the north-easterly Alize winds, making it ideal for windsurfing but a bit too wild for swimming. A walk along the ramparts that front the Atlantic Ocean, sheltering the medina behind their grand fortifications, is a great way to enjoy the sunset. Inside the vehicle-free medina, there are lots of craft shops, along with some really good food and produce shops in the lively souk. Look out for bottles of argan oil, a highly aromatic oil pressed from the nut-like centre of the yellow fruit of the argan tree, which grows exclusively in this part of Morocco. Argan oil has a quite pronounced and earthy flavour, not dissimilar to hazelnut oil. I like to use it when grilling whole fish over charcoal or on the barbeque as its strong flavour holds up extremely well; it also works beautifully in salad dressings. It is worth buying a bottle from one of the shops in the souk or from one of the reputable cooperatives on the road into town.

If you can, time your visit to coincide with the annual Gnaoua Music Festival, when international artists come

STAYING IN THE ATLAS MOUNTAINS

KASBAH DU TOUBKAL
Imlil, Asni
Tel +212 24 485 611
www.kasbahdutoubkal.com
Perched on a rocky outcrop facing Toubkal, the highest peak in North Africa, this is the best mountain retreat in the country. From the nearby village of Imlil, a scenic 90-minute drive south of Marrakech, guests ascend on the back of mules to the traditional kasbah, which enjoys the most breathtaking views of the High Atlas Mountains. Apart from enjoying the languid pace and exploring the mountains, this is the perfect setting to taste mechoui (a whole lamb slow-roasted in a beehive-shaped, sealed clay oven) served in big chunks with salt and ground cumin for seasoning. Walnut trees are prolific in this district, and the nuts appear in many guises on the plate, including salads, tajines and desserts.

to play with local Gnaoua musicians. A fusion of Berber, African and Arabic mystical traditions, Gnaoua music resonates strongly with the many indigenous cultures that connect with their spirituality through music and dance – powerful stuff, and very moving to watch.

On our first visit to Essaouira, we stayed in a rather basic riad in the medina, its claim to fame being that Jimi Hendrix once slept there. But my most recent visit revealed that things are looking up in the accommodation stakes, with a few new luxurious riads and small boutique properties catering to the discerning traveller. Rather than eat indoors, head for Place Moulay Hassan at the port, the town's social centre, where the fishermen display their catch in the late afternoon at small stalls along the waterfront. This is a great way to experience the raw and windswept nature of the place, while partaking of the best budget food in town. You choose the exact fish you want, then haggle amiably for the fairest price, and watch it being cooked right there on makeshift charcoal barbeques before being served simply with lemon, salt and bread.

The food of Morocco is delicious, shrouded in mystery and seductive to the palate, with complex spicing. The Arabs have long been leading spice merchants and this is most evident as you wander through the souks and see large sacks of ground spices, nuts, dates and olives in every hue. One seasoning that sets Maghrebi food apart is the spice mixture ras el hanout – literally meaning 'head of the shop', a name derived from the individual versions made by spice merchants, with each family recipe being a closely guarded secret. This aromatic blend comprises as many as 24 different ingredients, depending on the whims of its maker, and is an intrinsic ingredient in many tajines and soups.

The availability of alcohol in Morocco is more widespread than you might imagine in an Islamic country – at least in the cities, where a degree of flexibility is applied to the interpretation of the laws of the Koran. As a general rule, alcohol is available in restaurants and hotels, and a selection of Moroccan wines can be purchased in local wine shops for just a few dollars. Moroccan wines are made from local and imported grape varieties, which are grown in vineyards that stretch along the coastal plains between Casablanca and Tangier. Other wines are imported from France at highly inflated prices because of the prohibitive tax on alcohol, so it's worth getting accustomed to the local wines – my favourite standbys are the rose or gris varieties, especially Siroua or Guerrouane brands, which tend to work best with the flavours of the food.

Wherever you find yourself in this dynamic country, you will discover traditional foods, with recipes transmitted verbally from one generation to the next, as is the practice in so many other ancient cultures. According to the laws of Islam, food should never be wasted and should always be shared, so meals are generally eaten in the company of family and friends. Tradition also demands that the table be overflowing with a variety of dishes, a long-held custom stemming from a nomadic lifestyle. The popular saying of 'first you eat with your eyes' definitely applies here, and the custom is to take a small taste from each artfully decorated plate. It is never intended for everything to be eaten, for an empty plate implies a mean host, while the lavish generosity bestowed on visitors is a measure of the host's hospitality and a source of respect.

To all those people who have walked with me through Morocco, and who have shared their philosophy of abundance, I say 'Shukran' (thank you).

SLEEPING AND EATING IN ESSAOUIRA

L'HEURE BLEUE
2 Rue Ibn Batouta (at Bab Marrakech), Essaouira
Tel +212 24 783 434
www.heure-bleue.com
Just inside the medina walls, this is a sophisticated and welcome addition to the Essaouira scene. Lunch or dinner on the roof terrace here is mandatory when visiting this beachside town.

RESTAURANT FERDAOUSS CHEZ SOAUD
27 Rue Abd Essalam Labadi, Essaouira
Tel +212 24 473 655
Soaud's cooking is excellent, traditional food with a modern twist. Just let her devise a menu for you. Trust me – this woman cooks brilliantly.

SALMON CARPACCIO WITH PRESERVED LEMON AND CHILLI

This simple summer dish really shows off the versatility of preserved lemons, and with a gentle spike of chilli, both act as a foil to the salmon's voluptuous oiliness. The flavours of Morocco adapted to our modern way of preparation – stunning.

600 g sashimi-grade salmon fillet, skin and bones removed
1 teaspoon sea salt
½ teaspoon freshly ground black pepper
125 ml fresh lemon juice, strained
40 ml verjuice
1 preserved lemon, finely diced
2 small red chillies, finely sliced
2 teaspoons small capers, rinsed
1 tablespoon chopped oregano
1 tablespoon chopped parsley
1 tablespoon chopped chives
125 ml extra virgin olive oil
2 punnets micro watercress, snipped
6 teaspoons freshwater salmon roe

Slice the salmon into 5 mm slices and lay in a large dish in a single layer. Season with salt and pepper.

Mix the lemon juice, verjuice, preserved lemon, chilli, capers, fresh herbs and olive oil together to make a marinade and pour over the fish. Cover and refrigerate for 30 minutes. The fish will 'cook' during this time – if you leave it any longer the texture will be altered and the flavour will spoil.

Take the fish out of the refrigerator and leave to sit for 15 minutes before serving to allow the flavours to fully develop. Arrange the fish slices on serving plates to make a neat rectangle in the centre of the plate. Mix the watercress through the marinade and spoon over the fish. Dot with salmon roe and serve.

SERVES 6

LAMB, CHICKPEA AND HARISSA SOUP

This is an adaptation of the Moroccan harira, a hearty broth packed with flavours and textures. The pulses can vary according to the region, with lentils, beans, rice and chickpeas used in a range of combinations – my favourite version is from Fes. I adore the nutty flavour and texture of chickpeas and have mixed them with green lentils for this interpretation of the classic. For best results, use dried chickpeas, soak overnight and cook them before you start the soup. If you have any leftover roast lamb, add it to the soup a few minutes before serving.

1 head garlic
100 ml olive oil
5 tomatoes
2 teaspoons sea salt
1 teaspoon freshly ground black pepper
1 small brown onion, diced
500 g lamb shoulder, diced
2 teaspoons cumin seeds, roasted and ground
1.5 litres White Chicken Stock (see Essentials)
½ teaspoon saffron threads
200 g green lentils, rinsed and soaked in cold water for 30 minutes
2 tablespoons Harissa (see Essentials)
250 g cooked chickpeas
2 tablespoons shredded coriander leaves
1 tablespoon shredded mint leaves
1 tablespoon finely diced red onion
20 ml fresh lemon juice, strained
40 ml extra virgin olive oil

Preheat the oven to 180°C. Cut the top off the head of garlic, drizzle with a little olive oil and wrap in foil. Cut the tomatoes in half lengthways, drizzle with a little olive oil and season with salt and pepper. Roast the garlic and tomatoes for 30 minutes, or until soft and coloured. Unwrap and squeeze the roasted cloves of garlic from their skins. Discard the skins.

In a large saucepan, heat the remaining olive oil over moderate heat and fry the onion for about 10 minutes until softened, stirring occasionally. Remove and set aside.

Season the lamb pieces with salt, pepper and ground cumin, add to the pan and fry for about 10 minutes until lightly browned. Stir occasionally to prevent burning. Return the onion to the pan, add the stock, saffron, green lentils, roasted garlic and tomato and bring to boiling point. Stir in the harissa, reduce the heat and simmer for 20 minutes.

Add the cooked chickpeas and simmer for another 5 minutes. Taste and add more salt and pepper if necessary. Swirl in the coriander, mint, red onion, lemon juice and extra virgin olive oil and serve with crusty bread.

SERVES 4

ROASTED BEETROOT AND WALNUT SALAD

Salads are an integral part of any Moroccan meal – important appetisers that stimulate the palate and offer a vast array of textures and flavours. Whenever I decide to cook Moroccan food at home, it turns into something of a production because I always want to include all of the following dishes. I love the way their flavours bounce off each other.

1 bunch baby red beetroot
1 bunch baby golden beetroot
2 tablespoons finely diced red onion
1 teaspoon coriander seeds, roasted and ground
2 tablespoons chopped coriander leaves
2 tablespoons chopped mint leaves
75 ml extra virgin olive oil
50 ml walnut oil
50 ml fresh lemon juice, strained
sea salt and freshly ground black pepper
½ cup lightly roasted walnuts, chopped
handful of small beetroot leaves
20 ml rosewater

Preheat the oven to 180°C. Combine the red and golden beetroots and roast them whole for 20 minutes or until soft. Remove from the oven and peel off the skins when cool enough to handle.

Dice the beetroots, then add the red onion, ground coriander, coriander and mint.

In bowl, whisk both oils and the lemon juice, then season to taste with salt and pepper.

Toss the beetroot mixture, walnuts and beetroot leaves through the dressing to coat. Sprinkle with rosewater just before serving.

SERVES 4

CAULIFLOWER AND PINE NUT SALAD

I have very fond memories of a salad similar to this at La Maison Bleue in Fes. The spicy dressing works wonders with the texture of the cauliflower, making it alive and vibrant. Cut the cauliflower into tiny florets with very little stem.

½ cauliflower, cut into small florets
2 tablespoons pine nuts, roasted
1 tablespoon white sesame seeds, roasted
2 teaspoons finely diced preserved lemon rind
½ cup coriander leaves, chopped

RAS EL HANOUT DRESSING
20 ml fresh lemon juice, strained
½ teaspoon ground cumin
½ teaspoon ras el hanout
½ teaspoon Harissa (see Essentials)
70 ml extra virgin olive oil
sea salt and freshly ground black pepper

Bring a saucepan of water to the boil and cook the cauliflower florets for 2 minutes until softened.

Remove from the heat, strain, then refresh under cold water to stop the cooking.

To make the dressing, whisk the ingredients together in a bowl until emulsified then season to taste with salt and pepper.

To serve, toss the cauliflower with the pine nuts, sesame seeds, preserved lemon and coriander, add the dressing and toss to combine.

SERVES 4

CARROT AND ORANGE SALAD

This is one of the definitive tastes of Morocco and appears in myriad guises at every table right across the country. Instead of using the traditional grated carrot, I have opted for sweet baby carrots and left them whole.

1 bunch baby carrots, peeled
1 orange, peeled and segmented
1 teaspoon minced orange zest
50 ml fresh orange juice, strained
2 teaspoons fresh lemon juice, strained
25 ml orange blossom water
2 tablespoons castor sugar
½ teaspoon sea salt
¼ teaspoon freshly ground white pepper
½ teaspoon cumin seeds, roasted and ground
½ teaspoon ground cinnamon

Blanch the carrots in boiling salted water for 2 minutes, then drain and refresh under cold water to stop the cooking.

Mix together the remaining ingredients (except the cinnamon) in a bowl, add the carrots and toss to combine. Set aside for 30 minutes for the flavours to mingle. Sprinkle with cinnamon to serve.

SERVES 4

< CARROT AND ORANGE SALAD (LEFT); CAULIFLOWER AND PINE NUT SALAD (BACK); ROASTED BEETROOT AND WALNUT SALAD (FRONT); SMOKED EGGPLANT SALAD (RIGHT)

SMOKED EGGPLANT SALAD

Being eggplant, this naturally rates very highly in my salad stakes and is a much-loved favourite. It really pays to smoke the eggplants over hot coals if you can, as it makes an enormous difference to the flavour.

2 × 300 g eggplants (aubergines)
1 punnet Roasted Cherry Tomatoes (see Essentials)
100 ml olive oil
2 teaspoons minced garlic
3 tablespoons chopped parsley leaves
4 tablespoons chopped coriander leaves
1 teaspoon sea salt
½ teaspoon freshly ground black pepper
1 teaspoon cumin seeds, roasted and ground

Roast the eggplants over charcoal or hot coals if possible, otherwise roast in a hot oven until the skins are blistered and the flesh is soft. Leave until cool enough to handle, but still warm. Peel the eggplants, discard the skins and chop the flesh.

Peel the tomatoes, remove the seeds and mash coarsely.

Heat the oil in a pan and cook the garlic with the mashed tomatoes for 10 minutes. Add the chopped eggplant and remaining ingredients and cook gently for a further 10 minutes. Remove from the heat and allow to cool before serving.

SERVES 4

GRILLED CHILLI PRAWNS AND MECHOUIA

Mechouia is a delicious warm salad or stew of tomatoes and roasted capsicums – almost like a Moroccan ratatouille. It makes a wonderful accompaniment to prawns, but it would be perfectly acceptable to use Moreton Bay bugs, squid or chunks of fish instead.

40 ml olive oil
4 ripe tomatoes, roasted, peeled and seeded
2 teaspoons minced garlic
2 green capsicums (peppers), roasted, peeled and seeded
3 tablespoons chopped coriander leaves
½ teaspoon sweet paprika
1 teaspoon sea salt
½ teaspoon freshly ground white pepper
½ teaspoon cumin seeds, roasted and ground

CHILLI PRAWNS
20 ml extra virgin olive oil
1 teaspoon ras el hanout
2 small red chillies, minced
2 cloves garlic, minced
½ teaspoon sea salt
16 raw king prawns, shelled and deveined
4 lemon wedges

Heat the olive oil in a pan and cook the tomatoes and garlic for about 15 minutes until a puree forms. Mash with a spoon as they cook so they break down easily. Dice the roasted capsicums and add to the tomato puree. Add the remaining ingredients, cook for 10 minutes then allow to cool before serving.

To prepare the prawns, mix the oil with the ras el hanout, chilli, garlic and salt in a bowl. Add the prawns and toss until well coated. Cook under a hot grill for a few minutes until the prawns change colour.

Remove the prawns from the heat and serve with the mechouia and lemon wedges.

SERVES 4

SENEGALESE GINGER POUSSIN

I have had dinner a few times at the very stylish Riad Tamsna on a roof terrace in the depths of the Marrakech medina, sitting on big cushions under the stars with soft candlelight glowing from the low tables. One of their signature dishes is poulet yassa, and after tasting it on my first visit, I became completely hooked. This is my attempt to recreate it. It will serve four people as part of a shared table with other dishes, in true Moroccan tradition. As an accompaniment, you can't go past chunks of pumpkin seasoned with cumin, salt and ground chilli and dry-roasted until cooked.

20 g unsalted butter
1 teaspoon minced ginger
1 teaspoon minced garlic
4 × 400 g poussins
1 teaspoon sea salt
¼ teaspoon freshly ground black pepper
1 teaspoon ground cumin
2 teaspoons ground ginger
1 preserved lemon
olive oil, for pan-frying
8 golden shallots, halved
4 whole cloves garlic, peeled
few sprigs of thyme
2 tablespoons seedless raisins
200 ml White Chicken Stock (see Essentials), warmed
80 ml balsamic vinegar
1 tablespoon honey
2 teaspoons minced candied ginger

Preheat the oven to 190°C. Blend the butter with the ginger and garlic. Loosen the skin above the breasts of the birds and slide the butter between the skin and the meat. This will keep the chicken moist during cooking and season the meat at the same time. Truss their legs together with kitchen twine.

Mix the salt, pepper, cumin and ground ginger together and rub liberally over the skin of the birds.

Remove the flesh from the preserved lemon and discard. Cut the rind into fine slices and set aside.

Heat the oil in a heavy-based pan and saute the poussins for a few minutes each side until brown.

Remove from the pan. Add the shallots and garlic and sweat over moderate heat until softened but not coloured. Add the thyme, raisins and sliced preserved lemon then sit the birds on top.

Pour on the warm stock, transfer to the oven and roast, uncovered, for 25–30 minutes until the stock has evaporated and the birds are cooked (test at the thigh joints – the juices should run clear).

Bring the balsamic vinegar to the boil in a small saucepan and simmer until reduced by half. Add the honey and candied ginger, simmer for 2 minutes then remove from the heat.

Remove the birds from the oven and cut into quarters. Separate the leg and thigh joints, leaving them on the bone, then remove the breast fillets from the bone and slice each one in half diagonally.

Arrange the carved poussins on warmed plates and drizzle with the vinegar honey sauce. Serve with spiced baked pumpkin, buttered spinach or steamed rice.

SERVES 4

BERBER ROASTED POUSSINS WITH COUS COUS STUFFING

Typical of Berber cooking, tahmira is a spice rub used as a marinade to colour and flavour chicken. I have used cous cous as a stuffing, resulting in a self-contained parcel of elegance and mystery. This is best served simply with a salad of leafy greens tossed with a tangy lemon dressing. I also give each person a finger bowl of warm water with a splash of orange blossom water so hands can be kept clean as they tackle the small poussin carcasses.

4 × 500 g poussins, cleaned
100 ml White Chicken Stock (see Essentials)

COUS COUS STUFFING
40 ml olive oil
1 small brown onion, finely diced
2 cloves garlic, finely sliced
1 small red chilli, finely sliced
80 g merguez sausage, diced
2 red capsicums (peppers), roasted, peeled and chopped
2 tablespoons shredded parsley leaves
1 teaspoon sea salt
½ teaspoon freshly ground black pepper
100 g cous cous, cooked (see page 415)

TAHMIRA SPICE MIX
½ teaspoon saffron threads
60 ml extra virgin olive oil
1 teaspoon sweet paprika
2 teaspoons minced garlic
1 teaspoon freshly ground black pepper
2 teaspoons sea salt

To make the cous cous stuffing, heat the oil in a frying pan and saute the onion until softened. Add the garlic and chilli and fry for about 3 minutes until softened. Add the diced sausage and fry until beginning to colour. Stir in the roasted capsicum, parsley, salt and pepper, then remove from the heat, stir in the cooked cous cous and allow to cool completely.

Preheat the oven to 180°C and lightly oil a baking dish.

To make the tahmira, grind the saffron in a mortar and pestle (one with a smooth surface so you don't lose any – I use either a wooden or ceramic mortar for this) and mix into the oil with the remaining ingredients. Stir until combined.

Stuff the poussin cavities with the cous cous stuffing and skewer or tie with kitchen twine to secure. Rub the tahmira liberally over the surface of the birds, then lay them in the prepared baking dish with the chicken stock and roast for 25 minutes until cooked. During the cooking, the stock will evaporate, keeping the birds moist as they bake. Test at the thigh joint with a skewer and if the juices run clear, the meat is cooked. Remove the skewers or twine before serving.

SERVES 4

SEAFOOD PASTRIES

B'stilla (or pastilla) is a Moroccan festive pie, made in layers using the thin sheets of ouarka pastry. Traditionally pigeon or chicken is used, but I have been served a seafood b'stilla in both Fes and Marrakech over the years. I have sourced fresh sheets of tissue-thin brik pastry from a Melbourne supplier (Maison de Tunisie) which is very similar to ouarka pastry. Failing that, it is totally acceptable to use ready-made filo pastry sheets or make your own. These pastries can also be made smaller and served as snacks – just cut the pastry sheets down to size before assembling. I sometimes use cooked orzo instead of rice vermicelli and it is just as successful, absorbing the sauce as it reduces down.

200 g white fish fillet (jewfish, blue eye, ling, flathead), skin removed
200 g large raw prawns, shelled and deveined
200 g squid tubes, cleaned
200 g dried rice vermicelli
1 tablespoon finely diced preserved lemon rind
2 tablespoons chopped coriander leaves
2 tablespoons chopped parsley leaves
8 sheets brik pastry (or 16 sheets filo pastry)
250 ml vegetable oil
2 egg yolks

MARINADE
2 large cloves garlic
3 teaspoons sea salt
1 teaspoon ground turmeric
2 teaspoons freshly ground black pepper
2 teaspoons ground cumin
1 tablespoon Chermoula (see Essentials)
1 tablespoon Harissa (see Essentials)
1 tablespoon sweet paprika
60 ml fresh lemon juice, strained
100 ml olive oil
2 fresh bay leaves

To make the marinade, crush the garlic with 1 teaspoon salt to make a paste. Mix it with the remaining marinade ingredients in a bowl.

Cut the fish into large 2.5 cm chunks, cut the prawns in half crossways, and cut the squid lengthways into 1 cm wide strips. Add the seafood to the marinade then cover with plastic film and leave in the refrigerator for 1 hour.

Soften the vermicelli in boiling water for 1 minute, then drain and refresh under cold running water.

Cut the vermicelli into 2 cm lengths and set aside.

Carefully pour the seafood and its marinade into a frying pan and saute over moderate heat for 2–3 minutes until the seafood is translucent and about half-cooked. Remove the seafood with a slotted spoon and set aside.

Stir the vermicelli into the sauce in the pan and cook for a further 5 minutes or until the sauce has reduced and thickened. Remove from the heat, add the seafood, preserved lemon and chopped herbs and leave the mixture to cool for 30 minutes.

Fold the brik pastry sheets into quarters and then into triangles and snip about 2–3 cm off the non-pointed ends to make pastry rounds that will fit an 18 cm plate, with some overhanging the edges.

To make each pastry, rub a little vegetable oil onto the plate. Lay one pastry sheet over the plate, then place a second sheet on top. Spoon a quarter of the seafood stuffing onto the centre of the pastry and spread out evenly to the inner rim of the plate. Mix a little water with the egg yolks to make an egg wash.

Fold the first pastry layer up and around the stuffing, pleating the edges over and daubing with egg wash as you go. Carefully flip this first stuffed pastry layer over so it sits on the second pastry sheet. Repeat the process, brushing with egg wash. Flip the assembled pastry over onto the plate so the smooth surface faces upwards – it should be 12 cm in diameter. Brush with egg wash. Make the other three pastries in the same manner.

Heat the remaining vegetable oil in a frying pan to 180°C – it needs to be about 3 cm deep, enough to semi-deep-fry. Cook one pastry at a time. Slide each pastry into the oil, smooth side facing up, and fry for 3 minutes until golden. Carefully flip the pasty over in the oil and fry for another 3 minutes until golden. Drain on paper towel and keep warm in a 150°C oven while you fry the remaining pastries.

NOTE: If you are using filo pastry, allow four sheets for each pastry (two sheets for each layer) as it is more fragile than brik pastry. Brush with melted butter instead of egg wash and bake on a flat tray in a 180°C oven for 20 minutes until golden.

SERVES 4

BAKED HARISSA EGGPLANT

This is one of my favourite eggplant dishes, and makes a regular appearance on Sunday nights when friends drop in for an informal dinner. I serve it with several other dishes but it's always the first one to disappear. It goes well with all manner of things, from a simple grilled or roasted chicken, chermoula-baked fish or roast lamb, but as far as I'm concerned, it's unbeatable just on its own.

2 large eggplants (aubergines)
100 ml olive oil
5 cloves garlic, minced
1 tablespoon minced ginger
1 teaspoon cumin seeds, roasted and ground
1 teaspoon ras el hanout
100 ml honey
75 ml fresh lemon juice, strained
2 tablespoons Harissa (see Essentials)
sea salt and freshly ground black pepper
2 tablespoons parsley leaves, shredded

Preheat the oven to 200°C (400°F). Cut the eggplants in half lengthways and then into thick slices crossways. Heat a grill plate, brush each eggplant slice with oil, reserving 40 ml for later, and grill for a minute or so on each side. Remove from the grill.

Heat the remaining olive oil in an ovenproof frying pan and fry the garlic, ginger, cumin and ras el hanout for about 1 minute until fragrant. Add the honey, lemon juice and harissa and simmer for 2 minutes until slightly reduced. Season to taste with salt and pepper.

Add the grilled eggplant slices and toss to coat well. Put the pan in the oven and bake for 7 minutes. Remove from the heat, stir in the shredded parsley and serve.

SERVES 4

SPICED TOMATO AND CHICKPEA TAJINE

It really is worth making the effort to buy good-quality dried chickpeas and soak and cook them yourself. The difference in texture between the dried and tinned varieties is astounding (though it can be useful to have a tin in the pantry for an emergency).

1 cup dried chickpeas, soaked overnight
50 ml olive oil
1 white onion, finely sliced
4 cloves garlic, finely sliced
2 small red chillies, finely sliced
1 tablespoon minced ginger
1 teaspoon ras el hanout
1 teaspoon ground cinnamon
1 teaspoon sweet paprika
½ teaspoon saffron threads
100 ml White Chicken Stock (see Essentials) or water
1 tablespoon Harissa (see Essentials)
200 g Roasted Cherry Tomatoes (see Essentials)
1 teaspoon castor sugar
2 tablespoons small black olives, pitted
4 tablespoons cooked, double-peeled broad beans
4 tablespoons fresh peas
1 teaspoon sea salt
1 teaspoon freshly ground black pepper
3 tablespoons shredded parsley leaves

Cook the chickpeas in boiling water for 40 minutes or until soft. Strain, discarding the water.

Heat the oil in a wide-based pan and saute the onion, garlic, chilli and ginger for about 5 minutes until softened and fragrant. Stir in the ground spices, then add the saffron and stock and simmer for 3 minutes. Add the cooked chickpeas and harissa and simmer gently for 5 minutes.

Add the roasted tomatoes, sugar, olives, broad beans and peas and stir over heat for a few minutes until the peas soften. Remove from the heat and season with salt and pepper. Stir in the parsley and serve.

SERVES 4

SPICED TOMATO AND CHICKPEA TAJINE >

LEMON AND OLIVE CHICKEN TAJINE

This tajine is inspired by the Maison Arabe Cooking School, where I spent a day learning the ropes of Moroccan cooking under the watchful guidance of Mohammed and Aziza, the dada (cook). This particular combination would have to be the most well known of all the Moroccan tajines, but the flavours also work very well with lamb. Eating it at a table under an enormous fig tree with perfect blue skies above made the flavours sing like the sunshine. In Morocco cooks use smen, an aged butter made by flavouring clarified butter with salt and dried herbs, then leaving it to cure in earthenware pots for several weeks until its pungent flavour ripens. After a bit of experimentation, I have managed to replicate it by melting some blue cheese into ghee, which helps to give the dish its elusive character.

½ preserved lemon
4 chicken thighs, on the bone
1 red onion, grated
400 ml White Chicken Stock (see Essentials) or water
20 ml extra virgin olive oil
12 large black or green olives
1 tablespoon coriander leaves
1 tablespoon parsley leaves, roughly chopped

CHICKEN MARINADE
1 tablespoon ghee
2 teaspoons crumbled blue cheese
60 ml vegetable oil
20 ml fruity extra virgin olive oil
½ teaspoon sea salt
1 teaspoon freshly ground black pepper
1 dried chilli, crushed
1 teaspoon ground ginger
½ teaspoon saffron threads
4 cloves garlic, minced
1 tablespoon chopped parsley leaves
1 tablespoon chopped coriander leaves

Separate the rind from the preserved lemon and finely dice, reserving the lemon pulp.

To make the marinade, melt the ghee in a saucepan and stir in the blue cheese until combined.

Remove from the heat. Roughly chop the lemon pulp and add to the ghee with the remaining marinade ingredients. Stir thoroughly to combine. Add the chicken joints to the marinade, cover and set aside for 30 minutes at room temperature.

Heat a frying pan over moderate heat, add the chicken pieces and marinade and cook until starting to colour. Turn the chicken pieces over, stir in the grated onion and cook for 2 minutes. Add the stock and reduce the heat to low. Cover and simmer for 20 minutes or until the liquid has reduced by half.

Add the extra virgin olive oil, olives and preserved lemon rind and continue to cook for 5 minutes.

Check the seasoning and adjust if necessary. Sprinkle the coriander and parsley over the top and serve with steamed cous cous.

SERVES 4

CHERMOULA-BAKED SKATE WITH COUS COUS SALAD

Almost any type of fish can be prepared in this manner. I have recently started using skate wings – it is a sensational match to the complexity of the chermoula and the fish responds perfectly to this method of cooking. The cous cous salad is one of my 'at home' staples. I prefer to use Spiga brand Tunisian cous cous because its grains are larger and it has a great nutty texture and taste. If you use another brand or type, simply adjust the cooking time to suit the size of the grain. Be mindful that the best results for smaller grain (regular) cous cous are obtained by following tradition and steaming and fluffing the grains three times before serving.

2 skate wings, skin and bones removed
2 tablespoons Chermoula (see Essentials)
2 tomatoes, peeled, seeded and diced
1 tablespoon diced preserved lemon rind
2 tablespoons shredded coriander leaves

COUS COUS SALAD
300 ml cold water
100 g Spiga cous cous
50 ml fresh lemon juice, strained
200 ml extra virgin olive oil
1 teaspoon ras el hanout
1 teaspoon freshly ground black pepper
2 teaspoons sea salt
2 cloves garlic, minced
2 red bird's-eye chillies, minced
2 green onions, finely sliced
2 tablespoons finely diced preserved lemon rind
3 tablespoons pine nuts, roasted
1 punnet Roasted Cherry Tomatoes (see Essentials)
1 teaspoon minced lemon zest
2 tablespoons chervil leaves
1 tablespoon chopped parsley leaves
1 tablespoon chopped mint leaves
1 tablespoon coriander leaves

To prepare the fish, cut each wing into 3 cm wide strips following the natural line of the fish. Place the fish pieces in a single layer in a baking dish and spoon the chermoula over the top. Mix gently with your hands to ensure the fish is totally covered with the chermoula, then leave to marinate for 30 minutes. Preheat the oven to 180°C.

To prepare the cous cous salad, place the cold water in a saucepan, pour in the cous cous grains and bring to the boil. Whisk, then cover the pan and reduce the heat to very low so the grains cook by the absorption method. Continue to whisk every few minutes for about 18 minutes until the grains have absorbed all the liquid and have become fluffy. Remove from the heat.

Mix together the lemon juice, olive oil, ras el hanout, pepper and half the salt, then stir half the dressing through the cous cous to flavour and moisten. Add the remaining ingredients to the cous cous with the rest of the dressing and toss to combine thoroughly.

Bake the fish, uncovered, for 8 minutes – do not turn.

Spoon the cous cous salad onto plates, then sit the fish on top and spoon the juices over the fish.

Sprinkle the diced tomato, preserved lemon and shredded coriander over the top and serve immediately.

SERVES 4

SPICED SARDINES WITH FENNEL, GRAPEFRUIT AND WATERCRESS

Sardines are a prominent feature on menus in Essaouira. I created this salad from other ingredients I saw at the markets there, offering a clean and refreshing foil for the natural oiliness of the fish. If you are unable to get fresh sardines, you can substitute small blue mackerel, herring or bonito fillets, or swordfish steaks – just adjust the cooking time slightly.

16 sardines, scaled and gutted
1 teaspoon sea salt
40 ml olive oil
20 ml fresh lemon juice, strained
20 ml onion juice (strained juice of grated red onion)
2 teaspoons Harissa (see Essentials)
½ teaspoon ground cinnamon
½ teaspoon ground ginger
1 teaspoon cumin seeds, roasted and ground
1 teaspoon coriander seeds, roasted and ground
½ teaspoon cayenne pepper
1 teaspoon freshly ground black pepper

SALAD
1 ruby grapefruit
pinch of sea salt
1 small fennel bulb, finely shaved
1 tablespoon fennel fronds
2 green onions, finely sliced
40 ml extra virgin olive oil
8 green olives, pitted and sliced
2 tablespoons coriander leaves
large handful of watercress sprigs

Rub the surfaces of the sardines inside and out with salt. In a bowl combine the olive oil, lemon and onion juice, harissa and spices, then rub liberally over the fish. Marinate at room temperature for 1 hour before cooking.

To prepare the salad, peel and segment the grapefruit and save the juice. Combine in a bowl with the remaining salad ingredients and set aside while you cook the fish.

Place the sardines and marinade in single layer on a flat baking tray and cook under a hot grill for 4 minutes. Transfer the sardines to plates, pile the salad on top in the centre of the fish and serve.

SERVES 4

ALMOND AND RASPBERRY PASTILLA

This is my all-time favourite Moroccan dessert, with the classic flavour combination of almonds, cinnamon and orange blossom, and the raspberries giving it a lavish appearance. The recipe serves six people (I have found it too hard to reduce it down any further) so even if you are only cooking for four, make it as it is and enjoy the leftovers . . . if there are any!

250 g blanched almonds, roasted
50 g icing sugar
1 teaspoon ground cinnamon
8 sheets filo pastry
125 g unsalted butter, melted
500 ml milk
65 g castor sugar
1 stick cinnamon
60 g cornflour
250 ml thick (45%) cream
40 ml orange blossom water
1 punnet raspberries
1 tablespoon Cinnamon Sugar (see Essentials)

Preheat the oven to 175°C and line a baking tray with baking paper. Process the roasted almonds until finely ground and mix with the icing sugar and ground cinnamon.

Fold the pastry sheets in half and cut out six 8 cm rounds from each folded sheet, using a sharp knife and a bowl or small plate as a template. Continue until you have 48 pastry rounds. Discard the scraps.

Create six stacks on the baking tray. Start with one double sheet in each stack and brush with melted butter. Sprinkle with some of the almond mixture. Continue layering, with a double layer of pastry, butter and a sprinkling of almond mix each time, until you have seven layers. Finish each stack with the remaining pastry rounds and brush with butter. Bake for 20 minutes or until golden, then remove from the oven and transfer to serving plates.

In a saucepan, bring the milk, sugar and cinnamon stick to simmering point over medium heat. Whisk together the cornflour and cream, then stir into the simmering milk with the orange blossom water. Cook over gentle heat until the mixture forms a custard consistency and coats the back of a spoon. Remove from the heat, pass through a fine mesh sieve and discard the cinnamon stick.

Pour the warm custard over the pastry stacks. Top with raspberries, dust with cinnamon sugar and serve immediately.

SERVES 6

TOFFEE DATES WITH VANILLA CREAM

The variety of fresh dates in the Arab world is quite astounding. I made this dessert for dinner once when staying in a beautiful house in the Palmeraie area of Marrakech that had a garden full of date palms.

150 g gianduja (hazelnut) couverture chocolate
110 ml pouring (35%) cream
12 fresh dates
200 g castor sugar
50 ml water

VANILLA CREAM
350 ml pouring (35%) cream
½ teaspoon vanilla bean paste
6 large egg yolks
50 g castor sugar
2 g gelatine leaves, softened in cold water

Chop the chocolate into small pieces and place in a bowl. Heat the cream in a saucepan to simmering point then pour over the chocolate and stir until melted. Refrigerate until the ganache is firm, then transfer to a piping bag with a small nozzle attached.

Split the dates down one side and remove the stones. Pipe the firm ganache into the centre to fill the dates and press to close. Refrigerate until ready to serve.

To make the vanilla cream, place the cream and vanilla in a saucepan over gentle heat and bring to simmering point. Whisk the egg yolks and sugar in a bowl until pale and creamy. Stir in the hot cream and whisk to combine.

Sit the bowl over a pan of simmering water and cook, stirring, until the mixture reaches a thick custard consistency and coats the back of the spoon. Stir in the softened gelatine until dissolved. Pass through a fine mesh sieve and stand the bowl over ice to cool it quickly. Refrigerate for about 2 hours until set.

Heat the sugar and water in a saucepan over high heat and cook, without stirring, to a caramel colour. Working quickly (as the toffee will continue to cook and darken), dip each stuffed date into the pan using a fork, to coat with a thin layer of toffee. Rest on a flat tray lined with baking paper until set.

To serve, spoon some vanilla cream into the centre of each plate and arrange the toffee dates on top. Serve immediately.

SERVES 4

IN SEARCH OF PERFECT HUMMUS
THE MIDDLE EAST

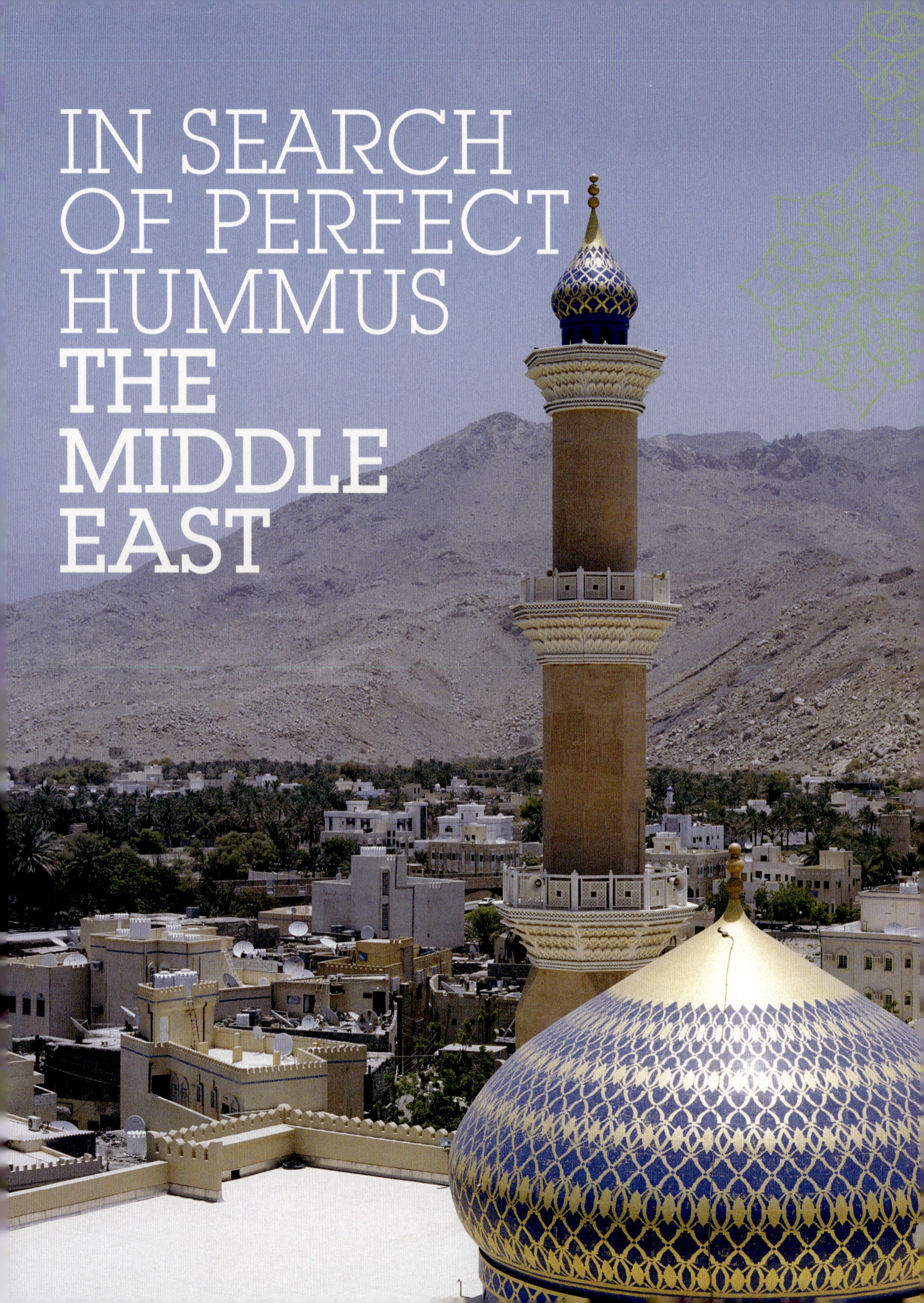

I have always been fascinated with Persian history and Arab food lore, and the impact it has had not only on the Middle Eastern region but across the world. Here food has a much greater significance than mere sustenance, as is demonstrated by the Arab propensity for hospitality and generosity. Bread is considered sacred and salt symbolic. Indeed, I was told that it is never an accident if food is served without salt, but rather a tacit warning that your host intends to kill you after you finish eating! Since I strongly believe that it is the cook's responsibility to properly season the food – anything less seems an insult – I couldn't help but smirk when I heard this. Such folklore offers insights into the rituals of the Middle Eastern table.

On our first trip to the Middle East, we visited the pocket of ancient land smack bang in the middle – Israel of today, Palestine of yesterday. In Tel Aviv, we stayed with our dear friend Andrew, who was working there at the time, and met up with Guy, a colleague from London who shares my enthusiasm for discovering local culinary secrets. Our first sunset drink was in the lounge of a seriously cool chill-out bar at Jaffa, one of the oldest operating ports in the world (now merged into Tel Aviv-Yafo). With a boardwalk that stretches for kilometres, it offers a dramatic backdrop to the city. We kicked back and gazed at the imposing Tel Aviv skyline, which also has some pretty interesting Bauhaus architecture and design when you get up close. I must say we were surprised by the heartbeat of this city: there's a sense of urgency, a need to enjoy every minute – maybe because the future seems so unpredictable. The vibrant restaurant and bar scene appears to be constantly evolving; the local clubs pulsate with the latest music; and traditional food is available from street carts and small hole-in-the-wall cafes all over town. The streets of the Neve-Tzedek neighbourhood are a shopper's paradise, filled with interesting stores, chic cafes and restaurants.

This is where the search for perfect hummus began – at Abu-Hasan, a hummus bar in central Tel Aviv – and we could never walk past the nearby Abulafia Bakery without succumbing to a bagel or some bread. During the same visit, we also discovered musakhan, a Palestinian savoury flatbread like a pizza, topped with minced chicken and seasoned with sumac (not dissimilar to Turkish lahmacun, made with minced lamb). We checked out the fabulous food delis at Levinsky Market, packed with smoked fish, pickled herrings and cured mullet roe, and stalls overflowing with fresh produce and spices. Tel Aviv also provided me with the most sublime falafel I have ever tasted – big, crisp and incredibly fresh. You'll find them at the falafel place at the Sheqem department store, on Ibn Gvirol Street. Since then, it has become my mission to taste hummus and falafel anywhere and everywhere, a duty I take very seriously.

Early one morning we took a taxi into the hills to Jerusalem, to spend the day with Andrew's friend, Yossi, a university professor who acted as our guide for the day. The landscape surrounding the city is incredibly spartan, so open and windswept. Visited by thousands of pilgrims each year, the walled Old City of Jerusalem is charged with religious significance. For Jews it is the holy site of Abraham's sacrifice; for Muslims, it is where Muhammed ascended to heaven; and for Christians, it is where Jesus was crucified and resurrected.

We happened to be there at Easter when it coincided with both Greek Orthodox Easter and Jewish Passover, so there were more people than usual squished into the narrow streets. We walked along Via Dolorosa, the street punctuated by the stations of the cross that Jesus passed on the way to Calvary. Standing at the Western Wall (once called the Wailing Wall), we let our hands glide over the smooth stones and noted the hundreds of furled pieces of paper in the crevices between the stone blocks – messages and prayers left by worshippers. The Temple Mount stands immediately above, on a high platform, with the golden Dome of the Rock and the most exquisite mosque next to it. Climb the steps to the roof of the Petra Hotel for the best view of the dome and its surrounding labyrinth of streets. Archaeological excavations have revealed streets built during Herod's time – the layers of history exposed like an open wound, each built on top of the other.

The Old City is divided into four quarters – Muslim, Armenian, Christian and Jewish, and the present city walls were built by the Turks during the reign of Suleiman the Magnificent. There are several gates, and we entered through Jaffa Gate, where we got distracted for a short while checking out the cluster of mobile caravans that make and sell falafel – clearly a bit of a fixation at the time! Once inside the walls, we walked through the Arab souk, a lively street market with lots of noise and action, where I bought a falafel gadget so I could have a go at making them myself. This simple little device scoops and shapes just the right amount of the mixture for each falafel, but no matter how much I try (and believe me, I've tried), somehow I never have the same deftness of hand as those who have done it all their lives.

In the Armenian quarter we found intricately designed ceramics, and in one of the narrow streets of the butchery section, in the Muslim quarter near the Damascus gate, we sat in a small cave-like room chiselled into the rock and ate the most divine hummus imaginable. The shop is humble, it has no name, and you need the guidance of a local to get you there, but this business has been passed down through the generations. Hummus is what they do – that's it, served with warm flatbread. This defining culinary moment has stayed with me ever since. I felt sure I had found the perfect hummus, and no others have been able to match the smooth creaminess and harmonious flavour of that one. Not that this stops me from continuing my search every time I visit the Middle East.

After spending several hours wandering through the narrow streets and paths of Jerusalem's Old City, listening to one story after another, and catching occasional glimpses of everyday life for those who live within these walls, we tried to get a taxi to take us to Bethlehem but it was not considered wise for us to visit at the time. So, as a special treat before dinner, Yossi drove us up the mountain behind the Hebrew University. With the soldiers and guard outposts of the West Bank ever so close, we gazed down to the Dead Sea in the distance, and watched another perfect sunset across the vast expanse of desert. We had dinner at Ocean, a gorgeous restaurant in the new city that is sadly no longer there, but I have fond memories of the beautiful feast we enjoyed, prepared by avant-garde chef Eyal Shani (now at Bruno restaurant in Tel Aviv). We ate St Peter's fish, which is smaller in size but has a similar texture and taste to sea bass, caught from the Sea of Galilee and baked whole with fennel and lemon in a wood-fired oven; lobster in a luscious tomato butter sauce; prawns grilled over citrus charcoal; blue bream cooked over hot coals; and a leg of lamb roasted with wild herbs. It was a revelation to find a menu showcasing non-kosher ingredients, and this was a spectacular meal – the flavour of every single ingredient shone through.

SLEEPING AND EATING IN TEL AVIV

HILTON TEL AVIV
Independence Park, Tel Aviv
Tel +972 3 520 2222
www.hilton.com
Great central location facing the Mediterranean and surrounded by a large park. You can walk along the lengthy promenade to Jaffa.

ABU-HASAN (ALI-KARAVAN)
1 Ha'dolfin Street (on the hill), Jaffa, Tel Aviv
Tel +972 3 682 0387
and
14 Shivtaie Israel Street, Jaffa, Tel Aviv
Tel +972 3 682 8355
Serving the best hummus in Jaffa for more than 40 years, these single-minded places open early morning and close when the hummus is finished.

HUMUS ASALY
73 Yafet Street, Jaffa, Tel Aviv
Tel +972 3 681 3435
A definite must if you want to eat excellent hummus.

LILITH
42 Maazeh Street, Tel Aviv
Tel +972 3 629 8772
This restaurant had just opened when we visited and offered sensational food with light, modern flavours. I have heard that it now has a cooking school attached, and the menus are strictly kosher – fish and dairy items only.

MARGARET TAYAR'S
4 Retsif Ha-Aliyah Shenei Street, Jaffa, Tel Aviv
Tel +972 3 682 4741
This seafood restaurant is enjoyed by locals and tourists alike and regularly tops the list of Ten Best Restaurants in Israel. Always call to check opening hours; reservations are essential. Margaret is Jewish Moroccan, so make sure you try her grilled or stuffed sardines.

ABULAFIA BAKERY
Yafet Street (across the road from Margaret Tayar's restaurant), Jaffa, Tel Aviv
You can't help but be drawn in by the aroma of freshly baked bagels and pita breads, each flavoured in different ways. There's even one type of bread that is just like the Indian rumali, or handkerchief bread – cooked paper thin in large sheets over a hot domed metal plate.

QUEENS OF FALAFEL
85 Yehudah Halevi, Tel Aviv
Tel +972 3 566 2050
Local women Orna and Ella have created hugely popular modern versions of this culinary classic.

COMME IL FAUT
Hangar 26, Old Port district, Tel Aviv
Fab cafe with organic food in this redeveloped waterfront area.

A few years later I worked with Israeli chef Moshe Basson at a Melbourne Masterclass. Born in Iraq, Moshe grew up in and around Jerusalem, where his parents ran a bakery in an Arab village – and where he planted his first eucalyptus tree in the courtyard of the family home. As we prepared for our presentations, swapping food and travel stories, he told me about the source of his kosher Middle Eastern food, with many of the ingredients collected from the wild. A disciple of the international Slow Food Movement and a noted chef in his homeland, Moshe maintains he was taught by the best chefs in the world – mothers. His restaurant, Eucalyptus, is in the centre of Jerusalem and, to honour his heritage, he planted a eucalyptus tree at the front when he opened. Moshe has created some complex dishes in his time; one that I will always remember is eggplant, onion and fig, each stuffed with minced spiced chicken and braised together until soft, then served with a tamarind fig sauce.

Experience has given me a new appreciation of kosher food. I hadn't realised it could be so sophisticated yet timeless, with the sun-drenched flavours of summer in every mouthful – there's so much more to it than chopped liver! In a way, it felt quite perverse to be focusing on food and pleasure in such a war-torn, fractured country. Then we looked around and realised that the Israelis certainly weren't allowing their lives to grind to a halt, inspiring in us an even deeper respect for the people of this troubled region. Sharing food at the table brings people together. Wouldn't it be something to see harmony and peace restored in this ancient land? Make hummus not war . . . If only life could be that simple.

Many say Beirut is not for the faint-hearted. When we visited for the first time in 2005, just weeks after former prime minister Rafik Hariri was assassinated in a massive car-bomb attack, some of our friends suggested we must have rocks in our heads to even think about going at a time like that. But these days, when is the right time? We flew over to meet up with our travelling buddy Andrew, who was very familiar with the area, having by then moved on from Tel Aviv. As it turned out, the timing was spot on. In the wake of the assassination, Beirut was undergoing rapid political change – and through Andrew and another friend, Brett, who was living there at the time, we met so many interesting people who shared stories of resilience and survival with us.

To get a sense of the city we wandered through the streets without a map, letting curiosity be our guide, and soon discovered that Beirut is beguiling as it is crazy. The place buzzes with young professionals who play as hard as they work, creating a hip and happening city.

The traffic, which is chaotic at the best of times, grinds to a complete halt during peak hour. Some of the old Mercedes taxis pre-date the civil war, though there are many new ones, so flagging a cab can be a case of pot luck. There is a madness to the architecture: some buildings are brand new with ultra-modern design, while others are pockmarked or mere skeletons that have been left standing shell-shocked against the horizon. There are reminders of war everywhere; the city is a living monument to the horror and waste of it all.

The buildings in East Beirut, around Gemmayzeh and Achrafieh, are the most fascinating: a real mix of grunge and ghostly monoliths, interspersed with some incredibly beautiful houses and gardens, and wonderful shops. This is also where we discovered the most diverse range of food outlets and restaurants. We decided it was the Darlinghurst of Beirut – anyone familiar with Sydney will know what I mean! Rue Monot comes alive at night; roller doors are pushed up to reveal hidden bars and sophisticated dance clubs. This is party central and boy, these people sure know how to party. The beats of world music could be heard everywhere, and there was such an air of friendliness that we never once felt any threat to our safety. Rather, we were embraced into the heartbeat of the city.

EATING IN JERUSALEM

FAMILIES RESTAURANT
Suq Khan es-Zeit Bazaar, Jerusalem
(near the Jaffa Gate, Old City)
Order the falafel and meze plates.

EUCALYPTUS
Safra Square, Building 4, City Hall, Jaffa Road, Jerusalem
Tel +972 2 624 4331
Home to chef Moshe Basson's indigenous food. A gatherer of wild foods across the region, he creates layers of flavours in his delicious home-style cooking. Look out for the eucalyptus tree out front.

The Corniche is a long road that skirts the city along the coastline from Downtown to the airport, lined with cafes, bars, amusement parks, private beach clubs (so *very* Beirut), bread sellers, and the occasional hawker. It's the most popular place to promenade in the entire city, and really comes alive late in the afternoon and over the weekend. During the day, when it was quieter, we would watch teenagers jumping off the rocks into the sea. We stayed at a hotel on the Corniche, overlooking the Mediterranean Sea near Pigeon Rocks. To start each day, we hit the fresh juice bars up the hill in Hamra, and the cafes and patisseries in Verdun for fabulous coffee.

For such a small country, Lebanon is full of treasures. It is possible to visit any part of it in a day, and everything is within easy reach of Beirut. Driving north out of the city, we took a detour from Jounieh up the mountainside to Harissa – we just had to go and check out a place with a name like that. A renowned pilgrimage site, there are several places of worship in the vicinity, including a gigantic white statue of the Virgin Mary at the peak, keeping a watchful eye over the coast, and a modernist Maronite church. Stopping here also gave us the opportunity to see iconic Lebanese cedar trees up close. Continuing up the coast, we reached the ancient city of Byblos, where we wandered through the ruins of past civilisations, particularly the intact crusader castle perfectly positioned above a shimmering harbour.

One of the reasons I wanted to visit Lebanon was to continue my search for the perfect hummus and falafel, something I'd started on an earlier visit to Jerusalem. We decided the best hummus was served at a seafood taverna in Byblos, along with a memorable fattoush salad; and the best falafel could be had at a street stall opposite the ABC Shopping Centre in Achrafieh, with nearby Al Mijana Restaurant coming a close second. I learnt that falafel are generally made with dried chickpeas in Israel, Syria, Lebanon and Jordan, and with dried broad beans in Egypt.

Every meal began with an assortment of meze, a tradition at which the Arab world excels. I was in heaven because eggplant had such a strong presence on every menu, prepared in one guise or another. My hunt for the best moutabal (a smooth smoky eggplant puree laced with garlic and lemon, similar to baba ghannouj) just about took over from hummus. Lebanon's national dish, kibbeh, also reeled us in, and we tasted many versions of this specialty. However it's served, the lamb meat is first pounded with burghul (cracked wheat) and seasonings

SLEEPING AND EATING IN BEIRUT

HOTEL ALBERGO
137 Abdel Wahab El Inglizi Street, Achrafieh, Beirut
Tel +961 1 339 797
www.albergobeirut.com
Beautiful auberge-style house in the centre of East Beirut, close to much of the nightlife and restaurants around Rue Monot.

INTERCONTINENTAL PHOENICIA HOTEL
Fakhr Ed Dine Street, Minet al-Hosn, Beirut
Tel +961 1 369 100
www.ichotelsgroup.com
On the Corniche overlooking the Mediterranean and close to the renovated Downtown area, this is a stylish modern hotel that was rebuilt after the civil war. Ask for a sea-facing room on the upper floors.

BREAD
Gouraud Street, Gemmayzeh, Beirut
Tel +961 1 566 506
This small, unassuming and genuine neighbourhood joint packed with locals is a firm favourite of mine. The breads are made in-house and the tiny kitchen produces deliciously light modern Mediterranean food. Terrific wine list too.

ISTAMBOULI RESTAURANT
Commodore Street, Hamra, Beirut
Tel +961 1 352 049
For the best cheese boreks and hummus.

DRAGONFLY BAR
Gouraud Street, Gemmayzeh, Beirut
(a few doors up from Bread)
Tiny but terrific place for champagne or cocktails before dinner, with great small meze plates for sharing. This place has a great vibe, very friendly service and just oozes atmosphere.

AL MIJANA RESTAURANT
Abdel Wahab El Inglizi Street, Achrafieh
Tel +961 1 328 082
Traditional Lebanese meze and grills – don't miss the famed Mijana hummus or the excellent falafel.

to give it a smooth and velvety texture. From there it can be served in various ways: raw (as in a tartare); rolled into balls or made into dome or oval shapes before being fried (the balls can be stuffed with pine nuts or the sweet fat from lamb tails, considered a real delicacy); grilled over charcoal; or cooked with a tahini or yoghurt sauce. Often we would order a few different styles of kibbeh, just to see which one tasted better. As I may have mentioned before, I take my culinary research very seriously!

The accompanying breads are to die for: kaake, flat rounds of sesame-crusted bread with a hole near the top so they resemble large handbags, and the simple but delicious saj, wafer-thin sheets drizzled with olive oil and sprinkled with za'atar – my personal favourite. Another terrific discovery was the sourdough breads at Bread Republic and its sister restaurant Bread, which boasts organic produce and excellent cooking. I became addicted to their labneh, thick, creamy yoghurt made from raw sheep's milk; drizzled with green peppery olive oil, it became a must with everything – I even ate it for breakfast with cucumber and tomato. Another taste sensation was the new-season almonds, so virginal white and fresh, with the same clean flavour I remember from Spain. And I can't leave out the divine kanafeh cheese pastries – I first had them in Turkey, but the Lebanese versions tasted even better to me.

As we drove east out of Lebanon, through the high mountain pass to Damascus, we realised we were following army trucks full of Syrian soldiers departing Lebanon, which certainly added a sense of drama to the journey. A word of warning: the border crossing can be quite tedious and time-consuming; you need patience and, if possible, a driver who speaks Arabic.

We arrived in Damascus at dusk, and laid out before us was a skyline dotted with white minarets illuminated with soft green light – the colour of Islam. The sheer beauty of it took my breath away. Considered by many to be the oldest continually inhabited city in the world, Damascus has long Christian and Islamic histories, and happily both cultures manage to coexist harmoniously in this modern age. As we crawled along at a snail's pace amid the frenzy of peak-hour, bumper-to-bumper traffic, weaving between battered yellow taxis, we had ample time to take in the atmosphere of the city. Damascus feels so ancient, as if a millennium of dust and grime has been baked onto the buildings – it would look amazing if it gave itself a bloody good wash! The Ottoman legacy left its mark on the city in the shape of the Takiyya as-Suleimaniyya mosque, a modest version of the grand mosques of Istanbul, with its signature minarets at each corner. Also of Ottoman origin (from Konya, in the Turkish region of Anatolia), the whirling dervishes have long been integrated into Syrian culture, and their performances are magical to watch.

To help us navigate our way around town, we hired a local guide called Raeda, who turned out to be insightful, informative, modern and ever so friendly. (In fact, we were always greeted with extraordinary friendliness, and treated with respect and generosity wherever we went in Syria.) There was so much to see, all jam packed in and around the old city, bounded by the remains of the Roman wall with several impressive gates (babs). We entered the ancient maze of souks through Bab Al-Jabiye (the main gate) that leads directly onto 'The Street Called Straight' (from the Latin Via Recta), where Greeks and Romans once trod. Today, rows of shops and a long undercover market with a semi-domed iron roof take up much of the street. We made a beeline for the renowned Bakdash, where ice cream made with mastic gum of various flavours is churned next to the counter in big stainless steel vats – my favourites were rose and pistachio. Holding centre stage in the old city is the Umayyad Mosque, one of the most significant religious buildings for Muslims. Previously the site of a Roman temple and then a Christian church before being converted to a mosque in the 8th century, the prayer hall houses a shrine dedicated to John the Baptist, who is revered by both Muslims and Christians. We stood in the vast limestone courtyard, equally fascinated by the groups of black-clad veiled women and the intricate mosaic tiles and domes of the building. Enticed by great food aromas perfuming the air around the mosque, we walked around its walls to discover some snack stalls huddled together in a covered lane just behind the mosque on Sharia al-Qaimariyya.

EATING IN BYBLOS

BAB EL MINA SEAFOOD RESTAURANT
Jbeil, Byblos Harbour (next to The Fishing Club), Byblos
Tel +961 9 540 475
www.babelmina.com
An hour's drive along the coast from Beirut, sit in the sun on the front terrace and enjoy a delicious lunch overlooking the old Roman ruins of the harbour. Their hummus, fattoush salad and fried baby squid are sensational.

Exploring outside the confines of the old city, we walked through the compact Souk Saroujah, along Handicrafts Lane, then on to the central square of Al Merjeh, passing through a local fruit and vegetable market at Sharia Shoukri as-Quwatli, where the produce looked much better and fresher here than that we'd seen in the souk. The area around Ahnouss and Sarajah squares also had terrific grocery shops. All manner of food shops lined the streets; in particular, our attention was caught by the sweet pastry shops around Al Merjeh – a real feast for the eyes. Every time we passed one of these shops, we couldn't resist going in to buy some delicacies: shabeyak (small crescent-shaped filo pastries made with pistachio nuts, almonds and orange blossom water) and ghoraibeh (gorgeous little shortbread biscuits) were both outstanding. Each street also seemed to have a bread seller, their bicycles loaded with simit, local loaves of sesame-crusted bread strung onto wooden sticks that are balanced precariously on the back. The sophisticated Abou Roumaneh neighbourhood is home to the more glamorous stores and restaurants.

We loved the routine of eating little and often throughout the day, savouring some small delicacy (such as the excellent falafels) whenever the mood struck, and stopping for refreshment at the fresh juice bars that are pure heaven and seem to be everywhere. At a shawarma stall, we had perfectly grilled chunks of spicy chicken with yoghurt sauce sandwiched between warm flatbread, then we strolled across the alleyway to Al-Nafura, one of the oldest cafes in town, for a shot of strong Arabic coffee. Raeda ordered some maamoul for us to try – these totally delicious semolina pastries are stuffed with either soft white cheese or sweet dates, and are perfect with coffee. This particular coffee shop is well known for its professional storytellers (hakawatis), who come by at sunset to recount tales from history. The story is never finished, so people will always return to hear more. But the best meal of the entire trip was at Zeitouna Restaurant, in the Christian quarter of Damascus – a local friend, Cesar, took us there when we explained we wanted to sample the very best of local cuisine. Set in a typical Andalous-style house with a large internal courtyard, the restaurant was jam-packed. After dinner I was given the royal tour, including the upstairs private rooms reserved for special events, and the kitchens with an open wood-fired oven and proper charcoal grills. Arab culture celebrates outdoor cooking, elevating mashwi (grilling) to an art form, with a similar social significance to the Australian barbeque culture. We saw many outdoor eating houses offering food that had been grilled over charcoal.

As we ate our way around Syria, we became aware of the regional subtleties of many dishes, and the myriad ways of preparing the dips and salads for meze. The descriptions may look identical on a menu, but the taste is often quite different. At one restaurant, the menu listed hummus twice: once as hummus and then as Beiruti hummus. The

SLEEPING AND EATING IN DAMASCUS

FOUR SEASONS HOTEL
Shukri Al Quatli Street, Damascus
Tel +963 11 339 1000
www.fourseasonshotels.com
Great central location in the downtown area, within easy walking distance to everything.

ZEITOUNA RESTAURANT
24 Zeitouna Street, Bab Sharqi, Damascus
Tel +963 11 543 5994
Beautiful courtyard restaurant serving traditional Syrian food – the standouts for me were the house-made Arabian lamb sausages and stuffed vine leaves.

BEIT JABRI
Sawwaf Street, Old City, Damascus
Tel +963 11 541 6254
www.jabrihouse.com
Casual cafe in an old Damascene house with friendly service, and great meze, juices and shish kebabs.

BAKDASH
Souk Hamidiyeh, Damascus
The best ice cream in the city.

AL-NAFURA
Behind the eastern gate of Umayyad Mosque, Damascus
A local institution dating back more than 200 hundred years, this atmospheric coffee house is located in a former bathhouse, and is renowned for its traditional storytellers.

waiter explained that Syrian hummus is more delicately flavoured (with only a little garlic and a pronounced lemony flavour) whereas the Beiruti version is spicier, with more garlic, pepper and cumin. Of course, this only added to the mystery of hummus and the range of possibilities on offer. The search must go on . . .

We decided to head north to Aleppo, a city that also claims to be among the oldest inhabited cities in the Middle East. Finding a car and an English-speaking driver proved incredibly easy, and we set off along a wide, modern highway, passing vistas that ranged from olive and fig trees and pistachio orchards to long stretches of desert. About an hour out of Damascus, we took a detour to the small village of Maalula. High up in the barren hills, this is one of the last remaining places where Aramaic (the language of Jesus Christ), one of the oldest continuously spoken languages in the world today, is still in daily use. We bought an Aramaic dictionary and language book as a memento, and so we could have a go at getting our tongues around the words. Continuing north, our journey took us past trees bent over and growing sideways due to the strength of the desert winds, and the traditional mud-brick beehive houses around Hama that offer protection from the elements and insulation from extremes of temperature.

We arrived in Aleppo at sunset. Amongst the many minarets that punctuate the skyline, we noticed churches and cathedrals of every denomination, all within close proximity. After dumping our bags at the hotel, we made our way to the souk, passing a fabulous street market near Bab Antakya, with handcarts overflowing with fresh vegetables, herbs and fruit. It is always so easy to see exactly what's in season when you come to places like this, and we bought some of the largest and juiciest strawberries imaginable to have for breakfast. The food shops in the souk covered every culinary nook and cranny: hessian bags full of shiny black coffee beans laced with cardamom pods; shiny purple eggplants; perfumed tomatoes; a sea of mint – perhaps the most used herb in the Middle East; the freshest walnuts; tubs of aromatic spices; and hanging ropes threaded with dried vegetables. Several shop owners offered us mint tea, which we gratefully accepted, with lots of light-hearted conversation and laughs thrown in. As you exit the souk to the east, you come face to face with the Citadel, an imposing landmark that dominates the city. We felt rather small as we went inside, and spent some time sitting in the amphitheatre, trying to imagine a past way of life. The street opposite the entrance is lined with antique shops and cafes – a great place to stop for a cold drink or a coffee while you watch the passing parade.

Our favourite part of Aleppo was Al-Jdeida (the Christian Armenian quarter), a short walk from the Old City. Some of the buildings of this district have been faithfully restored into elegant boutique hotels while retaining their charm and character, making it the ideal place to stay. While we were out exploring the town, we walked past some of the most dilapidated houses we had ever laid eyes on, but instantly appreciated that these streets had been walked upon for several thousands of years. Attracted by a frenzy of activity and delicious smells, we lined up with a bunch of locals at a falafel shop, where our curiosity was rewarded by one of the best falafel sandwiches ever, dripping with a tangy tahini sauce. Soon after, we discovered Sharia Yarmouk, a street filled with juice bars all lined up in a row – I will always remember Aleppo for its fresh watermelon juice.

SLEEPING AND EATING IN ALEPPO

BEIT WAKIL
Al-Jdaidah, Sissi Street, Aleppo
Tel +963 21 211 7083
www.beitwakil.com
This atmospheric hotel also houses a terrific restaurant – the food is refined (a modern version of traditional dishes) and the lamb sausages and meze are the best in town. There is also a lovely small basement bar – worth knowing about in a town short on places to have a decent drink.

BEIT AS-SISSI
Al-Jdaidah, Sissi Street, Aleppo
Tel +963 21 221 9411
The ratatouille with eggplant is a standout, as are the kebabs.

Our departure from Syria took us by road from Aleppo across the mountains to the Mediterranean coast, then down through Tripoli to Beirut. The coastal border checkpoint comprised a few low-slung shacks that could easily pass for a shanty town, but the farewell was as friendly as our other encounters in Syria, and we left the country as committed fans, deeply impressed by its people and its food. Anywhere that venerates eggplant to such a degree is worthy in my book! On returning to Beirut, I made a note in my diary that the city felt positively decadent and Western by comparison.

During a recent visit to Stockholm I had the opportunity to lunch with Donald Bostrom, a highly regarded Swedish photo-journalist and writer who has spent the past few decades travelling throughout the Middle East. He has photographed and written extensively about the region, its politics and its cuisine, and our fascinating conversation turned into a long lunch as we reminisced about the food, the warmth and generosity of the people, and the travesties that have turned the region into such a beleaguered place.

My time in the Middle East has left me with enduring and evocative memories; this is a region I feel immense affection and compassion for. I can't wait to go back, to experience more of that fabulous warmth and hospitality and to learn more about the sumptuous traditions and mysteries of the Arab table.

MY HUMMUS

After eating hundreds of bowls of hummus in all sorts of places across the Middle East, I have played around with the combinations to find the one that suits me best. My preference is for a sharp garlicky taste with the gentle warmth of cumin. Purists will peel the chickpeas after they have been cooked, a time-consuming task that results in the most perfect, ultra-smooth texture. I have seen women in Lebanon performing this daily ritual. Hummus can be served with other meze dishes, flatbread, grilled meats, kebabs, and of course with falafel.

300 g dried chickpeas
1 teaspoon bicarbonate of soda
100 ml tahini
4 cloves garlic, minced
60 ml fresh lemon juice, strained
2 teaspoons sea salt
1 teaspoon ground cumin
100 ml extra virgin olive oil
½ teaspoon chilli oil
2 teaspoons shredded parsley leaves

Cover the chickpeas with cold water, stir in the bicarbonate of soda and soak, covered, overnight.

Drain and transfer to a large saucepan, then cover with cold water and cook for about 30 minutes until soft. Drain, reserving a little of the cooking liquid. Set aside 2 tablespoons of the whole chickpeas for serving.

Place the cooked chickpeas in a food processor with the tahini, garlic, lemon juice, salt and cumin and blend until smooth. The paste will be quite thick so add just enough of the cooking liquid to soften, then slowly drizzle in the oil. Taste and adjust the seasoning if necessary.

Spoon the hummus onto a plate. Scatter the whole chickpeas over the top, then drizzle with the chilli oil and shredded parsley. This is best served at room temperature.

SERVES 10

LAMB WITH SPICED CHICKPEAS, FALAFEL AND HUMMUS

Lamb and chickpeas are natural partners on any Arab table. You could add some fresh ricotta or creamy feta to the chickpeas if you wanted, for a richer result.

1 teaspoon cumin seeds, roasted and ground
1 teaspoon sea salt
½ teaspoon freshly ground black pepper
½ teaspoon allspice
20 ml olive oil
2 × 8-rib lamb racks, *not* trimmed
6 tablespoons Hummus (see page 431)

FALAFEL
50 g dried chickpeas, soaked in cold water overnight
50 g dried broad beans, soaked in cold water overnight
2 teaspoons sea salt
1 teaspoon freshly ground black pepper
½ teaspoon ground coriander
½ teaspoon ground cumin
¼ teaspoon ground chilli
½ teaspoon bicarbonate of soda
1 tablespoon minced red onion
2 cloves garlic, minced
2 tablespoons chopped parsley leaves
2 tablespoons chopped coriander leaves
vegetable oil, for deep-frying

SPICED CHICKPEAS
40 ml olive oil
3 cloves garlic, minced
1 teaspoon ground turmeric
½ teaspoon ground chilli
1 teaspoon ground cumin
200 g cooked chickpeas
40 ml fresh lemon juice, strained
2 tablespoons finely diced roasted pimiento (piquillo pepper)
1 tablespoon minced lemon zest, blanched
1 teaspoon sea salt
½ teaspoon freshly ground black pepper
2 tablespoons finely chopped chives

Combine the cumin, salt, pepper, allspice and olive oil and rub into the lamb racks. Slow-cook by sealing in a cryovac bag or a double layer of zip-lock plastic bags and cooking in a pan of water held at 70°C for 10 hours (use a thermometer to monitor the temperature). While the lamb is cooking, prepare the chickpeas and the falafel.

To make the falafel, rinse the chickpeas and broad beans and pat dry with a tea towel. Peel the broad beans. Combine the chickpeas, broad beans, salt, pepper, ground coriander, cumin and chilli in a food processor and blend to make a smooth paste. Add the bicarbonate of soda, then tip the dough onto the work bench, add the onion, garlic, parsley and coriander and knead for 5 minutes, until firm. Roll the dough into small balls and stand on a flat tray until ready to cook.

To make the spiced chickpeas, heat the oil in a frying pan and saute the garlic, turmeric, chilli and cumin until fragrant. Add the chickpeas, toss until well coated with the spices then cook for 3–4 minutes. Add the lemon juice, diced pimiento and blanched lemon zest, season with salt and pepper and stir to combine.

Remove the lamb from the pan of water and leave to rest for 10 minutes. Carve the lamb loin from each rack and slice. Remove the soft luscious meat and fat from between the bones and cut into small dice. Stir the diced lamb and chives through the chickpeas.

To cook the falafel, heat the oil in a saucepan to 180°C and fry the balls, a few at a time, for 3–4 minutes until golden and crisp. Drain on paper towel.

To serve, spoon the hummus into bowl plates and arrange slices of lamb loin on top. Spoon the spiced chickpeas over the top, add a few falafel balls and serve immediately.

SERVES 4

ZA'ATAR CHEESE BALLS

Labneh is one of my favourite Arabic foods, so versatile and delicious. This simple combination makes a terrific starter at lunch or dinner, is wonderful served as a snack with drinks, and makes a great accompaniment to roasted baby beetroot. I use the voluptuous Shaw River yoghurt made from rich buffalo milk, the closest approximation to the traditional yoghurts of the Middle East. It's well worth tracking it down to make these cheese balls, otherwise use another reputable one.

500 g buffalo yoghurt
2 tablespoons Za'atar (see Essentials)
1 tablespoon shredded parsley leaves
1 tablespoon chopped chervil
1 teaspoon freshly ground black pepper
40 ml extra virgin olive oil

Put the yoghurt in a double-layer muslin bag, tie with string and hang overnight in the refrigerator over a bowl to remove excess moisture.

Place the za'atar, parsley, chervil and pepper in a bowl and mix well.

Roll the labneh into small balls, then roll in the za'atar mix until thoroughly coated. Arrange on a plate and drizzle with olive oil to serve.

SERVES 6–8

SPICED QUAIL VINE LEAVES

Rather than the usual dolmades-style rolls, I have adapted the idea and steamed the filling in dariole or pudding moulds lined with the vine leaves so when they are turned out, they have a defined shape and elegant appearance. It makes it very easy for serving as all the work has been done beforehand.

4 quails
1 head garlic
1.2 litres White Chicken Stock (see Essentials)
sea salt and freshly ground black pepper
½ teaspoon ground cumin
75 ml olive oil
1 red onion, finely diced
3 cloves garlic, minced
1 teaspoon ground turmeric
½ teaspoon ground cinnamon
½ teaspoon ground allspice
200 g medium-grain rice, soaked in water for 20 minutes then drained
2 tomatoes, peeled, seeded and finely diced
2 green onions, finely sliced
2 tablespoons shredded parsley leaves
2 tablespoons shredded mint leaves
30 ml fresh lemon juice, strained
24 preserved vine leaves
25 ml extra virgin olive oil, extra

TOMATO GINGER SAUCE
3 tomatoes, peeled and seeded
2 teaspoons small capers, rinsed
2 teaspoons minced ginger
2 cloves garlic, crushed
40 ml extra virgin olive oil
2 teaspoons red wine vinegar
sea salt and freshly ground black pepper

Preheat the oven to 190°C. Remove the quail breast and leg meat from the carcasses and set aside. Roast the quail bones and the head of garlic for 15 minutes. Transfer to a large saucepan and smash with a meat cleaver. Add the chicken stock and bring slowly to the boil, then simmer gently for 30 minutes. Remove from the heat, strain through a fine mesh sieve and discard the solids.

Lightly season the quail meat with salt, pepper and ground cumin. Heat 20 ml of the olive oil in a frying pan and saute the quail pieces, skin-side down, for 3 minutes then flip over and cook for another minute. Remove from the heat and allow to cool.

Heat the remaining oil in a wide-based pan and fry the onion and garlic until softened. Add the ground spices, then stir in the rice. Pour in 600 ml of the quail stock, reduce the heat to low and simmer gently, covered, for 15 minutes until the rice is tender and the stock has been absorbed.

Remove from the heat and stir in the tomato, green onion, parsley, mint and lemon juice. Season to taste with salt and pepper. Chop the cooked quail meat into small dice, stir into the rice and allow to cool.

To make the sauce, dice the tomatoes and place in a non-reactive saucepan. Stir over moderate heat for about 6 minutes until all the juices have evaporated. Add the capers, ginger and garlic and cook for 2 minutes, then stir in the oil and vinegar. Season to taste with salt and pepper. Set aside, and warm through gently when ready to serve.

To assemble the moulds, blanch the vine leaves in boiling water then drain and pat dry. Brush each mould with a little extra oil then line with the vine leaves (allow three leaves for each mould), starting from the centre and working out and upwards so that the entire inner surface is covered. Press the quail and rice filling into the moulds until full, press firmly to pack tight then fold the overhanging leaves over the top to close.

Place the assembled moulds on a steamer tray, then cover and steam over gently boiling water for 15 minutes until heated through.

To serve, turn the moulds upside down and tap gently so the vine-leaf parcels turn out onto plates. Spoon the warm tomato ginger sauce over the top and serve.

SERVES 8

SAFFRON LOBSTER ORZO WITH HARISSA OIL

This mouth-watering dish is from the repertoire of Lew Kathreptis, a dear friend, fellow chef and traveller who made this for dinner the first time I visited him in Dubai. He has an innate understanding and appreciation of Persian flavours, and his cooking has long been a source of inspiration to me.

300 ml Lobster Broth (see Essentials)
½ teaspoon saffron threads
2 cups cooked orzo
120 g mascarpone
40 g finely grated parmesan
2 quarters of preserved lemon, rind only, cut into fine julienne strips
1 teaspoon fresh lemon juice, strained
sea salt and freshly ground white pepper
200 g cooked lobster tail meat
120 g ghee
1 tablespoon finely chopped chives
2 teaspoons thyme leaves
½ teaspoon truffle oil
40 ml extra virgin olive oil
4 Parmesan Crisps (see Essentials)

LEW'S HARISSA
3 teaspoons caraway seeds
1 tablespoon cumin seeds
1½ tablespoons coriander seeds
7–8 chillies, seeded
1 tablespoon dried mint
70 ml extra virgin olive oil
3 red capsicums (peppers), seeded and chopped
½ head garlic, peeled and chopped
2 teaspoons salt

To make the harissa, roast all the seeds separately and grind with the dried chillies and mint. Pass the spice mix through a fine mesh sieve. Heat the olive oil over gentle heat and cook the capsicum for about 30 minutes until soft and caramelised. Combine the capsicum, spice mix, garlic and salt in a food processor and blend to a smooth paste. Refrigerate in an airtight container until ready to use.

Heat the lobster broth and saffron in a small saucepan, bring to simmering point and cook gently for 2 minutes. Add the orzo to heat through, then stir in the mascarpone. Season to taste with the parmesan, preserved lemon, lemon juice, salt and pepper, and keep warm.

Gently heat the cooked lobster in the melted ghee until warm.

Stir the chives, thyme and truffle oil into the orzo.

Mix 2 tablespoons of the harissa with the extra virgin olive oil to make harissa oil.

To serve, spoon a little harissa oil in the centre of each bowl plate. Place the orzo in the centre of the oil, allowing it to spread the oil to form a larger circle. Arrange the lobster on the orzo, spoon on the saffron lobster broth and top each serving with a parmesan crisp.

SERVES 4

FATTOUSH WITH A TWIST

I have adapted this classic Lebanese salad to my own style. Instead of tossing the bread through the salad in the usual manner, I have made wafer-thin layers between the salad, creating a sandwich effect with a wonderful textural contrast.

1 small red onion, finely diced
¼ teaspoon sumac
¼ teaspoon freshly ground black pepper
16 Roasted Cherry Tomatoes (see Essentials)
2 green onions, finely sliced
½ avocado, finely diced
2 red radishes, finely sliced
1 small cucumber, peeled, seeded and diced
1 punnet mache cress, snipped
12 baby cos lettuce leaves (picked from the heart of the lettuce), stems removed
1 tablespoon shredded coriander leaves
2 teaspoons shredded mint leaves
1 tablespoon shredded parsley leaves
1 tablespoon Dukkah (see Essentials)

BREAD WAFERS
2 rounds Lebanese bread
40 ml extra virgin olive oil
1 teaspoon sumac
1 tablespoon Dukkah (see Essentials)

SALAD DRESSING
25 ml red wine vinegar
25 ml fresh lemon juice, strained
1 teaspoon pomegranate molasses
140 ml extra virgin olive oil
1 teaspoon Za'atar (see Essentials)
½ teaspoon sea salt
¼ teaspoon freshly ground black pepper

To make the bread wafers, preheat the oven to 180°C. Separate each bread into two sheets, then cut out two 8 cm rounds from each sheet using a pastry cutter. Brush the bread rounds with olive oil and lay on a flat tray. Season each piece with sumac and dukkah, then lay another tray on top to flatten the bread and weigh it down during cooking. Bake for 10 minutes until the bread is crisp and golden. Cool on a wire rack.

To make the salad dressing, whisk all the ingredients together until emulsified.

To make the salad, mix the diced onion with the sumac and pepper. Add the remaining salad ingredients (except the dukkah), drizzle with enough dressing to moisten and toss to combine.

Spoon a little salad into the centre of each plate and drizzle with a little extra dressing. Sit a bread wafer on top, then continue layering until you have a stack with two bread layers. Spoon a little salad into the centre of the top wafer, sprinkle with dukkah and serve.

SERVES 4

FRIED LAMB'S BRAIN KIBBEH

Considered the national dish of Lebanon, kibbeh is always included at mealtimes in one guise or another. These torpedo-shaped patties of cracked wheat and minced lamb can be served raw like tartare or fried; some are moulded and left hollow in the centre, some are filled with the sweet-tasting tail fat from lamb, and others are stuffed with a variety of things, such as nuts and vegetables. Having tasted many different kibbeh preparations in Beirut, I decided my favourites were the fried ones with soft luscious centres, so this is a tribute to that style.

500 g minced lamb
160 g fine burghul (cracked wheat), soaked in cold water for 15 minutes
1 tablespoon grated red onion
½ teaspoon ground cumin
½ teaspoon ground allspice
1 teaspoon sea salt
1 teaspoon freshly ground black pepper
½ teaspoon sweet paprika
vegetable oil, for deep-frying
1 brown onion, sliced into fine rings
2 tablespoons plain flour, seasoned with salt and pepper

CREAMED EGGPLANT
300 g eggplant (aubergine)
½ teaspoon cumin seeds, roasted and ground
2 small cloves garlic, chopped
½ teaspoon sea salt
80 ml tahini
20 ml fresh lemon juice, strained
70 ml extra virgin olive oil

BRAIN STUFFING
2 sets lamb's brains, blanched and peeled
2 tablespoons pine nuts, roasted
1 tablespoon diced roasted red capsicum (pepper)
50 g firm feta, diced
1 teaspoon mild chilli powder
1 teaspoon sea salt
1 teaspoon freshly ground black pepper

To make the creamed eggplant, put the eggplant directly over hot coals or a gas flame and cook until the skin is blackened and blistered. Peel when it is cool enough to handle. Place the eggplant pulp in a food processor and blend with the cumin, garlic, salt, tahini and lemon juice until combined. With the motor running, gradually add the oil and blend until smooth. Leave at room temperature while you prepare the kibbeh.

To make the stuffing, cut the lamb's brains into 1 cm dice and mix with the remaining ingredients until combined. Roll into 12 small balls.

To make the kibbeh, place the lamb mince in a large bowl and slap handfuls of mince against the sides of the bowl – this softens the texture and makes it buttery smooth. Continue to slap the meat for about 20 minutes until it feels really soft and pliable. Make sure that all the excess moisture has been squeezed from the burghul and work it into the mince with the grated onion, cumin, allspice, salt, pepper and paprika until it makes a smooth paste. Refrigerate for 1 hour until firm.

Roll the kibbeh into 12 balls and then, working with one at a time, put the balls between two layers of greaseproof paper and flatten with a rolling pin to make disks about 6 cm in diameter. Put a ball of stuffing in the centre of each disk and fold the kibbeh over to make an elongated torpedo shape. Press the edges to seal and pinch off any excess.

Heat the oil in a large saucepan or deep-fryer to 180°C, add the kibbeh a few at a time and fry for 6 minutes until crisp and brown. Drain on paper towel.

Toss the onion slices through the seasoned flour, shaking off any excess. Fry in the hot oil for 2 minutes until crisp and golden, then drain on paper towel.

Spoon some creamed eggplant onto the centre of plates and arrange the kibbeh on top. Add some fried onion rings and serve.

SERVES 4

ZA'ATAR DUCK LIVERS WITH BLOOD ORANGE AND CRACKED WHEAT SALAD

Liver responds so well to spice, and this combination of ingredients never fails to impress. Make sure you buy livers from organic or free-range chickens that have been carefully removed from the bird, and use the larger lobes of the liver – it makes all the difference to the quality of the dish. If you wish, chicken livers can easily be substituted with equal success. The cracked wheat salad is an adaptation of tabbouli.

12 duck livers, cleaned
40 ml olive oil
3 cloves garlic, minced
1 teaspoon cumin seeds, roasted and ground
1 teaspoon coriander seeds, roasted and ground
½ teaspoon chilli powder
½ teaspoon freshly ground black pepper
3 blood oranges, peeled and segmented
20 ml orange blossom water
20 ml fresh lemon juice, strained
20 dandelion leaves
1 punnet mizuna cress, snipped
1 tablespoon Za'atar (see Essentials), plus extra to serve

CRACKED WHEAT SALAD
125 g burghul (cracked wheat), soaked in hot water for 15 minutes until soft
1 white onion, finely diced
3 ripe tomatoes, peeled and finely diced
2 cloves garlic, minced
75 ml extra virgin olive oil
2 teaspoons sea salt
1 teaspoon freshly ground black pepper
40 ml pomegranate molasses
4 tablespoons parsley leaves, finely shredded
2 green onions, finely sliced
seeds from 1 pomegranate

To make the salad, drain the cracked wheat into a bowl, add the diced onion, tomato and garlic and mix so the cracked wheat absorbs the tomatoes and their juice. Add the olive oil, salt, pepper and pomegranate molasses, kneading with your hands to combine. Set aside to allow the flavours to infuse.

Combine the livers with the oil, garlic, cumin, coriander, chilli and pepper and toss to coat well. Heat a heavy-based pan over high heat and sear the seasoned livers, tossing the pan so they flip and cook evenly. Cook for 2–3 minutes only – they need to remain pink inside. Remove the pan from the heat, add the remaining ingredients and toss the pan to combine.

Stir the parsley, green onion and pomegranate seeds through the salad and spoon onto plates.

Arrange the livers and any pan juices on top and sprinkle with a little extra za'atar to serve.

SERVES 4

SPICED CHICKEN ORGANS WITH ZHOUG

Jerusalem is known for its mixed grills, and the whole region takes pride in the art of barbequing over hot coals rather than gas. Organ meat or offal is also very popular and it makes a welcome change from the regular prime meat cuts. Zhoug is a fiery chilli condiment used extensively in the region.

skin from 1 chicken, cleaned (ask your butcher to do this)
vegetable oil, for deep-frying
60 ml olive oil
1 red onion, finely sliced
3 cloves garlic, minced
1 teaspoon sea salt
1 tablespoon ground cumin
1 teaspoon ground chilli
1 tablespoon ground coriander
2 teaspoons ground turmeric
¼ teaspoon freshly ground black pepper
4 chicken hearts, cleaned
8 chicken livers, trimmed
4 chicken giblets
4 small rounds of thin pita bread
4 tablespoons thick plain yoghurt

ZHOUG
120 g long red chillies, chopped
30 g small red chillies, chopped
6 cloves garlic, peeled and chopped
4 tablespoons chopped parsley leaves
4 tablespoons chopped coriander leaves
50 ml water
1 teaspoon cumin seeds, roasted and ground
pinch of ground cardamom
1 teaspoon sea salt
1 teaspoon freshly ground black pepper

To make the zhoug, pound the chillies and garlic to a rough paste in a mortar and pestle, then work in the fresh herbs and water. Pound the remaining ingredients into the paste, then refrigerate in a sealed jar until ready to use.

Stretch the chicken skin out on a wire rack and leave to dry for 6 hours or overnight. Cut into thin strips lengthways, then deep-fry in hot oil until crisp and drain on paper towel. Set aside until ready to use.

Heat the olive oil in a large cast-iron fry pan and saute the onion for 5 minutes until softened. Add the garlic and cook for another 3 minutes until coloured. Stir in the salt and spices, then remove from the pan and set aside.

Add the chicken organs to the same pan and fry over high heat for a few minutes until they are tender but not overcooked. Remove from the heat and combine with the onion mixture.

Grill the pita bread in the hot pan briefly, just enough to warm through. Lay each bread round on a serving plate, spread with zhoug then spoon the yoghurt into the centre. Pile the cooked chicken organs on top, add the chicken-skin crisps and serve.

SERVES 4

CHEESE AND HERB CIGAR PASTRIES

Although Moroccan in origin, these pastries (briouats) are popular and readily available in every country of the Middle East. They can be filled with meat or vegetables but I just love them with this cheese filling. Serve them with cocktails or as part of a meze course with salads and falafel.

75 g fresh ricotta, drained
75 g cheddar, finely grated
2 tablespoons mint leaves, chopped
½ teaspoon sea salt
½ teaspoon freshly ground white pepper
8 sheets brik (or filo) pastry
40 g unsalted butter, melted
1 egg white
vegetable oil, for deep-frying

In a bowl, mix the cheeses together with the mint and season with salt and pepper.

Cut each pastry sheet into two lengths about 12 cm wide and trim the edges (as the sheets are round). Working with a few pastry sheets at a time, keeping the rest covered with a tea towel, lay the sheets on a bench and brush the edges with butter.

With the short end closest to you, spoon the cheese mix in a thin layer two-thirds of the way along the pastry length. Roll over twice from the short end, then fold in the edges to seal in the filling and continue to roll up into a thin cigar shape. Brush the join with egg white so the pastry does not open during frying. Repeat with the remaining pastry and filling to make 16 pastries.

Heat the oil in a deep-fryer or large saucepan to 180°C and fry the pastries a few at a time for 2 minutes until crisp. Drain on paper towel. Serve immediately while they are still hot and crisp.

SERVES 8

PERSIAN SAFFRON CHICKEN RICE

This rice pilaf reminds me of Indian biryani, not surprising given the Persians and Arabs introduced this method of cooking rice to India during the Moghul reign. It is, by definition, a festive dish served at celebratory occasions, with a hint of luxury coming from the saffron. The rice is cooked twice – first parboiled then steamed so the flavours intermingle and the rice forms a crusty base. Like the base of a paella, this is the part that those in the know fight over.

3 chicken breast fillets
2 litres White Chicken Stock (see Essentials)
½ teaspoon saffron threads
2 eggs, lightly beaten
150 g thick plain yoghurt
2 teaspoons sea salt
1 tablespoon finely chopped chives
1 tablespoon chopped dill
1 tablespoon chopped coriander leaves
1 tablespoon chopped parsley leaves
2 tablespoons Saffron Butter (see Essentials), melted
2 tablespoons almond flakes, roasted

RICE PILAF
400 g basmati rice
2 teaspoons sea salt
40 ml olive oil
20 g unsalted butter
1 small white onion, finely diced
2 cloves garlic, minced
zest of 1 orange, blanched
½ teaspoon saffron threads, infused in 40 ml hot water
½ teaspoon ground cinnamon
½ teaspoon ground cardamom
2 teaspoons castor sugar
4 dried roses, broken into petals
2 tablespoons dried barberries
2 tablespoons chopped pistachios
30 g raisins
1 teaspoon freshly ground black pepper

Cut each chicken breast fillet into four strips lengthways. Heat the stock to boiling point, then add the chicken, cover with a lid and remove from the heat. Leave to cool (the chicken will cook through during this time and become meltingly tender). Remove the chicken from the stock and cut into large chunks.

Heat 100 ml water in a pan to simmering point, grind the saffron threads in a mortar and pestle and add to the hot water. Remove from the heat and leave to infuse for 15 minutes, until cool.

Whisk the eggs, yoghurt, salt and saffron liquid together in a bowl. Add the chunks of cooked chicken and stir to completely cover with the yoghurt. Cover and leave to marinate for 5 hours in the refrigerator.

To make the pilaf, soak the rice in cold water for 2 hours, changing the water after an hour. Wash the rice until the water runs clear. Bring 2 litres water to boiling point in a large saucepan and add the strained rice and salt. Reduce the heat and simmer for 4 minutes only, until the rice is two-thirds cooked – the grains should still have white chalky centres. Remove from the heat, pass through a sieve and wash with tepid water.

In a clean pan, heat the oil and butter and fry the onion, garlic and orange zest until softened. Add the saffron water, cinnamon, cardamom, sugar, rose petals, barberries, pistachios and raisins and stir to combine. Remove from the heat and season with pepper.

In a bowl, mix together the chives, dill, coriander and parsley.

To assemble the chicken rice, heat half the saffron butter in a wide-based pan until sizzling, then reduce the heat and add a quarter of the rice to cover the base of the pan. Working quickly, spoon on a third of the spiced fruit and nut mix, then a third of the yoghurt chicken, then a third of the herb mix. Repeat this process twice more, then cover the lot with the remaining rice. Dot a little more saffron butter across the surface.

Make a few holes in the rice mix with the handle of a wooden spoon to create steam vents (to ensure even cooking). Cover the pan with a tight-fitting lid – I wrap a damp cloth or foil around the lid to make sure no steam can escape. Cook over moderately high heat for 5 minutes, then reduce the heat and cook over gentle heat for 20 minutes. Do not lift the lid during this process.

When cooked, remove from the heat and check that the rice is cooked, but do not stir. Transfer the rice to a serving plate, being careful not to mix it up too much, and pour on the remaining melted saffron butter. Sprinkle with roasted almond flakes and serve.

NOTE: To make individual servings, brush pudding moulds or small bowls with melted butter. Carefully arrange the rice and chicken layers in the mould, pressing firmly to condense. Sit the moulds on a steamer tray, cover and steam for 5 minutes, then turn out onto serving plates and serve as above.

SERVES 6

ARCTIC CHAR WITH BURGHUL AND PARSLEY SALAD

I have adopted the 'confit' method of cooking the fish, as for coral trout with roasted prawn crust (see page 499), here adding a seasoned crust that has a distinctive Middle Eastern character. The slow, gentle cooking maintains the moisture and integrity of the fish's texture, giving it that melt-in-the-mouth quality. Fish looks deceptively raw or rosy when cooked confit-style, but don't worry – the heat is gentle enough to just set the protein without changing the colour of the fish flesh. Arctic char is now being farmed in the cold waters off the Tasmanian coast, with a relatively short season in early spring; if you can't find it, freshwater salmon from Victoria makes the best substitute.

60 g fine burghul (cracked wheat)
2 teaspoons minced lemon zest
½ teaspoon ground chilli
½ teaspoon sumac
1 teaspoon sea salt
2 teaspoons Za'atar (see Essentials)
2 teaspoons white sesame seeds, roasted
1 tablespoon chopped coriander leaves
1 tablespoon chopped parsley leaves
1 tablespoon chopped chives
4 × 150 g fillets Arctic char, cut from the middle of the fish, skin and bones removed
60 ml extra virgin olive oil
1 teaspoon sea salt, extra

PARSLEY SALAD
1 cup parsley leaves
2 tablespoons coriander leaves
1 small red onion, finely diced
½ long red chilli, seeded and finely diced
1 tablespoon white sesame seeds, roasted
40 g pine nuts, roasted
¼ teaspoon sumac
2 teaspoons fresh lemon juice, strained
20 ml olive oil
sea salt and freshly ground black pepper

YOGHURT TAHINI SAUCE
150 g thick plain yoghurt
1 tablespoon tahini
1 clove garlic, minced
½ teaspoon sea salt
30 ml fresh lemon juice, strained
¼ teaspoon freshly ground black pepper
¼ teaspoon sumac
40 ml extra virgin olive oil

To make the yoghurt sauce, whisk the ingredients together until combined. Keep refrigerated until ready to serve.

To make the parsley salad, toss the ingredients together to combine.

To make the crust, soak the burghul in cold water for 10 minutes then strain and squeeze out as much water as you can. Combine with the lemon zest, chilli, sumac, salt, za'atar, sesame seeds and chopped herbs.

Place the fish portions in a cryovac bag or a double layer of zip-lock plastic bags with the olive oil and extra salt and seal to secure. Heat a pan of water to 60°C and poach the fish in the bag for 10 minutes at a constant temperature. Remove from the water and leave to settle for 5 minutes, then remove the fish from the bag.

Lay the top surface of the fish onto the burghul crust and press gently to coat. Turn the fish pieces over and crust the other side.

Spread the yoghurt sauce onto plates then sit the fish on top and sprinkle with any extra burghul crust. Place a nest of salad alongside and serve immediately.

SERVES 4

STRAWBERRY AND ALMOND NAPOLEON

Strawberries are synonymous with Syria, hands down the most popular and readily available fruit in spring there. Whenever I go near one, I am reminded of the stunning strawberry displays we saw on the street carts of Aleppo – luscious, large and naturally ripened so they are red and juicy right through.

10 sheets filo pastry
120 g unsalted butter, melted
3 tablespoons castor sugar
4 tablespoons Almond Praline (see Essentials)
1 punnet strawberries, hulled and sliced
2 teaspoons icing sugar, sifted

STRAWBERRY SAUCE
250 g strawberries, hulled
50 g castor sugar
2 teaspoons fresh lemon juice, strained

ALMOND CREAM
70 ml milk
35 ml latte di mandorla
2 egg yolks
70 g castor sugar
2 g gelatine leaves, softened in cold water
1 teaspoon Frangelico liqueur
125 ml pouring (35%) cream, whipped

To make the strawberry sauce, blend the strawberries with the sugar and lemon juice until pureed.

Pass through a fine mesh sieve, pressing to extract as much juice as possible. Discard the solids.

Preheat the oven to 160°C and line a flat baking tray with baking paper. Place a sheet of filo on a bench and brush with melted butter. Sprinkle with sugar and top with another sheet of pastry. Repeat until the stack has five sheets, then repeat the process again so you have a second stack of pastry. Cut each pastry stack into 6 cm squares. You should have 16 squares in total – four for each serve (though I always make a few extra in case of breakages).

Place the pastry squares on the prepared baking tray (you will need to do this in batches). Cover with a sheet of baking paper and then another baking tray to compress the pastries as they cook. Bake for 8–9 minutes until crisp and golden. Remove from the oven and transfer to a wire rack to cool. Repeat until all the pastry squares have been baked. When cool, store in an airtight container until ready to use.

To make the almond cream, heat the milk and latte di mandorla in a saucepan to simmering point.

Whisk the egg yolks and sugar in a bowl for about 5 minutes until pale and creamy, then whisk in the hot milk. Sit the bowl over a pan of simmering water and continue to whisk until the mixture thickens and reaches a custard consistency. Stir in the softened gelatine and Frangelico and remove from the heat. Pass through a fine mesh sieve, then sit the bowl over ice until the mixture cools completely. Fold in the whipped cream then refrigerate for 2–3 hours until set. Spoon the almond cream into piping bag with a small fluted nozzle.

To assemble, spoon the strawberry sauce onto the centre of serving plates, pipe some almond cream in the centre and sprinkle with praline. Add a layer of sliced strawberries then cover with a pastry square. Repeat the layers three more times, finishing with a pastry lid. Dust the top with icing sugar to serve.

SERVES 4

BUTTERMILK PUDDING WITH TAMARILLOS AND MINT ICE CREAM

I just love the lightness and gentle acidity of these flavours, a perfect counterbalance to the richness of other foods. If tamarillos are not available, I often use fresh pomegranate seeds and strawberries mixed together, and sometimes even slow-roasted quince – all fruits that feature on the Arab table.

4 tamarillos
1 tablespoon demerara sugar

BUTTERMILK PUDDING
200 ml milk
400 ml pouring (35%) cream
40 g castor sugar
1 vanilla bean, split lengthways
8 g gelatine leaves, softened in cold water
340 ml buttermilk

MINT ICE CREAM
240 ml milk
25 g mint leaves, blanched
100 g castor sugar
3 egg yolks
1 teaspoon mint essence
240 ml pouring (35%) cream

To make the buttermilk pudding, heat the milk, cream, sugar and vanilla in a saucepan over gentle heat until just simmering. Stir in the softened gelatine until dissolved and remove from the heat. Allow to cool for 15 minutes then gently whisk in the buttermilk until combined. Pass through a fine mesh sieve. Pour into individual serving glasses or small dishes and refrigerate for about 4 hours until set.

To make the ice cream, heat the milk with the blanched mint leaves to simmering point over gentle heat. Whisk the sugar and egg yolks in a bowl until pale and creamy. Add the hot milk and whisk to combine. Sit the bowl over a pan of simmering water and cook until the mixture reaches a custard consistency and coats the back of a spoon. Remove from the heat and pass through a fine mesh sieve. Cool for 20 minutes, then stir in the mint essence and cream. Churn in an ice-cream machine until firm, then transfer to the freezer until ready to serve.

Peel the tamarillos and cut each one into five slices crossways. Lay the slices on a flat baking tray and sprinkle with sugar. Heat with a blowtorch (or under the grill) until the sugar has caramelised but the fruit still holds its shape. Allow to cool for 5 minutes.

Arrange the tamarillo slices on top of the buttermilk puddings, then add a small scoop or quenelle of mint ice cream and serve.

SERVES 4

OTTOMAN URBAN ISTANBUL

I marked the new millennium with an important discovery: the dramatic beauty of Turkey. Nothing quite prepared me for my first visit to Istanbul. As we flew over the city, the view was breathtaking: the elegant minarets of the Sultan Ahmed Mosque pierced the sky to the south of the Golden Horn, and to the north, the striking landmark of the Galata Tower rose above the medieval Genoese citadel. Istanbul is divided in three by the Bosphorus Strait, the dividing line between Europe and Asia, with the Black Sea to the north and the Marmara Sea (an offshoot of the Aegean) to the south. The old city is clustered onto the peninsula around Sultanahmet, to the west of the Bosphorus, while across the Golden Horn to the north lie the districts of Galata, Beyoglu, Harbiye and Taksim, the heart of modern Istanbul.

Driving from the airport through the arches of the 4th-century Byzantine aqueduct, I already had the impression that this was going to be one hell of an exciting town. As it turned out, Istanbul exceeded my expectations. I just love its intoxicating diversity, seductive lifestyle and sensual, exotic food. I love that everything has a contemporary twist, and that the city takes on a different personality in each of the four seasons. It has, quite simply, become one of my favourite cities in the world, and one that constantly draws me back.

While remaining true to its Ottoman heritage, Turkey embraces the contemporary world, resulting in an intriguing blend of Islamic tradition and secular modernity. Images of Ataturk, the founder of modern Turkey, are everywhere, reflecting the profound impact his forward-thinking social policies and sweeping reforms had on the people. Today, there's such a vibrant and optimistic feeling in the air; change is occurring at almost lightning speed, and there's a palpable appetite for innovation and modern design. I recently read Orhan Pamuk's *Istanbul: Memories of a City*, a personal and idiosyncratic exploration of the past 50 years of the writer's home city. For him, Istanbul 'has always been a city of ruins and of end-of-empire melancholy', a city struggling to find its identity after the collapse of the mighty Ottoman Empire. His book is a reflective and passionate testament to the beauty and mystery of Istanbul, and I find Pamuk's work all the more fascinating now that I've had a taste of the city's daily rhythms and am more familiar with the streets and buildings he describes.

The Ottoman Empire left a remarkable imprint on the face of Istanbul; its exquisitely crafted grand buildings are without parallel. In the historic district of Sultanahmet, the incredibly beautiful Hagia Sofia (Holy Wisdom) is the greatest example of Byzantine church architecture, completed in 537 AD and converted to a mosque in the 15th century, when minarets were added. The large dome and surrounding smaller domes rise majestically out of rather banal urban surroundings, creating a dramatic juxtaposition. For four centuries, the Ottoman sultans lived in the adjacent Topkapi Palace, enjoying a life of indulgence that the rest of us can only dream about. The palace sits on Seraglio Point, where the Golden Horn meets the Bosphorus, and was built as a cushioned paradise, with vaulted chambers, filigreed windows and marble bathhouses. We stopped for tea in the refined setting of

STAYING IN ISTANBUL

HILTON ISTANBUL
Cumhuriyet Caddesi, Harbiye
Tel +90 212 315 6000
www.hilton.com
A terrifically comfortable hotel with the best outlook in town, facing the beautiful Bosphorus. Think sixties retro and you have the style. Rooms have outdoor terraces, many with stunning views, and the location is ideal, close to Taksim and all the happening places.

A'JIA HOTEL
Ahmet Rasim Pasa Yalisi, Cubuklu Caddesi 27
Tel +90 216 413 9300
www.tablethotels.com
This secluded and quiet boutique hotel is a waterfront jewel.

BUYUK LONDRA OTELI
Mesrutiyet Caddesi 117, Beyoglu
Tel +90 212 245 0670
www.londrahotel.net
A civilised cheap and cheerful option, full of offbeat character.

BENTLEY HOTEL
Halaskargazi Caddesi 75, Harbiye
Tel +90 212 291 7730
www.bentley-hotel.com
Fabulous boutique hotel with a very hip design – great for an indulgent stay.

Konyali, its garden terrace cafe. But my favourite building in this cluster is the Sultan Ahmed Mosque, also known as the Blue Mosque for its brilliant-blue interior tiles. The perfect symmetry of its six minarets makes it one of the most mesmerising sights in the world.

Though new by comparison (it was built in the mid-19th century), Dolmabahce Palace, from where the Ottoman Empire was administered for almost 70 years, is sumptuous in its design and well worth a look. It faces the Bosphorus near Besiktas, the terminal for ferries to the Asian side of the city. The main road of Besiktas is also home to a thriving fresh produce market, where we found big chunks of tulum (a sheep's milk cheese not unlike feta), kaymak (clotted cream), yoghurt, spices, nuts, pomegranates and dried fruits, as well as an incredible array of just-picked vegetables.

A more recent visit took us across the Bosphorus to Kadikoy, where we marvelled at the produce markets that lined the pedestrianised main thoroughfare. It was heaven, and with its more languid pace, we felt as if we were wandering around a big village. We drooled over wooden boxes of just-picked figs, honey and yoghurt stalls, fresh nuts, an endless array of spanking-fresh fruit and vegetables, and the best fish display I've seen in Turkey – all accompanied by a soundtrack of lively hollering from the merchants. I love how the city has a completely different feel on this side of the water.

Istiklal Caddesi is considered the nerve centre of the modern city. This long pedestrian mall has a tram track that runs down the centre from Taksim down to gentrified Tunel, and is lined with shops, bars, restaurants and cafes, all vying for attention with the grand apartment blocks and churches along the way. Even in the depths of winter, you'll have to fight your way through the crowds. There is a never-ending stream of people, but that's an intrinsic element of Istanbul's energy, and at least it beats the dreadful traffic that puts the city in a state of almost constant gridlock. I also love the buzzy atmosphere along Cicek Pasaji, a glassed-over passageway just off Istiklal Caddesi. Originally a flower market, it's now lined with bustling cafes and bars, and is loud and boisterous. Our friend Andrew often takes us to one of the bars for a glass of raki (aniseed aperitif) with a couple of meze plates, before we all move on to a restaurant for dinner. During the day, it's great fun to visit Balik Pazari – the fish bazaar next to Cicek Pasaji – to check out the array of glistening fish.

Turkey's reputation for hospitality is legendary, and a visit to any shop, market, street vendor, cafe, restaurant or private home will confirm this. Wherever you go, you will be welcomed with warmth and sincerity, and the markets, alleys, streets and bars hum with a conviviality that is intoxicating. Wandering through the narrow back streets behind the imposing Galatasaray High School (built in 1481, and with a venerable history of educating the country's leaders), our friend Andrew led us through the corridors of a building and into an enclosed garden where there was home-made lemonade for sale. As we sat on wooden benches under lemon trees quenching our thirst with lemonade, we marvelled at this secret oasis in the heart of the city.

The ritual of taking a hamam (Turkish bath) is another of life's great treats, and a daily ritual for many of Istanbul's inhabitants – a time to socialise as much as anything else. After visiting a public bathhouse for a spell in the steam room, being lathered on a marble slab, then scrubbed to within an inch of your life, you emerge feeling virginally clean. We went in search of some of the more noted of Istanbul's hamams: the most famous and illustrious are situated close to the Grand Bazaar and, for my money, the best one is Cemberlitas Hamam, a few blocks from the bazaar. The atmosphere is amazing – very opulent and quite surreal.

The Ottomans combined the culinary traditions of the entire eastern Mediterranean with Arab, Persian and Asian influences, resulting in one of the world's most dynamic cuisines. A great way to get a handle on the amazing range of food available is to walk through the Grand Bazaar's labyrinth of interconnecting passageways that are covered with domed ceilings and decorated with ornate tiles. The bazaar is divided into sections, which helps when you know what you are looking for, and the main thoroughfare of Kalpakcilar Basi Caddesi is as wide as any European boulevard. It's worth a stop at Fez Cafe right in the centre of the bazaar for a cup of Turkish coffee or tea, for a brief respite from the frenetic atmosphere.

Not far from the Grand Bazaar, you'll find the Spice Bazaar, or the Egyptian Market, as it is also known – this is where you come for produce. Its narrow streets are packed to the rafters with wonderful displays of cheese, pastirma (cured dried beef) and sucuk (sausage), olives, eggs, yoghurt, pastries, nuts, vegetables, herbal teas and baskets of pungent dried spices. I bought a bag of powdered salep, an extract of orchid root that is used to give ice creams an elastic texture; it's also used in milk drinks as a thickener and, just for good measure, is considered an aphrodisiac. In between the rows of stalls, men wheeling ornate carts sell delicious morsels such as rounds of simit bread, which look like large bagels with a sesame seed crust, and bags of the freshest pistachios and almonds imaginable. If you need a caffeine fix, there's a terrific place on Tahmis Caddesi, one of the city's oldest coffee shops. At another local eatery, I became besotted with tavuk gogsu kazandibi, a savoury Ottoman pudding made with shredded chicken, milk, cream and rice flour, cooked like a flat sheet until browned and crisp on the bottom and mousse-like in the centre, then cut into rectangles and rolled into logs. It is one of the most delicious things I've ever tasted.

EATING IN ISTANBUL

CHANGA
Siraselviler Caddesi 87/1, Taksim
Tel +90 212 251 7064
www.changa-istanbul.com
Our favourite restaurant, with an interesting menu offering modern takes on Turkish classics. The cocktails are to die for, especially the satsuma caipiroska with a slice of bergamot. Definitely the most sophisticated place in town.

MUZEDECHANGA
Sakip Sabancı Caddesi 22, Emirgan
Tel +90 212 323 0901
www.changa-istanbul.com
About a 40-minute drive north along the Bosphorus, this immaculately designed space from the Changa team is located in the grounds of the Sakip Sabanci Museum, making it fab for a leisurely lunch on the terrace after viewing the latest international exhibition.

CIYA
Caferaga Mahallesi, Guneslibahce Sokak 43/44, Kadikoy
Tel +90 216 330 3190
The terrific regional home cooking here is worth the trip across to the Asian shore of the Bosphorus. At the meze kitchen, you spoon your choices onto a plate and then pay according to weight. At peak times, you can always wander around the nearby food shops while you wait for a table.

LEB-I DERYA
Kumbaraci Yokusu, 115/7, Beyoglu
Tel +90 212 293 4989
This uber-cool rooftop bar has wrap-around views of Istanbul and the Bosphorus. If their house cocktails don't do it for you, come for a terrific Turkish breakfast and take it from there.

HUNKAR
Mim Kemal Oke Caddesi 21, Nisantasi
Tel +90 212 225 4665
Traditional Turkish food cooked with flair: the crisp roasted lamb with eggplant puree blended with bechamel is not to be missed. A favourite haunt for the business set by day, it attracts a broader clientele at night.

CEZAYIR
Hayriye Caddesi 12, Galatasaray, Beyoglu
Tel +90 212 245 9980
www.cezayir-istanbul.com
Set in a fabulous building that used to be a school, with generous spaces and a happening bar, this is a real local. Try it during the cooler days of autumn and winter, and graze on the tapas plates.

SEYHMUZ KEBAP SALONU
Medrese Sokak 2, Cemberlitas
Tel +90 212 526 1613
For the best kebabs in town – in every imaginable style. This is a no-fuss local joint with tables on the footpath outside the shop. Head to the Grand Bazaar and ask for directions (it's near Beyazit and the jewellery stores).

MANGERIE BEBEK
Cevdet Pasa Caddesi 69, Bebek
Tel +90 212 263 5199
Seriously cool cafe in Bebek with a view of the Bosphorus – a real favourite. Delicious, non-fussy food, and they cook a mean steak too.

KIYI
Kefelikoy Caddesi 126, Tarabya
Tel +90 212 262 0002
www.kiyi.com.tr
One of our favourite fish restaurants on the Bosphorus, Kiyi is near the Black Sea, an hour's drive north of the city. Choose your fish from their catch of the day (displayed on ice), and nominate your preferred cooking method – simply grilled is often best.

Whenever we visit Istanbul, it is a ritual of ours to have an arrival dinner at Changa Restaurant, where Peter Gordon is consultant chef; 'changa' means mix in Swahili, and this is a perfect description for the eclectic range of dishes on the menu. Located in one of the city's few original Art Nouveau buildings, the restaurant successfully combines old and new, classic and modern. Among my favourite dishes is an eggplant dish (naturally) with a miso and sesame sauce, and lakerda, traditionally cured bonito with braised leeks and mint pesto – anything with lamb is always good. I tend to just ask them to cook for us so we can be surprised each time.

A chance meeting with restaurateurs Tarik Bayazit and Savas Ertunc (the team behind Changa and MuzedeChanga) during our first trip to Istanbul blossomed into a life-long friendship. On our most recent visit, before taking us into the depths of the bazaar to show us their favourite merchants, they took us to their favourite kebab shop, Seyhmuz Kebap Salonu, in a back street behind the bazaar. We sat at an outdoor table, and the boys asked the cook to make us every different type of kebab so we could see and taste the difference. The very impressive selection included: long skewered adana kebabs of minced lamb; seyhmus (a flat, plate-sized pattie consisting of two layers of minced lamb, with diced tomato and green chilli sandwiched in the centre, which is then fried like a pancake); sis kebab (cubes of lamb); urfa kebab (skewered meat and eggplant slices); and iskender kebab (lamb served on flat bread with tomato and yoghurt sauce). All incredibly delicious, and we found it impossible to stop eating. Intrigued by our curiosity and our appetite for their kebabs, the owners added several plates to our order, so it turned into a much longer lunch than we had anticipated. Puffed pide breads, which emerge from the wood-fired oven at the back of the shop, are usually torn

Further afield, we have had memorable stays along Turkey's stunning coastline. Here are a few of my favourite places to encourage you to explore beyond Istanbul.

THE AEGEAN COAST

MACA KIZI HOTEL
Turkbuku, Bodrum
Tel +90 252 377 6272
www.macakizi.com
One of the most stylish places you will find along the coast – the attention to detail is beyond compare, and the hotel also offers excellent food. The chef does a great modern spin on the classics, and a wood-fired oven in the garden means brilliant pizzas and pides for lunch.

ORFOZ
Cumhuriyet Cadessi 177/B, Bodrum
Tel +90 252 316 4285
www.orfoz.com/bodrum.htm
In my opinion, the wonderful seafood dishes at Orfoz are the main reason to visit Bodrum: the mussel pilav is a standout. Orfoz's parent restaurant is in Bozburun, further along the coast.

GIRITLI
Yalimevki, Turkbuku
Tel +90 252 377 5747
The best tables at this waterfront seafood restaurant are out on the wooden pier over the water. The meze plates are fantastic, so be sure to order one of each.

THE TURQUOISE COAST

BAHCE RESTAURANT
Anit Mezar Karsisi, 31, Kas
Tel +90 242 836 2370
This friendly family-run outdoor restaurant is set in a lovely garden and has some of the most delicious meze and fish dishes on the entire coast. All the eggplant salads are divine.

KEBAP HOSPITAL
Antep Sofrasi, Gocek
This modest outdoor place, a street back from the water's edge, has wood-fired ovens and charcoal grills. The lahmacun is unbeatable and the kebabs melt in the mouth – there's always a queue outside.

SAVILE RESIDENCE
Cukurbag Yarimadasi Bulent, Kalkavan Sok 18, Kas
Tel +90 242 836 4188
www.savileresidencekas.com
Staying at this fabulous little hideaway on the peninsula a few kilometres from Kas town centre is like having your own beach house. The lovely owners also cook delicious food, offering a different menu every night.

THE MEDITERRANEAN COAST

HILLSIDE SU HOTEL
Konyaalti, Antalya
Tel +90 242 249 0700
www.hillside.com.tr
Designer modern beachfront hotel. At night the chill-out lounge and bar comes into its own, as you relax on white beanbags on the sand and tune in to the sounds spun by the resident DJ – the ultimate beach club.

into smaller pieces to wrap the kebab with green leaves, herbs and tomato relish. I now make a pilgrimage here every time I'm in town, and am never disappointed.

Kurdish in origin, lahmacun is Turkey's answer to pizza: the thin base is topped with minced lamb and cooked in a wood-fired oven – utterly addictive, especially with a dollop of sheep's milk yoghurt. Another reason I love this country so much is their celebration of the humble anchovy (hamsi); it is a prized ingredient and features in so many of their dishes. Anchovy and eggplant! No wonder I have adopted this place as my second home and incorporated Turkish influences into my repertoire. Fished from the Marmara Sea and the Black Sea, the prime anchovies are preserved in salt and oil for future pleasure – a perfect package from nature. The best fillets are thick and not too salty, much like those prepared by hand in the south of France and the Basque region of Spain. Having driven almost the entire length of the Bosphorus to reach our favourite fish restaurant at Tarabya, one day I plan to take a boat and sail right up the Bosphorus into the Black Sea and cruise around for a while. I've heard of a market in the small town of Trabzon, on the south-eastern shore, that sells nothing but anchovies – and that alone is reason enough to make the trip.

Over the years, Tarik and Savas have introduced us to many intriguing ingredients; indeed, the customs guys at Sydney Airport are always most interested in what I bring back! I have acquired a taste for candied bergamot oranges (which give Earl Grey tea its distinctive flavour), and at the end of my last visit Tarik gave me a jar made by a small producer for their restaurant. I also like to bring back a bottle or two of bergamot oil – it makes a lovely light salad dressing and is great for drizzling over grilled fish – from a terrific shop in Bebek that sells delicious olive oils. Compressed sheets of sun-dried fruit puree such as amardine, an intensely fruity apricot leather, are used to flavour drinks or even added to braised meats or stews. And I am in awe of the incredible variety of olives in Turkey: glistening in large bowls, they are available in every shape, size and hue at the markets, and are offered at every eating house as a sign of welcome.

Our longtime travelling companion Andrew now lives in Istanbul, so we have someone else on the ground to fill us in on all the local knowledge – which is just as well, since restaurants and bars here come and go so quickly. Some only last one season and then reinvent themselves. The giddy pace of change is exciting and invigorating, and I love that my life is filled with so many Turkish delights from this sensual place.

FRIED ANCHOVY PASTRIES AND ANCHOVY CUSTARD

I have Adelaide doyenne Catherine Kerry to thank for passing on the recipe for these delightful pastries. When I worked with her at Petaluma Restaurant in the Adelaide Hills, we would often make them as a canape for lunch service. They brush the palate like a feather, making you lust after them all the more. If you don't have time to make the pastry, use the ready-made sheets of brik pastry that are available from North African food shops. To add an extra dimension of anchovy flavour, I serve the pastries with steamed anchovy custards, which also create a wonderful synergy between the textures. This makes the most delicious first course.

1 cup plain flour
70 ml cold water
30 ml extra virgin olive oil
12 anchovy fillets, drained and cut in half crossways
vegetable oil, for deep-frying
2 teaspoons Tapenade (see Essentials)

STEAMED ANCHOVY CUSTARDS
100 ml pouring (35%) cream
75 ml milk
3 anchovy fillets, chopped
½ teaspoon sea salt
¼ teaspoon freshly ground white pepper
2 eggs
1 egg yolk
2 teaspoons anchovy cream
30 ml extra virgin olive oil

To make the pastries, place the flour, water and oil in a mixer bowl with a dough hook and mix until a dough forms. Cover the bowl and rest for 30 minutes. Divide the dough into four pieces and roll out each piece on a floured surface until about 3 mm thick. Cut the dough into diamond shapes about 6 cm across (cut out three diamonds from each piece). Lay an anchovy fillet across the pastry, then roll the pastry up from the point to form cigars.

Heat the oil in a deep-fryer or pan to 180°C, then deep-fry the pastries a few at a time for about 3 minutes until golden. Drain briefly on paper towel and serve warm.

To make the custards, preheat the oven to 135°C and line a baking dish with a tea towel. Heat the cream and milk in a saucepan until it starts to simmer. Whisk in the chopped anchovy, then remove the pan from the heat and leave to infuse for 10 minutes. Season with salt and pepper to taste.

Whisk the eggs and yolk together until just combined (don't make them too fluffy), then add the anchovy cream and oil and whisk until combined. Add the egg mix to the hot cream and stir until combined.

Pass the custard through a fine mesh sieve and pour into demi-tasse cups or small ramekins.

Remove any bubbles that may appear on the surface to keep the custard as smooth as possible. Stand the cups in the lined baking dish and pour in enough boiling water to come two-thirds of the way up the sides of the cups. Bake for 20 minutes or until just set – they should have a slight wobble in the centre when tested. Remove the cups from the water bath and leave to settle for 5 minutes.

To serve, stand the cup or ramekin on a saucer, sit a small dollop of tapenade in the centre and lay an anchovy pastry across the top. Put the remaining pastries in the centre of the table for sharing.

SERVES 4

ANCHOVY AND OLIVE BOREK

I make no apologies for sharing several recipes based on my beloved anchovy, which holds pride of place in my repertoire alongside eggplant. It is such a versatile ingredient to use in cooking, and just a hint can change a dish from the ordinary to the sublime. These savoury pastries always remind me of the taste of spanking-fresh fish, direct from the water at the edge of the Black Sea.

6 sheets brik (or filo) pastry
24 large spinach leaves, blanched
1 egg yolk
40 ml olive oil

FILLING
100 ml extra virgin olive oil
3 brown onions, finely sliced
4 cloves garlic
1 teaspoon sea salt
1 teaspoon sugar
1 teaspoon freshly ground black pepper
50 ml balsamic vinegar
80 g black kalamata olives, pitted and chopped
1 teaspoon chopped rosemary
1 teaspoon chopped thyme
100 ml White Chicken Stock (see Essentials)
150 g anchovy fillets, chopped

To make the filling, heat the oil in a large frying pan and saute the onion, garlic, salt, sugar and pepper over gentle heat for 20 minutes until softened. Add the vinegar, olives, chopped herbs and stock and cook for another 20–30 minutes or until the mix is quite dry. Allow to cool slightly, then stir in the chopped anchovies.

Preheat the oven to 180°C. Cut each pastry sheet in half to give you 12 sheets. Working with two sheets at a time, cover the centre part of the pastry with a thin layer of blanched spinach leaves and spread the anchovy filling on top.

Mix a little water with the egg yolk, then brush the pastry edges with the egg wash. Fold in the sides then roll up the pastry into small finger-shaped rolls and lay on a flat tray.

Heat the olive oil in a frying pan and fry the pastries over moderate heat for 3 minutes until just starting to brown. Roll over and fry the other side for 2 minutes, then transfer to the oven and bake for 10 minutes until golden. Serve immediately or while still quite warm.

SERVES 4

SAFFRON AND LEMON BEEF PASTRIES

These pastry parcels are packed with flavour and need absolutely no adornment. They make the most delicious canapes, and can also be made a fraction larger and served as a starter with a small salad of crisp bitter greens and a pomegranate dressing. The tendons create a contrasting texture to the meat, and the trotter's role is to provide a natural gel for the sauce, which holds the whole thing together when cooked.

1 kg beef brisket
200 ml olive oil
1 teaspoon freshly ground black pepper
1 brown onion, finely diced
6 cloves garlic, minced
1 tablespoon minced ginger
1 red bird's-eye chilli, minced
1 tablespoon ras el hanout
1 teaspoon cumin seeds, roasted and ground
2 teaspoons coriander seeds, roasted and ground
2 dried chillies, roasted and ground
1 teaspoon sweet paprika
2 litres Beef Stock (see Essentials)
2 teaspoons saffron threads
300 g beef tendons
1 pig's trotter, blanched
1 tablespoon minced lemon zest
2 tablespoons shredded parsley leaves
2 tablespoons shredded coriander leaves
2 teaspoons sea salt
2 teaspoons freshly ground black pepper, extra
12 sheets brik pastry
1 egg yolk
vegetable oil, for deep-frying

Preheat the oven to 180°C. Brush the brisket with a little olive oil, sprinkle with pepper and place in a roasting pan. Bake for 10 minutes on each side to brown the meat, then remove from the pan and set aside. Reduce the oven temperature to 150°C.

In the same pan, heat the rest of the olive oil and saute the onion, garlic, ginger and chilli for about 4 minutes until fragrant. Add the spices and cook for a few minutes. Pour in the beef stock, bring to the boil and add half the saffron. Reduce to a simmer, add the browned beef brisket, tendons and trotter and cover with baking paper then foil. Transfer to the oven and bake for 5 hours or until the meat is very tender.

When the meat is ready, remove the brisket, tendon and trotter from the stock and rest on a tray for about 20 minutes until cool enough to handle. Discard the trotter. Peel the tendons, reserving the soft inner lengths, and shred the brisket into small lengths, discarding any fat, muscle tissue or skin.

Allow the stock to settle then skim the surface to remove the oil layer and any scum. Strain through a fine mesh sieve, pour into a saucepan and bring to the boil. Add the remaining saffron, reduce the heat and simmer until the sauce has thickened and reduced by half. Pass through a fine mesh sieve and discard the solids. Stir in the lemon zest and herbs, taste for seasoning and adjust with salt and pepper.

Mix the shredded brisket and tendon strips and lay in a baking dish or plastic container – the meat should be about 3–4 cm high. Press down to condense. Pour on enough sauce to just cover the meat, reserving the rest for another use. Refrigerate overnight to set – it will become firm, with the meat suspended in the jellied sauce (as in foreground of photo). Turn out onto a flat board and cut into small brick-shaped logs, about 8 cm long × 3 cm wide.

Cut each brik pastry sheet in half, trim off the rounded edges and lay a log of meat onto each sheet at the narrower end closest to you. Mix a little water with the egg yolk, then brush the pastry edges with the egg wash. Roll over once then fold in the sides and roll up to enclose.

Heat the oil in a large saucepan or wok to 180°C, add a few pastries at a time and deep-fry for 4 minutes until crisp and golden. Drain on paper towel, rest for 3 minutes then serve.

SERVES 12

SQUID, ROASTED RED CAPSICUM AND EGGPLANT SALAD

This salad is inspired by one of my favourite condiments – ajvar, an ancient Arabic relish that is common in southern Turkey and across the Middle East. I have also seen it used in Croatian and Serbian cooking, and Eastern European delis in Australia sell it in jars. I remember buying jars of this exotic relish long before I'd set foot in any of these countries and tasted it first hand. Everything has a way of naturally falling into place.

1 red capsicum (pepper)
250 g eggplant (aubergine)
60 ml extra virgin olive oil
1 small red onion, finely diced
3 cloves garlic, minced
1 long red chilli, minced
1 teaspoon castor sugar
50 ml fresh lemon juice, strained
2 teaspoons red wine vinegar
1 teaspoon sea salt
½ teaspoon freshly ground black pepper
4 tablespoons chopped parsley leaves
400 g squid tubes, cleaned and cut into thin strips lengthways
100 g wild rocket leaves, stems removed

Sit the whole capsicum and eggplant over direct flame or hot coals and cook until the skin has blistered, turning to blister all the surfaces evenly. Place in a plastic bag and leave to sweat for 20 minutes until cool enough to handle. Remove the charred skins and core of the capsicum and the stalk of the eggplant and cut the flesh into a coarse pulp.

Heat the oil in a pan and saute the onion, garlic, chilli and sugar until the mixture begins to colour and caramelise. Add the roasted eggplant and capsicum pulp and stir to combine. Season with lemon juice, vinegar, salt and pepper and stir in the parsley. Taste and adjust the seasoning if necessary.

Cook the squid for 45 seconds in a large saucepan of boiling water, strain and add immediately to the warm salad with the wild rocket leaves, tossing to combine and allowing the flavours to mingle while the squid is still hot. Pile onto plates and serve.

SERVES 4

PICKLED LAMB'S TONGUE AND FIG SALAD

In the past, I have partnered lamb's tongue with celeriac and horseradish, mustard fruits and also with mustard spaghetti (all delicious combinations), but I just love them with ripe figs, the symbolic fruit of Turkey. Vincotto and fig vinegar are available from specialist food stores. The inspiration for this photo was taken from Karim Rashid's Morphescape collection of tableware, a modernist interpretation of Istanbul's Ottoman skyline. I first came across these beautiful pieces at Changa Restaurant in Istanbul and then just had to buy some from the Karim Rashid store when I was next in New York.

4 ripe figs, cut into quarters
2 tablespoons shelled pistachios, chopped
1 small red onion, finely sliced
1 punnet mache cress, snipped
8 slices pancetta, grilled to make crisp wafers

PICKLED LAMB'S TONGUES
8 small lamb's tongues
50 ml olive oil
1 tablespoon diced fennel bulb
1 tablespoon diced onion
1 teaspoon minced garlic
1 teaspoon minced ginger
30 g diced speck or bacon
1 teaspoon brown mustard seeds
1 stick cinnamon
2 mace blades
5 whole allspice
1 clove
1 teaspoon black peppercorns
50 g palm sugar, shaved
200 ml rice vinegar
500 ml White Chicken Stock (see Essentials)
3 teaspoons sea salt

DRESSING
25 ml vincotto
25 ml fig vinegar
2 teaspoons Roasted Garlic Paste (see Essentials)
125 ml extra virgin olive oil
½ teaspoon sea salt
½ teaspoon freshly ground black pepper

To prepare the pickled lamb's tongues, soak the tongues for 24 hours in cold water with a pinch of salt, changing the water every 4 hours or so. Drain.

Heat the oil in a large, heavy-based pan over moderate heat and fry the fennel, onion, garlic and ginger until softened and fragrant. Stir in the speck and mustard seeds and cook for a few minutes, then add the tongues and toss to coat with the aromatics. Add the remaining ingredients and bring to the boil over gentle heat. Simmer for 2 hours or until the tongues are soft.

Take the pan off the heat and allow the tongues to cool completely in their pickling stock. Remove the cooled tongues and dislodge any spices attached to the meat. Peel the tongues and slice finely crossways just before serving.

To make the dressing, whisk all the ingredients in a bowl until emulsified.

Combine the sliced lamb's tongues, figs, pistachios, onion and cress in a bowl, add the dressing and toss to combine. Arrange the salad in neat piles on plates and top with the crisp pancetta to serve.

SERVES 4

CHANGA'S EGGPLANT SALAD WITH TAHINI AND MISO

Tarik and Savas, the owners of Changa in Istanbul, kindly sent me this recipe after I raved about it at the first dinner I ate at their restaurant. I order it every time I visit and its taste never diminishes or becomes boring. They serve it with crisp grissini-style breadsticks, but it also makes an ideal accompaniment to grilled lamb and meat kebabs.

1 kg eggplant (aubergine)
bread sticks, to serve

MARINADE
1 tablespoon red miso paste
20 ml sesame oil
3 teaspoons sunflower oil
70 ml mirin
45 ml light soy sauce
1 tablespoon tahini
3 teaspoons castor sugar
2 teaspoons white sesame seeds

MISO TAHINI SAUCE
2 teaspoons red miso paste
2 teaspoons sesame oil
65 ml sunflower oil
25 ml mirin
20 ml light soy sauce
2 teaspoons tahini
2 teaspoons castor sugar
2 teaspoons white sesame seeds, roasted
2 teaspoons honey
1 teaspoon pomegranate molasses
few drops of Tabasco sauce
1 teaspoon rice vinegar

Preheat the oven to 210°C. Slice the eggplant into thick chunks.

Mix all the marinade ingredients together, add the eggplant chunks and toss to coat. Leave to marinate for 5 minutes, then transfer the eggplant and marinade to a non-stick baking tray and roast for 20 minutes. Arrange the eggplant on a plate.

Whisk together the ingredients for the miso tahini sauce, spoon over the hot eggplant and serve with crisp bread sticks.

SERVES 4

FISH WITH TOMATO, GINGER AND DRIED LIMES

Available in Middle Eastern food stores, dried limes add a delicious complexity and mellow acidity to sauces. A herb pilav makes the perfect accompaniment to this fish dish. Introduced by the Persians, rice pilavs hold a prized position in the Turkish repertoire, thanks to the Ottoman chefs who created signature pilavs made rich with butter, nuts and spices. It's important to soak the rice grains in plenty of cold water then rinse thoroughly – this removes excess starch so the grains remain separate during cooking.

1 tablespoon minced ginger
4 cloves garlic, minced
1 teaspoon sea salt
30 ml Ginger Juice (see Essentials)
4 × 120 g salmon or jewfish cutlets
3 teaspoons Baharat Spice Mix (see Essentials)
25 g unsalted butter
30 ml olive oil
1 small brown onion, finely diced
2 small red chillies, finely sliced
4 ripe tomatoes, peeled and chopped
2 dried limes, pierced with a skewer
2 teaspoons brown sugar
160 ml Fish Stock (see Essentials)
½ teaspoon freshly ground black pepper
20 ml fresh lime juice, strained

HERB PILAV
200 g basmati rice
100 g unsalted butter
1 small white onion, finely diced
½ teaspoon ground allspice
1 teaspoon finely chopped fresh dill
3 green onions, finely sliced
450 ml White Chicken Stock (see Essentials), warmed to simmering point
2 teaspoons sea salt
1 teaspoon freshly ground black pepper
1 tablespoon chopped parsley leaves
1 tablespoon chopped basil leaves
1 tablespoon chopped mint leaves
1 tablespoon chopped chives
1 tablespoon fresh lemon juice, strained
2 tablespoons Fried Shallot Slices (see Essentials)

For the pilav, soak the rice in cold water for 1 hour, changing the water twice, then rinse until the water runs clear.

Melt the butter in a heavy-based saucepan and fry the onion, allspice and dill until fragrant, about 4 minutes. Stir in the green onions, then add the drained rice and stir until the rice is coated with the onion mix.

Add the warmed stock all at once, stir well and season with salt and pepper. Cover the surface with a sheet of baking paper cut to fit the pan. When the stock starts to bubble, cover with a lid, reduce heat to the lowest setting and leave to cook for 15 minutes, until the rice has absorbed all the liquid and the grains are soft.

Take off the heat and remove the lid and paper. Stir through the chopped herbs, lemon juice and fried shallots. Taste and adjust seasoning if necessary – it may need a little extra salt.

For the fish, pound the ginger, garlic, salt and ginger juice in a mortar and pestle to make a paste.

Dust the fish with half the baharat spice mix. Heat the butter and oil together in a heavy-based pan and fry the fish for 2 minutes on each side. Remove from the pan. Add the onion and chilli to the pan and fry until softened. Stir in the ginger garlic paste and fry for another 2 minutes until fragrant, then add the remaining baharat mix and stir to combine. Fry for a minute or two longer until the spice becomes fragrant.

Add the tomato, dried limes and sugar and cook for 5 minutes. Pour in the stock and simmer gently for 15 minutes until slightly reduced. Season with pepper, taste and adjust the seasoning if necessary – it may require a little salt.

Lay the fish cutlets on top and spoon the sauce over the top. Cover and simmer gently for 10 minutes until the fish is just cooked through.

Transfer the fish to plates and spoon on the sauce, discarding the dried limes. Add a squeeze of fresh lime juice and serve with the herb pilav.

SERVES 4

LAMB AND PISTACHIO MANTI WITH POMEGRANATE SALAD AND GARLIC YOGHURT SAUCE

Manti are the Turkish equivalent of ravioli, little pasta parcels that originate from Kayseri in central Turkey's Cappadocia region. I have teamed my adaptation of these with another classic – the widely available shepherd's salad that has sustained many a rural worker during their travels with their herds. Rustic by nature, I have given it an elegant facelift in this instance. The addition of pomegranate seeds is a personal whimsy.

40 ml olive oil
1 small white onion, finely diced
4 cloves garlic, minced
2 teaspoons ground chilli
1 teaspoon sumac
1 teaspoon ground allspice
250 g coarsely minced lamb
1 tablespoon tomato puree
100 ml Beef Stock (see Essentials)
2 tablespoons chopped mint leaves
1 tablespoon chopped parsley leaves
3 tablespoons shelled pistachios, chopped
1 teaspoon sea salt
1 teaspoon freshly ground black pepper
2 egg yolks, lightly beaten
2 tablespoons thick plain yoghurt
24 Shanghai won ton wrappers (or gow gee wrappers, or thin pasta sheets)
1 egg white
1 teaspoon sumac

GARLIC YOGHURT SAUCE
125 g thick plain yoghurt
40 ml fresh lemon juice, strained
2 cloves garlic, minced
1 small green chilli, minced
½ teaspoon ground cumin
2 tablespoons shredded mint leaves
1 teaspoon sea salt
½ teaspoon freshly ground black pepper

POMEGRANATE SALAD
60 ml extra virgin olive oil
2 teaspoons fresh lemon juice, strained
2 teaspoons fig vinegar
2 teaspoons pomegranate molasses
½ teaspoon sea salt
¼ teaspoon freshly ground black pepper
2 tablespoons diced tomato
2 tablespoons cucumber fine julienne strips
4 tablespoons pomegranate seeds
1 red radish, cut into fine julienne strips
1 tablespoon shelled pistachios, chopped
2 green onions, finely sliced
½ long green chilli, finely sliced
2 tablespoons shredded parsley leaves
4 large green olives, pitted and finely sliced >>

GINGERBREAD AND YOGHURT MERINGUE

This is a dessert from one of our first menus in London, inspired by my passion for decent gingerbread and the crates of cumquats I saw at the shops across the road in Soho's Chinatown. The magic happened when we combined these flavours and introduced another texture: the sweet acidity of the yoghurt meringue. You can always substitute candied orange or clementine if you don't have any candied cumquats to hand.

1 ginger blossom, finely sliced lengthways
100 ml Sugar Syrup (see Essentials)
12 Candied Cumquats (see Essentials)
2 tablespoons Almond Praline (see Essentials)

GINGERBREAD
175 g self-raising flour
2 teaspoons ground ginger
2 teaspoons ground cinnamon
110 g brown sugar
100 g unsalted butter
50 ml golden syrup
2 large eggs, beaten
175 ml milk
40 ml Sugar Syrup (see Essentials)

YOGHURT MERINGUE
25 g egg white (about 1 egg)
35 g castor sugar
2 tablespoons honey
30 g candied (sweet preserved) ginger, finely diced
1.5 g gelatine leaves, softened in cold water
150 g thick plain yoghurt

To make the gingerbread, preheat the oven to 150°C and line a 15 cm square cake tin with baking paper. Sift the flour, ginger, cinnamon and brown sugar into a bowl. Melt the butter with the golden syrup, then mix with the egg and milk. Stir the liquid into the dry ingredients until combined, then pour into the prepared tin. Bake for 40–45 minutes, leave in the tin for 5 minutes, then turn out onto a wire rack to cool. When the cake is completely cold, wrap it in plastic film and freeze for 2 hours.

Preheat the oven to 110°C. Cut four thin slices from the cake (use an electric slicer, if you have one) so you have long rectangular strips that are as wide as the depth of the cake. Reserve the rest of the cake for another use. Place the cake slices on a flat tray and dry in the oven. When half dry, brush with the sugar syrup and return to the oven to finish drying. While hot, wrap the cake slices around the outside of 6 cm ring moulds (like egg rings but with higher sides). Press the edges together for a couple of minutes until they seal and the cake cools into its shape. They should resemble hollow collars.

Cut the ginger blossom into fine slices lengthways and lay on a wire rack to dry out overnight. Preheat the oven to 110°C. Brush the ginger blossom slices with sugar syrup and and bake until dry and crisp.

Heat 150 ml of the liquid from the candied cumquats and simmer until it has reduced slightly and reached a syrup consistency. Allow to cool.

To make the yoghurt meringue, whisk the egg white and as it starts to stiffen, slowly add the sugar, continuing to whisk until firm and glossy. Boil the honey with 20 ml water in a saucepan until it reaches 120°C (use a sugar thermometer) then slowly pour into the meringue, continuing to whisk as you add the hot honey. Stir in the candied ginger and the softened gelatine.

Allow to cool to blood temperature then whisk in the yoghurt while the meringue is still warm.

Line the insides of each ring mould with a strip of baking paper. Spoon the yoghurt meringue into each mould until half full, then sprinkle with some of the praline. Allow to set in the refrigerator for 30 minutes. Fill each mould with the remaining meringue and refrigerate for 2 hours until firm.

To serve, remove the ring moulds from the meringues and slip the gingerbread collars over the meringue to encase them. Sprinkle with the remaining praline and arrange the candied cumquats on top. Stand a candied ginger blossom wafer up from the top of the meringue, drizzle the syrup around the sides and serve.

SERVES 4

APRICOTS WITH PISTACHIO CREAM

Apricots are an important ingredient for the entire Arab region. When they are prolific at the end of summer, they are dried in the sun for use throughout the year. For this quick dessert, I have teamed them with pistachios, another staple of the Turkish repertoire. You should be able to find whole candied citrus fruits, including clementines, at specialist food stores.

20 dried apricots
150 g castor sugar
30 ml orange blossom water
½ candied clementine, finely diced
2 tablespoons Pistachio Praline (see Essentials)
150 ml thick (45%) cream, lightly whipped

Soak the apricots in enough warm water to cover for 5 hours until softened. Strain, reserving 200 ml of the apricot water.

Heat the sugar and reserved water in a saucepan and boil for 5 minutes until the sugar has dissolved. Add the orange blossom water and softened apricots and poach over gentle heat for 15 minutes. Turn off the heat and allow the apricots to cool in the syrup. When cool, remove the apricots and cook the syrup until thickened and reduced by half. Cool completely before serving.

Gently stir the candied clementine and two-thirds of the pistachio praline into the whipped cream, being careful not to overwork. Spoon the cream into a piping bag.

Split each apricot in half without cutting all the way through to make a pocket. Pipe the pistachio cream into each apricot until the centres are full. Stand the apricots on plates, drizzle with the cooled syrup and sprinkle the remaining pistachio praline over the top.

SERVES 4–6

ROSE PETAL AND RASPBERRY CREAM

Like the classic 'fool' (simply whipped flavoured cream), this is an easy dessert to prepare, with a sense of elegance to it. Enjoy it during summer when raspberries are at their peak. To make it a little more lavish, I have stirred tiny meringue dots and rose-flavoured Turkish delight through the mousse before it is refrigerated, adding an unexpected crunch to the texture.

100 g castor sugar
½ teaspoon rosewater
20 ml fresh lemon juice, strained
125 ml raspberry puree, strained
250 ml pouring (35%) cream, whipped
4 tablespoons Meringue Dots (see Essentials)
4 pieces rose-flavoured Turkish delight, cut into 5 mm dice
200 g fresh raspberries
12 fresh (unsprayed) red rose petals
4 tablespoons Persian fairy floss

ROSE SYRUP
300 g castor sugar
150 ml water
40 ml rosewater
6 fresh (unsprayed) rose petals
4 dried roses, broken into petals

Stir the sugar, rosewater and lemon juice into the raspberry puree until dissolved. Gently fold in the whipped cream. Spoon or pipe the mousse into serving bowls or glasses and refrigerate for 2 hours until set.

To make the syrup, combine the ingredients in a saucepan and simmer for 20 minutes until slightly reduced and thickened. Pass through a fine mesh sieve, discarding the solids. Allow the syrup to cool completely before serving.

To serve, swirl the meringue dots and diced Turkish delight through the mousse and smooth the surface with a palette knife. Arrange the raspberries over the mousse, drizzle with the rose syrup and sit a few red rose petals and Persian fairy floss on top. Serve immediately.

SERVES 4

ORIGINAL SIN FRANCE

Paris has the distinction of being the first international city I ever fell in love with. I had an immediate emotional response to the city, and found myself in awe of its beauty, its history and its passion. I was working as a school teacher in Adelaide at the time, so travelling had to coincide with holiday breaks, which means winter in Europe. Paris at Christmas time is particularly beguiling: the shop windows are filled with opulent displays and the mood on the streets is convivial and celebratory. The festive food is amazing, and everything is washed down with some delicious wine or a glass of champagne. I visited Notre Dame Cathedral on Christmas Eve to observe mass, an experience that gives a true sense of meaning to the season. After Christmas, the pastry shops sell Galette des Rois (king's cake), to mark Epiphany and bring in the New Year. This sweet almond pastry is made in the pithivier style, complete with gold-cardboard crown cut-outs on top. Anyone can feel royal when they eat one of these, and the pithivier shape provided inspiration for what became a Paramount signature dish: five-spice duck and shiitake mushroom pie.

Paris, the eternal city of light, exudes serious style. It has an atmosphere that is so very different from anywhere else on earth. There are 20 arrondissements (neighbourhoods) within the Peripherique (a ring road that separates the city from its suburbs), and these come together like a bunch of small villages that spiral outwards from the centre near the Louvre Museum on the Right Bank of the Seine. This makes navigation really easy, and the super-efficient underground metro system makes it even easier to get around.

Falling in love with Paris means falling in love with its food and wine culture. Where to start? On that first visit, when French cuisine was regarded as the last word in style and elegance, I was like a kid let loose in a candy store. These days, the rest of the world has caught up and in many ways overtaken this prestigious position. But those first impressions have stayed with me, and stir up the same feelings every time I visit. To me, Paris symbolises love, romance, food, wine, civilised living, intellectual discourse and hedonistic pleasure.

Parisians seem to live by the notion that food is the reason for living. With food culture held in such high esteem by the city's inhabitants, it's easy to understand why we rarely go to a supermarket during our visits to Paris. That said, it's still a luxury to have the time to think about food, to be able to shop each day for it, to discuss it passionately and then to cook it. Like everywhere in the world, Paris is succumbing to an alarming trend toward pret-a-manger – prepared meals that can be zapped in a microwave. Quel horreur! For many, though, this has sparked a renewed interest in street markets and they are flourishing under increased sites and days of operation. Even staying in a hotel, you can make the most of this vibrant local food scene: buy ready-prepared items from the shops or markets so you can indulge in a private picnic in your room without any cooking. A crusty baguette from the boulangerie, some hand-made cheese from the fromagerie, saucisson, pate and celeriac remoulade from the charcuterie, and sweet pastries from the patisserie provide a complete taste experience. Then there are the chocolate shops – don't get me started on those.

Our French was rudimentary, but we quickly learnt how to order coffee (essential anywhere!), a croque monsieur sandwich or the set menu if all else failed. It was wonderful to be able to eat at cafes, bistros, brasseries and modest neighbourhood restaurants, right up to fine-dining places with Michelin stars. The Parisian restaurant scene is characterised by its unique and atmospheric bistros and brasseries, which continue to be a mainstay

STAYING IN PARIS

MONTALEMBERT
3 Rue de Montalembert, 6th arrondissement, Paris
Tel +33 1 45 49 68 68
www.montalembert.com
One of the smarter modern hotels in the city – comfortable, friendly and not too big. An open fireplace in the lounge area is a bonus during winter. Located in the ever-groovy Saint-Germain-des-Pres district, it's a short walk to all the sights.

APARTMENTS TO RENT
www.parisflats.com.au; www.rentapart.com
An apartment is perfect when staying for a week or more (and wanting to cook!).

ARTUS HOTEL
34 Rue de Buci, 6th arrondissement, Paris
Tel +33 1 43 29 07 20
www.artushotel.com
With a fab location right near Odeon, this hotel boasts modern design and a great village atmosphere.

for daily dining. In Les Halles, I adore suppertime at Au Pied de Cochon, where you can eat from the daily set-price menu without going broke, and indulging in the timeless grandeur of Le Grand Vefour. Near the busy train stations of Gare du Nord and Gare de l'Est is the always-bustling Brasserie Flo, where I can never resist ordering some smooth-as-silk pate and brioche. On the Left Bank, try a light salad and glass of wine at Les Deux Magots on Boulevard Saint-Germain (where I once sat next to Karl Lagerfeld and had fun texting all our fashion friends to make them envious); or revel in the Gallic charm and consistency of Allard, the definitive Parisienne bistro.

More recently, I became a big fan of Joel Robuchon's L'Atelier, which is also on the Left Bank, near Rue du Bac. The interior is decked out like a sushi bar (you sit at stools around a counter with the open kitchen in a glass box behind) with a distinctive Japanese aesthetic, but the food is unashamedly modern French, taken to a new, lighter level. Little plates appeared in quick succession as Margie and I sat and ordered as we went: white anchovies (Spanish boquerones) with an eggplant confit; scampi ravioli with truffle; a sinful grilled duck foie gras with roasted peach; and a perfectly cooked rouget (red mullet) fillet with olives, tomato and a dash of chilli. The waiters noted our appreciation and poured tastes of different wines for us to try with each dish. It was a sublime experience.

Born on 14 July, Margie is a Bastille baby. When we decided to celebrate her birthday in Paris one year, our visit coincided with the bicentenary of the French Revolution in 1989. It was a wild time to be there. We took a small studio room in the main street of Ile St Louis, one of the two islands in the River Seine. The street noise was constant but, as they say, you can sleep when you're dead! Spectacular fireworks were launched from the Eiffel Tower and all the bridges along the Seine, and street parties seemed to spring up everywhere. Every restaurant, bistro, cafe and bar was in a celebratory mood and we acquired a serious taste for champagne. We started the week with an extraordinary degustation menu at chef

PARIS FOOD MARKETS

What I love about Paris more than anything is seeing people doing their daily shopping for food at the many street markets, with their alluring displays and amazing diversity of fresh product. Parisians are obsessed with the provenance of their food. Exchanges are lively, and the vendors are generally happy to tell you all about the origins of the produce, what its season is and how to use it – always interspersed with a few laughs from the stall holders if your pronunciation is slightly out.

Rue Montorgueil, near Rue Montmartre, 1st arrondissement
The only existing street market left over from the old Les Halles days – look for the great espresso bar halfway along the street. Closed on Monday.

Marche des Enfants Rouges, 39 Rue de Bretagne, 3rd arrondissement
A Marais landmark, this is the city's oldest street market – now a wonderfully authentic farmers' market. Open daily.

Rue Mouffetard, 5th arrondissement
Daily local street market.

Boulevard Raspail, between Rue du Cherche Midi and Rue de Rennes, 6th arrondissement
Regular street market Tuesday and Friday; organic markets on Sunday.

Rue de Buci, off Boulevard Saint-Germain, 6th arrondissement
Daily street market.

Boulevard Richard Lenoir, 11th arrondissement
Held on Thursdays and Sundays, this market has a diverse array of produce.

Boulevard de Belleville, 11th arrondissement
This Saturday street market is one of my favourites for a taste of Asia.

Place d'Aligre (behind the Bastille and the new opera house), 12th arrondissement
Daily street market that's considered to have the best fresh produce in the city, with incredible variety; when in season, the tomatoes are a knock out.

Barbes Market
Boulevard de la Chapelle, opposite Lariboisiere hospital, 18th arrondissement
On Wednesday and Saturday, this side street is transformed into a North African souk.

Dejean Market
Rue Dejean, 18th arrondissement
Full of edible treasures, this market will transport you to Africa. Closed on Monday.

Alain Passard's renowned Arpege restaurant, where we struck up a friendship with our waiter and the sommelier during the course of the evening, and we all ended up sharing a bottle of wine from the year of Margie's birth. Somehow, dinner finished with breakfast at the legendary Cafe de Flore on Boulevard Saint-Germain.

As it happened, some friends of ours from Adelaide, Darrin and Maree, were spending the year travelling around France so they joined us in Paris for the rest of the week. Equally fond of food, we worked our way through the entire menu at La Maison du Chocolat, where everything is made with chocolate: silky hot chocolate in large cups, mousse, biscuits, ice cream, sorbet, the list goes on. I remember needing a very long walk afterwards. Then there was our daily pilgrimage to one of the Berthillon ice-cream shops on Ile Saint Louis – it was the height of summer after all, and their wild strawberry (fraise des bois) ice cream is a seasonal specialty. It was a week of enviable gastronomy.

EATING IN PARIS

L'ATELIER DE JOEL ROBUCHON
5 Rue de Montalembert, 7th arrondissement
Tel +33 1 42 22 56 56
Perfect small plates, ideal for the curious diner; reservations taken for lunch and 6.30 p.m. sitting only.

ARPEGE
84 Rue de Varenne, 7th arrondissement
Tel +33 1 47 05 09 06
www.alain-passard.com
At this Michelin three-starred restaurant, chef Alain Passard cooks ethereally light food: his vegetable infusions are gorgeous and all his entrees with foie gras are to die for.

GUY SAVOY
18 Rue Troyon, 17th arrondissement
Tel +33 1 43 80 40 61
Traditional French cuisine, showcasing the finest seasonal ingredients. I remember a brilliant dish of mussels pan-fried with tiny fresh mousseron mushrooms in their natural juices. Guy Savoy called it 'de la terre et de la mer' (literally, from the earth and the sea), and the flavours were a perfect embodiment of that.

RESTAURANT D'HELENE AND SALON D'HELENE
4 Rue d'Assas, 6th arrondissement
Tel +33 1 42 22 00 11
I love the street-level salon here: it has a more casual feel, warm and informed service, and great tapas-style tasting plates from innovative Basque-born chef Helene Darroze. The upstairs restaurant is more formal – and significantly more expensive.

404
69 Rue des Gravilliers (off Boulevard Sebastapol), 3rd arrondissement
Tel +33 1 42 74 57 81
The great family-style Moroccan food here is the best in town, with wonderful tajines. Mourad Mazouz made his name here before going on to carve out a niche in London with Momo and Sketch.

DONG HUONG
14 Rue Louis-Bonnet, 11th arrondissement
Vietnamese menu with authentic Asian flavours – always jam-packed with locals.

AU PIED DE COCHON
6 Rue de Coquilliere, 1st arrondissement
Tel +33 1 40 13 77 00
www.pieddecochon.com
Quintessential Parisian bistro that's open 24 hours.

BRASSERIE FLO
7 Cour des Petites-Ecuries, 10th arrondissement
Tel +33 1 47 70 13 59
www.flobrasserie.com
The specialty at this old-style brasserie is choucroute for two – a mound of sauerkraut with boiled ham, bacon and sausage.

LES DEUX MAGOTS
6 Place St-Germain-des-Pres, 6th arrondissement
Tel +33 1 45 48 55 25
www.lesdeuxmagots.fr
Once the haunt of the intelligentsia – Jean-Paul Sartre and Simone de Beauvoir were regulars – this is now a place to see and be seen. Nab a pavement table and watch the world go by.

ALLARD
41 Rue St-Andre-des-Arts, 6th arrondissement
Tel +33 1 43 26 48 23
This is the place to come for classic bistro dishes of snails, foie gras or frogs' legs.

LE GRAND VEFOUR
17 Rue de Beaujolais, 1st arrondissement
Tel +33 1 42 96 56 27
This lavishly decorated restaurant is a temple to French gastronomy. Specialties include lamb with star anise and Breton lobster. Save room for one of the spectacular dessert plates.

Cruising the city after dinner when the streets were quieter, we would drive by all the famous landmarks and sights, the sensational architecture brilliantly illuminated under the night sky and looking even more spectacular than during the day. One of my favourite squares is the 17th-century Place des Vosges in the heart of the Marais, with its serenity and perfectly symmetrical arcades. A few minutes walk from the square on the other side of St Paul metro is a hidden pocket of interesting specialty food shops, such as Izrael (the best spice shop in Paris), an olive oil shop and another that sells smoked salmon and cured fish products.

Each arrondissement seems to be stamped with a unique personality, which is reflected in its food culture. The Latin Quarter has a maze of small back streets that are home to many of the city's Moroccan and Tunisian restaurants, sandwiched between book shops and antique furniture stores around Rue Saint Jacques and Boulevard Saint Michel. African food shops can be found in the 10th arrondissement, off Rue du Faubourg Saint Denis, and also up in Belleville, in the 19th arrondissement, where the Arabs compete with the Vietnamese for space. For paper-thin Breton crepes, head to the 14th, behind Boulevard Montparnasse and around Boulevard Raspail; the Algerian, Senegalese and Middle Eastern shops are clustered near Montmartre, with its Barbes and Dejean markets and halal butcher shops; and the Eastern European Jewish shops are in the Marais, in the 4th arrondissement. Chinatown, in the 13th arrondissement, just beyond Place d'Italie, makes me feel right at home – it's just like Chinatown anywhere, only the signs in French make it even more exotic. The Vietnamese have made their home where the 11th meets the 19th, near Belleville, with a most diverse array of shops, bars and eating places.

Even though this city lives and breathes food, there are so many more dimensions to it, just waiting to be discovered. Apart from excelling in architecture, art and design, Paris is also a retail-therapy paradise. It is simply impossible to visit and not shop! I love to check out the inspired designs at the cutting-edge Colette store on Rue Saint Honore, find a bargain in La Samaritaine department store right by the Pont Neuf, browse and drool through the gourmet-

SPECIALTY FOOD STORES IN PARIS

PIERRE HERME PATISSERIE
72 Rue Bonaparte, 6th arrondissement (at Saint Sulpice)
Tel +33 1 43 54 47 77
The most celebrated patissier in France. It's worth a pilgrimage to any of his stores for the most sensational pastries imaginable, which all look like jewels – and the packaging is just as stylish.

LADUREE
16 Rue Royale, 8th arrondissement
Tel +33 1 42 60 21 79
21 Rue Bonaparte, 6th arrondissement
Tel +33 1 44 07 64 87
www.laduree.fr
For simply the best macaroons in the world and one of the loveliest rooms to take afternoon tea – a total Parisian indulgence.

BERTHILLON
31 Rue Saint-Louis-en-L'Ile, 4th arrondissement
Tel +33 1 43 54 31 61
Renowned Parisian ice-cream shops scattered around Ile Saint Louis and beyond, with the best hand-made ice creams and sorbets. There's a huge list of flavours – the chocolate ice cream is the smoothest and creamiest you will ever eat, but you must try the fraise des bois in summer.

IZRAEL
30 Rue Francois-Miron, 4th arrondissement
Tel +33 1 42 72 66 23
This amazing spice shop in the Marais is jam-packed with intriguing produce, and sources spices and olives from around the world.

LA FERME SAINT HUBERT
18 Rue Vignon (a side street behind Fauchon, off Place de la Madeleine), 8th arrondissement
Tel +33 1 45 53 15 77
Fabulous cheese shop stocking regional specialties, plus a small restaurant with a cheese menu.

MARIAGE FRERES
13 Rue des Grand-Augustins, 6th arrondissement
Tel +33 1 40 51 82 50
www.mariagefreres.com
One of my favourite tea houses – afternoon tea in the salon is one of the necessary pleasures of Paris.

LA MAISON DU CHOCOLAT
225 Rue du Faubourg St Honore, 1st arrondissement
Tel +33 1 42 27 39 44
www.lamaisonduchocolat.com
Robert Linxe's empire now has branches worldwide selling the finest hand-made French chocolates, but a pilgrimage to one of the five Paris stores is a must for chocoholics.

food floor of Galeries Lafayette, the boutique food shops around Place de la Madeleine or the luxury stores around the Champs Elysees. I also have a bit of a weakness for perfume, and the perfume shops in Paris are the best in the world. If I had another life, I think I would like to be a perfumier, using my olfactory senses in a different way.

And if it all gets too much, you can always spend a day being pampered and sipping mint tea at Hammam de la Grande Mosquee, a terrific Arab bathhouse in the 5th arrondissement, near Place Monge. (Check your days first, though: it's women-only on Monday, Wednesday, Thursday, Friday and Saturday; and men-only on Tuesday and Sunday.)

Paris in early summer is unbeatable but to make the most of our time in France, we decided it was time for some rural experiences. As we quickly discovered, travelling around France automatically involves food and wine, and it has long been asserted that the heart of French gastronomy lies not in the cities, but in the countryside. Heading west to Normandy, following the path of the Seine, we got to eat runny, ripe Camembert and Livarot cheeses, and to stock up on the best butter in the world. We continued west to the rugged peninsula of Brittany, with its abundant seafood. The local salt-marsh Fines de Claire oysters were some of the best-tasting I've ever had, and the tiny black mussels were so sweet and full of sea flavour.

Heading south-east of Paris, our perception of French food continued to expand after a short visit to Dijon, the home of mustard. After spending some time in the local shops we enjoyed a simple but delicious roadside picnic of sliced ham and mustard on baguette. Our visit coincided with Easter – and spring lamb, normally a rare and highly prized treat, has a starring role in the festive celebrations. I recall eating tiny cutlets cooked perfectly pink, with a salad of bitter greens including dandelion, land cress and witlof.

One of my favourite culinary memories is a side-trip we took to Lyon, home to the great burgundies of the world, in January 1983. There we made the pilgrimage to a gastronomic shrine to modern French cooking – Paul Bocuse's flagship restaurant, L'Auberge du Pont de Collonges, a few kilometres from our base in Lyon. The meal was an incredible series of firsts for us: truffle; succulent bone marrow wrapped in braised radicchio leaves; chicken cooked in pig's bladder then pierced at the table to release its rich aromas; appreciating the etiquette of cheese service, as a prelude to dessert; and surrendering to the carefully designed flow of a degustation menu. Sure, this requires trust, but the benefits can be outstanding. In fact, we enjoyed our meal so much that we returned the next night to taste the things we missed the first time around. I remember it had been snowing and, to my mind, the best thing to do in such weather is to eat, drink and stay warm by the fire. The experience of dining at Paul Bocuse's restaurant was so profound that it planted the seed for our entry into the professional culinary world and restaurant life. It started the dream. In those days, acclaimed French chefs were pretty vocal about the importance of premium produce and the commitment to excellence, a call to arms that has since resonated around the world with chefs and cooks who share these same values. Black winter truffles from Perigord, for example, are one of life's must-haves, with their elusive and earthy pungency. It pays to be in France during the short season from December to February, to eat Bresse chicken roasted with truffles under its skin or added to a broth (as we were lucky enough to have at L'Auberge du Pont de Collonges). I remember getting excited once when I saw them at the markets in the middle of the year – only to find that while the summer ones look fantastic, they have almost no taste.

Lyon proved to be a food-lover's paradise and, at the time, we thought we had hit the jackpot. This was also where we experienced the home cooking of Lyonnais women in traditional bistros and small auberges (inns), making us envious of the region's rural bounty. Menus were often dispensed with in favour of the set menu of the day, which might include such rustic dishes as sausage baked in brioche, breakfast waffles and potato galette. Walking

EATING IN AND AROUND LYON

L'AUBERGE DU PONT DE COLLONGES
40 Quai de la Plage, Collonges au Mont d'Or, near Lyon
Tel +33 04 72 42 90 90
www.bocuse.fr
An extraordinary dining experience is assured at Paul Bocuse's Michelin three-starred restaurant.

BERNACHON
42 Cour Franklin-Roosevelt, Lyon
Tel +33 04 78 24 37 98
The truffles at this traditional French chocolaterie are to die for.

around town one day, we discovered we were staying right near Bernachon, a beautiful chocolate shop, so we ate chocolate truffles as snacks throughout the day and took a couple of boxes with us when we left. We quickly decided that we must come back when it was warmer, to fully appreciate the diversity and beauty of France.

On our next trip we explored Burgundy and the Loire Valley. Heading south-east from Paris, we drove our little deux chevaux through the hills to the heart of the chablis region, Auxerre and Epoisses, where we sampled some gorgeously stinky ripe Epoisses de Bourgogne cheese, then on to Gevrey Chambertin, Nuits Saint Georges, Meursault and Beaune, beginning a life-long passion for pinot noir wines. Intoxicating times indeed! Just to the west, the Loire Valley boasts stunning chateaux and grand estates, and the muted tones of the countryside change dramatically with each season. We discovered sancerre wines, and lingered in the main towns of Orleans and Tours, as well as the smaller country town of La Fleche in the Western Loire, which has a terrific produce market on Sunday mornings – if you're here in autumn, check out the locally grown garlic and chestnuts. Some of France's finest goat's cheeses are also made in this region, and many small producers sell direct from their farms.

Further south, we spent a few weeks exploring the rugged landscapes of the Auvergne region, staying in the Ardeche Valley, a few kilometres from Aubenas. What a contrast: limestone hills, stark granite outcrops and picturesque medieval villages perched precariously on the edges of precipices. Our modest lodgings were in a converted stone barn down the paddock from the main farmhouse. The barn sat in the middle of a cherry orchard above the river, a tributary of the Rhone. We were able to buy river trout from the fishermen to cook for dinner, many of the farms sold their hand-made cheeses, and we would walk along the lane each morning to buy freshly baked bread from the boulangerie. We passed the time lazing in the garden, taking long walks or driving to nearby villages to find produce, drinking bottles of local vin de pays wine – and cooking. This was a hiatus in my working life: idyllic months living in Europe between closing the door on the teaching profession and returning to Australia to take up the challenge of restaurant life. It gave me time to think and ponder and plan.

We drove south through Provence and the Cote d'Azur, stopping at Carpentras and Arles, whose markets overflowed with tiny green puy lentils, walnuts and fabulous sausages perfumed with garlic. The hills were covered in wild lavender, savoury, verbena and sunflowers – aromas that define the region and add a distinctive flavour to the lamb raised on these pastures. A detour west along the coast, almost to the Spanish border, brought us to the rustic town of Collioure, just before Port-Vendres. Our reason for visiting was a predictable one: the best anchovies in France are produced here – laboriously processed by hand, just as they are in Spain's Basque region at the Ortiz factory. If you are ever in this area, try and get hold of a tin of Anchois Desclaux, the best brand, which come in round blue tins. Once you have tasted a premium product such as this, where you can literally taste the care that's gone into it, there is no going back. Sadly, it is becoming a dying art, and the viability of the industry is also threatened by over-fishing. Banyuls-sur-Mer, on the other side of Port-Vendres, is the source of another of my favourite tastes from this region. Banyuls red wine vinegar is made from grenache grapes, and a splash in a salad dressing or added to baked fish can make all the difference.

Back in Provence, we soon realised that Provence is to France what Tuscany is to Italy: eternally popular and everyone's favourite. Many farmhouses have been carefully restored and converted into luxury accommodation, some with cooking schools attached. The food along the coast has a strong Mediterranean influence and bears a strong resemblance to coastal Italian and Spanish cuisine, relying heavily on seafood, tomatoes, garlic, artichokes, herbs and olive oil. Pistou is stirred into Provencale soups and, across the Italian border, Genoa

STAYING IN PROVINCIAL FRANCE

GITES RURAUX
www.gite.com
www.rentagite.com
Country houses for rent.

VILLA FLORENTINE
25 Montee Saint-Barthelemy, Lyon
Tel +33 4 72 56 56 56
www.villaflorentine.com
Luxurious respite that's perfectly located in the old town overlooking the Roman amphitheatre.

is home to pesto; both sauces are made with basil, garlic and oil, and perfectly capture the taste of summer.

One of the greatest and most sought-after of all French products would have to be champagne. As Oscar Wilde memorably said, 'Only those with no imagination cannot find a good reason to drink champagne.' For me, the world is definitely a better place for having champagne in it. Tucked away to the east of Paris, in the Marne Valley, the hilly terrain of the champagne zone stretches from the main city of Reims and winds down to Epernay and the smaller surrounding villages such as Bouzy, Dizy, Ay and Hautvillers that sit within the appellation. (Of course, all sparkling wine made outside the designated champagne region is just that – sparkling wine!) These fertile lands are carpeted with vineyards; in fact, the whole place just lives and breathes champagne, and it's impressive to see an entire community working collectively toward a single purpose. The method of producing the delicate effervescent bubbles that have tickled our collective palates and imaginations for generations was first perfected in the early 18th century by Dom Perignon, a Benedictine monk at the Hautvillers Abbey, near Epernay. At the time, wine making was an intrinsic part of monastic life and religious duty. Requiring unparalleled attention to detail in its production, champagne elicits fervent support from the people who live in this exclusive region – maybe that's why they all seem so convivial.

In his classic survey, *The Food of France*, Waverley Root states that the champagne region presents us with 'the anomaly of being the only important wine region in the country which has not produced on its own soil an appropriate cuisine to accompany its wine'. As a cook, that does not bother me in the least, since the region has given us a wine so versatile it can be matched with foods from all over the world. Naturally, regional dishes of the Marne have evolved to preserve local honour, largely following the philosophy that prestige has to carry through from the glass to the plate, so items of luxury have found a permanent place on the tables of the champagne region. It is common – and expected – that menus will feature caviar, lobster, truffle, foie gras and the like. The restaurants in Reims and Epernay feature cuvees from all the champagne houses on their wine lists, and it is quite natural to serve champagne throughout the entire meal.

In our early restaurant days, Margie and I were invited for a private tasting at the house of Bollinger in the small village of Ay. We sat in a glass atrium in their very impressive 19th-century mansion, the sun was streaming in, and one of the Bollinger heirs was offering tastes of several vintages at 10 o'clock in the morning – now that's what I call a great way to kick start the day! Lunch at a local restaurant followed, naturally with more champagne. Bollinger remains one of the only family-owned and -operated champagne houses, and was our house champagne at Paramount for many years. We also had an invitation from Moet et Chandon to stay at their exclusive Chateau de Saran country estate, a few kilometres from Epernay. It was all completely over the top: afternoon tea on the terrace with champagne, a sumptuous dinner with liveried service and a showcase of several fine vintages. The next day began with a drive through the surrounding vineyard-covered hills, followed by a tour of the Moet et Chandon cellars, a massive maze-like network of chalky limestone tunnels that originated in Roman times and provide the perfect climate for ageing and fermenting champagne.

Having developed a high regard and immense affection for the champagne region over the years, I was thrilled when, in 2004, Dom Perignon's chef de cave, Richard Geoffroy, invited London chefs David Thompson, John Campbell, Rainer Becker, Andrew Turner and me to challenge their champagne with our myriad food styles and flavours. Our mission was to provide a tasting menu for dinner at the chateau, followed by a different menu for lunch the next day at Trianon, the lovely pavilion opposite the main gates of the maison. This was no mean feat, given we were plied with champagne (DP, of course) from the moment we stepped onto the private jet that flew us across the Channel. After a lovely lunch, we went straight to the chateau kitchens to prepare our many dishes for dinner that night (our glasses were kept topped up throughout). We sat at the table with Richard and his select team to taste whatever vintage they thought would best complement each dish. Sometimes it took a few different tries to reveal the perfect match. Such a tough job – one that I could happily do every day for the rest of my working life . . .

Chefs' dinner menu

Marinated scallops with yuzu, seaweed and imperial Oscetra caviar
Tuna sashimi with ginger blossom, toasted sesame and shiro miso
Pork, scallop and roasted cashew salad
Steamed chicken, lobster and foie gras with eggplant and spiced orange
Salmon mi-cuit, spiced lentils and ballantine of foie gras

David came out with all guns blazing, in true Thai style – he served all these dishes together, in the vain hope of causing perplexity:
Oysters with sweet fish sauce and deep-fried shallots
Clear chicken soup with ceps and Thai basil
Charolais beef stir-fried with green curry
Cured sea bass and red shallots
Raspberry ripple
Strawberry and pink grapefruit trifle, Campari jelly

Lunch menu at Trianon
Blood sausage, crispy cured pork, beetroot and artichoke foam
Port-marinated foie gras, pistachio bread, lemon curd and balsamic glaze
Roasted diver scallop, cauliflower puree, raisins and candied cauliflower
Salted salmon, pork hock, green mango and salmon roe salad
Rib-eye beef, ceps and fried garlic
Apricot tart with creme fraiche ice cream
Coconut jasmine blossom jellies

I get a real kick out of matching flavour profiles with the many different styles of champagne. The possibilities are virtually endless, and extend way beyond the conventional territory of oysters, caviar, shellfish, mousses, terrines, fines herbes and emulsion sauces to ingredients like soy sauce, ginger, galangal, sesame, miso, peanuts and cashews, roasted coconut, yuzu, basil, green chilli, shiso and white pepper. Exciting times indeed.

I leave it to champagne matriarch Madame Lily Bollinger to have the last word on this magical drop that embodies the excellence of French cuisine: 'I drink it when I'm happy and when I'm sad . . . I trifle with it if I'm not hungry and drink it when I am. Otherwise I never touch it – unless I'm thirsty.' A votre sante!

SIMON'S BLACK TRUFFLE SANDWICHES

I have not given quantities here. The idea is a very simple one and the amount you make is dependent on the number of people you are preparing for and, more importantly, the amount of fresh winter black truffle you have. Simon, a dear colleague, makes these for us at Christmas when the first batch of French winter black truffles arrive, so Christmas in Sydney has come to be associated with this little taste of luxury. If you have lashed out and bought a fresh truffle, make sure you buy the very best French butter as its flavour is of paramount importance in these sandwiches. A 50 g truffle should be ample to satisfy eight people without making you a pauper. Of course, black truffles of equal measure from Manjimup in Western Australia are now appearing on our market in June and July, so you can treat yourself twice a year if you are a truffle lover.

good-quality sourdough bread
Lescure 'demi sel' French butter
black truffle, shaved
sea salt

Preheat the oven to 200°C. Cut the bread into very thin slices, remove the crusts and cut into even-size fingers. Toast the bread lightly on one side only.

Lay the slices toasted-side down and slather the non-toasted side liberally with butter. Smother half the buttered slices with truffle slices then sprinkle with salt. Cover with the remaining buttered slices to make sandwiches and lay on a flat baking tray.

Bake for 3–4 minutes until you smell the truffle aroma. Serve immediately.

AN EXTRAVAGANT OYSTER PLATE

During our Paramount days, we offered a 'six-pack oyster plate' – each oyster from a different region and prepared in its own manner. In Australia, we have Sydney rock oysters, ocean-dwelling Pacifics and native Angasi oysters; because each species is grown in different parts of the country across various seasons, each has a unique flavour. This dish is an extravagant gesture, and one that takes time to prepare, but your efforts will be truly appreciated by oyster lovers. Adjust the quantities according to the number of serves you are preparing.

OYSTER AND SHIRO MISO BROTH
250 ml Dashi Stock (see Essentials)
2 teaspoons shiro (white) miso paste
1 teaspoon mirin
1 teaspoon sake
20 ml light soy sauce
2 teaspoons Ginger Juice (see Essentials)
1 Angasi (or Belon) oyster
shiso cress, snipped
kinome leaf (optional)
chopped chives

Bring the dashi stock to simmering point then whisk in the miso paste until dissolved. Pass through a fine mesh sieve and season with mirin, sake, soy and ginger juice.

Put the oyster in the bottom of a small serving cup or shot glass and pour the miso broth over the top. Add a leaf of shiso cress and kinome and a sprinkle of chopped chives.

TEA-SMOKED OYSTER WITH GREEN MANGO AND MINT
very finely shredded green mango
mint leaves, finely shredded
finely shredded makrut lime leaf
coriander cress, snipped
Green Chilli Dressing (see Essentials)
1 Angasi or Pacific oyster, in the shell
Tea-smoking Mix (see Essentials)
small betel leaf
roasted peanuts, crushed

Mix the green mango with the mint, lime leaf, cress and chilli dressing. Leave to marinate while the oysters are smoked.

Lay the oysters in their shell in a steamer tray. Line a wok with foil and sit over a high heat. Add the tea-smoking mix and as it starts to smoke, sit the steamer tray over the wok and cover with a tight-fitting lid. Smoke for 3 minutes – just enough to warm the oysters and impart a slight tannin tea flavour.

Remove the tray from the wok, allowing the burnt offerings to cool before discarding.

Add the tea-smoked oyster to the green mango salad and toss to combine. Arrange the oyster and its salad on a betel leaf and sprinkle with crushed peanuts. >>

FROM BACK TO FRONT: OYSTER AND SHIRO MISO BROTH; TEA-SMOKED OYSTER WITH GREEN MANGO AND MINT; SALT AND PEPPER OYSTER FRITTER WITH FENNEL AND BLACK BEAN; OYSTER WITH CUCUMBER WASABI JELLY AND LIME GRANITA; OYSTER WITH GREEN TEA NOODLES AND SEAWEED; OYSTER AND PICKLED SHIITAKE MUSHROOM WON TON >

MEN 3.3.3 elBulli

<< SALT AND PEPPER OYSTER FRITTER WITH FENNEL AND BLACK BEAN

tissue-thin fennel shavings
finely shredded daikon radish
daikon cress, snipped
red shallot, finely sliced
vegetable oil, for deep-frying
1 large Pacific oyster
egg white
Black Pepper Salt Crust (see Essentials)

BLACK BEAN LIME DRESSING

5 g salted black beans, rinsed
1 golden shallot, minced
½ teaspoon minced ginger
¼ teaspoon freshly ground black pepper
2 drops of sesame oil
3 teaspoons light soy sauce
2 teaspoons mirin
2 teaspoons fresh lime juice, strained
25 ml extra virgin olive oil

To make the dressing, place all the ingredients in a bowl and whisk until combined.

Mix the fennel, daikon, cress and shallot with enough black bean dressing to moisten.

Heat the oil to 180°C in a saucepan or small wok. Dip the oyster in the egg white, then coat in the black pepper salt crust. Fry the oyster fritter for 50 seconds until crisp, then drain on paper towel.

Arrange the fennel and black bean salad in a small serving spoon and sit the oyster fritter on top so it remains crisp.

OYSTER WITH CUCUMBER WASABI JELLY AND LIME GRANITA

Cucumber Wasabi Jelly (see Essentials)
finely diced cucumber
finely diced avocado
wasabi flying fish roe
1 Sydney rock oyster
shiro (white) soy sauce
creme fraiche

LIME GRANITA

100 ml sauvignon blanc
25 ml verjuice
25 ml fresh lime juice, strained
40 ml Sugar Syrup (see Essentials)
½ teaspoon minced makrut lime zest

To make the lime granita, mix the ingredients together in a bowl until combined. Pour into a shallow tray and freeze for 5 hours, stirring with a fork every hour. Don't let it sit in the freezer for too long or it will become too icy – the texture should remain quite slushy.

Chop the cucumber jelly into small dice and mix with the diced cucumber and avocado so there is an even amount of each. Add ¼ teaspoon wasabi flying fish roe.

Brush the oyster with soy sauce to season. Spoon enough cucumber jelly mix into a small spoon, then sit the oyster on top. Place a tiny dollop of creme fraiche on top of the oyster then spoon on a little of the lime granita.

OYSTER WITH GREEN TEA NOODLES AND SEAWEED

1 Sydney rock oyster
Ponzu Soy Mayonnaise (see Essentials)
green tea noodles (cha soba), cooked
sesame seaweed salad
threads of Pickled Ginger (see Essentials)
snipped chives
Sterling caviar

Shuck the oyster, reserving the strained juice. Add a little oyster juice to the mayonnaise for extra flavour.

Toss the noodles with the mayonnaise, seaweed salad, pickled ginger and chives. Toss the oyster through the mayonnaise to lightly coat.

Arrange the noodles in a small serving spoon and sit the dressed oyster in the centre. Top with a tiny dollop of caviar.

OYSTER AND PICKLED SHIITAKE MUSHROOM WON TON

slices of Pickled Shiitake Mushrooms (see Essentials)
fresh water chestnut, finely diced
Chinese black bacon, cut into tiny julienne strips and grilled until crisp
1 Pacific oyster
2 won ton wrappers
vegetable oil, for deep-frying

Drain the pickled mushrooms to remove any excess liquid, then mix the mushroom slices with the water chestnut, crisp ham sticks and oyster.

Cut the won ton wrappers into rounds, using a 6 cm pastry cutter. Lay a wrapper on the bench, wet the edges with water, then spoon the oyster and mushroom stuffing into the centre. Cover with another wrapper and press the edges together to seal, making a won ton pillow.

Heat the oil to 180°C in a saucepan and fry the oyster won ton for 1 minute. Flip over and fry for another 30 seconds. Drain on paper towel.

TOMATO SOUP WITH CRAB AND HORSERADISH SANDWICHES

The purity of flavour of the stock infused with the clear tomato water makes this a delightful soup, perfect for warm-weather eating. Tomatoes and crab both have a definitive sweetness to them, making them ideal partners in various preparations. I season the soup with the French fleur de sel from Brittany as it has a distinctive iodine 'sea' taste that makes it just right here.

2 × blue swimmer crabs, cleaned and chopped into quarters
1.6 litres Fish Stock (see Essentials)
2 small red chillies, sliced lengthways
6 large ripe tomatoes, roasted
500 ml Tomato Water (see Essentials)
2 teaspoons fleur de sel or other sea salt
8 small red cherry tomatoes, blanched and peeled
8 small yellow plum tomatoes, blanched and peeled
2 teaspoons chervil leaves

CRAB SANDWICHES
1 baguette, sliced into thin rounds
40 ml extra virgin olive oil
200 g picked crabmeat
2 teaspoons grated fresh horseradish
2 tablespoons Alioli (see Essentials)
2 teaspoons snipped chives
2 teaspoons chervil leaves
½ teaspoon sea salt
¼ teaspoon freshly ground white pepper

Combine the chopped crabs, fish stock, chilli and roasted tomatoes with their juices in a large saucepan. Bring to simmering point over gentle heat, so the flavours have time to infuse and develop. As soon as it reaches simmering point, reduce the heat to the lowest setting so the surface of the stock is hardly moving and cook gently for 30 minutes. Pass through a fine mesh sieve, pressing to extract as much juice as possible. Discard the solids.

Heat the tomato water in a saucepan and simmer gently until reduced by a third. Add the essence to the strained soup and bring back to simmering point. Season with salt, taste and adjust if necessary.

To make the sandwiches, preheat the oven to 160°C. Brush the bread slices with olive oil and lay on a baking tray in a single layer. Bake for 15 minutes until crisp and lightly golden.

Mix the crabmeat with the remaining ingredients in a bowl until combined. Lay half the toasts on the work bench and cover with the crab mix. Cover with the remaining toast slices and press to secure, making neat sandwiches.

Divide the peeled tomatoes among the bowls, ladle on the hot soup and sprinkle with chervil leaves. Arrange the crab sandwiches in a neat stack on a plate next to the soup and serve.

SERVES 4

GOOSE LIVER PARFAIT WITH SAUTERNES JELLY AND PICKLED PORK SALAD

This assembly is a celebration of texture. I have fond memories of some brilliant charcuterie plates I have shared in France and here in Australia, at restaurants where they take the time to prepare each component in the time-honoured manner. You can buy pickled pork hock from your butcher and walnut sourdough from any decent sourdough bakery these days, which cuts down the preparation time somewhat. In place of the Iberian ham, you could use slices of cured goose (or duck) breast, made in the style of prosciutto, if you prefer.

8 wafer-thin slices walnut sourdough, crusts removed
20 ml walnut oil
4 slices Iberian ham, cut in half lengthways

SAUTERNES JELLY
210 ml sauternes
3 g gelatine leaves, softened in cold water

LIVER PARFAIT
185 g unsalted butter
2 small white onions, diced
3 small cloves garlic, sliced
50 g speck, diced
60 g fatty pancetta, diced
1 tablespoon thyme leaves, chopped
400 g goose livers, cleaned
50 ml cognac
25 ml Banyuls vinegar
2 teaspoons sea salt
1 teaspoon freshly ground white pepper
75 ml pouring (35%) cream

PICKLED PORK SALAD
80 g pickled pork, boiled for 3 hours until the meat is soft and pliable
1 thick slice walnut sourdough, crusts removed and cut into 5 mm cubes
20 ml walnut oil
½ small stick celery, finely sliced
½ punnet celery cress, snipped
4 cornichons, finely sliced on the diagonal
1 red shallot, finely diced
1 teaspoon aged balsamic vinegar
½ teaspoon sea salt >>

<< To make the jelly, heat the sauternes in a saucepan to simmering point then stir in the softened gelatine until dissolved. Allow to cool completely.

To make the parfait, heat 20 g of the butter in a frying pan and saute the onion and garlic until softened. Add the speck, pancetta and thyme and cook until it starts to colour. Remove from the pan.

Heat another 20 g of the butter in the same pan and saute the livers for 2 minutes each side until they begin to brown. Add the cognac and vinegar and cook for another minute until the alcohol has burned off, then remove the pan from the heat. The livers should still be very rare and pink in the centre. Put the livers and their juices and the pancetta mix in a food processor, add the salt and pepper and blend until smooth.

Roughly chop the remaining butter. With the motor running, add the butter, piece by piece and then add the cream and pulse just until combined – don't overwork the parfait at this stage or it will split. Taste and adjust the seasoning if necessary. Pass the parfait through a conical sieve, pushing through small amounts at a time so as not to overwork the mixture.

Spoon or pipe the parfait into serving dishes or little pots until three-quarters full. Refrigerate for an hour until set. Pour the cooled (but not set) sauternes jelly on top to fill the pots, then cover and refrigerate for another hour or two, until the jelly is firm.

To prepare the pickled pork salad, preheat the oven to 150°C. Shred the meat from the pickled pork hock. Toss the bread cubes through half the walnut oil, lay on a baking tray and toast in the oven for about 10 minutes until crisp, to make crunchy croutons. Keep the oven on at this temperature for the walnut bread wafers.

Mix the shredded meat with the croutons, celery, cress, cornichons and shallot and add the remaining walnut oil, balsamic vinegar and salt to lightly coat.

Lay the walnut sourdough slices on a baking tray and brush with walnut oil. Toast in the oven until crisp. Place a slice of ham on top of each toasted wafer and return to the oven for one more minute so the ham is gently heated, bringing out its flavour.

To serve, set each little parfait pot on a plate with a small pile of pickled pork salad and a small stack of ham and walnut bread wafers to the side.

SERVES 8

CORAL TROUT WITH ROASTED PRAWN CRUST AND FENNEL SALAD

This fish featured on a menu I prepared for a Veuve Cliquot champagne lunch in Sydney in 2005. The low cooking temperature allows the protein in the fish to set while retaining its inherent moisture, leaving the flesh quite translucent and jewel-like – a method that lends itself perfectly to tropical fish. Other warm-water reef fish, such as red emperor, gold band or scarlet snapper, or the rosy flesh of cool-water fish like Arctic char or ocean trout can be used in place of the coral trout.

4 × 100 g coral trout slices, cut from the middle of the fish, skin removed
40 ml olive oil
1 teaspoon sea salt
4 teaspoons freshwater salmon roe

ROASTED PRAWN CRUST
100 g jasmine rice, roasted and ground
40 g dried prawns, roasted and ground
2 dried scallop roes, ground
2 tablespoons shredded mint leaves
2 tablespoons chopped chives
½ teaspoon ground chilli
1 teaspoon sea salt
1 teaspoon freshly ground white pepper

FENNEL SALAD
30 ml fresh lemon juice, strained
30 ml rice vinegar
2 teaspoons anise liqueur
2 teaspoons ground star anise
½ teaspoon sea salt
½ teaspoon freshly ground black pepper
100 ml sunflower oil
2 small fennel bulbs, shaved
1 cucumber, peeled and shaved into thin ribbons
4 green onions, finely sliced
1 tablespoon shredded mint leaves

Put the fish in a cryovac bag or a double layer of zip-lock plastic bags with the oil and salt, then seal to secure. Cook in a pan of water held at 60°C (use a thermometer to monitor the temperature) for 11 minutes. Remove from the water and leave to settle for 3 minutes.

To make the prawn crust, mix the ingredients together in a bowl until combined.

While the fish is cooking, make the fennel salad. Whisk the lemon juice, vinegar, anise liqueur, ground anise, salt, pepper and oil until emulsified. Mix the fennel, cucumber, green onion and mint together in a bowl, add some of the anise dressing and toss gently. Leave to marinate for 5 minutes before serving.

Remove the fish from the bag and place on a tray with the prawn crust. Roll both sides of the fish in the crust to coat.

Arrange the fennel salad on plates and lay the fish on top. Drizzle a little extra dressing around the fish, sit the salmon roe on top and serve.

SERVES 4

ROQUEFORT MOUSSE WITH VEAL SWEETBREADS, HAZELNUT AND PEAR

Veal sweetbreads have become something of a rarity these days, a luxury item well worth their value and far superior to the smaller ones from lamb. You will need to order them from your butcher a few days ahead. In the final year of Paramount, we served this as a cheese course before dessert on one of our tasting menus, but it also makes a wonderful starter. If you don't have time to make the cheese mousse, then you could simply add small chunks of Roquefort to the salad to get a similar flavour profile and balance.

4 veal sweetbreads, blanched and peeled
½ cup plain flour
½ teaspoon sea salt
½ teaspoon freshly ground black pepper
½ teaspoon ground cumin
1 egg, beaten
½ cup panko (Japanese breadcrumbs)
40 g unsalted butter
50 ml olive oil
2 golden shallots, finely diced
60 g hazelnuts, roasted and chopped
½ nashi pear, sliced into thin julienne strips
1 tablespoon chervil leaves
12 small red radicchio leaves, trimmed
4 slices flat pancetta, cut in half to make 8 short strips and grilled until crisp

ROQUEFORT MOUSSE
175 ml milk
125 g Roquefort, crumbled
2 g gelatine leaves, softened in cold water
85 ml pouring (35%) cream, whipped

HAZELNUT TRUFFLE VINAIGRETTE
2 teaspoons verjuice
3 teaspoons Forum cabernet vinegar
¼ teaspoon fresh black or white truffle, minced
40 ml extra virgin olive oil
3 teaspoons hazelnut oil
few drops of white truffle oil
½ teaspoon sea salt
¼ teaspoon freshly ground black pepper

To make the mousse, heat the milk to simmering point then pour over the cheese and whisk until smooth. Add the softened gelatine and stir until dissolved. Pour the mix through a fine mesh sieve and refrigerate until cool. Gently fold in the whipped cream until combined. Spoon the mousse into small dariole moulds and refrigerate for about 3 hours until set.

To make the vinaigrette, whisk all the ingredients together until emulsified.

Break the sweetbreads into 2 cm chunks then roll in flour seasoned with a little salt, pepper and cumin. Dip each piece in egg and then coat with the panko crumbs, shaking off any excess. Heat the butter and oil in a frying pan and fry the sweetbreads for 3 minutes, then turn over and fry for another 3 minutes until cooked through and golden. Drain on paper towel.

To assemble the salad, mix the shallots, hazelnuts, pear strips, chervil and radicchio in a bowl with a little of the vinaigrette. Lay a few sweetbread fritters on each plate and pile the salad on top.

Dip the cheese moulds in hot water to loosen and turn out onto each plate next to the salad. Drizzle a little extra dressing over the cheese, lay the crisp pancetta wafers across the top and serve.

SERVES 4

PEPPERED TUNA NICOISE

Inspired by long and languid summer days along the Mediterranean coast, this is one of my regular 'at home' salads, especially when I want to prepare something light and flavoursome. Any sashimi bar at the fish market or a quality fishmonger will be able to cut the tuna in this manner for you.

300 g sashimi-grade yellowfin or bluefin tuna, cut into 4 rectangular logs
40 ml olive oil
1 teaspoon sea salt
2 teaspoons freshly ground black pepper
½ teaspoon cayenne pepper
vegetable oil, for deep-frying
2 teaspoons small salted capers, rinsed and patted dry with paper towel
½ red capsicum (pepper), roasted and peeled
½ yellow capsicum (pepper), roasted and peeled
6 baby beans, blanched and finely sliced
1 tablespoon chopped chives
2 tablespoons chervil leaves
1 punnet rocket cress, snipped
½ punnet parsley cress, snipped
½ punnet celery cress, snipped
4 anchovy fillets
4 hard-boiled quail eggs, shelled

BLACK OLIVE TAPENADE
100 g small Ligurian black olives, pitted
3 anchovy fillets
1 clove garlic
1 teaspoon small salted capers, rinsed
½ teaspoon smooth Dijon mustard
pinch of cayenne pepper
½ teaspoon freshly ground black pepper
75 ml extra virgin olive oil

ANCHOVY DRESSING
2 teaspoons anchovy cream
1 teaspoon Roasted Garlic Paste (see Essentials)
30 ml Banyuls vinegar
100 ml fruity extra virgin olive oil
½ teaspoon freshly ground black pepper
½ teaspoon sea salt

To prepare the tuna, mix the oil with the salt, pepper and cayenne. Roll each tuna log in the spiced oil until well coated. Wrap each log in a long length of plastic film, to make about eight layers around the tuna. Tie both ends to secure, making sure there are no air pockets inside the plastic.

Bring a saucepan of water to simmering point, turn off the heat and float the tuna parcels in the hot water for 2 minutes, rolling with a spoon. Remove from the water and sit the tuna parcels on ice until cool. The tuna should remain raw and uncooked, the heat being just enough to allow the seasoning to stick to the surfaces.

Heat the oil for deep-frying in a saucepan to 150°C and gently fry the capers until crisp but not brown. Drain on paper towel to dry out.

To make the tapenade, blend all the ingredients except the oil in a food processor to make a paste.

With the motor running, slowly add the oil in a thin steady stream until the tapenade is quite smooth.

To make the dressing, whisk all the ingredients together until emulsified.

Slice the roasted capsicums into very fine lengths then dice finely. Mix the diced capsicum with the bean slices, chives, chervil and cress leaves. Add enough dressing to just moisten the salad.

To serve, smear a little anchovy dressing onto the centre of each plate. Sit a teaspoon of tapenade in the centre. Unwrap the tuna, cut into slices and arrange on each plate in a circle around the tapenade, overlapping the slices like a collar. Place the cress salad in the middle on top of the tapenade. Lay an anchovy fillet across the salad and sit a quail egg on top. Drizzle with a little extra dressing, sprinkle with the fried capers and serve.

SERVES 4

BIRD BATH

We created this consomme-style soup for our 'Sublime' tasting menu in London and have served it on many auspicious occasions since. The idea was adapted from the practice of pressing the juices from roasted bones of duck that was made famous by La Tour d'Argent restaurant in Paris more than a century ago. We applied the same 'pressing' principle to raw bones after meticulous cleansing, which produces a golden elixir with great clarity and an intense depth of flavour. In London I used a combination of partridge, chicken and quail but the bones of any small birds can be used. In Australia, I would replace the partridge with pheasant or guinea fowl, as these birds are easier to obtain here. For an even richer result, a small amount of squab can be used – but sparingly, or its gamey flavour will dominate.

2 fresh snow (white) fungus, torn into small petals

BIRD DUMPLINGS
100 g chicken thigh fillet, chopped
1 egg white
20 g foie gras, chopped
200 g partridge (or quail) breast meat, minced
1 teaspoon oyster sauce
1 teaspoon light soy sauce
1 teaspoon minced ginger
1 teaspoon minced garlic
1 teaspoon minced coriander roots
1 teaspoon sea salt
½ teaspoon freshly ground white pepper
1 teaspoon whole green peppercorns
2 green onions, finely sliced
24 won ton wrappers, cut into 6 cm rounds
rice flour, for dusting

BIRD ESSENCE
1.5 kg bones – carcasses of partridge, quail and chicken
1.7 litres water
40 ml light soy sauce
2 teaspoons mushroom soy sauce
3 teaspoons fish sauce
40 g dried scallops, finely chopped
40 g Chinese black bacon, finely sliced
2 tablespoons chopped green onion tops
1 scant teaspoon jasmine tea leaves

To make the bird essence, clean the bones thoroughly, removing all traces of fat, blood and innards. Wash the bones twice under cold running water, drain and then chop the bones into small pieces with a cleaver. Don't leave the bones to soak as this dilutes the essential flavour.

Put the remaining essence ingredients, except the tea leaves, in a large bowl and stir to combine. Cover with silicone paper or baking paper and then foil to seal the bowl.

Sit the bowl over a large saucepan of gently boiling water and steam for 3 hours. Make sure the bottom of the bowl is not in contact with the boiling water. Remove the bowl from the heat and strain the soup through a fine mesh sieve, pressing to extract all the juices. Discard the solids.

Leave to settle overnight in the refrigerator and remove any residual fat that may have risen to the surface. When ready to serve, reheat the soup just to simmering point and float jasmine tea leaves on top. Turn off the heat and leave to infuse for 5 minutes. Strain the soup through a sieve lined with three layers of muslin cloth to ensure maximum clarity. Taste and adjust the seasoning if necessary.

To make the dumplings, place the chopped chicken meat and egg white in a food processor and blend until smooth. Add the foie gras and pulse until just combined, so the mixture is mousse-like.

Mix the minced partridge meat in a bowl with the oyster and soy sauces to season.

Pound the ginger, garlic, coriander root, salt and pepper in a mortar and pestle to make a paste.

Combine the paste with the minced partridge, chicken mousse, green peppercorns and green onion slices.

Lay the won ton wrappers on a bench and sit a small spoonful of the stuffing in the centre of each one. Wet the edges with water, fold in half then fold the ends in to meet and press together, to form a tortellini shape. Stand the dumplings in a single layer on a flat try dusted with rice flour until ready to cook.

When ready to serve, poach the prepared dumplings in boiling water for 3 minutes until cooked, then remove carefully with a slotted spoon. Divide the dumplings among serving bowls and add the torn snow fungus petals. Ladle on the hot bird essence and serve immediately.

SERVES 6

ANISE FISH FONDUE WITH SAFFRON MAYONNAISE

This robust and flavoursome broth takes its lead from the traditional bouillabaisse, a classic of the French repertoire. The fish used for the stock base is the most important factor, and I like to use bony rock fish and red mullet along with crab to extract the richest possible flavour. Ask your fishmonger to thoroughly clean and gut the whole fish for you to ensure there are no trace elements of blood remaining on the bones or gills. Serve this with generous chunks of crusty French baguette to soak up all those delicious juices.

500 g black mussels
4 × 60 g slices snapper or red emperor fillet, skin on
1 flathead fillet
4 red mullet (rouget) fillets, pin-bones removed
olive oil, for brushing
sea salt and freshly ground black pepper
vegetable oil, for deep-frying
8 sea urchin roes
500 ml Tempura Batter (see Essentials)
1 tablespoon shredded parsley leaves

FISH BROTH
12 raw king prawns
60 ml olive oil
1 small leek, diced
1 green onion, diced
1 small fennel bulb, diced (reserve the fronds)
1 small carrot, diced
3 small red chillies, sliced
5 cloves garlic, chopped
1 tablespoon thyme leaves
2 tablespoons chopped parsley leaves
2 teaspoons ground fennel seeds
2 blue swimmer crabs, cleaned and chopped into quarters
100 ml tomato puree
6 ripe tomatoes, peeled
2 rock fish or rock cod, gutted and chopped
2 red mullet (rouget), gutted and chopped
1 small flathead, gutted and chopped
2 red spot whiting, gutted and chopped
1 teaspoon saffron threads
100 ml Pernod
sea salt and freshly ground black pepper

SAFFRON MAYONNAISE
½ teaspoon saffron threads
50 g sourdough bread, crusts removed
1 tablespoon diced roasted pimiento (piquillo pepper)
1 small red chilli, chopped
2 cloves garlic, chopped
1 teaspoon smooth Dijon mustard
1 egg yolk
1 teaspoon sea salt
½ teaspoon freshly ground black pepper
175 ml extra virgin olive oil

To make the fish broth, peel the prawns and reserve the heads and shells. Devein and butterfly the prawns, then refrigerate until ready to serve.

Heat the oil in a large saucepan and gently saute the leek, green onion, fennel, carrot, chilli and garlic for 15 minutes until softened. Add the thyme, parsley and ground fennel and sweat over heat for another 5 minutes. Stir in the reserved prawn heads and shells and the crabs and cook for another 5 minutes.

Add the tomato puree and tomatoes and stir over moderate heat for 10 minutes. Add all the chopped fish, saffron and Pernod then pour in enough water to just cover the fish (about 2.5 litres – more can be added later if necessary). Bring to the boil over gentle heat and simmer for 1 hour. Turn off the heat and leave the broth to settle for 20 minutes.

Strain the broth through a conical sieve, pushing firmly to extract as much of the fish juice as possible. Discard the solids. Bring the strained broth to simmering point in a clean pan and season to taste with salt and pepper. If the broth appears too thick, dilute with a small amount of water at this stage.

To make the saffron mayonnaise, soak the saffron threads in 150 ml hot fish broth for 5 minutes. Tear the bread into small pieces, pour on the saffron stock and leave for 15 minutes until softened. Place the saffron bread in a food processor with the pimiento, chilli, garlic, mustard and egg yolk and blend until smooth. Season with salt and pepper. With the motor running, gradually add the olive oil until the mayonnaise thickens. Refrigerate until ready to serve.

Steam the mussels in a covered frying pan until the shells open. Transfer to a bowl of iced water then remove the mussels from their shells and trim off the beards.

Heat 500 ml of the broth in a saucepan and poach the snapper, flathead and prawns over gentle heat for about 5 minutes until cooked. Lay the red mullet fillets on an oiled tray, brush with olive oil and season with salt and pepper. Cook under a hot grill for 6 minutes.

Heat the vegetable oil in a large saucepan to 180°C. Dip the sea urchin roes into the tempura batter to coat, shaking off any excess. Fry in the hot oil for 40 seconds, just until the batter becomes crisp. Drain on paper towel.

To serve, divide the fish, prawns and mussels among serving bowls and ladle the hot soup over the top. Sprinkle with shredded parsley and fennel fronds and sit the sea urchin tempura on top. Add a generous dollop of saffron mayonnaise to each bowl, serving the rest separately to share at the table.

SERVES 4

STEAMED HALIBUT AND FOIE GRAS WITH SOY GINGER CONSOMME

I love the different species of fish drawn from the cold waters of the northern hemisphere, and halibut is definitely one of the stars. The other flavours and textures introduced in this dish play a great supporting role and don't override the inherent character of the fish. If halibut is unavailable, use sole, flounder, brill or even deepwater flathead. The foie gras can only be steamed inside the fish if it is raw (impossible in Australia as the importation of the raw product is forbidden) so if you are using the semi-cooked foie gras that's available in Australia, then you will need to omit it from the steamed parcel. Instead, for the closest approximation, briefly sear a slice of semi-cooked foie gras on both sides in a hot pan and sit it on top of the fish parcel as you serve it.

2 tablespoons enoki mushrooms, trimmed
2 teaspoons shredded Pickled Ginger (see Essentials)
1 tablespoon snipped chives
1 punnet onion cress (rock chives), snipped
4 pieces Fish Crackling (see Essentials)

SOY GINGER CONSOMME
6 dried shiitake mushrooms
150 ml warm water
250 ml Dashi Stock (see Essentials)
250 ml White Chicken Stock (see Essentials)
75 ml Ginger Juice (see Essentials)
25 ml mirin
50 ml light soy sauce
50 ml fish sauce
12 cm length of skin from smoked salmon

MUSHROOM DUXELLES
60 ml olive oil
2 tablespoons finely diced brown onion
3 cloves garlic, minced
6 fresh shiitake mushrooms, stems removed, caps finely sliced
12 chestnut mushrooms, finely sliced
6 oyster mushrooms, finely sliced
1 teaspoon chopped thyme
sea salt and freshly ground black pepper

HALIBUT PARCELS
4 large Chinese cabbage (wombok) leaves, stem removed
4 × 120 g halibut squares, sliced in half
4 × 30 g slices foie gras

To make the consomme, soak the dried mushrooms in the warm water for 30 minutes in a large saucepan. Add the remaining ingredients and bring to simmering point over gentle heat. Simmer very gently for 1 hour until the flavours have infused – the surface should barely move or bubble. Pass through a fine mesh sieve, then taste and adjust the seasoning if necessary.

To make the mushroom duxelles, add the oil to a heated pan and fry the onion and garlic until softened. Add the mushrooms and thyme and cook over moderate heat for about 10 minutes until the mushrooms have softened. Season to taste with salt and pepper, then set aside to cool.

For the halibut, blanch the cabbage leaves in boiling water then refresh in iced water. Squeeze to dry out and remove any excess moisture. Lay the leaves on the bench and sit a slice of halibut in the centre of each one. Spoon half the mushroom mix on top and lay a slice of foie gras on top. Spoon the remaining mushroom mix on top so the foie gras is encased within, then sandwich together with the remaining fish slices.

Wrap the cabbage around the fish firmly to make secure parcels, tucking the sides in. Wrap each fish parcel in plastic film, twisting the ends to secure. Lay the fish parcels on a steamer tray, cover with a lid and steam over gently boiling water for 12 minutes, until the fish is just cooked. Remove the plastic wrapper and cut each parcel in half crossways. The foie gras should be pink.

To serve, sit the two slices next to each other in bowl plates, cut-side up, and ladle the consomme around the fish. Scatter the enoki mushrooms, pickled ginger and chives in the broth and lay the onion cress and fish crackling on top of the fish.

SERVES 4

VANILLA STRAWBERRY VACHERIN

Some of the most flavoursome strawberries in the world are the Mara des Bois from France, which we had supplied to us in London during the summer months. It is vital that you look for the reddest, juiciest, most flavoursome strawberries to make this dessert. The combination of flavours is a classic in French cuisine and a universal favourite.

100 ml creme fraiche
200 ml thick (45%) cream
40 g icing sugar, sieved
¼ teaspoon vanilla extract
4 tablespoons Strawberry Sauce (see Essentials)
2 punnets ripe strawberries, hulled and sliced
icing sugar, to serve

MERINGUES
50 g egg white
50 g castor sugar
50 g icing sugar, sieved
8 g cornflour

VANILLA ICE CREAM
2 vanilla beans, split lengthways
500 ml milk
6 large egg yolks
150 g castor sugar
500 ml pouring (35%) cream

To make the vanilla ice cream, scrape the seeds from the vanilla bean into the milk in a saucepan, then add the beans and bring to a simmer over very low heat. The slower the infusion, the better the flavour. Whisk the egg yolks and sugar in a bowl until pale and creamy, then whisk in the hot milk mixture.

Stand the bowl over a saucepan of gently simmering water and cook, stirring, until the mixture reaches a custard consistency and coats the back of a spoon. Strain through a fine mesh sieve into a clean bowl and discard the vanilla beans. Allow to cool. The custard should be speckled with the minute vanilla seeds. Stir the cream into the cooled custard, then churn in an ice-cream machine until firm. Store in an airtight container in the freezer until ready to serve.

To make the meringues, preheat the oven to 50°C (not fan-forced) and line a flat tray with baking paper or a silicone mat. Whisk the egg whites in an electric mixer until soft peaks form. With the beaters running, gradually add the sugar and icing sugar and continue to whisk until glossy and firm. Stir in the cornflour until just combined.

Spoon the meringue mix into a piping bag with a small round nozzle and pipe dots about 2.5 cm in diameter with little peaks, created by flicking your wrist as you lift the piping bag away.

Put the meringue dots in the oven and bake for 30 minutes until set. Turn off the heat, leave the oven door ajar and allow the meringues the cool in the oven. They should remain white throughout the process – if they colour, then the oven heat is too high. Store in an airtight container until ready to serve.

Gently whip the creme fraiche, cream, icing sugar and vanilla until firm.

To assemble, place a scoop of ice cream in the base of each glass coupe or bowl, then spoon on a little strawberry sauce. Make layers with meringue, cream and strawberry slices, finishing with a few strawberry slices and a meringue on top. Dust with icing sugar and serve.

SERVES 4

<< Place your chosen moulds in the freezer.

To make the caramel ice cream, bring the cream and milk to simmering point in a saucepan. Whisk the egg yolks and 150 g of the sugar in a bowl until pale and creamy, then whisk in the hot cream mixture. Stand the bowl over a pan of simmering water and cook, stirring, until the mixture reaches a custard consistency and coats the back of a spoon. Set aside.

In another saucepan, boil the water and remaining sugar over high heat, without stirring, to make a caramel. Add a little of the custard to the caramel as soon as it reaches the desired colour (be careful – it will bubble and expand, so have everything ready!). Whisk the caramel back into the custard, then pass through a fine mesh sieve into a bowl and allow to cool. Churn in an ice-cream machine until firm. Spoon the caramel ice cream into the mould until it is a third full, then freeze for 2 hours until firm.

To make the honeycomb ice cream, bring the milk to simmering point in a saucepan. Whisk the egg yolks and sugar in a bowl until pale and creamy, then whisk in the hot milk. Stand the bowl over a pan of simmering water and cook, stirring, until the mixture reaches a custard consistency and coats the back of a spoon. Pass through a fine mesh sieve into a bowl and allow to cool. Stir the cream into the cooled custard, then churn in an ice-cream machine. When the ice-cream is firm, stir in the honeycomb, then spoon it into the mould until two-thirds full. Return the mould to the freezer for 2 hours.

To make the hazelnut chocolate ice cream, shave the chocolate into the milk in a saucepan over gentle heat until the chocolate has melted completely and the milk reaches blood temperature. Whisk the egg yolks and sugar in a bowl until pale and creamy, then whisk in the hot chocolate milk. Stand the bowl over a pan of simmering water and cook, stirring, until the mixture reaches a custard consistency and coats the back of a spoon. Pass through a fine mesh sieve into a bowl and allow to cool. Stir the cream into the cooled custard, then churn in an ice-cream machine until firm.

Spoon the hazelnut chocolate ice cream into the mould until full, ensuring the top is smooth and even. You should now have three layers of ice cream of equal thickness. Freeze the moulds for at least 5 hours or overnight before turning out.

To make the gaytime gold dust, blitz all the ingredients together in a blender to make a fine crumb. Store in an airtight container in the refrigerator until ready to serve.

Dip each mould into a bowl of hot water for a few seconds, then turn the ice cream out into a bowl of gaytime crumbs. Turn in the crumbs to coat the surfaces, then stand the ice cream on a cold serving plate and serve immediately.

SERVES 20

LAVENDER PANNA COTTA WITH TOFFEE APPLES AND HAZELNUT MERINGUE

I created this dessert to partner an 18-year-old ancient reserve single malt, which we served alongside – a magical union that was cause for much comment. Each of the elements in the dessert can be prepared beforehand, leaving the final assembly until you are ready to serve.

LAVENDER PANNA COTTA
2 tablespoons chopped fresh lavender
65 g castor sugar
340 ml thick (45%) cream
165 ml milk
4 g gelatine leaves, softened in cold water

HAZELNUT MERINGUE
1 cup ground hazelnuts
2 tablespoons cornflour
1 cup castor sugar
60 g egg whites

HAZELNUT PRALINE
100 g castor sugar
25 ml water
2 teaspoons hazelnut oil
75 g hazelnuts, roasted and skinned
2 teaspoons chopped fresh lavender

HONEY TOFFEE APPLES
20 g butter
4 golden delicious or pink lady apples, each cut into 8 crescents
250 g castor sugar
75 ml water
2 tablespoons lavender honey
60 ml liqueur tokay

To make the panna cotta, combine the lavender, sugar, cream and milk in a saucepan, stir and bring very slowly to the boil. The slower the infusion, the better the flavour. Add the softened gelatine and stir until dissolved. Pour through a fine mesh sieve into a jug, then pour into eight 150 ml dariole moulds. Refrigerate for at least 8 hours until set.

To make the meringue, preheat the oven to 150°C and line a baking tray with baking paper. Mix the hazelnuts with the cornflour and two-thirds of the sugar in a bowl. Whisk the egg white until just beginning to firm (but not stiff) then slowly add the remaining sugar and whisk until soft peaks form. Gradually fold the meringue into the dry ingredients, then spoon into a piping bag and pipe 5 cm circles on the lined baking tray. Pipe six small dots also. Bake for 20 minutes until set and firm. Cool on a wire rack, then store in an airtight container until ready to use.

To make the praline, combine the sugar and water in a saucepan and boil without stirring until it forms a caramel. Grease a baking tray with hazelnut oil, then cover with roasted hazelnuts and lavender. Pour on the hot caramel and allow to cool and set. Scrape the caramel from the tray and break into pieces. Feed small amounts into a food processor with the motor running and blend until a fine crumb forms. Keep refrigerated until ready to use (otherwise it will become too sticky).

To make the toffee apples, preheat the oven to 180°C and butter a baking dish. Place the apple slices in the dish in a single layer. Combine the sugar and water in a saucepan and cook, without stirring, until it forms a caramel. Stir in the honey then pour over the apple. Bake for 8 minutes until the apple slices soften and take on a toffee colour. Flip them over and cook for another 5–8 minutes. Remove the apple slices from the baking dish while still warm and store in airtight containers on baking paper.

Reheat the caramel remaining in the pan to simmering point, add the tokay and cook for a few minutes until it becomes syrup-like. Strain and allow to cool before serving.

To serve, place the meringues on a plate and arrange a few apple slices evenly on top. Turn out the panna cotta from its mould and sit on top of the apple. Spoon on the toffee sauce, sprinkle with praline and sit a small meringue dot on top.

SERVES 8

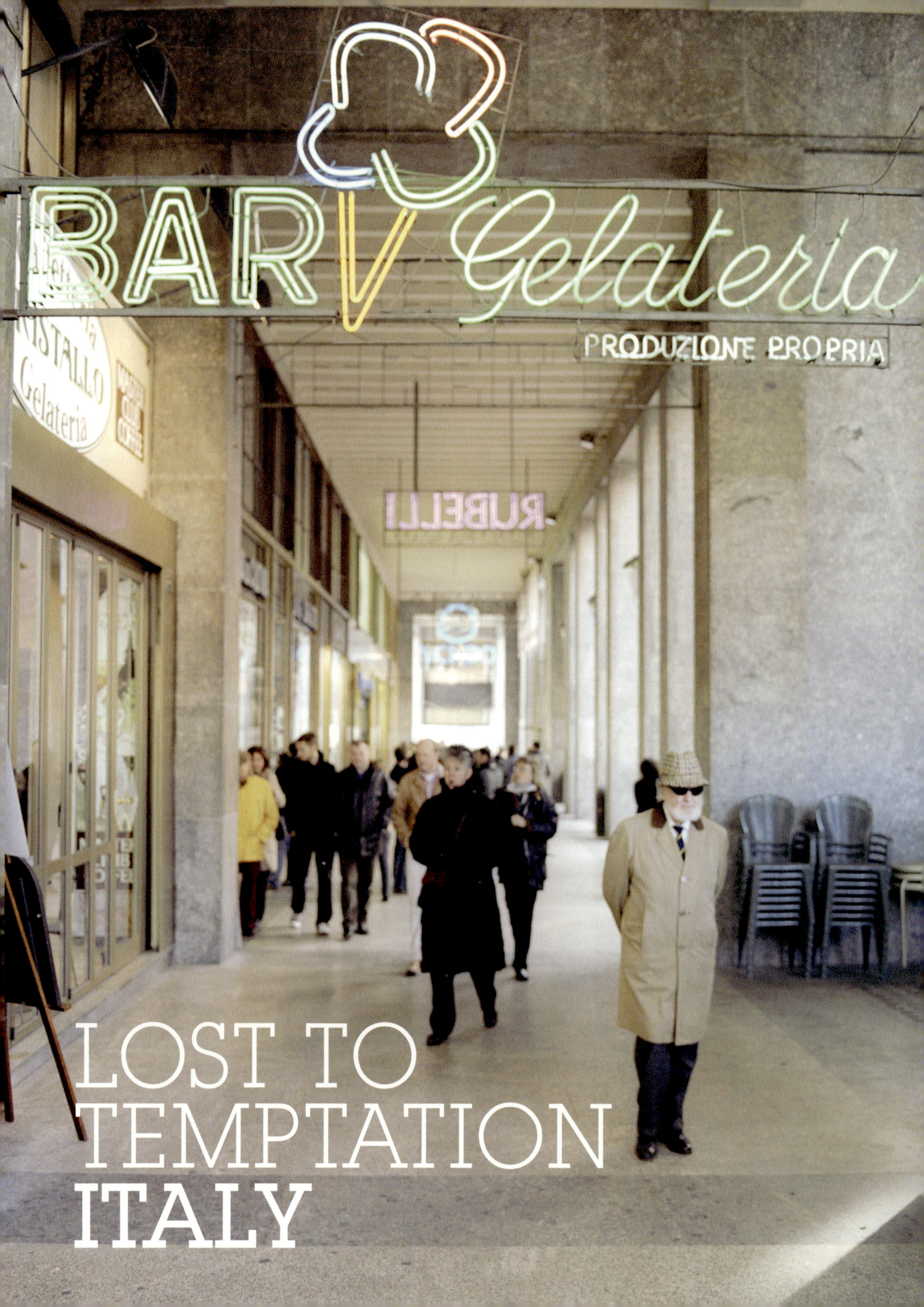

LOST TO TEMPTATION ITALY

There is nothing more intoxicating than the Italian landscape – except perhaps its food. While it may appear that Italy has one unified cuisine, exemplified by spaghetti bolognese, pizza, veal parmigiana and the like, this is simply not the case, and a visit to any part of the country quickly reveals its incredible diversity. Even with some degree of homogenisation (think mass-produced pasta, sauces, factory-made salami and cheese and much more), there remains a staunch preference for authentic regional cooking. I have noticed that Italians tend to have little curiosity for food from outside their country or region; they prefer to eat what they know. Unlike Britain, France, Spain and Portugal, where cultural and food traditions have been influenced by colonial history and the waves of immigration that ensued, Italy seems almost to shun outside influences, and fights hard to maintain the purity of its culinary tradition. Italians are wildly passionate about food, about *their* food. Indeed, Italy is the birthplace of the Slow Food Movement, a reaction against the commercial methods of food production that are wreaking havoc on artisanal traditions worldwide. There is much to learn from the unhurried way of life the movement promotes – truly La Dolce Vita.

Once in Rome, we asked a hotel concierge to suggest a good restaurant that served local Roman food and he sent us off in a taxi to a small family-run place that specialised in mushrooms. The entire menu was based around fungi – it was heaven. The restaurant was a small and modest; mama was doing the cooking while papa took care of the tables and poured the wine. We felt like we were sitting in a home rather than a restaurant.

We were staying near the Borghese Gardens above the Spanish Steps and spent many happy hours wandering along Via Condotti and the surrounding streets, stopping for coffee at Antico Caffe Greco or having a Campari with freshly squeezed blood orange juice and some bruschetta at one of the cafes and bars that line Piazza Navona. Our early-morning visits to Campo dei Fiori, the central square with its thriving produce market, demonstrated that the daily act of shopping for food lies at the heart of existence here; food is entirely bound up in pleasure and the people share a deep respect for the bounty of each season.

Our friend Jonathon lives in the Eternal City for most of the year, sensibly returning to Sydney during our summer to avoid the worst of the European winter. He cooks with his heart and soul, with great flair and imagination, and the best food in Rome is often served on his terrace – a boy after my own heart. Ask Jonathon about the food of his adopted city and you'll get a response like this:

'Having lived in Rome for more than two decades, I have been to more than my fair share of good restaurants across Italy, but it's often the simplest eating experiences that provide the true thrills. I've missed a train on purpose for an extra portion of steamed wild asparagus at Delle Belle Donne in Florence. I've watched newlyweds posing for the photographers at Castel Dell'Ovo in Naples,

SLEEPING AND EATING IN ROME

HOTEL LOCARNO
Via della Penna 22, Rome
Tel +39 6 361 0841
www.hotellocarno.com
My theory is when in Rome, be extravagant! And there's nowhere better to do this than the Locarno, a stylish hotel right near Piazzo del Popolo in the centre of town.

LORD BYRON HOTEL
Via G. de Notaris 5, Rome
Tel +39 6 322 0404
www.lordbyronhotel.com
This place is a stone's throw from the Borghese Gardens – don't miss sunset drinks on the roof terrace.

LILO AL PIEDONE
Between Piazza della Minerva and Via del Corso, Rome
A great local trattoria.

ANTICO CAFFE GRECO
Via Condotti 84, Rome
Tel +39 6 679 1700
This tiny space packed with locals day and night is among the most venerable cafes in the world – a Roman landmark.

FERRARA
Via del Moro 1a, Trastevere, Rome
Tel +39 6 5833 3920
www.enotecaferrara.it
A terrific enoteca (wine bar) with really decent food.

FORNO DI CAMPO DEI FIORI
Campo dei Fiori 22, Centro, Rome
Tel +39 6 6880 6662
Some of the best pizzas in town, especially the basic pizza bianca ('white' pizza, simply topped with salt and olive oil).

while sitting at a dockside table in one of the rough-and-tumble trattorias, eating fried generations of neonati (literally newborns – tiny translucent fish, smaller than whitebait, with a very limited fishing season). In Bologna, the never-ending antipasti at Da Silvio makes it hard to think about anything else, and if you want hopeless romance mixed with happy tastebuds, then opt for a sunset plate of coda di rospo (a top-heavy fish with an extremely ugly face) on the waterfront at Do Mori on the Giudecca side of Venice.

In Rome, the best food is honest and uncomplicated. There are people who literally swoon from the pizza bianca, baked around the clock at the Forno di Campo dei Fiori, while others get weak-kneed from the crisp filetto di baccala (deep-fried salted cod fillet) served each evening out of the hole-in-the-wall establishment in the nearby Largo dei Librari, smack bang in the middle of all the cheap clothes shops in Via Giubbonari. But I suppose the sign of a great eatery is a place where you go regularly, with any number of friends, and where you have never been let down. Trattoria da Francesco in Piazza del Fico is noisy, chaotic, theatrical, delicious. Run at high speed by a dry-witted family, it's hard to get a table after 9 p.m. (though at lunchtime, with a totally different staff and menu, it's a bit easier). Their grilled steak on the bone is unbeatable (also the fillet steak in balsamic vinegar), as are the heavenly thin-crust pizzas, the foccacia with thick-cut raw ham, and the flawless panna cotta with a small spoonful of acacia honey on top. For a slightly upmarket, better-behaved version of the same, Maccheroni in Piazza delle Coppelle is a good bet. Much traditional Roman cuisine is based on Jewish recipes. While the famous (and famously expensive) restaurants in the Ghetto are okay, La Botticella in Vicolo del Leopardo, serves some terrific, hearty classics of mixed Roman origins: pigeon wrapped in bacon; tripe; deep-fried artichokes; stuffed zucchini flowers; coda alla vaccinara (oxtail in thick tomato sauce); and a pasta sauce they invented called La Botticella, which is essentially a red pesto with wild herbs. Meanwhile, politicians, actors, artists and the like gather at Pierluigi (since 1938) in Piazza dei Ricci, for perfect pasta served with a variety of creative sauces like prawns and zucchini – sounds strange, tastes great; grilled radicchio; fritti di paranza (seafood platter); and soppressa di polpo, which is best described as octopus salami, and is one of the tender surprises of Rome.'

You can see why I love him to bits – and it's through passionate and generous advice like this that I find the true essence of any city.

Our good friends Keith and Alan live on the Adriatic Coast, beneath the limestone peak of Monte Conero, on the outskirts of Sirolo, about half an hour's drive south of Ancona (where there is little reason to linger). Sirolo is a charming medieval town – a rare find in this day and age – and the fine pebbly beaches along this stretch of the coast are breathtakingly beautiful when you get away from the main areas, with cliffs, caves, secluded beaches and sheer drops to the sea. With mutual friends David and Peter, we made a special trip one year to celebrate David's 40th birthday at Keith and Alan's villa. It was a house party that was to last for days – full of madness, mayhem and much hilarity, with the daily routine revolving around food, wine and more wine. What's to complain about?

EATING ON THE ADRIATIC COAST

DA GIACCHETTI
Via Portonovo 1, Portonovo (near Sirolo)
Tel +39 071 801 384
Outdoor terrace on the pebbly beach with excellent seafood plates.

GIUBBI
Albergo Ristorante Belvedere
Via Redipuglia n.1, Staffolo (near Ancona)
Tel +39 0731 779 261
www.giubbi.com
About 30 kilometres south-west of Ancona, this restaurant in the hills offers traditional Marche dishes, including gnocchi with nettles and a deliciously rich meat sauce called graminghe that's served with thick worm-like maccheroni pasta. Graminghe is made from offcuts and leftover heels of prosciutto, salamis and anything piggy (though no smoked meats), which are minced into a pot with garlic and chilli flakes and cooked down with tomatoes then finished with a dash of cream. Chef Ilde also offers cooking classes.

We would wander into the town square each morning for an espresso to kick-start the day, enjoying the spectacular view out to sea from the cafe terrace along the medieval ramparts. Then we would check out the food market – a bunch of trucks, vans and handcarts in a car park at the back of the town square. At the norcini (specialist pork butchers), I tasted porky bits I had never seen in Australia, along with various styles of prosciutto, pancetta and coppa made from the sweet meat of local pigs, and we took home some salsiccia di cinghiale (wild boar sausages) and mazzafegati (pork sausages stuffed with liver and orange) to cook for lunch. Back in the square, we munched on porchetta (spit-roasted pig with wild fennel and herbs), which was delicious, even at 10 o'clock in the morning. I tell you, I was in pig heaven.

Italy seduces with its food shops and markets – every town, city and village embraces the ritual of daily shopping. Now there's nothing Alan likes more than a spot of shopping, and we soon became partners in crime, visiting alimentaris (grocers) and anywhere else of gastronomic interest. There was an abundance of baby fennel, broad beans, asparagus and baby artichokes, and the sardines were sensational, so they too made a regular appearance for lunch. The Marche region is also truffle territory – the white ones are stiff competition for those from Piedmont – and November is the time to indulge. Being close to Abruzzo, which is renowned for its fiery food, we were also able to stock up on red chillies and capsicums – essential for our group of spice addicts.

While Keith is a brilliant home cook, Alan never usually sets foot in the kitchen and admits to being scared of 'that beast' (as he calls the stove), but one afternoon when the rest of the household was taking a siesta, he decided he wanted to learn to cook something he could make by himself. I showed Alan how to bake a cake, thinking he could never go wrong with Elizabeth David's foolproof chocolate and almond cake recipe. All went smoothly, with me standing at his shoulder offering a little tip here and there. As he put the cake in the oven to bake, we agreed to come back in 45 minutes to see if it was cooked. I went out for a swim and came back to the kitchen a little early, just in case (you can never be sure when trying out a different oven), only to find Alan sitting cross-legged on the floor in front of the oven, watching the bloody thing bake! It is a priceless memory. To this day, I think of him every time I put a cake in the oven. Of course, the story is the source of so much amusement among us all that he has never lived it down – but, to his credit, Alan has cooked that cake countless times since, and it is always done to perfection!

EATING IN MILAN

TRATTORIA DA PINO
Via Cerva 14 (near the Duomo), Milano
Tel +39 02 7600 0532
Sit at shared tables with locals for authentic local food and a casual ambience.

For David's actual birthday dinner, we drove around the other side of Monte Conero to Portonovo, a seaside village to the north of Sirolo. We ate at Da Giacchetti, a restaurant right on the pebble beach, with white-clothed tables set out under the stars and romantically lit with candles in paper bags – it was a heavenly setting. The kitchen staff cooked up an extravaganza from locally caught seafood: starters included baby octopus seared and served with a potato salad; tender squid; and a lemony carpaccio of gilt-head bream. This spread was followed by angel-hair spaghetti with clams; gnocchi with artichokes and scampi tails; and a feathery-light fritto misto. A rich chocolate-fudge birthday cake completed the banquet, then we all headed back to the villa for a nightcap of grappa.

The next night saw a feast in Keith and Alan's garden, courtesy of their good friend Ilde from Giubbi restaurant in the village of Staffolo, who occasionally comes to visit and can never resist cooking for them. Ilde arrived in the early afternoon to crank up the wood-fired oven, which assumed prime position at one end of the garden, and the burning logs soon developed a decent heap of hot coals, essential for the night's cooking. She rolled pizza dough into fine sheets and set up an array of ingredients on a table near the oven. When the oven was ready for cooking, Ilde whipped up three different types of thin-crust pizza: one perfectly simple with olive oil, anchovies and tomato; another with mixed herbs and a smattering of fresh mozzarella; and another with artichoke hearts and ham. Needless to say, they were absolutely delicious – perhaps the best pizza I have ever eaten, washed down with a local light red wine, the odd vodka and lots of laughs.

During our stay we had endless conversations about food and cooking, and I can't resist sharing a few of the villa's favourite recipes with you, in Keith's own inimitable words (see pages 532–3). Vivid memories of these tastes transport me to those blissful days on the mountain and I am certain that food cooked with this kind of love and humour tastes all the better for it. I am also convinced that there is something in the water in Italy that encourages such emotional and expressive outpourings about food!

Up north in Lombardy, Milan considers itself the style centre of the country, and a walk around the streets near the Duomo quickly confirms the city's penchant for the latest fashion. The clubs, bars and restaurants around Corso Como are packed with glamorous locals, and we spent much of our time at pavement terraces or bars, eating toasted prosciutto sandwiches, ultra-fresh rocket salads and fabulous risottos. At drop-dead gorgeous Lake Maggiore, to the north-west of Milan, we stayed with the family of a friend, Vito. Their house was perched high on the mountain above the lakeside town of Stresa, and boasted an uninterrupted view of the snow-capped Alps along the border with Switzerland. We often sat on the roof terrace with a bottle of wine and whiled away the afternoon siesta playing board games or cards. One day we took a boat out onto the lake to visit Isola Bella, a magical setting with white swans gliding past the lush gardens.

We ate deliciously simple home cooking, prepared by Vito's mother and based around local Lombardy produce. Every meal was shared with the whole family (three generations!) and whoever happened to be visiting. There would always be a soup, then a pasta or risotto dish, followed by polenta or another secondi, and finishing with fruit. It was here we had our first taste of pecorino di fossa (hard, slightly salty sheep's milk cheese matured in caves), and also the sweet mascarpone sometimes served with fruit for dessert. I also remember being offered various local salamis and cured meats, such as bresaola, to taste – for me, one of the best things about travel is tasting something at its place of origin.

We made our way across to Verona, where Margie's cousin Christine lives. An authority on local history, Christine offered to show us the sights – both cultural and culinary. Verona was the setting for Shakespeare's *Romeo and Juliet*, and although Romeo and Juliet were fictitious characters, the two families did exist. We stood below the tiny balcony of the house which once belonged to the family Shakespeare called the Capulets, and which has come to symbolise the star-crossed lovers. We explored beautiful Baroque and Gothic cathedrals, and walked around the impressive Roman arena. Along the way we ate a sublime porcini risotto at a modest osteria (inn). As you might expect, given that the silky grains of carnaroli and vialone nano are farmed nearby, the risotto was perfectly creamy, beautifully seasoned and packed full of flavour. Carnaroli grains absorb more liquid during cooking and produce a creamier risotto, while the slightly longer grains of vialone nano rice soak up less liquid and retain a firmer, nuttier texture. Because the fertile soils of the surrounding Veneto region yield abundant crops of vegetables, these are often the stars of the table here, with meat playing a minor supporting role. We tasted strongly flavoured asiago cheese and ate cotechino sausage with a lovely salad made from young radicchio leaves. I also came to appreciate the herbal, astringent and slightly medicinal flavour of Campari – although alcoholic, its bitterness stimulates the appetite and aids digestion, so I choose to regard it as a tonic. With its heady mix of spices, herbs and bergamot, it makes a perfect summer aperitif when mixed with the freshly squeezed juice of blood oranges, or if they are not in season, ruby grapefruit.

Hoping to avoid the throngs that congregate in and around the sidewalk cafes of the iconic Piazza San Marco, we visited Venice in late summer, when the fever pitch of the tourist season was nearing its end. The city sits like an open jewel box amid its filigree of canals, the reflected light making the buildings look like clusters of precious gems emerging from the water. Thankfully there are no cars – locals use the waterways in the same way as they do roads, with equally interesting traffic rules. Since we had a car and didn't want to leave it in Chioggia (at the southern end of the Venetian lagoon), we took the vehicle ferry to the Lido, the long narrow island that sits between the lagoon and the Adriatic Sea. Swimming in the sea

EATING AND DRINKING IN VENICE

VINI DA GIGIO
Cannaregio 3628A, Fondamenta San Felice, Venice
Tel +39 041 528 5140
Terrific traditional Venetian food – the squid dishes are my favourite.

HARRY'S BAR
San Marco 1323, Venice
Tel +39 041 528 5777
The atmospheric bar that's the birthplace of the Bellini and Carpaccio.

AL GATTO NERO
Fondamenta della Giudecca 88, Burano, Venice
Tel +39 041 730 120
This trattoria serves superb seafood and picture-perfect desserts.

was a delight, making the dog days of summer in Venice bearable as we didn't feel hemmed in by the old city walls. I must say, hanging at the beach Italian style is a unique experience: everyone promenades in their best clothes, then they disappear into cute little wooden cabins that are a fixture at the Lido, and emerge in fashionable bathers. Ever so civilised! From where we were staying, it was a short vaporetto (waterbus) ride across the canal to Piazza San Marco, and it was fascinating to glide past gondolas and an endless parade of houses and palazzos, some fallen into disrepair or even abandonment.

As our accommodation had a small kitchen, we would head into the Rialto Market (next to the famous bridge of the same name) in the early morning to gather supplies: fresh fish from the pescaria, a bunch of flowers along the way, then on to the vegetable section – a cornucopia of stalls, all offering vibrant and tempting fresh produce. Our favourites were different-coloured capsicums for roasting and to make peperonata, eggplants (of course) and the many varieties of bitter-tasting radicchio from Verona or Treviso that we used for salads, together with tiny bulbs of fennel. I cooked really straightforward food, happy to just play with such perfect ingredients: we enjoyed the simplicity of grilled fish with a salsa verde or a lemon dressing, and tomatoes with such intense flavour that we ate them unadorned except for a drizzle of extra virgin olive oil and a pinch of sea salt. Ripe summer fruits played a starring role as well, with juicy melons, peaches and strawberries cut up and served with mascarpone and a splash of sweet wine. Along the way, I worked at mastering the art of risotto. When we ate out, we chose modest local places and ate simple, rustic dishes. In search of a quintessential Venetian experience, we stopped off at Harry's Bar late one afternoon for their signature Bellini, made from white peach juice and prosecco, and drank it Italian style – standing at the bar with a plate of ham and melon. On discovering that tiramisu originated in the Veneto, we set ourselves the onerous task of finding the best by ordering it everywhere we went. My favourite was at Al Gatto Nero, a long-established trattoria at Burano, one of the islands in the lagoon. The winning tiramisu had perfect purity of flavour and ever-so-elegant presentation.

As much as I adore Italian cities for their buzz and sense of style, it's just as thrilling to drive around the country and visit the smaller towns and villages – though dealing with Italian traffic is certainly an experience!

The coastline that runs along the western side of Italy is dramatic and spectacular, and we wished we had longer to linger and explore the area more thoroughly. However, on this particular trip we wanted to spend some time in Tuscany, so after the obligatory photo opportunity standing next to the leaning tower of Pisa and an impromptu picnic of bread, some olives, a chunk of parmigiana and some locally produced, fruity olive oil, we headed inland. We drove into Florence just on sunset, propelled along by the peak-hour rush, and marvelled the gorgeous young things hanging off the backs of vespas – even on motorbikes, the Italians manage to look glamorous! We found a modest pensione with generous

SLEEPING AND EATING IN FLORENCE

GALLERY HOTEL ART
Vicolo dell'Oro 5, Florence
Tel +39 055 27 263
www.lungarnohotels.com
A small stylish hotel near the Ponte Vecchio. Ask for one of the upstairs rooms overlooking the river.

I FRATELLINI
Via dei Cimatori 38, Florence
Tel +39 055 239 6096
This hole-in-the-wall place serves the best panini in town.

DOLCI E DOLCEZZE
Piazza Beccaria 84, Florence
Tel +39 055 234 5458
The place to come for cakes, pastries and sweet treats – great in the afternoon with a glass of prosecco.

FESTIVAL DEL GELATO
Via del Corso 75 (right near Piazza dell Repubblica), Florence
Tel +39 055 239 4386
A daily stop here for a gelato fix is mandatory.

BALDOVINO
Via San Giuseppe 22, Florence
Tel +39 055 241 773
Classic Tuscan trattoria with gorgeous wood-fired pizzas.

windows that opened onto a busy street near the Mercato Nuovo. Florence is a celebration of Renaissance art and architecture, and everywhere there are reminders of the era of Michelangelo, Caravaggio and Botticelli. Across the Arno River, we wound our way up the hill to Piazzale Michelangelo, stopping to gaze at the dramatic panorama of the city and across to the beautiful town of Fiesole on the distant hill. Florence looks just as it must have centuries ago, the imprint of modern life hidden behind the architectural beauty of its monuments and buildings. Our intention had been to stay here and study at one of the language schools for a couple of months, but we bailed at the last minute, preferring the broader experience of spending time in several places. Before we left though, we did manage to eat some excellent pizza and fabulous salads, work our way through many bottles of chianti and do the rounds of the city's gelato bars every day – perfect food for hot summer days.

As we drove south to Siena, we became immersed in the burnt-umber tones of the Tuscan landscape, with vineyards and olive groves carpeting the hills in every direction. On our way, we stopped off at the fortified medieval village of San Gimignano perched up on a hill. Leaving the car outside the city walls, we walked around the cobblestone lanes, tasted some local wine at one of the wine shops, then hightailed it out of there to escape the tourist crush. Siena is an enchanting place, but we went there with one express purpose: to taste the local delicacy, panforte, a confection of honey, spices, candied fruit and almonds. One barista told us that it was originally made as a kind of energy bar for the crusaders travelling to the Holy Land. On the road into town we passed a couple of factories that make panforte for export, and then we sampled different varieties in Siena's cafes and espresso bars. The two most popular are nero, a darker sweetmeat with a pronounced tang of bitter almonds, and light-coloured margherita, which is gorgeous, golden and spicy – my favourite. Siena also gave us our first taste of panzanella salad, made with ripe tomatoes, garlic, bread and olive oil.

RENTING A VILLA IN ITALY

Is there anyone who doesn't dream of tasting the good life in an Italian villa? To live the dream – for a week or two anyway – check out these websites:
www.elsovillas.com
www.elegantresorts.com.au
www.cvtravel.net

As our time in Italy came to an end, we headed north to Bologna, a truly gastronomic city. At the heart of a region renowned for the production of Parmigiana Reggiano (parmesan cheese), Parma ham and balsamic vinegar, Bologna is a place steeped in tradition, and food takes pride of place with many shop windows. One morning, we sat at one of the cafes in the main square, Piazza Maggiore, and watched the city come alive, before taking a stroll through the covered Mercato delle Erbe to drool over the stunning array of fresh produce. It was hard to go past the huge rounds of mortadella sausage, golden strands of tagliatelle pasta smothered with a rich meat ragu, and tortellini stuffed with ricotta and sage. Dinners of cotechino sausage, pigs' trotters stuffed with sweetbreads and feathery light fritto misto (a selection of fried food), all washed down with deliciously fruity lambrusco wines had us groaning at the table.

Travelling around Italy has shown me how vast and rich its culinary heritage really is, and how the food of each region reflects its unique characteristics. As the produce can be so specifically local, Italy rewards the curious traveller, and I can't wait to visit the Mediterranean islands of Sicily, the Aeolians and Sardinia. With their Arab-Moorish influences, I imagine these rugged outposts will add a different cultural dimension to the Italian food experience. Part of this particular dream is about to be realised as I write. I am about to embark on an impromptu trip to Sicily, picking up a snappy sports car on arrival in Palermo and driving into the sunset – pure bliss. Like so many countries, Italy has had a profound effect on my work and the way I think about food. I haven't nearly finished yet. There's so much more that I have to explore.

SLEEPING AND EATING IN SIENA

PICCOLO HOTEL IL PALIO
Piazza del Sale 19, Siena
Tel +39 577 281 131
This modest hotel is great because it is about 10 minutes' walk from the main square, making it quieter and better for sleeping than being smack bang in the centre of everything.

TAVERNA DEL CAPITANO
Via del Capitano 6 (not far from the cathedral), Siena
Tel +39 0577 288 094
Grab a table in the garden area if it's warm and order the local specialties, such as ribollita (Tuscan bread and vegetable soup) and any of the pasta dishes.

PRAWN AND FREGOLA SALAD

An ancient grain from medieval times, fregola is an ancient semolina pasta (like cous cous) native to Sardinia, where durum wheat is the island's main crop. It is generally coarser in texture than cous cous, however, and is also toasted, giving it a nutty, wheaty flavour. Fregola is available from selected food stores and health-food shops.

200 g fregola
50 ml olive oil
1 teaspoon shellfish oil
2 cloves garlic, sliced
1 red bird's-eye chilli, sliced
40 g fatty pancetta, finely diced
16 raw prawns, shelled, deveined and butterflied open
1 punnet cherry tomatoes, halved
1 small fennel bulb, finely diced
250 ml Prawn Stock (see Essentials)
1 teaspoon sea salt
1 teaspoon freshly ground black pepper
4 cooked artichoke hearts, quartered
25 ml fresh lemon juice, strained
2 tablespoons shredded parsley leaves

Cook the fregola grains in a large saucepan of boiling water for 10 minutes until just al dente, then strain.

While the fregola is cooking, heat the olive and shellfish oils in a frying pan and saute the garlic, chilli and pancetta until softened and beginning to colour. Add the prawns and saute for another 2 minutes until the prawns change colour. Remove the prawns and set aside.

Add the tomatoes, fennel and fregola to the pan and toss together. Pour in the stock, bring to the boil then reduce the heat and simmer for 6–8 minutes until slightly reduced. Season to taste with salt and pepper and stir in the prawns, artichoke hearts, lemon juice and parsley. Toss over heat for a minute, then serve immediately.

SERVES 4

OCTOPUS, ANCHOVY AND CELERY SALAD

Choose the tiny octopus that has not been beaten in a cement mixer as you will find its texture is more tender and far superior. Simply remove the head and beak from the body and tentacles before cooking. I also cut each one in half beforehand as this makes it easier for serving.

400 g baby octopus, cleaned
50 ml olive oil
1 teaspoon sea salt flakes
1 teaspoon freshly ground black pepper
2 tablespoons small black olives, pitted and halved
4 inner sticks celery, finely sliced crossways
8 anchovy fillets, cut in half crossways
1 tablespoon shredded parsley leaves
1 punnet celery cress, snipped
12 witlof (chicory) leaves, taken from the heart, trimmed
handful salad burnet sprigs or wild rocket leaves

ANCHOVY VINAIGRETTE
40 ml fresh lemon juice, strained
2 teaspoons anchovy cream
100 ml extra virgin olive oil
sea salt and freshly ground black pepper

To make the vinaigrette, whisk the ingredients together until emulsified.

Toss the octopus with the oil, salt and pepper until coated. Saute on a hot grill plate or in a frying pan for 2 minutes, then flip over and cook for another 2 minutes until tender.

Mix the octopus with the dressing and remaining salad ingredients and toss to combine. Arrange on plates and serve.

SERVES 4

OCTOPUS, ANCHOVY AND CELERY SALAD >

BUFFALO MOZZARELLA WITH BEETROOT AND HORSERADISH

Mozzarella made with buffalo milk is packed with flavour, aroma and character – truly an ingredient that needs little messing with. Victoria's Shaw River mozzarella is a premium product that bears little resemblance to the mass-produced, plastic-wrapped cow's milk mozzarella that is found in every supermarket. To complement the essential characteristics of the cheese, I opt for a robust, peppery green extra virgin olive oil – Joseph's First Run or a luscious Sicilian oil like Ravida would be my preferred choice.

2 × 1 cm thick slices sourdough bread
100 ml peppery extra virgin olive oil
4 buffalo mozzarella
½ teaspoon coarsely ground black pepper
1 punnet red chard cress, snipped
½ punnet mustard cress, snipped

BEETROOT REMOULADE
3 medium beetroot
100 ml extra virgin olive oil
3 teaspoons Banyuls (or red wine) vinegar
3 teaspoons smooth Dijon mustard
1 tablespoon finely diced cornichons
1 tablespoon grated horseradish
½ teaspoon sea salt
½ teaspoon freshly ground black pepper

BEETROOT JELLY
200 ml beetroot juice (from pureed and strained beetroot)
50 ml Banyuls red wine vinegar
3 g gelatine leaves, softened in cold water

To make the remoulade, preheat the oven to 200°C. Put the beetroots in a roasting pan and roast for about 25 minutes until soft. Allow to cool slightly then remove the peel and grate coarsely. Whisk the remaining ingredients in a bowl until incorporated, then add the grated beetroot and mix thoroughly. This tastes best when served warm, not refrigerator cold.

To make the beetroot jelly, heat the juice and vinegar just to simmering point then stir in the softened gelatine until dissolved. Pass through a fine mesh sieve and cool. Pour into a small tray to give the jelly a depth of 1 cm. Refrigerate for 2 hours until set. When ready to serve, cut the jelly into 1 cm cubes.

To make crunchy croutons, preheat the oven to 170°C. Remove the crusts from the sourdough slices and cut the bread into 1 cm dice. Toss with a little olive oil to lightly coat then lay on a baking tray and bake for 10 minutes until golden and crisp.

Cut each mozzarella ball into four even slices. Arrange the slices on a plate, slightly overlapping each other to make a circle in the centre of the plate (leave a hole in the centre for the remoulade).

Drizzle the cheese liberally with olive oil and sprinkle with black pepper.

Spoon the beetroot remoulade into the centre, so the cheese is still visible. Scatter the beetroot jelly cubes and crunchy croutons on the plate around the cheese, arrange the cress on top of the remoulade and serve.

SERVES 4

BAKED SARDINES WITH SWEET AND SOUR EGGPLANT

This salad, known as caponata in Italy, is a staple of an antipasto selection and makes a great accompaniment to most types of seafood or as an inclusion in a picnic basket. The tantalising flavours are pure Sicilian.

1 tablespoon sultanas
40 ml white wine (I would use pinot grigio or soave)
30 ml olive oil
3 tablespoons fresh breadcrumbs (from decent Italian bread)
1 tablespoon pine nuts, lightly roasted
4 anchovy fillets, chopped
12 small Ligurian black olives, pitted
2 tablespoons shredded parsley leaves
2 teaspoons chopped oregano leaves
1 teaspoon minced lemon zest
1 golden shallot, minced
2 cloves garlic, minced
¼ teaspoon grated nutmeg
¼ teaspoon chilli powder
½ teaspoon freshly ground black pepper
12 sardines, butterflied open
4 fresh bay leaves
40 ml fresh lemon juice, strained
50 ml fruity extra virgin olive oil
50 g pecorino cheese, finely grated

SWEET AND SOUR EGGPLANT
75 ml extra virgin olive oil
1 brown onion, diced
4 cloves garlic, minced
1 stick celery, sliced
6 tomatoes, peeled and roughly chopped
150 ml Tomato Pasta Sauce (see Essentials)
2 tablespoons castor sugar
125 ml red wine vinegar
2 tablespoons salted small (Aeolian) capers, rinsed
10 small black olives, pitted
1 red capsicum (pepper), roasted, peeled and sliced
1 yellow capsicum (pepper), roasted, peeled and sliced
2 × 200 g eggplants (aubergines), diced and deep-fried
sea salt and freshly ground black pepper

To prepare the eggplant, heat the oil and saute the onion for about 5 minutes until softened, then add the garlic and cook until softened. Add the celery and cook for another minute, then stir in the tomatoes and cook for 3 minutes. Add the tomato sauce, sugar, vinegar, capers, olives and capsicum slices. Simmer for 5 minutes, then stir in the fried eggplant and season to taste with salt and pepper.

Soak the sultanas in the wine for 1 hour, until plump. Heat the olive oil in a frying pan and gently fry the breadcrumbs until crisp and golden.

Preheat the oven to 175°C. In a bowl, mix together the sultanas and wine, fried breadcrumbs, pine nuts, anchovies, olives, parsley, oregano, minced lemon zest, shallot and garlic. Season with the nutmeg, chilli and pepper.

Lay the butterflied sardines flesh-side up and spoon some of the stuffing along the centre of each fish. Fold over to enclose the filling and lay the stuffed fish in a heavy-based baking dish interwoven with bay leaves. Pour on the lemon juice and extra virgin olive oil. Throw any extra filling over the fish and sprinkle with pecorino. Bake for 15 minutes until the sardines are cooked. Discard the bay leaves.

To serve, make a small nest of eggplant salad in the centre of each plate, lay the baked sardines on top and drizzle with the pan juices.

SERVES 4

PAPARDELLE WITH CAVOLO NERO SALSA

The dark moody cavolo nero leaves, a staple of Tuscany, are plentiful during winter, so go for the small sweet leaves of this cabbage relative. Here, I use it to make something akin to salsa verde to give a gossamer-thin coating to the wide ribbons of pasta. Garlic and anchovy seem such natural flavour partners with this vegetable and the whole thing is as easy as pie to make. The salsa is also an excellent accompaniment to rare roast beef, particularly if you replace the parmesan with gorgonzola.

100 g papardelle
120 g cooked tuna, flaked (I use a reputable brand of tinned cooked tuna, such as Ortiz or Sirena)

CAVOLO NERO SALSA
150 g small cavolo nero leaves
2 large cloves garlic, chopped
30 g diced pancetta
1 small red chilli, sliced
8 white anchovy fillets (boquerones)
1 tablespoon anchovy cream
1 cup parsley leaves
1 tablespoon salted baby capers, rinsed
½ teaspoon sea salt
½ teaspoon freshly ground black pepper
120 ml extra virgin olive oil
40 g grated parmesan cheese

To make the salsa, blanch the cavolo nero leaves and half the garlic in boiling water for 3 minutes. Drain and blend in a food processor until smooth. Fry the pancetta with the chilli and remaining garlic until crisp then add to the cavolo nero and blend until combined. Add the white anchovy fillets, anchovy cream, parsley and capers and pulse until combined. Season with salt and pepper. With the motor running, slowly drizzle in the oil to make a puree. Add the cheese and pulse until just combined.

Cook the pasta in a large saucepan of boiling water until al dente. Drain and toss with the flaked tuna and cavolo nero salsa until the pasta is lightly coated with the sauce. Serve immediately.

SERVES 4

ANGEL-HAIR PASTA WITH BOTTARGA AND SEA URCHIN CREAM

Bottarga is the smoked roe of mullet, and is something of a delicacy in many parts of Italy. When combined with sea urchin roe, it gives the hot pasta a distinct and luscious taste of the sea. Bottarga is available from some fishmongers, fish markets and select food specialists. It needs to be shaved very finely on a sharp mandoline to get tissue-thin shavings that simply melt into the hot pasta.

50 g sea urchin roe
2 teaspoons pouring (35%) cream
sea salt and freshly ground black pepper
200 g angel-hair pasta (spaghettini)
20 ml extra virgin olive oil
25 g unsalted butter
1 teaspoon minced garlic
60 g bottarga, finely shaved
40 ml fresh lemon juice, strained
3 tablespoons chopped chives

Pulse the sea urchin roe and cream together in a blender until smooth, being careful not to overwork. Season with a little salt and pepper to taste.

Cook the pasta in a large saucepan of boiling water until al dente.

While the pasta is cooking, heat the oil and butter in a frying pan and saute the garlic until softened.

Strain the pasta and toss into the pan with the garlic butter, then remove from the heat and add the shaved bottarga, lemon juice, chives and sea urchin cream. Toss until the pasta is coated with the cream and everything is evenly distributed.

Arrange on plates using a fork to twirl the pasta and serve immediately.

SERVES 4

ANGEL-HAIR PASTA WITH BOTTARGA AND SEA URCHIN CREAM >

ROASTED PUMPKIN, SAGE AND GOAT'S CHEESE RAVIOLI

These flavours and textures just sing together, and the colours always remind me of lazy autumn days in the Italian sunshine. The pasta dough is inspired by Marcella Hazan's potato gnocchi. She insists that the addition of eggs gives a lighter result, and she's absolutely right. The pasta dough deteriorates and becomes inflexible as it cools due to the starchiness of the potato, so you need to be organised and have the stuffing ready before you make the dough.

40 g parmesan cheese
12 sage leaves, deep-fried

PUMPKIN STUFFING
1 head garlic
40 ml extra virgin olive oil
600 g peeled pumpkin, cut into large chunks
½ teaspoon sea salt
½ teaspoon freshly ground black pepper
1 tablespoon sage leaves, finely shredded
150 g fresh goat's cheese
50 g parmesan cheese, grated

SAGE BUTTER
200 g unsalted butter, softened
2 cloves garlic, minced
½ cup chopped sage leaves
½ teaspoon sea salt
½ teaspoon freshly ground black pepper

POTATO PASTA DOUGH
800 g semi-waxy potatoes (desiree, dutch cream or spunta)
2 teaspoons sea salt
350 g strong bread flour (00 grade)
rice flour, for dusting (optional)

To make the pumpkin stuffing, preheat the oven to 180°C. Cut the top off the head of garlic, sit on a square of foil and drizzle with a little olive oil. Wrap up to secure and bake for 30 minutes until softened. Remove from the heat and when cool enough to handle, squeeze the garlic out and discard the skins. Reduce the temperature to 175°C.

Lay the pumpkin on a baking tray, drizzle with olive oil and season with salt and pepper. Bake for 30–40 minutes until softened. Remove from the heat and allow to cool. Blend the pumpkin and roasted garlic in a food processor until smooth. Taste and adjust the seasoning if necessary. Stir in the shredded sage, crumbled goat's cheese and grated parmesan.

To make the sage butter, blend all the ingredients together. Refrigerate for 1 hour before using.

When ready to serve, heat the butter in a pan until it just begins to colour.

To make the parmesan shards, preheat the oven to 180°C. Make small piles of grated cheese on a flat tray lined with baking paper. Bake for 8–10 minutes until the cheese melts and starts to colour. (If you want a neat round shape, stand a round pastry cutter on the tray and sprinkle the cheese inside the cutter to cover the surface.) Transfer to a wire rack to cool and store in an airtight container between layers of baking paper until ready to serve. You want to make one large or two small shards for each serve.

To make the pasta dough, cook the potatoes whole in boiling salted water until cooked. Remove from the water and leave until just cool enough to handle (the potatoes must be kept reasonably hot while making and forming the dough). Peel the potatoes and pass through a mouli or potato ricer. Add the sea salt and flour and work the dough to form a ball.

Divide the dough in three batches, keeping the rest covered with a cloth to prevent drying. Pass through the rollers of a pasta machine, dusting with rice flour if necessary to prevent sticking.

Do this about three times to make the dough cohesive and pliable. Continue to roll each pasta sheet from the widest setting through to the second-lowest setting. Cut the pasta sheets into eight rounds using pastry cutters – you need four that are 9.5 cm in diameter for the bases and four that are 11 cm in diameter for the lids.

Spoon some pumpkin stuffing into the centre of the four smaller rounds, then cover with the larger rounds so they resemble puffed pillows, pressing the edges together firmly to seal. Lay on a flat tray lined with baking paper to prevent sticking until ready to cook.

Bring a saucepan of water to boiling point, add a pinch of salt and cook the ravioli for 4 minutes, until they float to the surface. Carefully remove from the water with a slotted spoon and set one on each serving plate.

Spoon on the sizzling sage butter, top with the parmesan shards and fried sage leaves and serve.

SERVES 4

GRILLED FISH WITH GREMOLATA RISOTTO

This preparation is the essence of an Italian summer repast – its clean, fresh flavours remind me of al fresco moments along the Adriatic Coast. The gremolata really lifts the rice to an ethereal level, making it a perfect partner for simply cooked fish. The risotto also works well with tender poached veal.

4 × 125 g red emperor (or trumpeter, blue eye, hapuku, snapper or jewfish) fillets, skin on
20 ml olive oil
1 teaspoon sea salt
½ teaspoon freshly ground black pepper

GREMOLATA
4 cloves garlic
2 tablespoons parsley leaves
2 teaspoons lemon zest

GARLIC AND PARSLEY RISOTTO
1 bunch parsley, chopped (stems and leaves)
100 ml extra virgin olive oil
2 teaspoons sea salt
1 teaspoon freshly ground black pepper
500 ml fish stock
2 cloves garlic, minced
160 g Carnaroli rice
100 ml water
3 teaspoons fresh lemon juice, strained

To make the gremolata, chop the garlic, parsley and zest together until finely minced. Set aside.

For the risotto, blanch the chopped parsley in boiling water for 10 seconds, remove with a mesh spoon and plunge into iced water to stop the cooking. Reserve 75 ml of the cooking liquid. Remove the parsley from the ice and squeeze to remove any excess water. Blend with the reserved cooking water, 40 ml extra virgin olive oil, and salt and pepper to taste. Pass the parsley oil through a fine mesh sieve and discard the solids.

Heat the stock in a saucepan to simmering point. In a wide-based pan, heat the remaining oil over moderate heat and gently fry the garlic until softened. Add the rice and stir to coat the grains. Add the hot stock, one ladle at a time until the rice is cooked and all the stock has been absorbed.

Preheat the oven to 150°C. While the rice is cooking, brush the fish fillets with olive oil and season with salt and pepper. Lay, skin-side up, on a flat tray and cook under a hot grill for 5–6 minutes until just cooked. Remove from the heat and rest in the oven for a couple of minutes until the rice is ready.

Remove the rice from the heat and stir in the lemon juice, half the parsley oil and half the gremolata, then season to taste with salt and pepper.

Spoon the risotto onto serving plates, sit the fish on top and sprinkle with the remaining gremolata. Drizzle the remaining parsley oil around the rice and serve.

SERVES 4

Here are some words of wisdom from my friend Keith, who lives on Italy's Adriatic Coast: a discourse on cooking with broad beans, artichokes and tomatoes, following the flow of the seasons. I have left the recipe ideas just as he wrote them, as a brilliant example of intuitive cooking and creative ways of making the most of an abundance of fresh produce.

MASHED BROAD BEAN DIP

If we have lots of willing hands around to shell the beans and skin them (so all you're left with is the yummy green centre), then we make loads of paste by blending the beans with mint leaves, parmesan, salt and pepper. While it whizzes around in the blender, add glugs of virgin olive oil until it gets to the consistency of porridge.

Use fresh on bruschetta, or as a sauce on penne/tortiglioni pasta, with a dusting of parmesan (add a little hot pasta water if the paste seems too dense). The paste lasts forever frozen and is an absolute life saver for last-minute pasta!

BROAD BEAN AND MINT SOUP

We also do a broad bean and mint soup, which is basically hot stock, a potato, the shelled beans and a bunch of mint added to an onion and garlic that have been sweated in olive oil. When the potato is cooked, blend and pass through a colander, then put everything back in the pan, season and add a handful of parmesan before serving with bruschetta.

OUR CARCIOFI (BABY ARTICHOKES)

When the season starts, the poor infants are murdered at birth and delivered to our back door by the basketful, so we take it in turns to rip off a few outer leaves; a quick bath of cold water and vinegar to flush out the eerie wigs, and then they are thrown into a padella (frying pan) of hot oil with garlic, parsley and peperoncino and fried for a few minutes. This is followed by a splash of white wine, a stock cube, salt and black pepper, slightly covered so they steam in the wine vapour till it evaporates . . . deeeeeeeeeeeeelish!! At the beginning of the season we just consume kilos of carciofi like this. Then we have to invent new dishes to use the excess . . . if we're up to it. A lasagne with the sliced, cooked babies, a light bechamel and we have a stinky cheese here that is buried in a well for months so it smells like mould called formaggio del fossa, crumbled, with a glug or two of tartufo (truffle) oil . . . yummy!!! Or the fresh lasagne pasta chopped up into schizo bits (maltagliati . . . meaning 'badly cut') with a sauce of fried sausage, baby carciofi, a little panna (cream) and parmesan. Of course we also get them preserved under oil, but that's the job for an old girl from the village. We will boil up a chopped-up leg or shoulder of lamb, with loads of onions and all the spices for a tagine, leave it till the next day then pop the cooked leg in the oven with the cooked carciofi and the reduced liquids for half an hour till sizzling and slightly browned. Yummy with cous cous.

When we get the teenagers (middle to end of season), we rip off the outer, harder leaves, chop off the spiky heads (a Bart Simpson cut) and stuff the centres with a mix of parsley, garlic, chilli, salt and black pepper then stand them up in a pan, shoulder to shoulder – like soldiers – and fry them gently in olive oil, then add a few glugs of white wine, cover and steam till the wine has evaporated and they get very slightly burned or browned.

HAVING OUR WAY WITH TOMATOES

Luckily tomato time coincides with the invasion of guests, so we can dish out industrial-size bowls of our pomodoro concoctions at lunch (which usually vanish in a minute) so our hungry campers need only prosciutto and melon, salads and fruit to satisfy them after the pasta course. Then it's usually a coma for the afternoon as we have been known to drink lashings of vino bianco.

This is the absolute favourite with the family and kids. It was first performed for us in Sirolo by our Napolitano secretary.

Take tons of cherry tomatoes sliced in half and sizzle them in olive oil in a closed pan with loads of garlic (in better homes they seed the toms). Reduce the bubbling goo till it's sticky (you can cheat a little by adding a few gollops of bought passata), and add a little salt, black pepper, sugar, handfuls of basil leaves and optional chilli. Then add the hot cooked pasta (rigatoni or tortiglioni) and stir, throwing in handfuls of grated Pecorino Romano, and when everything is all coated and sticky, cover the lot with a smoked Scamorza cheese that has been chopped into tiny cubes, so the Scamorza kind of melts as the pasta arrives on the table . . . we like that!

My favourite is a recipe from our sister Furio: she chops and seeds her cherry toms as she's got class. You gather a bunch of every herb you can find in the garden – rosemary, sage, bay, thyme, marjoram, oregano and basil . . . chop all, except the basil, as fine as you can with a mezzaluna and put into a heatproof pasta bowl. Heat olive oil till it begins to smoke and pour onto the herbs – such fun as they cook immediately, then in goes your cooked spaghetti, the cherry toms, the torn basil and handfuls of parmesan. Stir everything and if the mess gets too sticky add a little hot pasta water . . . so yummy.

When we are overcome with an excess of cherry tomatoes we bottle them. So easy as we cheat by half-filling preserving jars with the toms, tomato passata, a teaspoon of sugar and salt, and a handful of basil, then fill them up with more toms and passata till the jars are full. Then we close the lids and boil the jars in a huge tub for an hour and leave to cool. Still tastes great on pasta in the middle of winter when we can't get fresh basil.

The round and ribbed tomatoes are destined for salads and creamy mozzarella . . . the plum and odd-shaped tomatoes we use for making sugo – which in our house is easy. Cook mountains of them chopped with onion, garlic and celery with *no* water, slowly, slowly till you have a reduced mush which you zap when cold and pass through a colander to remove the skins, add a little salt, black pepper and sugar (brings out the flavour).

Fresh, frozen or bottled, it's a life saver. For instance, my family devours kilos of mussels, steamed and then tossed in the sugo with chopped parsley. Or we slow-cook a piece of meat overnight in the sugo, so you have a great pasta sauce the next day and a lump of tender meat for seconds . . . so clever are the Italians!

QUAIL WITH PROSCIUTTO, FIGS AND GORGONZOLA

One of my favourite Italian taste memories is a dish served by Armando Percuoco at Sydney's Buon Ricordo, which involves wrapping fresh figs in prosciutto and baking them in a creamy blue cheese sauce. I have used those ingredients and his inspiration as a starting point for this dish, which elaborates on another Italian classic – saltimbocca. The flavours and textures are in perfect balance and harmony.

4 large quails
½ teaspoon freshly ground black pepper
¼ teaspoon sweet paprika
120 g Gorgonzola Piccante
4 teaspoons Caramelised Onions (see Essentials)
8 whole sage leaves
12 slices prosciutto
20 ml olive oil
sea salt and freshly ground black pepper
4 fresh figs
25 g unsalted butter
1 teaspoon finely chopped sage
150 ml pouring (35%) cream
20 ml extra virgin olive oil
2 teaspoons aged balsamic vinegar
4 small radicchio leaves, finely shredded
½ punnet sorrel cress, snipped
½ punnet rocket cress, snipped

To prepare the quails, preheat the oven to 180°C. Split each bird down its backbone and butterfly open, then carefully remove all its bones except its leg bone using a small paring knife. A compliant butcher may do this for you. Dust the quail with pepper and paprika to lightly season.

Cut four small rectangular logs from the gorgonzola, about 5 mm in diameter.

Spread the caramelised onion in a thin layer over the inside of each quail and lay the cheese on top. Roll the birds over to conceal the stuffing, then press a sage leaf onto the skin on both sides and wrap each quail in two slices of prosciutto – so it resembles a rolled sausage.

Heat the oil in an ovenproof frying pan and saute the quail parcels for 3 minutes until brown on one side. Flip over, then transfer the pan to the oven and cook for another 5 minutes. Remove, season with salt and pepper, then leave to rest for 3 minutes. Keep the oven on for the figs.

Cut a cross in the top of each fig to open slightly and stuff a small piece of cheese in the centre. Press gently to seal. Dice the remaining cheese for the sauce. Using the remaining prosciutto, wrap one slice firmly around the base of each fig. Sit the figs in a small ovenproof dish so they fit snugly together.

Melt the butter in a pan, add the chopped sage, cream and remaining cheese and cook over gentle heat just until the cheese has melted into the sauce. Pour the sauce over the figs and bake for 4 minutes.

Whisk the oil and vinegar together to make a vinaigrette and season with salt and pepper to taste.

Toss through the radicchio and cress to lightly coat.

Slice each quail sausage into four pieces crossways. Stand a baked fig in the centre of each plate and place the quail pieces, cut-side up, around the fig. Drizzle a little sauce over the fig, arrange the salad on top and serve.

SERVES 4

SLOW-BRAISED LAMB NECK WITH WHITE TRUFFLE NOODLES AND PORCINI

This combination of flavours just screams Italy to me. If you are lucky enough to have some fresh white truffle at your disposal (its season is November in Italy) shave a little over the top when serving. This dish came about in London when we discovered the intensely perfumed truffle flour (Tartufalba's Farina con aroma di tartufo) and started playing with flavours and textures that would complement it. I have also made it with milk-fed kid (baby goat) meat, so if you happen to have a source of this tender young meat, then by all means give it a go.

4 × 180 g milk-fed lamb necks
½ teaspoon sea salt
½ teaspoon freshly ground black pepper
½ teaspoon dried porcini powder
80 ml extra virgin olive oil
12 white asparagus spears
150 ml Pepper Sauce (see Essentials)
2 teaspoons fresh green peppercorns
1 punnet celery cress, snipped

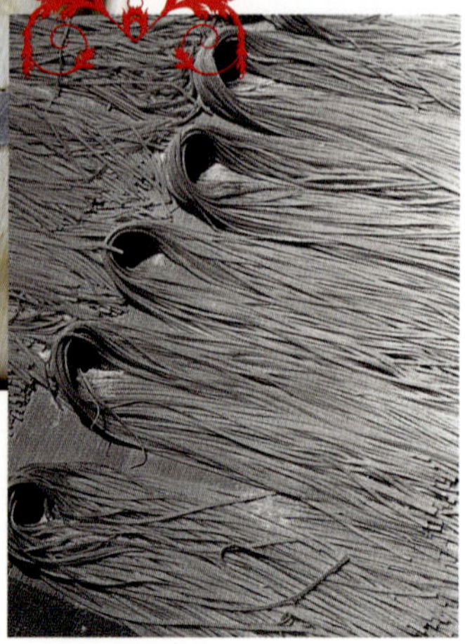

WHITE TRUFFLE NOODLES
80 g strong bread flour (00 grade)
20 g white truffle flour
pinch of sea salt
1 egg
3 teaspoons extra virgin olive oil

MUSHROOM PEPPER CRUST
1 tablespoon ghee
1 small brown onion, minced
3 cloves garlic, minced
1 teaspoon ground cumin
1 teaspoon ground coriander
½ teaspoon dried porcini powder
1 teaspoon sea salt
½ teaspoon freshly ground black pepper

TRUFFLE MUSHROOMS
25 g dried porcini mushroom slices
20 ml extra virgin olive oil
1 clove garlic, minced
1 teaspoon minced lemon thyme
1 teaspoon white truffle oil
60 g chanterelle mushrooms, cleaned and sliced
1 tablespoon chopped chives
1 teaspoon sea salt
½ teaspoon freshly ground black pepper >>

<< To prepare the lamb, mix the salt, pepper and porcini powder and rub into the lamb. Seal the lamb necks and olive oil in a cryovac bag or a double layer of zip-lock plastic bags. Cook the lamb in a pan of water held at 70°C for 7 hours (use a thermometer to monitor the temperature). Remove the bag from the water and leave to settle for 15 minutes before opening. While the lamb is cooking, prepare the other components.

To make the truffle noodles, mix both the flours with the salt. Knead the egg and oil into the flour until it forms a firm dough, kneading for about 5 minutes. Wrap in plastic film and rest for 1 hour.

Roll the dough into a length and cut into four pieces. Roll each piece of dough until flattened then pass through the rollers of a pasta machine, starting at the widest setting and passing through each setting to make thin sheets of dough. Pass each sheet through the spaghetti cutters on the pasta machine and hang for 15 minutes over a wooden stick.

Bring a large saucepan of water to a rapid boil and cook the noodles for 3 minutes until al dente. Drain and refresh under cold running water, then drain again. Shake to remove any excess moisture, then toss the noodles through a little olive oil to prevent them sticking. Set aside until ready to serve.

Remove the tougher stems from the asparagus and peel the stalks up to just below the tip. Cut each stalk into six slices on the diagonal, then cook in a pan of boiling water for 5 minutes until tender. Refresh under cold running water, drain and set aside.

To prepare the mushroom pepper crust, melt the ghee and saute the onion and garlic over gentle heat for about 15 minutes until softened. Spread onto a silicone mat or a sheet of baking paper to make a thin layer and allow the mix to dry out. Leave in a warm place or in the oven overnight (with just the pilot flame on). When dry, blend in a food processor to make a fine powder, then mix with the cumin, coriander, porcini powder, salt and pepper.

To prepare the truffle mushrooms, soak the porcini slices in 100 ml warm water for 30 minutes until softened. Drain, reserving the porcini water for another use. Chop the softened porcini into small pieces.

Heat the olive oil and saute the garlic for 2 minutes until softened, then add the chopped porcini, lemon thyme, truffle oil and chanterelle mushrooms and cook for another 3 minutes until the mushrooms have softened. Remove from the heat and stir in the chives, salt and pepper.

Heat the pepper sauce until simmering.

Roll the lamb necks in the mushroom pepper crust to season and lightly coat. Heat a pan and brush with oil, then quickly sear the lamb, rolling in the pan, for 4 minutes so the crust sticks to the meat. Remove from the heat and slice each lamb neck into four or five slices crossways.

Combine the mushrooms, truffle noodles, asparagus and green peppercorns and arrange like a nest in the centre of each plate. Place the lamb slices on the noodles and ladle the hot pepper sauce over the top. You can arrange a couple of the white asparagus slices on top of the lamb if you wish, then sprinkle with celery cress and serve.

SERVES 4

PRALINE CHOCOLATE PARADISE

This dessert is easy to assemble once you have the basic components prepared. It can also be made in one log in a rectangular cake tin if you prefer, in which case it simply needs to be turned out and cut into slices.

1 Chocolate Fudge Cake (see Essentials), cut into 1 cm thick slices
1 cup Almond Praline (see Essentials)
4 Butterscotch Almond Clusters (see Essentials)

CHOCOLATE GANACHE
400 ml pouring (35%) cream
500 g Valrhona Manjari chocolate, chopped
60 ml Mandarin Napoleon liqueur

To make the ganache, heat the cream in a saucepan to simmering point and pour over the chopped chocolate and liqueur. Stir until combined and smooth, then allow to cool to room temperature.

Slice the cake into 5 mm thin sheets. Grease six 200 ml dariole moulds and line with baking paper. Start with a layer of cake, cut to the diameter dimensions of the moulds. Press onto the base to cover then spoon on a layer of ganache to make a 5 mm thick layer. Sprinkle with a fine layer of praline and refrigerate for 20 minutes to allow the ganache to set. Repeat the layers until you have three layers of ganache and finish with a layer of cake to seal. Allow to set in the refrigerator for few hours before turning out.

Dip the moulds into hot water to turn out the cake. Stand the moulded cakes on a flat tray and pour some of the softened ganache over the top to coat the outside surfaces. Refrigerate until the ganache icing has set. Trim the base to remove any excess.

Sit a chocolate paradise cake in the centre of each plate and sprinkle with praline. Stand a butterscotch almond cluster on top and serve.

SERVES 6

PEACH AND PINK GRAPEFRUIT TRIFLE WITH CAMPARI JELLY

This alluring dessert looks quite dramatic when assembled in elegant art deco champagne coupes, instantly revealing its many layers and making it a cinch to serve, as all the hard work has been done beforehand.

500 ml Sugar Syrup (see Essentials)
400 ml moscato
zest and juice of 1 pink grapefruit
4 yellow peaches
4 × 4 cm rounds of Genoise Cake (see Essentials)
1 pink grapefruit, peeled and segmented

PINK GRAPEFRUIT BAVAROIS
65 ml milk
zest of ½ grapefruit
2 egg yolks
75 g castor sugar
45 ml fresh pink grapefruit juice, strained
2 teaspoons Campari
2 g gelatine leaves, softened in cold water
125 ml pouring (35%) cream, whipped

CAMPARI JELLY
65 ml fresh pink grapefruit juice, strained
25 ml Campari
90 ml Sugar Syrup (see Essentials)
3 g gelatine leaves, softened in cold water

MERINGUE CLOUDS
25 g egg white (about 1 egg)
25 g castor sugar
25 g icing sugar, sieved
4 g cornflour >>

<< Heat the sugar syrup, moscato, zest and juice in a saucepan to simmering point. Add the peaches and cover with baking paper to ensure they remain submerged. Simmer for 15 minutes until softened, then remove from the syrup and allow to cool. Peel the peaches then cut in half and remove the stones.

Soak the genoise cake rounds in the syrup for 10 seconds to soften, then press into the base of coupe glasses or serving bowls. Slice the peaches and arrange in a layer over the cake.

To make the bavarois, heat the milk and grapefruit zest over gentle heat to simmering point. Whisk the egg yolks and sugar until pale and creamy. Whisk in the grapefruit juice and Campari until combined. Add the hot milk and sit the bowl over a pan of simmering water and continue to cook, stirring, until the mixture thickens to a custard consistency. Stir in the softened gelatine until dissolved and remove from the heat. Pass the mix through a fine mesh sieve and discard the solids. Sit over ice to cool.

Whip the cream until thickened. When the custard mix has cooled, fold in the whipped cream until combined. Spoon the grapefruit cream over the peaches until the glasses are three-quarters full.

Refrigerate to set while you continue.

To make the jelly, heat the juice, Campari and sugar syrup in a saucepan until it starts to simmer. Add the softened gelatine and remove from the heat, stirring until dissolved. Allow to cool completely.

Cut the grapefruit segments into thin slices and arrange on top of grapefruit cream in an even layer. Pour the cooled (but not set) Campari jelly over the top to fill each glass. Refrigerate for 2 hours or until ready to serve.

To make the meringue clouds, whisk the egg whites with electric beaters and when soft peaks form, gradually add the castor sugar while continuing to beat. Whisk until stiff peaks form.

Gently fold in the icing sugar and cornflour until combined.

Bring a saucepan of water to just below simmering point – the surface should barely move and not bubble. Using two dessertspoons, shape the meringue to make quenelles (so they resemble cumulus clouds) then float on top of the water and cook for 2 minutes. Roll each cloud over with a spoon and cook the other side until set. Remove with a slotted spoon and drain on paper towel.

Lay a meringue cloud on top of the jelly layer of each trifle and serve immediately.

SERVES 4

HAZELNUT CROQUANT SEMIFREDDO

An Italian version of parfait, semifreddo is a frozen confection that requires no churning, making it an ideal dessert to prepare at home. Hazelnut and chocolate are made to go to bed together and the crunchy croquant effect created with the honeycomb and praline elevates it to a perfect menage a trois. Pectin powder, commonly used when making jams and preserves, is available from supermarkets, health-food stores and specialty food stores.

25 g Almond Praline (see Essentials), finely crushed
50 g Honeycomb (see Essentials), finely crushed
40 ml maple syrup

SEMIFREDDO
600 ml thick (45%) cream
2 large eggs, separated
100 g icing sugar, sieved
50 ml Frangelico liqueur
120 g gianduja (hazelnut) chocolate, melted
75 g Almond Praline (see Essentials)
75 g Honeycomb (see Essentials), crushed into small pieces

CROQUANT WAFERS
65 g castor sugar
1 g pectin powder
50 ml fresh orange juice, strained
35 g unsalted butter
15 g glucose
25 g plain flour, sifted

To make the semifreddo, whisk the cream just until soft peaks form. Whisk the egg yolks with half the icing sugar until pale and creamy, then whisk in the Frangelico and cooled melted chocolate.

Whisk the egg whites until stiff then gradually add the remaining icing sugar, continuing to whisk until glossy. Fold the cream into the chocolate mix then gently fold in the egg whites, praline and honeycomb. Spoon into eight 150 ml dariole moulds and freeze for 8 hours or overnight.

To make the croquant wafers, place the sugar, pectin, orange juice, butter and glucose in a saucepan and bring to the boil, whisking to combine. Remove from the heat and cool, then stir in the flour. Refrigerate for 1 hour until the mixture becomes firm.

Preheat the oven to 175°C and line a flat baking tray with baking paper. Using a palette knife, spread the wafer mix evenly over the prepared baking tray to make a thin layer. Bake for 5–6 minutes until golden. While still hot, cut the wafers into your preferred shape using a sharp knife (if left to cool it will crack and be uneven). Store the wafers between sheets of baking paper in an airtight container until ready to serve.

Stand each mould in a bowl of hot water for a few seconds then invert a frozen semifreddo onto each plate. Mix the praline and crushed honeycomb together and sprinkle over the semifreddo, then drizzle with maple syrup. Lay a croquant wafer across the top and serve.

SERVES 8

ESSENTIALS

ALIOLI

This mayonnaise is used with so many dishes throughout Spain, from seafood and salads to stews and paella. Any leftovers can be refrigerated for up to 5 days.

1 head garlic
¼ teaspoon sea salt
20 ml fresh lemon juice, strained
1 egg yolk
20 ml red wine vinegar (I use Forum cabernet)
¼ teaspoon freshly ground white pepper
¼ teaspoon Spanish sweet paprika
160 ml fruity extra virgin olive oil

Preheat the oven to 180°C, wrap the garlic in foil and roast for 30 minutes or until soft. Squeeze the garlic from the cloves and mix to a paste with the sea salt in a mortar and pestle. Blend the garlic mixture with the lemon juice, egg yolk, vinegar, pepper and paprika in a food processor. With the motor running, slowly drizzle in the oil in a thin, steady stream until the sauce emulsifies and thickens.

To make **saffron alioli**, infuse ¼ teaspoon saffron threads in the vinegar over gentle heat until warmed. Leave to cool then proceed with making the alioli.

MAKES 200 ML

ALMOND PRALINE

75 g blanched almonds
1 teaspoon hazelnut oil
200 g castor sugar
50 ml water

Preheat the oven to 160°C. Roast the almonds for 10 minutes or until golden. Brush a baking tray with the oil and spread the nuts onto the tray. Put the sugar and water in a saucepan, bring to the boil and cook until it becomes a caramel colour – do not stir or it will crystallise. Pour the hot caramel over the nuts and leave to cool. When cold and set, break into pieces using a cleaver or mallet and blitz in a food processor until it forms fine crumbs. Store in an airtight container in the refrigerator for up to a month.

To make **hazelnut** or **pistachio** praline, substitute the same quantity of either roasted hazelnuts (with skins rubbed off) or shelled pistachios for the almonds.

MAKES 300 G

ANCHOVY MAYONNAISE

8 cloves garlic
2 large eggs
8 Ortiz anchovy fillets, chopped
25 ml sherry vinegar
1 teaspoon fresh lemon juice, strained
300 ml extra virgin olive oil
½ teaspoon sea salt
½ teaspoon freshly ground white pepper

Preheat the oven to 180°C, wrap the garlic cloves in foil and roast for 30 minutes until soft. Boil the eggs for 2 minutes only. Squeeze the garlic from the skins into the bowl of a food processor and blend with the warm shelled eggs and anchovy fillets. Add the sherry vinegar and lemon juice then, with the motor running, slowly drizzle in the oil until the sauce emulsifies. Season, then taste and adjust if necessary. Refrigerate until ready to use. Keeps for up to 5 days.

MAKES 350 ML

BAHARAT SPICE MIX

Almost every spice blend used in the Arab world and Middle Eastern cooking is known as baharat, which literally means 'spices'. Each blend varies from region to region, family to family, but the overall flavour of baharat is not dissimilar to allspice. Baharat is generally used as a seasoning for marinades, preserves, meat and vegetables.

2 tablespoons black peppercorns
1 tablespoon coriander seeds
1 stick cinnamon
20 cloves
1 tablespoon cumin seeds
seeds from 4 green cardamom pods
1 teaspoon ground cassia
2 teaspoons freshly grated nutmeg
2 tablespoons ground paprika

Grind the whole spices to a fine powder and then mix in remaining spices. Store in a sealed jar for up to a month.

MAKES 8 TABLESPOONS

BEEF STOCK

A rich stock made from roasted beef bones, shanks and veal knuckles that forms the basis of good sauces and soups and gives a great depth of flavour.

1 kg beef bones
1 kg split shanks
2 kg veal knuckles
500 ml red wine
5 tomatoes
2 brown onions, chopped
1 large carrot
handful of parsley
2 teaspoons black peppercorns
1 sprig thyme

Preheat the oven to 200°C. Place the bones in a baking dish and brown in the oven for 30 minutes. Transfer the bones to a large stockpot (there should be room to spare). Remove any fat from the baking dish and deglaze with the red wine, then tip the wine and juices into the stockpot. Roast the tomatoes, onions and carrots in the baking dish for 30 minutes until softened, then add to the stockpot with the remaining ingredients and cover with cold water. Bring to the boil, then reduce the heat and simmer gently for 6 hours, skimming regularly to remove any scum.

Carefully remove the bones, then strain the stock through a conical sieve and discard the solids. Strain the stock again through a fine mesh sieve. Skim any excess fat from the surface with a ladle, then allow to cool completely before refrigerating (for up to 5 days) or freezing (for up to 2 months).

MAKES 3 LITRES

BLACK PEPPER SALT CRUST

6 tablespoons sea salt
3 tablespoons freshly ground black pepper
190 g rice flour

Dry-roast the salt and pepper together in a cast-iron frying pan over gentle heat for about 5 minutes until aromatic, stirring often. Cool, then grind in an electric spice grinder to make a fine powder and mix with the rice flour until evenly combined. Store in airtight container until ready to use. Keeps for up to a month.

MAKES 300 G

BLACK PEPPER STIR-FRY PASTE

Inspired by the Nonya cooks of Melaka, this is a complex, fragrant paste that gives extra kick to a dish.

5 stalks lemongrass
6 small red chillies
8 cloves garlic
4 coriander roots
5 makrut lime leaves
75 ml vegetable oil
1 tablespoon freshly ground black pepper
25 ml fish sauce

Chop the lemongrass finely with a knife (to make the paste finer when processed), then chop the chillies, garlic, coriander roots and lime leaves.

Blend together in a food processor with the oil. Add the pepper and fish sauce and continue processing until you have a fine paste. Check for taste and adjust if necessary. Store in the refrigerator for up to a week.

MAKES 200 G

BLACK-INK NOODLES

3 large eggs
2 teaspoons squid ink
2 teaspoons olive oil
320 g strong bread flour (00 grade)
pinch of sea salt
rice flour, for dusting

Blend the eggs, squid ink and oil in a food processor, then add flour and salt and blend until the dough forms a ball. Wrap in plastic film and refrigerate for 1 hour.

Cut the dough into four pieces, then flatten by hand or with a rolling pin. Pass each piece of dough through the rollers of a pasta machine, starting on the widest setting and working your way through each setting until you reach the finest. Dust the dough with rice flour before moving onto the next setting to prevent sticking (rice flour is used as it is free of gluten, which could toughen the dough at this stage).

Hang the sheets of dough over a broom handle or the back of a chair to dry for 10 minutes – this makes it easier to cut. Pass the dough through the spaghetti cutters on your pasta machine, then hang the noodles over a broom handle or the back of a chair for 30 minutes or until ready to cook.

Bring a large saucepan of water to a rolling boil, then add the noodles and allow the water to return to the boil. Cook for 2 minutes, then remove the noodles with a sieve and drain. If not eating immediately, refresh the noodles under cold running water to stop the cooking, then drain and toss lightly with a little oil to prevent sticking. To reheat, immerse the noodles in boiling water for 10 seconds, then drain.

MAKES 450 G

BLOOD ORANGE CURD

Made in the same manner as the classic lemon curd, this recipe can be adapted to use any citrus juice.

5 egg yolks
100 g castor sugar
2 teaspoons finely grated blood orange zest
110 ml blood orange juice
125 g cold unsalted butter, diced

Whisk the yolks, sugar and zest together in a bowl until pale and creamy. Add the juice and whisk until combined. Stand the bowl over a pan of simmering water and cook until it starts to thicken, stirring constantly. Still stirring, gradually add the cold butter piece by piece, adding each piece as the previous one melts into the curd. When the last piece of butter has been added, remove the bowl from the heat and set over a bowl of ice to stop the cooking. Allow to cool, then store in an airtight container in the refrigerator for up to 5 days.

MAKES 250 G

BLOOD PLUM SAUCE

250 ml water
250 g castor sugar
25 ml brandy
20 ml creme de cassis
25 ml anise liqueur
½ vanilla bean, split
½ stick cinnamon
2 cloves
1 whole mace
600 g blood plums, halved and stones removed

Put all the ingredients except the plums in a large stainless steel saucepan, bring to the boil, then simmer for 20 minutes. Add the plums to the syrup and cook over gentle heat for 1 hour or until the plums have lost their shape and become mushy. Press through a conical sieve, extracting as much liquid as possible and discarding the solids. The sauce can be used right away or refrigerated in a sealed jar for up to a month.

MAKES 600 ML

BOOZY CUMQUATS

500 g cumquats, washed
500 g castor sugar
750 ml Pedro Ximenez sherry
2 teaspoons vanilla extract

Blanch the cumquats in boiling water for 2 minutes, then drain and cool. Place them in sterilised glass jars, then add the sugar, sherry and vanilla and seal. Tip the jars back and forth and upside down so that the sugar dissolves in the sherry. Tip the jars in this same way every couple of hours for the first few days then store in a dark cupboard for 2–3 months until the cumquats have softened, matured and become boozy. These will keep for up to 6 months, though once opened they should be refrigerated.

MAKES 2 × 600 ML JARS

BREAD WAFERS

1 sourdough baguette
1 clove garlic, cut in half
extra virgin olive oil

Wrap the baguette in plastic film and freeze until half-frozen. Preheat the oven to 140°C. Using an electric slicer or a very sharp bread knife, slice the bread into wafer-thin slices crossways or on the diagonal (depending on the result you want). Rub the bread slices with the cut edge of the garlic then brush both sides of the wafers with extra virgin olive oil. Lay the slices on a flat baking tray and bake for 15–20 minutes until crisp and light golden. Cool on a wire rack then store in an airtight container.

MAKES 30

BROWN CHICKEN STOCK

This is a richer stock than its white counterpart, the roasted bones and vegetables lending more colour and flavour to the stock.

3 kg chicken carcasses
250 ml red wine
12 tomatoes
40 ml vegetable oil
2 brown onions, chopped
3 large carrots, chopped
2 heads garlic, cut in half
5 green onions, chopped
1 knob ginger, sliced
2 bay leaves
1 teaspoon black peppercorns
handful of parsley
5 litres White Chicken Stock (see page 559)

Preheat the oven to 200°C. Place the chicken carcasses in a baking dish and brown in the oven for 30 minutes to render some of their fat. At the same time, roast the tomatoes in another dish for 20 minutes until coloured and softened.

Heat the oil in a large stockpot and cook the onion, carrot, garlic, green onion and ginger until fragrant, then stir in the bay leaves, peppercorns and parsley. Transfer the chicken carcasses to the stockpot. Remove any fat from the baking dish and deglaze with the red wine, then tip the wine and juices into the stockpot, along with the roasted tomatoes. Bring to the boil, then simmer gently, uncovered, for 3–4 hours, skimming frequently to remove any fat and scum.

Strain the stock through a conical sieve, pressing firmly to extract as much liquid as possible, then discard the solids. Strain the stock again through a fine mesh sieve. Skim any excess fat from the surface with a ladle, then allow to cool completely before using, refrigerating (for up to 5 days) or freezing (for up to 2 months).

MAKES 4 LITRES

BUTTERSCOTCH ALMOND CLUSTERS

pinch of cream of tartar
20 ml water
100 g castor sugar
30 g brown sugar
20 ml glucose
25 g unsalted butter
150 g slivered almonds, lightly roasted
20 small (petit-four size) patty cases

Dissolve the cream of tartar in the water and add to a small saucepan with the sugars, glucose and butter. Stir over gentle heat until the sugar dissolves, then increase the heat to high and bring to the boil. Boil until it reaches 145°C (use a sugar thermometer to check). Put a single layer of almonds in the patty cases and pour the hot butterscotch on top. Stir with a chopstick to make clusters and leave to cool completely. Remove the almond clusters from the paper cases and store in an airtight container for up to 2 days.

MAKES 20

CANDIED CUMQUATS

500 g cumquats, washed
3 green cardamom pods, cracked
Sugar Syrup (see page 557)
2 teaspoons orange blossom water

Put the cumquats in a large saucepan and cover with cold water. Bring to the boil over high heat then drain. Repeat twice, so the fruit is brought to the boil three times. Put the cumquats and the cardamom in a large saucepan and cover with sugar syrup. Simmer gently for 2–3 hours until the syrup has thickened and the fruit is translucent. Add the orange blossom water then transfer the fruit and syrup to a sterilised glass jar, seal and allow to cool. Store in the refrigerator for up to 3 months.

MAKES 1 × 750 G JAR

CARAMELISED ONIONS

Caramelised onions are especially good made with the sweet, golden Kununurra onions from the Kimberley region of Western Australia, which appear in spring, otherwise the red Spanish onions are also good. Serve these as a condiment, use as a tart filling or as a topping for toast or bruschetta.

125 ml olive oil
4 onions, finely sliced
25 g brown sugar
40 ml red wine vinegar

Heat the olive oil in a wide, heavy-based pan over moderate heat and cook the onions until softened and starting to change colour. Add the sugar and vinegar and cook for another 30 minutes until caramelised and sweet. Allow to cool and store in airtight container in the refrigerator, where they will keep for 2–3 weeks.

MAKES 400 G

CHAT MASALA

'Chat' is an Indian term for appetisers, palate teasers or small morsels eaten as a snack. This spice mix is used to flavour fried pastries, various potato preparations and tomato-based salads.

1 teaspoon black peppercorns
1 teaspoon cumin seeds
½ teaspoon ajwain seeds
3 cubeb
½ teaspoon dried pomegranate seeds
seeds from 3 green cardamom pods
1 teaspoon ground black salt
1 teaspoon amchoor powder
1 teaspoon ground ginger
¼ teaspoon asafoetida powder
1 teaspoon chilli powder

Grind the whole spices to a fine powder and then stir in the remaining spices. Store in a sealed jar. Keeps for 2 weeks, but is best used soon after being made.

MAKES 2 TABLESPOONS

CHERMOULA

A distinctive Moroccan marinade that adds a depth of spicy herbaceous flavour and character to fish, meats and vegetables.

1 teaspoon cumin seeds
2 large dried chillies
½ teaspoon saffron threads
50 ml fresh lemon juice, strained
1 red onion, minced
2 teaspoons minced garlic
½ teaspoon ground paprika
½ teaspoon freshly ground black pepper
½ teaspoon freshly ground cinnamon
1 teaspoon sea salt
1 cup coriander leaves, finely chopped
1 cup parsley leaves, finely chopped
125 ml olive oil

Dry-roast the cumin seeds and dried chillies separately over gentle heat until fragrant. Cool, then grind to a fine powder. Place the saffron threads and lemon juice in a small pan, then bring slowly to simmering point to bring out the colour and flavour. Cool, then mix all the ingredients together. Refrigerate for up to 2 days.

MAKES 200 ML

CHILLI CARAMEL

250 g palm sugar
juice and finely grated zest of 1 makrut lime
100 ml Tamarind Liquid (see page 557)
100 ml fish sauce
20 ml fresh mandarin juice, strained
2 small red chillies, sliced into fine rounds
40 g Fried Shallot Slices (see page 550)

Heat the palm sugar and lime zest in a saucepan over moderate heat until caramelised, then add the tamarind liquid and fish sauce. Simmer for 5 minutes, then stir in the lime and mandarin juices and the sliced chilli and cook for another 2 minutes. Stir in the fried shallots, remove from the heat and allow to cool. Taste for balance – you may need to adjust depending on the type and quality of the palm sugar used and the strength of the tamarind liquid. Store in the refrigerator for up to 5 days.

MAKES 400 ML

CHILLI JAM

One of the most essential items in my pantry, whether at home or in the restaurant. I love this for its strong, addictive personality and complex yet refined flavour. This recipe is tried and true and does not work if you reduce the amounts (many have tried, and all have failed!), so think big and just go for it. You'll find it gets used up quickly.

1.5 kg long red chillies, chopped
300 g small red chillies, chopped
8 brown onions, chopped
15 large cloves garlic, chopped
1 litre vegetable oil
300 ml Tamarind Liquid (see page 557)
125 g palm sugar, shaved

Place the chillies, onion, garlic and oil in a food processor and blend to a smooth paste. Cook the paste in a wide, heavy-based frying pan over low heat until dark red – this will take up to 12 hours of continuous slow cooking and occasional stirring. Stir in the tamarind liquid and palm sugar and cook very slowly for another 2 hours. Spoon into jars, then cover with a film of oil and seal. Refrigerate for up to 3 months.

MAKES 2 LITRES

CHILLI LEMONGRASS PASTE

5 long red chillies, chopped
2 cloves garlic, chopped
2 tablespoons chopped lemongrass
2 tablespoons chopped galangal
7 tablespoons chopped red shallots
2 teaspoons sea salt
2 teaspoons kapi (Thai shrimp paste)

Pound the ingredients together in a mortar and pestle to make a fine paste. Transfer to an airtight container, cover with a film of oil and store in the refrigerator for up to 3 days.

MAKES 250 G

CHILLI SALT CRUST

This gives a superfine and seasoned coating to seafood and tofu when deep-frying.

3 large dried chillies, broken
1 tablespoon sea salt
1 teaspoon black peppercorns
1 teaspoon Spanish sweet paprika
50 g rice flour

Put the chillies, salt and peppercorns in a frying pan over very low heat and roast slowly for about 5 minutes until fragrant. Cool then grind to a fine powder. Stir in the paprika and rice flour until combined. Store in an airtight container for up to 2 weeks.

MAKES 75 G

CHILLI TURMERIC PASTE

10 small dried chillies, soaked and drained
5 small yellow or orange chillies
8 cloves garlic, chopped
1 teaspoon sea salt
1 tablespoon chopped turmeric
1 stalk lemongrass, minced using a Microplane
3 teaspoons chopped galangal
5 red shallots, chopped
3 teaspoons kapi (Thai shrimp paste)

Pound the chillies and garlic with the salt in a mortar and pestle until smooth. Add the remaining ingredients and pound until the paste is smooth. Keeps for 3 days in the refrigerator.

MAKES 250 G

CHINESE FIVE-SPICE POWDER

An essential spice mix used in Chinese cooking. Although it varies from region to region and maker to maker, it is characteristically highly aromatic with a well-balanced aroma and flavour.

5 star anise
1 tablespoon fennel seeds
1 tablespoon Sichuan peppercorns
2 teaspoons cloves
1 teaspoon ground cassia
1 teaspoon freshly ground cinnamon

Grind the whole spices to a fine powder, then pass through a fine mesh sieve and discard the husks. Stir in the ground cassia and cinnamon. This is best used soon after making, but can be stored in a sealed jar for up to 2 weeks.

MAKES 4 TABLESPOONS

CHINESE MASTER STOCK

This stock should never be thrown out – as long as it is brought to a boil every week and is kept refrigerated in a sealed container, it will grow better and richer with age and can be kept topped up. Just make sure that every time you cook meat in it you strain the stock through a fine mesh sieve before refrigerating it, to keep it free of any particles that may cause bacteria to grow. This master stock gives a rich, reddish-brown, lacquered appearance and a wonderful flavour and aroma to meat and poultry. As the process of red-braising is a very gentle one, it also gives anything cooked in it a tender, velvety texture.

3 litres White Chicken Stock (see page 559)
300 ml dark soy sauce
250 ml light soy sauce
100 ml Shaoxing rice wine
40 g yellow rock sugar
2 star anise, broken
2 pieces cassia bark
1 teaspoon fennel seeds
1 teaspoon Sichuan peppercorns
1 black cardamom pod, cracked
2 pieces dried tangerine peel
2 red bird's-eye chillies, split
4 slices ginger
2 slices galangal
3 pieces liquorice root

Bring all the ingredients to the boil in a large stockpot. Simmer gently for 1 hour, then strain through a fine mesh sieve and discard the solids. Allow the stock to cool completely before refrigerating in a sealed container.

MAKES 3.5 LITRES

CHOCOLATE FUDGE CAKE

The quantities for this cake can easily be doubled or tripled. The cooking time will remain pretty much the same if the depth of the tin is constant – just make sure the tin is wider rather than deeper when making a larger batch. This cake is baked with a water bath on the shelf below to ensure gentle, moist cooking.

100 g dark couverture chocolate
100 g unsalted butter
3 large eggs, separated
150 g castor sugar
50 g plain flour, sifted

Preheat the oven to 160°C. Grease and line a 30 cm × 24 cm cake tin that is 5 cm deep. Shave the chocolate into a bowl and melt it gently with the butter over a pan of simmering water, then set aside to cool a little.

Whisk the egg yolks and 75 g of the castor sugar in a bowl until light and frothy. Whip the egg whites in another bowl until stiff peaks form then, while still beating, slowly add the remaining sugar. Stir the melted chocolate mixture into the egg yolk mixture, along with the flour, then gently fold in the stiff egg whites. Pour the cake batter into the tin, then cover the exposed surface with baking paper to prevent a crust forming during cooking.

Place in the oven with a baking dish of water set on the shelf below. Cook for 20 minutes or until the centre is set (if a skewer comes out clean, the cake is cooked). Remove from the oven and put the tin on a wire rack to cool. Peel off the top layer of baking paper and turn the cooled cake out onto the wire rack. Remove any paper still attached to the cake. When the cake has cooled completely, wrap it carefully in plastic film and store at room temperature until ready to use.

MAKES 1 CAKE

CINNAMON SUGAR

For maximum flavour, make this as you need it, and buy your ground cinnamon from a reputable spice dealer.

1 tablespoon castor sugar
2 teaspoons ground cinnamon

Mix together and use as required.

MAKES 1½ TABLESPOONS

CORIANDER PESTO

100 ml peanut oil
25 g raw peanuts, blanched
1 small green chilli, chopped
2 teaspoons finely chopped ginger
4 cloves garlic, chopped
1 cup (firmly packed) Thai or holy basil leaves
¼ cup (firmly packed) Vietnamese mint leaves
1 cup (firmly packed) coriander leaves
1 teaspoon shaved palm sugar or jaggery
2 teaspoons fish sauce
2 teaspoons fresh lime juice, strained

Heat the oil in a frying pan and fry the peanuts over moderate heat until golden. Strain the peanuts, reserving the oil, and allow to cool. Blend the cooled peanuts in a food processor with the chilli, ginger and garlic. Add the herbs and half the reserved oil, and blend to a smooth paste. Blend in the palm sugar, fish sauce and lime juice and process until the herbs are finely chopped. With the motor running, gradually pour in enough of the remaining oil to make a smooth paste. Spoon into a sterilised glass jar, cover with a film of oil and seal. This keeps, refrigerated, for a week, but is best used soon after it is made.

MAKES 200 ML

CREME FRAICHE PASTRY

I have used this short, flaky pastry to make my signature five-spice duck and shiitake mushroom pies in a past life, and for many other pies since. I don't recommend it for tart cases, as it is too short and will slip down the sides of the tins during cooking.

125 g cold unsalted butter
200 g plain flour
1 teaspoon sea salt
125 g creme fraiche

Chill the bowl and blade of a food processor in the refrigerator. Chop the butter into chunks and, while still cold, blend with the flour and salt in the food processor until the mixture resembles breadcrumbs. Add the creme fraiche and pulse until just incorporated. Don't overwork the dough at this stage or the pastry will be difficult to handle when rolling. Form the pastry into a ball by hand, then wrap in plastic film and refrigerate for 2 hours.

Roll and cut the pastry as required. Keep the pastry as cool as possible when working with it – you may need to return it to the refrigerator as you roll and cut as it can become temperamental during handling. Any leftover pastry can be frozen for later use.

MAKES 450 G

CUCUMBER JUICE

1 large cucumber
water

Peel the cucumber and roughly chop the flesh. Blend the flesh with a little water in a food processor. Pass the juice through a fine mesh sieve and discard the pulp. Refrigerate for up to 3 days.

MAKES ABOUT 250 ML

CUCUMBER WASABI JELLY

250 ml Cucumber Juice (see preceding recipe), strained
50 ml verjuice
1 teaspoon wasabi powder
5 g gelatine leaves, softened in cold water
1 tablespoon wasabi flying fish roe (tobiko)

Heat the juice and verjuice in a saucepan to blood temperature only, then whisk in the wasabi powder. Don't let it boil or it will lose its vibrant colour.

Stir in the softened gelatine until dissolved and allow to cool. When cool, and just as it starts to set, stir through the wasabi roe until evenly distributed. Pour into moulds and refrigerate until firm. This will keep for up to 3 days in the refrigerator.

MAKES 300 ML

DARK CHOCOLATE GANACHE

100 ml pouring (35%) cream
125 g best-quality dark couverture chocolate, shaved

Heat the cream in a saucepan to simmering point. Pour the hot cream over the shaved chocolate in a bowl and stir until thoroughly combined. Cool then refrigerate for up to 5 days.

MAKES 200 ML

DASHI STOCK

An essential base stock used in many Japanese preparations. The quality of the water does affect the outcome, so it's worth using bottled still or spring water.

6 cm piece dried kombu seaweed (kelp)
1 litre still mineral water
50 g dried bonito flakes

Place the kombu and water in a large saucepan and bring slowly to the boil. When simmering, stir in the bonito flakes and remove from the heat. Allow to sit for 45 minutes to infuse, then strain and use as required. This will not keep, so use it the same day it is made.

MAKES 1 LITRE

DUCK LIVER PATE

90 g unsalted butter
1 small white onion, finely diced
2 small cloves garlic, chopped
25 g bacon, diced
30 g pancetta, diced
2 teaspoons thyme leaves
200 g cleaned duck livers
25 ml cognac or brandy
2 teaspoons red wine vinegar
1 teaspoon sea salt
1 teaspoon freshly ground black pepper
40 ml pouring (35%) cream

Heat 20 g of the butter in a frying pan and saute the onion and garlic for about 4 minutes until softened. Add the bacon, pancetta and thyme and saute until it starts to crisp and colour. Remove from the heat and tip into a bowl. Return the pan to the heat, melt another 20 g of butter and saute the livers over moderately high heat for 1 minute until they start to brown, then flip over and cook for another minute. Add the cognac and vinegar and cook for 1 minute until the alcohol has burned off. Remove the pan from the heat – the livers should still be pink in the centre.

Put the livers and their pan juices into a blender with the bacon mix, salt and pepper and blend until smooth. With the motor running, add the remaining (cold) butter piece by piece, then add the cream all in one go and pulse just until incorporated – do not overwork. Taste and adjust the seasoning if necessary. Store in the refrigerator in an airtight container, covered with a film of melted butter to prevent oxidisation. Keeps for 3 days.

MAKES 350 G

DUCK STOCK

This is a great stock to have on hand for making a soup or sauce. Make it when you have cooked duck for another dish – the bones have far too much flavour to throw out.

2 duck carcasses
100 ml Shaoxing rice wine
vegetable oil, for frying
1 brown onion, chopped
½ head garlic
2 green onions, chopped
4 slices ginger
1 bay leaf
½ teaspoon black peppercorns
handful of parsley
2.5 litres White Chicken Stock (see page 559)

Preheat the oven to 200°C. Place the duck carcasses in a baking dish and brown in the oven for 30 minutes to render some of their fat. Remove the carcasses and fat and deglaze the pan with the Shaoxing wine.

Heat a little oil in a stockpot and saute the onion, garlic, green onion and ginger until fragrant, then stir in the bay leaves, peppercorns and parsley. Transfer the duck carcasses to the stockpot. Remove any fat from the baking dish and deglaze with the Shaoxing wine then tip the wine and juices into the stockpot. Cover with stock, bring to the boil, then simmer gently, uncovered, for 3 hours, skimming frequently.

Strain the stock through a conical sieve, pressing firmly to extract as much liquid as possible, then discard the solids. Strain the stock again through a fine mesh sieve. Skim any excess fat from the surface with a ladle, then allow to cool completely before using, refrigerating (for up to 5 days) or freezing (for up to 2 months).

MAKES 2 LITRES

DUKKAH

Originally from Egypt, this fragrant spice and nut mix can be served with bread and olive oil or used in salads, sprinkled over boiled or poached eggs or served with black sausage and offal.

2 tablespoons sesame seeds
3 teaspoon cumin seeds
1 tablespoon coriander seeds
15 g hazelnuts
½ teaspoon salt
¼ teaspoon freshly ground black pepper

Roast the sesame seeds, cumin and coriander seeds and hazelnuts separately in a pan over low heat until aromatic and lightly coloured. Cool. Rub the hazelnuts to remove their papery skins then grind until fine. Grind the coriander and cumin seeds together and mix with the ground hazelnuts, sesame seeds, salt and pepper. Store in an airtight container for up to 2 weeks.

MAKES 4 TABLESPOONS

FISH CRACKLING

skin from 1 ocean trout or salmon fillet

Scrape the inside of the skin to remove all traces of fish flesh, then scrape the outside surface to ensure all scales have been removed. Wash the cleaned skin in cold water then stretch it out onto a wire rack and sit it on a shelf above the stove or in a warm dry place and leave to dry for up to 30 hours.

Lift the dried skin off the rack and cut into strips crossways. Store the dried strips in an airtight container until ready to use – they will keep for up to 2 weeks. To cook, deep-fry the strips in hot oil for 2 minutes until they become crisp, then drain on paper towel.

SERVES 10

FISH STOCK

Use good-quality, fresh, cleaned fish heads and bones as they affect the stock's flavour and clarity; any deep-sea white-fleshed fish is ideal.

heads and bones of 2 large fish
6 green onions, chopped
1 knob ginger, sliced
1 teaspoon white peppercorns
500 ml dry white wine

Wash the fish heads thoroughly to remove all blood, then remove the gills as they will make the stock bitter. Put all the ingredients in a stockpot and cover with cold water. Bring to a boil, then simmer gently for 2 hours, skimming frequently to remove any scum.

Strain the stock through a conical sieve, pressing to extract as much liquid as possible, then discard the solids. Strain the stock again through a fine mesh sieve. Cool completely before refrigerating or freezing; keeps for 3 days in the refrigerator or 1 month in the freezer.

MAKES 4 LITRES

FRIED GARLIC SLICES

Garlic cloves can be sliced finely and cooked in the same manner as fried shallots (see below).

FRIED LEEK STRIPS

Leeks can be cut into 7 cm sticks then finely sliced lengthways and cooked in the same manner as fried shallots (see below).

FRIED SHALLOT SLICES

Made from the smaller Asian red shallots, these crisp, wafery slices are sprinkled over stir-fries, noodle dishes, curries and so on. They can be bought ready-made from Asian food stores, but are easy to make at home.

red shallots, peeled
vegetable oil, for frying

Finely slice the shallots lengthways. Heat a 4 cm depth of oil in a wok or heavy-based pan, add the shallots and cook over moderate heat until golden brown, stirring occasionally for even cooking – the shallots should float freely in the oil as they cook. Remove the pan from the heat immediately and pour the hot oil through a sieve into a stainless steel bowl. Spread the fried shallots on paper towel to drain and cool (reserve the flavoured oil for other cooking). Store the fried shallots in a sealed container for up to 3 days.

GAME STOCK

A luscious stock that makes an ideal base for a wickedly rich sauce to serve with game birds or poultry.

vegetable oil, for frying
4 red shallots
5 cloves garlic
a few green onion tops
4 slices ginger
3 bird's-eye chillies
fresh green peppercorns, crushed
black peppercorns, cracked
roasted bones and wings from 4 squabs or pigeons
roasted bones and wings from 3 quail
50 ml Shaoxing rice wine
2 litres Brown Chicken Stock (see page 546)

Heat a little oil in a large heavy-based saucepan and saute the shallots, garlic, green onion tops, ginger, chillies and pepper until softened. Add the roasted bones, and deglaze the pan with rice wine. Pour in the stock and simmer for about 30 minutes until reduced by two-thirds. Pass through a fine mesh sieve and discard any solids. Strain again through a filter cloth. Keeps in the refrigerator for up to 3 days.

MAKES 800 ML

GARLIC PEPPER PASTE

Inspired by Thai flavours, this paste is best used within a day of being made.

12 cloves garlic
2 small red chillies
2 tiny green bird's-eye chillies
2 tablespoons chopped coriander root
2 tablespoons chopped young ginger
1 tablespoon chopped grachai
2 tablespoons fresh green peppercorns
1 teaspoon white peppercorns, cracked
25 ml vegetable oil

Chop the garlic and chillies and pound in a mortar and pestle with the coriander root, ginger, grachai and peppercorns to make a rough paste. Add the oil and continue to pound until the paste becomes smooth. A blender can be used but this will give the paste a different texture.

MAKES 150 ML

GENOISE CAKE

A classic sponge that can be used in many different dessert preparations.

4 egg yolks
90 g castor sugar
90 g plain flour
½ teaspoon vanilla extract
30 g melted butter, cooled
3 egg whites

Preheat the oven to 160°C. Grease and line a 20 cm × 28 cm shallow rectangular tin with baking paper.

Beat the egg yolks and half the sugar until pale and creamy. Fold in the flour, vanilla and melted butter. Whisk the egg whites to a soft peak and, with the motor running, slowly add the remaining sugar until the whites have become firmer, but not too stiff. Gently fold the whites into the cake batter, then pour the batter into the tin. Bake for 10–15 minutes until the batter is set (a skewer should come out clean). Cool on a wire rack before storing in an airtight container for up to 3 days.

MAKES 1 CAKE

GINGER JUICE

2 ginger roots, minced
cold water

Put the minced ginger in a food processor with just enough cold water to wet it. Blend for a minute or two, then press through a fine mesh sieve to extract as much juice as possible. Reserve the ginger pulp for flavouring a stock or sauce. Pour the juice into a jar and refrigerate for up to 5 days. Shake well before using.

MAKES ABOUT 75 ML

GINGER VINAIGRETTE

50 ml fresh lime juice, strained
50 ml Ginger Juice (see above)
20 ml rice vinegar
few drops of Tabasco sauce
½ teaspoon Roasted Garlic Paste (see page 555)
2 teaspoons minced red shallot
½ teaspoon black sesame seeds
2 teaspoons fish sauce
2 teaspoons mirin
2 teaspoons vegetable oil
60 ml fruity extra virgin olive oil
sea salt and freshly ground black pepper

Whisk all the ingredients together in a bowl until emulsified. Store in a sealed container in the refrigerator for up to 2 days.

MAKES 200 ML

GLASS WAFER MIX

These wafers can be served in the same way as tuiles to give added texture to a dessert. The mixture keeps perfectly in the refrigerator for 2 weeks, but becomes hard when cold so needs to be brought back to room temperature before use.

50 g unsalted butter
45 g glucose
90 g castor sugar
45 g plain flour

Melt the butter and glucose in a bowl over a pan of simmering water. Mix the sugar and flour in another bowl, then pour in the melted butter and glucose and stir to incorporate. Allow to cool before proceeding. At this stage the mixture can be kept for a month in the refrigerator or several months in the freezer.

Preheat the oven to 180°C and line two baking trays with baking paper. Roll the mixture into small balls, using a teaspoonful for each. Place two balls at a time on a baking tray, well spaced, and bake for 5 minutes or until caramel-coloured. Remove the tray from the oven, then allow the wafers to cool for 15–20 seconds. While warm and pliable, cut each wafer into rounds using a pastry cutter (unless otherwise specified, use an 8 cm pastry cutter). Allow the wafers to cool and firm on the tray, then transfer them to an airtight container until ready to use. Cook another two wafers on the second baking tray to keep the process going while one batch cools. Store in an airtight container for up to 2 days.

MAKES ABOUT 25 WAFERS, DEPENDING ON SIZE

GREEN CHILLI DRESSING

This fiery Thai nam jim should be used within 2 hours of being made as it relies on its punchy freshness for maximum effect and flavour.

3 large coriander roots
1 large clove garlic
2 teaspoons chopped galangal
3 tiny green bird's-eye chillies
40 g palm sugar
finely grated zest of ½ makrut lime
90 ml fresh lime juice, strained
1 teaspoon makrut lime juice, strained
30 ml fish sauce

Pound the coriander, garlic, galangal and chillies in a mortar and pestle until smashed into a medium-fine paste. Make a sugar syrup by bringing the palm sugar and 20 ml water to simmering point. Add the sugar syrup to the paste and pound, then add the lime zest, juices and fish sauce. Taste and adjust if necessary.

MAKES 175 ML

HARISSA

Harissa is a fiery Tunisian condiment used to enhance salads and cooked fish and meats, and an automatic addition to cous cous. Test the water, so to speak, and then use it accordingly.

75 g large dried chillies, chopped
2 teaspoons cumin seeds
¼ teaspoon caraway seeds
2 large cloves garlic, minced
1 teaspoon sea salt
50 ml tomato puree
60 ml olive oil

Soak the chillies in a little water for 2 hours, then drain. Dry-roast the cumin seeds over gentle heat until fragrant. Cool, then grind to a fine powder with the caraway seeds. Puree the chillies, garlic and 100 ml water in a food processor, then blend in the spices, salt and tomato puree. With the motor running, slowly pour in the oil. Spoon into a jar, then cover with a film of oil and seal. Refrigerate for up to 1 month.

MAKES 250 ML

HAZELNUT PRALINE

see Almond Praline

HONEYCOMB

360 g castor sugar
120 g glucose
60 ml water
15 g bicarbonate of soda

Line a baking tray with baking paper and place in the refrigerator. Combine the sugar, glucose and water in a large saucepan, bring to the boil and cook until it turns a caramel colour. Add the bicarbonate of soda and whisk quickly – it will explode in volume – then pour onto the prepared tray and allow to cool and set. Break into shards and store in an airtight container in the refrigerator for up to a week.

MAKES 500 G

LAKSA PASTE

A classic paste featured in Nonya cooking. Apart from using it to make laksa soup, I also use it as a stir-fry paste and a marinade for barbequed meats or fish.

2 teaspoons belacan (Malaysian shrimp paste)
1 teaspoon dried prawns
2 dried bird's-eye chillies
1 teaspoon coriander seeds
2 red shallots, chopped
4 cloves garlic, sliced
1 teaspoon minced lime zest
1 stalk lemongrass, finely sliced
1 teaspoon chopped galangal
1 teaspoon chopped turmeric
4 red bird's-eye chillies
25 g candlenuts
2 coriander roots, chopped
1 teaspoon ground turmeric
1 tablespoon coriander leaves
1 tablespoon Vietnamese mint (laksa) leaves
120 ml vegetable oil

Dry-roast the belacan, dried prawns, chillies and coriander seeds separately over gentle heat until fragrant. Cool, then grind to a fine powder in a spice grinder. Place in a blender along with all the other ingredients and process to a smooth paste. Spoon into a jar, then cover with a film of oil. The laksa paste can be kept in the refrigerator for up to 2 weeks.

MAKES 250 ML

LEMON CARAMEL

This tangy caramel syrup can be made using any citrus fruit – oranges, blood oranges, grapefruit or limes. I use it with fruit or ice cream or to give added intensity to a dessert using the same flavour.

250 g castor sugar
50 ml water
juice and finely grated zest of 3 lemons

Bring the sugar and water to the boil in a saucepan over high heat and cook without stirring until a pale caramel forms. Reduce the heat to moderate, add the juice and zest and cook for a further 15 minutes until the mixture is syrupy. Pour the caramel into a stainless steel bowl to stop the cooking process. Allow it to cool completely before using or storing in the refrigerator, where it will keep for 2 weeks.

MAKES 350 ML

LIGHT CRAB STOCK

8 tomatoes
3 raw blue-swimmer crabs
2 litres Fish Stock (see page 550)
2 stalks lemongrass, minced
6 makrut lime leaves, shredded
1 teaspoon minced lime zest
6 coriander roots, minced
4 green onions, finely chopped
2 teaspoons minced ginger
12 white peppercorns, cracked
40 ml fresh lime juice, strained
30 ml fish sauce

Preheat the oven to 200°C and roast the tomatoes for 20 minutes until coloured and softened. Remove the carapace and dead man's fingers from the crabs and rinse crabs under cold water. Crack the claws and break the crabs into pieces with a mallet. Combine the stock, tomatoes, crabs, lemongrass, shredded lime leaves, lime zest, coriander root, green onion, ginger, peppercorns and lime juice in a stockpot and bring to the boil over moderate heat. Reduce to a mere simmer and cook gently for 45 minutes. Add the fish sauce, taste and adjust if necessary. Strain the stock through a fine mesh sieve, pressing firmly to extract all the liquid. Discard the solids. Allow the stock to cool and refrigerate for up to 2 days or freeze for up to a month.

MAKES 2 LITRES

LIME SYRUP

Make in the same manner as Lemon Caramel (see left), using 4 limes in place of the lemons.

LOBSTER BROTH

Make in the same manner as Light Crab Stock (see above), using lobster shells and claws instead. Roast the lobster shells in the oven for 8 minutes before adding to the stock.

MERINGUE DISKS

50 g egg whites (about 2 eggs)
50 g castor sugar
50 g icing sugar
1 teaspoon cornflour

Preheat the oven to 40°C and line a baking tray with baking paper. Whip the egg whites until stiff peaks form then, while still whisking, slowly add the sugar to make a stiff meringue. Sift the icing sugar and cornflour together and fold into the meringue. Using a large round nozzle on a piping bag, pipe the mixture onto the prepared tray and spread into the desired round size. Bake for 1 hour or until dry.

Open the oven door and leave to cool in the oven for 30 minutes, then store in an airtight container for up to 3 days.

MAKES 20–24 MERINGUE DISKS

MERINGUE DOTS

50 g egg whites (about 2 eggs)
50 g castor sugar
50 g icing sugar
1 teaspoon cornflour

Preheat the oven to 40°C and line a baking tray with baking paper. Whip the egg whites until stiff peaks form, then while still whisking, slowly add the sugar to make a stiff meringue. Sift the icing sugar and cornflour together and fold into the meringue. Pipe little peaked drops of the mixture onto the prepared baking tray and bake for 25 minutes until dry. Cool the meringues on a wire rack for 30 minutes, then store in an airtight container for up to 3 days.

MAKES 2 CUPS

MINT YOGHURT SAUCE

A favourite from India, where it is known as podina. There are many varieties and interpretations of this recipe, which goes particularly well with fried food, spiced meats and pastries.

2 tablespoons coriander leaves, chopped
4 tablespoons mint leaves, chopped
2 small green chillies, chopped
2 teaspoons diced red onion
1 teaspoon minced ginger
2 teaspoons fish sauce
1 teaspoon fresh lime juice, strained
250 ml thick plain yoghurt

Blend all the ingredients except the yoghurt to a paste in a food processor. Add the yoghurt and pulse only until the mixture comes together. Do not overwork or the yoghurt will split and make the sauce too thin. Refrigerate for up to 2 days.

MAKES 250 ML

NUOC CHAM

This Vietnamese chilli dipping sauce is served with pastries, grilled meats, barbequed pork and all manner of things. It is best used the day it is made.

2 cloves garlic, minced
2 small red chillies, minced
40 ml fresh lime juice, strained
60 ml fish sauce
40 ml coconut vinegar or rice vinegar
60 ml Sugar Syrup (see page 557)

Stir all the ingredients together in a bowl and leave for 30 minutes to allow the flavours to infuse before serving.

MAKES 200 ML

OXTAIL STOCK

This rich, unctuous stock can be used in various soups and sauces – it is especially good for making a Vietnamese-inspired pho. Ask your butcher to chop the oxtails into pieces for you.

2 oxtails, cut into pieces
1 brown onion, quartered
4 cloves garlic
1 large carrot, quartered
100 ml port
2 teaspoons black peppercorns
4 sprigs thyme
3 sprigs parsley
4 litres White Chicken Stock (see page 559)

Preheat the oven to 200°C and roast the oxtail, onion, garlic and carrot in an oiled baking dish for 30 minutes or until brown and crisp. Transfer to a large stockpot. Deglaze the baking dish with port, then add the port and juices to the stockpot with the peppercorns, thyme, parsley and stock. Bring to a simmer over gentle heat and continue simmering, very slowly, for 5 hours, skimming occasionally to remove fat and scum.

Carefully remove the oxtail and allow to cool (the meat can be removed from the bone and used in another recipe). Strain the stock through a conical sieve, pressing to extract as much liquid as possible; discard the solids. Strain the stock again through a fine mesh sieve, then allow to cool completely and refrigerate overnight to settle. Remove any fat or sediment that may have risen to the surface, and refrigerate for up to 5 days or freeze for up to 2 months.

MAKES 3 LITRES

PARMESAN CRISPS

Preheat the oven to 160°C. Using a circular template cut out of baking paper, grate parmesan in rounds onto a baking tray lined with non-stick baking paper. Bake for 5–6 minutes until melted and beginning to crisp. Remove and leave on the sheet to cool, then lift off gently with a spatula. Store in an airtight container between sheets of baking paper to keep them separate. Use the day they are made.

PEPPER SAUCE

This sauce should be used sparingly as its flavour is intense and its character slightly viscous. It can be flavoured with mustard, porcini, foie gras, beetroot or even brandy and cream if you plan to serve it with a classic pepper steak.

vegetable oil, for brushing
½ brown onion, chopped
1½ large cloves garlic, sliced
2 small sprigs thyme
2 teaspoons black peppercorns
1 teaspoon Sichuan peppercorns
50 ml brandy
100 ml shiraz or other full-bodied red wine
1 litre Beef Stock (see page 545)
freshly ground black pepper

Stand a stockpot over moderate heat, brush with a film of oil and fry the onion, garlic, thyme and peppercorns until the onion has softened and the mixture is fragrant. Add the brandy and, when hot, carefully touch the surface with a lit match to flame it, then add the wine. Cook gently until reduced by a third, then add the stock and bring to the boil. Reduce to a simmer and cook for 1 hour, or until reduced by a third again, skimming occasionally.

Strain the sauce through a conical sieve and then again through a fine mesh sieve. Skim again, then taste and add ground black pepper to refresh the peppery flavour. Cool. Reheat gently as required. Keeps for 5 days in the refrigerator or several weeks in the freezer.

MAKES 600 ML

PICKLED BAMBOO SHOOTS

500 g bamboo shoots, trimmed
125 ml rice vinegar
90 g castor sugar
25 ml fish sauce

Blanch the bamboo shoots in boiling water three times, refreshing each time under cold water. Slice the bamboo finely, using an electric slicer or mandoline. Bring the vinegar and sugar to the boil in a saucepan and simmer over medium heat for 5 minutes to reduce slightly. Add the fish sauce, then pour the hot vinegar over the sliced bamboo. Allow to cool, then cover and refrigerate for 2 days before using – it will keep in the refrigerator for up to 2 months. Strain the bamboo shoots from their liquid before using.

MAKES 500 G

PICKLED CARROT STRIPS

50 ml coconut vinegar
15 ml fresh lime juice, strained
35 ml fish sauce
25 ml sesame oil
25 ml Shaoxing rice wine
40 ml Sugar Syrup (see page 557)
2 large carrots, cut into fine julienne strips

Mix together the vinegar, lime juice, fish sauce, sesame oil, rice wine and sugar syrup, then pour over the carrot strips to cover. Store in the refrigerator for up to a month. Strain the carrot from its liquid before using.

MAKES 100 G

PICKLED CUCUMBER

125 ml fresh lime juice, strained
45 ml fish sauce
25 ml Sugar Syrup (see page 557)
1 long cucumber, peeled, seeded and cut into fine julienne strips

Mix the lime juice, fish sauce and sugar syrup together. Pour over the cucumber and leave to pickle for 4 hours before using. This pickle is best used the day it is made. Strain the cucumber from its liquid before using.

MAKES 100 G

PICKLED GINGER

150 g young ginger, peeled
175 ml rice vinegar
1 teaspoon fish sauce
1 teaspoon fresh lime juice, strained
1 teaspoon Sugar Syrup (see page 557)

Trim the knobs of ginger to a uniform size, then slice extremely finely, using either a fine-bladed knife, a cleaver or a mandoline. The slices should resemble tissue paper. Pack the ginger into jars. Combine the remaining ingredients and pour over the ginger to cover. Mix well, then seal and refrigerate for up to 2 months. Strain the ginger from its liquid before using.

MAKES 125 G

PICKLED SHIITAKE MUSHROOMS

75 ml vegetable oil
2 teaspoons Sichuan peppercorns
5 small dried chillies
50 g castor sugar
50 ml rice vinegar
25 ml light soy sauce
1 tablespoon finely shredded ginger
15 fresh shiitake mushrooms, stems discarded, caps finely sliced

Heat the oil in a wok, add the peppercorns and chillies and cook until blackened. Add the sugar, vinegar, soy sauce, ginger and mushroom slices. Remove from the heat, then cover and leave overnight in the refrigerator. Keeps for up to 2 weeks. Strain the mushrooms from their liquid before using.

MAKES 375 G

PICKLED VEGETABLES

Toss these crunchy pickles with noodles or serve with soy-braised chicken.

50 g castor sugar
70 ml rice vinegar
2 small red chillies, finely sliced
1 teaspoon sea salt
1 teaspoon chilli oil
125 ml boiling water
1 tablespoon finely shredded mint leaves
1 carrot, cut into fine julienne strips
1 cucumber, peeled and seeded, then sliced into fine julienne strips
2 cups cauliflower florets, blanched
½ daikon radish, cut into fine julienne strips

Combine the sugar, vinegar, chilli, salt and chilli oil in a bowl and pour on the boiling water. Stir until combined. Pour the hot pickling mix over the vegetable strips. Allow to cool, then cover and refrigerate. Leave to pickle for 1–2 days before serving. Keeps for up to 2 weeks. Strain the vegetables from their liquid before using.

MAKES 500 G

PISTACHIO PRALINE

see Almond Praline

PONZU SOY MAYONNAISE

2 egg yolks
20 ml fresh lime juice, strained
25 ml Cucumber Juice (see page 549)
25 ml ponzu soy sauce
1 teaspoon Japanese rice vinegar
1 teaspoon wasabi paste
finely grated zest of 1 makrut lime
1 teaspoon minced Pickled Ginger (see third recipe on this page)
1 teaspoon fish sauce
1 teaspoon sesame oil
125 ml fruity extra virgin olive oil
25 ml lemon oil

Blend all the ingredients except the oils in a food processor. With the motor running, slowly pour in the combined oils until thickened and emulsified. Taste and adjust the seasoning if necessary. Keeps in the refrigerator for up to 3 days.

MAKES 250 ML

POWDERED SCALLOP ROE

Make this any time you have fresh scallops with large roes that aren't needed in the dish you're making. Lay cleaned scallop roes on a flat tray lined with baking paper and leave to dry out overnight in a warm place (on a shelf above the stove or in the oven with the pilot light on). The roes will shrink to about a quarter of their original size. When dry, use an electric spice grinder to grind the roe into a fine powder. Keeps in an airtight jar for about a month.

PRAWN STOCK

Use the heads and shells from fresh raw prawns to make this rich, fragrant stock. Once cooled, it is best kept frozen unless it is to be used immediately.

6 tomatoes
1 kg raw prawn heads and shells
100 ml Shaoxing rice wine
50 ml vegetable oil
1 brown onion, chopped
6 cloves garlic, sliced
3 slices ginger
2 slices galangal
1 stalk lemongrass, finely sliced
2 red bird's-eye chillies, chopped
1 teaspoon Sichuan peppercorns
1 teaspoon fennel seeds
1 star anise
2 makrut lime leaves, chopped
3 litres Fish Stock (see page 550)

Preheat the oven to 200°C and roast the tomatoes for 20 minutes until coloured and softened. Heat a large wok, add the prawn heads and shells and toss over high heat until they start to colour. Deglaze the wok with Shaoxing wine and remove from the heat. Heat the oil in a stockpot and saute the onion, garlic, ginger, galangal, lemongrass, chilli, peppercorns, fennel seeds, star anise and lime leaves over moderate heat until they start to colour and become aromatic. Add the prawn heads, shells and their juices, tomatoes and stock and bring to the boil. Simmer gently for 2 hours, skimming frequently to remove any scum.

Strain through a conical sieve, pressing to extract as much liquid as possible, then discard the solids. Strain the stock again through a fine mesh sieve. Allow to cool completely, then use or freeze immediately; it will keep for several weeks frozen.

MAKES 2.5 LITRES

RASPBERRY SAUCE

250 g raspberries
40 g castor sugar
1 teaspoon fresh lemon juice, strained

Blend the raspberries, sugar and juice together in a food processor until smooth. Pass through a fine mesh sieve and discard the seeds. Keep refrigerated for up to 2 days.

MAKES 200 ML

RED MASALA PASTE

A paste inspired by the masala blends of the Chettinad region of south India.

2 teaspoons coriander seeds
½ teaspoon cumin seeds
seeds from 1 cardamom pod
¼ teaspoon black peppercorns
½ teaspoon ground turmeric
½ teaspoon chilli powder
¼ teaspoon sea salt
15 ml malt vinegar
25 g ghee
2 small cloves garlic, minced
½ teaspoon minced fresh ginger
1 red chilli, minced
2 red shallots, minced
2 teaspoons Tamarind Liquid (see page 557)

Dry-roast the whole spices over gentle heat until aromatic. Cool, then grind to a fine powder. Combine with the ground turmeric, chilli powder and salt and stir in the vinegar to make a paste. Heat the ghee in a frying pan over moderate heat and cook the garlic, ginger, chilli and shallots until fragrant. Add the spice paste and fry until it begins to colour, then stir in the tamarind liquid and let the paste absorb it. Remove from the heat and allow to cool. Store in the refrigerator for up to a week.

MAKES 100 ML

ROASTED CHERRY TOMATOES

200 g cherry tomatoes (about 20 tomatoes or 1 punnet)
2 teaspoons extra virgin olive oil
½ teaspoon sea salt
½ teaspoon freshly ground black pepper
½ teaspoon castor sugar

Preheat the oven to 140°C. Cut the tomatoes in half and sit, cut-side-up, on a flat baking tray. Drizzle with oil and season with salt, pepper and sugar. Lightly roast for 20–25 minutes until starting to caramelise. Remove from the oven and allow to cool. The tomatoes should hold their shape and not collapse.

SERVES 4–8

ROASTED GARLIC PASTE

1 head garlic
½ teaspoon olive oil

Preheat the oven to 180°C. Slice the tips off the head of garlic and drizzle with the olive oil. Wrap in foil and roast for 30 minutes until soft. Allow to cool, then unwrap and squeeze the soft garlic paste out from its skin. Store the paste in an airtight container in the refrigerator for up to 2 days.

MAKES 1 TABLESPOON

SAFFRON ALIOLI

see Alioli

SAFFRON BUTTER

Use as a flavouring to enrich sauces – stir it in at the last minute.

50 ml Tomato Water (see page 558)
1 teaspoon saffron threads
250 g unsalted butter, softened

Bring the tomato water to a boil in a small saucepan, add the saffron and infuse for a few minutes only. Remove from the heat and allow to cool. Whip the butter in a food processor, then blend in the cooled saffron liquid until incorporated. Refrigerate in a sealed container for up to 2 weeks, or freeze for several months.

MAKES 250 G

SAMBAL BAJAK

Because it has been cooked, this sambal is quite gentle on the palate. Used mainly in Indonesian cooking, it is popular with rice dishes such as nasi goreng.

30 g belacan (Malaysian shrimp paste)
20 long red chillies, chopped
6 candlenuts
1 tablespoon minced ginger
1 tablespoon minced garlic
10 red shallots, sliced
6 makrut lime leaves, shredded
50 ml vegetable oil
30 ml Tamarind Liquid (see page 557)
250 ml coconut milk
30 g palm sugar
40 ml fish sauce

Dry-roast the belacan over gentle heat until fragrant. Place the belacan, chilli, candlenuts, ginger, garlic, shallots, lime leaves and oil in a food processor and blend to a smooth paste. Cook the paste over gentle heat for 10–15 minutes until softened. Add the remaining ingredients, bring to the boil then simmer for 30 minutes until a thick paste has formed and a layer of oil is still evident. Stir the oil into the sambal and remove from the heat. Cool completely, then refrigerate in a sealed jar for up to 2 months.

MAKES 300 ML

SHELLFISH STOCK

Make in the same manner as Prawn Stock (see opposite), using crab and lobster shells in place of prawn shells.

SHIRO MISO FLAKES

100 g shiro (white) miso paste

Spread a thin layer of miso paste onto a baking tray lined with baking paper. Leave in the oven for 3 hours with only the pilot light on (any more heat and it will burn). When the miso has dried and become toasty, crumble into small pieces and keep in an airtight container until ready to serve. To make a finer powder, grind the dried miso flakes in a spice grinder. Store in an airtight container for up to 2 weeks.

MAKES 2 TABLESPOONS

SICHUAN SPICE SALT

1 tablespoon Sichuan peppercorns
1 tablespoon white peppercorns
2 tablespoons sea salt

Dry-roast the peppercorns and salt together in a pan until fragrant. Cool, then grind to a powder. Pass through a fine sieve and store in a sealed jar. Best used within about 2 weeks.

MAKES 4 TABLESPOONS

SOY PORK JELLY

see Soy-braised Pork (below).

SOY WASABI DRESSING

40 ml light soy sauce
30 ml rice vinegar
2 teaspoons Chinese black vinegar
15 ml fresh lime juice, strained
2 teaspoons fish sauce
1½ teaspoons castor sugar
1½ teaspoons wasabi powder
20 ml water
¼ teaspoon freshly grated wasabi root, if available
good pinch of freshly ground black pepper
⅓ teaspoon sesame oil
40 ml light olive oil
2 teaspoons wasabi oil

Whisk all the ingredients together in a bowl until emulsified. Refrigerate for up to 3 days.

MAKES 180 ML

SOY-BRAISED PORK

2 tablespoons sea salt
2 kg piece pork belly
3 green onions, chopped
6 slices ginger
50 ml light soy sauce
60 ml mirin
60 ml Shaoxing rice wine
40 ml fish sauce

Rub the salt into the pork and refrigerate on a tray, covered, for 3 hours. Bring a stockpot of water to the boil and blanch the pork belly for 2 minutes. Remove the meat from the pot and refresh immediately under cold running water. Repeat this process twice, blanching the pork three times altogether. Put the pork in a large bowl, skin-side down. Mix together the remaining ingredients and pour over the pork. Cover with baking paper, then seal the bowl with a large sheet of foil. Place the bowl over a large saucepan or steamer of gently simmering water and steam the pork for 8–9 hours, topping up the water in the steamer as necessary. The pork will shrink during the cooking process.

Carefully remove the pork from the bowl and discard any pieces of ginger or onion stuck to the meat. While the meat is hot, remove any bones, then lay the pork on a tray and leave to cool for 30 minutes. Cover with a sheet of baking paper then sit another baking tray on top to weigh it down. Refrigerate for 4 hours until the meat is cold and compressed.

Strain the cooking liquid through a fine mesh sieve, then refrigerate until set. Remove and discard the fatty layer, but reserve the **soy pork jelly** for another use (the jelly keeps for 1 week in the refrigerator or 2 months in the freezer). Cut the pork into cubes or slices once it is cold – the meat will tear while it is still warm.

MAKES 1 KG

SPICED EGGPLANT PICKLE

Another essential in my larder. I serve this vibrant, spicy pickle with curries, dosas (rice pancakes) or parathas (flaky Indian bread).

6 large dried chillies
1 tablespoon minced garlic
2 teaspoons minced ginger
1 teaspoon ground turmeric
1 tablespoon brown mustard seeds
500 g small eggplants (aubergines), washed
200 ml vegetable oil
65 g palm sugar, shaved
2 teaspoons sea salt
100 ml malt vinegar
1 teaspoon garam masala

Soak the chillies in hot water for about 30 minutes until soft. Drain, reserving the water. Place the chillies, garlic, ginger, turmeric and mustard seeds in a food processor with a little chilli water and blend to a paste. Slice the eggplants into 1 cm thick rounds. Heat the oil in a frying pan, add the spice paste and stir for a few minutes to release the flavours. Add the eggplant and cook until soft, stirring occasionally. Add the palm sugar, salt and vinegar and simmer over gentle heat until thick. Remove from the heat and stir in the garam masala. Cool. Spoon into jars, then cover with a film of oil and seal. Keeps for 2 months. Once opened, store in the refrigerator.

MAKES 500 ML

SPICED TOMATO CHILLI PICKLE

An adaptation of a kasaundi, which is served as a condiment with breads and fish dishes in India. This has the sweet, sour and spicy flavours so characteristic of Indian preserves. I find it most versatile and also use it as a base for sauces.

1 tablespoon brown mustard seeds
125 ml cider vinegar
2 tablespoons cumin seeds
125 ml vegetable oil
pinch of freshly ground cloves
2 teaspoons ground turmeric
2 tablespoons minced ginger
10 cloves garlic
10 red bird's-eye chillies
2 kg ripe tomatoes, peeled and quartered
75 g palm sugar, shaved
60 ml fish sauce

Cook the mustard seeds in the vinegar over moderate heat for 10 minutes, then set aside for 2 hours. Dry-roast the cumin seeds over gentle heat until fragrant. Cool, then grind to a fine powder. Heat the oil in a large heavy-based frying pan, add the ground cumin, cloves and turmeric and fry over gentle heat until fragrant. Remove the pan from the heat. Place the mustard-seed mixture, ginger, garlic and chillies in a blender and process until smooth, then add to the oil and spices with the tomato. Cook for 1 hour over gentle heat, stirring frequently. Add the palm sugar and fish sauce and cook for a further 30 minutes. Taste and adjust if necessary. Spoon into jars, then cover with a film of oil. Keeps in the refrigerator for up to 2 weeks.

MAKES 500 ML

STRAWBERRY SAUCE

250 g strawberries
40 g castor sugar
1 teaspoon fresh lemon juice, strained

Blend the strawberries, sugar and juice together in a food processor until smooth. Pass through a fine mesh sieve and discard the seeds. Keep refrigerated for up to 2 days.

MAKES 200 ML

SUGAR SYRUP

500 ml water
500 g castor sugar

Combine the water and sugar in a saucepan and and stir over moderate heat to boiling point. Simmer for 5 minutes, then remove from the heat and allow to cool completely. Store in an airtight container in the refrigerator for up to a month.

MAKES 800 ML

SUSHI RICE

This is short-grain rice that has been cooked by the absorption method, then seasoned with vinegar, spread out and fanned to cool it down as quickly as possible.

1 cup short-grain rice
1 cup water
1 cm piece dried kombu seaweed (kelp)
30 ml sake
50 ml Japanese rice vinegar
½ teaspoon sea salt
1 tablespoon castor sugar

Soak the rice in double its volume of cold water for 5 minutes, then drain and repeat. Drain the rice again and leave it in the colander for 15 minutes. Put the rice into a large saucepan with the water and kombu, cover with a tight-fitting lid and bring to the boil over medium heat. When the water starts to boil, increase the heat (do not remove the lid) and boil for 4 minutes, then reduce heat and continue to cook for 5 minutes or until the rice has absorbed all the water. Remove from the heat, splash the sake over the rice and stir until the rice puffs up. Lay a piece of muslin over the rice, replace the lid and leave to stand for 10 minutes.

Meanwhile, heat the vinegar and salt in a non-reactive pan over low heat until the salt has dissolved – don't let the vinegar boil. Add the sugar and whisk to combine.

Tip the hot rice into a large wide bowl or tray, spreading it out evenly. Stir through the seasoned vinegar, lifting the rice to cool it down quickly and distribute the vinegar uniformly. Be careful not to add too much vinegar or the rice will become mushy. Continue lifting and stirring the rice, fanning it at the same time (or leave near a fan and stir occasionally) until the rice cools to body temperature. The rice needs to be used as soon as it reaches this point; if it gets cold, the grains will become hard.

SWEET CHILLI SAUCE

500 ml white vinegar
250 ml water
750 g castor sugar
1 large clove garlic, finely sliced
1 stalk lemongrass, minced using a Microplane
3 coriander roots, minced
2 makrut lime leaves, finely shredded
finely grated zest of ½ makrut lime
2 teaspoons minced ginger
4 large red chillies, sliced into fine rounds

Heat the vinegar, water and sugar in a wide-based saucepan to boiling point. Add the remaining ingredients and simmer for 20–25 minutes until reduced by half – the mixture should coat the back of a spoon. Cool and store in a sealed container in the refrigerator for up to a month.

MAKES 1 LITRE

SWEET GINGER DRESSING

80 ml fresh lime juice, strained
20 ml Ginger Juice (see page 551)
30 ml Yamamoto sweet ginger vinegar
30 ml aged rice vinegar
25 ml fish sauce
20 ml mirin
¼ teaspoon chilli oil
¼ teaspoon sesame oil
50 ml sunflower oil
20 ml extra virgin olive oil
⅓ teaspoon freshly ground black pepper

Mix all the ingredients together until emulsified. Store in an airtight container in the refrigerator for up to 5 days.

MAKES 270 ML

SWEET TAMARIND DRESSING

30 g palm sugar, shaved
200 ml Tamarind Liquid (see below)
40 ml Sugar Syrup (see left)
150 ml fresh lime juice, strained
30 ml Ginger Juice (see page 551)
50 ml fish sauce
25 ml sesame oil

Heat the palm sugar and tamarind liquid together over gentle heat just until the sugar has dissolved. Allow to cool then whisk with the remaining ingredients. Store in the refrigerator for up to a week.

MAKES 500 ML

SWEET-AND-SOUR PICKLE

3 red bird's-eye chillies, chopped
1 small dried chilli, broken
4 small cloves garlic, chopped
80 ml vegetable oil
120 ml light soy sauce
200 ml cider vinegar
300 ml Sugar Syrup (see left)

Heat the chillies and garlic in the oil over gentle heat to infuse. When it starts to simmer, add the remaining ingredients and gently simmer for 15 minutes. Strain, discarding the solids, and allow to cool. Store in an airtight container in the refrigerator for up to a month.

MAKES 700 ML

TAMARIND DRESSING

This dressing is slightly more tart and astringent than Sweet Tamarind Dressing (see below left) – it is made in the same way, omitting the sugar syrup.

TAMARIND LIQUID

The most refined way to use tamarind is to make tamarind liquid, getting maximum flavour without the coarse, fibrous texture of the pulp. Simmer 1 part tamarind pulp to 3 parts water for 30 minutes or so, then pass through a coarse mesh or conical sieve. Discard the fibre and seeds. If the liquid seems too thick or pasty, stir in a little extra water. Store in the refrigerator for up to a month.

TAPENADE

I use large fleshy olives (either black or green) to make this Mediterranean condiment.

250 g black or green olives, pitted
2 small cloves garlic, minced
60 g anchovy fillets
25 g salted Aeolian capers, washed
1 tablespoon fresh green peppercorns
1 tablespoon chopped parsley leaves
¼ teaspoon chilli powder
150 ml extra virgin olive oil

Blend all the ingredients together to make a fine paste, adding the oil gradually. Keep in the refrigerator for up to 2 weeks.

MAKES 500 ML

TEA-SMOKING MIX

1 tablespoon oolong tea leaves
1 tablespoon jasmine tea leaves
zest of 1 orange
2 pieces dried tangerine peel
2 tablespoons jasmine rice
2 tablespoons brown sugar
3 star anise, broken
2 teaspoons Sichuan peppercorns
3 pieces cassia bark

Mix all the ingredients together and store in an airtight container for up to a month.

MAKES 10 TABLESPOONS

TEMPURA BATTER

150 g sifted plain flour
2 tablespoons cornflour
1 teaspoon sea salt
½ teaspoon sansho pepper
1 teaspoon wasabi powder (optional)
1 egg yolk
250–275 ml ice-cold soda water

Combine the flour, cornflour, salt, pepper and wasabi in a bowl. When ready to cook, add the egg yolk to the flour mix, pour in the cold soda water and mix roughly using a chopstick. This batter should not be smooth – a lumpy appearance is what you are looking for – and it must be used within an hour.

MAKES 500 ML

TOFFEE APPLE SLICES

10 g butter
2 golden delicious apples, each cut into eight slices
125 g castor sugar
40 ml water
2 teaspoons golden syrup
25 ml Calvados

Preheat the oven to 180°C and butter a baking dish. Place the apple slices in the dish in a single layer. Combine the sugar and water in a saucepan and cook until it forms a caramel. Stir in the golden syrup and Calvados then pour over the apples. Bake for 8 minutes or until the apple slices soften and take on a toffee colour. Flip the slices over and cook for another 5–8 minutes. Remove the apple slices from the dish while still warm and lay on a tray lined with non-stick baking paper. Strain the sauce and cool. Store in the refrigerator for up to 3 days.

MAKES 16 SLICES

TOMATO ESSENCE

see Tomato Water (below).

TOMATO PASTA SAUCE

This typical pasta sauce (Italian pomodoro) is best made when tomatoes are at their peak. Good-quality canned tomatoes can be substituted if decent, very ripe fresh ones are not available.

50 ml extra virgin olive oil
2 brown onions, diced
4 cloves garlic, chopped
1 kg very ripe tomatoes, peeled and chopped
1 tablespoon castor sugar
50 ml tomato puree
2 teaspoons sea salt
1 teaspoon freshly ground black pepper

Heat a wide-based saucepan over moderate heat, add the oil and fry the onion and garlic for 5 minutes until softened. Add the chopped tomatoes and sugar and bring to the boil. Reduce the heat, add the tomato puree and simmer for 25 minutes until the tomatoes have broken down and become very soft. Season with salt and pepper, taste and adjust if necessary. Transfer the sauce to a blender and puree until smooth. Store in a sealed jar in the refrigerator for up to 2 weeks.

MAKES 1 LITRE

TOMATO WATER

This is an exquisite way of adding the intense flavour of summer's best tomatoes to sauces and the like, and a great way of extending their season. Both the water and the essence keep best frozen in ice-cube trays.

5 kg tomatoes

Pulp the tomatoes, then drain in a jelly bag or a double layer of muslin suspended over a bucket for 24 hours. To keep the liquid clear, do not push or force the pulp through the bag.

To make reduced **tomato essence**, bring the tomato water to a boil and simmer until reduced by half. This increases the sweetness slightly and intensifies the flavour.

MAKES ABOUT 1 LITRE

TRUFFLE BUTTER

This is the perfect way to keep truffle – nothing goes to waste and the truffle flavour is preserved in the butter, being released when it cooks.

offcuts of shaved fresh truffle – as many as you can get your hands on
125 g unsalted butter
2 cloves garlic, minced
1 tablespoon shredded parsley leaves
½ teaspoon sea salt

Place all the ingredients in a bowl and blend with a stick blender or spoon until smooth. Wrap in plastic film and roll into a sausage shape, so you can cut off slices as you need them. Keeps in the refrigerator for up to 2 weeks.

MAKES 125 G

TURMERIC WATER

2 knobs turmeric, minced

Put the turmeric in a food processor with just enough cold water to wet it. Blend for a minute or two until crushed and pulpy, then press through a fine mesh sieve to extract as much liquid as possible. Discard the solids. Transfer to a jar and keep in the refrigerator for up to 5 days.

MAKES ABOUT 75 ML

VEGETABLE STOCK

This versatile stock can be made ahead of time. Use it as a base for a vegetable curry, add it to a stir-fry or enrich it with coconut milk to make a sauce or soup.

1 head garlic
6 dried shiitake mushrooms
500 ml warm water
25 ml vegetable oil
1 brown onion, chopped
2 carrots, finely sliced
1 stick celery (with leaves), chopped
1 tablespoon minced ginger
5 green onions, sliced
3 red bird's-eye chillies, sliced
2 teaspoons black peppercorns
2 teaspoons Sichuan peppercorns
1 tablespoon minced fresh turmeric
2 litres water
1 stalk lemongrass, finely sliced
50 ml fish sauce

Preheat the oven to 180°C. Wrap the garlic in foil and roast for 30 minutes until softened. Unwrap and separate the cloves. Meanwhile, soak the dried mushrooms in the warm water for 15 minutes until softened.

Heat the oil in a stockpot. Add the onion, carrot, celery, ginger, green onion, chilli and roasted garlic and cook over gentle heat for about 15 minutes until softened. Add the mushrooms and their soaking liquid, the black and Sichuan peppercorns, turmeric and water and bring to a boil. Simmer for 30 minutes, then add the lemongrass and fish sauce and simmer for a further 15 minutes. Strain the stock through a fine mesh sieve, then discard the solids. Allow to cool. This will keep for 5 days in the refrigerator or 1 month in the freezer.

MAKES 2 LITRES

VIETNAMESE FIVE-SPICE MIX

1 teaspoon ground anise seeds
1 teaspoon ground cloves
1 teaspoon ground cinnamon
1 teaspoon powdered garlic
1 teaspoon ground ginger

Mix the spices together and store in an airtight container for up to 2 weeks.

MAKES 5 TEASPOONS

WHITE CHICKEN STOCK

1 chicken carcass
1.5 kg free-range or organic chicken
6 slices ginger
handful of green onion tops
2 teaspoons white peppercorns, cracked
500 ml dry white wine

Wash the chicken carcass and chicken in cold water to remove all blood. Combine all the ingredients in a stockpot and cover with cold water. Bring to a boil over gentle heat and simmer slowly for 2 hours, skimming frequently to remove any scum.

Carefully remove the chicken carcass and the chicken; strip the meat from the chicken and keep for another use, then discard both carcasses. Strain the stock through a fine mesh sieve. Allow to cool completely, then remove any fat that rises to the surface. Keeps for 3 days in the refrigerator or 1 month in the freezer.

MAKES 4 LITRES

WHITE PORK STOCK

I make this fragrant, Asian-inspired stock as a base for soups, to add to a stir-fry, or for slow-braising to extract maximum flavour during cooking.

2 kg pork bones
1 pig's trotter
75 ml Shaoxing rice wine
handful of green onion tops
100 g chopped fennel bulb
2 tablespoons sliced ginger
1 teaspoon white peppercorns, cracked
2 bay leaves

Bring a stockpot of water to the boil and blanch the pork bones and trotter for 2 minutes. Remove from the pot, plunge into cold water then drain. Return the blanched bones to the rinsed-out pot with the remaining ingredients and pour in 5 litres of cold water. Slowly bring to a boil, then reduce the heat and simmer gently for 2 hours, skimming frequently to remove any scum.

Strain the stock through a fine mesh sieve, and discard the solids. Allow the stock to cool completely, then skim the surface of any excess fat. Keeps for 3 days in the refrigerator or 1 month in the freezer.

MAKES 4 LITRES

XO SAUCE

75 g dried scallops
75 g Chinese black bacon
75 g dried prawns
75 ml vegetable oil
1 red bird's-eye chilli, minced
½ red capsicum (pepper), seeded and diced
2 large cloves garlic, minced
1 small brown onion, minced
1 large dried chilli, ground
¾ cup Fried Shallot Slices (see page 550)
¾ cup Fried Garlic Slices (see page 550)
½ teaspoon sea salt
½ teaspoon castor sugar

Steam the dried scallops and bacon separately for 30 minutes until really soft. Shred into very fine pieces with your fingers. Place the dried prawns in a spice grinder and grind to a floss. Heat the oil in a large frying pan, add the chilli, capsicum, garlic, onion and ground chilli and cook slowly for 30 minutes. Add the shredded scallops and bacon, ground prawns, fried shallots and fried garlic and cook for another 15 minutes. Add the salt and sugar and cook for 5 minutes, then taste and adjust the seasoning if necessary. This will keep in the refrigerator for up to a month.

MAKES 500 ML

ZA'ATAR

When making za'atar, look for dried wild thyme (hyssop) from Greek or Middle Eastern food stores for the best flavour.

2 teaspoons dried wild thyme (hyssop)
2 teaspoons sumac
2 teaspoons white sesame seeds, roasted
2 teaspoons sea salt

Mix all the ingredients together in a bowl. Store in an airtight container for up to 2 weeks.

MAKES 2 TABLESPOONS

GLOSSARY

achiote paste
Made from ground annatto seeds, vinegar and seasonings, this paste is a vibrant orange–red colour with an earthy flavour, and is available from food shops that stock Mexican and Latin American food products.

anchovy cream
A creamy paste made with anchovies, vinegar and olive oil. I use the organic Italian Sommariva brand, which is available from specialty food stores.

anise liqueur
A sweet liquorice-flavoured liqueur. I like the Spanish 'Anis de la Asturiana' brand, available from merchants who stock Spanish wines. If you can't find it, use Pernod, Sambuca or ouzo instead.

Asian celery
With slender stalks and a more pungent flavour than Western celery, Asian celery looks like outsized coriander. It is available from Asian food stores.

banana blossom
Dark-purple closed flowers of the banana tree that are in fact immature bananas before they develop into fruit. Used in salads, they can be found at Asian food stores.

banana leaves
The long green leaves of the banana tree are stripped from their central hard rib and sold by weight as a wrapper for cooking or as a platter for serving. To make them pliable, dip in hot water before use. Available from Asian food stores and some greengrocers.

Banyuls vinegar
A finely tuned red wine vinegar, sourced from grenache grapes of the Banyuls wine region of Languedoc-Roussillon in southern France. Available from specialty food stores.

belacan (Malaysian shrimp paste)
This pungent paste is made from pounded, salted and fermented shrimp, dried and pressed into rectangular cakes. Dry-roast over low heat for a more mellow flavour. Available from Asian food stores.

betel leaves
These glossy deep-green, heart-shaped leaves are sold in bunches and have a slightly bitter taste. Available from Asian food stores that sell fresh produce.

bone marrow
Soft, nutritious fat found inside beef bones. These days it is considered a delicacy, so you will need to order it from your butcher in advance. Ask your butcher to chop the marrow bones, then use a skewer to extract the raw marrow from the centre.

bonito flakes
Also known as katsuobushi, these are bonito shavings that have been smoked and dried. Available from Japanese food stores – the larger shavings are a little more expensive, but worth it for the flavour.

candied (sweet preserved) ginger
Tender young ginger stems preserved in a sweet syrup, used predominantly in desserts. Available from selected food stores and most Chinese grocers.

candlenuts
Cream-coloured soft nuts with a high oil content used in Singaporean, Nonya and Malaysian cooking. Keep refrigerated once open to avoid deterioration. Available from Asian food stores.

cape gooseberries
Small round orange-coloured fruits with a papery husk that is peeled away. In Australia, they come into season during winter and are available for about 3–4 months.

caviar
Sterling caviar is top-quality American caviar sourced from farmed white sturgeon according to traditional Russian methods. Available from luxury food stores.

chickpea flour
Also known as besan, chickpea flour is mainly used for thickening sauces and making pakoras or fritters. Available from Indian and health-food shops and other selected food stores.

chilli powder
There are many types of chilli powder on the market, with varying degrees of heat and colour. Kashmiri chilli powder is mild, but adds a vibrant red colour. One of the fieriest on the market is Blue Tongue from Thailand, which is often available at Thai food stores. A little goes a long way, and other, milder chilli powders can be substituted if you can't find this particular variety.

Chinese black bacon
Look for long slender packets of lup yook in any Asian or Chinese grocery store. Each packet contains strips of semi-dried pork belly cured with sweetened dark soy sauce.

Chinese black vinegar
Brewed from malt and sticky rice, this vinegar has low acidity and a gentle sweetness. Sold as Chinkiang vinegar in Asian food stores and some supermarkets.

Chinese hot chilli sauce
This vinegar-based chilli sauce with a gentle kick is available from Chinese and Asian food stores.

Chinese sausage
Lap cheung are thin red pork sausages that have been wind-dried. The best ones are found hanging in Chinese butchers, but they are also sold vacuum-packed in Asian food stores.

Chinese sesame paste
A Chinese version of tahini, with a rich nutty flavour that comes from roasting the sesame seeds before grinding them into a thick paste. Available from Chinese food stores.

cloud-ear fungus
Also called black fungus or wood-ear fungus, this is a staple in Asian cooking. Its soft and crinkly flesh absorbs flavours and adds great texture. Available fresh from greengrocers or dried in packets from Asian food stores (the dried version needs to be reconstituted in warm water for 30 minutes before use).

coconut juice
This is the colourless sweet liquid from the centre of fresh coconuts – always shake a coconut before buying to make sure it is full of juice. Carefully crack the coconut over a bowl to collect the juice, then strain and refrigerate for up to 3 days. Young coconut juice from green coconuts is particularly delicious, and is sometimes available chilled or frozen at Asian stores.

coconut oil
Commonly used in south Indian and Sri Lankan cooking, coconut oil is extracted from fresh coconut. It solidifies when cold and has a creamy white appearance. Available from Indian food stores.

coconut palm heart
The tender hearts of the coconut palm stem are available fresh in Asia and tinned elsewhere.

coconut palm sugar
Gula melaka is the Malaysian name for these cylindrical cakes of caramel-coloured sugar. It has a unique flavour, like coconut caramel, and is a popular addition to desserts. Available from Asian food stores.

coconut vinegar
Sourced from the sap of the coconut tree, this fragrant vinegar has low acidity and a cloudy appearance. You'll find it at Asian food stores.

cream
Various types of cream have different properties, depending on their fat content: pouring (35%) cream is suitable for whipping, while thick (45%) cream can be cooked successfully. Very thick or double cream (up to 55%) is great to serve straight from the refrigerator but is unsuitable for cooking as the high fat content causes the cream to split on heating.

cress
Sold in small punnets, these hydroponically grown salad leaves and herbs are available in many varieties, including red garnet, swiss chard, red chard, daikon, tatsoi, mizuna, mache, celery, rocket, watercress, sorrel, coriander, basil and shiso. Simply snip off the small sprouts and use as required. Available from selected greengrocers.

dried barberries
These sour dark-red berries are used in Persian and Arabic cooking. They are available from specialty spice suppliers.

dried Chinese anchovies
Also known as ikan bilis, these are small salted whole fish that have been dried. They are available from Asian food stores.

dried lemongrass powder
Powdered dried lemongrass is available from specialty spice shops. Its flavour dissipates quickly, so buy small quantities as required.

dried liquorice root
From the feathery wild liquorice plant, the dried root has a gentle, sweet flavour and is used in Chinese cooking and herbal medicines. Available from Chinese food stores and herbalists.

dried lime-leaf powder
Powdered dried makrut lime leaf is available from specialty spice suppliers.

dried porcini powder
Italian porcini mushrooms that have been dried then ground to a fine powder. Available from specialty food stores, or buy dried porcini slices and grind them as required.

dried prawns
Used to add flavour and texture to Asian dishes, dried prawns can be dry-roasted and ground, or soaked in warm water to soften before use. Available from Asian food stores.

dried scallop
Known in China as conpoy, dried scallop is considered a delicacy (which is reflected in the high price tag). Soak in warm water or steam until softened, then shred and add to stocks or sauces for intense flavour. Available from Chinese food stores and herbalists.

dried shiitake mushrooms
Available from Asian food stores, these dried mushrooms need to be reconstituted in hot water before use; the tough stalks are generally discarded, although they can be used to flavour stocks.

edamame
These young soy beans are sold frozen in Asian stores. Boil them whole for 2 minutes only, then refresh in cold water and remove the beans from their pods.

fermented fish sauce
Strongly flavoured and purple-grey in colour, fermented fish sauce is thicker and more pungent than regular fish sauce due to heavier fermentation. Called nam pla raa in Thailand, mam tom in Vietnam and padek in Laos, it is available from food stores that specialise in South-east Asian products.

fig vinegar
Made in Limoges in France, this intense fruity vinegar has low acidity and a complex, balanced flavour. It can be found at specialty food stores.

finger limes
Native to Australia, these wild limes are, not surprisingly, finger shaped. To use, cut them in half lengthways and scrape out the lime pearls. Finger limes are in season from February to May and can be sourced from specialist greengrocers.

fleur de sel
A pure white sea salt from Brittany in France. It is more expensive than other brands because of its flavour and perfectly formed crystals. Available from specialty food stores.

fondant
Ready-prepared fondant is available from specialist suppliers of dessert products.

Forum cabernet vinegar
Forum is a Spanish range of wine vinegars and this one, made from rich cabernet grapes, has excellent balance and flavour. Available from specialty food stores.

fruit purees
I use Boiron frozen fruit purees, a French brand sold in 1 litre tubs for restaurant service, with varieties including coconut and lychee. If unavailable, puree the required fruit (fresh or frozen) yourself, then pass through a sieve before using.

garam masala
This rich and aromatic Indian spice blend varies from region to region. Make sure you buy it from a reputable spice merchant, as its fragrance diminishes quickly.

garlic chives
Sometimes called Chinese chives, these dark-green slender stems with a flower bud at the tip have a hint of garlic flavour. Buy them from Chinese food stores that sell fresh produce.

gelatine leaves
Transparent and colourless, these fragile sheets are available in various weights – from 1 g right up to 10 g, hence the need to specify the exact weight in recipes. Whatever brand you buy, check its strength by weighing one leaf before proceeding with recipe. Soften the leaves in cold water for 2 minutes, then squeeze to remove excess water before stirring into hot liquid.

ginger blossom
Also called myoga or wild ginger bud, these small pink blossoms of young ginger are used in Japanese and Nonya cooking. In Australia they have a short season during February and March; in other parts of the world, they are imported from Japan.

glucose
A sugar in liquid form that's used in desserts to give a silken texture. Soften in a bowl over a pan of hot water before adding to other ingredients. Available from supermarkets and specialty food stores.

gold and silver leaf
Used to adorn desserts, ice creams and cakes, these fragile, edible leaves are sheathed between layers of paper and require extremely careful handling. Available from specialist suppliers of dessert products.

hot bean paste
Sometimes called chilli bean paste or toban jiang, this thick spicy sauce is made from dried broad beans and chillies fermented in earthenware tubs. Used in Sichuan cooking, it is available from Chinese food stores.

Iberian ham
The sweet ham of Iberian black pigs fed on acorns, which gives the cured meat its distinctive flavour. Choose from Jabugo, Serrano and Bellota. Thankfully, this is now imported into Australia and is available from specialty food stores and premium butchers.

jaggery
Commonly used in Malaysian and Indonesian cooking, jaggery is a dark palm sugar that can be sweeter than other Asian palm sugars. Sold in blocks, the required amount is shaved off before using. Available from Asian food stores.

Japanese grilled eel fillet
Japanese unagi (freshwater eel) is marinated in a sweet teriyaki-like glaze before being grilled. Available from Japanese food stores and selected fishmongers.

Japanese rice vinegar
Fermented from rice, this mellow vinegar is an essential ingredient in Japanese cooking. Available from Japanese and some Asian food stores, selected supermarkets and health-food shops.

jellyfish *see* salted jellyfish

jicama
A tuber vegetable similar in appearance to a turnip, with brown papery skin and creamy white flesh. A staple of Mexican and Latin American cooking, it is known as yam bean in Asia. Water chestnuts make a good substitute. Available from selected greengrocers and Asian food stores.

kapi (Thai shrimp paste)
Pungent paste made by pounding salted and fermented shrimp. Available from Thai and Asian food stores.

kinome leaves
Available fresh in very limited supply from specialist Japanese grocers, these tiny dark-green feathery leaves from the sansho tree have an intense peppery flavour. There is no substitute, so simply omit if unavailable.

latte di mandorla
Sweetened almond milk imported from Italy. Sold in bottles at selected food stores.

liquorice essence
Used in desserts to give a distinctive, smooth liquorice flavour. Available from specialty suppliers.

liquorice paste
This thick, intensely flavoured paste is mostly used in desserts, and is available from specialty suppliers. It is possible to make it yourself by chopping shop-bought liquorice sticks into small pieces and dissolving in a little milk over gentle heat until smooth. Strain before using.

long-leaf (saw-tooth) coriander
These elongated leaves with serrated edges, a pungent aroma and distinctive flavour are available from Asian food stores that sell fresh produce.

lotus root
Sausage-shaped tuber with creamy white flesh and holes through its length – its unique consistency is starchy and crunchy at the same time. Scrub the surface lightly, then slice into thin rounds to reveal its inner lacy pattern. Available from Asian food stores and selected greengrocers.

lotus seeds
Sold in dried form, and with a similar appearance to shelled peanuts, lotus seeds are used in both savoury and sweet Asian dishes. Available in packets (or tinned in sweetened syrup) from Asian food stores.

makrut lime leaves
Also known as kaffir lime leaves, these dark-green double leaves with a pronounced lime flavour are widely available from Asian food stores and selected greengrocers.

micro watercress *see* cress

miso paste
Made from fermented soybeans, sometimes with rice or barley added, miso is high in protein and has a rich, salty flavour. Red miso, or akamiso, is more pungent than white shiro miso, and so is used in hearty soups and braises. Both are available from Japanese stores and some supermarkets.

mitsuba leaves
Also known as Japanese parsley, this salad leaf has a mild peppery flavour and soft texture. Available from selected greengrocers.

mizuna
Feathery green salad leaf with a gentle mustard flavour. Available from most greengrocers.

mustard oil
Aromatic oil used in Bengali and northern Indian cooking, and for making pickles and chutneys. Available from Indian food stores and health-food shops, it needs to be stored in the refrigerator.

nori *see* seaweed

onion cress
This goes by various names, including onion, shallot or chive cress and rock chives. Grown in punnets, it has slender green stems with tiny black seeds at the tip.

orange blossom water
Perfumed water used in Arabic and Middle Eastern cooking, available from selected supermarkets and Middle Eastern food stores.

pandanus leaf
Used in Asian cooking, this long, slender green leaf has a distinctive flavour and aroma. The juice is also used as a colouring for desserts. The leaves are available fresh (or dried in packets – with reduced flavour) from Asian food stores, as is the juice.

passionfruit juice
To add passionfruit flavour without the seeds, cut passionfruit in half, remove the pulp with a spoon, then press through a fine mesh sieve into a bowl, squeezing out as much juice as possible. Discard the seeds. Use straightaway or freeze in small portions for later. One ripe passionfruit yields about 2 teaspoons juice.

Pedro Ximenez sherry
PX is a black sherry from Jerez, Spain. With its raisin and candied orange notes, it makes the perfect partner for chocolate desserts. Available from specialist wine suppliers.

perilla leaves *see* shiso leaves

Persian fairy floss
Also known as pashmak, this sweet floss is used to decorate desserts. It comes in various flavours, including vanilla and pistachio. Available from specialist food stores.

pickled garlic
Peeled garlic cloves that have been pickled in vinegar and brine. Available from Asian and specialty food stores.

pickled grachai
Used in Thai cooking, this ginger-like rhizome is rarely available fresh, but can be bought in jars from Asian food stores.

pickled young tamarind leaves
Available in jars from Asian food stores, these leaves make a tasty addition to soups, salads and stir-fries. Rinse before using.

pimiento
These red bell-shaped Spanish capsicums (peppers) are also known as piquillo peppers. Grown in Navarra, northern Spain, they are roasted, peeled and packed in a brine solution.

pomegranate
The seeds and juice of this fruit are used in Asian, Middle Eastern and Mediterranean cooking. Buy whole pomegranates in season (late summer to the end of autumn) and scrape out the seeds, discarding the bitter pith and thick leathery skin. The red seeds can be used whole or squeezed to make a delicious juice.

pomegranate molasses
A thick, dark syrup with a gentle acidic flavour. Use it in the same manner as lemon or vinegar when making a salad dressing or sauce. Available from Middle Eastern and specialty food stores.

pomelo
Found throughout South-east Asia, this looks like a very large grapefruit with a thick spongy skin. The fruit can be either yellow or pink and has little juice, but its flesh is a prized ingredient in many Asian salads. Available from fruit shops and Asian food stores.

ponzu soy sauce
A lightly brewed Japanese soy sauce, with lemon or yuzu added during the fermentation process, giving the sauce a distinct citrus flavour. Available from Japanese food stores and health-food shops.

potato flour
Fine white flour that is used to make dim sum pastries and some tempura-style batters. Available from Asian food stores.

preserved lemon
These are whole lemons split and packed in salt and lemon juice and left to soften for more than a month. They are readily available at food stores if you don't have the time or inclination to make yourself. Generally only the skin is used, which is finely chopped and added to salads, soups and tajines.

ras el hanout
Ras el hanout (literally 'head of the shop') is a complex and distinctive mix of spices and herbs originating in the Meghribi villages of north Africa. The blend varies according to who makes it, but most versions include 20 or so spices. Ras el hanout is used with meat, game, poultry, rice and cous cous, and is available from specialty spice suppliers.

roasted pimiento *see* pimiento

rose apple
Also known as water apple, this crisp and juicy fruit with a rose-pink skin is used in Malay, Indonesian and Thai cooking. Available from specialist fruit suppliers during late winter and early spring.

rosewater
A distillation of rose petals with an intense fragrance and flavour, this is available from Middle Eastern, Indian and specialist food stores.

salam leaves
A member of the cassia family, these Indonesian bay leaves are used fresh or dried in the soups, curries and sauces of Java and Sumatra. They are completely unrelated to the Western bay leaf, so don't be tempted to use these as a substitute. Available from Asian food stores.

salted black beans
Also known as fermented black beans, these have a distinctive salty, rich taste and pungent smell. They are available from Asian food stores and some supermarkets.

salted dried radish
Shredded daikon radish that has been salted and dried. Rinse before adding to salads, soups and stir-fries. Available from Japanese and Asian food stores.

salted duck eggs
Not to be confused with 1000-year-old preserved eggs, these eggs should be steamed whole for 30 minutes before use. The flavour is mildly salty and is delicious in salads and curries. Available from Chinese food stores.

salted jellyfish
Salted and sun-dried strips of jellyfish provide a crunchy, elastic texture and absorb the flavours they are cooked with. Buy in packets from Chinese food stores, and reconstitute in water before using.

salted yellow beans
These salted and fermented soy beans add a unique pungency to soups and sauces. Available in bottles from Asian food stores.

sansho pepper
Related to Sichuan pepper, sansho pepper is sourced from the prickly ash tree and has a zesty lemon flavour. Use sparingly, as it can cause numbness to the palate. Available in small bottles from Japanese food stores.

sea urchin roe
The soft orange roe from inside the black spiky shells of sea urchins. This delicacy of Japanese cooking can be served raw or (briefly) cooked, and is sold in small wooden trays at specialist fishmongers.

seaweed
Hijiki, wakame, arame, kombu and nori are all dried seaweed. Kombu is used when making stocks and simmered dishes, while nori sheets are roasted and used in sushi preparations. The remaining varieties need to be soaked in cold water to reconstitute before being used in salads, soups and braises. Available from Japanese stores, health-food shops and specialist food stores.

sesame oil
Available from Asian food stores, roasted sesame oil (also known as black sesame oil) is a dark, intense oil with a pronounced nutty flavour.

sesame seaweed salad
A ready-made salad of green seaweeds (ogo, wakame and sea lettuce) pickled in vinegar, mild chilli and sesame. Available from Japanese food stores and selected fishmongers.

shellfish oil
An aromatic oil made by infusing olive oil with roasted lobster, crab or prawn shells. Ready-prepared shellfish oil is available from specialty food stores.

shichimi togarashi
Seven-spice chilli mix used to season Japanese noodle dishes, soups and grilled meats. Available in small bottles from Japanese food stores.

shiro (white) soy sauce
Made exclusively with wheat, this pale honey-coloured sauce is prized in Japanese cuisine for its delicate flavour. It darkens with age, so should be used as soon as possible. Available from Japanese food stores.

shiso leaves
Known as perilla in South-east Asia and shiso in Japan, these leaves come in green and purple varieties, and taste like a cross between mint and basil, with the purple leaves having the stronger flavour. Used in pickles, salads, tempura and rice dishes, and as a wrapper for grilled meats, they are available at specialist greengrocers and Japanese food stores. *See also* cress

Shaoxing rice wine
Sometimes called Chinese cooking wine or yellow rice wine, this essential pantry item for Chinese cooking is available from Chinese and Asian food stores.

shrimp paste *see* belacan and kapi

snow fungus
A delicate white fungus that absorbs the flavours it is cooked with; break it into smaller petals before adding to sauces or soups. Available dried from Chinese food stores or fresh in small punnets from specialty greengrocers.

squid ink
The black ink from the small sacs found inside squid or cuttlefish. It can be purchased from specialty food stores or fishmongers.

sticky rice
Used extensively in Asian cooking, sticky rice is available in white, black or red varieties. The short grains have a sweet flavour and chalky appearance; as they cook, they swell and become sticky. Available from Asian stores and some supermarkets.

sweet ginger vinegar
Imported from Japan under the Yamamoto brand, this delicate vinegar is used in salad dressings or to accompany sashimi.

tatsoi leaves
This small green salad leaf related to bok choy and Chinese cabbage is available from selected greengrocers.

urad dal
Also known as black gram, this has an earthy flavour and is very popular in Indian curries. When split, the outer casing comes off to reveal a creamy white centre – this is known as split black gram dal, and is used for making dosa, idli and various breads in south Indian cooking. Available from Indian food stores and selected supermarkets.

vanilla bean paste
Made by scraping out the contents of vanilla beans and mixing to a paste with sugar. The flavour is more intense than vanilla extract so use it sparingly. Available at specialty food stores; keep refrigerated after opening.

wakame *see* seaweed

wasabi flying fish roe
The sac containing the tiny roe or fish eggs from flying fish (also known as tobiko) is rubbed with fresh wasabi to give the roe a pale green colour and gentle wasabi flavour. Imported from Japan, this is available from specialty food stores or fishmongers.

wasabi leaves
Fresh wasabi leaves are quite difficult to come by, but if you do manage to find them, shred a few and add to a salad for tangy, peppery flavour. There is no substitute, so simply omit if unavailable.

wasabi oil
This flavoured oil, imported from Japan under the Yamamoto brand, should be used sparingly as it has a pronounced pungency. Available from specialty food stores.

water spinach
A popular Asian leafy green vegetable used in stir-fries and salads. Also known as kangkung, water convolvulus or ong choi, it is readily available from Asian food stores and greengrocers.

wheat starch
Similar to cornflour, this very fine flour is used in many dim sum pastries, and is available from Asian food stores.

yam bean *see* jicama

young coconut juice *see* coconut juice

yuzu
Highly perfumed Japanese citrus fruit with a distinctive flavour. Yuzu is not available fresh in Australia, but you can buy bottles of preserved juice from Japanese food stores.

ACKNOWLEDGEMENTS

So many people have inspired my work, my life and my abiding passion for travel and the enduring rewards it brings. To Margie, who has been with me every step of the way over the past thirty years, for sharing the journey, for giving resonance to every experience. You have given me such enormous fulfilment, words cannot describe it. Thank you for believing in my dreams, for giving me the faith, courage and support to reach for the stars, and for always being there for me. You make everything possible.

Enormous thanks to my publisher and dear friend Julie Gibbs, for your constant faith and courage, your astute observations and investment in my dreams and work. To my photographer Anson Smart, it has been a dream ride working with you on the road and in the studio – your divine pictures have captured the very essence of my work. To Anna Last, for your guidance and enthusiastic styling assistance, and for your expert eye in gathering the amazing array of props that have given my food its powerful impact. A special thanks to Jessica, for assistance with preparing the dishes for the food photography. To Alison Cowan and Rachel Carter for editorial prowess, precision and patience – wow, what a team! To my graphic designer Jay Ryves, of Future Classic, your vision and artwork has brought my words alive and given them a magical visual impact – thank you. Thanks also to Sue Van Velsen, for keeping everything on track and masterminding the book's production.

To my many friends around the world who have shared in these adventures and treasured moments, my world is a better place for knowing you all and you have opened my eyes to so many wonders and experiences. To Alan, Keith and Jonathon, your generosity with your words and insights into Italian life are very much appreciated. A special thanks to a couple of my travelling buddies, Melinda Lawrence and Jason Minty, for your generosity in sharing some of your travel snaps with me for this book – you have captured some beautiful images on our adventures. To Eduardo Gonzales, who introduced me to the heartbeat of Spain and shared in many adventures across its length and breadth over the years. To Julie McIntosh and Sarah Hoyland at Classic Safari Company, who gave me the scope and opportunity to explore India, Morocco and South Africa through my work.

To Andrew Wood, of *Divine* magazine, and Scott Wasley, of wine and sherry importers The Spanish Inquisition, whose sherry workshops opened my eyes to the possibilities of matching food to the diverse flavour profiles of sherry in all its variety, for giving me the momentum to further Spanish pursuits, and the introductions to make it happen. The relationship has come full circle as Scott now supplies Universal with premium sherries, Spanish and Portuguese wines.

A very special thank you to Jessica Muir and Ian Atkinson, for helping me to breathe life into these words and for giving a physical presence to the culinary imaginings and ideas I have conjured up during my travels. I could not have achieved this without your creative energy, care and passion; together we make an enviable, dynamic team. To every one of my team at Universal, directed by the talented management of Jessica Muir, Liz Carey and Paul Guiney – my Universal angels – thank you for your dedication, loyalty and commitment to pushing the boundaries, and for helping to make it all possible.

Many thanks to the following, for supplying such beautiful props for the photography.

Anibou, +61 2 9319 0655; www.anibou.com.au

The Art of Wine & Food, +61 2 9363 2817; www.artwinefood.com.au

The Bay Tree, + 61 2 9328 1101; www.thebaytree.com.au

Chee Soon & Fitzgerald, +61 2 9360 1031; www.cheesoonfitzgerald.com

Cloth, +61 2 9699 2266; www.clothfabric.com

Dedece, +61 2 9360 2722; www.dedece.com

Dinosaur Designs, +61 2 9698 3500; www.dinosaurdesigns.com.au

Husk, +61 3 9528 7411; www.husk.com.au

Ici et la, +61 2 9699 4266; www.icietla.com.au

Le Bonbon, +61 2 9369 3067; www.lebonbon.com.au

Lynette Cunnington – Chinese Art & Furniture, +61 2 9326 2227; www.chineseart.com.au

Major & Tom, +61 2 9557 8380; www.majorandtom.com.au

Miljo, +61 2 9387 7143; www.miljoshop.com

Mrs Red & Sons, +61 2 9310 4860

Mud Australia, +61 2 9519 2520; www.mudaustralia.com

No Chintz, +61 2 9386 4800; www.nochintz.com

Ondene, +61 2 9362 1734; www.ondene.com

Orson & Blake, +61 2 9326 1155; www.orsonandblake.com.au

Papaya, +61 2 9386 9980; www.papaya.com.au

Parterre Garden, +61 2 9363 5874; www.parterre.com.au

Planet, +61 2 9698 0680; www.planetfurniture.com.au

Ruby Star Trader, +61 2 9518 7899

Simon Johnson, +61 2 8244 8288; www.simonjohnson.com.au

Space Furniture, +61 2 8339 7588; www.spacefurniture.com.au

Top 3 by Design, +61 2 9388 9699; www.top3.com.au

Waterford Wedgwood, +61 2 9899 2877; www.waterford.wedgwood.com.au

INDEX

LANTERN

Published by the Penguin Group
Penguin Group (Australia)
250 Camberwell Road, Camberwell, Victoria 3124, Australia
(a division of Pearson Australia Group Pty Ltd)
Penguin Group (USA) Inc.
375 Hudson Street, New York, New York 10014, USA
Penguin Group (Canada)
90 Eglinton Avenue East, Suite 700, Toronto, Canada ON M4P 2Y3
(a division of Pearson Penguin Canada Inc.)
Penguin Books Ltd
80 Strand, London WC2R 0RL England
Penguin Ireland
25 St Stephen's Green, Dublin 2, Ireland
(a division of Penguin Books Ltd)
Penguin Books India Pvt Ltd
11 Community Centre, Panchsheel Park, New Delhi – 110 017, India
Penguin Group (NZ)
67 Apollo Drive, Rosedale, North Shore 0632, New Zealand
(a division of Pearson New Zealand Ltd)
Penguin Books (South Africa) (Pty) Ltd
24 Sturdee Avenue, Rosebank, Johannesburg 2196, South Africa

Penguin Books Ltd, Registered Offices: 80 Strand, London, WC2R 0RL, England

First published by Penguin Group (Australia), 2008

10 9 8 7 6 5 4 3 2 1

Design by Jay Ryves, Future Classic © Penguin Group (Australia)
Illustrations by Jay Ryves, Hazel Lam and Al Goh, Future Classic

Photographs on Contents page (right), pages 80 (left) and 81 by Jason Minty; facing page 1, pages 17, 156, 338, 343, 346, 347, 352, 357 and 363 (left) by Katie Pashley; pages 6 (right) and 39 by Soraya Zamen; pages 28, 75, 114, 118 (left) and 125 by Cefn Ridout; pages 40 (left), 69 (right), 80 (right), 96 (right), 100 (all except far right), 110 (left), 115, 118 (right), 134 (left), 145, 204, 244 (left), 262, 264, 267, 269, 271, 282 (right), 304, 310 (left and centre), 318 (right), 375 (left), 376, 381 (left), 400, 402, 405, 406, 409, 411, 414, 419 (right), 430 (right), 431, 435 (right), 459, 463, 470 and 474 (right) by Christine Manfield; pages 49 (right), 162 and 254 by Margie Harris; pages 62, 69 (left), 85, 106, 110 (right), 111 and 123 by Alison Cowan; pages 88, 96 (left), 99, 100 (far right), 123 (right), 444, 447, 474 (left) and 477 by Melinda Lawrence; pages 128 and 134 (right) by Rebecca Rosconi; page 151 (left) by Brooke Hendrik; page 158 by Aun Koh (Lonely Planet Images); page 182 by Michael Coyne (Lonely Planet Images); page 288 by Ann Cecil (Lonely Planet Images); pages 295 and 300 by Kate Ford; page 454 by Katie Kaars; all other photographs by Anson Smart.

Styling by Anna Last
Typeset by Post Pre-press Group, Brisbane, Queensland
Colour reproduction by Splitting Image, Clayton, Victoria
Printed and bound in China by 1010 Printing International Limited

National Library of Australia
Cataloguing-in-Publication data:

Manfield, Christine.
Fire : a world of flavour / Christine Manfield.
Camberwell, Vic. : Penguin Australia, 2008.
9781920989392 (hbk.)
Includes index.
Cookery, International.

641.59

penguin.com.au